The Grand Spas of Central Europe

ALSO BY DAVID CLAY LARGE

Munich 1972: Tragedy, Terror, and Triumph at the Olympic Games

Nazi Games: The Olympics of 1936

And the World Closed Its Doors: One Family's Abandonment to the Holocaust

Berlin

Where Ghosts Walked: Munich's Road to the Third Reich

Germans to the Front: West German Rearmament in the Adenauer Era

Contending with Hitler: Varieties of German Resistance in the Third Reich (editor)

The End of the European Era: 1890 to the Present (with Felix Gilbert)

Between Two Fires: Europe's Path in the 1930s

Wagnerism in European Culture and Politics (co-editor)

The Politics of Law and Order: A History of the Bavarian Einwohnerwehr, 1918–1921

The Grand Spas of Central Europe

A History of Intrigue, Politics, Art, and Healing

David Clay Large

ROWMAN & LITTLEFIELD
Lanham • Boulder • New York • London

Published by Rowman & Littlefield
A wholly owned subsidiary of
The Rowman & Littlefield Publishing Group, Inc.
4501 Forbes Boulevard, Suite 200, Lanham, Maryland 20706
www.rowman.com

Unit A, Whitacre Mews, 26-34 Stannary Street, London SE11 4AB

Copyright © 2015 by Rowman & Littlefield

All rights reserved. No part of this book may be reproduced in any form or by any electronic or mechanical means, including information storage and retrieval systems, without written permission from the publisher, except by a reviewer who may quote passages in a review.

British Library Cataloguing in Publication Information Available

Library of Congress Cataloging-in-Publication Data
Large, David Clay.
 The grand spas of Central Europe : a history of intrigue, politics, art, and healing / David Clay Large.
    pages cm
 Includes bibliographical references and index.
 ISBN 978-1-4422-2236-6 (cloth : alk. paper) — ISBN 978-1-4422-2237-3 (electronic) 1. Health resorts—Europe, Central—History. 2. Europe, Central—Social life and customs. 3. Europe, Central—Politics and government. I. Title.
 RA846.L37 2015
 613'.122094—dc23
                                                         2015017468

∞™ The paper used in this publication meets the minimum requirements of American National Standard for Information Sciences—Permanence of Paper for Printed Library Materials, ANSI/NISO Z39.48-1992.

Printed in the United States of America

For Hans Rudolf Vaget, Native Son of Marienbad

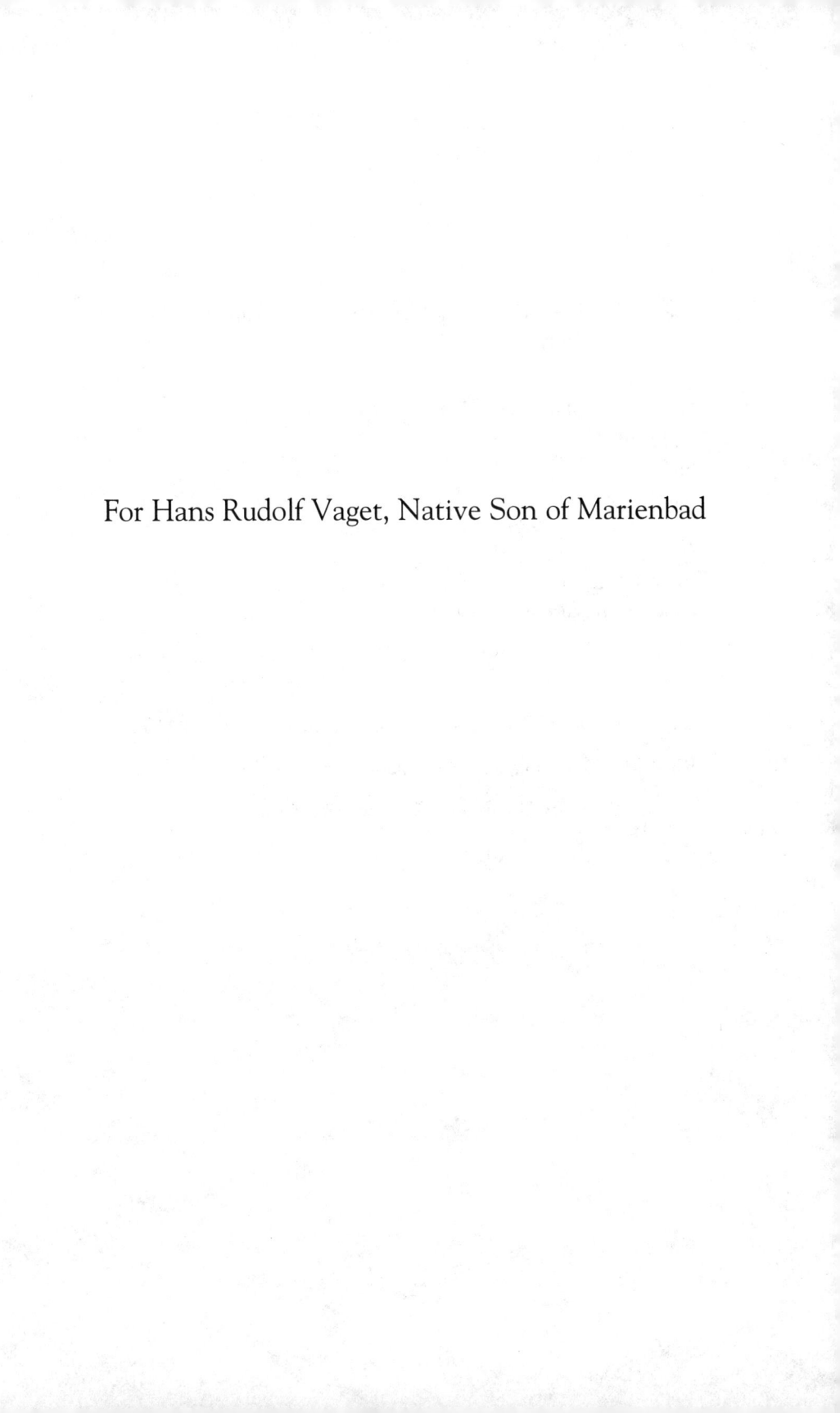

Thousands have lived without love, not one without water.

—W. H. Auden

Fons Levit Inalidos
Animum Qui Vertit Ad Artem
Emendat Mores
Excolit Ingenium

(Just as the bubbling spring revives and helps the sick body, it leads the mind to art and ennobles the customs and spirit.)

—Inscription at Elisabethbrunnen, Bad Homburg

Captain Renault: What in heaven's name brought you to Casablanca?

Rick: My health. I came to Casablanca for the waters.

Captain Renault: The waters? What waters? We're in a desert.

Rick: I was misinformed.

—*Casablanca*

Contents

	Introduction	1
Chapter 1	Spas and Spa Culture from the Greco-Roman World to the Grand Tour	11
	The Ancient West	12
	Decline and Resurrection	29
	The Grand Tour	42
Chapter 2	Baden-Baden: The "Summer Capital of Europe"	51
	Becoming Baden-Baden	52
	Faites Votre Jeu: The Age of Bénazet	61
	August Granville's Baden-Baden	69
	The "Jewish Question"	79
	Getting There	81
	The Revolutions of 1848–1849	84
Chapter 3	Muses in the Waters	91
	Two Titans at the Fountains: Goethe and Beethoven	92
	Scribble, Squander, Soak: Romantic-Era Writers in Baden-Baden	108
	The Sound of Music	115

Chapter 4	Roulettenburg: Russian Writers at the Grand German Spas	137
	Troubled in Soul (and Bowels): Nikolai Gogol in Baden-Baden	138
	Ivan Turgenev's Path to the West	141
	Turgenev versus Tolstoy	146
	Ménage à Trois on the Oos	151
	Fedor Dostoevsky in German Spa Land	158
	Showdown in Baden-Baden	172
	Do Svidaniya to Deutschland	175
Chapter 5	Politics on the Promenade	181
	A Line in the Water	182
	The German Question(s)	188
	Five Balls over the Waters: Bismarck's Alliance System	206
	Vicky, Willy, Nicky, Bertie, and Franz Josef	211
Chapter 6	Modernization and Its Discontents	225
	Innovations	226
	Medicalization: "It's Not Just about the Waters Anymore!"	237
	A Jewish Space	246
	Taking the Waters with Marx/Twain	255
Chapter 7	Trouble in Paradise: Spa-Town Life from World War I to the Triumph of Hitler	269
	The Grand Spas at War	269
	German Spa Towns and the Weimar Republic	287
	Rump Austria	298
	Slouching toward Berlin: Karlsbad and Marienbad in the Twenties and Thirties	308
Chapter 8	Brown Waters: Grand Spas under the Third Reich	319
	Nazis and Spas	319
	"Germany's Visiting Card"	325
	"Ein Volk, Ein Reich, Ein Führer"	338
	A Coda: Badenheim 1939	350
	Wartime	351

Chapter 9	A New Beginning	367
	Postwar	368
	Recovery	374
	Epilogue: The Grand Spas Today	391
	Acknowledgments	407
	Principal Sources and Suggestions for Further Reading	411
	Index	435
	About the Author	465

Netherlands
Hamburg
Szczecin
Bremen
Elbe R.
Poznań
Germany
BERLIN
Düsseldorf
Bad Ems
Bonn
Dresden
1
Bad Homburg
2
Belgium
Frankfurt
5
Karlsbad
Rhine R.
3
PRAGUE
6
Luxembourg
Wiesbaden
Marienbad
Czech Republic
Stuttgart
France
4
Baden-Baden
Danube R.
Linz
VIENNA
Munich
Salzburg
Baden-bei-7
Wien
8 Bad Ischl
Liechtenstein
Innsbruck
9 Bad Gastein
Graz
Switzerland
Austria

Introduction

In recent years the word "spa"* has become ubiquitous, almost as unavoidable as "sustainable." Thus it should come as no surprise that there are "sustainable spas"—places like Dune Echo Village in Pondicherry, India, where you can get your deep-muscle massage and colonic evacuation while simultaneously saving the planet. Yet these "green" health resorts are merely the surface of the pool when it comes to the spa phenomenon in our time. According to a Global Spa Summit held in 2007 at the Waldorf-Astoria Hotel in New York City, the international spa industry raked in forty billion dollars the previous year. Today there are more than ten thousand spa locations in the United States alone, and this figure does not include beauty parlors offering "spa" treatments, airport "XpresSpas," or those countless backyard hot tubs marketed, rather cheekily in my view, as "spas." The International Spa Association is happy to report that spas are increasingly displacing golf resorts as the venue of choice for corporate retreats. "Golf isn't relaxing," notes a sales director for Canon Industries, "it's very competitive and adds more to the

---

*Many people assume that the term "spa" derives from Belgium's premier water-cure town, Spa, which adopted the moniker in the fourteenth century, perhaps taking it from the Latin phrase "Salus per Aqua," which was sometimes used in abbreviated form in Roman imperial times. Yet it's also possible that the term is a derivation of the Walloon word for "fountain," *espa*. In any event, the popularity of Belgium's Spa as a water-cure refuge in the sixteenth and seventeenth centuries seems to have generated a broader usage of the word for any mineral-spring complex catering to health pilgrims.

stress." Spas, on the other hand, "provide a good chance to network and talk in a relaxed atmosphere."

The spa treatments to which stressed-out businesspeople and health seekers of all sorts flock these days vary wildly from standard thermal-spring bathing to wallowing in "beer baths" (Czechoslovakia), practicing underwater shiatsu (Thailand), rolling in herb-scented hay (Zermatt, Switzerland), being scrubbed with sea salt and Javanese spices (Vienna), getting massaged with linen-wrapped hot stones while listening to *Greensleeves* (Santa Barbara, California), sitting for hours in lithium-laced pools (Chinati Hot Springs, Marfa, Texas), enduring the "back, sack, and crack" male Brazilian wax treatment (London), or having your face slimed by giant African snails (Russia). Should you prefer a purely armchair healing experience, I recommend Fay Weldon's novel *The Spa* (2007), which showcases a moat-encircled retreat in the northern English countryside available only to high-achieving ladies who pay a small fortune for a few days of Botox, aromatherapy, and group testimonials à la Chaucer.

As lively and variegated as today's international spa scene may be, however, it is really just a faint echo of a much more potent and vital natural-cure culture based on "healing waters" that prospered in Europe from pre-Roman times to the First World War, with a long coda stretching into our own day.

There were always, of course, other forms of natural health therapy in addition to the healing waters, including herbal remedies and the so-called air cure, which relied on the putative therapeutic properties of dry desert or mountain air to treat respiratory afflictions like tuberculosis—witness the seven-year "cure" undertaken by the fictional Hans Castorp in Thomas Mann's novel *The Magic Mountain* (1924) or the tubercular Doc Holliday's real-life struggle to prolong his days as a gunslinging dentist by moving from Atlanta to the American Southwest in the 1880s. (Recent research indicates that the high-elevation air cure may actually be useful in treating drug-resistant strains of this disease, since reduced atmospheric pressure inhibits the ability of M. *tuberculosis* to survive and multiply.)

But it is hot water, not dry air, which is of central concern in this narrative, in which we will meander through the convoluted world of hydropathy and balneology (as the "science" of therapeutic bathing is called).

The story of thermal spas is important—not least in the history of medicine and personal health. We may think that we are long past the days when the water cure stood at the forefront of medical treatment, but that is not the case. Until only very recently, conventional internal medicine in the industrialized world could not offer much alternative to the benefits of taking the waters. In many instances, "healing waters" provided as much symptomatic relief as (if not more than) any other remedies then available for arthritic, respiratory, digestive, and nervous ailments. Of seventeenth-century medicine it has been said: "Nearly all men died of their remedies and not of their diseases." Later on, the use of electrified beds to drive tapeworms from the body in late nineteenth-century European hospitals suggests, for example, that modern technology was not necessarily a blessing. True, for major afflictions such as cancer or occluded arteries, water therapies could be something of a curate's egg—not nearly what they were cracked up to be. Yet even in the dire straits of mortal illness there was (and is) much to be said for the spa treatments' placebo effect—and at least with healing water, the cure was not (generally) more painful than the disease.

Moreover, in an age of increasingly industrialized conventional medicine, there is also something to be said for a medical equivalent of "slow food": unhurried, hands-on, relatively low-tech care in which the body is considered more a garden to be tended than a machine to be fixed. This is the sort of care once practiced in medieval almshouses like Paris's Hôtel Dieu and, more lastingly, in Europe's great thermal-spring spas.

Along with various ancillary diversions, it was genuine faith in the power of the thermal waters to heal that kept people coming back to the spas season after season, generation after generation, independent of medical outcomes. In this regard, spa waters were like the sacred spring at Lourdes—and perhaps in some cases also a bit like Samuel Johnson's definition of second marriage: "the triumph of hope over experience."

The phenomenon of taking the cure at thermal-spring resorts can be—and indeed has been—addressed from a variety of perspectives. I have chosen in this book to focus on the spa towns (*Kurorte*) of Central Europe—and more particularly, on those few legendary locales that can properly be called "grand."

Why this approach? Why the major luxury resorts of Central Europe? Certainly there were and are historically important spas elsewhere in the world: one thinks foremost of England's Bath, Malvern, and Cheltenham; France's Vichy, Evian, and Aix-les-Bains; and of course Spa in Belgium. The United States had the elegant Saratoga Springs Resort in New York State; the famed sanatorium in Battle Creek, Michigan, run by health-food guru John Harvey Kellogg;* and my own favorite thermal spa, Montana's century-old Chico Hot Springs, where they have a sign asking guests to please not pee in the pool.

It was in Central Europe, though, where over the course of the nineteenth century the water-cure culture reached its zenith in terms of refinement, global resonance, and internal diversity. When Bath, Aix-les-Bains, and Spa were starting to fade, the grand Central European Kurorte—places like Baden-Baden, Wiesbaden, Bad Ems, Bad Homburg, Bad Gastein, Baden-bei-Wien, Bad Ischl, Karlsbad, and Marienbad—were enjoying a flowering that, in varying degrees of intensity, lasted until the 1920s. Moreover, the diverging fate of the Central European spa towns in the post–World War II era and the partial comeback that virtually all of these places have managed in recent times make them an especially worthy subject for the student of contemporary European social and cultural history.

What, more specifically, can a history of these grand spas teach us? Well, among other things, it tells us about changing theories of the body and bodily needs; fads in health care and personal hygiene; evolving views on the connections between prevailing lifestyles and physical and mental health; the translation of court etiquette and sophisticated urban manners to smallish rural retreats; relations between the social classes, especially between the fading aristocracy and ambitious middle classes; ever-changing divertissements and new ways of keeping health pilgrims entertained; modes of travel, journeying to the resorts first by horse-drawn coach, then by train, and finally by fabulous motorcars. Finally—perhaps less glamorously but fascinating all the same—the history

---

*Kellogg's Battle Creek Sanatorium, which attained great popularity and influence in the early twentieth century, imposed a strict low-fat diet based on whole grains, fiber-rich food, and (above all) nuts. Another requirement was frequent enemas, often administered with yogurt. In its use of hydrotherapy and electrotherapy, Kellogg's institution resembled major European spas, but its (literal) nuttiness in dietary matters went beyond what most Europeans would have tolerated. Nor would Kellogg's total ban on alcohol have gone over well in Europe, where beer and wine were regarded as a food group. The Battle Creek "San" is deliciously satirized in T. Coraghessan Boyle's comic novel *The Road to Wellville* (1993).

of grand spa culture reveals the commingling of wealth and fame with petty spite, prejudice, and endless intrigue.

Unlike in the grand spas' salad days, today these faded European dowagers must compete for custom with slicker and trendier places all over the planet, above all in Asia. (Not surprisingly, China is coming on strong in the global spa world, now boasting water resorts that compare in opulence with the most sumptuous of those in Thailand and Indonesia.) Nonetheless, the grand spa towns of Central Europe remain the destinations of choice for thousands of people who (like me) want some centuries-old history to go along with their soaks, massages, and high-powered enemas.

The famed Central European spas at the center of this narrative were by no means the norm, even in their home territory. Nineteenth-century Germany alone had more than three hundred registered Kurorte. The vast majority of these locales were small, unprepossessing places lacking luxury hotels, monumental bath palaces, fancy restaurants, and glittering casinos. They served *Früstuck*, not "breakfast" or "*petit déjeuner.*" Their clientele consisted primarily of middle- and lower-middle-class families from the surrounding region who came to be cured, not to play. Generally, there was not a princeling, nor even a novelist, in sight. These places appear in my discussion only to provide points of comparison with the major Kurorte.

For me, what is of singular interest about the grand spas is precisely their capacity to attract patrons of social, political, and cultural distinction, often from foreign lands, who did not come to these locales solely to heal—or sometimes to heal at all. Far from being only about wellness, the grand spas in their heyday amounted to their world's equivalent of today's golf and tennis resorts, conference centers, business retreats, political summits, fashion shows, theme parks, and sexual hideaways—all rolled into one. People, especially wealthy people, went to the grand spas almost as much for social and cultural sustenance as for a possible cure for their gout or arthritis. Many restless husbands went to the water-cure resorts to get away from their wives. (As Goethe told his friend Eckermann, he had to find "a little sexual adventure" each time he went to Karlsbad, or he would "die of boredom.") On the other hand, some men and women went to the spas to *find* spouses, for among their other attractions, the grand spa towns functioned as marriage markets for the cash-strapped aristocracy and socially ambitious middle classes.

Moreover, in the cultural domain, apart from offering a rich diet of musical and theatrical fare to their guests, the grandest spas were places where culture was actually created. Attracting as they did some of the greatest poets, novelists, playwrights, and composers of their day, the spas of Central Europe spawned countless works of art, literature, and music. Fortunately for the spa historian, some of the literary works generated in these cultural hothouses also *featured* them in their settings, thereby providing a wealth of lore on the manners and morals of the water-cure society. As the more literate of modern-day visitors to Baden-Baden, Wiesbaden, Karlsbad, or Marienbad surely know, taking along Turgenev, Tolstoy, Twain, Dostoevsky, Flaubert, or Goethe greatly adds to the richness of the experience.

I have duly included the stories of these and many other celebrated artists in this journey through the history of the grand Kurorte. Baden-Baden, the focus of my second chapter, became known as "Europe's Summer Capital" in part because it was a world-class cultural mecca that attracted the likes of Nicolo Paganini, Franz Liszt, George Sand, and Victor Hugo. Yet Baden-Baden was hardly alone in having its thermal baths—and glittering casinos—graced with the muses of literature, music, drama, and (less prominently) painting. Karlsbad and later Marienbad were favored summer haunts for Goethe—retreats where the poet sometimes worked but mostly played and carried on those sexual dalliances that were so necessary to his mental equilibrium and artistic temperament.

It was in Karlsbad that Goethe encountered a fellow cultural titan (and frequent spa-goer), Ludwig van Beethoven. That great composer never did find a cure for his most pressing afflictions at any of the grand spas he patronized, but Beethoven did discover there an inspirational environment for his music. He had a lot of company. An array of prominent artists—Frédéric Chopin, Richard Wagner, Hector Berlioz, Johannes Brahms, Gustav Mahler, Alfred de Musset, and Gérard de Nerval, to name just a few—produced some of their best work in the grand Kurorte of Central Europe.

Although neither Goethe nor Beethoven were devotees of casino gambling, games of chance constituted a principal attraction for many of the regular patrons, including the artistic patrons, at the grand spas. This was famously true of those Russian literary giants Fedor Dostoevsky and Leo Tolstoy, who carried on disastrous affairs with Madame Roulette at various German Kurorte. On the other hand, their countryman Ivan Turgenev managed to settle in for years on end at Baden-Baden without losing a single kopek at the tables. Instead, Turgenev lost his heart to a French woman who had also landed in Baden-Baden—and then fell in love with the glamorous spa town itself, which, for him, embodied the Western sophistication and progressive spirit grievously lacking in his native country. Chronicling the widely divergent experiences among Russian literary figures in German spa land sheds some watery light on the momentous rift between Westerners and Slavophiles in nineteenth-century Russian culture.

Yet another side trip along this journey involves politics—more specifically, high-level politics and diplomacy. Just as today's political leaders, when gathering, say, for a conference on world poverty, will likely choose Davos over Port-au-Prince, nineteenth-century European potentates repaired to the major spas of Mitteleuropa to solve, and sometimes to aggravate, the pressing problems of their day. As with cultural achievement in spa territory, the practice of international politicking and summit diplomacy can be illuminated by watching it unfold on the promenades of the grand spa towns.

Because this narrative follows the evolution of the major Central European Kurorte not only in their role as centers of healing but also as arenas of political, social, and cultural conflict, it offers a darker picture of spa life than one might expect from a history of luxury thermal bathing. The spa towns certainly promoted themselves as sheltered havens from real-world discord, and many patrons definitely did seek them out for blissful escape. Yet instead of finding conflict-free zones, they typically encountered locales where, by dint of confined space, the tensions and acrimonies of the times actually loomed larger. Just as the spas were all too often unable to deliver on their promise of physical cures, their offer of an island of peace in an ocean of tumult likewise proved illusory more often than not.

One of the darker sides of the Central European spa saga in modern times has to with the role played by Jews on the narrow but glittering grand Kurort stage. Their part was not always that of the victim or malefactor. Nor was it marginal. Especially during the water-cure heyday, Jews figured prominently in all aspects of grand spa life—as doctors, hotel and restaurant owners, ordinary residents, and patrons. They were crucial to the "medicalization" and modernization of the major spas at the fin de siècle. Wealthy Jews enjoyed a privileged status at the top Central European spas even as anti-Semitism was gaining traction across the region. But this condition could not last, and, like a malignant Doppler effect, the raucous noises of the new era—jackboots hitting pavements and shouted racist slogans—swept into the Kurorte, a little belatedly but just as loudly. Soon, places that had once crowed about their cosmopolitanism boasted about being "judenrein" (cleansed of Jews).

My narrative of grand spa life in Mitteleuropa would certainly have been more upbeat had I stopped at the First World War, which is the ending point for most portraits of these places. Yet the great spa towns' decline and partial revival over the course of the twentieth century is just as important and intriguing as the water-cure resorts' apogee in the late nineteenth century. Thoroughly caught up in the swirling currents of "total war," empire-shattering revolution, economic collapse, ideological division, and the radical transformation of conventional medicine, the grand spas offer yet another aperture—a many-faceted kaleidoscope—through which to view the ever-changing imagery and narrative of our times.

My decision to continue this grand spa journey well past the usual point of disembarkation and to pause for extended periods at rather less fetching and edifying roadside attractions is one of the many ways in which this trek is a personal one.

Most accounts of Europe's major thermal-spring resorts are exercises in nostalgia—eulogies for a lost world of glamour and grace that became a casualty of the Great War along with the sprawling empires and aristocratic society that sustained the spas. This book is emphatically not such an exercise. At the same time, however, my determination to undertake a project like this reflects a weakness on my part for faded luxe of the sort conjured up by once-grand hotels (Istanbul's Pera Palace, for example); historic trains (Europe's *Orient Express* and America's *Super Chief*, the latter carrying its own barber shop); great ocean liners (above all the RMS *Caronia*, offering only first class)—and grand spas. I considered doing a book on the historic Central European Kurorte at the very beginning of my academic career, but I am glad that I kept putting off this task until I was substantially older, on the southern side of my seventh decade. Paul Theroux once observed that it is "only with age that you acquire the gift to evaluate decay." There is much more to the grand spas' history than decorous decay, but encroaching decrepitude is part of the story here—a part with which I can now truly identify.

In choosing this topic I was also animated by a consideration that historians all too often ignore or undervalue and that I myself discounted in my callow youth: Would the subject in question afford, even demand, research junkets to pleasant and pampering places? I can say without hesitation that in this regard the Friedrichsbad in Baden-Baden represents a major improvement over the German Federal Archives in Koblenz, where over the years I have spent many an hour conducting research (and trying not to breathe in too much dust).

Having finally decided to get my spa project off the ground and to focus on the grand Kurorte of Central Europe, I had to determine exactly which locales this category might justifiably include and how much emphasis to place on each venue. These decisions were admittedly somewhat arbitrary. Other historians, when examining the historic European spa phenomenon, have ranged across the entire continent—and thrown in Great Britain for good measure. Even a study focused on the Kurorte of Mitteleuropa might well feature different spas than I do or have included the grand baths of Budapest, above all the splendid thermal pools at the Hotel Gellért, the model for Wes Anderson's film *Grand Budapest Hotel* (2014). But I wanted to limit myself to spas belonging (historically) to German-speaking Central Europe. In the end, I came up with a venue selection small enough to allow an examination of each locale in some detail (albeit with no claim to comprehensive coverage) and broad enough to illustrate the diversity of Kurort history and style.

This is a personal history not only in its idiosyncratic selection of locales to feature and topics to raise but also in its—for want of a better word—intimacy. Historians typically try to keep an objective distance from their subject matter, eschewing any (obvious) injection of opinion or personal experience. Such separation from the subject at hand is clearly necessary for historical understanding and judicious assessment. In this project I have hewed to the distance code most of the time, but I do not hesitate, on occasion, to let fly with my curmudgeonly crotchets and to bring in personal stories. The epilogue is almost as much a travelogue as a history.

Finally, I have followed my own lights in matters of style and presentation. My predilection for informal prose, along with an aversion to academic in-speak, will be evident throughout. Absent too is any grand theorizing of the sort that, in the words of John Searle regarding the work of Jacques Derrida, "gives bullshit a bad name."

As I said, I first got the idea to undertake a spas project many years ago. The notion came to me in—where else?—a grand spa. It happened that I had a full day to kill in the Frankfurt area before flying out and decided to spend it in nearby Bad Homburg, which a friend had highly praised. I was enthralled by the elegance and easygoing languor of the place. Sitting in the ornate Kaiser-Wilhelms-Bad with a gin and tonic, I said to myself, "Silly boy, why don't you do a book that would give you an excuse to come here more often?" This, finally, is that book.

CHAPTER ONE

~

Spas and Spa Culture from the Greco-Roman World to the Grand Tour

When a well-traveled Russian gentleman named Nikolai Karamsin paused to take the waters at Baden in Switzerland during a Grand Tour through Central and Western Europe in 1799, he was following in an ancient tradition: that of stopping off at a famed mineral-water resort to cure his ailments, socialize with fellow bathers, and enjoy some lively cultural divertissements.

But for all its antiquity, a pedigree dating back to the classical Greeks and Romans, the hallowed ritual in which Karamsin was participating was in his day just getting back on its feet after having been knocked about for centuries by changing cultural mores and perspectives on what it meant to be "well." There were times when it appeared that the great water-cure institutions perfected by the ancients had vanished entirely, never to return. On the other hand, it was precisely over the long and highly fluid period between the Greco-Roman era and the Grand Tour heyday of the late eighteenth century that virtually all the ingredients in latter-day spa culture came together. A tour of our own—actually, more of a romp—through this two-thousand-year stretch is in order before we settle into a more leisurely amble through the Central European spa landscape of recent times.

The Ancient West

Challenged with identifying the liquid of choice in the ancient Greco-Roman world, many of us might choose wine, but we'd be wrong: *water* was the fluid that made Western classical civilizations go.

There was nothing unusual in this: water was the oil of life in *all* the early civilizations (just as it is in our own, as we've come to learn with increasing dismay). Obviously, people everywhere in the ancient world *drank* water, rank and unsafe as it often was. Yet water was also widely used for religious, medicinal, hygienic, and cosmetic purposes. A few examples will illuminate this phenomenon.

The Essenes, an ancient Judaic sect associated with the Dead Sea Scrolls, bathed in cold water at the start of each day to purify their bodies and souls. Any Jew who wished to enter the temple was likewise required to undergo a ritual bath. Jewish women bathed in stone-lined mikveh chambers after menstrual periods or childbirth to purify themselves before resuming sexual relations with their husbands. Famously, King David first laid eyes on the beautiful Bathsheba as she was taking her morning ablutions in her father's garden.

During the Purna Kumbh Mela festival, a Hindu rite dating back over two millennia, masses of pilgrims gathered every twelve years—and still gather—at the confluence of the Ganges and Yamuna Rivers to wash away their sins by bathing in sacred waters. (That these pilgrims often picked up various infectious diseases in the bargain, or sometimes even drowned, did not prevent the Mela from becoming the largest human gathering in the world, with more than eighty million participants in recent times.)

Like the Ganges, the Nile River was said to possess miraculous powers—powers not just to bring life to the parched land through which it flowed but also to heal wounds, cure diseases, and make barren women fecund. Ptolemy II sent his daughter Nile River water when she married to ensure fertility. In Cleopatra's time the Egyptian state licensed public baths that charged hefty fees. These baths served primarily hygienic functions—and although they might leave a customer cleaner, they could be downright nasty and dangerous. Egyptian bath attendants routinely assaulted patrons and made off with their clothing. One customer claimed that his bath steward emptied a jar of boiling water over him, "scalding my belly and my left thigh to the knee, so that my life was in danger."

In ancient Scythia, every bit as dirty and dangerous as Egypt, nomadic horsemen and women called "Amazons" by the Greeks used cold water to wash their heads but preferred sweat-lodge-like chambers to bathe their bodies. According to Herodotus, the Scythians tossed handfuls of cannabis seeds onto red-hot stones inside their felt-covered teepees, yielding a potent vapor that steamed off encrusted filth and made the bathers "shout with joy."

Yet among all the ancient civilizations, it was the Greeks, and then even more so the Romans, who made the most of water and water baths as curative agents—as paths not just to cleanliness, beauty, or fecundity, but to better health and even psychic improvement. Characteristically, they developed protoscientific theories about how and why water worked to heal the body and mind. Over time these classical Western civilizations came to conduct their bathing regimens in elaborate facilities that, looking back from our comfortable lounge chair in, say, Baden-Baden's sumptuous Friedrichsbad, we can identify as the definitive progenitors of our modern water-cure culture.

For the Greeks, the notion that bathing in open water or in tubs could be transformative was amply present in Homer's great sagas. In the *Odyssey*, Odysseus assuages the aches and pains of travel in a special bath drawn for him by the sorceress Circe. At another stop in his travels, when visiting the palace of King Alcinous, Queen Arete orders a bath to be prepared for her distinguished guest. The bath in question is luxuriously hot, involving a copper tub placed over a blazing fire. Young Odysseus emerges from his ablutions virtually reborn, "looking more like a god than a man." Likewise, Odysseus's son Telemachus, having been personally bathed and oiled by Polycaste, the youngest daughter of King Nestor, steps forth from this service looking "handsome as a young god."

In the *Iliad*, it is Hector's turn to experience the transformative power of water—albeit not in a tub. He heals his war wounds by bathing in the sacred waters of the River Xanthus. And then there is Hector's nemesis, Achilles: his mother tried to make him immortal by immersing him in the River Styx, only to botch the job by holding onto his heel.

While for Homer's legendary heroes, bathing seems to have induced primarily physical transformations, for Archimedes, that great Greek mathematician of the third century BCE, a dip in the tub facilitated intellectual revelation. As the story goes, Archimedes figured out how to determine the volume of irregular shapes while splashing in his bath. "Eureka, I've found it!" he reportedly cried, then ran naked through the streets shouting the good news.

Crucially for the development of nascent spa culture, the ancient Greeks also took to the waters for their day-to-day health, convinced by influential physicians that varying forms of hydrotherapy constituted the best treatment for all manner of ailments. Hippocrates, often called the father of medicine, made a serious study of what in his day was already a flourishing hydropathic culture. He was an advocate of regular immersions in hot and cold waters, believing, along with many of his colleagues, that this practice could bring the body's "humors" into proper balance. Moreover, while he prescribed cold baths for fevers, he was convinced that warm baths could enhance the digestive process by softening abdominal muscles.

On the other hand, Hippocrates clearly had his reservations about the growing practice of *drinking* medicinal waters. In his seminal work, *De aere, aquis et locis* (*On Air, Water and Local Conditions*), he argued that all "hard and salty" mineral waters, laden with such ingredients as iron, silver, copper, and sulfur, were very difficult to digest and likely therefore to engender extreme constipation. Hippocrates's intervention shows that battles among physicians over the relative merits of this or that hydrotherapy were present at the very dawn of spa culture.

Galen, the last of the great Greek physicians, was perhaps the most prominent water-cure advocate of his day. Depending on the disease that needed to be addressed, this mighty healer distinguished between partial and complete baths and between warm and cold treatments. Intriguingly, Galen also encouraged opium consumption while bathing. The two therapies taken together constituted for him a glorious panacea, effective for "headaches, vertigo, deafness, epilepsy, apoplexy, poor sight, bronchitis, asthma, coughs, the spitting of blood, colic, jaundice, hardness of the spleen, kidney stones, urinary complaints, fever, dropsy, leprosy, menstrual problems, melancholy, and all other pestilences."

Like virtually all aspects of daily life in ancient Greece, securing medical treatment, including the various water treatments, was wrapped in religiosity and sacred ritual. Cultish practice, albeit semisecularized later on, would remain an important aspect of spa culture down through the ages.

Where there were religious cults there were, of course, gods and goddesses. The premier god of medical healing in the ancient Greek world was Asclepius (fifth century BCE), son of Apollo and Coronis. Conveniently, Asclepius had five lovely daughters acting as his assistants: Hygeia, responsible for cleanliness and sanitation; Iaso, a specialist in convalescence; Aglaea, goddess of beauty, adornment, and hair care; Aceso, expert in ointments, unguents, herbs, and antiaging creams; and Panacea, goddess of universal remedy and therefore patron saint of the entire spa movement.

Not surprisingly, given this battery of talent behind it, the Asclepius cult, staffed by both priests and physicians, spread quickly through the entire ancient Greek imperium.* Soon patients in need of serious medical attention, or perhaps just a cosmetic tune-up, had only to repair to the nearest Asclepius center, easily identifiable by a statue of the medical god holding a serpent-entwined staff.

Why the snake? Live snakes, some poisonous and some not, were used in the healing process, and in fact a typical Asclepius facility was crawling with serpents as well as priests and doctors, a potent (and sometimes lethal) combination. Adding to the excitement was the ready availability of opiates at Asclepius facilities such as Epidaurus. As one authority has written: "The medical priests [of Asclepius] administered opium to those who visited Epidaurus to seek a cure for illness. The sick slept in the sanctuary of the temple, the priests procuring healing dreams for them."

Because the Asclepius cures were sometimes worse than the diseases, the healing centers had their own cemeteries. These were always situated on the peripheries so that patients need not be overly troubled by reminders of unsuccessful cures. (In this practice, too, modern spa towns would borrow from the ancients.)†

---

*The Asclepius cult in ancient Rome was most prominently represented by a third-century BCE temple on an island in the River Tiber. This island has served as a healing center ever since. Today it is home to the Fatebenefratelli Hospital, run by the Hospitaller Order of St. John of God.

† Malvern in England contains, in my view, one of the saddest spa-town graves of all time: that of Charles Darwin's eldest daughter, Annie, who died in 1851 at age ten from tuberculosis following an arduous cure regimen directed by Dr. James Gully, who had also treated Darwin himself. Darwin was so devastated by Annie's death that he could never return to Malvern, but he did not lose faith in the water cure: he simply took his custom to other British spas.

There is yet another way in which ancient spa culture anticipated the modern: judgments regarding the efficacy of the various curative treatments were deeply entwined with the power of suggestion, with the placebo effect of feeling better because you *wanted* to feel better and because the doctors *told* you that you were better. In the Asclepius cult, for example, priests guided all phases of healing with revelations and signs from resident oracles, who also informed the patients when they could stop their daily regimens of baths and bloodlettings and simply go home. Perhaps, like Alexander the Great when consulting a famed oracle regarding his parentage (his mother was said to have mated with a snake, but he preferred Zeus as a progenitor), curists bribed the oracular interpreters to get the results they wanted.

No doubt most patients were happy enough to leave the healing centers, but there must have been some early Munchausen types who actually *relished* the often strenuous therapeutic rituals, not to mention the narcotic drugs on hand. It may not have been Munchausen syndrome or drugs, but *something* kept the writer Aelius Aristides for *thirteen years* at the famed Asklepion at Pergamum (which still functions today as a hydropathic healing facility).

Upon completing their cures, early spa patrons, again like modern ones, were expected to dig deeply into their pocketbooks. Payments depended on the patients' purses, but wealthy curists typically gave handsome gifts to adorn the facilities, sometimes adding to major amenities like open-air theaters, such as the large and acoustically sophisticated amphitheater at Epidaurus.

The presence of playhouses, along with eating halls and gaming rooms, rapidly became de rigueur not just at the Asclepius centers but also at the gymnasia—those elaborate sporting venues where wealthy young men engaged in rigorous physical exercise followed by drinks, a snack, a round of dice or knucklebones, and inevitably a cleansing, curative bath. The baths attached to the gymnasia typically were cold—cold immersions being considered healthier and manlier than hot ones, a conviction that some Romans (not to mention headmasters at Victorian boarding schools) later came to share.

At the gymnasia men generally played nude, just as they did in the ancient Olympic Games. Oily, sweaty wrestling matches often segued into oily, sweaty sex. In addition to invigorating trysts, there might also be stimulating discussions about the latest theatrical production or lectures by noted philosophers, who themselves were not loath to join in the fun.

Many Greek cities (at least in Attica) also boasted public baths independent of the gymnasia. At all such public facilities strict hygienic regimes prevailed, involving, in addition to bathing, vigorous rubdowns with scented oils and scrape-downs with edged bronze implements called strigils. Professional "bath men" or slaves brought along by the bathers rendered these services. (Resourcefully, the bath attendants often collected in little vials the gunk they scraped off the bodies of famous Olympic athletes and sold this stuff to female fans as face cream.)

Unlike the gymnasia, many of the public bathhouses possessed heated tubs, a luxury that young Athenian swells could quickly get used to. As for the rival Spartans, they looked with contempt on water baths of any sort, hot or cold. Although they developed a primitive vapor bath and dipped newborn infants in wine, Spartan men insisted for the most part upon retaining their virile grime and stink. (The Spartans found themselves banned from the Olympic Games in 424 BCE because, true to form, they could not resist breaking the "sacred truce" that was supposed to keep the games free of the otherwise incessant internecine warfare. Yet the Spartans' disgusting hygienic habits could well have been another reason for kicking them out.)

In ancient Greece water and wine went together—quite literally, since wines typically were diluted with water before being consumed. At their gymnasia and public baths, Greek men liked to drink wine, lots of wine, while soaking in the tubs. Although full-scale inebriation was frowned upon at the baths, prudish sobriety was even more scorned. Men who insisted on drinking *only* water were thought to radiate a noxious odor. When two notorious water drinkers, Anchmolus and Moschus, entered the public baths, everyone else got out.

If the Greeks, rather quietly, pioneered many aspects of modern spa practice, the Romans, not quietly at all, brought the water-cure culture to its ancient-world apogee from the second century BCE to the fall of the Western Empire in the late fifth century CE. Indeed, the Roman imperial spa world at its sophisticated height would not be approached again in magnificence until the grand thermal spring resorts of Central Europe attained *their* pinnacle of fame and influence in the nineteenth century.

The Romans' therapeutic bathing culture, like that of the Greeks, included artificially heated pools as well as natural mineral springs both hot and cold. While in a technical sense the latter institutions would have to be considered the nearer precursors of the great mineral-spring healing resorts of nineteenth- and twentieth-century Europe, the entire bath culture of ancient Rome ultimately fed into the modern spa phenomenon.

Artificially heated public baths, called *thermae*, and mineral spring baths, whose most opulent examples were termed *aquae*, played an absolutely central role in the civilization of ancient Rome. While the grandest thermae were built in the Eternal City itself, most of the aquae, dependent on the whims of nature, flourished outside the capital, the earliest ones close by, the later ones springing up, so to speak, all across the expanding empire. As Mary Beard puts it in her history of Pompeii, "Wherever the Romans went, so too did Roman baths."

For bathing rituals, amenities, and architecture, the great thermae erected in the capital were particularly formative. Like the infamous gladiatorial contests, most of these grand public institutions existed through the largesse provided by various Caesars to their subjects. As a point of contact between bread-and-circus benevolence and popular culture, however, the baths were considerably more positive than the carnage in the Colosseum. But just like that great arena, the largest of the public bath complexes provided important blueprints for grand buildings down through the ages. For example, the Baths of Caracalla helped inspire not only many later spa buildings but also monuments of twentieth-century American travel such as the old Pennsylvania Station and Grand Central Station in New York City.

Within Rome itself, the first of the great public baths was established by Marcus Agrippa (c. 64 BCE–12 BCE), a statesman, general, and close colleague of Octavian, the future Caesar Augustus. This complex, erected in around 25 BCE, put to shame the earlier public baths of the Republican era, which had charged small fees, as well as the more opulent private "bathrooms" found in some villas and palaces. The city of Rome's inventory of fee-charging public baths numbered 170 in a census of 33 BCE but had climbed to over 1,000 some 175 years later, when Pliny the Elder was writing his epochal *Natural History*, which included much lore on healing waters. About a hundred major aquae, scattered around the growing empire, were also recorded in Pliny's time.

Since most of these commercial bathing facilities were rather paltry affairs, often little more than brothels with a slimy tub or two, the first of the grand municipal endowments must have impressed even jaded Romans. Yet the standards of opulence and cleanliness set by Agrippa's public bath were soon trumped by ever grander establishments associated with the emperors Nero, Titus, Domitian, Trajan, Caracalla, and Diocletian. (Trajan's Baths, by the way, recycled in their foundations the walls and vaults of Nero's never-completed "Golden House.")

Nowadays, the Baths of Caracalla stand as the most famous of the ancient Roman baths because this complex's expansive ruins are easily accessible to tourists and archeologists alike. Of course, there are no longer any bathers to be seen at the evocative ruins, but one still finds prostitutes and con men lurking about, just as one did in the ancient era.* Tellingly, Mussolini's fascist regime hoped to use the Caracalla ruins as the venue for wrestling matches at the 1944 Rome Olympics—but, alas, those games had to be canceled on account of a rather less playful contest going on around the world at the same time. In more recent years, the Caracalla ruins have provided a perfect setting for al fresco grand opera, most notably productions of Verdi's *Aida*, replete with horses, chariots, camels, and the obligatory hordes of Nubians. As for the even larger Baths of Diocletian, the huge site they once occupied now houses Michelangelo's church of Santa Maria degli Angeli e dei Martiri, as well as the National Museum of Rome. Located nearby, fittingly, is the highly educational Museo della Terme.

Although the great Roman thermae varied somewhat in size and opulence, all had a number of basic features integral to the bathing culture of the capital and other imperial cities. At the center of these sprawling complexes stood the bath buildings proper, consisting of dressing rooms (*apodyteria*); a gently heated vaulted chamber called the *tepidarium*; a cold plunge pool known as the *frigidarium*; and finally the immensely comfortable *caldarium*, a rotunda lit by the sun and heated both by solar power and vapors circulating beneath the floor. Surrounding these primary

---

*Many years ago, I myself was the credulous victim of a well-known scam at the Baths of Caracalla. A fellow claiming to be a sales representative for Ermeneglio Zegna accosted me outside the baths, giving me a sob story about having run out of petrol and needing money to get to an important meeting. In exchange for about $30 worth of lira, he presented me with a "genuine" Zegna jacket, worth at most half that.

facilities were smaller structures where favored patrons could bathe in private, along with a large bronze swimming basin kept at optimal temperatures by a wood-burning furnace (*hypocaust*) located directly below it. For the very hardy, there were also extremely high-temperature *sudatoria* that brought out a good sweat, similar to our contemporary steam rooms or Turkish baths.

Next to the bathing facilities were Greek-inspired palaestrae or gymnasia, where the naked, sweating bathers could get even sweatier by engaging in various forms of vigorous exercise. Also as in Greece, but on a much grander scale, patrons had access to on-premises eating halls, taverns, gaming rooms, massage parlors, barber and depilatory shops, libraries, museums, and medical services equipped with all the latest herbs, potions, unguents, and *narcotica*. (As in Greece, opiates were widely available at the Roman baths, where they were used much as they are today—both for medicinal and recreational purposes.)

Unlike the smaller Republican-era commercial baths, not to mention the Greek gymnasia, the grand imperial thermae did not draw their water from wells or cisterns but from huge aqueducts, themselves great marvels of ancient engineering. The combination of technical skill and civic vigor necessary to keep this entire operation afloat was unique to the Roman Empire. To be able to participate in this magnificent culture constituted a major part of what it meant to be a Roman.

But which Romans are we talking about? The first thing to be said about the patrons of the thermae (and also the aquae) is that they were more diverse than the generally well-off and exclusively male clientele of the Greek gymnasia. Because the great Roman public baths were free, even the poor could enter them. Slaves were admitted as well—generally as attendants of their masters but sometimes, surprisingly, also as customers. Unlike in Greece, women soon gained access to the baths, and for several centuries there was even mixed-gender bathing, another sign, perhaps, of an unprecedented sexual freedom that recent classical scholars have identified as a prerogative of Roman women. The females in question certainly included prostitutes, but "respectable" married and unmarried women frequented the baths as well. The women varied in age from coltish nymphets to bewhiskered crones. Old or young, married or not, the women in the mixed baths undoubtedly cavorted with their male counterparts, and perhaps with each other, in what some frescoes atop the wall of a changing room in a public bathhouse at Pompeii clearly show as "athletic sexual intercourse" (Mary Beard's phrase). Most of these scenes involve conventional twosomes, but there is also a ménage à trois and even (I can vouch for this myself) a foursome engaged in a truly contortionist maneuver.

Like the Greeks—yet again, even more so—the Romans combined wine drinking with bathing. This was famously true at Pompeii, which was a major center of Roman wine cultivation. Furious drinkers, the Pompeiians used the baths both to sweat out previous binges and to fortify themselves for more bingeing to come. According to one contemporary observer, after a thorough preheating, Pompeii bathers, "without putting on a stitch of clothing, still naked and gasping, [would] seize hold of a huge jar . . . and, as if to demonstrate their strength, pour down the entire contents . . . vomit it up again immediately, and then drink another jar. This they repeat two or three times over, as if they were born to waste wine and as if wine could be disposed of only through the agency of the human body."

Finally, the Roman baths were good places in which to pull the plug, as it were, when one was ready to go. Marcellinus (d. 468 CE), a Roman general and patrician who ruled over Dalmatia, laid himself down in a very hot public bath after fasting for several days. As the last breaths steamed out of him he babbled to his friends about the sumptuous pleasure he was experiencing.

Unsurprisingly, such bathhouse adventures were not to everyone's taste, and the entire culture of public bathing, especially public mixed-sex bathing, came under increasing criticism. Conventional wisdom among classical scholars has it that Emperor Hadrian, a notorious spoilsport, put an end to the practice of coed bathing at some point between 117 and 138 CE. However, newer research, making use of previously untapped Christian sources, suggests that mixed-gender bathing continued in a few places all the way up to the early fifth century.

While some baths banned women entirely in the post-Hadrian era, many others added separate facilities for women. The complexes with separate gender facilities typically located the female wing close enough to the men's to allow common use of the expensive *hypocaust*—and probably also to facilitate some sneaking back and forth. Baths wishing to remain open to both sexes but lacking segregated gender facilities could accommodate Hadrian's decree by mandating separate bathing hours for men and women. At these places, the general rule seems to have been for women to bathe in the morning and men in the afternoon. As in so much of classical scholarship, however, the surviving documentary evidence regarding precisely who did what and when and with whom at the Roman baths is about as substantial as a bar of soap in hot water.

Owing to the diversity of their clientele, Roman public baths are often said to have been great social levelers. One scholar has described them as "a hole in the ozone layer of the [Roman] social hierarchy." There could be some truth in this. Nudity undoubtedly helped bring all the bathers down to a common denominator, and it can't have been pretty. The bodies of the poor may actually have been marginally less hideous than those of the bloated rich, for whom self-restraint at the table usually meant frequent vomiting. Yet this leveling business should not be oversold. Social distinctions still made themselves manifest. Wealthy patrons appeared at the thermae with retinues of slaves and could opt for the costly private bathing facilities if they so chose. The rich could also afford to bring their own fancy bath kits, so as not to have to share strigils with the plebes. And, as in modern gyms, where floor-to-ceiling mirrors often constitute the most important piece of equipment, the self-regarding atmosphere at the Roman thermae seems to have been anything but harmoniously egalitarian. Contemporary stories set in these institutions are filled with sharp observations about competitive preening, jealousy, and mean-spirited joking about fellow bathers' hunchbacks, harelips, goiters, bunions, clubfeet, and other unfortunate afflictions. The poet Martial wrote a revealing piece about a bather who laughed at another man's hernias, only to discover that he had developed a nasty bleeder-button of his own.

Anything as pleasurable and opulent as the thermae predictably aroused disapproval and even scorn among self-appointed guardians of an older and sterner morality. Keepers of the guttering Republican flame naturally fell into this category. Typically, they saw the thermae as perfumed imports from decadent Greece, a civilization that tellingly lacked a word for "incest." To an old scold like Seneca, for whom the good life was equivalent to an ascetic one, the great baths were yet another sign of how far imperial Rome had strayed from the virtuous ways of the republic.

Sweating, Seneca averred, should be achieved not by hot baths but by good hard work, as was the way in the glory days of Scipio Africanus. In Scipio's day, Seneca added, Roman warriors may have smelled bad due to infrequent ablutions, but that "bad" smell was in reality the manly odor of "the camp, the farm, and heroism." Now that spic-and-span bathing establishments had been introduced, he concluded, men were "actually fouler than of yore."

Although Seneca's criticism of the baths was based primarily on lofty moral considerations, he seems also to have been animated by a personal grudge with which even the more libertine among us might sympathize:

> I live over some baths. Imagine the assortment of sounds, which make me hate the very power of hearing. When the muscle boys are exercising and pumping the lead weights, when they are working out, or pretending to, I hear their grunting. . . . Finally imagine the hair-plucker with his strident, shrill voice, never holding it in, except when he's plucking someone's armpit and making his client yelp instead.

Pliny the Elder, too, commented on the fall from virtue represented by the sumptuous imperial baths. He noted that old Fabricus (an austere republican who had held office in the late third century BCE) would have been shocked by all "these displays of luxury . . . and women bathing with men." In another passage, Pliny wondered what the austere Roman leaders of Cato's time would have thought about "boiling baths" in which men cavorted together with women who were so shameless as "to expose their pubes (*pectines*) to public view."

It should be added that even the thermae devotees themselves occasionally showed some understanding that their kind of voluptuous bathing could, instead of improving their health, actually have deleterious effects. A first-century CE Roman tombstone includes the following Stoic irony in its inscription: "Wine, sex and baths ruin our bodies, but they are the stuff of life—wine, sex and baths."

While to austere champions of the erstwhile republic the faux-clean imperial thermae fostered a degenerate culture of shameless hussies and noisy muscle boys, for Christian critics, initially impotent but increasingly influential, Roman-style bathing, especially mixed-gender bathing, was an affront to God. Clement of Alexandria (150–215 CE), who was one of those early Christians who provided clear evidence for mixed bathing, also offered the first surviving Christian condemnation of it. He insisted point blank that "bathing for pleasure" was impermissible in the eyes of God. Naturally, what Clement believed about baths held true also for sex, which in his view must be practiced solely for procreation. Although, unusually for an early Christian (or for a good many later ones, come to think of it), Clement advocated equality between the sexes, he blamed what he saw as the growing licentiousness of Roman bath culture squarely on women, who went so far as "to dine and get drunk while bathing." Warming to his topic, Clement went on to fulminate against women who stripped naked in front of their male slaves and then gave the latter "permission for lusty, fearless touching."

What more needed to be said? Actually, it turned out, quite a lot more, but there is no need here to chronicle the growing chorus of Christian indignation regarding "impure" bathing practices that lasted until the fall of Rome and well beyond.

While the bathing rituals at the great Roman thermae were believed to have therapeutic as well as hygienic value, the practice of taking the waters at the mineral spring aquae was naturally bound up with yet more ambitious claims regarding medicinal efficacy. For this reason, the aquae were also easier to defend. On the other hand, the promise of healing could generate its own forms of excess, such as bathing overly long or drinking enormous quantities of mineral water. Having chastised those who spent an *entire day* sitting in the baths, Pliny went on to lambaste those who bragged about the heroic amount of mineral water they drank. "I have seen some already swollen with drinking to such an extent that their rings were covered by skin, since they could not void the vast amount of water they had swallowed."

As it developed over the years, Rome's inventory of mineral springs and attendant water-cure therapies grew into an enormous hydropathic industry—and one that catered to far more than real or imagined afflictions of the body. Some of the more renowned springs were quite close to the capital. Nearby Aquae Cutilae, for example, was famous for its exceptionally cold waters, which Celsus (a second-century CE philosopher and critic of early Christianity), along with Pliny, touted for their efficacy in treating stomach disorders. Aquae Albulae, situated between Rome and Tivoli, was according to Pliny the place to go to heal all manner of wounds, although Augustus went there for his rheumatism.

In fact, it is primarily for this last affliction that the Albulae spring complex, later renamed "la Solfatara," is still used today.

The most famous—or infamous—water-cure resort in Italy proper was undoubtedly Baiae, located on the north shore of the Bay of Naples. Baiae's spectacular beauty was one of its main draws—just as "location, location, location" would be instrumental to the popularity of many grand spas later on. Even more crucially—and here, too, is a hint of the future—Baiae became the hydropathic venue of choice for ancient Romans because of an array of sideshows that had little to do with healing. But before moving on to those other attractions, as the Romans themselves quickly did, I should note that Baiae's therapeutic powers won high praise from the usual suspects: Celsus spoke rapturously of the sulfurous sweat baths "in the myrtle groves above Baiae"; Strabo said Baiae's hot thermal springs were suited to the needs of even the most fastidious curists; and the voluble Pliny gushed, "Nowhere . . . is water more bountiful than in the Bay of Baiae or with more variety of relief."

One suspects that these authorities were getting carried away with themselves. While the prospect of relief from serious illness or just aches and pains undoubtedly prompted many a good Roman to make the trek down to Baiae, what really enticed people, especially wealthy people, to stay on a regular basis and to turn this lovely place into the empire's hottest vacation retreat, littered with opulent second homes and all the other amenities that rich people needed, was a play scene whose decadence impressed even the likes of Tiberius, Caligula, and Nero. (No doubt if that latter-day "emperor of Viagra," Silvio Berlusconi, had been around then, he too would have been down at Baiae, swinging along with his teenage tarts in an ancient version of his bunga-bunga parties.) During the peak summer season, drunken revelers moved from one swimming party to the next, never bothering to get dressed.

Naturally, like the grand thermae back in the capital, Baiae had its detractors. Varro, a sanctimonious scholar, fumed that at this supposed place of healing, "unmarried women are common property, old men behave like boys, and lots of young boys act like young girls." As an added frisson, a fatal attraction so to speak, Baiae offered the exciting possibility of being buried alive in pumice, for Mt. Vesuvius loomed over the region and might erupt at any moment—as of course it did in 79 CE, putting an abrupt end to many a frivolity.

As I mentioned earlier, wherever the conquering Romans went in the barbarian world, they took their bath culture with them—much as, some two millennia later, American military service families abroad would invariably import little pieces of Peoria. This "wherever-they-went" claim with regard to the Romans should be taken quite literally. In an amazingly short period, the Roman legions built—or, more often, built onto—thermal bathing facilities in every corner of their far-flung empire. Some of those distant outposts were to become household words in the later European spa world: Aix, Vichy, Aachen, Baden (German-speaking Switzerland), Baden-Baden (Germany), Wiesbaden (Germany), and Bath in England.

Ancient Bath, though not belonging to the Central European spa culture at the heart of this book, deserves some commentary here because its Roman-era incarnation was especially impressive (as are its partially excavated ruins today). These extant ruins and the many artifacts found in them provide us with some of our best clues regarding what life must have been like in such a far-flung spawn of Mother Rome. Characteristically, the thermal spring system that became Rome's westernmost spa had long been in use by native peoples before the legions penetrated southern Britain under Julius Caesar in 55–54 BCE. (Caesar himself, by the way, never went to the springs at Bath, though he loved to take the waters during his march through Gaul, and his famous motto might well have been amended to read, "I came, I saw, I bathed." It is only fitting that in 1894 the city of Bath erected a statue of this great water-culture imperialist next to the ruins of the Roman baths.) As for pre-Roman Bath, we know from archeological evidence that the springs there were being used some seven thousand years ago by Paleolithic hunters, who undoubtedly took pleasure in lazing about in the hot waters after chasing down an elusive great elk. The Celts are also known to have frequented these springs, which they considered sacred to their primary goddess, Sulis.

Bath's first recorded mention as a salubrious spring dates back to a delightful legend probably concocted by Geoffrey of Monmouth, a twelfth-century Welsh cleric. According to this tale, a Celtic prince named Bladud, who had been banished by his father for having contracted leprosy, took up pig farming in the region around Bath. Unfortunately, Bladud's pigs also caught the dreaded disease (the prince was undoubtedly lonely), with the result that Bladud seemed washed up as a swineherd. One day, however, he noticed that his pigs were shedding their leprous symptoms after wallowing in some hot mineral waters. The prince accordingly plunged in himself, emerging miraculously cured. He promptly returned home, took control of his father's kingdom, and built a new capital next to the healing spring. Caer Baden, he called the place. (Predictably, the charming Bladud story was eventually dismissed as "ridiculous" by rationalist historians in the eighteenth century, and local boosters came to favor an exclusive focus on the Romans as the true founders of Bath.)

The springs at Caer Baden remained important to Celtic tribes for both medicinal and religious reasons. The tribes believed that the waters could exert their healing powers only after the reigning goddess, Sulis, had been placated with gifts, generally in the form of coins. Sensitive as they were to native religious customs, the Romans slaughtered the Druid priests at Caer Baden but retained the goddess Sulis, twining her with their own goddess Minerva to create the double-duty deity Sulis Minerva. After putting down a bloody revolt led by the "Amazon" warrior-queen Boudicca in 60 CE, the Romans built a new temple at the springs dedicated to Sulis Minerva. They named their fortress town Aquae Sulis.

The bathing facility that gradually evolved next to the temple at Aquae Sulis was one of the most elaborate in Rome's Western Empire. Much like the aquae back home, it consisted of a sprawling complex of hot and cold pools, covered with timbered roofs and connecting tiled walkways. Three different springs channeled the waters to the pools via a complicated system of lead and copper piping. An equally sophisticated set of flues and chimneys allowed hot air from wood-burning hypocausts to circulate beneath the treatment rooms. Initially male and female bathers (the ladies coming mostly from local stock) could take the waters together, but the ban on mixed-gender bathing by Emperor Hadrian seems to have put a damper on this happy practice. Rather than instituting separate hours for men and women, as many Roman spas did in the post-Hadrian era, Aquae Sulis sensibly built additional facilities for women so that both sexes could bathe at the same time (and perhaps find ways to do it together, as of old).

Like their counterparts stationed elsewhere around the empire, Roman citizens and their hangers-on residing at Aquae Sulis did not repair to the springs solely to salve their aches and pains or perchance to socialize: they also went there to request recompense from their water goddess for some slight or injury done to them. Aggrieved curists could have the resident temple scribe compose a letter to Sulis Minerva detailing the offenses against them, naming the offenders, and suggesting appropriate punishments—say, blinding, impotence, or beheading. The letters, inscribed on sheets of pewter, were tossed into one of the pools, along with an appropriate offering to the goddess. Because many of these pewter-sheet curses survived the slow deterioration of the imperial bathing complex and also the sloppy excavation efforts beginning in the eighteenth century, we have a revealing window into the social life of this prominent Roman-era spa. Among other edifying facts, we learn that the ancients did not take lightly offenses to their honor or purse: steal a lady's shoes and the requested punishment might be death; question a man's virility and castration was just the ticket.

Closer to home—and closer also to the home in this book—lay a small settlement in the gentle Oos Valley a few miles east of the mighty Rhine called Aquae by the Roman legionnaires who founded the place in 74–75 CE. No doubt earlier peoples had used the hot spring waters upon which some Roman soldiers had conveniently stumbled a few years earlier, but we have no clear evidence of this. Since this bucolic little valley had no strategic use to the invading Romans, it must have been those wonderful hot waters that induced them to construct a wooden fortress there, which they soon replaced with a much more elaborate marble-coated administrative structure and the full complement of enclosed pools, steam rooms, workout facilities, and recovery/recreation stations essential to any Roman spa. What apparently justified such an elaborate outlay was not only the local waters' exceptional heat (at 67 Celsius, they were the hottest yet to have been found) but also their highly salubrious minerals, including sodium, chloride, fluoride, lithium, calcium, and potassium. Moreover, the springs were magnificently *abundant*, spewing out some eight hundred thousand liters per day.

Not surprisingly, Aquae soon became a very popular rest and recreation venue for legionnaires operating in the area. In a testament to the soldiers' belief that they received genuinely useful treatment for their afflictions, or at least a pleasant respite from their unceasing battles against the barbarians, legionnaires donated sculptures of their favorites gods and goddesses to the complex. Sometimes an entire military unit pooled its resources to endow a very large monument. Soldiers' dependents, administrators, and, with time, the various service providers that congregated around any Roman military post also made use of the baths and contributed to their glorification.

Under Emperor Trajan (r. 98–117 CE), Aquae attained enough local stature to become the capital of an administrative district of considerable size, stretching from the Rhine in the west to the Black Forest in the east. Over the next century, growth continued at a modest pace, the baths getting sufficient regular use to require new additions, steady maintenance, and, in the third century, extensive restoration work. A plaque found in the ruins of old Aquae dedicated to Emperor Caracalla (r. 211–217 CE) suggests that he may personally have had a hand in the restoration effort; it is probable, in fact, that the bathing complex which Caracalla visited while fighting the Alemanni tribe in 213 CE was Aquae. Alas, the success in 260 CE of those same Alemanni in breaking through the Limes (the fortified line protecting Roman territory), overrunning Aquae, and forcing a permanent Roman retreat from the area ended the first blossoming of spa amenities at what would later become Baden-Baden.

Decline and Resurrection

Within the Roman imperial spa world, Aquae was one of the earlier casualties of Rome's long decline and fall. Soon hundreds of other water-cure outposts of imperial Rome would meet the same fate. As early as the sixth and seventh centuries, the sumptuous spas that had so recently given succor to Romans everywhere were already turning into vegetation-covered ruins—Piranesi etchings in the making.

Truth to tell, though, many of the Roman aquae and thermae had begun to rot from within even before their degeneration into picturesque ruins. Like the Olympic Games under Roman administration, the baths became ever sleazier and more debased. Lackadaisical hygiene turned the bathing pools into enormous petri dishes—perfect incubators of infectious disease. Matters were hardly helped by the proclivity of Roman soldiers to treat the baths as regular trysting venues, where they generously passed on their favorite sexually transmitted diseases, principally that dreaded "Pox Romano," gonorrhea, to the local ladies. For some critics of Roman bathing, the very heat of the thermal waters had been problematical; they attributed the empire's decline in part to a malign influence of hot baths on men's testicles.

One is not supposed to use the term "Dark Ages" anymore, but in the three or four centuries following the Western Roman Empire's official collapse in 476 CE, the public bathing culture across Europe was exceedingly dim. As the imperial bath complexes fell into ever greater desuetude, the practice of large-scale public bathing declined sharply without ever disappearing entirely—unlike that other classical funfest frowned on by pious Christians, the Olympic Games, which after years of decline were banned by Emperor Theodosius in 391 CE, seventy-eight years after Emperor Constantine had converted to Christianity and decreed toleration for that religion in the empire.

The fact that the Roman baths and spas, like the Olympic Games, were seen by Rome's new Christian rulers as vestiges of pagan decadence was undeniably a major factor in their precipitous decline. St. Jerome (347–420 CE), an influential theologian and translator whose youthful escapades with free-spirited Roman girls left him with a lasting suspicion of the opposite sex, became censorious of the Roman baths due to their alleged hotting-up effect on women, who in his view were quite hot enough by nature already. For Jerome, the baths fostered promiscuity by warming the female blood and also by making ladies more attentive to their physical attractions, whose sole purpose anyway was to entrap unwary men. Rather than cultivating beauty, a good Christian woman must, in his view, "make haste to spoil her natural good looks."

Christian antipathy was not the whole story here, however. The Gothic tribes who sacked and pillaged their way across the Western Roman Empire admired some classical institutions, but the baths were not among them. If these Goths washed themselves at all, they did so in rivers or lakes. Not only did the barbarians smash up beautiful tubs and pools, they wrecked the great aqueducts that fed them.

In the end, though, the major cause for the erosion of ancient Rome's bathing and water-cure culture cannot be attributed to the workings of barbarians or Christians: it followed naturally from the atrophy of the intricate infrastructure that had made all this possible in the first place. Relative social stability and political centralization, good roads, bountiful state and private coffers, tolerant mores, and, above all, sophisticated engineering skills had kept the baths and ancient spas going; when those things fell by the wayside, so, too, did the Roman water culture.

Yet even in the darkest days not *all* sumptuous bathing went down the drain. Ironically, while the great Roman public bathing complexes were returning to nature, wealthy clerical leaders still splashed about in opulent *private* baths. No enemy of luxury, at least for himself, Bishop Victor of Ravenna adorned the bathroom in his episcopal palace with dazzling mosaics and marbles. Even more impressive was a "secret" bathroom in the Vatican called the Stufetta del Bibbiena, so named after Cardinal Bibbiena, a worldly Renaissance-era cleric who in 1516 commissioned Raphael to decorate his bathroom in the papal apartments with erotic frescoes emulating recently excavated Roman ruins. The cardinal and later various popes could soak in a hot tub while gazing at a still-life *Satyricon* featuring naked nymphs and satyrs, most notably randy old Pan himself, who could be seen leaping out of the bushes with an enormous erection.

All along, albeit less resplendently, many monasteries maintained extensive bathing facilities for their inmates. Monastic bathing was not undertaken for bodily pleasure, much less for erotic bliss—or so it was claimed. In any event, while we can surely say that cleanliness was *not* next to godliness for the vast majority of early medieval Christians, it certainly could be so for God's stand-ins and pious servants.

Meanwhile, back in Rome, one of God's top ventriloquists was taking a very different approach than Cardinal Bibbiena to the city's ancient bathing legacy. Pope Sixtus V, the most hard-line of all the Counter-Reformation popes, hated pagan relics so passionately that he took special pleasure, and great pains, in destroying them. Among the ruins he attacked were those of the Baths of Diocletian, upon whose destruction he spent 5,339 scudi. It was on the site of Diocletian's frigidarium that Michelangelo placed his Santa Maria degli Angeli. And it was in this same splendid church that, some three-hundred years later, Pope Pius IX (he of "Syllabus of Errors" fame and the last pontiff to unite himself in spiritual and temporal power) opened the "Roman Exposition of All Arts Created by Catholicism" (December 1868–July 1870). The purpose of this exposition was to document Catholicism's triumph over paganism as well as Pio Nono's own bitter opposition to the new Italian state, political liberalism, and that modern cultural permissiveness which, in his eyes, recalled the decadence of Diocletian.

We properly attribute the rebirth of faded classical glories to the Italian Renaissance, but in the realm of public bathing for pleasure and health, this revival, or partial revival, began earlier, in the High Middle Ages. Thus Jules Michelet's famous bon mot about the medieval period—"*mille années sans un bain*"—is more witty than accurate. In another of those ironies with which the history of spas abounds, the Roman-era public baths and corollary water-cure culture were in part rescued by the same agency, militant Christianity, which had helped to bring it all down. More specifically, the crusaders, who set out to expel Islam from the Holy Land, returned from their misbegotten missions with several good things, among them the Turkish *hamam*. As this Near Eastern import gradually became a fixture in Western and Central Europe, it underwent some alterations derived from earlier Roman customs. To the Turkish and Arab practice of sprawling on benches in superheated chambers, the Europeans added squatting in tubs and also pouring flagons of heated water over their heads: early versions of the shower douche. Like the Roman aquae, the medieval bathhouses boasted tables covered with medicinal herbs, unguents, and potions—not to mention bottles of hungry leeches and little suction-cup devices for controlled bloodletting. Over time, the medieval bathing and water-cure culture became highly organized. Bath attendants and bath doctors received specialized training; bath professionals formed their own guilds in many towns; and to become a master bathman one had to perform a *Meisterstück* of bath caregiving.

Because it was an arduous operation to maintain a medieval bathhouse—businesses and households had no running water, not to mention *heated* running water—fees for the use of these facilities could be steep. This meant that it was the bourgeoisie who mainly frequented the urban commercial baths. In the German region, however, extra bath money, called *Badegeld*, which was added regularly to workers' salaries, made it possible for the lower orders to bathe from time to time. This *Badegeld*, by the way, can be seen as a precursor to the paid spa visits included in the beneficent medical insurance packages provided to most West German workers in the second half of the twentieth century.

Even more crucial to the recovery of a full-fledged bathing and water-cure regime was the avidity with which medieval entrepreneurs set about reopening and refurbishing some of the long-moldering Roman spa complexes. In the case of Aquae Sulis, which had never died out entirely, this refurbishment started early, with late seventh-century Saxons not only making some improvements to the baths but also adding a monastery, thus continuing that facility's tradition of attending simultaneously to body and soul. It was the Saxons, too, who gave this place a new name, Hat Bathu, from which the town's modern name derives.

Belgium's Spa had to wait considerably longer for its medieval facelift, which, in 1326, coincided with the discovery of some new chalybeate springs by an ironmonger from Liège. Baden in Switzerland and its similarly named German equivalent, whose Roman-era facilities were likewise never entirely abandoned, both enjoyed a modest renaissance in the twelfth century, setting them up for later fame.

Meanwhile, down in Italy, warm baths slowly came back in vogue. (In that country, the late-medieval baths were often called *stufato*—"stews"—slang for brothels.) A mid-fourteenth-century water-cure authority, Gentile di Foligno, argued strongly that cold baths were deeply unhealthy, although, characteristically, that maniac puritan Savonarola would countenance only frigidly cold treatments during his short-lived "divine republic" in Florence. At the same moment, Savonarola's superiors in Rome were putting out orders to ban public bathing entirely in an unsuccessful effort to curb the spread of syphilis.*

Especially in Germany, where public nudity never was (and still is not) a major hang-up, *Volk* of both sexes often took their cleansing and healing ablutions together sans coverings of any kind, except perhaps on their heads. In sixteenth-century Baden, an *Armenbad*, or bath for the poor, allowed mixed bathing until the Jesuits, who had gained great influence in the area, stepped in to ban the practice. The Germans, it should also be said, did not have to wait for the Crusades to revive forms of public cleansing and healing water culture; earlier on they had borrowed hot vapor baths from the Russians, who themselves had not needed the Romans to know about hot steam baths. In 973, an Arab diplomat was pleasantly surprised to find refreshing saunas in Saxony and Bohemia, rudimentary harbingers of Karlsbad and Marienbad.

---

*This action by the church brings to mind efforts by San Francisco health authorities in the 1980s to halt the spread of AIDS at gay bathhouses. Although a court order outlawed only the renting of private rooms at the baths, many of the houses decided to shut down.

Over in Aix-la-Chapelle (Aachen), Emperor Charlemagne bathed in the revived Roman baths together with hundreds of friends, male and female alike. Other evidence of men and women ablating together in a *Schwitzbad* comes from a series of miniature engravings contained in the *Sachsenspiegel* of the Hussite era.

As always, public bathing in the nude had its detractors. One of the most noted of these was the Italian Renaissance scholar and book hunter Poggio Bracciolini, who among other accomplishments discovered Lucretius's ancient poem *On the Nature of Things* in an impoverished Benedictine abbey in Germany. More importantly for our purposes, Poggio left behind an extensive account of a visit he made in 1495 to the medieval baths at Baden (Switzerland). Poggio was no provincial puritan, but what he witnessed in Baden shocked him. As he wrote to a friend in Florence, he saw "old women as well as younger ones going naked into the water before the eyes of men and displaying their private parts and their buttocks to the onlookers." A lattice-like barrier separating the men's and women's sections did not prevent the two sexes from ogling each other, drinking together, and even touching each other. "Amazingly," Poggio continued, "men watched their wives being handled by strangers and were not disturbed by it; they paid no attention and took it all in the best possible spirit."

Although Poggio could have used a medicinal tune-up himself, he could not bring himself actually to take the waters at Baden. After all, he wrote, "it seemed to me ridiculous that a man from Italy, ignorant of their language, should sit in water with a lot of women, completely speechless." On the other hand, Poggio was Renaissance man enough and Italian enough to see some salutary echoes of pagan Rome in the bathing rituals at Baden. Some of the women, he could not help noticing, were "good-looking and well-born and in the manner and form like a goddess." These lovelies floated with arms outstretched on the water, "until you might think they were winged Venuses." The very prettiest among them playfully asked the males gazing down on them from above to throw them pennies, which the men, including Poggio himself, obligingly did. Our Italian scholar was also impressed by how much good old-fashioned *fun* these Swiss-Teutons were having—playfully grab-assing and fondling one another, drinking heavily but not quarreling or cursing. Here was a form of natural, sensual living that Poggio believed his own land had lamentably lost:

We are terrified of future catastrophes and are thrown into a continuous state of misery and anxiety, and for fear of becoming miserable, we never cease to be so, always panting for riches and never giving our souls or our bodies a moment's peace. But those who are content with little live day by day and treat any day like a feast day.

How weird it was! Epicurean values were alive and well *north* of the Alps, and most alive of all in the north's watery emulation of Poggio's Roman forebears.

Yet in truth, if Poggio had taken the trouble to look more carefully around his native land, he would have discovered that plenty of people were still splashing about in public, albeit not in the nude and perhaps not with such lusty abandon as these primitive Teutons. Even some of the old Roman thermal aquae, such as venerable Aquae Albulae at Tivoli and the hot springs at Pozzuoli near Naples, were again in use, though in sadly dilapidated condition.

The Italian Renaissance's primary contribution to hydropathy was the recovery of ancient lore on healing waters and the considerable refinement of that teaching. One of the chief figures here was the Swiss polymath Paracelsus, who, like the ancients, believed that human health depended on harmony between man and nature. Touting various waterborne minerals as powerful medicinal agents, he prescribed thermal-spring waters as the perfect antidote to afflictions like goiters. (Today there is a statue in Bad Gastein dedicated to this influential natural healer, who spent some time in that storied spa.)

What bothered many of Paracelsus's colleagues, most notably the well-known Italian physician Andrea Bacci, was that the whole phenomenon of water-based hygiene and curative bathing had lost whatever "scientific" underpinning it had possessed among the ancients and was now almost exclusively in the hands of laymen. Bacci argued vociferously that balneology was a rational discipline that only trained physicians could understand. "How many [people] today," he asked plaintively, "go the baths on a doctor's advice rather than at the suggestion of some layman?" He and his colleagues pushed for a rigorous regimen at the baths where all aspects of the experience—which venue to visit, which therapies to pursue, what to eat and drink—could be closely supervised by medical specialists. But this ideal of a perfectly controlled hydropathic environment, which would be echoed by spa doctors down through the ages to our own day, remained largely a pipe dream.

Not only were the "revived" water-cure establishments in the sixteenth and seventeenth centuries frequented by patrons doing pretty much their own thing, these facilities themselves typically fell far short of the hygienic and therapeutic ideals envisaged by the contemporary balneologists.

We can get a sense of the spa-going experience prevailing in late sixteenth-century continental Europe via accounts left by that great French philosopher and essayist Michel de Montaigne. In 1580–1581 Montaigne undertook a lengthy journey animated in part by a desire, a *fervent* desire, to rid himself of the extremely painful kidney stones that had been torturing him for years. Nowadays kidney stones can be broken up using ultrasound waves or drugs, but in Montaigne's day, and for well over three hundred years thereafter, taking the waters was just about the only solution for this affliction—though of course it was no real solution at all.

Montaigne's search for waters that might help him pass his painful stones took him to spas in Switzerland, Italy, and his own country. It must be said that Montaigne, despite the seriousness of his quest, was not a very serious or dutiful patient; he was a playful and irreverent one, like many of those curists of his day whose independent behavior aroused the ire of contemporary balneologists. Montaigne was certainly quite unimpressed by the spa doctors he encountered, each of whom insisted that only *his* particular combination of treatments would work. "Of twenty consultations," the Frenchman snorted, "there were not two in agreement, each doctor damning the other and accusing him of murder."

Montaigne put his independent streak on display at Plombières-les-Bains, his very first medicinal stop. On the theory that if one dose is good, several doses must be better, he drank *nine* glasses of purgative mineral water rather than the prescribed one or two. But then, in an inexplicable reversal of this willful overdose strategy, he bathed only every other day rather than the recommended two or three times a day. At the Lucca baths in Italy, he bathed in and drank from the healing waters on the same day rather than on alternate days as ordered. Moreover, he refused to carry around the special bottle in which patients were supposed to urinate in order to keep precise track of their outflow.

"*C'est une sotte costume,*" he sniffed, "*de conter ce que on pisse.*" At Viterbo in Italy, Montaigne did not take the waters at all, having been put off by a previous patient's furious graffito cursing the doctor who had sent him to this useless place.

Meanwhile, his disdain for keeping track of his pissing notwithstanding, Montaigne was often more attentive to his bowels than to the usual touristic attractions. We learn from his travel journal that on one particular Tuesday at Baden, the water he drank caused him "three stools," and that two days later another dose brought impressive results "both in front and behind." Then—and this must have been both highly gratifying and highly painful—he tells us he voided a stone "as big and long as a pine nut, but as thick as a bean at one end, and having, to tell the truth, exactly the shape of a prick." Moments of relief like this aside, Montaigne's condition did not improve as a result of his mineral water baths and purgations; indeed, not only did his stones not break up, but he also came down with a bad toothache, heaviness in the head, and eye trouble—all of which he blamed on the waters. "I began to find these baths unpleasant," he laconically tells us.

Montaigne would have fared no better had he taken his medicinal baths in England's Bath. If anything, the therapeutic scene at Bath in the late sixteenth century, and for many years thereafter, was considerably less appetizing than on the Continent, which is why many English of that era preferred to go abroad rather than to take the waters at home. The once-green thermal pools of Roman-era Bath had become, for want of regular cleaning, an opaque brown. Queen Elizabeth I visited Bath in 1597 to take the cure but was quickly driven away by the feculent odors. Some seventy years later, in 1668, Samuel Pepys went to Bath for the waters. Although he found the town pleasant enough, the overcrowded Cross Bath, into which he bravely plunged along with several companions, gave him pause. "Only methinks it cannot be clean to go with so many bodies together in the same water," he observed coyly in his diary. The water in this famous pool also proved uncomfortably hot, at least for him: "Strange to see how hot the water is, and in some places, though this is the most temperate bath, the springs so hot as the feet [are] not able to endure. But strange to see when women and men herein, that live all the season in these waters, that cannot but be parboiled, and look like Creatures of the Bath."

We know from other sources that the bodies lazing about at Bath in these years were not only numerous but often horribly diseased: covered in suppurating wens, bulging buboes, and angry boils. Nevertheless, in a testament to that era's high tolerance for physical hideousness, not to mention its lack of curative alternatives, ailing bodies, even royal bodies, kept coming to Bath. In 1663 Charles II, newly restored to the throne, took his wife Catherine Braganza to Bath to cure her infertility. Catherine not only failed to get pregnant but almost died of skin poisoning. She might as well have bathed in the putrid Thames.

A full century later, when Bath had become a great center of fashion, the thermal pools remained infamous for their uncleanliness. Tobias Smollett's alter ego Humphry Clinker believed that no one but a lunatic would subject himself for extended periods to the "stench and filth" of the main spa at Bath, even if the waters there might be "of some service" in the treatment of "diabetes, diarrhea, and night sweats."

Over in Spa, however, the hygienic situation was considerably better—and by the seventeenth century that out-of-the-way little town had developed such a reputation as a medical wonderland that health pilgrims from all over Europe made arduous journeys to get there. In 1619 a Frenchman named Pierre Bergeron insisted that the magical elixir bubbling up from the springs at Spa could "extenuate phlegm; remove obstructions in the liver, spleen, and the alimentary canal; dispel all inflammations; comfort and strengthen the stomach and the nerves; purge wateriness and the peccant humors of choler, phlegm, and melancholy; are laxative and diuretic." As if this were not enough, the miraculous Spa waters could also "staunch, provoke, consume catarrhs, dry the too-humid brain, cure paralyses, and resolutions of nerves, and contractions and convulsions; benefit head colds, migraines, apoplexies, ophthalmias, vomitings, obstructions, serosities, dropsy, inflammation of the liver and kidneys, chlorosis, vermin, retention, calculus, gravel, ulcers, leprosies, etc., and finally render women fecund."

Even with a panacea as potent as the waters of Spa, one could not expect to be put right overnight. It might take weeks or months for any signs of improvement (real or imagined) to become manifest, and during that extended period the heath pilgrim understandably needed some diversions or entertainments to fill out the long and demanding days. As early as the seventeenth century, major spas met this need with a prodigious array of social activities—distractions that later grand spas would try to emulate, each adding its own particular refinements. Our seventeenth-century chronicler Pierre Bergeron was just as effusive about Spa's entertainments as about its waters, though he also saw a ridiculous side to some of the amusements. Noting that ladies and gentlemen taking the waters at Spa required a social regime that might help "banish all care, anxiety, and melancholy," he added:

> From this follow all kinds of games and pleasures, concerts, dances, ballets, feasts, tilting at the ring, love affairs, serenades, philosophical discussions, promenades, and buffooneries; the beauty, charm and gracefulness of the ladies in their various dresses and finery as nymphs and fairies; the romantic gallantry of the cavaliers, the soldierly swaggering and rodomontades in the Spanish manner; the varying guise and singularity of dress, the pell-mell language of so many nations, the gibberish of the local people, the poetic stanzas; the drolleries and laughter of some, and the foolishness and stupidity of others, the complaisance and reserve of these, the frankness and naiveté of those, the harmonies, the quarrels, then the disagreements among the ladies, and a thousand other varieties whose nature and art they enjoy cultivating at Spa.

In his description of early seventeenth-century Spa, Bergeron archly suggests that many of the pilgrims went there "under the pretext of taking the waters." For some folks, taking the cure was primarily an excuse for hying off and having a grand time, preferably without their spouses. The downside of this, as Bergeron also noted, was that while a gentleman might leave Spa with his liver on the mend, he might also go away with a new venereal disease or two. And even those ladies who had not hoped to "become fecund" via the waters at Spa might have become so nevertheless.

At almost exactly the same time that Pierre Bergeron was assessing the scene at Spa, an English traveler named Thomas Coryat stopped at Baden (Switzerland) during a lengthy trek around Europe. Coryat kept a meticulous journal during his travels, and that diary, though old-fashioned in its orthography and turns of phrase, is rife with jaundiced attitudes about the Continent's weird and wanton ways that are still current among some hard-core British Eurosceptics. As for his stop in Baden, Coryat was not animated by a desire to cure any physical malady like asthma or kidney stones. He was just curious about what went on at this resort whose waters had been attracting a well-heeled clientele since the fourteenth century. Coming from the land of Bath, Coryat had nothing against public bathing per se, but like Poggio Bracciolini before him, he was shocked by the partial nudity of the bathers (at this point both men and women wore covering below but not above the waist) and even more by the fact that men and women bathed together without benefit of matrimony:

> Also I have noted another strange thing amongst them that I have not a little wondered at. Men and women bathing themselves together naked from the middle upward in bathe: whereof some of the women were wives (as I was told) and the men partly bachelars, and partly married men, but not the husbands of the same women.

Working himself into a lather of outraged morality, Coryat went on to report that the *husbands* of these frolicsome female bathers could often be found standing "hard by the bathe in cloathes, and beholding their wives not only talking and familiarly discoursing with other men, but also sporting after a very pleasant and merry manner." Did not these husbands realize that although their wives might go into the baths "with the effigies of a male lambe characterized upon her belly, the same might within a few howers grow to an horned ram (according to a merry tale that I have sometimes heard) before she should return again to my company." Coryat himself was a bachelor, but he assures us that if *he* were with a wife in such a place, "truly I should hardly be persuaded to suffer her to bath herselfe in one and the selfe same bath with one onely bachelar or married man with her, because if she was faire, and had an attractive countenance, she might perhaps cornifie me." Yet in the end, what so deeply riled Coryat and others about Baden—that is, its atmosphere of sexual license—was precisely what helped to make the Germanic baths popular not only among German speakers but among Europeans generally.

If Belgium's Spa and Switzerland's Baden certainly enjoyed "destination resort" status in the seventeenth and eighteenth centuries, these places increasingly faced stiff competition from more recently emergent Central European Kurorte (spa towns).

Among the first of these to make a name for itself across international boundaries was Karlsbad in Bohemia, located about 130 kilometers west of Prague. Historian Simon Winder has argued that "Bohemia's two great contributions to Europe have been to do with the manipulation of water—whether in lager or in spas." True enough, but in Karlsbad's case, it was the thermal-spa water, not the stream water mixed with hops and yeast, that generated renown early on.

Like nations, spa towns with pretensions to grandeur seemed to need foundation myths to buttress their pedigrees; Karlsbad was no different. According to useful legend, the hot springs there were discovered when Habsburg emperor Charles (or Karl) IV stumbled upon them while stag hunting in 1347. After his hunting hounds fell into a pool of hot water, he happily followed them in, despite the fact that his dogs had been badly scalded. Although the story is apocryphal, Charles did establish a community around the springs (hence the name Karlsbad), and the waters did turn out to be hot enough to parboil legions of late medieval and Renaissance-era health pilgrims, who typically spent up to ten hours a day in the baths. Curists at Karlsbad initially took the waters only externally; not until 1520 did a local physician propose, much to the horror of his colleagues, that the waters there might be profitably *drunk* as well as wallowed in.

Like getting old, the *Trinkkur* (drink cure) as practiced at Karlsbad was not for sissies. At this fabled spa the regimen called for a dose of up to eighteen glasses of mineral water on the first day of treatment. The obedient patient was expected to increase the daily dose until he had emptied forty glasses into his protesting gut. To keep track of their progress and prevent miscounts, curists carried an abacus-like device called a *Trinkuhr* (literally, drink clock). An English spa physician named Dr. Tilling, who visited Karlsbad in the middle of the eighteenth century, claimed in a published report to have consumed *fifty* glasses of mineral water in *two hours*, with only beneficent results. Looking back on this heroic deed 150 years later, another English physician commented wryly: "That [Dr. Tilling] should have drunk so much and so often, and expressed himself the better for the performance, excites the wonder of every intelligent reader. It may be added that, if the doctor was such a wholesale drinker of mineral water himself, he would doubtless prescribe tasks to his patients that few of them could perform without repugnance or pain." (By the early nineteenth century, Karlsbad doctors had decreased the daily water dose to twelve or fifteen glasses, and in the 1890s they brought the prescription down to a mere *four glasses a day*—such being the falling-off in fortitude of later generations.)

Not only did early-days Karlsbad patients have to put down heroic quantities of water, they were also forbidden the compensatory pleasure of consuming beer, sugar, or butter on grounds that these items could compound their maladies. Uncooked fruit, classed as a poison, was also disallowed. According to a tenacious Karlsbad legend, an impetuous Englishman, "with the daring of his race," ate two cherries after drinking a glass of Sprudel and fell dead on the spot.

Whether visiting patients "took" their waters by the glassful or externally in a *Sitzbad*, from the early seventeenth century on, Karlsbad attracted the high and mighty from all over the Habsburg Empire and eventually from Europe as a whole. Czar Peter the Great of Russia visited Karlsbad in 1711. Suffering from exhaustion, depression, and constipation, Peter hoped the famed waters would clear out his system while the amiable atmosphere would lift his spirits. A letter he wrote to his wife from Karlsbad, however, suggests that he was *not* impressed by the ambiance: "The place is so merry that you might call it an honorable dungeon, for it lies between such high mountains that one scarcely sees the sun. Worst of all, there is no good beer." On the other hand, the waters at Karlsbad must have had their desired effect, for soon Peter experienced "a violent looseness" in his bowels. No doubt the "violence" of this bowel-loosening owed something to the fact that the Czar mistook his physician's order to drink three *glasses* of mineral water an hour to mean three *pitchers* of the stuff. At any rate, Peter's experience at Karlsbad (and later at Baden-Baden) inspired him to order a vast *banya* (bath) building program at home. When asked whether his country might also need to import Western physicians, Peter replied, "No, no, for Russians banyas are enough."

The Grand Tour

At the time Peter the Great was taking the waters at Karlsbad, legions of lesser-known figures were stopping off at major Western and (sometimes) Central European spa towns as welcome interludes on their Grand Tours around the Continent. Such tours were undertaken by people of diverse nationality—Russians, Poles, Americans, Brazilians—but it was the English who were the most frequent and intrepid of the Grand Tourists in an era when "tourist" still connoted high class and style—not the clueless mediocrity it does today. The quintessential Grand Tour, whose heyday lasted from the late seventeenth century to the French Revolution, functioned as an educational rite of passage for its privileged participants. (Not all were privileged, though: impecunious but knowledgeable young men, known as bear leaders, could get a free trip to the Continent by serving as tutors and secretaries for the Grand Tourists.)

For Englishmen, the principal purpose of the Grand Tour was to smooth down some rough edges by exposing the young squires to the Continent's great works of art and architecture, fashionable polite society, and Romance languages. However, like that approximate twentieth-century equivalent, the junior year abroad for American college kids, the learning experience often took a back seat to having one hell of a good time. If anything, young Georgian-era English aristocrats were considerably better at debauchery than mid- to late twentieth-century American frat boys, and their Grand Tours sometimes showcased drunken loutishness of truly heroic proportions. To cite just three examples: A group of ten young English bucks who thoroughly trashed a Milan *albergo* one night in 1787 were found to have consumed during that single eventful evening some *thirty-six* magnum bottles of burgundy, claret, and champagne. Following a collision in Vienna in 1786 between a fiacre and a carriage carrying three well-oiled English "gentlemen of distinction," one of the young Brits pounced on the cabbie and knocked all his teeth out. In 1827, when the salad days of the Tour were long gone by, a drunken mob of young Englishmen blocked the entrance to a Parisian church on Christmas Eve, cursing and beating some poor locals who were merely trying to attend midnight Mass. Naturally, in addition to all the drinking there was also the obligatory whoring. To get in proper spirit for an educational trip to Pompeii, an English "milord" typically prefunctioned in one of the myriad brothels of Naples. Thus, along with crates of portable Continental culture, English Grand Tourists also often came home with a bad case of the clap.

This is where the spas came in. In a classic study of the Grand Tour, Christopher Hibbert notes that "the [Grand] Tourist's itinerary was largely governed by the waters he wished to taste, the baths he wished to visit and the princelings to whom he wished to present letters of introduction." What Hibbert does not sufficiently emphasize here is the *absolute necessity* of the spa experience as a mending operation, an all-but-compulsory pit-stop where burnt-out travelers could attempt needed repairs on their ravaged bodies and hopefully recharge their batteries before plunging full-time back into debauch. Alas, given the rather less-than-Spartan quality of the eighteenth-century cure regimen, these stops were generally not as restful or palliative as one might have hoped. Nonetheless, at the spas the tourists were not (generally) confining their liquid intake to alcohol, and every hour they spent sitting in a hot bath was (mostly) an hour free of fornication.

Although hard living undoubtedly took its toll on some travelers during their Grand Tours, many stayed healthy enough, with or without visits to the spas, to make very productive use of their time abroad. For historian Edward Gibbon, the Tour proved a splendid climax to a rigorous classical education, setting him up for his great work on the decline of the Roman Empire; for Thomas Coke, the future first earl of Leicester, study of Palladian architecture in Italy inspired the construction of a magnificent neo-Palladian mansion in Norfolk, plus an outstanding collection of classical sculpture; for the artist William Kent, close inspection of great Continental gardens led to the creation of fine cultivated tracts back home that had a huge influence on landscape design around the world. Moreover, with respect to the Grand Tourists' spa visits in particular, it should be noted that at least *some* of them seem actually to have been healthful. The Earl of Carlisle described his routine at Spa in the summer of 1768 as follows: "I rise at six; I am on horseback at breakfast; play at cricket at dinner; and dance in the evening until I can scarcely crawl to bed at eleven. This is the life for you."

Down at Aix-les-Bains in southeastern France, another favorite Grand Tour pit stop, the cure regimen was more focused directly on the waters—and for good reason. The water-cure culture had been taken especially seriously in France since the early seventeenth century, when King Henri IV appointed his own physician as superintendent of baths and mineral fountains. In subsequent centuries, an organized national spa industry teamed up with a powerful tourism lobby to ensure that the water cure continued to garner significant support in the highest reaches of government. Aix, which in the eighteenth century was more fashionable than rival Vichy, profited greatly from the government support. Not incidentally, during the French Revolution, this spa (along with Belgium's Spa and Germany's Baden-Baden) provided a welcome haven for aristocrats fleeing the guillotine in Paris. Like Spa, Aix claimed to be able to cure just about any and every affliction known to man (and woman): "[A]ll affections of the nerves, such as convulsions, palsies, numbness, trembling, gouts, sciaticas, contractions, swellings, distempers of the bowels, stomach-aches, spleen, inveterate head-aches, vertigoes, nephritical distempers, cold affections of the womb, stoppage or flux of the menses, barrenness, abortions, and scabs of all sorts." Aix's claim to remedy infertility brought it many female visitors, including foreign ladies, but the doctors there were careful to warn that ladies must not undertake the more aggressive treatments due to "the relative feeble constitution of women, whose organic functioning is so easily activated and in whose nature nervousness predominates."

Ladies, nervous or not, were very much part of the Grand Tour scene—and, their "feeble constitutions" notwithstanding, they were just as likely as men to take the waters during their treks. Indeed, British ladies sometimes undertook health-related excursions to the Continent on their own, without male accompaniment, because, as Brian Dolan has noted in his study of Englishwomen on the Grand Tour, "Travelling abroad for the sake of one's health was one of the few legitimate reasons women in Enlightenment England could use to escape domestic circumstances. Such was the attraction of these liberties that many sought shelter in the temple of health who did not require Hygeia's services."

Not all Grand Tourists, male or female, ended up including a pit stop at a spa on their travels. Henry Swinburne, a skeptical English traveler, was not about to undertake a cure whose powers, he was sure, "existed nowhere but in the idea or roguery of doctors." That great English romantic, William Beckford, who combined physical fastidiousness with deep eccentricity, had hoped to take the waters at Spa but thought otherwise after seeing the huge, sweaty crowds at the main bath. And perhaps the most famous Grand Tourist of all, Lord Byron, preferred a manly swim across the Hellespont to a dainty dip at some spa. (Perhaps, too, Byron did not wish to expose his malformed right foot to fellow bathers.)

If it had been just health-giving waters and good times that the English Grand Tourists were after, they could, of course, simply have stayed at home: Britain had plenty of its own spas, and by the Tour's heyday in the eighteenth century, Bath, the country's largest spa, was positively flourishing despite its unhygienic waters. Indeed, in this period, Georgian Bath was undoubtedly the most fashionable and influential spa in the world.

Much of the credit for turning Bath into the fashion center of eighteenth-century England was due to one man: Richard "Beau" Nash. A former Royal Guards officer turned small-time lawyer, thief, and gambler (careers, as we know, with much in common), Nash moved from London to Bath in 1702 in hopes of finding a profitable card game. Bath offered its visitors plenty of opportunity to gamble even before its splendid casino materialized later in the century. Nash, an accomplished card sharp, figured he could quickly replenish his pocketbook, sadly depleted due to increasing expenditures on fine clothes and fast women, by a bit of gaming among the gullible curists and provincials at Bath.

Surprising himself and everyone who had known him in his former existence, Nash ended up staying on in Bath and becoming its master of ceremonies, an unpaid and unprestigious position that he exploited to remake the then-dowdy town in his own peacock image. Immediately upon taking up his new post, Nash set about ridding the streets of garbage, beggars, and overly aggressive whores and refining the social life by banning public sword bearing among the gentlemen and improper attire among the ladies. He improved the cultural scene by importing noted musicians and actors from London. Nash also opened a hospital for the treatment of rheumatic diseases and, in 1706, built an elegant new structure atop one of the thermal springs where curists could meet "in civilized company" and knock back a few glasses of the mineral-rich water. He called this facility the Pump Room.

For the next century or so, Bath's Pump Room, with its daily chamber-music concerts and steady parade of celebrities and socialites, would become virtually synonymous with high fashion and refined elegance. It was the Pump Room that Daniel Defoe had in mind when, on a visit to Bath in 1724, he described the town as "a resort of the sound, rather than the sick." Over the years, the Pump Room took on a slightly risqué image as a "school for scandal" (in Richard Sheridan's famous phrase), a gilded academy where legions of swells spent a happy semester or two. Passing through this academy at the tail end of its heyday in the early nineteenth century, the young American scientist Benjamin Silliman, an austere moralist, was predictably scandalized: "Bath," he wrote, "is probably the most dissipated place in the kingdom. It is resorted to by many real invalids, but by far the greater number belong to that class who wear away life in a round of fashionable frivolity without moral aim or intellectual dignity."

Along with its frolicsome Pump Room, eighteenth-century Bath became deservedly famous for its Palladian-style architecture, of which it offered some of the finest examples outside Italy. A young architect named John Wood arrived in Bath in 1716, attracted less by the blossoming social scene than by the region's deposits of pale limestone, which he believed was the perfect construction material for magnificent buildings—indeed, the stuff from which he might create a grand neoclassical city in the style of Italy's own Andrea Palladio. Wood succeeded beautifully in this aspiration, transforming a relatively squalid provincial burg into an airy Georgian town, replete with some of the most esteemed neo-Palladian buildings in the world. In addition to a series of stately houses and commercial buildings around Queen's Square, he designed the Royal Mineral Water Hospital for Rheumatic Diseases. He also designed, but did not live to see completed, the King's Circus, a gracefully curved three-tiered terrace combining Doric, Ionic, and Corinthian motivs. The completion of this magnificent structure was achieved by Wood's son, John Jr., who then added his own masterpiece, the Royal Crescent, to Bath's neo-Palladian topography. By the time the two Woods had put their stamp on the place, Bath was as prominent for its architectural beauty as for its waters.

Over the course of the eighteenth century, just about everybody who was anybody in English society, and many Continental grandees as well, passed through Bath. Artists and writers, too, were attracted to the town, and some of them, like Thomas Gainsborough, Thomas Carlyle, and Walter Savage Landor, lived there for a time.

The writer who eventually became most intimately associated with Bath was Jane Austen (this despite the fact that she lived there for only a small part of her life and was happy to leave it: contemporary culture tourists who go to Bath to "walk in the footsteps of Jane Austen" could most accurately emulate their heroine by following her quickly out of town).

After spending agreeable holidays in Bath in 1797 and 1799, Austen's family moved there in 1800, when Jane was twenty-five. The move was her parents' decision, not Jane's, and it may have been motivated by

Reverend and Mrs. Austen's hope not only to improve their own uncertain health but also to find a suitable husband for their still unmarried daughter. In addition to its other amenities, Bath had become Britain's premier marriage market. As one might imagine, independent-minded Jane was not at all anxious to be hitched to a mate of her parents' choosing, and her anger over the prospect of being put on show in Bath seems to have colored her reaction to settling in the city. In a letter written shortly after the family move, she described Bath as "all vapour, shadow, smoke, and confusion."

Although Austen soon recovered from her initial disorientation and developed a keen eye for Bath's social rituals, its mating games, and Pump Room flirtations, she always retained a measure of resentment against a place that had been forced upon her and that within the span of her eight-year stay began noticeably to slide downhill from the pinnacle of fashion it had become earlier. Austen's mostly jaundiced view of Bath is evident in the two novels she chose to set (or partially set) there: *Northanger Abbey* and *Persuasion*. The former features an innocent young girl, Catherine Morland, enjoying a holiday in Bath in the late 1790s; whereas *Persuasion*'s world-weary Anne Elliot feels imprisoned there, consigned to an early spinsterhood in a town that, like Anne herself, is past its prime. By the time Austen left the handsome spa town that now memorializes her with a "Jane Austen House," she had come to hate the place so much that she never returned. When she needed to take the waters at a spa, she went to Cheltenham.

Increasingly, though, Austen repaired to English seaside towns (Lyme Regis was a favorite) rather than to inland spas when she wanted a physical tune-up or holiday break. She was not alone in this. Indeed, one of the causes of Bath's decline in the nineteenth century was the rise of ocean-bathing resorts such as Brighton and Weymouth, places that offered a more vigorous "cure" and vacation experience than the traditional spas. The intensifying rush to the seaside in Britain was facilitated by the new Great Western Railway, which promoted excursions to English coastal resorts much as America's Milwaukee and St. Paul Railroad would later promote visits to Yellowstone Park.

Someone once said of baseball's Chicago Cubs: "Any team can have a bad century." England's Bath can be seen as something like the Chicago

Cubs of the spa world: having had some very good years in the 1700s, it went on to have a very bad century in the 1800s.

For Continental spas, especially those in Germany, matters turned out quite differently, though not immediately. With the exception of Bad Pyrmont in Lower Saxony and, to a much lesser degree, Baden in the Margravate of Baden, German spas showed up less prominently on the itineraries of Grand Tourists because traveling across that region in the eighteenth century was especially expensive, inns along the way were often crude, the "most savage banditti in Europe" were said to plague local roads, and one might have to speak German, which few foreigners could, or indeed wanted to. Yet the German region's relative paucity of international-class spas was soon to change, and that change was to begin first and foremost with the little settlement on the River Oos that the Romans had called Aquae, the conquering Germans called Baden, and the world as a whole eventually came to know as Baden-Baden ("so nice you had to say it twice").

CHAPTER TWO

Baden-Baden

The "Summer Capital of Europe"

Thomas Coryat, the early seventeenth-century English traveler who left us his colorfully jaundiced impressions of Baden in Switzerland, also stopped briefly in Germany's Baden during his tour of the Continent. Apparently he did not take the waters there, and he had little to say about the place save to complain that he had a devil of a time finding it. If he *had* stayed there he probably would not have found much to like. True, this German Baden had slowly begun to recover its identity as a water-cure venue in the late Middle Ages, when visitors from nearby Strasbourg began coming over regularly to take the waters. Yet pig farming, not people curing, remained the main industry, and an eyewatering odor of swine shit filled the air. As late as Coryat's time the town possessed only four thermal baths in working order (down from twelve in the Roman era), and even those were in sad shape. If one accepts the verdict of another contemporary chronicler, the local hotels were nothing to write home about either: "Mediocre meals with poor wines, a lack of almost all creature comforts, inadequate housekeeping, and poor service."

Germany's Baden would remain relatively obscure for another two hundred years, figuring only marginally in seventeenth- and eighteenth-century Grand Tour itineraries. Despairing over the sad state of the town, Margrave Karl Friedrich was anything but cheered by a report on the place he received in 1774 from one of his aides. This assessment spoke grimly of the "backwardness and uncleanliness" of Baden's bathing facilities. In response, the margrave established a new bathing commission with a mandate to revitalize the town as a cure center. In search of ideas to fulfill this mandate, the commission's chief made a study trip to Bad Pyrmont in Lower Saxony. This seemed a sensible move. For most of the eighteenth century, Pyrmont had reigned as Germany's premier water-cure resort, its best answer to England's Bath and Belgium's Spa. Like those places, it attracted its share of aristocrats and princelings and had also become an important intellectual center, a true hotbed of German *Aufklärung*, or "enlightenment." Ironically, though, at the time the margrave's man arrived in Pyrmont in search of some enlightenment on spa management, that place was already beginning to lose its luster—slipping into a gradual decline that eventually would leave it in the shadow of several other, more up-to-date German spas, including that bedraggled little burg in the Margravate of Baden that was hoping to become the next Pyrmont. In any event, the Baden makeover project envisaged by Karl Friedrich did not look very promising in the 1770s because the margrave lacked the financial resources to do much for his principal spa town. All he could manage were some small rewards, a few *douceurs*, for those bath attendants who worked especially hard to clean up the pools and keep the pig ordure at bay.

Crucially, though, this situation would soon start to change, and to change so rapidly that within a few decades Baden would not so much want to copy Pyrmont or to catch up with Switzerland's Baden but to *distinguish* itself from that Swiss resort so as not to lose its own luster by confused misidentification. Germany's Baden reinvented itself as Baden-Baden, double the power and prestige of any other Baden. The rise of Baden-Baden (as I'll call it now, even though the official name-change did not occur until 1932) helped to propel the growth in stature of German-region spas in general—a development which in turn played its small part in the larger story of Germany's political ascendancy in the nineteenth century. As if to crown its emergence as one of the grandest spa towns in the world, Germany's double-Baden would self-confidently assume yet another new moniker: "Summer Capital of Europe."

Becoming Baden-Baden

Revealingly, Baden-Baden owed its initial emergence as a "destination" Kurort to political and social developments well outside its own bucolic environs—indeed, to events outside the German region itself. Like modern Germany, which owes so much to France (both to French achievements and to French foibles), Baden-Baden would not have become what it is today without *la grande nation*.

France's first great gift to Baden-Baden came via the French Revolution of 1789–1799, that enormous cataclysm that tore apart the sociopolitical fabric not only of France itself but also of neighboring territories. As the revolution progressed—or perhaps regressed—from its relatively moderate constitutional beginnings to an all-out crusade against the Ancien Régime, representatives of that old order, principally aristocrats and high-level clerics, increasingly faced the choice of accepting "revolutionary justice" (i.e., the guillotine) or beating a path out of France. Not surprisingly, those who could do so often chose the latter option, although escape was not always easy. The choice of a safe haven was governed by many factors, but two of the most important were proximity and comfort.

Baden-Baden, roughly a day's trip from the Alsatian border, easily met this first requirement, and by the late eighteenth century it was making at least a tentative start toward satisfying the second. The town already had one of its signature structures, a wooden *Promenadenhaus* (promenade house) for dancing and other amusements. This building, which went up across the little Oos River from the village proper, was connected to the town by a long lane flanked with imposing oak and chestnut trees (Kastanienallé, later Lichtentaler Alle). This lovely avenue, which became another of the spa's signature attractions, was perfect for daily constitutionals and the early evening *passeggio*. The creation of the Promenadenhaus and Kastanienallé shows city boosters were mindful that a "modern" Kurort could not be merely about healing waters but also must offer healthful exercise and opportunities for putting on the style. Revealing, too, is the participation of the margrave's government in Baden-Baden's improvements. Although the margrave remained strapped for cash, he was able to scrape together enough funds to assist in the advancements. In addition to sponsoring construction projects, Margrave Karl Friedrich appointed a spa director who had to be a registered physician. A few years later, in order to address the money problem, the margravate began imposing a tax on all spa visitors, with the revenues earmarked for infrastructure improvements. Such state engagement would be central to the rise of the entire German spa industry in the nineteenth century, helping it to prosper while rival British spas like Bath, sticking tenaciously to the private-enterprise model, began seriously to languish.

Baden-Baden's political patrons, Margrave Karl Friedrich and his successors, were happy to welcome those English guests who were pouring out of their country every summer (England, as everyone knew, did not *do* summer) in search of a better grade of cure. But the margrave was also very attentive to his French guests because, through blood ties and taste, his family was deeply connected to the French nobility. This became a key factor in attracting French aristocrats to Baden-Baden as the guillotine scaffolds began sprouting up all over their homeland.

Whatever its attraction to French nobles fleeing the guillotine, the émigrés in question did not expect to stay long in their new "home." The fury of the revolution would soon dissipate, they thought. Failing that, the radical Jacobins would be sent packing by native counterrevolutionaries working with neighboring foreign powers that feared and hated the new order as much as the refugees. But the revolution did not quickly peter out; on the contrary, it gained traction and became ever more radical in response to the threat of domestic counterrevolution and foreign invasion. For the émigrés, the hope of returning to France anytime soon quickly faded.

Faced with the prospect of a longer-term residence abroad, along with a diminution of the funds brought from home, the French aristocrats who had fetched up in Baden-Baden had little choice but to try something they had done precious little of before: support themselves using whatever native skills and wits they might possess. For some, this challenge spelled destitution, but others proved surprisingly adroit at making a living. In most cases, the path to solvency (and sometimes even riches) in Baden-Baden involved putting to use resources the nobles already had: knowledge about and a feeling for luxury goods. In relatively short order, French aristocrats marooned in Baden-Baden established fine jewelry lines, manufactured exquisite perfumes and soaps, and distilled heady liquors. It helped that these were precisely the kind of high-end products that were much in demand in a socially ambitious water-cure resort like Baden-Baden. The town could now add fancy French luxury items to its inventory of attractions—and the ready availability of such glamorous goods eventually became de rigueur for any first-class spa.

Soon after they had settled in Baden-Baden, the émigré aristocrats received unwanted company from home in the form of an invading revolutionary army. France had gone to war against Austria in June 1792 and, after suffering reverses in the early fighting, not only had expelled the invaders but, beginning later that year, dispatched its own crusading armies into foreign territory, including the German states. Despite their claims to be agents of liberation, bringing *liberté*, *egalité*, and *fraternité* in their baggage trains, the French soldiers did all the things invading armies usually do: they billeted on the backs of the natives; they looted far and wide; they raped indiscriminately; and they murdered civilians whose only offense, as one French lieutenant admitted, "was not to give up promptly what little money they might have had."

Yet while many towns suffered grievously from the French invasion, Baden-Baden avoided this fate despite the margrave's having thrown in his lot with the Austrians. From 1790 to 1796, the town's main complaint was a steady falloff in cure guests—from a count of 554 in 1790 to a miserable 52 in 1796. When an advance guard of the Corps Moreau reached Baden-Baden on July 4, 1796, residents (and émigrés) feared the worst. Panic engulfed the hitherto peaceful little town. Yet the panic soon proved unfounded. After allowing some plundering in the outskirts of town, General Moreau, who took up quarters in a local inn called the Salmen, ordered his men to behave themselves. The general, it turns out, was already in negotiations with Karl Friedrich's agents regarding an armistice and reversal of allegiances. Tellingly, the negotiation process involved hearty dinners and frequent visits to the baths, with the happy result that, unlike many other towns in the area, Baden-Baden escaped significant despoliation. Equally telling, though, was the hasty conversion of Baden-Baden's largest building, the Neue Schloss (New Palace), into a hospital for the injured soldiers of both armies. Over the next century and a half, principal structures in many German spa towns, including bathhouses, would all too often have to harbor badly injured soldiers as opposed to gouty or otherwise indisposed civilians.

Not only did France's revolutionary expansionism leave Baden-Baden physically intact, it greatly spurred the town's progress toward greater renown as a Kurort. From December 1797 to April 1798, a major diplomatic conference took place in nearby Rastaat with the object of working out compensation for German princes who had lost lands to France on the left bank of the Rhine. The Congress of Rastaat failed to accomplish much in terms of diplomacy, but the diplomats did not fail to take note of the attractions of Baden-Baden, to which they regularly repaired after fruitless sessions at the bargaining table. The diplomats were beguiled not only by the thermal waters but by the availability of gambling tables and an extremely alluring physical environment—a terrain of deep woods, meandering streams, waterfalls, mysterious grottos, weird rock formations, and gently rolling hills that harmonized perfectly with prevailing romantic tropes concerning landscape aesthetics.

Baden-Baden's natural splendors featured prominently in a local newspaper, the *Rastaater Congressblatt*, published during the Congress by a local promoter named Aloys Schreiber, who also put out the first comprehensive guidebook to the city. In this book, Schreiber praised all the "must-see" beauties and attractions of the region, sights that could provide the visitor "with pleasant goals for his various daily excursions and walks."

Among the Rastaat conferees who made their way to Baden-Baden was First Consul Napoleon Bonaparte, who had assumed overall command of France's military operations after his successful foray into Italy in 1796. Napoleon's visit to Baden-Baden was brief, and despite a penchant for long, hot baths (which he took in part to soothe his painful hemorrhoids), apparently he did not take the waters. On the other hand, Napoleon's decision to grace the town with his august presence added further to Baden-Baden's luster, at least among the French. Soon a host of other notables, many of them French, would descend on Baden-Baden and, unlike Napoleon, end up staying there for long periods and partaking of all the town's amenities, including a new brothel staffed largely by imported French prostitutes.

Baden-Baden's French connection was further strengthened by some timely nuptials. In 1806, desiring to harness the state of Baden (recently transformed from a margravate to a duchy) firmly to his own fortunes, Napoleon, now emperor of France, orchestrated a marriage between his adopted daughter, Stéphanie de Beauharnais, and Karl Louis, the grandson of Karl Friedrich of Baden. For good measure, Napoleon promoted Duke Karl Friedrich to the status of grand duke and gave him a prominent role in the newly constructed Confederation of the Rhine, an assemblage of sixteen German satellite states that revolved around Paris in a wobbly orbit. The union between Stéphanie and Crown Prince Karl Louis of Baden proved no more blissful than that between France and its new German client states—the couple lived apart most of the time—but was beneficial to Baden-Baden because the coquettish and beautiful Stéphanie saw fit to summer frequently in the spa town, where she built a charming little palace. She called the town her *"buen retiro."*

Stéphanie and Karl Louis were together at least enough to produce three daughters (a son died in infancy), who themselves made strategic marriages that helped promote Baden-Baden's growing status as a watering hole for royalty. Stéphanie's first daughter, Princess Luise Amelie, managed to hook Prince Gustav of Vasa, not a terribly big fish. Her younger sister, Princess Josephine Friederike Luise, married Prince Karl Anton of Hohenzollern-Sigmaringen, the scion of the junior Catholic branch of that great Prussian dynasty. This was a more impressive catch. Meanwhile, the youngest daughter, Princess Marie Amelie Elisabeth Karoline, snared William Alexander Anthony Archibald Douglas-Hamilton, Eleventh Duke of Hamilton. All this meant that in addition to the well-established French connection, the Grand Duchy of Baden, and hence Baden-Baden, enjoyed dynastic ties both to Prussia and to Britain.

Sweden and Bavaria were drawn into the mix, too, owing to dynastic marriages involving two of Karl Friedrich's sisters: Friederike with King Gustav IV of Sweden and Karoline with King Maximilian Joseph I of Bavaria. Moreover, Queen Elisabeth Ludovika, the wife of Prussian King Friedrich Wilhelm IV, frequented Baden-Baden for her health, further making the spa *hoffähig* (court-acceptable) among European royalty.

And if all this were not enough, there was also a royal *Russian* connection, for back in 1793 yet another sister of Karl Friedrich, Luise, had married Crown Prince Alexander of Russia, who would become czar in 1801. This Russian connection would eventually prove even more important for Baden-Baden than the French one, as generations of Russians, and not just royals and aristocrats, came to treat this smallish German spa town as a kind of second dacha.

Russia, of course, was Napoleon's target in his ill-fated eastern crusade of 1812. His disastrous retreat from Moscow proved to be the beginning of the end for Napoleon and his empire, though the actual demise did not come until Waterloo in 1815.

The protracted meeting called to sort out the mess left behind by the "Corsican upstart"—the Congress of Vienna—had enormous implications for the future of Europe and the world. What primarily interests us here, though, is the congress's impact on the Kurort Baden-Baden, which turned out to be even more significant than that of the smaller meeting at Rastaat some seven years earlier. Baden-Baden, which lies about halfway between Paris and Vienna, proved to be a perfect way station for diplomats coming and going between France and Austria. The diplomats paused at the spa to carry on informal discussions, to rest up after the tedious bickering in Vienna, and to gird their loins for yet more bickering to come. Having once tasted Baden-Baden's delights, many of these movers and shakers returned to the spa regularly while at the same time talking up the place among their friends and relatives, most of whom were fellow aristocrats. This meant that Baden-Baden, although eventually "democratizing" along with the other grand Central European spas, was in the early nineteenth century a veritable nest of blue bloods. As for the Grand Duchy of Baden, it emerged from the Congress of Vienna negotiations in surprisingly good shape for a state that had sided with Napoleon. Czar Alexander I, with his marital connections to Baden, personally intervened to keep the state intact.

Baden-Baden, however, could not have become so *couru* with the carriage crowd without dramatically improving its facilities—without, that is, undertaking yet another round of civic improvements that convincingly elevated it above its competitors across Germany and Central Europe. Some of this new makeover was the work of private entrepreneurs, but most of it, as before, derived from the largesse of Grand Duke Karl Friedrich and his successor, Karl Louis. When it came to Baden-Baden's bath culture and its accoutrements, these small-scale rulers acted very much like latter-day Caesars.

In 1804, Karl Friedrich charged his court building director, Friedrich Weinbrenner, an influential architect who had trained in Italy, with the construction of a new Museum Politechnikum to house artifacts from the ruins of Roman-era Aquae. Because the new museum was situated above a major thermal spring, the building's west wing boasted a *Trinkraum* (drinking room), while the east wing embraced the historic *Quellenhaus* (spring house) that drew on the town's primary thermal source. In 1819, in place of an older and dilapidated bathing complex, Weinbrenner designed a more elaborate, Doric-columned *Trinkhalle* that augmented the town's neoclassical look. This building's historicist design notwithstanding, the new Trinkhalle boasted state-of-the-art equipment, the dernier cri in pumps, pipes, and spigots. Moreover, the facility dispensed not only good old-fashioned natural spring water but also artificially carbonated "Karlsbad water," a soon-to-be-trendy concoction pioneered by a Bohemian spa doctor named W. W. Kölreuter.

Also in the spirit of the times, in 1824 Weinbrenner transformed a recently secularized religious building, the sprawling *Jesuitenkolleg* (Jesuit College), into the swanky *Kur- und Conversationshaus* (hereafter Conversation House), replete with dance hall, reading room, sitting room, gambling den, and full-service restaurant. Where sworn-to-poverty Jesuits had once prayed, schemed, and indoctrinated, wealthy curists now waltzed, gluttonized, drank, and read their favorite literary works—often the products of romantic writers who were fellow guests at the spa.

Unlike England's Bath and Belgium's Spa, Germany's Baden in the eighteenth century had possessed no free-standing theater, but that changed in 1805–1806 following a decision by the city council to construct a playhouse "for the purpose of enhancing pleasure and elevating [Baden-Baden's] status." The theater was originally projected to cost 1,500 gulden, a hefty enough sum at the time, but cost overruns brought the final bill to 7,534 gulden, a huge outlay indeed. Because the high cost of construction stretched town coffers, city fathers felt justified in approaching Grand Duke Karl Friedrich for an annual subsidy of fifty gold florins to keep the new theater operating. Karl Friedrich consented to the subsidy—although, with his own purse pinched from funding ambitious construction projects in his capital of Karlsruhe, he insisted that the moneys be paid out of revenues from the town's gaming activities.

While Karl Friedrich and his court builder were seeing to the "enhancement" of Baden-Baden as an up-and-coming Kurort, two private citizens from Tübingen set out to remedy a serious deficiency in the town's hospitality infrastructure—the lack of a major, international-class hotel. (Existing hostelries like the Salmen, Hirsch, and Sonne were simply not up to snuff.) Aware that Baden-Baden could not be the first-class destination resort it hoped to be without a place to park fastidious foreign visitors, the well-known Tübingen publisher Johann Friedrich Cotta and his business partner, Johann Ludwig Klüber, purchased another recently secularized building, the former Kapuzinerkloster, and proceeded at vast expense to turn it into a grand hotel. Naturally, they hired the ubiquitous Weinbrenner to provide the design. Cleverly, Weinbrenner kept parts of the old structure intact while converting the spaces to completely new purposes: the former prayer room became the hotel's "ball, music and conversation center," the front choir became a stage, and the rear choir, a gaming and billiard room. Installing eighteen majestic Doric columns, Weinbrenner transformed the old nave and transept into a huge cross-shaped dining room. (As for the food served in that gargantuan restaurant, we know that it was copious and quite heavy by our standards: one did not shed pounds by dining at Cotta's.)

When it was completed in 1809, Cotta's Badischer Hof boasted fifty guest rooms as well as an adjoining garden-surrounded *Badehaus* equipped with thirty polished-stone tubs. There was even a thermal bath for the horses. Yet while Baden-Baden's new grand hotel may now have been ready to receive visitors, the hotel's owners, Cotta and Klüber, were not ready to act as successful hoteliers; they didn't know what they were doing and made a complete hash of the business. The Badischer Hof did not fully reach its potential until after the two Johanns sold their holdings in 1830. (The hotel remains in operation today, but it is far from the grandest hostelry in town.)

By the time the Badischer Hof had reached its prime in the middle of the nineteenth century, other hotels and tourist facilities were sprouting up all around town. There was good reason for this: visitor numbers were climbing steadily. Back in 1800, Baden-Baden had attracted only 391 guests, but in 1812, despite the ongoing war in Europe, the number was up to 2,500. In 1820, five years after the end of the Napoleonic Wars, 5,100 visitors came to town, two-thirds of them foreigners; the total number of guests rose to 7,500 in 1825. Five years later, despite a new revolution in Paris (always an important feeder city for Baden-Baden), the guest count was 10,300, and in another half-decade it reached 15,500. Baden-Baden's growing popularity was fueled mainly by satisfied customers spreading the word—what happened in Baden definitely did *not* stay in Baden—but an energetic publicity machine did its part as well. Here is how Baden-Baden's *Morning Paper for Sophisticated Classes*, a newspaper published by Cotta, touted the spa town in July 1830:

The bathing time here begins in May and ends in October. But among the eight to ten thousand strangers, who visit Baden-Baden every year, there are barely two thousand really using the baths. Many people are here just to relax or to look for new amusements and to associate with their informal sojourn all the conveniences and pleasures of the cities from which they came. Therefore, the resort, where one formerly found only insignificant dwellings with modest, middle-class furnishings, completely changed within approximately twenty years. Elegant houses, equipped with magnificent appointments and conveniences, party grounds, brilliant soirées, concerts, balls, restaurants which compared with those in Paris, and other innovations which came up one after another. In areas where before lonely strollers or harmonious groups were walking, one now meets luxurious carriages and horses, fine hired buggies, elegant equestrians of both sexes, some riding very valuable horses, and some on donkeys, which are especially chosen for children and timid ladies. This, too, is characteristic of the changes in the community—that the number of children and women usually surpasses that of the men, giving the spa life a more attractive diversity and the town itself more the character of a larger city which suddenly develops [in the summer] only to disappear again for six months.

Faites Votre Jeu: The Age of Bénazet

Among the "new amusements" alluded to by Cotta's paper was the one that did more than any other ancillary attraction to transform Baden-Baden into a "grand spa"—gambling. It is fitting that this should have been so. Gambling, after all, had been an integral part of Roman bath culture and had helped fuel the growth of famous water-cure towns like Bath and Spa. There seemed to be something about the public bathing rituals that called for good food, good wine, good sex—and a good round of rolling the bones. But of course gambling, like wine and sex (not to mention haute cuisine), can become an addiction, a habit with a possible darker side. Over the years, gambling would become a highly contentious issue in the life of the grand spas.

As for Baden-Baden, a resort city that one day would vie with Monte Carlo for the title of "top casino town in Europe," the early experience with gambling was not terribly auspicious. As the nineteenth century dawned, a few local hotels, including the Salmen, Sonne, and Sonnenplatz, provided private gaming rooms for their guests. For this privilege the hotels paid a small tax to the municipal government. During the first years of the new century, a Frenchman named Paul Chevilly maintained a public gaming concession in the original Promenadenhaus. In 1809, when the Grand Duchy of Baden decided to allow Baden-Baden to award a second gaming concession for the newly renovated Jesuitenkolleg, some townspeople protested vehemently: gaming, they insisted, was injurious to public morals. But immoral or not, the second gaming concession went through because it had the backing of the local spa director, Dr. von Sternhayn, who, it turned out, had his own investments in the gaming tables and other amusements at the new Conversation House. More importantly, Grand Duke Karl Friedrich, whose exchequer was proving inadequate to fund all the improvements to make Baden-Baden a top contender in the European spa world, came to see gambling as the proverbial golden-egg-laying goose. After all, every new gaming concession involved a hefty up-front fee plus taxes on earnings—the proceeds split between the duchy and the municipality. Soon those eggs dropped by the goose of gambling indeed proved golden. As the *Morning Paper* gushed in 1820, "There was no lack of money for [civic] improvements, since the very considerable fees paid by the gambling operators were being used for these purposes by direction of the highest officials."

It was to reach the stage where such encomiums were sufficiently justified that the grand duchy decided to focus on large public *Spielbänke* (casinos) with exclusive—and very expensive—operational privileges. The above-mentioned 1809 concession inaugurated this program. Initially the idea was to have just one big concession, but when a pair of ambitious French gentlemen, both ex-colonels, applied for this privilege, the city council, with state approval, decided to grant *two* licensees. Thus, in 1809 a Monsieur Payer became the lessee of a concession in the Conversation House for a fee of 700 Louis d'ors, while a compatriot, L. Cheville, gained the right to establish roulette wheels in the Promenadenhaus for the same fee.

Yet within short order these facilities also proved inadequate. Thus, Weinbrenner's brand new Conversation House, built in 1824, added a large casino under the direction of another French concessionaire, Antoine Chabert, who paid an annual fee of 27,000 gulden for the right to pick the pockets of an ever-growing number of players. Chabert's gaudy casino, featuring a red coffered ceiling and crystal chandeliers, was much more imposing than any of the gaming rooms that preceded it. Chabert himself was also a showy piece of work. A Strasbourg native who got financially (and physically) fat as a corrupt army supplier during the Napoleonic wars, he sprinkled golden powder in his mutton-chop whiskers and ended up impressing even fellow arrivistes by his gaucherie. If this sounds Balzacian, there is good reason for it: Chabert was one of the models for Balzac's Père Goriot in the novel of the same name. But unlike old Goriot, Chabert had gone on to make additional piles of money by investing in casinos in Paris's Palais Royal, that den of urban iniquity where one could find anything one wanted in the realm of the pleasurable.

Once resettled in Baden-Baden, Chabert, along with upgrading the local gambling milieu, introduced the novel practice of drinking coffee in the late afternoon—an intelligent move because it fortified patrons for long nights at the gaming tables. Finally, in another cagey move, Chabert brought in musical virtuosi like the dazzling violinist Nicolo Paganini to perform at his casino. Dutifully keeping casino guests happy during moments away from the tables, these artists were the forerunners of glittery twentieth-century Las Vegas entertainers—the Wayne Newtons and Elvis Presleys of their day.

Some of the artists who graced Baden-Baden were themselves gamblers. I'll have much to say down the line about the gambling experiences of writers and musicians at Baden-Baden and other grand Central European spas. At this point, though, I'll just dust off an apposite observation by the German poet Johann Peter Hebel, the first writer of rank to regularly take the waters—and roll the bones—at Baden-Baden. With respect to gambling, Hebel is noteworthy also because he was a frequent *winner*, surely a rarity:

> In Baden I was playing the great game for another five days, not only at the table but also at the bank, being so happy at the latter that I could not only live at no cost to me during these five days but also show off. When I, for instance, tipped the domestics, I said: "It is not your fault that I am not a Count, but you should not suffer because of that." Nothing is more pleasant than contrasting experiences. I spent the evenings among the coachmen and footmen of those Counts and Barons with whom I had enjoyed lunch.

In July 1830 France experienced another revolution, something that was becoming a habit. For the French, the "July Revolution" meant the advent of a new regime under King Louis Philippe. For Baden-Baden, the upheaval meant the beginning of a whole new chapter in its gambling history—the "Age of Bénazet."

Jacques Bénazet, who took over from Chabert as Baden-Baden's chief gambling impresario in 1838, owed his spectacular career in that German spa town in good part to King Louis Philippe. That monarch, famed (and also derided) for his bourgeois aesthetic and accountant mentality, regarded gambling as wasteful and unproductive, even though it generated quite a bit of revenue for the French state. Under the king's prodding and after scores of prominent Frenchmen had lost their shirts, the Chamber of Deputies closed down casino gambling across France, effective December 1837. Bénazet, who had been supervisor of gaming in Paris and was part owner of two major gambling clubs there, foresaw Louis Philippe's ban to be France's loss and Germany's gain: he promptly shifted his sights to Baden-Baden, where he knew Chabert's lease at the Conversation House was about to expire. The latter gentleman, realizing that he lacked the deep pockets to compete with Bénazet for the Baden concession and also that the gaming licenses he continued to hold in other German spas, principally Wiesbaden and Bad Ems, would keep him well away from poverty's door, voluntarily vacated his Conversation House lease. By offering more than double what Chabert had been paying (40,000 as opposed to 19,000 gulden), Bénazet had little trouble convincing the new ruler, Grand Duke Leopold, that he was the right man to run the tables at Baden-Baden.

Bénazet arrived in Baden-Baden in early 1838 with more than just deep pockets. He had an outsized personality and a pedigree to match (or appear to match) his riches. Still young looking in his early sixties, Bénazet tinted his bushy hair with "China water" and eschewed a conventional beard, opting instead for a handlebar mustache and one of those ugly little growths under the lower lip we call today a "soul patch." Born of poor, illiterate day laborers in a small village in the Pyrenees, Bénazet managed to become a lawyer and, more importantly, the son-in-law of a wealthy ship owner from Bordeaux. Deploying his wife's money, he moved to Paris and began to make his own fortune in the newly opened stock exchange. From there it was on to the gambling business and other lucrative ventures like brothel management and politician purchasing. He was equally enterprising in tweaking his résumé to make it more attractive to Grand Duke Leopold and his officials. Upon his arrival in Baden, he claimed to be a descendant of the last Moorish king of Grenada. When that lineage did not seem to strike just the right chord, he bought a pedigree from a "heraldic institute" in Brussels identifying him as the scion of an ancient and noble French line hailing from Toulouse. In sum, even more than Antoine Chabert, Jacques Bénazet, Baden-Baden's new king of gambling, was a true child of Balzac's *La Comédie Humaine*.

Over the next decade Bénazet not only modernized Baden-Baden's gambling halls but also set about upgrading and renovating the entire town. This definitely needed doing, despite all the improvements made earlier in the century. When Bénazet arrived, the place must have seemed still pretty provincial to a man coming from Paris. It had only 564 houses and a population of 14,500 souls, every ninth of whom was a domestic servant. There were twenty-one butchers and sausage makers, attesting to the town's ongoing love of the swine. Turning first to his main business of gambling and sensing that the First Empire aesthetic Chabert had created at the Convention House in the 1820s was already passé, Bénazet brought in a famed theater painter from Paris, Pierre-Luc-Charles Ciceri, who redecorated the gambling rooms in the neobaroque style of his theatrical sets. Then, using profits from his gaming empire, Bénazet paid for the construction of a second Trinkhalle, an imposing district administrative office, and a branch railway line. With Bénazet's largesse, the city built better roads and an up-to-date sewer system, mundane but absolutely crucial improvements. Hardly less crucially in terms of tourist appeal, the Frenchman saw to the transformation of the town's pokey little band into a real orchestra—one capable of playing the demanding works of Richard Wagner and Hector Berlioz (eventually under the baton of that latter maestro himself).

Berlioz, of course, was a Frenchman like Bénazet, and things French—language, food, décor, clothing, cosmetics, and so on—which had long been fashionable in Baden-Baden now became so omnipresent that a visitor there might have imagined himself in a French *ville*—albeit an unusually upscale one. At the beginning of every cure season a small army of milliners, couturiers, pedicurists, hairdressers, perfumers, and corset makers arrived from Paris to set up shop. Beginning in 1842, a Parisian painter named Jean-François Utz came to town for several summers to photograph prominent personalities employing the new daguerreotype system.

To ensure that his compatriots and other Europeans of the right sort were aware of this little Rhine-region bijou, Bénazet launched a publicity campaign featuring the talents of well-known foreign journalists. The scribes were brought to Baden-Baden on lavish junkets paid for by the entrepreneur—and, as handsomely subsidized travel writers often do, they wrote articles extolling a place they allegedly had just happened to stumble upon. Journalist Eugéne Guinot came up with the phrase that became Baden-Baden's signature tagline: "Europe has only two capitals: in the winter, Paris; in the summer, Baden-Baden." Bénazet was content with seeing Baden-Baden's capital status confined to the summer; he spent his own winters in Paris.

One famous, or infamous, sometime Paris resident who visited Baden-Baden during Bénazet's time was Lola Montez, that grandest of all "grand horizontals," best known to history for her tempestuous relationship with King Ludwig I of Bavaria, a relationship so scandalous that it contributed to the king's abdication in 1848. According to court gossip, "Lola," who was actually born Eliza Gilbert in Ireland, gained access to the king's heart (and purse) by bursting into his study one fine afternoon and cutting open her blouse to prove to him that the formidable bulges he had admired under her garment were "nature's work alone." But Lola's conquest of Ludwig came only after a long line of similar conquests, a dizzying journey up the ladder of European society and culture—the ladder in question being more like a stack of bunk beds.

Among Lola's bunkmates was Alexandre Dumas, père; the noted journalist Alexandre Dujarier; musician Franz Liszt; and, albeit only in the fertile mind of novelist George MacDonald Fraser, the immortal Harry Flashman. It was during her affair with Liszt that Lola first visited Baden-Baden. She had gone with her musician lover to Bonn for a Beethoven festival in August 1845. While there she attracted considerable attention by dancing naked on a tabletop at a private dinner. Finding Bonn hopelessly boring, Lola, along with Liszt, fled up the Rhine to Baden-Baden, about which she had heard great things. Baden-Baden did indeed prove livelier than Bonn, although the bar here was not terribly high. While Liszt, suffering from jaundice, took the waters, Lola frequented the gaming tables, not so much to gamble as to meet men.

We do not know whether Lola had any luck on that score, but we do know that she managed thoroughly to scandalize Baden-Baden, as she had Berlin, Warsaw, and Bonn before—and would Munich soon after. Scandalizing Baden-Baden took some doing, but Lola proved up to the challenge. One evening at a roulette table, she showed her dancer's agility by casually throwing a leg over the shoulder of the man standing next to her, a move that distracted not only the gambler but also the croupier. Shortly thereafter, in the great hall of the Conversation House, she raised her skirt up to her crotch in order to impress an admirer. The resulting outcry from the ladies got her expelled from town. (By this time, Liszt had grown tired of Lola's antics: he fled the city while she was napping in their hotel room. Before departing, he left money with the owner to pay for the furniture he was sure she would smash upon discovering his absence.) After being booted out of Baden-Baden, Lola went back to Paris for a while before descending on Munich and the helpless Ludwig.

In October of that same year, a very different foreign guest visited Baden-Baden: William Gladstone, future prime minister of Britain. One of Gladstone's obsessions was rescuing and Christianizing "fallen women"—women a little like Lola Montez (who, by the way, eventually did throw off her wanton ways and convert to Christianity, but only after becoming so old and unattractive that she could no longer ply her favorite trade). It was, in fact, to rescue a fallen woman that Gladstone ventured to Baden-Baden, although the woman in this case was his sister, Helen, who had fallen into drugs and alcohol rather than prostitution. After first trying a cure at Bad Ems, Helen had moved on to Baden-Baden because some of the doctors there were known to be quite liberal with their prescriptions for laudanum, her pain reliever of choice. According to an anguished letter written by William to their mother, Helen was polishing off 150 drops of laudanum per day, enough to kill her if she kept this up for very long. "She is poisoned much in body, and, more in mind by use of that terrible drug," reported William.*

On one occasion brother William stood by while Helen, held down by burly orderlies, suffered the application of dozens of leeches to her

---

*Gladstone's experience with his sister's laudanum abuse did not prevent him from using the drug himself when he entered Parliament. In hopes of increasing his rhetorical powers, he habitually put a few drops in his coffee before addressing the House.

trembling body. Another bad moment came when she locked herself in her room and drank down a bottle of eau de cologne. Despite pleading with Helen for days on end, Gladstone was unable to coax his sister to return with him to London. She eventually returned on her own a couple months later, having been threatened with disinheritance by her father. As for William, he had been so preoccupied with his sister during his stay at Baden-Baden that there would have been no time to take the waters or gamble even if he had wanted to (which, given his prudery, he most surely would not have). He would leave that kind of thing to his hated rival, Benjamin Disraeli, a passionate gambler and high liver who became a regular guest at Spa.

Bénazet's Baden-Baden may have been too louche for the likes of Gladstone and perhaps not louche enough for la Montez, but state and local officials were certainly grateful for the beneficence that the great Frenchman showered on their town. Yet with time, the sheer scope of Bénazet's ambitions, not to mention his outsized ego, began to rankle. His plan to build the largest thermal bath since Caracalla in the Valley of the Oos was just too grandiose for local sensibilities, and Karlsruhe vetoed it. City officials whom Bénazet thought he'd bought and paid for shockingly rejected his scheme to construct elaborate bathing facilities around a number of smaller thermal springs to which he owned the rights. Miffed, Bénazet spent more and more of his time in Paris. When he died in 1848, he had managed so thoroughly to estrange himself from "his" town that the local press hardly took notice of his passing. He was duly buried in a local cemetery, but nine years later, per wishes of his family and with no objections from his immediate neighbors, living or dead, his remains were exhumed and transferred to Paris's Cimitère Montmartre. They rest there today alongside the graves of Heinrich Heine, Hector Berlioz, and Jacques Offenbach, all sometime guests and/ or performers at Baden-Baden.

Jacques Bénazet's death did not spell the complete end of the age of Bénazet in Baden-Baden, for a son, Édouard, took over his father's unexpired gambling leases in 1848. I will have more to say about Édouard and the further evolution of gambling in Baden-Baden later on, but for now, the passing of Jacques Bénazet offers an excellent opportunity to take stock of the spa town during the 1830s and 1840s.

August Granville's Baden-Baden

By the late 1840s, Baden-Baden, which had earlier witnessed riots in opposition to the spread of gambling, seemed to have reconciled itself to the presence of lavish casinos and to the expansion of tourism. The town's few remaining pig farmers abandoned their swine and turned their attention to the tourists, who had the advantage of being generally just as fat and often far less intelligent than the pigs. In the lucrative summer seasons, many homeowners moved to the upper floors of their dwellings in order to rent out lower spaces to visitors. As was (and is) often the case in newly minted tourist towns, lots of young people who once might have become artisans, manual laborers, or farmers instead took jobs in hotels and restaurants or opened souvenir shops full of Black Forest cuckoo clocks and other kitschy bric-a-brac. This being a water-cure town, a good part of the permanent population worked at the baths in some capacity—as cleaners, attendants, administrators, therapists, nurses, and doctors.

We can get a good sense of the scene in Baden-Baden during the mid-1830s from an exceptionally comprehensive and colorful portrait of the place penned by a naturalized British physician, A. B. Granville, who in that era dutifully visited *all* the major Central European spas in order to produce his magnum opus, *The Spas of Germany* (1837).

Augustus Bozzi Granville, it turns out, was a colorful character himself. Born in Milan in 1783, he studied medicine to avoid military service under Napoleon. After practicing medicine in Greece, Turkey, Spain, and Portugal, Granville joined the British navy. In the process, much like the redoubtable Joseph Conrad, he learned English well enough to write fluently and copiously in that language. Eventually he fetched up in London, where, between writing books on cholera prevention and the "Sumbul," a "new Asiatic remedy of great power against nervous disorders, spasms of the stomach, hysterical affections, paralysis of the limbs, and epilepsy," he performed the first recorded medical autopsy on an ancient Egyptian mummy. A contemporary portrait of Granville shows a handsome young man cradling a human skull in his lap.

Granville studied the spas of Central Europe for the same reason he wrote about cholera and the "Sumbul": to remedy "woeful ignorance and prejudices" on the part of his fellow Englishmen, laypeople and physicians alike. The ugly truth, as he saw it, was that the English people of his day did not sufficiently appreciate the healing power of mineral waters, especially when those waters were located in a foreign land like Germany. The fault for this lay principally with those benighted British physicians, who enforced a conspiracy of silence when it came to the God-given glories of German mineral springs: "There is no doubt that the great blessing offered by Providence to man, suffering under bodily disease, in the sanative power of mineral waters, particularly those of Germany, has been withheld from the people of this country longer than from any other nation," huffed Granville. The English doctors perpetuated this ignorance among their patients in part to conceal their own ignorance, in part because "of a singular skepticism on the part of [British] medical men as to the power of mineral waters in curing disease"—a skepticism carried to the extreme of pooh-poohing every suggestion that a patient might best be served by getting his ailing body posthaste to Germany. At most, a British doctor might propose a local spa—say, Tunbridge Wells or Bath—when only a German Kurort—say, Baden-Baden—would do.

With respect to the competence of the physicians employed in the better German spas, Granville could be almost as effusive as the propaganda coming out of Germany itself. "I'm not going to stand up for every physician I have met at the several spas recently visited; but this I will say for the majority of them . . . that a more learned, or better instructed class of medical men is not easily to be found, either in England or elsewhere."

Baden-Baden, the first Kurort Granville visited on his fact-finding trip through Central Europe, had its fair share of learned practitioners, among them a certain Dr. Kramer, whom Granville assiduously interviewed, and also a peripatetic Englishman named Hutton, who was in residence only during the summer season. As for the doctors' patients at the spa, Granville at first wondered where they might be keeping themselves, for in walking the pretty village streets he saw only folks who looked fit and healthy. He concluded, as others had done before him and many more would do in the decades to come, "that the larger number of those who go thither [to Baden-Baden] have other objects in view than the pursuit of health." Those "other objects," of course, were the things that made Baden-Baden the "summer capital of Europe."

Still, there must have been *some* sick folk in town, and to locate them and learn about their treatment regimens, Granville repaired not to a local hospital (there wasn't one yet) but to the various hotels possessing private access to the major springs. There, he hoped, he would find "the true invalids who add to the renown of Baden."

Granville did find those elusive patients and did learn quite a lot about the qualities of the thermal waters they were "taking," the various treatment procedures they underwent, and the doctors who supervised those treatments. His account of the Baden-Baden cure and its complicated infrastructure is a treasure-trove of information on the medical side of life in this flourishing Central European Kurort.

In Granville's time, the total quantity of *Quellen*, or sources, at Baden-Baden was back up to twelve—the same delightful dozen that had been available to curists in the Roman era, though this would not again be so until the late eighteenth century. As always, the most important and bountiful of these springs was the *Ursprung*, or "original spring." It flowed from crevices in the quartz cliffs above town at the powerful rate of seven and a quarter million cubic inches every twenty-four hours. In additional to being plentiful, the Ursprung water was very hot: 153 1/3 degrees, according to a measurement Granville took directly at the source. The thermal stream plunged back underground before bubbling up again at the above-mentioned Museum Politechnikum, by which time it had lost half a degree of heat.

Some of this water went immediately into a large fountain inside the museum's portico, which was decorated with fragments recovered from the ancient Roman baths. Anyone with a handy cup could drink free of charge from this fountain. Yet one might well ask: Who would want to? Aside from being superhot, this water stank to high heaven. The stink derived not from sulfur, as most people assumed, but from a nasty substance called *Badeschleim* (bath slime)—a species of "vegeto-animal matter" that grows in the reservoirs of all mineral hot springs, though more in some than in others. There was so much of this gunk in the Ursprung water that every glass of it, if left to stand for a few seconds, produced a darkish layer at the bottom much like wine sediment but not nearly as palatable. Nonetheless, as Granville noted, people lined up to drink cup after cup of the Ursprung water without even making a face.

Another portion of the Ursprung flowed into a large reservoir just to the left of the museum portico. Townspeople filled buckets of water from this steaming pool to take home for various domestic uses, "including every culinary operation." Most of the Ursprung waters, however, did not remain at the Politechnikum; they flowed on through underground pipes to those finer hotels that had purchased rights to use this precious fluid in their own private baths.

By the time the waters reached the hotels they had (thankfully) lost another two degrees of heat but naturally still contained the Badeschleim and other ingredients that made them distinctive (and, according to local boosters, near-miraculous in their capacity to cure "rheumatism, gout, and vascular obstructions"). Those health-giving ingredients included salts, sulphate, muriate, carbonate of lime, magnesia, iron, and carbonic acid gas.

Among the several hotels served by the Ursprung, Granville preferred the Coeur de Zöhringer, a newish establishment offering "every luxury a patient can desire." The bathing facilities at the Zöhringer, like those at the other hotels, were closely supervised by a resident physician as well as the municipal police. The thicket of regulations governing the behavior of proprietors, attendants, and the bathers themselves had been established by the town's cure director some twenty years earlier and were strictly enforced. The same was true of the rules regarding bathing fees, though these could vary according to the quality of the hotel (at the Zöhringer, an ordinary bath cost twenty-four kreuzer and a douche thirty-six kreuzer—fees Granville found "moderate" for so classy a place).

Given the high heat of Baden-Baden's waters, patients hoping for a cure there were advised to take only *one* bath a day. As Granville noted coyly: "One Baden warm bath is exciting; two of them in one day would be productive of dangerous irritation." In fact, indiscriminate use of the local waters had sometimes resulted in more than irritation. During Granville's time a rich merchant, having apparently overdone his bathing regimen, was found dead in his tub one fine evening. Meanwhile, a lady lost the use of her arms and legs as a result of taking *three* hot baths in succession. Moreover, there were some patients—those with enlarged livers or weak hearts—who "must abstain [entirely] from the hot bath at Baden if they care for their safety."

For patients with sound constitutions, though, and for curists willing to risk possible side effects like loss of limb use and death, Baden-Baden's waters could not be more beneficent, contended local spa doctors. The best time to reap such benefits, counseled Kramer, was before eating rather than after, lest one of those nasty side effects come into play. "I can hardly state how many have suffered from neglecting this brief injunction," noted the doctor. Finally, regarding the local waters, Kramer warned that their high heat and powerful chemicals made them unsuitable for normal bathing by the unsick. "Those who are not ill, and merely wish for a *bath*, had better not trifle with the *Ursprung*."

Granville learned much about the dos and don'ts of the water cure at Baden-Baden from his frequent talks with Dr. Kramer, who was not only the town's most prominent physician at that time but also *conseilleur privé* to the Grand Dukes of Baden. Moreover, Kramer had written extensively on hydrotherapy and best-practice techniques for spa doctors. He in turn had been influenced by a galaxy of noted water-cure advocates, including Herman Boerhaave (1668–1738), Samuel-Auguste Tissot (1728–1797), and, above all, Vincent Priessnitz (1799–1851).

From Boerhaave, a famous Dutch physician who had instructed Peter the Great, Linnaeus, and Voltaire, and who is often described as the founder of the modern academic hospital, Kramer (and thus Granville) learned to see the skin not so much as a protective barrier for the body's muscles and internal organs but as a sieve through which the tiny chemical agents in mineral water could usefully pass. Water could open obstructed pores because it was such an effective solvent. Once inside the body, mineral-rich thermal waters were free to do all their wonderful work, which for Boerhaave included curing gout, a disease from which he suffered himself off and on throughout his life.

The celebrated Swiss physician Tissot, another polymath, became famous in the world of balneology for his vigorous advocacy of cold baths, which he prescribed as a cure for most maladies, including migraine headaches, but also as an antidote to evil habits like masturbation, which he insisted caused blindness.

Finally, we have Vincent Priessnitz, a self-taught healer from Bohemia who became the most important prophet of hydropathy in the nineteenth century. Priessnitz devoted most of his life to promoting what came to be known as "natural cure"—a combination of beneficent waters, healthy food, good air, and serious exercise—over conventional medicine. This was a crusade that would become much more contentious after Priessnitz's death, but even in his own lifetime this autodidact had to defend his *Naturheilkunde* against charges of quackery lodged by university-trained physicians. With respect to water therapy, Priessnitz pioneered several practices that became staples in many nineteenth-century spas (including Malvern, where they proved so ineffective in Dr. Gully's treatment of little Annie Darwin, and later at John Harvey Kellogg's famed sanatorium at Battle Creek, Michigan). The water-cure techniques prescribed by Priessnitz included, in addition to the usual hot and cold baths, wet-sheet packing and hot wraps of body parts, vigorous rubdowns with hot towels, and steam baths. These were to be reinforced by a routine of early rising, early bedtimes, vigorous walks, and plain food. Overall, this approach worked well enough to earn Priessnitz the epithet, "Nature's Doctor."

Armed with wisdom gleaned from Priessnitz and others, along with insights gained from his own time in the trenches with Baden-Baden's valetudinarians, Kramer put his patients through all the paces they would have expected of him. Their routines included not just regular baths but also wet wraps, rubdowns, saunas, longish walks, and five carefully monitored meals per day.

In Kramer's time at Baden-Baden the baths and saunas were typically *not* taken in the nude, unlike in days of yore and also later on in the twentieth century, when coed nude bathing would become not only common but even *mandatory* at the city's famed Friedrichsbad.

As for those long walks, they were becoming part of the regimen at all the major Central European spas and indeed an important dimension of an increasingly popular body-movement cult that saw exercise as necessary to physical and mental well-being. While this may seem axiomatic to us today, serious exercise did not catch on until the late eighteenth century, and most of the folks who started walking for their health still could not swim. Spas helped spread the ideal of healthy walking by making it *fashionable* to move one's own feet rather than relying exclusively on the feet of one's horses. At grand spas like Baden-Baden in this era, even ladies were encouraged to walk, and to facilitate that practice they were advised to "dress down" into outfits that actually allowed them to move their legs. Baden-Baden and its rivals also popularized walking in groups, which not only made the excursions more fun but encouraged laggards to keep up, something that armies had discovered long ago.

Even for the slowpokes, the walking part of Kramer's spa regimen at Baden-Baden must have seemed more attractive than the dietary demands. The "plain food" championed by Priessnitz and acolytes like Kramer was definitely *not* the sort of rib-padding, tasty fare one would have found at Cotta's restaurant in the Badischer Hof. According to Granville, who put together a list of "allowed" and "forbidden" beverages and foods for curists at Baden-Baden and other Central European spas, a patient might legitimately enjoy, in the beverage department, barley water but not beer, broth but not punch, and cocoa but not tea; in the food category, asparagus was allowed but not anchovies, greens but not goose, fish but not fat (animal), and oatmeal but not onions. Strangely enough (by our lights), red meat, as long as it was not salted, smoked, or too fatty, was "much recommended." No doubt many curists stuck to the dreary diet prescribed by Kramer and his cohorts; but many more must have snuck off to Cotta's as often as they could.

Admittedly, then, the food dished out to Baden-Baden curists in the mid-nineteenth century was not early Alice Waters. On the other hand, it *was* largely "local and seasonal," there not being much choice in the matter. And with time, spa food would get much better and eventually play a small part in the epochal sea change from ancien to nouvelle cuisine.

One therapy that Kramer especially favored, even though it lacked sanction from his august mentors, was the mud bath. Although mud baths are thousands of years old, they did not become a trusted tool in the spa doctors' medical kit until the early nineteenth century, when, according to a dubious Dr. Granville, there was a "mania" for this therapy at all the German spas. We do not know why Dr. Kramer valued mud baths so highly, but it might have been because once a patient was packed tightly away in one of the casket-like tubs, he or she could be left exclusively in the care of a lowly bath attendant.*

At the time Dr. Granville dropped in on Dr. Kramer, the latter had been practicing for over twenty years in Baden-Baden. Interestingly

---

*A few years ago, while taking a mud bath in the Napa Valley, I was left to the tender mercies of an attendant who took special delight in packing my private parts with the very hottest clumps of the foul-smelling goo. I still bear the scars today.

enough, those twenty years had taught the spa doctor that, although his *chère source* was indeed wonderful, it was not quite the panacea that he had originally thought it to be. He acknowledged to Granville that at times he had been "disappointed" with the result of his treatments, concluding that some of his patients might have been better served by simply staying at home.

No doubt Kramer confided such doubts about the usefulness of his work only to intimates like Granville; certainly this kind of talk would not have gone down well with his superiors or the salespeople at Baden-Baden, whose promotional pitches never contained any caveats about the spa's "healing waters"—not to mention possible side effects like loss of limb use or death. And in any event, Baden-Baden's draw was based on a lot more than its wonderful waters. A curist might indeed have dealt with this or that medical affliction just as well by staying at home, but only by personally visiting this Black Forest refuge could he or she experience the delights of Europe's summer capital.

Baden-Baden's diversions in the 1830s and 1840s were quite varied and sometimes arduous. As Granville noted censoriously, echoing earlier critics of European spa life, in this little city nighttime "was turned into day, and invalids often destroy[ed] at night the good they had done themselves in the day by drinking and bathing in the water." Put in the less censorious words of a contemporary publicist, the bathing season at Baden-Baden "might best be described by a short French phrase: 'C'est toujours jour de fête.'"

One saw the daily fête most prominently on the public promenade, that colonnaded boardwalk whose shaded precincts afforded, in Granville's scornful assessment, "a hundred excuses for the assemblage of the many thousand idlers, who devote just one hour, in every four-and-twenty, to that great object, health; and two-thirds of the remaining time to pleasure and dissipation." Realizing that many, if not most, of their guests had indeed come for pleasure rather than health and in the process were typically spending some two million florins every season (in Baden one could pay with florins, kreuzer, francs, or gulden), the town fathers left no stone unturned and no vice untapped in their ongoing effort to keep those florins flowing.

The above-discussed gambling concessions, of course, constituted an obvious means of separating a fool from his florins. In his report on

Baden-Baden, Granville did not have much to say on this subject, save to observe "with deep sorrow" that the gaming circles there included "the daughters of Englishmen, who pressed around the tables to stake their *petite pièces*," allowing themselves to be "elbowed by some rude fellow-gambler, who probably had as little character as he had money to lose."

Naturally, not *all* tourists at Baden-Baden were foolish or greedy enough to gamble, and for these folk there had to be an array of other divertissements. The spa town's reading rooms provided a relatively harmless form of entertainment, especially for the ladies who flocked to them at midday, though not so much to read as to gossip about "the latest scandals, duels, and the extraordinary adventures of the preceding day."

Shopping provided the ladies with another fairly painless entertainment—painless, perhaps, except to the pocketbook. By Granville's time, Baden-Baden boasted many *"merchandes de mode"* and *"boutiquiers"* offering luxury goods of the sort produced by those noble émigrés who had been marooned in the town by the French Revolution. Yet as Granville could not help noticing, the shops seemed "to address themselves to the English only." The store names might be French, and even the owners French, but the goods therein typically carried descriptions written in English so as not to befuddle those English ladies who made up the bulk of the clientele.

In his observations regarding Baden-Baden's shops, Granville was unwittingly touching on a much larger issue: the English touristic invasion of the Continent and the consequent gradual displacement of the French language by English as the most popular means of communication. In the 1830s, that displacement was not yet occurring across the board—French held on as the language of choice for many spa patrons, especially aristocratic spa patrons, for a good number of years. Yet for the *grande langue*, the writing was literally on the wall in those English-language explanations at the better Baden shops in the mid-nineteenth century.

A crucial part of every guest's day in Baden-Baden, whether that visitor be male or female, a serious curist or just a tourist looking for a good time, was a stroll on the public promenade. According to Granville, the guests of lesser social distinction tended to walk in the early afternoon, while the "exclusives" showed themselves at five o'clock on the planks before retiring to a "diner prié or the table-d'hôte par excellence at Chabert's."

The dining room at this particular establishment featured floor-to-ceiling mirrors like those at the Gallerie des Glaces at Versailles—perfect for studying the reflected visages of one's neighbors, or even better, oneself. While attending one of those exclusive dinners at Chabert's, Granville was simultaneously charmed and put off by the presence of some two-hundred women tucking into their tournedos. Had not Lord Byron himself reminded us that no pretty woman should ever be seen eating? Yet here were legions of lovelies, "exhibited, at one view, absorbed in that vulgar performance." Often vulgar, too, was the conversation of these ladies (and gentlemen), whose comments, "if founded on facts," suggested that "the morality of many of the temporary inhabitants of this watering-place must be of a very low standard, and licentiousness would seem to be tolerated to a degree, surpassed only by that of the larger capitals of Europe."

Like those larger cities of Europe, little Baden-Baden witnessed during the summer season various balls and grand parties. Sumptuous balls were a high point of the bathing season at all grand spas, belonging as they did to "*la mode de vie*" of the aristocrats who frequented the baths. As a French historian notes in a recent study of the spa-going European nobility, "grand balls were without doubt the most favored form of conviviality [among aristocrats] at the thermal springs." At Baden-Baden, the grandest of the balls were held at the Conversation House, while smaller, more intimate affairs took place in private villas or rented halls at the major hotels.

Our dogged researcher Granville attended a *bal paré* (full-dress ball) at the Conversation House, which "brought under the same gilded roof for a few hours all the beau monde of Baden." Music was provided by two groups: the regimental band from the garrison at Rastaat and the resident orchestra of Baden. The attendees were by no means exclusively aristocratic, but all had at least to *look* the part, for a liveried lackey at the door had the authority to turn away anyone who "presented himself in a costume deemed less than respectable." But alas, sniffed Granville with characteristic scorn, this preoccupation with the "external man" meant that, along with the "*sommités aristocratiques* of almost every nation in Europe," one also encountered "the Zeros and the Rogues from the same countries, in no inconsiderable number." As for the women at the balls, the presence of the Dowager Duchess Stéphanie and her daughter Princess Marie proved to be no guarantee "that the purest of their sex, only, [were] admitted." Moreover, the epithet "*paré*" seemed misapplied, for most of the ladies wore a demitoilet. In the confusing Babel of languages, "one could distinguish the superior number of the English among the company," but these Brits, like the citizens of other countries, typically fell back on fractured French when they could not make themselves understood in their own languages. After a few hours, many of the ladies had broken into an inelegant sweat, while the men, even the tough hussars among them, looked thoroughly beaten down. Yet on and on they went into the small hours of the morning, some revelers becoming "positively *sick* with exertion."

Along with gaming and dancing, Baden-Baden offered theatrical spectacles as a diversion. Later on, this spa town would become an important center of theater (as it also would of orchestral music and even opera), but at the time of Granville's visit, the local theater scene was still fairly provincial. To the visiting Englishman's skeptical eye, most of the performances seemed "burlesque," and most of the performers "indifferent" in ability. Yet there were occasional stars, such as the appropriately named German actor Wilhelm Kunst. He treated the "gay folks of Baden" to a "*Grosses Trauerspiel* in five acts *nach* Shakespeare: *Hamlet Prinz von Dänemark*." The play was in German, not in the excellent translation by Schlegel but in a stilted version by a local nonentity named Schröder. Yet the translation probably did not matter much: although Baden-Baden was located in a German-speaking land, most of the foreign visitors knew only a few phrases in that language, and "*Sein oder nicht sein—das ist die Frage*" (To be or not to be—that is the question) was probably not one of them.

The "Jewish Question"

One question that Granville completely ignored in his portrait of 1830s Baden-Baden was what the Germans later would call "the Jewish question." Because Jews came to play important roles in all the major Central European Kurorte, especially in the second half of the nineteenth century, it is appropriate here to investigate their standing in Germany's breakout grand spa as it began its climb to prominence.

Actually, in the early nineteenth century a kind of Jewish question was already evident in Baden-Baden and indeed across the German region, because the French Revolution had brought with it heightened appeals for the emancipation of German Jews. Yet unlike in France, in the German states the new order did not bring full emancipation anywhere. The Grand Duchy of Baden, it turns out, adopted the most progressive measures, but even these fell short of full equality. In that state, the granting of full settlement and citizenship (*Niederlassung und Bürgerrecht*) privileges was left in the hands of the municipalities, and none of them was willing to give Jews the same rights as Gentiles. The reason offered by Baden's new constitution of 1808 for withholding full civic rights to Jews was that these people had not yet reached "the level of education and employment-preparedness displayed by Christians." (This was a perfect Catch-22 argument, since by continuing to deny Jews equal access to education and employment their "readiness" for full citizenship could be indefinitely postponed.) Nonetheless, it was a testament to how bad conditions had been for German Jews in the Middle Ages and Early Modern period that many of them celebrated the new order, some even going so far as to greet Napoleon as a secular messiah.

By 1812, the year Napoleon retreated from Moscow, Baden-Baden's Jewish population was substantial enough for the poet Hebel to include "Juden" among the groups which were notably present around town. Jews were certainly present at the so-called *Armenbad* (bath for the poor), an old institution in the gift of the margraves that served "poor people, injured military veterans, and Jews." Somewhat earlier, in the late eighteenth century, one of the town's thermal springs, hitherto known as the Quelle zum Greifvogel, had been renamed the Judenquelle in local parlance. It was called thus, explained a municipal authority, "because it contains the water [flowing] to the bathhouse which serves the Jews." The bathhouse in question was undoubtedly located in the Gasthaus Hirsch, an establishment still in existence today, albeit much expanded (and no longer catering primarily to Jews).

The Hirsch hotel pointed to the existence of Jewish *visitors*, not just residents. It is probable that visiting Jews wealthy enough to stay at the Hirsch may also have gambled at the one casino in town not operated by a Frenchman: the Spielbank Oppenheimer, named for a Jewish banker from Berlin of that name. By 1816 the number of Jews visiting Baden-Baden had grown to the point that the State Bathing Authority sanctioned the opening of a second "Jewish hostelry," called "Zum Roß."

This establishment remained in business through the season of 1837 and perhaps beyond. Lodgings like the Hirsch and the Roß were much in demand because they were the only localities where religious Jews could obtain kosher food. On the other hand, more secular Jews, especially the wealthier ones, often ignored their faith's dietary strictures and stayed at the top "Christian" hotels, provided they could get in. In general, they seem to have been able to gain admittance, for in the "summer capital of Europe" at this time, capital typically spoke louder than race, at least in the domain of tourist-oriented commerce. Down the road, alas, even this level of self-interested "tolerance" would not always be on hand.

We know virtually nothing about the above-mentioned Jewish gambling concession owned by Herr Oppenheimer (not even the concessionaire's first name), but we have much more information about another Jewish entrepreneur who played an important role in the life of Baden-Baden in the first half of the nineteenth century: David Raphael Marx. Herr Marx (no relation to Karl) was a book dealer and book printer from Karlsruhe. In 1816 he opened in the Conversation House the Reading Institute, which included a bookstore and lending library. In a testament to the importance of book reading in that era, the Baden Ministry of the Interior granted Marx's operation an annual subsidy of one thousand gulden, drawn from gambling revenues. In return, Marx not only set up a library with appropriate reading matter but also laid in a large supply of newspapers and magazines. Naturally, Marx advertised his establishment in French.

The Reading Institute became a central meeting point for Baden-Baden's cosmopolitan clientele, especially the females. At midcentury, according to a local paper, one could find there "Russians, Chinese, French, English, Peruvians, Austrians, Danes, Spanish, Americans, Jews, Arabs, and Persians." Later on, even Queen Victoria showed up at Marx's establishment, noting in a diary entry for April 1, 1872: "I walked down to D. Marx's shop where there are all sorts of pretty things and I made several purchases." As for Herr Marx himself, he converted to Lutheranism on March 21, 1848, and accordingly gained full citizenship rights.

Getting There

Depending on where they came from, most of the foreign visitors to Baden-Baden in the first half of the nineteenth century found that the journey thither required some genuine effort. The place was a bit out of the way—close to the navigable Rhine but not quite on it. Until the mid-1840s, the only way into the town was by road. In this era there were four main routes: one coming from France via Strasbourg; one from the Lower Rhine via Leopoldshaffen; another from northern Germany via Karlsruhe; and one leading from the west through Stuttgart. Our English visitor Granville had made the trip by ascending the Rhine on a large river steamer from Rotterdam to Biberach; changing there to a smaller steamer bound for Leopoldshafen; boarding a coach to Karlsruhe; and finally going on down to Baden-Baden by diligence. He does not say how long the trip took, but just for the Continental parts it must have required several days.

Granville made very clear that he was just one of many Englishmen to visit that spa town in the 1830s. Actually, he was a part of something much larger: the first wave of mass tourism to hit the European continent. In the post-Napoleonic period, most of Britain seemed to be traveling for pleasure. As Anthony Trollope astutely noted, Britain was the only country wealthy enough to have its middling classes—professionals and even tradesmen—venturing abroad in significant numbers.

In the 1820s and 1830s, many of those Continent-bound British travelers chose the Upper Rhine as their destination. This group was as diverse as the rest of the pack, ranging in rank, as William Thackeray put it in a delightful story, *The Kickleburys on the Rhine*, "from the ambassador who spends his leave here, to the apprentice who arrives for a couple of weeks' fun." As was true for Baden-Baden itself, a good part of the Upper Rhine Valley's lure in the age of romanticism had to do with the aura of mystery and sensual longing clinging to the region: all those crumbling cliff-top castles; vine-covered hills; fairy-tale villages; and, of course, the Lorelei—that riverside cliff haunted by a golden-haired girl whose beauty and siren's song caused, according to legend, many a seaman to crash and die on the rocks. For steamboat travelers, passage through the swirling currents at the base of the Lorelei was invariably an occasion for whistle-in-the-dark singing and extensive quaffing of the hillside product, meaning that passengers going on to Baden-Baden would have had an inspirational foretaste of the attractions awaiting them at the spa.

In the mid-1840s, travel to and from Baden-Baden underwent a huge change—part of a broader transition that affected not just travel but entire ways of seeing, thinking, and experiencing time. This sea-change was the coming of the railroad era, which, in the words of one of its most perceptive historians, Wolfgang Schivelbusch, created "a revolutionary rupture with [all] past forms of experience." With rail travel, people experienced spatial relationships (at least on land) in a brand new way—not in terms of animal capacities but in those of what a large powerful *machine* could do. What the "iron horse" could accomplish in comparison to an organic one was truly amazing: twenty to thirty miles-per-hour average speed for the early trains in England, or about three times the speed of stagecoaches. Seen from the window of a train, objects on the land seemed to fly by in a blur, virtually "killing space," as the poet Heinrich Heine put it (unfortunately, killing lots of animals, too, poor creatures that tarried too long on those strange iron tracks). Heine noted that it now took only four and a half hours to go from Paris to Orléans or even Rouen. Just imagine, he chimed, what would happen when the new rail lines to Belgium and Germany were completed!

That innovation came quickly. The first steam-powered railway line in Germany opened in 1835, covering the short distance between Nuremberg and Fürth. By the early 1840s, lines connected the growing German network to that of France. In 1844 the Baden State Railway opened a small station at Oos, near Baden-Baden, on the Rhine Valley Railway. Passengers bound for Baden-Baden changed to horse-buses for the final short trip to the spa town. Just one year later a branch rail line was added, along with a new station in the center of town. Baden-Baden was now completely connected by iron rails to the outside world. By 1860, following the inauguration by Napoleon III of the Paris-Strasbourg railroad, Baden-Baden boosters could brag that it took a mere *twelve hours* to get from Paris to their town. The folks making that trip would be yet more diverse than the earlier stagecoach crowd, which, though containing a fair sample of bourgeois adventurers, was still predominantly upper crust. Baden-Baden never became an Everyman's retreat, but the railroads helped significantly to broaden and democratize its patronage.

If the rail journey to Baden-Baden was much faster, easier, and even more democratic than the stage rides of yore, train travel was not necessarily without stress and discomfort. On the contrary, that time-killing speed could be disorienting for many travelers, as was also the feeling of being propelled like a bullet across high bridges and through dark tunnels. One particularly upsetting implication of the daring speed was the high possibility of very ugly carnage if something went wrong. "It is really flying," observed a brave pioneer on the maiden trip of George Stephenson's steam locomotive in England in 1829, "and it's impossible to divest yourself of the notion of instant death to all upon the least accident happening." Even if one avoided cataclysmic death, there was a good chance of falling prey to "railway spine," a fibromyalgia-like affliction that typically continued long after disembarkation. Along perhaps with a painful back, some of those early rail travelers to Baden-Baden undoubtedly suffered from stress and anxiety, but fortunately for them, "nervous disorders" were among the very afflictions the awaiting "cure" was designed to fix.

The Revolutions of 1848–1849

Three years after the railway revolution arrived in Baden-Baden, a revolution of the more conventional political variety hit the town: the Revolutions of 1848–1849, yet another gift from France. This upheaval—actually, a wave of upheavals, engulfing most of Europe—started in February in Paris, when the coupon-cutting monarch Louis Philippe finally outlived his welcome. The deposed king ended up back in exile in England, where he arguably should have stayed all along. In the meantime, like the French revolutions of 1789–1799 and 1830, this one spread almost immediately to Germany.

Being on the French border, the Grand Duchy of Baden was among the first of the German states to become caught up in the heady spillover from Paris. The stirring French ideas fell on fruitful ground in Baden because various liberal, radical-democratic, and even socialist elements there had long been frustrated by the Grand Duchy's failure to live up to the progressive hopes kindled in the region by the first great French Revolution. As in other German states, a host of organizations and salons reflecting those hopes, among them various *Turnvereine* (political-gymnastics clubs) and *Schützenvereine* (shooting clubs) sprouted up across the land. As historian James Sheehan notes, "With the possible exception of the months immediately after the First World War, there is no other period in German history so full of spontaneous social action and dramatic political possibilities." Little Baden-Baden, with its close ties to France, shared fully in this moment of great expectations, joining in the insistent calls for press freedom, jury trials, arms for the people, and a national German parliament.

Up in Karlsruhe, feeling the heat, Grand Duke Leopold quickly capitulated. Because this ruler had always been rather more progressive than most of his cohorts, his agile donning of the red-black-gold colors of revolution was perhaps less painful than similar moves by other German leaders. On the other hand, Leopold was no democrat, and those who worried that his adroit change in political coloration might be merely tactical were soon proved correct. Yet for the moment, all was unity, brotherhood, and love. Townspeople bedecked their houses in the revolutionary colors and, with the grand duke presiding, celebrated the new era with a grand feast at the Holländische Hof restaurant. A delegation of happy democrats presented Leopold with an official thank-you letter for his support.

But the spirit of togetherness soon proved ephemeral, as did the grand duke's goodwill. There had always been significant differences of vision among the opponents of the old order, and those differences began to assert themselves more prominently once the new crowd tasted actual power. As in other German states during these momentous days, the most critical divide arose between moderate liberals and radical democrats; the former were essentially constitutional monarchists, while the latter pushed for a democratic republic on the model of the United States (whose own inadequacies in the democracy department often eluded these German visionaries). Two fiery Baden radicals, Friedrich Hecker and Gustav von Struve (he dropped the embarrassing "von" in 1847) led the charge for democracy in Baden. Having walked out of a national preparliamentary gathering in Frankfurt to protest that congregation's pusillanimity, Hecker and Struve sought to turn Baden and southwestern Germany into a springboard for "real revolution" across the divided region. They mobilized an enthusiastic band of several thousand rebels and proclaimed a republic.

Cleverly sensing that he was no longer wanted, Duke Leopold fled to Switzerland. From there he appealed for help from nearby Hesse, whose ruler, fearing a possible spread of the republican contagion to his own state, was only too happy to oblige. The Baden rebels fought bravely but were quickly outmatched by the Hessians and by Badenese troops loyal to Leopold. By the end of April 1848, Hecker and Struve's republican dream was dashed. Later that year Hecker would be chased into exile and Struve packed off to jail.*

Tellingly, throughout all this chaos, a bronze statue of Grand Duke Leopold standing in the central square of Baden-Baden remained untouched. In fact, that statue would remain steadfastly in place until World War II, when it fell victim to the Hitler government's insatiable need for metals to make arms.

Looking ahead to that ugly future, I should note that in one important respect the turmoil of 1848–1849 foreshadowed what was to come. Along with an upsurge of nationalism, 1848 brought a new wave of anti-Semitism and anti-Jewish violence to the German region, and that violence was especially pronounced in the state of Baden. Behind this violence, which was strongest in the rural regions of northern Baden, was a traditional hatred of the Jews as economic middlemen thought to prey on the peasantry, along with an age-old religious bigotry that portrayed the Jews as the "killers of our Savior, Jesus Christ." In relatively progressive Baden, another motivation lay in the fears of many ordinary citizens, conservative by nature, that the revolution might finally bring full emancipation to the Jews. As a result of massive populist anti-Semitic pressure from below, the new liberal state parliament backed away from forcing local municipalities like Baden-Baden and Freiburg to grant Jews full privileges of citizenship.

Meanwhile, the national parliament that had assembled in Frankfurt with hopes of creating a unified, constitutional Germany was being pulled apart by internal divisions over what kind of nation the reformers wanted and also what size. In the spring of 1849, the unwieldy assembly that had been meeting in St. Paul's Church slowly dispersed, conservatives and moderates leaving voluntarily, frustrated radicals needing a kick in the pants by King Friedrich Wilhelm IV of Prussia. Earlier this same monarch had turned down the Frankfurt parliament's offer of leadership over a new constitutional Germany, saying he could not accept "a crown from the gutter." In May 1849 he sent a Prussian army

---

*After his release from jail in 1849, Struve, like Hecker, went into exile, in his case in the United States. There he continued to fight for reform. An abolitionist and Lincoln backer, Struve was among many German "Forty-Eighters" who fought for the Union in the Civil War. Yet his heart remained in Germany, and when Prussia offered him an amnesty in 1863, he returned to that state, where he found a new cause in militant vegetarianism. He died in Vienna, Austria in 1870, age sixty-four.

down to Baden, where it quickly and bloodily suppressed a new uprising by angry radicals desperately trying to restart the German revolution. The suppression of this last-ditch rebellion effectively ended Germany's spirited but deeply flawed campaign to create a new nation from below with (generally) liberal ideals. When Germany did become a unified nation a quarter-century later, the unity would be imposed from above with the aid of "iron and blood," and the nation thus created would at its core be far from liberal.

But what, we might ask, did all of this mean for the fate of Baden-Baden as an international water-cure and gambling resort? Revolutions have a way of frightening people, and the ones in 1848–1849, though ultimately abortive, did scare potential visitors away from the spa. For several months patronage at the baths and Spielbänke dropped off significantly. Gambling took a harder hit than bathing because the German radicals, like political radicals in many other places, tended to be highly censorious when it came to "social vices" that injured ordinary people. There were calls from the radical faction in the new Baden government for a suppression of gaming. Up in Frankfurt, that call seems to have been heard, for the would-be national parliament grandiosely ordered the closing of all casinos in Germany. Although the Frankfurt parliament's decrees generally proved unenforceable—Nanny Frankfurt lacked a stick—a group of vigilantes acting in the name of "the Reich" marched over to nearby Bad Homburg and shut down its tables.

Even after the 1848–1849 revolutions collapsed and conservatives reasserted control, gambling remained endangered because the top Prussian authorities, who had led the restoration effort, harbored their own reservations about gaming. In May 1849, contingents of Prussian soldiers, having killed or chased away the last of the Baden radicals, camped along the Kastanienallé and billeted in Baden-Baden residences. The Grand Duchy of Baden was fast becoming a Prussian satellite state.

Under these conditions, Édouard Bénazet, the recently installed concessionaire at the Conversation House and new kingpin of Baden-Baden gaming, became concerned enough for the future of his livelihood to make a dramatic gesture of his own. In May 1849 he shut down gambling at the tables he controlled and ordered the entire Conversation House closed to visitors. He did not intend to impose this draconian order for long: the point of his move was to show everyone in authority what conditions in town would be like without the "lifeblood" of gaming. Local worthies quickly got the point. Fearful of losing the upcoming summer season, they implored Bénazet to reopen his halls. They also desisted, at least for a time, from efforts to cramp his style.

In certain ways, though, Bénazet's style did become cramped because after 1849, the Prussian ruling house, which earlier had been represented only sporadically in Baden-Baden, made that spa town one of its favorite summer havens. Crown Prince Wilhelm, the future king of Prussia and emperor of Germany, had led the Prussian troops that "restored order" in Baden in 1849. He became quite attached to Baden-Baden and was one of those Hohenzollerns who returned there regularly over the years. "I came to you as an enemy, but next time I'll come to you as a friend," he is reported to have said upon pulling out of town in 1849. Alas, when he made good on that promise to return later on, he brought along his wife, Augusta, an archprude who hated gambling and refused to set foot in the Conversation House. Bénazet worried that Augusta might convince her husband to call for an end to gambling in Baden tout court—a worry that was hardly unfounded because Wilhelm, once he became emperor, did indeed decide to ban casino gambling across the entire Reich. In the meantime, although he did not try to cut off Baden-Baden's lifeblood, the Prussian crown prince proved to be anything but a party animal during his frequent visits to the town. He shunned the fast international set, preferring the company of fellow soldiers quartered at nearby Rastaat. Even more threatening to Bénazet's world were some of the old troopers in the prince's retinue, who despised everything that "Europe's summer capital" stood for. For example, Wilhelm's adjutant general, Prince Kraft von Hohenlohe-Ingelfingen, let it be known that, for him, the fashionable strollers on the Grand Promenade were nothing but "the scum of Parisian society." Bénazet knew that he had to step carefully lest the sun go down permanently on Baden-Baden's long summer day.

The summer sun did not go down for good at Baden-Baden—at last report, it still rises there every day during the season—but there would definitely be darker times to come. So let us leave the town for the moment with a nostalgic *mise en scène* penned by an English diplomat, Sir Horace Rumbold, detailing what he witnessed on the Grand Promenade in 1856:

In the motley crowd that thronged the board walk, or sat in closely packed rows round the kiosk where the band was playing, or lounged by the shop of Mellerio the jeweler, or flirted and tattled at the tables under the trees, every type and class and nation was represented. We had there a perfect epitome of European society in all its shades and gradations: German royalty, French art and literature, Parisian fashion and frailty; the greatest ladies from London, Vienna, and St. Petersburg cheek by jowl with the fairest sinners from Berlin or the Quartier Breda; the impassive *croupier* and the fevered, broken gambler side by side; English blacklegs jostling Frankfurt Jew stock-brokers; lanky Baden dragoons mixed with stalwart Croats of *Benedek infanterie* and the boyish-looking recruits of the Prussian regiments; and, for *couleur locale*, a sprinkling of the wonderful hats, red waistcoats, and long, silver-buttoned coats of the Schwarzwald peasantry, and yet more wondrous huge butterfly head-dresses of their womankind. The air was full of laughter, of shrill female voices, of the clatter of a thousand tongues in a dozen different languages, hushed now and then by the marvelous harmony that floated across from Koennemann's faultless Kapelle. The atmosphere was loaded with tobacco smoke, or with subtler and more grateful perfumes as some pretty women glided past through the ever-shifting throng; the glare of the gas fell crudely on the many-colored multitude in all its variety of dress and ornament, here and there lighting indifferently on a rouged cheek or a sweet girlish face, flashing off a diamond trinket in some pink, shell-like ear, or giving relief to a bright patch of colour or to features strongly marked. It was a gaudy, bewildering, yet strangely intoxicating scene—essentially of the earth earthy—but set in such lovely surroundings, that when the soft moon stole over it from above the ruins of the *Alte Schloss*, tipping the tall trees with silver and marking their shadows on the quiet lawn and walks beyond, one could only revel in its singular beauty, and he must have been a churl indeed, or a pedant, who could moralize over, instead of giving himself wholly up to, its magic charm.

CHAPTER THREE

Muses in the Waters

It is never easy to account for the role of place in the creation of an artistic work, yet sometimes setting can be just as influential as inspiration from fellow artists, living or dead. In the pages that follow I trace the importance of the Central European spa scene in the lives and work of a few selected writers and musicians. Painters spent time at the spas, too, but in their domain the Kurorte generated fewer works of lasting value; and, with the notable exception of architects and landscape designers, visual artists did not have much impact on the spas themselves or on the contemporary perception of them.

For writers and musicians working in the late eighteenth and nineteenth centuries, the grand Kurorte had a function similar to the splendid coffeehouses in fin de siècle Vienna. The Viennese coffeehouses were (to quote a recent academic study) "locales of spectacle, consumption and sexual license on the one hand, and on the other [incubators] for the gestation of new political, social and creative ideas." So, too, were the spas, in spades. The writers and musicians who congregated in the Kurorte every summer did not call what they did "networking," but this is as good a term as any for their activity. Of course, they did other things as well. Some actually took the waters. Some plunged into (often disastrous) love affairs. Some played at roulette (equally disastrously). Some seem to have just sat around and stared at the walls. But the fact that many *worked* as well as *networked* was of no small importance to the cultural life of Europe in the nineteenth century.

Two Titans at the Fountains: Goethe and Beethoven

For Goethe, Germany's most prominent man of letters, the grand spas of choice were in Bohemia, principally Karlsbad, Teplitz, and Marienbad. A creature of habit, Goethe visited these places some twenty times between 1785 and 1823, his stays typically lasting from fifteen to nineteen weeks.

In 1814, however, Goethe thought he might break his routine with a visit to Wiesbaden, about which he had heard promising things from friends. In 1810 the Frankfurt-area spa had added a new *Kurhaus* and casino to its amenities, which also included a charming landscape. Its clientele was said to be especially cultivated. But was it affordable? Cautiously, the ever-thrifty poet inquired of a knowledgeable acquaintance: "Would you please send me a description of Wiesbaden, along with an estimation of what one person with a single servant might expect to lay out for a visit of four to six weeks?" Aware both of Goethe's solid financial resources and penny-pinching proclivities, the friend confidently replied, "It's doable!" Goethe accordingly made his pilgrimage to Wiesbaden that summer but was shocked by the cost of everything: "One quickly learns here that the coin is round [i.e., has to do a lot of rolling]!" he reported back. In fact, although the poet could not have known it, he had arrived in Wiesbaden when it was still relatively cheap, for it had not yet emerged as a world-class health resort, a true rival to Baden-Baden.

As for Baden-Baden, that grand spa *almost* got the opportunity to add Goethe to its list of illustrious guests. In 1816 Joachim Cotta, co-owner of the Badischer Hof, invited the great man to come down for a visit. Because Cotta was offering to put the poet up for free and the invitation had the backing of Goethe's patron, Duke Carl August of Saxe-Weimar, Goethe finally agreed to come. Cotta accordingly readied his best suite of rooms for the impending visit. But on the journey down to Baden-Baden, Goethe's coach threw a wheel and tipped over. Badly shaken, the poet took the mishap for a sign from heaven that he was not meant to go to Baden-Baden after all. He promptly returned to Weimar—and to his routine of summer visits to the Bohemian spas.

Initially, Goethe restricted his Bohemian cure custom to Karlsbad, the oldest, largest, and most storied of the region's spas. But he had been in no hurry to go there. He did not make his first visit until the summer of 1785, staying for forty-five days. He was then thirty-six years old, hardly a young man given that life expectancy for males in Central Europe at that time was a mere thirty-eight.

Goethe went to Karlsbad for reasons that made perfect sense given his interests, character, and state of health. The writer was a highly sociable man, interested omnivorously in the arts, natural science, and politics. He was hobbled by the usual gout along with some nasty stomach problems. And, perhaps most important, he was possessed of a very active, almost insatiable libido. Thus it is hardly strange that Goethe visited Karlsbad to improve his health, socialize with fellow notables, botanize and geologize, do some writing, and enjoy a stimulating tryst or two—not necessarily in that order. His ability to realize at least some of these goals on that first trip helps explain why spa visits became an important part of his life.

Before following Goethe on his maiden excursion to Karlsbad, let's take a brief look at the grand Bohemian spa he chose to honor with his presence. By the late eighteenth century, Karlsbad had clearly established itself among the first rank of Central European Kurorte. The town had suffered a terrible fire in 1759 but recovered quickly, replacing flammable half-timbered houses with solid stone edifices of many stories. City walls that had previously limited urban growth were not rebuilt after the fire, allowing expansion into the hinterlands. A tax on visitors provided funds for a fancy new theater, among other innovations. As for its clientele, Karlsbad continued to "collect crowned heads" (fortunately still connected to their bodies) following the historic visit of Czar Peter the Great in 1711–1712. In 1721 Empress Elizabeth Christine, wife of Habsburg Emperor Charles VI, descended on the Kurort with a large retinue that included her four-year-old daughter, Maria Theresa, who would go on to become one of Austria's most illustrious sovereigns.*

Eleven years later, Maria Theresa returned to Karlsbad in the tow of her father Charles, who loved to luxuriate in the local baths. Charles

---

*The bar here was not very high. Due to generations of inbreeding, the Habsburg family tree, like those of many other European dynasties, was rife with deformed branches and misshapen fruit. A famous case was Emperor Ferdinand I (r. 1835–1848). Born hydrocephalic, he suffered also from frequent epileptic fits. Although he was never formally declared incapacitated, a regent's council ran the government. Ferdinand, meanwhile, became famous for uttering one coherent sentence, "I am the emperor, and I want dumplings," and for entertaining himself by wedging his ample bottom into a wastebasket and rolling around on the floor.

enjoyed Karlsbad so much that in subsequent summers he often chose to govern his unwieldy realm from the comforts of his palatial villa at the spa. Yet comfortable as Karlsbad undoubtedly was, it was also a serious healing center, especially after the arrival in 1775 of Dr. David Becher. This august physician and chemist personally analyzed the region's mineral water and instituted a rigorous cure regimen featuring daily two-hour hot baths and several rounds of the various mineral-water fountains, where curists typically knocked back twenty to thirty glasses of the highly salty product. (The salt content of the Karlsbad waters was so high that Becher could distill large quantities of the stuff and market it as a separate export item.)

The great Dr. Becher may not have been known to Goethe when the latter set out for Karlsbad, but Becher would certainly have heard of the German writer. Eleven years earlier Goethe had become an instant literary celebrity by virtue of his novel *The Sorrows of Young Werther*, a story of impossible romance and suicide that caused a wave of copycat self-destruction across Germany by lovesick young men. One year after the success of *Werther*, Goethe took up residence in Weimar, the duchy with which he would remain associated as a resident artist and statesman for the rest of his life. Duke Carl August ennobled him, thereby facilitating his access to the kind of high society that congregated in Karlsbad every summer.

No sooner had Goethe's coach turned into Karlsbad's market square on July 4, 1785, than a trumpeter stationed atop a nearby tower sounded a fanfare of welcome. This was a greeting reserved for guests of distinction, though the honor of being "blown in" (as Goethe put it) faded somewhat when the honoree was pressed to fork over a handsome tip for the privilege. Then came more tips for the wagon driver and customs man, plus much palm greasing for the porters who carried Goethe's monstrous trunks into Der Weiβe Hasen Hotel, his home for the next month and a half. Upon checking in and signing the *Kurliste* (a necessary procedure allowing other important guests to know who among their kind was in town), Goethe dutifully paid the recently instituted cure tax required of all visitors, high and low. A hotel lackey then divested him of another tidy sum in exchange for a box of the handwritten visiting cards that guests dispatched in advance to other guests whom they intended to visit. Thus, within a few minutes of arriving in town, Goethe had already begun to hemorrhage money at a rate that was likely to make any actual bloodletting down the line seem tame by comparison.

The Kurliste to which Goethe added his name included a number of Weimar friends with whom the poet expected to socialize; also on the list was a close lady friend named Charlotte von Stein, with whom he hoped to socialize rather more intimately. (The fact that Frau von Stein was seven years his senior and the mother of eight was not a drawback in his eyes; she was highly intelligent as well as beautiful, and in any event, Goethe had nothing against "mature" female companions.) Conveniently, Frau von Stein, sans husband and brood, was quartered just next door at the Drei rote Rosen guesthouse.

Goethe immediately plunged into the Karlsbad social scene with Stein, taking her to dances in the Böhmischer Saal and the Sächsischer Saal. Just as his gout did not impede his dancing, his chronic stomach pains did not prevent him from dining regularly at local restaurants, where he and his date devoured heavy Bohemian dishes washed down with local beer and imported French wines.

As an intrepid social animal, Goethe hardly confined his attentions to Stein. Finding himself in a heady cosmopolitan environment, he took full advantage of the scene before returning to Weimar. He avidly hobnobbed with a coterie of Polish grandees in the retinue of Prince Adam Czartoryski, a general and writer of some distinction. He rubbed shoulders as well with the circle around a wealthy German count named Moritz Brühl—although for Goethe it was not Moritz but the count's wife, Tina, who was the chief attraction. Neglecting Stein, Goethe began swooning after the dazzling Tina, who, albeit not as intellectually brilliant as Stein, was ten years her junior and had "*Holz vor der Hütte*" (was well stacked). The poet's own brilliance did not prevent him from being surprised—and hurt—when Stein suddenly cut short her cure and returned to Weimar. Not long thereafter the Brühls also left, forcing Goethe to make do for the remainder of his stay with Princess Isabella Lubomirska, an aged sister of Prince Czartoryski's. Suddenly missing Stein, Goethe wrote her self-pityingly: "Everything became so empty here after your departure. Lost in reverie about you, I have wandered several times up the steps of the Drei rote Rosen. Otherwise, I just soldier on, drinking [my allotments of water] and bathing on alternate days."

But what about work? Eventually, Goethe would find ways of getting some significant writing done during his spa visits, yet his early stays at Karlsbad were marked by good intentions and meager results: a few slight poems for friends and some dabbling on his novel in progress, *Wilhelm Meister*. The truth was, as he admitted later, his spa visit had pitched him into a "*Fainéantisme über aller Beschreibung*" (laziness beyond all description).

On the other hand, his stay at Karlsbad did have useful consequences for his work because, as he insisted, "the waters really are beneficent and the [fact of] being around people all the time has been good for me. [Here] one sheds many of the rust spots that have built up due to an excessively lonely existence." To Carl August he wrote: "From granite [rock formations] through the whole of creation up to women, everything has contributed to make my stay here pleasant and interesting." Upon returning home he felt "freer of mind" and ready to plunge back into serious reading and writing. In sum: "I'm going to keep going to Karlsbad for sure. I owe a whole new level of being to this water source."

Goethe indeed returned to Karlsbad the following summer, but he seems to have spent most of his time during this visit preparing for a lengthy (and hugely formative) sojourn to Italy, which he commenced immediately upon leaving the spa. Karlsbad did not figure again in his travels until 1795, ten years after that first salubrious visit. This trip was prompted primarily by a new ailment, kidney stones (shades of Montaigne). For this thirty-six-day stay at the spa, Goethe took rooms in a different boarding house, Zum Grünen Papagei. He got the cost down to seven gulden a week by some hard bargaining. "We haggled like Jews," he reported proudly.

As was the case during his first visit, Goethe's physical troubles did not limit his social life at the spa, which, for its part, had become even more sophisticated in the intervening years. The expanded local theater now offered Mozart operas along with more homely fare. Goethe, too, was more seasoned, and he now had a fiancé back in Weimar, Christiane Vulpius, whom he had met in that city. She would remain his steady companion for the rest of his life, bearing him a son and finally becoming his wife in 1806. (Alas, she died ten years later). Endowed with worldly tolerance and a good sense of humor, Christiane playfully nicknamed her lover's penis "Herr Schönfuss" (Mr. Pretty Foot)—perhaps because it got around so much. Although Goethe tended to dismiss his spa liaisons as mere "*Augelchen*" (oglings), the women in question were often formidable intellects in their own right, and his interest in them seems to have embraced their brains as well as their bodies.

On the other hand, the poet's undeniable regard for the whole woman was not necessarily apparent in the salacious leers he visited upon these ladies. A thirty-something married woman named Friederike Brun, over whose ripe features Goethe's eyes had roamed with particular persistence, was initially put off by the attention. "At first I was pained by his glances . . . which were those of an appraising observer without faith in human worth . . . who wanted only to add more portraits to his gallery of beauties, and who viewed the world as one big peep-show." After managing to spend some quality time with Brun, however, Goethe was able to prove the nobility of his intentions, and by the end of his (and her) cure she could write: "I visit him daily and never miss an opportunity to be with him."

As for the "cure" part of his 1795 Karlsbad stay, Goethe once again was a dutiful patient. He consulted his doctors, drank his daily allotments of salty water, and took his thermal baths. While this regimen did not rid him of his stones, he believed that the combination of medical treatments and social-cultural stimulation at the spa was doing him a world of good. So pleased was he with his cure that his failure once again to do any serious writing during his stay did not overly trouble him. "I haven't worked at all," he wrote a friend. "Distractions have made exclusive claims on my time." But he found a bright spot in this dolce far niente, even beyond the dolce: "Although, distracted by the press of people, I wasn't able to attend to any of the work I had brought along, this very sociability actually gave me new insights into the world and its personalities." Thus Goethe could recommend Karlsbad to a friend and fellow artist, Friedrich Schiller: "One could travel a hundred miles and not see so many [interesting] people, and at such close quarters [as at Karlsbad]."

Karlsbad's charms notwithstanding, Goethe did not grace the place with his presence again until 1806. On this visit, too, his cure regime rendered him too lethargic to work productively, though it simultaneously heightened his desire for rigorous play and the "little love affairs" that, in his view, "alone [made] a cure visit bearable—otherwise one would die of boredom." His daily routine, he bragged in a letter to Christiane, was a model of strenuous, healthful activity: "One gets up at five o'clock, goes to the drinking fountains in all kinds of weather, climbs mountains, changes clothes, receives visitors, and ventures out into society. One does not shrink from rain, cold, wind, or drafts and feels throughout wonderfully well." The "society" was especially rich and plentiful that year, with some 542 registered cure guests.

The fact that not far away Napoleon's troops were laying waste to Central German towns, including Goethe's own Weimar, did not dampen the party spirit at Karlsbad. Goethe wrote to his old flame, Charlotte von Stein, about a new crop of aristocratic Polish, Russian, Prussian, and Austrian beauties who "dazzled" at various grand balls and dinners. The loveliest of these ladies, a personage Goethe codenamed "Pandora" in his diary, did not cross the poet's path until the last day of his cure (July 31). The most he could do with Pandora was walk with her for an hour or so, and the most she could do with him was talk his ear off. But the codename Pandora proved prescient, for the lady in question was nineteen-year-old Amalie von Levetzow, and the "Pandora's Box" she had brought along with her to the spa included her one-year-old daughter Ulrike. In 1806 Goethe "ogled" Amalie; fifteen years later it would be Ulrike who would catch his eye—and much more than that.

Goethe may indeed have rushed up and down mountains in all weathers at Karlsbad in 1806, but his physical infirmities, including the gout, were getting worse, and it is telling that from that year on there would no longer be any extended hiatuses in his spa-going routine. Feeling the need for a variety of treatments, Goethe henceforth broadened his cure destinations to include other Bohemian Kurorte, namely Teplitz, Franzensbad, and, above all, Marienbad. Whichever spa he chose, though, he continued, as best he could, to mix the business of health with the pleasure of social contact.

It is therefore not surprising that when another lady friend of Goethe's, Bettina von Arnim, suggested in 1810 that he might want to meet the great Ludwig van Beethoven during one of his cures, the poet expressed principled agreement. "Give Beethoven my heartfelt greetings and tell him I would make sacrifices to have his acquaintance," he wrote back. As for a possible meeting site, Goethe proposed Karlsbad, "where I go every year." When informed by Bettina of Goethe's desire to meet him, Beethoven, for his part, also showed interest, for he greatly admired the older man (twenty-one years his senior). The musician was, however, a little vague regarding the details of a possible get-together, as was only befitting of a mercurial man of genius. As one of Beethoven's biographers has noted, "The two supreme egos of German culture were clearly feeling each other out, neither wanting to seem too solicitous."

But if a Goethe-Beethoven meeting were to occur at all, it made good sense that it should happen at a grand spa. Like Goethe, Beethoven took the waters regularly as he aged. He did not do so to dally with the ladies or to gamble—he hated dancing and appears not to have known one playing card from another. No, he went to the spas in hopes of alleviating his manifold ailments, which included migraines, colitis, catarrh, hepatitis, diarrhea (from which he suffered so chronically that it became known as "Beethoven's disease"), flatulence, stomach pains, piles—and, most horrifying of all for a musician, encroaching deafness. Typically he took his cures at small spas close to his home in Vienna, but in 1811 he went to Teplitz, whose waters he was told might restore his hearing or at least stave off further deterioration. Teplitz was also close to Karlsbad, where art collector and patron Antonie Brentano (thought by some to be the woman of his dreams, his "Immortal Beloved") was taking a cure.

Alas, unlike Goethe, Beethoven found no love in Bohemia, nor did he find a cure for his hearing disorder or other maladies. Yet, also unlike the poet, he *did* find occasion to get a lot of work done at the spa. In that summer of 1811, between regular soakings in the thermal springs and trips to the drinking fountains, he managed to compose the incidental music for two plays (August von Kotzebue's *King Stephen* and *The Ruins of Athens*) as well as to start sketching his Seventh and Eighth Symphonies.

Meanwhile, the musician and poet kept circling each other warily, like seasoned cultural heavyweights. The circling remained purely epistolary for quite a while: Goethe wrote Beethoven proposing that the latter visit him at some point in Weimar; Beethoven asked Goethe to comment on the music for his play *Egmont*, which he promised to send forthwith.

We can thank the Bohemian spa scene that these two titans eventually *did* come together in person. The time was late summer 1812 and the place was Teplitz, where both men happened to be taking their annual cures. Like Dodge City, this Bohemian spa was not big enough for both these outsize personalities—or rather, it was not so big that they could have avoided each other even had they wanted to. Of course, they *were* prepared in principle to meet, and meet they did on at least four separate occasions.

The most notable of these encounters came when the two artists fell together during a walk down a garden path near the Teplitz Chateau. We might assume that this extended meeting between these cultural behemoths threw off brilliant intellectual sparks. But apparently it did not. Like a pair of Miami Beach pensioners, the forty-one-year-old Beethoven and the sixty-three-year-old Goethe focused their conversation, such as it was, on their respective ailments and treatments. At one point Beethoven also gave vent to a simmering envy of Goethe's omnipresent celebrity. When the poet coyly expressed irritation over the attention he was attracting from passers-by, Beethoven quipped: "Don't let it trouble Your Excellency; perhaps the greetings are intended for me."

Although the two geniuses exchanged no profundities about life and art, one telling incident *did* occur on that garden path in Teplitz. The story goes (as told by Beethoven in a letter to Bettina von Arnim) that the walkers encountered Empress Maria Ludovika of Austria and her entourage during their stroll and that, while Goethe politely doffed his hat and bowed low to Her Highness, Beethoven not only held his head high but crammed his headgear down around his ears. This incident has been widely interpreted as emblematic of Goethe's fawning loyalty to the Old Regime and Beethoven's upright championship of the new democratic ideas coming out of France. But even if this episode occurred in the way Beethoven described it (we have no independent corroborations), the political ideology of the two principals was considerably more complicated and malleable than the simple dichotomy of that day would suggest.

Yet at the same time, it must be said that both Goethe and Beethoven came away from their ambulatory tête-à-tête in Teplitz with impressions of each other that harmonized rather well with the popular stereotypes that were coalescing around both these figures. Although Goethe stated in his diary after his first meeting with Beethoven that he had "never met a more intense, more energetic, and more impassioned [*inniger*] artist," in a later letter, following the garden path incident, he qualified his praise, offering a portrait of a brilliant but angry, undomesticated creature not fit for human society. "His talent amazed me. Unfortunately, however, he is an utterly untamed personality, not all wrong if he finds the world detestable, but [with his rude behavior] not making it more enjoyable for himself or others." Beethoven, meanwhile, viewed Goethe's assiduous hobnobbing with vacationing bluebloods (all chattering excitedly about Napoleon's ongoing invasion of Russia) as behavior unbecoming a true artist. "Why mock the follies of virtuosi," he asked, "when poets, who should be the prime instructors of their countrymen, throw everything aside for the sake of glitter?"

Whatever their differences in personality and politics, these two great artists remained united in their physical infirmities and their increasingly desperate efforts to alleviate these troubles via healing waters. After his fruitless forays to Bohemia in 1811–1812, Beethoven returned to his earlier routine of summering in bucolic wine- and water-cure villages surrounding the Austrian capital. His favorite among these places was Baden (now called Baden bei Wien), which lay just south of Vienna in a lovely river valley flanked by vineyard-covered hills.

Like so many Central European spas, large and small, Austria's Baden had a Roman past, though what gave it cachet in the early nineteenth century was its status as a summer residence for several members of the Habsburg family, most notably Emperor Franz I. (Baden was also the hometown of Katharina Schratt, a noted actress who became Emperor Franz Josef's longtime mistress and confidante.) In the second half of the nineteenth century, Baden would become a favorite cure resort for wealthy Viennese Jews, some of whom built luxurious villas in the town. Still later, following World War II, Baden would serve as the headquarters of Soviet occupation forces in Austria. From the Romans to the Russians, the lure of Baden lay principally in its thermal Quellen, notable for their very high sulfur content. (The downside of this healthful bounty was an atmosphere smelling perpetually of rotten eggs, as if the earth were constantly passing gas, which in fact it was.) When Beethoven began summering regularly in Baden in the early 1820s, the town had just undergone extensive reconstruction in the so-called Biedermeier style following a devastating fire. To his credit, the maestro performed a concert in Karlsbad to benefit the burned-out victims of this conflagration—a "poor concert for the poor," as he called it.

Biedermeier suggests homey comfort, but there was nothing comfortable about the personality and habits of Ludwig van Beethoven, either in Baden or anywhere else. Other artists, including Goethe, might use their repeated cures to socialize or simply unwind, but for Beethoven, these annual getaways were a time for serious, sustained work—along with increasingly agonized efforts at healing. Associating the spring and summer months—his spa time—with creative growth, the musician typically sketched out his compositions during this period, allotting the "leafless" fall and winter months back in Vienna to the more mundane task of turning these sketches into finished compositions. Naturally, this sketching work involved lots of trial and error passages at the piano, whose keyboard the master pounded ever more fiercely the deafer he became. Complaints from neighbors about excessive "noise" obliged the composer to shift his quarters constantly—some fifteen times in Baden alone. One of those stops was so the so-called *Kupferschmiedhaus* (coppersmith house), where Beethoven lodged for two summers in 1822 and 1823. It was in this spartan dwelling that the composer, struck suddenly by a musical inspiration but lacking any paper on which to write it down, resorted to the next best surface to hand: a wooden shutter. A cure guest quartered across the street witnessed this droll incident and, once Beethoven had moved on, opportunistically purchased the note-covered shutter from the musician's landlord. A year later, when Beethoven returned to Baden in order to complete the sketches for his Ninth Symphony, he was able to regain his quarters at the Kupferschmiedhaus only after reimbursing the landlord for "damages" done to the window shade. (This fabled object has long since disappeared, perhaps as ash up some fool's chimney, but an imagined reproduction of it can be seen on a wall at the Kupferschmiedhaus, which is now a museum calling itself *Das Haus der Neunten*—"the House of the Ninth." Along with the shutter, the museum features a rather alarming waxwork figure of the composer, replete with wild hair and frowning visage, poring over the score of *Die Neunte*.)

Beethoven's repeated stays in bucolic Baden were bedeviled not only by whining neighbors and greedy landlords: the local waters and spa doctors were doing little to alleviate his infirmities, including his horrifying hearing loss, which became near total in the last years of his life. Complaining that his increasing deafness was being "made worse by the doctors," and that his personal physician back in Vienna had stupidly advised him to avoid wine but *failed* to warn him off the local asparagus, which aggravated his diarrhea, he seriously contemplated suicide. Unable to put a quick end to his misery, he wandered the area's dusty roads alone, disheveled and distraught, and issuing curses and occasional loud screams that he himself could not hear. But alarmed passersby *could* hear these imprecations, and in 1823, during one of his lonely treks from Baden to Wiener Neustadt, the long-suffering musician was denounced to the police as a *Lump* (bum) and incarcerated for vagrancy. This, it should be noted, was Beethoven's second run-in with the local authorities. Two years earlier he had been lunching at a Baden eatery, Zum Schwarzen Adler, when he learned that an inexpensive room might be available just across the street in the Rathausgasse; not wanting to miss out on this opportunity, he rushed off without paying his bill, leading to his arrest for what the police called *Zechprellerei* (bilking). He was eventually released after proving his identity and settling the bill.

Beethoven, it seems, could not catch a break in Baden, but he kept coming back year after year almost until his death in 1827. Undoubtedly he returned so often not for the thermal waters but because he loved to wander through the local hills and valleys. On the eve of one of his sojourns to Baden, he wrote: "How delighted I shall be to ramble for a while through bushes, woods, under trees, through grass and around rocks. No one can love the countryside as much as I do. For surely woods, trees and rocks produce the echo which man desires to hear?"

Beethoven never did find a "cure" for his afflictions (who, in the end, ever does?), but he did find inspiration in that beautiful (albeit sulfurous) environment for his musical genius. Although it is difficult to assess with precision the impact of his stays in Baden (or anywhere else, for that matter) on his art, musicologists often point to the third slow movement of his String Quartet in A minor, op. 132, as the strongest evidence of a palpable connection between his curing and his composing. Writes one authority: "[This piece] portrays the experience of healing and recovery in a way that is not found in any other works by Beethoven or his predecessors, namely through the use of the Lydian mode and the creation of a chorale melody that serves as a basic prayer and is then elaborated in variations." Yet if this work betrays the most "obvious" connection between place and product, many of his other compositions surely drew as well on his experiences at the spas, especially Baden, where he famously kept notepaper at hand for sudden inspiration during those long walks in the hills.

Goethe, too, was able eventually to combine his cures at Karlsbad and other Bohemian spas with some serious artistic work; indeed, the spa scene arguably fostered that work by encouraging the writer, who was not getting any younger, to meditate on the complicated relationship between aging, artistic creativity, and physical passion (or lack thereof). It was in Karlsbad in April 1808 that he made the first sketches for what would become his tragic novel, *Die Wahlverwandtschaften*. Two months later, still in Karlsbad, he completed the first section of this work; and by the time he left the spa in late August he had a rough draft of the whole book in his travel satchel. Goethe's next stop was Franzensbad. On the way there, contemplating his work in progress, in which the tedious requirements of marital propriety ultimately triumph over the insistent demands of the heart and senses, Goethe came up with the idea for a kind of artistic antidote: his poem, "Das Tagebuch," where unbridled sensuality happily wins out not only over marital conventions but also over advancing years.

Erotic love and old age: twining them on the page was one thing; fusing them in real life was quite another. Yet Goethe was not the sort of man to duck a challenge like this, which was nothing less than the classic challenge of the *Lebenskünstler*: to make life imitate art. It is telling, too, that Goethe would make his last stand for passionate love at a spa, ever the province of Eros. The spa in question was not Karlsbad, where Goethe had in earlier days enjoyed many an invigorating fling, but Marienbad, which had displaced Karlsbad in the poet's affections during his declining years. The hustle and bustle of Karlsbad, it seems, had eventually become more enervating than energizing for the aging artist, who had also come to doubt the curative properties of that spa's fabled waters. "The doctors want me to go to Karlsbad," he wrote in 1812, "but I don't like going there anymore because I've lost my faith in the place."

Unlike historic Karlsbad, Marienbad was a recent creation—albeit a very ambitious one full of aspirations to grandeur. The region's thermal springs had been long in use—most notably by soldiers during the Thirty Years War—but there were no physical structures there until the late eighteenth century. In the early nineteenth century a German physician from the monastery of Tepl built a boardinghouse called the Golden Balls next to a local thermal spring known as Marienbad, or Mary's Bath. According to legend, the spring in question was so named because a soldier of the Thirty Years War who had healed his wounds there affixed a picture of the Virgin to a nearby tree. The implication was that Mary herself took ablutions there, though doubtlessly not in tandem with the troops. Mary's imprimatur notwithstanding, "Marienbad" did not become an officially recognized place-name until 1810. Then, over the course of the next few years, a Czech landscape gardener named Vaclao Skalnik transformed the wild, woody, and rock-strewn countryside into gentle parkland so fetching that, as Skalnik himself modestly claimed, the new town could easily "have been confused for the Garden of Eden."

Rather than confusing Marienbad for Eden, Goethe, who first visited the town in 1820, saw something akin to an American frontier village (never mind that he had never set foot in America). "I had the impression that I was in the wilds of North America, where one builds towns in three years," he wrote. Yet Goethe could see genuine promise in this instant Arcadia, and he was right to do so. Marienbad would go on to become perhaps the most beautiful and fabled of all the grand Central European spas—its very name evocative of mystery, secret love, shadowy meetings, dreamy visions, and fragile, transient, glamour. Very soon, sooner than most of its peers, it became one of those places (rather like Venice) whose future was in its past, whose raison d'être was to glance back forever at "last year"—as the famously beguiling film by Alain Resnais has it.

Such a place was made to order for a man like Goethe, who was determined to act as if the present really *was* the past, to behave as if the geezer he had become was simultaneously the gay blade he once had been. That the poet tried to jump-start this human alchemy by falling head over heels in love with a young girl was hardly new—the illustrious pedigree here includes Abelard and Heloise and Dante and Beatrice, to name only two famous "May-September" romances—but Goethe took this hoary concept into ambitious new territory. Ulrike von Levetzow was only *seventeen* when Goethe re-encountered her in Marienbad, while he was *seventy-three*: this was more on the order of a January-December arrangement. But the writer was so smitten he could not help himself. Assured by his doctor that there was no *medical* reason why he could not hold up his end of the bargain, he pursued Ulrike relentlessly, popping up by her side every time she tried to take the waters. He presented her with pretty rocks he had collected during his geologizing; and when she showed no interest in these treasures, he salted his finds with Viennese chocolates. He used some lines of his own to cheer himself on: "Great passions are mortal illnesses. What might cure them makes them only more dangerous than before. . . . So, lively brisk old fellow / Don't let age get you down / White hairs or not / You can still be a lover." Hoping the Marienbad waters might be an elixir of eternal youth, he gulped more and more of the stuff while going lightly on the wine and local beer. True, he had by now become hard of hearing, rheumy of eye, and a bit lame, but observers noted a new spring in his step as he lurched after the young girl. And who knew? Perhaps there was some lead left in the old Pretty Foot pencil after all . . .

Alas, Ulrike was not about to find out. Having never taken the trouble to read his books, seeing in him not the creator of *Faust* but a grandfatherly fellow with bad teeth, a downward turning mouth, and wattles, she remained more repulsed than flattered by his attentions. Refusing to accept the clear message inherent in her polite but firm rebuttals, Goethe went ahead and proposed marriage to her in 1823. Or rather, he had Duke Carl August pop the question on his behalf and throw in as sweeteners high positions at court for both Ulrike and her mother, along with an annual pension of two thousand thalers for the new Frau Goethe should her husband predecease her, which was more than likely given the fifty-six-year age difference. This offer was sorely temping (especially to Frau Levetzow), but in the end, Ulrike was not to be had for love or money. Through her grandmother, Ulrike refused Goethe's (and the duke's) entreaties. Yet still the poet persisted in his demented pursuit and made such a nuisance of himself that Frau Amelie von Levetzow packed Ulrike and her two sisters off to Karlsbad. Goethe immediately followed, taking rooms directly above theirs in their new refuge. After a few days the Levetzows had had enough. They fled again, this time making clear they did not wish to be followed. In the past, Goethe had left his share of ladies in the lurch. Now it was his turn to be alone and bereft.

While there is undoubtedly a measure of poetic justice in Goethe's fate, it is hard to avoid discerning a strong element of pathos in this story as well—a very human pathos that calls more for a sigh than a snicker. (Thomas Mann captured the poignancy of the problem well when he wrote of "a gruesomely comic and highly embarrassing situation, at which, nevertheless, we laugh with reverence.") Goethe himself soon came to understand that he had set himself up for his crushing fall through a toxic combination of vanity and vulnerability; but, characteristically, he also blamed his artistic sidekicks, those muses who had once propelled him to great heights only gleefully to bring him down. On the coach that took him from Bohemia back to Weimar, he composed one his finest and most personal poems, "The Marienbad Elegy." Its last stanza, in the translation by Edgar Alfred Browning, reads:

> To me is all, I to myself am lost,
> Who the immortals' fav'rite erst was thought,
> They, tempting, sent Pandoras to my cost,
> So rich in wealth, with danger far more fraught,
> They urged me to those lips, with rapture crown'd.
>   Deserted me, and hurl'd me to the ground.

If Goethe's last love in Marienbad has an impressive literary pedigree, the trope it encapsulates—an elderly man's "unseemly" passion for a far younger person—has enjoyed a rich literary afterlife as well. One thinks immediately of Thomas Mann's own Gustav Aschenbach and Tadzio in *Death in Venice*; Vladimir Nabokov's Humbert Humbert and the pubescent sex bomb Lolita; and, even closer to home, Martin Walser's *Ein Liebender Man*, a fine novel in which a modern master of German letters sympathetically revisits the foibles of his most illustrious literary forebear.

Not surprisingly, the poignancy of the Goethe-Ulrike story was not lost on those who had a strong commercial stake in its longevity, namely, the keepers of the flickering Marienbad flame. Already in the late nineteenth century city promoters saw to it that a priapist obelisk was strategically placed next to the park bench where Goethe and Ulrike once sat—he inching closer, she inching away—and for good measure inscribed on the monument Goethe's "Wanderer's Song at Evening," which captured the quiet beauty of the place on a warm summer night. Implicit here was the suggestion that you, wandering health pilgrim, might wish to capture a bit of the Marienbad mystique yourself by falling hopelessly and stupidly in love with a fellow curist. Alternatively, you might simply want to drop a few coins (as I did) at the municipal historical museum located nearby on Goethe Platz. (Too bad, though, that you can't see the original Goethe bench with its inspirational obelisk. Those are long gone, and a bronze statue of the poet erected in 1932 was melted down for munitions by the Nazis in World War II. In 1993 a new bronze statue crafted by a local artist went up on the same site. There is also a "Goethe-Sitz" in the woods, a bench where the poet rested on his frequent walks.)

Goethe, the *ur*-Marienbad love pilgrim, never returned to the spa after the Ulrike debacle; not surprisingly, the place had lost its charm for him. He died nine years later, in 1832. As for Ulrike, she would have done well to marry the aged poet and take that pension offered her by Duke Carl August. She died unmarried at age ninety-five, having outlived her ardent suitor by some sixty-seven years. She could have raked in *134,000 thalers!*

Scribble, Squander, Soak: Romantic-Era Writers in Baden-Baden

Having snared Goethe, at least for a while, Marienbad, along with Karlsbad and Teplitz, would go on in later years to reel in a bountiful catch of famous artists and thinkers, some of whom hastened there to "walk in the footsteps" of the author of *Faust*. Friedrich Nietzsche was one of these culture tourists; so was Franz Kafka. But in the first two-thirds of the nineteenth century, it was less the Bohemian and Alpine-Austrian water-cure resorts than the grand Black Forest spa of Baden-Baden that served as the primary stomping ground for writers whose romantic aesthetic was giving definition to an age. (I say "primary" here because some of the leading Austrian writers of this era, figures like Franz Grillparzer and Johann Nepomuk Nestroy, preferred closer-to-home spas such as Bad Gastein and Bad Ischl.) Defining romanticism is famously akin to nailing Jell-O to a wall: this movement or "school" being so amorphous, populous, and diverse that at times the only qualification for admission seems to have been possession of a beating heart, or Heart. I am interested here only in those romantic artists whose hearts beat for a substantial period in nineteenth-century Baden-Baden. Unfortunately—or more likely, just the opposite—I won't be able to include *all* these figures; there are far too many of them.

As noted in the previous chapter, Germany's grandest water-cure resort figured importantly in the history of romanticism due in part to the efforts of the hotelier Johann Cotta; later on the gambling impresario Jacques Bénazet took up the mantle as the chief benefactor in town. Romantics by nature but lacking significant creative talent themselves, both men took delight in surrounding themselves with accomplished practitioners. Being in the hospitality line, both men also understood that it made good business sense to populate their premises with art celebrities, which the romantic era obligingly generated in abundance.

Johann Peter Hebel, the highly talented poet whom Johann Cotta comped at his brand new Badischer Hof in 1810, proved a perfect recruit. Not only did he improve his health at the baths and (amazingly) fatten his pocketbook at the Spielbank, he wrote widely distributed poems and articles praising the spa's many attractions: great food, scintillating conversation, salubrious waters, distinguished guests, and, not to forget, the "exhilaration" of gaming. In a letter he allowed to be disseminated by Cotta, Hebel gushed that in Baden-Baden "one lives in a completely different world," suffused with "glamorous high living, laziness, gambling for money, professors, and even comedians." Apart perhaps from the inclusion of "professors," Cotta's blurb, along with his own presence in town, was just the thing to draw in the crowds.

Not all Cotta's recruits were as glamorous or adept at publicity as Hebel. Ludwig Tieck, often called the father of German romanticism, first visited Baden-Baden at Cotta's invitation in 1810, just like Hebel. Dwarfish, crippled by gout, and extraordinarily ugly, Tieck was also morbidly shy and socially awkward. And, as was perhaps only fitting for a fellow who looked like he might live under a bridge in some dark Teutonic forest, Tieck was an avid collector of fantastical tales every bit as nightmare-inducing as those of the Brothers Grimm. Unlike the Grimms, Tieck also created a host of Gothic-style stories of his own. Some of these works were later published in a three-volume anthology aptly titled *Phantasus* (1812–1817), which proved to be a milestone in the Gothic revival. Finally, Tieck provided some of the best German translations of Shakespeare and Cervantes, certifying his reputation as a leading literary scholar of the day. Baden-Baden constituted the perfect refuge for this troubled genius. It provided relief (though no cure) for his gout, a quiet (and expense-paid) haven in which to work, and a landscape seemingly made to order for his vivid romantic imagination.

Baden-Baden's reputation as a nest of romanticism was augmented in the 1830s and 1840s by an influx of noted French writers belonging to that aesthetic persuasion. In addition to the pull factor exerted by Baden's scenic charms—all those crumbling castles and vineyard-covered hills—this French invasion benefited from a push-factor exerted by King Louis Philippe and his government. The coupon-cutting king's regime may have been open for business, but it was not open for cutting-edge culture. Under the "Crowned Pear," as Honoré Daumier famously satirized Louis, Paris, *even* Paris, could sometimes seem provincial and boring—especially when, as we know, there was no longer any casino gambling allowed. Yet there was, we also know, plenty of high-stakes gambling in Baden-Baden, courtesy in large part of Jacques Bénazet, who, like Cotta before him, enjoyed hosting important artists at his fabled establishment. Being French, Bénazet naturally put out the welcome mat to *artistes* of his own nationality, which is why the muses in the waters at Baden-Baden during his day were almost as likely to be French as the croupiers at his Conversation House.

The French had been descending in significant numbers on Baden-Baden well before Jacques Bénazet added so notably to the local attractions. With regard to the influx of French littérateurs, an important pioneer, Alfred de Musset, arrived in town some three years before Bénazet set up shop. This flamboyant poet and dramatist had been contemplating an excursion to Baden-Baden for some time when, in 1835, a love affair gone suddenly sour prompted him to seek out the Kurort as a hospice for his lovesick heart. For the previous two years Musset had been caught up in a tempestuous affair with none other than George Sand, the eccentric feminist writer notorious for dressing in men's clothes, smoking stogies, and putting frail, artistically inclined young lovers through their paces. Eventually, Frédéric Chopin would flutter into her web, but before him came Musset. In December, he and Sand (who had just abandoned her husband and two children) set out on what was supposed to be a romantic journey through Italy but ended in misery when both travelers became ill in Venice. Sand came down with a severe case of dysentery that left her bedridden for weeks on end. Musset, repelled by her condition, abandoned his partner in favor of a local prostitute, gambling dens, and endless absinthe consumption. One night he announced coldly to his stricken lover: "George, I must beg your pardon. I do not love you. In fact I never was in love with you." Musset soon came to regret his callousness when the tables were turned and it was *he* who was flat on his back, laid low by one of the dangerous fevers so common to Venice. As Sand relates in one of her "Lettres d'un Voyageur," which she published the following year in the *Revue des Deux Mondes*, Musset almost succumbed to his illness: "Thus your body, as tired and enfeebled as your spirits . . . *like a lovely lily stooped to die*." At death's delirious door, Musset imagined he was already across the threshold. Writes Sand: "Memory, perception, all the lofty functions of the intellect, so acute in you, became disturbed and dispersed like clouds by a gust of wind. You sat up in your bed shouting, 'Where am I, O my friends? Why have you lowered me alive into the grave?'" Sand kept her lover out of the grave by remaining at his bedside day and night, nursing him like Florence Nightingale. Eventually she brought in a handsome young Italian doctor named Pietro Pagello to help. Naturally, while tending to Musset, Pagello fell in love with Sand. By the time Musset was well enough to leave Venice, his former lover and her new Italian *amoroso* had set off on a romantic walking tour of the Veneto. Musset, cursing the terrible unfairness of it all, fled to Baden-Baden.

Perhaps he ought to have known that spas, whatever their usefulness in assuaging or curing physical maladies, are hardly the best places to go for a broken heart. Allied with Cupid as they are, chock full of couples and coupling, they tend to accentuate the despair and self-pity of poor lonely hearts recently jilted, denied, or cut adrift. Goethe discovered this in Marienbad; a century later, Kafka would discover it in the same spa— as no doubt did many lesser folk over the years. So it is not surprising that, rather than finding relief from his agony in Baden-Baden, Musset found only more despair and distress. Unable to get Sand out of his mind (he had unwisely included a copy of her book *Lelia* in his travel kit, along with his silk shirts and patchouli oil), he wrote her an agonized letter cursing the place he'd wished might bring him peace: "I had hoped for a moment of calm, but there is none of that here. What do I care about all these trees, all these mountains, all these *Germans* who pass by gushing their pompous nonsense [*galimatias*]? They say it is beautiful here, that the streets are charming, the Promenade agreeable, that the women dance, the men smoke, drink and sing, and even the horses take delight in galloping. [But] this is not really life, all this, it is simply the noise of life [*le bruit de la vie*]." No, Musset goes on melodramatically, "I won't get healthier, I won't even try to live, I would rather die from my love of you than go on living. . . . Oh, my love, I have a favor to ask. At sunset, one fine evening, go out alone into the countryside, sit down in a green pasture, and think about your poor child, who is dying."

Sand responded with some romantic claptrap of her own, but one senses that her heart was not fully in it (she had already ditched her doctor friend for another lover) and that she was simply putting on the style: "I'm writing from a small town where I've gone walking, alone, sad, broken in spirit from reading your letter from Baden-Baden. What is all this? Why do you always forget, now more than ever, that these feelings of yours must change? Live well, my poor child! Oh, without my own poor children, how gladly I would throw myself in the river!" Instead of the nearest river, Sand threw herself into more love affairs, most notably her nine-year liaison with Chopin.

Musset, for his part, threw himself into a frenzy of sustained gambling at Baden-Baden, as if a major victory at that "bastardized Parthenon" (his term for Bénazet's Conversation House) would compensate for his defeat in love. But he did not win at the tables. He lost all the money he had with him except for two thalers, which, central-casting romantic that he was, he gave away to a beggar child. Destitute, he made his way back to Paris, never to return to the Valley of the Oos.

Yet, like so many artists who had tarried in Baden, Musset was moved enough by his experiences at the spa to compose a poetic testament to his visit. Ironically entitled "Une bonne fortune," the long poem is anything but a paean to the grand old Kurort. It argues in essence that while fashion requires all stylish Parisians to descend on "this small village" every summer to seek happiness and health, they will find neither. Drinking healthful waters may be the professed raison d'être of the place, Musset says, but the Conversation House with its roulette tables is the "true" local shrine. There the "ivory balls roll from morning until night," whispering sweet "maybes" that almost always "turn out to be never."

Alfred de Musset was anything but an advertisement for German spa life, but his unhappy example did not prevent others of his ilk from following closely in his footsteps. Among these was the poet Gérard de Nerval, who visited Baden-Baden in 1838 and, like Musset, left a revealing account of his experiences. If anything, Nerval was even more flamboyantly romantic than his predecessor. He suffered the requisite nervous breakdowns and had endless dark dreams of ghosts and goblins. He preferred the spirit world to the material one. "This life is a hovel and a place of ill-repute," he wrote. "I am ashamed that God should see me here." To avoid overexposure to the Almighty, he stayed cooped up in his garret for weeks at a time. Appropriately, he eventually strung himself up from a window grating one autumnal evening in 1855, leaving a note to his aunt instructing her not to wait up for him "because the night will be black and white."

In the meantime, Nerval made a name for himself both with his brilliant protosurrealist poetry and by his antic behavior. For a time he kept a pet lobster named Thibault, which he took for walks in the Palais Royal on the end of a blue silk ribbon. He liked to say that Thibault was much preferable to a dog or a cat; he was a sérieux, peaceful creature who knew "the secrets of the deep." More importantly for his exploration of Germany and Baden-Baden, Nerval knew the language of the region and was an accomplished translator of Goethe's *Faust*, poems by Heinrich Heine, and other German works. Among the French romantic writers who saw fit to sojourn in the Black Forest spa, Nerval was undoubtedly the best equipped to appreciate what he encountered.

Perhaps because of his linguistic competence and deep knowledge of German literature, Nerval had a feeling for Baden that Musset did not. But when it came to gambling, he was just as clueless as his countryman. No sooner had he arrived at the spa than he lost virtually all his money at the tables. Because he was not there at the invitation of Jacques Bénazet, who was just then assuming control over the Conversation House, Nerval, unlike some later artistic gamers, had no admiring benefactor to cover his debts, much less take him in off the streets. "Faute d'argent, c'est douleur sans pareille," he observed—hardly the first or last poor sod to do so.

Without even the funds to return to Paris, Nerval wandered through the environs of Baden-Baden, reveling in the English-style parks, garden paths, and imposing stone bridges over the little Oos—as well as, farther out, the murky grottoes, darkly wooded hills, and hermit cabins. The contrast between "wild" nature and sedate urbanity filled him with awe (the standard for awe was lower then). Lacking the wherewithal to gamble, he carefully observed the play at the Conversation House, taking particular delight in a droll scene around the Grand Duke of Hesse, who every day bet exactly 12,000 gulden at *Trente et quarante*, sometimes winning but more often losing his entire stake. Behind the duke's chair stood a grim lackey, who shooed away anyone who came too close to his master. "Mein Herr, you are bothering the prince," the lackey would warn. Nerval also crashed a masked ball and pressed his face against the window of the Waldhorn Restaurant, where diners gorged on delicacies no less refined than in the best Parisian bistros. Once again, our poet was amazed by the contrast between what transpired in town and the scene just across the Oos, where swine (real ones) ambled along the dusty roads. He dutifully recorded all these impressions in a diary he later published as *Loreley, souvenirs d'Allemagne* (1852). His final verdict on this lovely spa town was so positive that local boosters began using it for promotional purposes: "One has to *visit* Switzerland, but one should *live* in Baden-Baden." (When one takes into account the typical French opinion of Switzerland, however, this praise loses some of its power.)

Interestingly enough, there is no mention whatsoever of thermal springs in Nerval's reminiscences. Like many of his countrymen, especially the artists among them, he had not gone to Baden-Baden to take the waters (if he had wanted to do that, he could just as well have stayed in France). Apart from gambling, what attracted him and his compatriots to Baden-Baden was primarily its physical aesthetic and "spiritual" ambience. It is worth emphasizing, once again, that in those days the Rhineland and Black Forest regions constituted *the* quintessential *terroir* of romanticism for the French and English as well as for the Germans. During his extended visit to the area, Nerval got (figuratively) drunk on the ambience and (literally) drunk on Black Forest *Kirschwasser* (an awful thought, actually).

Nerval was a figure of some stature in the literary world of the day, but his fame paled in comparison to that of another French littérateur who frequented Baden-Baden in the romantic era: Victor Hugo. The famed author of *The Hunchback of Notre-Dame* visited the spa for the first time in 1839 during the course of a journey down the Rhine. The river and its haunting landscape had fascinated him since childhood, when, according to a biographer, "night after night he gazed at the picture above his bed of an old ruined tower [on the Rhine], the source in his daydreams of so many somber images." The imagery eventually worked its way into *Le Rhin, letters à un ami* (1852), his scintillating collection of travel *pensées* that (as a blurb for the latest French edition chirps) "gave to the religion of Romanticism its center of worship and pilgrimage." Put in another way, Victor Hugo did for the Rhine what Mark Twain did for the Mississippi.

While in Baden-Baden, Hugo fetched up at Lichtental, that most magical of places. He loved the area so much that he came back in 1865, this time, now even more famous, taking quarters in the luxurious Bären Hotel, which the *Journal des Débats* described as "a favorite rendezvous for elite foreign society in Baden." As the *Débats* made clear, Hugo was traveling en famille, with his wife and two children. He and his family could have come by train, but Hugo, a notorious hater of the railways, chose a commodious horse-drawn coach instead. At the conclusion of his one-week stay, he gallantly presented to the Bären's proprietor an illustrated copy of *Les Misérables*, bound in Moroccan leather. This ceremonial presentation notwithstanding, Hugo's visit to Baden-Baden was really nothing more than an ordinary family vacation—the sort of thing that any well-to-do bourgeois paterfamilias might have organized. The Hugo experience in Baden-Baden should remind us that artists went to the grand spas not only to create, copulate, gamble, and schmooze—but also simply to relax.

The Sound of Music

Before the days of clacking typewriters, novelists and poets worked in relative silence apart from the occasional cry of frustration or joy; musicians, on the other hand, by definition operated in a world of sound, and in the nineteenth century the frequent presence of Europe's finest music makers at the grand Kurorte of Germany and Austria ensured that these places were full of the sounds of music. There had been music of some sort in the spas for centuries, but demand for regular musical entertainment increased dramatically in the nineteenth century with the greater emphasis on *drinking* medicinal waters along with—or sometimes in lieu of—bathing in them. Curists making their regular rounds of the various thermal-spring fountains liked to be distracted, and suitably upbeat music proved the ideal accompaniment to that ritual. Moreover, where better to escape the longueurs of hot summer afternoons—or, for that matter, long summer evenings—than at daily open-air concerts in the leafy "cure parks" or at nightly performances in formal concert halls? Gambling entrepreneurs like Baden-Baden's Jacques and Édouard Bénazet understood that of all the muses, the goddess of music was the most useful in terms of attracting custom, especially when the music makers in question were themselves major cultural celebrities. Central Europe had its full share of such figures, many of whom were more than willing to make extensive visits to the spas, particularly if their expenses were covered by local patrons. In addition to performing for guests, many of these visiting *Musiker*, echoing the great Beethoven, used their time at the spas to compose new works.

Although all the grand Central European Kurorte could boast lively musical scenes from the early nineteenth century to World War I, Baden-Baden undoubtedly enjoyed prominence in this domain, as it did in so many others.

Among the many great musicians who helped put Baden-Baden on the musical map of Europe, Franz Liszt stands out as a crucial pioneer. I mentioned earlier that Liszt had come to the spa in 1845 in the company of sexpot Lola Montez, but on that occasion, sick with jaundice and exhausted from his recent performances in Bonn, the musician gave no public concerts. Yet he *had* publicly performed on his very first visit to Baden-Baden five years earlier and on two subsequent stays in 1841 and 1843. These visits were sponsored by the enterprising Jacques Bénazet, who knew a prime attraction when he saw one. And no performer of that era had a greater pull than Franz Liszt. Part of his appeal derived from his incredible virtuosity at the piano. Like Mozart, he was a child prodigy pushed by an ambitious father, but unlike Mozart he had a long career that involved hundreds of public performances before large audiences. Also unlike Mozart, Liszt was strikingly handsome and stylish—qualities that made him, at least among the ladies, one of the greatest heartthrobs in the history of music. At the height of "Lisztomania," Franz's female fans wore bracelets made from piano strings he had broken; they carried little vials containing the dregs of his wine; they preserved his cigar butts as sacred relics; and when he left a glove onstage, they tore it to pieces and passed around the fragments.

Fully aware of his mesmerizing presence, Liszt began each performance in the same way: he would stride forcefully across the stage, his long black (later white) mane flowing behind him; upon reaching the piano he would pull off his grey kid gloves and drop them dramatically to the floor, then pause for several seconds as if in prayer while he gazed raptly at the keyboard. Even before he had finished putting his instrument through its paces, alternately caressing and furiously pounding the keys, his audiences, or at least the females among them, often lost control of their emotions. Keith Richards's descriptions of the early Rolling Stones could almost have been written by Liszt about his performances a century or so earlier: "The scene was dripping with sexual lust . . . [and] suddenly you're on the end of it. It's a frenzy . . . and you took that for granted every night."

As far as we know, Liszt did not take bevies of fourteen-year-olds up to his hotel room after his performances. Rather, he was a serial philanderer, and his taste ran to more mature women, often of aristocratic lineage, just like the patrons who had fostered his career early on. Along with Lola Montez, his paramours included George Sand (who loved to sit under his piano as he played); Italian heiress and political activist Cristina Belgiojoso, who famously kept the mummified body of one of her lovers in a cupboard; the notorious courtesan Marie Duplessis,* of whom he said, "Without knowing her, she put me into the vein of poetry and music"; and, most enduringly, Countess Marie d'Agoult, who bore him three children out of wedlock.

One of those children, Cosima, would go on to marry the conductor Hans von Bülow, only to cuckold him with his best friend Richard Wagner before finally divorcing Bülow and marrying Wagner.

Liszt was already much in demand as a performer when Bénazet lured him to Baden with a handsome honorarium. The performer was happy enough to include Baden-Baden on his tour (which also included Wiesbaden) because the worldly grand spa scene was perfect terrain for this "Jupiter of the keys." Shortly before his arrival, the *Badeblatt* could self-satisfyingly crow: "We've learned with great satisfaction that yet another succulent artistic pleasure awaits us, as it so often has in recent years due to an elite European public that rejects mediocrity while offering valuable recognition to true talents." On this occasion, Liszt gave two concerts in the Conversation House—performing works by Rossini, Donizetti, and Schubert as well as some of his own early compositions, such as *Taran-*

---

*Duplessis, who inspired Alexandre Dumas, fils's novel and play *La dame aux camélias* and Giuseppe Verdi's opera *La Traviata*, had her own Baden-Baden moment when, at age twenty-two, she visited the spa in hopes of curing her tuberculosis. There she caught the eye of a wealthy seventy-seven-year-old count, who made her his mistress for a time. According to one shocked commentator, "Marie Duplessis, for the sake of money, submitted to the intimate caresses of a man old enough to be her grandfather." Goethe should have been so lucky.

telles napolitaines and *Grand galop chromatique*. These concerts were a huge success, not least (again) with the ladies, whose hearts, rhapsodized the *Badeblatt*, were "coaxed right out of their bodies" by the maestro's playing.

By popular demand, Liszt returned to Baden-Baden the following season. As usual, he exploited the occasion to rub shoulders with royalty and the bluest of blue bloods. In a letter to one of his lady friends, he boasted of meeting Countess Narishkin and attending a *"réunion intime"* with Prince Friedrich of Prussia, Stéphanie, Dowager Duchess of Baden, and Princess von Wasa. In the evenings he could be seen on the Grand Promenade with one or two of his aristocratic friends—another demonstration, if one were needed, that he had truly arrived.

So popular had Liszt become, in fact, that he undoubtedly could have returned every season to Baden-Baden had he so chosen. But (as with some rock stars) the demands of constant touring began to wear on him, and increasingly he preferred to focus on composing rather than performing. His relationship with Baden-Baden reflected this change. Although in subsequent years he occasionally dropped in at the spa to see friends and get a physical tune-up, he more typically allowed himself to be represented there through his compositions, which the local orchestra dutifully performed virtually every season. In May 1880, however, he returned to Baden-Baden for an extended stay in connection with an annual music event sponsored by the Allgemeiner Deutscher Musikverein. Liszt was the initiator of this series, and it was he who had selected Baden-Baden as the site for the association's seventeenth annual festival. Befitting his regal status, Liszt took quarters in a grand suite at the Europäischer Hof normally reserved for Prince Gorchakov, the state chancellor of Russia. On the day of his arrival, he was received by no less a personage than Empress Augusta, wife of Emperor Wilhelm I of Germany. The high point of the festival's first day was a performance of Liszt's own *Christus* oratorio, which pious Empress Augusta had personally requested. On the second day, Liszt stepped aside in favor of works by the late Hector Berlioz, who, as I'll shortly make clear, was even more of a Baden-Baden personality than Liszt himself. According to the *Badeblatt*, demand for tickets to these concerts was so great that hundreds of people had to be turned away. Why all the excitement? No doubt people wanted to pay their respects to the recently departed Berlioz and the aged Liszt, who would appear only one more time at the spa before dying in 1886. But another draw may have been the festival's final selection: the Prelude and Liebestod to *Tristan und Isolde* by Richard Wagner.

In 1862, Richard Wagner briefly considered settling in Wiesbaden. He liked the Rhine region in general, and Wiesbaden itself, which he had visited a couple of times with his first wife, Minna, had a good local theater (his opera *Tannhäuser* was performed there in 1852). Wagner sometimes had his doubts about the grand spas, though. He was not a fan of the elaborate cure rituals, which he found boring and torturous. Nor was he attracted to the grand spas' prime diversion: gambling. He had no need of the risk of roulette because he was taking plenty of chances as it was with his revolutionary compositions and his bold quest to establish a new theater for the production of his musical dramas. Nevertheless, Central Europe's grand Kurorte figured notably in his career—and one of them, Baden-Baden, even sought to become the site of his ambitious new theater.

Wagner's first trip to a major Kurort was to Karlsbad, which he visited in 1835 to witness a performance by the local opera company of François-Adrien Boieldieu's *La Dame Blanche* (which he found wretched). His earliest *cure* visit was to Teplitz (or Töplitz, as it was often spelled then). Even more than most geniuses, Wagner sacrificed his health for his art, working himself to exhaustion day after day. At Teplitz he hoped to receive treatment for those two ailments that often afflicted men who spent too much time at their desks and failed to watch their diets: hemorrhoids and bad bowels. He repaired to the Bohemian spa in 1842 with Minna, who hoped to improve her own health via that Kurort's "fine air and baths." Health concerns notwithstanding, Wagner did not do much curing at Teplitz; he was too busy working on the score of *Tannhäuser*, which at that point he still called *Der Venusberg*. He returned to Teplitz the following summer to seriously take the waters but discovered that he really didn't have the constitution of a successful curist; he was just too restless and too bent on working rather than on following the languid cure rituals. As he related in his memoir, *Mein Leben* (*My Life*):

> I seized the opportunity of drinking the mineral waters, which I hoped might have a beneficial effect on the gastric troubles from which I had suffered ever since my vicissitudes in Paris. Unfortunately the at-

tempted cure had a contrary effect, and when I complained of the painful irritation produced, I learned that my constitution was not adapted for water cures. In fact, on my morning promenade, and while drinking my water I had been observed to race through the shady alleys of the adjacent Thurn Gardens, and it was pointed out to me that such a cure could only be properly wrought by a leisurely calm and easy sauntering. It was also remarked that I usually carried about a fairly stout volume, and that, armed with this and my bottle of mineral water, I used to take rest in lonely places.

Undaunted by his less-than-satisfactory experience at Teplitz, Wagner (again with Minna) went to Marienbad in 1845. The "stout volume" he had carried around in Teplitz was Grimm's *German Mythology*. In Marienbad he was careful to take along books he thought might be compatible with "the easy-going mode of life which is a necessary part of this somewhat trying treatment." Alas, the books in question, Wolfram Eschenbach's collected poetry and the anonymous epic poem *Lohengrin*, excited him to such a degree "that I had the greatest difficulty in overcoming my desire to give up the rest I had been prescribed while partaking of the water of Marienbad." We owe to Wagner's insubordination as a spa patient the first sketches of *Die Meistersinger* and the outline of his opera *Lohengrin*. Again, to quote his memoir:

> Suddenly the whole of my *Meistersinger* comedy took shape so vividly before me that inasmuch as it was a particularly cheerful subject, and not in the least likely to over-excite my nerves, I felt I must write it out in spite of the doctor's orders. I therefore proceeded to do this and hoped it might free me from the thrall of the idea of *Lohengrin*, and this longing so overcame me that I could not wait for the prescribed hour for the bath, but when a few minutes elapsed, jumped out and, barely giving myself time to dress, ran home to write out what I had in mind. I repeated this for several days until the complete sketch of *Lohengrin* was on paper.

Four years later, Wagner added revolutionary political engagement to his portfolio of radical musical adventurism. Hoping that a more democratic governmental system might clear the way for his "music of the future," he threw himself into the revolutionary actions of 1848–1849 in his native Saxony. He went so far as to deliver a rabble-rousing speech before the Fatherland Association, an organization dedicated to unifying the German states as a republic. The failure of that revolution forced Wagner into exile in Switzerland. (It is too bad, by the way, that unlike many German "Forty-Eighters," Wagner did not choose the United States for his exile: He might then have made Chicago or Minneapolis—both cities courted him—the site of his theater, and his subsequent work and thinking might have been shaped by sensible American midwesterners rather than by rabid German nationalists.)

Exile proved painful for Wagner. For one thing, his health, already bad, became even worse. Suffering terribly from erysipelas (an infectious skin disease, causing fierce itching and fevers) and constipation, he sought a cure for these maladies at Albisbrunn, a small hydropathical establishment near Zurich. The Swiss doctor put him through a brutally severe regimen that Wagner described as "water torture." He soon fled the place, as itchy and stopped-up as when he arrived.

More important, exile was hell for Wagner because he saw himself as a quintessentially *German* artist and desperately wanted to make his mark on his native land. But he could only return to German soil if a residence-ban imposed by King Johann of Saxony and recognized by all the other German rulers were lifted. As it turned out, Wagner's route back to Germany passed through, of all places, Baden-Baden, a Kurort about which the composer knew next to nothing.

In 1860, Baden-Baden hosted a major conference among European potentates (more on this later). This meeting proved important to Wagner because, along with King Johann, two highly influential ladies who backed his bid to return to Germany would be there: Princess-Regent Augusta of Prussia and her daughter, Grand Duchess Luise of Baden. Pressed by Wagner from afar, the two women presented his case to King Johann, who, largely in deference to them, made a partial concession to the composer: Although the king would not allow Wagner back into Saxony, he would make clear to his peers that he "had no objections to [Wagner's] visiting other German states for artistic purposes, so long as [these states] had nothing against [his appearances] there."

King Johann's partial concession ultimately paved the way for Wagner's settlement in Bavaria in 1864 at the invitation of King Ludwig II. It was largely through Ludwig's patronage that Wagner was eventually able to build his long-desired theater in the little Bavarian town of Bayreuth. We can say therefore that the road to Bayreuth went through Baden-Baden. In fact, a year before he moved to Bavaria (Munich, to be exact), Wagner, accompanied by Minna, paid a personal visit to the famed Black Forest Kurort. His purpose was to thank Princess Augusta for her intercession with King Johann. Thus, while Minna (in Wagner's words) "gave herself over to the exciting seduction of roulette-playing," he met with Augusta in Baden's grandiose Trinkhalle. Much to his dismay, the princess seemed rather put off by this tête-à-tête, no doubt seeing Wagner's insistence on a personal audience as impertinent. According to the composer's own description of the meeting, she claimed to have done little on his behalf and showed "indifference" to his concerns. "For the time being," he wrote, "I left this much-praised paradise of Baden without taking along a friendly impression [of the place]."

Yet two years later Wagner was back in this very same unfriendly "paradise." The occasion for this second visit was an invitation from his Parisian friend Marie von Kalergis-Moukhanoff, niece and ward of Russian state chancellor Count Nesselrode. A onetime student of Chopin, Marie had become a passionate champion of Wagner, declaring: "I believe in three infallibilities: in churchly affairs, the Pope; in politics, Bismarck; in art, Wagner." Rather like Liszt, Wagner could count on (and sometimes abuse) the love and support of devoted women. Where Wagner differed from Liszt was his proclivity to misuse the love of *men*, too: one thinks above all of poor King Ludwig II, whose infatuation Wagner exploited for all it was worth. As for Marie von Kalergis, she dutifully met Wagner at the train station in Baden-Baden and offered to show him around town. Although he claimed not to be suitably attired, Wagner allowed himself to be dragged along with her to a dinner party at the villa of Marie's good friend Pauline Viardot-Garcia, a noted opera singer and pianist. In *Mein Leben*, Wagner says little about this Viardot-Garcia dinner, save to mention that he met the Russian writer Ivan Turgenev there as well as Marie's husband, Moukhanoff, and that Marie tried diligently to generate "bearable conversation." Wagner cannot have been very impressed by the scene in Baden-Baden, for he immediately fled to Zurich (which, we might add, may not have been much of an improvement: the

Viennese like to say of this Swiss city that it is "twice as big but half as lively" as Vienna's sprawling Central Cemetery).

Wagner returned to Baden-Baden over the years but was never impressed enough by these experiences to say anything about them in his memoirs. Nonetheless, that spa town became highly impressed with *him*, the local orchestra increasingly including his compositions in its repertoire of musical offerings. One of the reasons Wagner enjoyed favor in Baden-Baden was the presence there of another fervent backer, the music writer Richard Pohl, who in the mid-1860s left Weimar to become the editor of the *Badeblatt*. In this capacity, Pohl campaigned tirelessly for Wagner as well as for his other two music idols, Franz Liszt and Hector Berlioz. Pohl, in fact, envisaged a theater featuring the compositions of these three geniuses.

Wagner respected Liszt and Berlioz but, as we know, wanted to establish a theater that featured exclusively his own works (well, Beethoven might be allowed in from time to time). In the mid-1860s, his new Maecenas, "Mad" King Ludwig II, offered to build him a magnificent theater in Munich, but the people of that city would have none of it: they had become fed up with Wagner's living high off the hog at state expense and his scandalous affair with Cosima von Bülow (all too reminiscent of King Ludwig I's ill-fated affair with Lola Montez). After Munich fell by the wayside, Wagner set his sights for a time on Berlin, for, with Prussia's victory over Austria and Bavaria in 1866, it seemed that the Prussian capital was the proper place for an artist who increasingly saw his work as a national project. But Otto von Bismarck, the architect of German national unity, had no use for Wagner or his dream of feeding at the national trough. In the end, therefore, the composer fell back on poor Ludwig, who was willing to finance a theater in little Bayreuth, on the eastern edge of his kingdom. Bayreuth may not have amounted to much, but precisely for that reason Wagner could be top dog there, the only real show in town.

Wagner had already decided on Bayreuth when word came in 1871 that a considerably more impressive town, Baden-Baden, was anxious to build him a theater. The initiative for this had come from Richard Pohl, who had convinced the mayor that a Wagner theater on the banks of the Oos would add significantly to the region's luster. The town council agreed and officially extended the offer to Wagner. Whether the composer was at all tempted to accept this offer we do not know, but in any event his polite no-thank-you letter came soon enough. In it he cited his desire to situate his *Festspielhaus* within the confines of Bavaria as the major reason for his choice of Bayreuth. Had it not been for this issue, he added unctuously, Baden-Baden would have been the "first place" to be considered.

One doubts this very much. Apart from his own less-than-enthusiastic impressions of the Kurort, that town's status as an *international* watering hole, with all kinds of frivolous diversions, made it distinctly unsuitable for his purposes. Not only did Wagner want a place where he would stand out as the chief attraction; he also wanted a venue compatible with his personal concept of musical drama as a highly serious, quasi-religious enterprise. As I mentioned above, Wagner additionally envisaged his theater as a German national project, or, as he put it, "the artistic sister to German unification." Bayreuth might be made to serve these purposes (the town had once belonged to Prussia), but Baden-Baden, as a cosmopolitan resort where people came to pamper their bodies and divert their minds, surely could not.

It would not be long, however, before Wagner came to regret his choice of Bayreuth—and, perhaps, also his hasty rejection of Baden-Baden. The premier Bayreuth Festival in 1876, featuring the first-ever performance of all four operas making up the *Ring des Nibelungen*, was (mostly) an artistic success but at the same time a commercial disappointment and (in the composer's view) a political failure. Germany's greatest statesman, Bismarck, did not show up, nor did the Reich's military heroes, Albrecht von Roon and Helmuth von Moltke. Rows of empty seats testified to the festival's failure to pull in the large crowds Wagner had counted on to cover his costs. The composer put the blame for this fiasco squarely on Bayreuth. In the letter he wrote the following summer from Bad Ems, where he had gone to nurse his bruised spirit along with his ailing body, he wrote:

> This much at least I have been forced to recognize—and the certainty of this knowledge will remain with me to the end—namely, that it is not my work which has been "judged," but Bayreuth. My work will be performed everywhere and attract large audiences, but people will not

be prepared to return to Bayreuth. I can blame the town only insofar as I *myself* chose it. Yet it was a great idea: with the support of the nation I wanted to create something entirely new and independent in a place which would fast achieve importance as a result of that creation—a kind of Washington [D.C.] of art. [But] I had too high an opinion of our upper classes. As a favor to me (and also, in part, out of mere curiosity) they put up for once with the immense inconvenience of Bayreuth, but they now recoil from the idea of repeating that experience.

In the end, one cannot help wondering whether Wagner, writing this letter while taking the waters at Bad Ems, might not have been kicking himself for having spurned Baden-Baden, where attracting the upper classes on a regular basis would *never* have been a problem. As for Wagner's actual choice, Bayreuth, it did manage to hang on over the years, but always with the assistance of generous financial benefactors—not only the abused Ludwig II but also that zealous Wagner fan Adolf Hitler, during whose twelve-year "Thousand-Year Reich" Bayreuth finally did become a true national project.

German spa life may not have agreed very much with Wagner, but for Hector Berlioz, often called the French Wagner because of his pioneering work in program music, German Kurorte, especially Baden-Baden, proved to be perfect soil for his artistic flowering. As he himself attested, Germany in general was considerably more receptive to his musical ideas than anywhere else, including the composer's native France. "There are rascals in Germany," he once wrote, "but one must confess that there is in that country much more cordiality and a deeper feeling for art than in the rest of Europe. I have been treated [there] with understanding, respect, and affection, which touches me to the bottom of my heart. Moreover . . . it is only owing to this dear country that I keep alive." Thus it is not surprising that Berlioz felt more at home in, say, Baden-Baden, Wiesbaden, or Weimar than in his native land.

Hector Berlioz became a veritable fixture in the cultural life of Baden-Baden during the ten-year period between 1853 and 1863 due largely to the efforts of Édouard Bénazet, who had taken over the spa's Conversation House following his father Jacques's death in 1848. Édouard's tenure as casino king was destined to be rockier than papa Jacques's, but he was just as determined as his dad to convert gambling gold into artistic treasure. Having studied for a time at the Conservatoire in Paris, Édouard Bénazet was especially interested in music and thoroughly knew his way around the innovative work of Berlioz, which was more than one could say for most French music critics or for the cultural establishment around France's new dictator, Napoleon III. Realizing that Berlioz needed a sympathetic audience and a generous benefactor, Bénazet invited the maestro to come to Baden-Baden and perform a concert of his own choosing in August 1853.

Leaping at the opportunity, Berlioz decided on an ambitious program consisting of the first two parts of his *Damnation de Faust*; fragments of his dramatic symphony *Roméo et Juliette*; and the *Carnaval romain* overture. A program like this could not be pulled off in a small space with a few players. Luckily, Bénazet was not a small-minded impresario: he converted most of the Conversation House into a concert hall, even moving out the roulette tables and suspending gambling for the time being. To augment the local orchestra, he imported dozens of musicians from Karlsruhe, whom he paid and put up at his own expense.

An audience of about six hundred well-heeled (and well-healed?) curists thoroughly enjoyed the performance, which indeed was such a success that Bénazet offered Berlioz the opportunity to take over direction of Baden's annual music festival starting the following year. Berlioz was only too happy to oblige. As he wrote later in his memoirs:

> M. Bénazet, manager of the casino at Baden, has several times invited me to organize the annual festival there, and has let me have everything I could want for the performance of my own works. His munificence in this respect has far surpassed anything ever done for me by those European sovereigns whom I have most reason to be grateful to. "I give you carte blanche," he said again this year. "Get the artists you need from wherever you please and offer them whatever terms you think will satisfy them. I agree to everything in advance."

For Berlioz, then, Édouard Bénazet's Baden was an artist's dream come true, and he kept coming back for repeat installments every year as long as he could. Adding to the allure of Baden-Baden was the chance to expose works that were as yet too daring for Paris. Such was the case with the first fragments of his opera *Les Troyens* and his symphony *Harold en Italie*.

And apropos dreams, none other than the dazzling Pauline Viardot-Garcia sang the roles of Cassandra and Dido from *Les Troyens* in 1859 (the full version of the opera premiered four years later). For this 1859 performance, Berlioz conducted an enormous orchestra made up of players from Baden-Baden, Karlsruhe, Weimar, and even Strasbourg—all (once again) paid and put up by Bénazet. Viardot-Garcia also sang in a performance in 1856 of parts of Berlioz's trilogy *L'enfance du Christ*. At the composer/conductor's request, profits from this concert went to victims of a disastrous flood in France. Berlioz earmarked proceeds from the following year's concert, which featured a potpourri of his own works, for the construction of a new municipal hospital in Baden-Baden. Clearly, Berlioz was fast becoming as much a local icon as Bénazet himself.

But the crowning moment for Berlioz in Baden-Baden was still to come. In 1862, again at Bénazet's behest, Berlioz was invited to open a grand new theater at the spa commissioned by the impresario. Erected just southeast of the Conversation House, the two-story theater, designed for the performance of opera, symphonic music, ballet, and drama, was built in the Florentine Renaissance style, replete with a sculptured pediment featuring the muses of poetry, music, and painting, and a fresco boasting the arms of the Grand Duchy of Baden flanked by medallions of Goethe and Schiller. As was only fitting, Berlioz elected to inaugurate this impressive structure with a new offering of his own: the premier performance of his third (and last) opera, *Béatrice et Bénédict*.

Perhaps less fitting was the nature of this particular opera. Based on Shakespeare's comedy *Much Ado about Nothing*, it might have seemed an odd accompaniment to a grand theatrical opening. But Berlioz certainly did not mean this as an insult to Baden or Bénazet: he loved Shakespeare and delighted in trying to match the bard's bawdy wit by inserting little jokes of his own into the story, which he characteristically altered by making the central protagonists not Hero and Claudio, but those hard-hearted satirists of love, Béatrice and Bénédict. He also added an entirely new character, a grotesquely asinine chapel master named Somarone, who introduces a wedding ode for Hero and Claudio with a rather trite allusion to the time-honored coupling of sexual climax and death: "*Mourez, tenders époux, mourez, mourez, mourez!*"

Berlioz himself seems to have thought this was pretty funny, and probably the audience did so as well, for the production was a huge success. The local press hailed the show as a great gift to Baden-Baden at an important moment in its cultural history. A year later Berlioz published the official score of the opera with a dedication to Édouard Bénazet: "Without you, [this score] would simply not exist."

As the Berlioz scholar Peter Bloom argues, Berlioz's time in Baden-Baden "became one of the happier chapters of his life, and serves as a small corrective to those accounts that would accentuate only the despondency of his last decade." But this does not mean that the composer's days at the spa town were filled with nothing but cheer (a cheer, by the way, that he sometimes seems to have buttressed with opiates). As I have repeatedly emphasized, spas are not necessarily the most cheerful of places. Dedicated as they are to health and rejuvenation, they tend to make people, especially elderly people, hyperconscious of their infirmities, incapacities, and mortality.

Such was certainly the case with Berlioz, who, like Goethe, tried during his spa visits to fend off the ugly realities of aging by pursuing ever younger women—which, alas, had the perverse effect of making him feel all the older. At age sixty, during his work on *Béatrice et Bénédict*, Berlioz fell madly in love with a young girl named Amélie. Although Amélie claimed to love him in return, the composer had trouble believing that such a beautiful young thing could truly fall for an old codger like himself. One summer day in 1862 a friend of his, Ernest Legouvé, found him sitting alone below the old castle at Baden-Baden contemplating a letter from Amélie he had just received. The letter reiterated Amélie's love, but Berlioz remained unconvinced. When Legouvé asked him why this was so, Berlioz responded forlornly, "I am sixty." "What does that matter," countered Legouvé, "if she sees you as thirty?" Berlioz: "Look at me. Look at my sunken cheeks and grey hair, look at these wrinkles . . . I am sixty. She cannot love me—she does not love me."

Berlioz would undoubtedly have suffered such moments of insecurity anywhere, but arguably they were all the more intense in a place where the reigning ethos was rejuvenation through restorative waters and healthful living. Goethe and the French romantic writer Chateaubriand may have had the self-assurance to imagine that, as Legouvé put it, "their genius endowed them with perpetual youth," but not Berlioz. And, as it turned out, the composer's doubts were justified. A year later, when he returned to Baden-Baden to conduct a repeat performance of *Béatrice*, Amélie had died, her youth notwithstanding.

Two years later, in 1865, Berlioz had to turn down an invitation from Bénazet to direct that year's music festival. He was simply too sick to travel. *Béatrice et Bénédict* proved to be his swansong, at least for Baden-Baden. He died in 1869, never having made it back to the place where he had enjoyed his happiest days.

Just after Berlioz finished his pleasurable decade of sojourning in Baden-Baden, Johannes Brahms settled into the spa town for an on-again, off-again ten-year stay of his own. For him, the chief attraction there was his old friend (and flame) Clara Schumann, who, following her husband Robert's death in 1856 had moved with her seven children into a small cottage in Lichtental. Having a passel of kids underfoot did not prevent Clara from establishing a notable artistic salon that attracted the likes of Viardot-Garcia, Turgenev, waltz king Johann Strauss II, pianist-composer Anton Rubinstein, French illustrator Gustav Doré, and German neoclassicist painter Anselm Feuerbach. Not surprisingly, Clara's salons involved music making along with the usual elevated talk. "Recently I gave a little party where it was quite gemütlich," Clara wrote in a June 1863 letter, "Madame Viardot and I played [piano] together and she sang." It was not long before Brahms, too, was socializing and performing at Clara's salons. "He [Brahms] came and went as he pleased, the table was always set for him," wrote Clara.

Brahms also became a regular participant at similar soirées hosted by Pauline Viardot-Garcia in her rather more imposing lodgings nearby. But the musician did not limit his time in Baden-Baden to socializing and informal sit-ins at the piano. Like Beethoven, he preferred to sketch out his compositions during spring and summer getaways in bucolic settings. While in summer residence at the small house he rented close to Clara's cottage in Lichtental, he threw himself into serious compositional activity. (Oddly for an artist so notoriously prickly toward any criticism of his work, he regularly showed these sketches to Clara, who, no musical slouch herself, had the confidence to pass severe judgment on some of them.)

In the summer of 1869 Brahms worked long and hard on preliminary versions of his String Quartet op. 51, no. 2, and finished the *Liebeslieder* waltzes for vocal quartet and piano duet. Brahms biographer Malcolm MacDonald hypothesizes that these waltz songs, which represented "a refined apotheosis of domestic music-making," might well "have been the outward expression of his current daydreams about the beautiful Julie Schumann [Robert and Clara's third daughter], whom he was seeing every day at her mother's house."

More generally, MacDonald suggests that the Black Forest landscape around Baden-Baden was instrumental in pushing Brahms in a more "romantic" direction in his work, reflected above all in his Trio in E-flat major, op. 40, for piano, violin and horn. This composition, MacDonald argues, owes much to "the highly poetic surroundings of the Black Forest around Baden." This argument seems all the more plausible given the fact that Brahms was in the habit of composing musical passages in his head during daily walks from his summer home in Lichtental to Baden's Old Castle. (On the other hand, there is no evidence that Brahms ever composed anything while sitting in a thermal bath—and in fact, he seems not to have "taken the waters" at all during his summers in Baden-Baden.)

If Brahms's regular summer interludes at the Black Forest spa town were highly productive and full of stimulating social contacts, they were demonstrably not as "happy" as those of Hector Berlioz. Throughout his life Brahms was subject to extended bouts of severe melancholy—today he would probably be diagnosed as a "chronic depressive." In part, these dark periods derived from anguish over his art—or rather, the reception of his art, particularly by modernist musicians and critics. No question about it: Brahms had a poisonous relationship with the New German School around Liszt and Wagner.

Early in his career he actually met Liszt in Weimar. During a performance by Liszt of his Sonata in B minor, young Brahms fell sound asleep and snored. Brahms apologized profusely afterwards, but the haughty virtuoso never forgave him. As for Wagner, he dismissed Brahms's work as "traditionalist"—about the worst thing he could say about a fellow musician.

Unquestionably, though, Brahms's melancholia stemmed also from another factor: a deeply unsatisfactory love life. Although handsome and (as far as we know) a capable enough sexual performer, he never managed to marry. He had protracted liaisons with one "respectable" woman after another but (again, as far as we know) only ever slept with prostitutes. Brahms's Baden-Baden interlude provided no relief from this forlorn pattern. Although he moved there while still carrying a torch for Clara

Schumann, he soon developed a mad passion for her daughter Julie, who showed him plenty of kindness but no reciprocal passion.

In 1869 Julie announced her engagement to an Italian count she had met on a trip to Italy. Brahms was devastated. When Julie duly married her count in a ceremony at Baden-Baden a few months later, Brahms responded by writing a piece of music that he (painfully) chose to see as a celebration of his own fantasy coupling with Julie. As Clara confided in her diary the day after the wedding: "Johannes brought me a wonderful piece . . . the words from Goethe's *Harzreise*, for alto, male chorus and orchestra. He called it *his* bridal song. The piece seems to me neither more nor less than the expression of his own heart's anguish. If only he would for once *speak* so tenderly!"

Perhaps Clara was right: if only Brahms could have *talked* like he composed (he was famously curt and acerbic), he might have had more luck with the ladies. On the other hand, he might not have enriched the world so magnificently with the fruits of his anguish. Indeed, we may be selfishly gratified that Baden-Baden provided no "cure" for Brahms's lonely heart. Like so many lovesick sojourners at the grand spas, he discovered that the romantic ambience aggravated rather than abated his pain.

Brahms did not gamble at Baden-Baden, but many of the other musicians who frequented that grand spa could not resist the tables at Bénazet's Conversation House. Operetta composer Jacques Offenbach (a frequent visitor also at Bad Ems) came to Baden-Baden for two summers in 1868 and 1869 to take the waters for his gout and to direct the theater that Bénazet had built close to his casino. The proximity of theater and casino proved deadly for Offenbach: virtually every evening he made a beeline from podium to roulette table, where he lost heavily. His "system" consisted in choosing with surefire accuracy the color or number that always failed to come up. So infallible was his approach that the casino in Bad Homburg offered to comp him lavishly if he would only move there and put on clinics for other system suckers.

Johann Strauss II was another compulsive gambler—and habitual loser. During earlier visits to the spa in the late 1860s he had lost relatively small amounts of money, but when he returned in the summer of 1872, flush with cash from recent appearances in Boston and New York, he managed to dump his entire American proceeds on the tables at Bénazet's. Ironically, when Strauss wasn't losing at the tables, he was strolling along the Lichtentaler Allee with Emperor Wilhelm I, whose Reich-wide ban on casino gambling would come into effect only two months later. The waltz king was among the last grand losers at the grand spa.

Baden-Baden, with the signal advantage of the Bénazets as patrons, might have attracted more noted musicians than any other Central European Kurort, but it was hardly the only elite spa whose hills were alive with the sound of music. The leading spas of Habsburg Austria, then still considered the world capital of music, drew in their share of famous composers, conductors, and players. Musical citizens of the Habsburg Empire were particularly prone to compose and cure in "K und K" territory. In 1825 Franz Schubert sought out Bad Gastein to work on his A minor sonata as well as his extensive Sonata in D major. That spa also served as inspiration for his *Gasteiner Symphonie* in C major, one of his best works. For Hungarian Franz Lehár, of *Merry Widow* fame, the spa of choice was Bad Ischl, sometimes referred to as Europe's *musikalischer Umschlagplatz* (revolving door, or hive of activity) because of the number of famous musicians who passed through. Lehár loved the place so much that he settled there in an imposing villa. Johann Strauss II was another Ischl fan. He summered regularly there from 1892 to 1898. Like Lehár, he bought a stately villa in town, where he divided his time between composing and hosting lively musical get-togethers.

Alpine Austria also figured prominently in the life of Johannes Brahms, who chose Bad Ischl as his favored haven in the early 1880s and then again during his declining years between 1889 and 1896. Ischl had come to prominence in the late nineteenth century as the summer residence of Kaiser Franz Josef; the aging Brahms liked it for the same reason the kaiser did: its great scenic beauty and tranquility. (In truth, the kaiser also loved Ischl for its abundance of wild game, a feature that impressed Brahms not in the least.) It was in Ischl that the old maestro composed the last dozen or so of his major works.

In the summer of 1896, as Brahms was composing his final piece of music, the *Eleven Chorale Preludes for the Organ*, he noticed that he was losing weight and feeling distinctly out of sorts. The portly musician, who had been in good (physical) health for all his adult life, agreed to consult a physician at Ischl as long as the doctor did not tell him anything "unpleasant." Obligingly, the spa physician diagnosed a mild case of jaundice, although he suspected liver cancer. Since Karlsbad, more than Ischl, was the place to go for jaundice, the local doctor proposed that Brahms go to Bohemia for a water cure. Brahms duly went there in the fall of 1896. Although he enjoyed the Karlsbad scene well enough, he found, not surprisingly, that the waters there were doing nothing for his "jaundice." He died a few months later, insisting to the end that he was merely going through a bad patch and was rapidly shedding weight in a deliberate attempt to trim down.

While he was still living (and composing) in Ischl in the early 1890s, Brahms spent considerable time with a young musician who was in many ways his nemesis: Gustav Mahler. Although the Bohemian-born Mahler can be considered a late romantic, his work has much more in common with Wagner's "music of the future" than with Brahms's more classic romanticism. During his stays at Bad Ischl, Mahler was prepared to tolerate Brahms even though he considered him a musical dinosaur. (Later, quite unkindly, he would dismiss Brahms as a "puny little dwarf with a narrow chest" who would "scarcely be able to keep his feet [if hit] by a breath from the mighty lungs of Richard Wagner.") In July 1894, Mahler wrote to a friend saying he had encountered Brahms in Ischl and found him "interesting." Two years later he was somewhat more ambivalent about the old man:

> In the next days I'm making an excursion to Ischl, where I always see Brahms. Here I can truly say, along with *Faust*: "From time to time I enjoy seeing the old fellow." He's a knotty and tough old tree, but he bears ripe sweet fruit. It's a pleasure to see the strong, leafy growth. But "we" don't fit well together, and our "friendship" holds up only because I, the young buck, pay him the requisite respect and show him only that side of me that I think will please him.

A friend and sometime lover of Mahler, violist Natalie Bauer-Lechner, observed in an unpublished memoir that while Brahms always cordially welcomed Mahler in Ischl, the latter did not derive much in the way of intellectual or artistic stimulation from their encounters because Brahms "shied fearfully away from any mentally challenging effort apart from his own compositional work." Perhaps this was so, but it is more likely that Mahler, believing that Brahms had nothing to say to him artistically, simply neglected to engage the old man.

What *did* engage Mahler in Ischl was above all the natural beauty, which often found its way directly into his music. Sounds of nature—bird calls, animal howls, country songs, and rushing water—would be woven intricately into his compositions. Like Brahms, Mahler came up with ideas for his music while communing with nature, but in his case the communing was almost heroically vigorous, involving long hikes and bike rides through the entire Salzkammergut. For him, such serious physical exercise was absolutely essential to his psyche, beset as he was with nervous anxiety and hyperkinetic restlessness. In notes to friends from Ischl and the surrounding region, Mahler wrote rhapsodically about multiday treks across mountain passes and alongside alpine lakes and streams. Yet, his restless athleticism notwithstanding, Mahler also found time to sit in the local baths, his favorite being a long-gone facility run by a Viennese doctor specializing in "hydrotherapy and massage." There Mahler got regular rubdowns for his aching muscles and (dubious) treatment for early symptoms of the heart disease that would cause his untimely death in 1911.

Like so many artists who frequented the grand spas, Mahler also found release (though perhaps not much stimulation) through hobnobbing with the many aristocratic grandees who summered in Ischl. For Mahler this socializing was especially important, for as a Jew brought up in Bohemia, rubbing shoulders with the crème de la crème of Austrian Christian society suggested that he might be "making it" after all. Or perhaps not. Although, after converting to Catholicism in 1897 and becoming director of the Vienna Court Opera in that same year, Mahler certainly attained the summit of Austrian musical life, he never felt in the least secure. In her memoirs, his widow, Alma (a piece of work in her own right*), recalled him lamenting: "I am thrice homeless: as a native of Bohemia in Austria,

---

*One of the great femme fatales of the twentieth century, Alma Mahler (née Schindler) went on to marry the great German architect Walter Gropius and then Austrian writer Franz Werfel, all the while carrying on affairs with many prominent men, including painters Gustav Klimt and Oskar Kokoschka. Her salons in Vienna and later New York became legendary. Although in Mahler and Werfel she had married Jews, Alma herself harbored strong anti-Semitic tendencies. After her death in 1964, she attained true immortality via a song by satirist Tom Lehrer, who crooned, "Alma, tell us, all modern women are jealous."

as an Austrian among Germans, and as a Jew throughout the whole world. Everywhere an intruder, never welcomed."

Yet such laments came later. Mahler's letters from Ischl give no evidence of such angst. At this point in his life he was still consulting spa doctors for his physical maladies rather than—as he would do in 1910—seeing Sigmund Freud for his psychic suffering. Freud, ever helpful, told him that he secretly wished his wife to be as chronically infirm as his mother (she had died of heart disease when he was a youngster) and, on top of that, he was seriously anal retentive.

By the time Mahler was seeking psychiatric help for his emotional anxieties, he was no longer spending summers in Ischl. At the turn of the century he began summering at Maiernigg on the Wörthersee in Carinthia, where he eventually built a villa. He repaired there as often as he could to compose but also to escape the relentless anti-Semitic attacks that plagued his years in Vienna. Bad Ischl, Kaiser Franz Josef liked to say, was welcoming to everyone, even Jews. Maybe Mahler should have kept that place as his summer refuge. Yet had he done so, he would not have found it safe for long.

CHAPTER FOUR

Roulettenburg

Russian Writers at the Grand German Spas

Russians had been coming to the grand Central European spas in significant numbers ever since Peter the Great arrived at Karlsbad in 1711. In the nineteenth century, it was especially the major German Kurorte that attracted Slavic visitors because in Russia itself these places were considered not only the most advanced medically but also the most stylish and sophisticated. For a full century, from the post-Napoleonic era to the First World War, everybody who was anybody in the Russian upper classes just *had* to spend summers hopping between Baden-Baden, Wiesbaden, Bad Homburg, and Bad Ems.

Each of these Kurorte also featured another attraction that drew in the Russians: casino gambling. Of course, visitors from other nations gambled, too, but the Russians became famous for the flair and recklessness they brought to the table—the roulette table in particular. "Show a Russian a roulette wheel," it was said, "and he will spin it." (Or, more acerbically: "Show a Russian a revolver chamber, and he may well spin that too.") Undoubtedly, the most notorious Russian roulette player (of the nonlethal variety) was Countess Sophie Kissileff, who gambled at Bad Homburg in the early 1850s. She was said to gamble only once a day: from 11:00 a.m. to 11:00 p.m. Neither a divorce order from her irate husband nor a papal edict (she was Catholic) could induce her to stop playing. When she eventually ran out of money, she had enriched the Homburg casino to the tune of about four million dollars (in today's money).

Countess Kissileff might have been the most notorious Russian gambler to hit German spa land in the second half of the nineteenth century, but she did not figure importantly in the spas' cultural life or in our understanding of the grand Kurort scene of that era. This distinction goes to a group of Russian spa patrons who also happened to be serious writers—and who, more than the writers of any other region, except possibly Germany/Austria itself, mined the spa terrain for valuable literary gold.

Some of these Russian writers—quite ruinously—also tried to mine the German spas in the more conventional way—by gambling. Leo Tolstoy and Fedor Dostoevsky both came down with virulent cases of ludomania in the German spas as if these places were fever-breeding swamps (which is exactly how these writers eventually came to see them). It was Dostoevsky who coined the memorable term "Roulettenburg" for the German spa-casino world that ensnared so many of his countrymen, himself included. Yet the Russian writer who lived longest and most productively in German spa land, Ivan Turgenev, managed to avoid gambling entirely. So did Nikolai Gogol. "Roulettenburg" may have been a particularly Russian place, but it was not the same place for all the illustrious Russian writers who experienced it.

Troubled in Soul (and Bowels): Nikolai Gogol in Baden-Baden

The first major Russian writer to spend significant time at the German spas in the nineteenth century was Nikolai Gogol. But *was* Gogol, born in Ukraine in 1809, truly a Russian? Although Ukraine was then part of the Russian Empire, many Ukrainians, Gogol included, liked to think of themselves as a breed apart (as so many Ukrainians do today). On the other hand, while Gogol may have started out as a Ukrainian patriot and in his early years as a writer focused on Ukrainian folklore and Cossack heroes, he ended up a fiery champion of the Russian Empire. (In this regard, he bears some similarity to the Georgian, Joseph Stalin, another ethnic outsider turned Russian imperialist.)

Gogol's national identity might have been subject to debate, then and now,* but his reasons for taking the waters in Germany remain clear

---

*When a lavish film adaptation of Gogol's Cossack saga *Taras Bulba* opened in Moscow in 2009, it instantly became part of an ongoing culture war between Russia and Ukraine.

enough. As mentioned earlier, gambling was not among them. He despised gaming of all sorts. Interesting, too, is the fact that Gogol confined his German spa sojourns to Baden-Baden, which he visited four times between 1836 and 1844. Most Russian patrons of the German Kurorte, including the writers, liked to spread their custom among several venues—Wiesbaden, Bad Homburg, and Bad Ems being the other top choices.

Gogol's first two trips to Baden-Baden, in 1836 and 1837, were animated purely by health concerns. Even as a child he had been a hypochondriac, a timid and physically repulsive little creature—the very antithesis of the Cossack warriors he later wrote about. "He was a trembling mouse of a boy, with dirty hands and greasy locks, and pus trickling out of his ear," wrote Vladimir Nabokov in an (otherwise) admiring biography. "He gorged himself with sticky sweets. His schoolmates avoided touching the books he had been using." Matters did not improve for Gogol in early adulthood. He became obsessed with his long, pointy nose, which supplanted that pus-dripping ear as his most notable anatomical feature. References to smells and sensitive proboscises would find their way into his literary work, not just his fantastic short story "The Nose" (1835) but also his dark masterpiece, *Dead Souls* (1842). As for his health, the young man developed a precocious case of gout and painful hemorrhoids—fruits of his ongoing gluttony and far too much time sitting around on his ample bottom. Moreover, he suffered from what we would today call irritable bowel syndrome—an unhappy oscillation between severe constipation and diarrhea. One week the poor fellow could barely produce a pebble, and the next he was a human fire hose. Baden-Baden, Gogol was told, was the best place to go in order to get this problem under control, for no one knew bowels and bowel movements better than the Germans.

And Baden *did* provide Gogol some relief from his miseries, largely because the spa doctors there put him on a strict diet and made him take daily walks, which he actually came to enjoy. The fact that he relapsed into his old habits as soon as he went home after his first visit had the happy consequence of requiring a return trip the following summer.

The director of the film, which was financed by the Russian Ministry of Culture, said the movie showed that there was "no separate Ukrainian." On Gogol's birthday, Russian prime minister Vladimir Putin hailed the author of *Taras Bulba* as "an outstanding Russian writer." Ukrainian president Viktor Yushchenko, on the other hand, declared Gogol unambiguously Ukrainian. "He no doubt belongs in Ukraine. Gogol wrote in Russian, but he thought and felt in Ukrainian."

His last two stays at the spa (1843, 1844), however, were motivated as much by business interests as bad bowels. Gogol contributed regularly to a literary journal called *Europa*, which in 1841 had shifted its headquarters from Paris to Baden-Baden (itself a sign of that little town's growing stature in the world of letters). The journal's editor, a German named August Lewald, spoke Russian and was committed to promoting Russian literature across Europe. To that end, he invited writers like Gogol to visit him personally and discuss possible contributions to the periodical. Thus it was that Gogol spent much of his time during his last two Baden visits chatting with Lewald and other *Europa* contributors. He also started work on a planned second part to *Dead Souls*. Baden-Baden, the writer believed, suited his creative needs perfectly because it provided both tranquility and stimulation.

Perhaps he should have stayed there. When he finally repatriated to Russia, following extended travels and stays elsewhere in Western and Central Europe, he fell under the influence of a starets, or itinerant holy man, who convinced him of the sinfulness of his imaginative literary work. Already prone to religiously motivated guilt and much weakened in mind and body due to a regimen of extreme asceticism prescribed by his guru, Gogol burned part two of *Dead Souls* along with some other unpublished manuscripts in an orgy of self-purgation on the night of February 24, 1852. That destructive act accomplished, he took to his bed in Moscow, refused all food, and after nine days suffered a gratifyingly painful death.

Ultimately, then, Gogol's experiences in Baden-Baden proved more important to his artistic career than to his health. Editor Lewald, true to his mission, promoted the young writer at every opportunity. In 1844, *Europa* serialized Gogol's now-famous Ukrainian saga *Taras Bulba*. In his introduction, Lewald correctly noted that while Gogol was among the most important authors then working in Russia, many of his countrymen tended to dismiss him because of his Ukrainian roots and preference for folkloric themes. Moreover, added Lewald with insight, Gogol's more recent work, biting satirical gems such as "The Inspector General" (1836), "The Overcoat" (1842), and, above all, *Dead Souls* showed the Russian people *how they really were*, not how they would have liked to be seen by the rest of the world.

Critical attacks at home on *Dead Souls*, which, at the insistence of the censors, was published originally under the anodyne title *The Adventures of Chichikov*, made Gogol more anxious than ever to stay abroad. However, instead of Baden-Baden, his favorite haunt now became Rome, a true city of dead souls, whose capacious catacombs, multilayered ruins, and priest-filled streets harmonized well with his latter-day abandonment of satirical send-ups of the Russian establishment in favor of religious orthodoxy and passionate imperial Russian patriotism. In amiable Baden-Baden, the pale, sickly, and corpulent Gogol had hardly been a party animal, but in his later years he became even more hermetic and paranoid, going out of his way to pick fights with literary rivals, whom he accused of everything from moral perfidy to stealing from his work.

One of Gogol's favorite targets was Ivan Turgenev, another devotee of the Baden-Baden scene. In his embittered last years, Gogol rarely missed an opportunity to lambaste the younger writer as a Germanized traitor to Mother Rus (a charge that Fedor Dostoevsky would later replicate, with a vengeance). Nevertheless, Turgenev had the good grace to concede that Gogol had been an influential pioneer, both in his work and in his pilgrimages to Western Europe. "We have all crawled out from Gogol's overcoat," Turgenev observed in a eulogy to his influential literary forebear.

Ivan Turgenev's Path to the West

Ivan Turgenev might have trodden in Gogol's footsteps in his own pilgrimages to Baden-Baden, but this fabled spa came to play a very different and much more important role in his life and work. Ultimately it became not just a second home but a "real" home—or as real a home as this restless soul could ever find. Turgenev's relationship with the Black Forest spa town, more intense than not only Gogol's but any other Russian writer's, cannot be understood without some familiarity with his family background, education, worldview, and personality.

Born in 1818 into an old Russian family with extensive country properties in Orel province (Central Russia) and a townhouse in Moscow, Turgenev could have led the life of a typical rural squire, shuttling between townhouse and provincial estate, philandering in the city with other nobles' wives and sleeping with serf girls down on the farm.

Turgenev's father, a somewhat feckless former cavalry officer, did just that—and so, in fact, did young Turgenev for a time. (A dalliance with one of his family's house serfs produced a daughter, Paulinette, whom Turgenev sent to France to be educated but otherwise largely ignored.) Turgenev's abusive and domineering mother, Varvara Petrovna Lutovinova, a wealthy heiress who controlled the family purse strings, had no objection to her son's impregnating a servant girl or to any of his other sexual liaisons as long as they didn't turn serious enough to threaten her jealous hold over him, which she sought to reinforce with occasional beatings and a stingy allowance. Not surprisingly, getting out from under "Mama" Petrovna became an imperative for young Ivan, who in any case had little use either for country living or for some dreary bureaucratic job in Moscow or St. Petersburg, which was his mother's life plan for him.

Yet Petrovna's plan seemed to be young Ivan's ineluctable destiny as he embarked on his university studies, first for one year at Moscow University and then for three years (1834–1837) at the more prestigious University of St. Petersburg. The Russian imperial capital, Peter the Great's "Window to the West" on the Gulf of Finland, was for Turgenev a significant improvement over backward-looking Moscow, but he soon found the capital city's court-dominated society and heavily censored intellectual life as oppressive and insufferable as its damp, foggy climate. For him, St. Petersburg was tolerable only because he expected to use it as a stepping-stone to that wider Western world that had fascinated Czar Peter and countless other knowledge-hungry Russians over the years. Turgenev set his sights particularly on Germany, that paradise of *Dichter und Denker* where a serious student of life could find, as he put it, "true enlightenment" (not to mention a refuge from maternal tyranny).

By promising to write home often and neither to gamble nor to lose his heart to some predatory Fräulein, Turgenev secured his mother's sanction for an extended period of study at the University of Berlin, then the world's greatest center of learning. The understanding between mother and son was that Ivan would return to Russia after his studies and take up a post in one of the imperial ministries, thereby fulfilling his destiny.

Turgenev himself fully expected to follow this path and indeed did so for a number of years. Yet his recent stay in Germany had exerted such a powerful impact on his outlook that he now felt like an alien—a "Westernized" alien—in his own land. Looking back some years later at this transformative experience in his own life and interpreting his personal odyssey as an episode in the ongoing ideological battle in Russia between "Westernizers" and "Slavophiles," he famously wrote: "I plunged into the German sea which was to purify me, and when I emerged from the waves I discovered myself a Westerner." Turgenev's plunge into the great German sea would ultimately turn into an extended swim—and most of that swimming, or perhaps I should say bathing, would take place in Baden-Baden.

During his stay in Germany, Turgenev had fallen under the influence of Hegel, whose abstruse philosophy he understood to involve a call for progressive sociopolitical change (other followers understood it in exactly the opposite fashion). As a budding Left Hegelian, Turgenev found much to fault in his homeland once he returned there in 1838 and dutifully took up a civil service post in St. Petersburg. Yet in truth, one did not have to be a Left Hegelian to find fault with the Russia of Czar Nicholas I, whose oppressive rule was summed up in his archconservative credo, "Orthodoxy, Autocracy, Nationality." To enforce this (in his eyes) holy trinity, Nicholas established a secret political police unit—the dreaded Third Section of His Imperial Majesty's Own Chancery—whose mandate was to nip in the bud any "subversive" activities, even if this required fomenting subversion so as to have something to crush. Not that genuine challenges to the existing order of things were lacking. On the domestic front, Nicholas's core project was the defense of serfdom, which, like America's "peculiar institution" of slavery, was increasingly coming under attack both at home and abroad. Among the domestic critics was Turgenev, who, despite being a serf owner himself, vowed to release his "souls" once he gained control over the family estate.

The longer Turgenev stayed in Russia, the more he pined to get away and travel around in Central and Western Europe as he had done during his student days at the University of Berlin. But his job in the civil service greatly limited his mobility. Moreover, getting official permission to travel extensively in the West was not easy under Nicholas I, whose reign had been challenged at the very outset by a revolt (the Decembrist uprising) of young military officers introduced to constitutional ideals during their occupation of post-Napoleonic France.

Circumscribed in his ability to travel abroad, Turgenev did the next-best thing: he regularly attended the St. Petersburg Opera, where much of the repertoire was Italian, French, and German, and many of the star performers were guest artists imported from Western Europe. Among these foreign stars was a young diva of Spanish ancestry named Pauline Viardot-Garcia. Turgenev first heard her sing Rosina in *Il Barbiere di Seviglia* in 1843 and was head-over-heels transfixed, as so many men were, by this dark-eyed beauty's Gypsy-like exoticism. (According to the German poet Heinrich Heine, "La Garcia's" animal magnetism was such that one felt, when watching her perform, "as though the monstrous plants and animals of India and Africa were about to appear before your eyes . . . and you would not be surprised to see a leopard or a giraffe or even a herd of young elephants stampede across the stage.") Turgenev, it is safe to say, was mentally transported by La Garcia not so much to India or Africa as to Paris, where the diva lived with her wealthy impresario husband, Louis Viardot. For the time being, though, he had to content himself with hanging around Pauline and her husband during Pauline's extended performance runs in St. Petersburg. The trio came to enjoy each other's company immensely.

In 1845 Turgenev resigned his civil service post, offering as justification eye problems that required immediate attention by a physician in Paris. But his real problem was with his lovesick heart, for which he believed the only "cure" was quality time with Pauline in France. The Viardots, for their part, encouraged him to visit them in Paris and at their country house in Courtavenel, south of the capital. Turgenev's relatively meager allowance, however, combined with those bothersome restraints on foreign travel imposed by the government, limited him to visits of short duration. Moreover, as capricious fate would have it, the object of those visits was often not available because she was off on work-related travels of her own.

Turgenev's dream of spending long periods abroad with his beloved Pauline would have to wait until his mother died (that occurred in 1850) and the oppressive regime of Czar Nicholas I came to an end. That second blessed event arrived in 1855 with Nicholas's death (which, oddly enough for a Russian ruler, occurred naturally, without the help of poisoning or stabbing). Nicholas died just as Russia was about to admit defeat in the Crimean War, that savage imperial bloodbath which helped to set the stage for the even more murderous imperial conflicts to come. In pitting Russia against Britain and France, the Crimean War drew a curtain between East and West, another anticipation of the future. Serfdom, too, contributed to that division, since its perpetuation in Russia well after its disappearance in Western and Central Europe tended to confirm convictions there (and to some degree at home as well) that the Czarist autocracy was inordinately benighted, closer in spirit to the despotic Orient than to the civilized West.

As it turned out, Russia's humiliating defeat in the Crimean War, attributable in large part to socioeconomic and technical backwardness rooted in serfdom, helped to bring about an unexpectedly quick end to that age-old institution. Alexander II, Nicholas's successor, made the elimination of serfdom a priority for his new regime. But if freeing the serfs and other progressive reforms launched by the incoming czar allowed liberal-minded Russian intellectuals like Turgenev to hope that their nation might now become more like the West, that very possibility horrified conservatives. A bitter ideological struggle over Russia's future at home and in the world—indeed a war over the national soul—dominated the country's intellectual and political life for the rest of the century. (In fact, in some ways it continues today.) Although the main theater of that internecine war would always be in Russia itself, ancillary beachheads were established in places abroad where Russians congregated. Not least among those foreign battlefronts was German spa land, especially Baden-Baden.

Turgenev's personal path to Baden-Baden began just as the young landowner, having given up his civil service post, was launching his literary career with a collection of stories titled *A Hunter's Notes*. Published in Moscow in 1847, this little book created a furor because it was among the first literary works in Russia to treat peasants as sympathetic human beings rather than as mute animals. The book's implicit attack on serfdom clearly marked Turgenev as a voice for Western-oriented reform. In 1852 he solidified this position with his eulogy for Gogol, whose satirical jabs at obtuse and corrupt Russian officialdom had greatly offended Czar Nicholas. Outraged by Turgenev's praise for this onetime gadfly, the czar personally ordered the writer's arrest and imprisonment for one month, to be followed by permanent exile on his rural estate.

The czar's demise in 1855 brought a quick end to Turgenev's internal exile, since Alexander II was not inclined to enforce it. At this point the budding writer could have gone back to St. Petersburg and rejoined its growing community of progressive, pro-Western intellectuals. Yet Petersburg held no attraction for him, not when the love of his life, Pauline Viardot-Garcia, was in France. Health issues also played a role in his determination to abandon Russia in favor of France. A hypochondriac from early on, Turgenev imagined that he had every disease known to man. In reality he had only a few, though they were bad enough. Like Gogol, he suffered even as a young man from "bowel complaints," which in turn brought on bouts of neuralgia and depression. Never one to suffer in silence (nor one to hide his literary gifts under a bushel), he told anyone who would listen that he had become "a human ant heap poked about by children," a "shed falling to pieces," and a "fish rotting in the thaw." Afflictions of this magnitude, he averred, could be treated effectively only in the West. In the end, though, it was less these maladies than his aching heart that took him to Western Europe in the mid-1850s.

Naturally enough, Turgenev's first destination in his Western travels was France, where he immediately reestablished relations with Pauline and her husband (who, by the way, was *honored*, not outraged, by the Russian's infatuation with his wife). Yet France turned out to be only a temporary haven for Turgenev because within a matter of a few years, the Viardots shifted their residence to Germany—more precisely, to Baden-Baden. One should hardly be surprised that Turgenev would end up there, too.

Turgenev versus Tolstoy

Ivan Turgenev first laid eyes on the German spa town that would become his principal exile abode in the summer of 1857. His visit was not occasioned by his bad bowels (he'd gotten that attended to in Paris), nor even by the siren call of Pauline (she and her husband had not yet moved there), but by a plea for help from a fellow Russian writer, Leo Tolstoy. Before getting Turgenev safely settled in Baden-Baden, I need therefore to say something about the Turgenev-Tolstoy relationship and explore the revealing encounter between these two artists in the famous German Kurort.

Turgenev had been introduced to Tolstoy by mutual friends in St. Petersburg in 1855. The latter was just back from the Crimean War, where he had served with distinction as an artillery officer. His Crimean experience provided the fodder for a collection of war stories titled *Sevastopol Sketches*. This riveting collection, along with three short autobiographical novels (*Childhood, Boyhood, Youth*) based on his upbringing at Yasnaya Polanya, his family's vast estate in the Tula region of Russia, made the handsome young noble an instant celebrity on the Petersburg literary scene. While Tolstoy's country-estate background was similar to Turgenev's—he, too, seduced serf girls—the two men could hardly have been more different in personality (and, later on, in outlook).

Whereas Turgenev was shy, gentle, reticent, and moderate in his habits, Tolstoy was extroverted, disputatious, mercurial, and given to extreme behavior. Of course, no one, least of all Tolstoy himself, could have foreseen that this swashbuckling young ex-military man enjoying his first literary success would, after creating two seminal masterpieces of Russian literature, trade brilliant imaginative fiction for tedious political/religious tract writing, and spend his last years as a notorious "holy fool" preaching pacifism, brotherly love, primitive Christianity, anarchism, abolition of private property, teetotaling, and vegetarianism to flocks of like-minded dreamers who gathered around him on a country estate he was determined to give away. Yet well before his transformation into a would-be messiah, Tolstoy showed signs pointing in that direction. Describing Tolstoy's mind-set and personality following a stopover by the younger writer at his digs in Paris, Turgenev presciently observed: "Tolstoy speaks of Paris as Sodom and Gomorrah. He is a blend of poet, Calvinist, fanatic, and landowner's son—somewhat reminiscent of Rousseau—a highly moral and at the same time uncongenial being." Tolstoy, for his part, claimed to respect Turgenev's work but secretly (and later not-so-secretly) regarded the older man as hypercivilized, all too soft and comfortable—fundamentally, not truly "Russian" at all.

In the spring of 1857, Tolstoy, to Turgenev's relief, left Paris and traveled on to Switzerland and Germany, meeting along the way a wealthy French banker named Ogier, who praised the glories of Baden-Baden as a restful pit stop for a man on the move. On the spur of the moment, Tolstoy decided to accompany his new French friend to the spa. He did not do so, however, to take the fabled waters. Despite a rather dissipated lifestyle, he was in reasonably good health (apart, that is, from the chronic gonorrhea he had first contracted at university and then refreshed periodically thereafter), and in any event could not imagine wasting time sitting around in hot waters when he could be out drinking, whoring, and, above all, gambling. No, it was Baden-Baden's magnificent casino, not its thermal springs, that brought the swaggering young Russian aristocrat to the Valley of the Oos.

Upon arriving in town, Tolstoy found the place filled with fellow Russian aristocrats: Prince Obolensky, Prince Trubetzkoy, Prince Menshikov, Count and Countess Stolypin, and Count Narishkin, to name just a few. Some of these worthies were in Baden largely to gamble, but few of them, it is safe to say, did so with such fierce dedication as Tolstoy. On his very first evening at the spa, July 12, he beat a path to the famous roulette tables at Jacques Bénazet's Conversation House. On that maiden tryst with Madame Roulette, the writer had time to lose only a few francs. Determined to get the better of his new mistress, Tolstoy returned to Bénazet's early the next morning and played straight through until nightfall. According to a diary he kept during his visit, he lost regularly early on but managed to recoup his losses at the end of the day. That night he admitted in a letter to his cousin, Countess Alexandra Tolstoy, that he had been obliged to eat in and was "quite ill" with exhaustion. Yet rather than sensibly walking away with his winnings, he went right back to Bénazet's the next morning, once again playing straight through the day until 6:00 p.m. This time there was no last-minute success. "Everything lost," he confided to his diary. Destitution did not induce sobriety. On the contrary, Tolstoy hit up his banker friend Ogier for a small loan of two hundred francs, which he immediately lost at the tables. Imposing yet again on the enabling banker, he secured a second loan of three hundred francs, large enough for him to play a little longer before all was gone.

Now there was nothing for it but to turn elsewhere for infusions of cash. He wrote everyone he could think of: his cousin Alexandra; an older brother, Sergei; the poet and editor Nikolai Nekrasov; and finally—Turgenev. Tolstoy's despair-filled pleas for help were highly alarming: Might he resort in his anguish to that other, more homegrown, form of roulette? Cousin Alexandra duly dispatched some funds. Turgenev, who at this moment was vacationing nearby at a village on the Rhine, also sent money, which he'd had to borrow himself. Along with the cash came an admonitory letter containing its own measure of self-pity: "If you only knew how difficult I find things and how sad I am! Take a lesson from me: Do not let life slide through your fingers." Noting in his diary that "Ivan is very severe with me," Tolstoy proceeded to send his friend's loan down the same Conversation House drain that had claimed all the previous loans.

Deterred neither by this latest setback nor by Turgenev's admonitions, Tolstoy dispatched a new cri de coeur to his writer friend. Now thoroughly alarmed by the message's self-lacerating tone, Turgenev decided that he had best go personally to his friend's side in this hour of crisis. He had wanted in any case to see Baden-Baden, about which he had heard such wonderful things from his French friends.

Turgenev arrived in Baden-Baden on July 31, checking in at the Holländische Hof for a three-day stay. Tolstoy rushed over to the hotel, and the two writers embraced warmly, with much cheek kissing in the Russian style. Very soon thereafter Tolstoy pleaded for yet another loan, promising Turgenev that he would use the money only to settle his accounts at the spa. Naively, Turgenev handed over a wad of bills and repaired to his room for a good night's sleep. Tolstoy, of course, ran immediately back to the roulette table at Bénazet's, confident that he now had a system with which to have his way with the house whore. It took Tolstoy less than an hour working his new system to accomplish his usual feat: transfer the small pile of chips in front of him to the mountainous stack next to the croupier.

Characteristically, the writer gave himself over to an orgy of self-loathing after this disaster, but, equally characteristically, he raged just as vehemently at the people around him, who in his eyes were complicit in his misfortune. "I am a bum, surrounded by bums," he scribbled in his diary. Presumably, he included banker Ogier and Turgenev among the bums who had abetted his disgrace. And then there were all those degraded hussies at the gambling tables who had disrupted his concentration with their wanton smiles. How was a man to work his system in such an atmosphere?

When he had initially made his decision to stop over in Baden-Baden, Tolstoy intended to move on from there to Holland and eventually to England for an extended stay. Now, completely destitute, he had no choice but to return to Russia, where in any case family troubles were calling for his attention.

Not surprisingly, Tolstoy's disastrous experience at Baden-Baden put him off German spas. There would be no more Roulettenburg for him.

He did visit the Bavarian spa town of Bad Kissingen in 1860, but not to gamble. He went there to inspect the village school as part of a larger study project on the German educational system. (In the end, he concluded that the rote discipline and strict regimentation prevailing in the German schools were "barbaric" and likely to produce "morally deformed children.") At Bad Kissingen he met with a nephew of Julius Froebel, the founder of the kindergarten system, whom he lectured on the superiority of Russian village schooling and the virtues of the untamed Russian peasantry, "a mysterious and irrational force from which one day would spring an entirely new organization of the world." At the Bavarian spa, Tolstoy also met briefly with his oldest brother Nikolai, who was trying fruitlessly to cure a mortal case of tuberculosis. Sergei, the brother he had touched up earlier, showed up as well, begging for money. Sergei gambled even more disastrously than Leo in German spa land. Tolstoy felt incapable of helping either sibling. "I'm no use to anyone," he melodramatically despaired in his diary.

Tolstoy would continue to oscillate between self-abasement and self-deification for the rest of his life, but when it came to the German spa scene, he remained consistently negative. His unhappy experience in Baden-Baden provided the material—and perhaps the impulse—for his depiction in *Anna Karenina* (1877) of the unnamed Kurort where Princess Kitty Shcherbatsky's parents take her for a cure. (Her actual disease, of course, is a broken heart.) Kitty herself comes to like the spa well enough, as does Kitty's mother, who admires the shopping and brilliant European social scene, but Prince Shcherbatsky, reflecting Tolstoy's own view, is deeply put off by all the posturing, artificiality, Germanic regimentation, and, above all, a "monstrous conjunction" between the waltz-playing orchestra, robust-looking bath attendants, and legions of "slow-moving, dying figures from every corner of Europe."

By the time he wrote *Anna Karenina*, Tolstoy had come to see places like Baden-Baden, where "a glittering façade masked inner decadence," as all too typical of the European West in general. Although in *Anna Karenina* the writer takes both sides in the ongoing Westernizer-Slavophile debate, it is clear that he considers German spa land a domain that all good Russians should avoid like the plague rather than flocking there in large numbers, supposedly to restore their health while in actuality putting at risk their very Slavic souls.

Ménage à Trois on the Oos

Ivan Turgenev, while sharing with Tolstoy a love of Russia's landscape and (at a distance) its smelly peasantry, continued to prefer his nomadic existence abroad to life in his erstwhile homeland. He returned to Russia periodically but never stayed for long. (On one of his later returns, in 1878, he tried to reconnect with Tolstoy at Yasnaya Polyana. But Tolstoy, full of pious gravitas, wrote off his onetime benefactor as someone who "only plays at life.") No, Turgenev would remain in exile, and in 1863 he decided to make Baden-Baden, whose charms had caught his eye during his mission of mercy to Tolstoy in 1857, his new refuge. He had always been an admirer of things German as well as things French, and Baden-Baden seemed to him to combine the best of both. But even more important, Pauline and Louis Viardot had shifted *their* center of operations to the German spa town the year before.

In choosing Baden-Baden as their new home, the Viardots showed considerable acumen. Pauline had more or less blown out her voice in the grand opera houses of Europe and was ready for semiretirement. In Baden-Baden she could still perform, both as a singer and pianist, albeit on a somewhat less demanding stage. The town had a credible orchestra with which she could work, and when not performing she could give music lessons to the bored offspring of the rich curists who descended on the place every summer. Louis Viardot, for his part, had come to hate France's despotic new ruler, Napoleon III, and was more than ready to leave his native country. In Baden-Baden he could continue to manage Pauline's career, what was left of it, and thumb his nose at "Napoleon the Little" (Victor Hugo's phrase) from the safety of Germany.

Then, too, neither of the Viardots was getting any younger (Louis was already in his sixties), and the grand old Kurort offered just the kind of amenities that folk of their age cohort and financial status prized: tranquil beauty, tree-lined paths, luxury hotels, fragrant gardens, concerts and theatrical productions, fine restaurants featuring the light and tender wines of the region, cafés famous for their creamy cakes—and, of course, easy access to opulent mineral-bathing facilities and expert spa doctors should the need arise to undergo a cure, which, given all those wines and cakes, it probably would. From the proceeds of the sale of their country house in France, the couple built themselves a pretty Swiss chalet–style villa in a parklike setting across the Oos from the town center. Louis brought over his fine collection of paintings, which he installed in a purpose-built gallery on the property. (Later, he deeded his collection to Baden-Baden, which was able through his largesse to lay the groundwork for what would become an impressive municipal art museum.) Soon Louis added to this sprawling compound a recital hall and small theater for his still-ambitious wife.

For Pauline Viardot-Garcia, though, there was something missing in this cozy new nest: the third partner in the amiable (and now most likely platonic*) ménage à trois that had kept her amused for several years in France. Pauline had come to genuinely love Turgenev and thrived on his company. Also, now that his purse-string-pinching mama was gone, the writer had quite a lot of money at his disposal. Perhaps he could help finance some of her projects (in fact, he was eventually to do just that). As for Louis, he, too, missed Turgenev, though perhaps not quite so intensely as his wife did. Like Pauline, Louis had come to enjoy being around the tall, gray-bearded Russian writer, with whom he could chat about politics, business, and other manly matters and who, *very* usefully, could help absorb some of the heat thrown off by the aging diva in their midst.

Thus both Viardots were pleased when Turgenev used their residency in Baden-Baden as an excuse to move there himself. Undoubtedly, the Russian knew that his friends, Pauline especially, hoped to exploit his proximity for their own purposes, but that didn't seem to bother him. He had felt lonely in France without them, and in any event Baden-Baden seemed as good a fit for him as for them. In fact, this pretty place was arguably an even *better* fit for Turgenev, who now suffered from a host of health problems that he hoped could be reduced in severity, if not cured outright, by the waters and other medical wonders available at the spa. Always a big eater, he had recently contracted a bad case of that glutton's curse, gout, along with painful lumbago. On top of that, he continued to suffer from the laryngitis and bronchitis he had initially come down with in the foggy cold of St. Petersburg.

A few years earlier, in 1859, he had tried to cure these afflictions at Vichy, France's premier spa, but he found the place inferior in every

---

*There is some debate in the literature about whether Turgenev's relationship with Pauline Viardot-Garcia was *ever* sexual. My guess is that the affair was not without its sexual moments early on, for both these figures had a randy side. Early physical passion may have tapered off with time, as it often does.

way to what he had seen of the German Kurorte. In Vichy's defense, it should be said that Turgenev's bad experience there was partly his own fault. Foolishly electing to stay in one of the town's few bargain hotels, he had been kept up all night by a barrel-organ player under his window. At dinner in his hotel, one of his tablemates, a typical French "vulgarian," loudly shared his certain knowledge that Russian peasants invariably sold their children into the harems of the Tartar Khans. "Of course, I wasn't able to persuade him otherwise." Having experienced that awful hotel, everything else in Vichy struck Turgenev as awful: the weather (it rained incessantly), the pretentious architecture, the "sickly yellow river" running through the center of town.

Baden-Baden, by contrast, proved delightful—so much so that Turgenev became an overnight Baden booster, writing letters to literary friends full of praise for his new abode and exhorting them to visit. Among the friends he tried to coax to the Valley of the Oos was Gustav Flaubert, whom Turgenev had met in Paris in February 1863. Flaubert was himself a spa aficionado, though his *ville d'eau* of choice was Vichy, which he had visited repeatedly over the years for his many afflictions, including an impressive array of venereal diseases he had contracted from prostitutes, male and female, on his travels in the Levant. (Unlike Turgenev, Flaubert liked to brag about his sexual exploits. During a bibulous dinner party with Turgenev and the French writer Edmond de Goncourt in 1876, Flaubert reminisced fondly about having casually buggered a girl with "an ice-cold backside" in a hut in Upper Egypt. Shocked, Turgenev allowed that he could "only ever approach a woman with emotion, a feeling of respect and surprise at my good fortune.")

Turgenev's sense of good fortune in having found Baden-Baden pulses through his first appeal (April 18, 1863) to Flaubert to join him there:

> I'm leaving Paris in a week's time to go and settle in Baden. Will you not come there? There are trees there such as I've seen nowhere else—and right on the tops of the mountains! The atmosphere is young and vigorous and it's poetic and gracious at the same time. It does a power of good to your eyes and to your soul. When you sit at the foot of one of these giants, it seems as if you take in some of its sap—and it's good and beneficial. Really, come to Baden, even if it were only for a few days. You will take away with you some wonderful colors for your palette.

Flaubert, who was not known to care much for trees, or for that matter the state of his soul, did not take up Turgenev's initial invitation nor any of the others that followed with some regularity in subsequent years. He was not even enticed by the cozy prospect, which Turgenev dangled before him in a letter of May 6, 1871, that if the Frenchman came to Baden, the two fellows could doss down together "like moles hiding in their holes." Later on in that same year, Turgenev finally gave up: "I won't summon you to Germany anymore; I understand your reluctance to set foot here."

One would have thought that Turgenev might have appreciated Flaubert's "reluctance" to come to Germany a bit earlier. France had declared war on Prussia in July 1870 and then proceeded to get trounced by a hastily assembled alliance of German states (more on this in the next chapter). The new German Reich that emerged from the war added insult to injury by annexing the French provinces of Alsace and Lorraine. A proud Frenchman like Flaubert would hardly have wanted to visit Germany at this moment, much less hunker down there like a mole.

Turgenev may have failed to lure Flaubert to Baden-Baden, but he had plenty of other visitors to the comfortable Louis XIII–style chateau he built for himself in 1864 on a large lot next to the Viardots' compound.* (Before that, Turgenev's Baden-Baden residence had consisted of the lower floor of a plain house in Schillerstrasse, where he was said to live "as modestly as a university student"—though, one trusts, not quite so squalidly.) Among the visitors from Russia was I. A. Goncharov, author of *Oblomov*, perhaps the greatest celebration of sloth-like lassitude in the history of literature. (In the first 150 pages of this long novel, the eponymous protagonist never leaves his bed; eventually he musters the energy to move to his couch; the novel inspired a wonderful new word: "Oblomovism"). The German writer Theodor Storm also dropped in. Turgenev liked to squire his visitors around the pretty little town, praising the place with all the ardor of a welcome-wagon lady. On a number of occasions he threw off his natural shyness to participate in Pauline's theatrical productions, showing himself to be quite the thes-

---

*This house proved rather too grand for Turgenev's financial resources, and he soon had to sell it. Fortunately, Louis Viardot bought the property and allowed his friend to continue to live there. Today, the building is privately owned and open only to group tours. But the intrepid single tourist can, by negotiating a narrow lane running behind the residence, admire the spacious gardens and an ornamental iron gate with a "T" motif designed by the writer.

pian. Even his health was improving, as Baden's gentle climate turned out to be just the ticket for his nagging respiratory ailments, while the hot baths proved soothing for his gout. (Turgenev was rather less keen on *drinking* mineral water, although, as he wrote Flaubert later on, he considered this practice "less obvious an illusion" than the purported value of international literary conferences, "*which won't and can't produce any result.*") Putting some additional weight on his tall frame, he self-mockingly called himself "Badenbourgeois."

Yet not all was sweetness and light for Turgenev in Baden-Baden. As a local celebrity, he was often bothered by tourists banging on his door, wanting to share with him a drink or two along with their insights on the human condition. More important, it proved impossible, even here, perhaps *especially* here, for Turgenev to escape the turmoil and rancor emanating from Russia. On February 19, 1861, Czar Alexander II signed the order abolishing serfdom in Russia. Like President Lincoln's Emancipation Proclamation two years later, this long overdue measure brought shouts of joy and praise but also considerable confusion and bitter recrimination in its wake. A set of very complicated rules and regulations surrounding the new law completely bewildered the peasants. Some were actively hostile to the program, seeing it as just another landlord's trick. As for those landlords, they generally felt betrayed by the young "Czar Liberator," seeing his most famous reform as an unforgivable crime against "true Russia."

To complicate matters for Turgenev, all this turmoil over the end of serfdom was bubbling up just as his ambitious new novel, *Fathers and Children* (1862), blazed across the Russian literary scene. Dealing as it did with generational conflict over the nature and proper course for Russia, *Fathers and Children* hit a sensitive nerve, to put it mildly. Leftist radicals were insulted by Turgenev's unflattering portrait of an arch-westernizing young doctor (Bazarov), while conservatives bristled at the author's ironical treatment of Pavel Kusanov, an aging traditionalist dandy. Although the novel is now widely recognized as Turgenev's masterpiece, at the time it came under a storm of criticism in the author's homeland.

Turgenev was no less swept up in this storm by dint of being far away in Baden-Baden. On the contrary, his decision to live abroad provided additional ammunition to those fellow Russians who wished to portray him as a traitor to his country, a literary Judas. In Baden-Baden itself, the talk among the visiting Russians was all about *Fathers and Children* and its local celebrity author. Much of that talk was predictably hostile, for Turgenev, a Russian landowner himself, was seen to have attacked the economic underpinnings of a way of life that included those annual cures at German grand spas.

The largely negative reaction to *Fathers and Children* by critics in Russia, and even more by Russians stopping off in Baden-Baden, was very much on Turgenev's mind as he set about to write his next novel, *Smoke* (1867), which, not by accident, is set in that very same Kurort among the upper-crust Russian swells who regularly summered there. If *Fathers and Children* had contained a measure of what the Germans call *Nestbeschmutzung* (soiling one's own nest), *Smoke* turned out to be a full-scale dump, albeit a highly artful one, a finely calculated dropping that could only have been delivered by a gifted ironist with intimate knowledge of the nest he was beschmutzing. Although Turgenev's fellow Russians are the prime target in *Smoke*, Baden-Baden itself comes in for some satirical scrutiny—treatment that reflects a rather more critical attitude to the author's adoptive home than he had harbored early on.

This is not the place for a detailed dissection of *Smoke*, which, like Tolstoy's *Anna Karenina*, is at bottom a complicated love story. But unlike *Anna Karenina*, Turgenev's little novel is hardly known today, and, given the subject of this study, I'd be remiss if I didn't tarry a bit with the author as he looks in on Baden-Baden and its querulous community of Russian curists. The book opens with a snapshot of the spa town on a typical summer afternoon:

> On the 10th of August 1862, at four o'clock in the afternoon, a number of people were crowding in front of the famous *Conversation* at Baden-Baden. The weather was lovely; everything around—the green trees, the light-coloured houses of the cozy town, the undulating hills—lay spread out in festive abundance in the rays of the gracious sunshine; everything smiled with a kind of blind and trustful charm, and the same vague but kind smile hovered on human faces, old and young, ugly and handsome. Even the painted and powdered Parisian *cocottes* did not disturb the general impression of rejoicing and serene content. . . .
>
> Everything . . . went on in its usual way. The orchestra in the pavilion played selections from *La Traviata*, a waltz of Strauss, and then *Tell Her*, a Russian song, instrumented by an obliging conductor. In the gambling

halls the same familiar faces crowded around the green-baized tables with the same dull and greedy look of something between amazement and exasperation—an essentially predatory look which the gambling fever imparts to all, even the most aristocratic, features.

Turning his attention to the local Russians, Turgenev lines up the all usual suspects—most of whom proved to be spitting images of real figures of the day and were easily identifiable to contemporary Russian readers.

> In their usual way our amiable compatriots gathered around the Russian tree—*l'arbre russe*; they approached it haughtily and negligently, in fashionable style; they greeted one another majestically, with elegant ease, as befits beings who are at the very summit of modern culture. But once they had met and sat down, they had absolutely nothing to say to one another and fell back either upon pitiful tittle-tattle or the hackneyed, flat, and extremely impudent jokes of a hopelessly stale French ex-journalist, a babbler and buffoon, with wretched Jewish shoes on his puny little feet and a contemptible little beard on his ignoble little face. He served up à ces princes russes all kinds of insipid rubbish out of the old almanacs *Charivari* and *Tintamarre*, and the *princes russes* went off into peals of grateful laughter as though involuntarily recognizing the overwhelming superiority of foreign wit and their own utter incapacity to invent anything amusing. And yet they numbered among them all the *fine fleur* of our society, all "the best and most fashionable people." Among them was Count X, our incomparable dilettante, a deep and musical nature, who "recited" songs so divinely, though in truth he could not play two notes correctly without first prodding the piano keys at random with a forefinger, and sang like an inferior gypsy or a Parisian hairdresser. There was also our delightful Baron Z, a Jack of All Trades—writer, administrator, orator, and card-sharper. There was Prince Y, a friend of the people and of the Church, who in the happy old days of state monopolies amassed an enormous fortune by selling vodka mixed with dope; and the brilliant general O. O., who had conquered somebody, restored order somewhere, but now did not know what to do with himself or what to say for himself; and R. R., an amusing stout man who imagined himself to be very ill and very intelligent, while in truth he was strong as an ox and dull as a post.

Like *Fathers and Children*, *Smoke* takes us into the raging "Whither Russia?" debate, but in this latter novel the conflict is all the more concentrated and claustrophobic due to the tiny foreign stage on which it plays out. One of the protagonists, Grigory Litvinov, a gentle and mildly progressive student of agronomy and economics, is pulled willy-nilly into pitted verbal battles between zealous arch-Westernizers, fatuous old generals, and embittered Slavophiles full of bile over Czar Alexander's treachery. Turgenev himself identifies most closely with another figure, Potugin, who, while seeing the potential pitfalls in rapid westernization, is much more critical of the Slavophiles' neomedieval cant, religious obscurantism, Great Russian imperialism, and naive faith in the "untutored instinct of the Russian peasantry." The Slavophiles insist that Russia is God's gift to humankind, but Potugin declares that, *au contraire*, "Russia for ten whole centuries has created nothing of its own, either in government, in law, in science, in art or even in handicraft." If Russia were suddenly to disappear from the face of the earth, cries Potugin, this would be no loss to civilization because even that nation's "most famous products—the samovar, woven bast shoes, and the knout—were not invented by us."

Fedor Dostoevsky in German Spa Land

Where there's *Smoke* there's fire. Perhaps because he had lived so long in exile, Turgenev was caught off guard by the firestorm of criticism his new novel ignited in Russia. Among his fiercest critics was a fellow Russian writer, Fedor Dostoevsky. Like Tolstoy, Dostoevsky would come begging to Turgenev in Baden-Baden when he lost his peasant-style shirt gambling at the tables of Roulettenburg. And also like Tolstoy, he would unhesitatingly bite the hand that once fed him.

At the time Dostoevsky denounced *Smoke* as an insult to Mother Russia, he was already well along on a personal and intellectual odyssey that had taken him through youthful political radicalism, arrest and imprisonment in 1849 for his involvement with a secret society of utopian-socialist dreamers, mock execution (he was standing in front of a firing squad when his death sentence, already commuted by the czar, was laughingly called off—ha, ha!), four years' hard labor in Siberia followed by six years of penal servitude in the military—and finally, the elaboration of a revised worldview informed by Christian Orthodoxy, fierce Russian patriotism, and a deep appreciation for the darker side of the human psyche.

Not surprisingly, perhaps, Dostoevsky's arduous odyssey had a profound effect on his health as well as on his mental outlook. Among the many myths about this great writer is that his lifelong battle with epilepsy began when he endured that mock execution in 1849. Although apparently no epileptic fit occurred at that moment, God knows it might have. A contending myth, started by a relative and perpetuated by Freud, has it that Dostoevsky's first epileptic seizure came in 1839 when he learned of his father's murder at the hands of his serfs. Yet while Dostoevsky may indeed have felt complicit in his father's death, this episode did not engender a seizure. According to his most authoritative biographer, the late Joseph Frank, the writer's first epileptic attack occurred sometime in 1850, at the outset of his exile in Siberia; it was marked by "shrieks, loss of consciousness, convulsive movements of the face and limbs, foaming at the mouth." For the next six years, Dostoevsky averaged one of these terrible fits every month. Later on the episodes tapered off, but he lived in fear of relapses for the rest of his life. (He suffered a major fit during the honeymoon following his first marriage; this set the tone for the rest of the marriage.) Less horrifically, but certainly bothersome, were afflictions he had picked up along the way to losing his youthful optimistic outlook: chronic obstructive pulmonary disease, a bad liver, dropsy, fevers, and the inevitable hemorrhoids.

Although Dostoevsky would eventually seek treatment for all these ailments in German spas, health problems were not his primary motive for visiting the Kurorte. His main motive was to gamble. That fateful impulse, however, was initially embedded within a larger, less problematic aspiration he shared with so many of his educated fellow countrymen: the desire to travel to the European West.

Dostoevsky tells us in *Winter Tales on Summer Impressions*, his short (and not very reliable) account of his first European journey in the summer of 1862, that he had been "dreaming of [a trip to Europe] for almost forty years," and, further, that he set off on that trip with great expectations regarding the fabled lands he intended to visit. In reality, however, he carried within him prejudices about the West that he had been incubating during his torturous but spiritually revelatory time in Siberia. And, as is often the way with prejudices, these were confirmed, even hardened, by actual experience. This was especially true of his confrontation with Germany, a land much admired by many educated Russians but a place that Dostoevsky decided to despise with all the fervor of his Slavic soul. "It is not for his fairness that he is famous," observes Saul Bellow in his foreword to the American edition of *Winter Notes*. (True enough, but one wonders whether this bigoted, anti-Semitic, self-obsessed, and foul-tempered genius had to be *such* a nasty piece of work.)

Dostoevsky traveled by train through Germany on his way to Paris on the first leg of his 1862 European trip. His brief stopover in Berlin did not bode well for the rest of his passage through the land of *Dichter und Denker*. Walking the streets, he discovered to his horror that all the people looked *German*! How disgusting! He immediately rushed away, "carrying in my soul the deepest conviction that it required special pains to accustom oneself to Germans, and that, unless you were used to them, it would be extremely difficult to stand them in large masses."

Additional stops in Dresden and Cologne did nothing to brighten Dostoevsky's view of the *Nyemsty* (literally, "mute ones"). "In Dresden I extended my poor judgment [of the Germans] to German womanhood. No sooner had I gone out into the street than I could imagine nothing more repulsive than the Dresden type of woman." Nor was he impressed by the magnificent Cologne Cathedral, which he had been expecting to admire, but which ended up just pissing him off: "It seemed to me like mere lace, lace and nothing but lace, a knickknack from a haberdashery shop resembling a paperweight for a writing desk about five hundred feet high." (To be fair to Dostoevsky, fairer than he was to the Germans, I should note that he *did* come to admire the Cologne Cathedral when he saw it a second time on his way home to Russia.)

The big Russian chip on Dostoevsky's shoulder was plainly in evidence when he was compelled to pay a toll at Cologne's famous iron bridge over the Rhine. In the visiting Russian's jaundiced view, the pompous jackass taking tolls at the bridge radiated an aura of boastful Germanic superiority and contempt for lowly Russian tourists: "I thought . . . his eyes were all but saying, 'You see our bridge, miserable Russian, and you see that you are a worm before our bridge and before every German person because you people don't have any such bridge!'" Throughout this caricature of the Germans, Dostoevsky was also quite consciously presenting an unflattering caricature of himself as the ugly Russian abroad, a scowling chap with a "bad liver" and an even worse attitude. Nonetheless, he meant every word he said.

Dostoevsky's next stop in Germany was Wiesbaden, the great spa town slightly southwest of Frankfurt where Goethe, Wagner, Mendelssohn, Balzac, and many other notables had taken the waters earlier in the century. By the time Dostoevsky got there, the grand resort was hosting some fifteen thousand cure guests annually, about the same number as Baden-Baden. Revealingly, the writer says nothing in *Winter Notes* about his brief stopover at the Kurort, giving the impression that he went from Cologne immediately on to Paris. But we know he paused at Wiesbaden from evidence on his passport and other travel documents, along with correspondence with his brother Mikhail.

A stop at Wiesbaden for Dostoevsky would have made good sense given his manifold health problems, and in fact he had cited ill health as his primary reason for travel to Europe on his passport and visa applications. Moreover, on the eve of his departure he wrote a letter to another brother (Andrey) offering a similar justification for his trip: "I am a sick, a chronically sick man. . . . My health is so wretched that I'm now . . . going abroad until September to cure myself."

If "taking the waters" had really been on Dostoevsky's mind as he set off for Europe, the Kurort he descended upon in late June 1862 had plenty of highly regarded thermal springs from which to choose. A. B. Granville, our intrepid English investigator of the entire German spa scene, judged the waters in Wiesbaden comparable to those in Baden-Baden in quality—so long as one chose the major springs used by the best hotels as opposed to the secondary Quellen exploited by the lesser hostelries. Along with its healing waters and fine hotels, Wiesbaden, like all the grand German spa towns, offered daily orchestral concerts and nightly theatrical productions during the season. According to a popular guidebook of the time, the spa town also provided "games of chance of all kinds." Shortly before Dostoevsky arrived in town, a magnificent new *Kursaal* (cure center) called the Wiesbadener Brunnen had opened its doors. This facility had been advertised extensively in the *St. Petersburg Times*, and for good reason: wealthy Russians had long been an important component of Wiesbaden's clientele.

But Dostoevsky was not a typical Russian spa visitor nor even a typical Russian-*writer* spa visitor. Unlike Turgenev and Tolstoy or even Gogol and Goncharov, he had no family money and was forced to live by his pen. This was both a source of grievance and pride. He declared at one point that if the pampered Turgenev had been forced to write all day and all night just to survive, like *he* did, the effort "would probably kill him."

Given the paucity of documentation for Dostoevsky's first visit to Wiesbaden, one cannot speak with any certainty either about his motives for stopping at the resort or his routine during his stay. It is highly doubtful, though, that he took the waters. Lacking the financial resources necessary for thermal bathing, not to mention luxury hotels or fine restaurants, it is probable that he went to Wiesbaden to *make* money rather than to spend it. And where better to reap a quick financial windfall than at the spa's famed gaming tables? But if replenishing his depleted pocketbook was indeed Dostoevsky's chief reason for visiting Wiesbaden, his stopover was an utter failure. We know this because of two anguished letters sent to him by his brother Mikhail. "For God's sake, don't gamble anymore," Mikhail writes in the first letter. "How can you gamble with our luck?" A month later Mikhail complains: "After your short stay in Wiesbaden your letters have taken on a purely businesslike tone, no longer saying anything about your trip or your impressions." On subsequent visits to the German spas, Wiesbaden and others, Dostoevsky would not be so tight lipped about his experiences there, including his disastrous experiences at the green tables. And there *would* be subsequent visits because, that first disaster notwithstanding, Dostoevsky had caught the gambling bug in a very big way.

Dostoevsky's next trip to Central and Western Europe came just one year later, in the summer and fall of 1863. Health issues were his stated reasons for this excursion, too: he said he was seeking "advice from European specialists on epilepsy." To help finance his journey, he secured a grant from St. Petersburg's "Society for the Support of Needy Writers and Scholars." But the main purpose behind this trip was to gamble in Germany and to rendezvous in France with a young Russian woman he had met in St. Petersburg in 1862. The woman in question, Apollinaria Suslova, was a student at the university and a pioneering feminist. Her eventual husband (not Dostoevsky) opined that Suslova "resembled Catherine de Medici. She could have lightheartedly committed a crime. She could have killed. She was one who would have enjoyed firing from her window at the Huguenots on St. Bartholomew's Eve."

The husband may have been exaggerating a bit in imagining Suslova happily slaughtering Huguenots, but there is no question that she had a sadistic side, especially in her treatment of men. Like Baudelaire's infamous mistress, Jeanne Duval, Suslova seems to have been a coquette of the first order, exploiting her considerable sexual charms to torment and humiliate her male partners. Her favorite method of torturing Dostoevsky was to deny him sex over extended periods. (In her defense, it should be noted that Dostoevsky seems to have been something less than a gifted swordsman, sometimes proving unable to hold up his end even when he did get the chance.) Freud argues in "Dostoevsky and Parricide" that, psychologically speaking, gambling is equivalent to male masturbation—a desperate substitute for sexual gratification. Whatever this theory's value as a general proposition, Freud may be on to something in the case of Dostoevsky in the company of Suslova. In any event, his liaison with her was to prove almost as disastrous as his coupling with the goddess of gambling.

The writer's second tryst with Madame Roulette was even more fraught than the first, largely because of an added complication: in order to embrace this demanding temptress as well as the one awaiting him in Paris, he had abandoned his first wife, Marya Dimitrievna, languishing back in St. Petersburg and dying of tuberculosis. The writer told himself that he was stopping at Wiesbaden only to win money to send home to the ailing Marya and other needy relatives. The reality is that he hoped for a gambling windfall large enough to solve *all* his financial problems in one fell swoop.

The even deeper reality is that he was now so ensnared by his ball-spinning (and ball-busting) inamorata that he could not quit her no matter how the romance proceeded. The delusions of gambling come through loud and clear in a letter he wrote his brother Mikhail after quickly winning three thousand francs via a sure-fire system: "Tell me, after that [win] how is it possible not to be carried away, why should I not believe that happiness is in my grasp if I stick rigorously to my system? And I need money, for myself, for you, for my wife, to write a novel. . . . Yes, I have come here in order to save you all and to save myself." (By the way, Dostoevsky's vaunted system consisted of nothing more than "holding myself in at every moment and not getting excited no matter what the play. . . . [With that approach] it's impossible to lose.")

With a predictability that matched the unpredictability of the roulette wheel's spinning ball, the writer soon lost all his early winnings—and then proceeded to lose more and more cash as he desperately sought to return to winning form. To his credit, he did send some of his initial earnings to his wife via her sister, but not long thereafter, rather less to his credit, he begged his sister-in-law to return the money to him because he was flat broke. It goes without saying that his long sessions at the gambling table left him no time (or money) to consult any of the local specialists regarding his epilepsy or to soothe his hemorrhoids in the hot baths.

Matters got even worse when Dostoevsky reconnected with Suslova in Paris and then traveled on with her to that greatest of all gambling Meccas, Baden-Baden. Once the couple arrived at the spa town with its opulent casino, Dostoevsky had to contend with *two* temptresses simultaneously. Suslova, for her part, remained alluring even though—as she did not hesitate to inform her partner—she had recently been jilted by a hot Spanish lover in Paris and required Dostoevsky's support, emotional and financial, to get over this terrible loss. Thus, in the writer's love-clouded eyes, a profitable stopover at Bénazet's was necessary to fund not only his own needs and those of his wife back home but also those of a demanding (albeit sexually stingy) lover by his side.

Apart from Baden-Baden's fabled casino, there was another reason why Dostoevsky chose this particular spa to recoup his fortunes. He wanted to meet with the town's most illustrious Russian resident, Ivan Turgenev. The contact was important to Dostoevsky because Turgenev, still Russia's leading writer, had agreed to contribute a short story called "Phantoms" to Dostoevsky's struggling literary journal, *Time*. Yet the younger writer was somewhat ambivalent about meeting Turgenev because, like Tolstoy, he considered the squire of Baden-Baden a lightweight who had lost contact with his inner Russian. Moreover, Dostoevsky was desperately afraid that Turgenev might get wind of Suslova and spread word about her among the gabby Russian curists in town, thereby setting tongues wagging back home as well. Yet another reason for Dostoevsky's edginess was that by the time the two writers actually met at Turgenev's house, the younger man had become so preoccupied with gambling that he had neglected to read a draft of "Phantoms" that Turgenev had sent him for his comments. Although aware that he had committed a faux pas in not reading "Phantoms," Dostoevsky did not appreciate how deeply he had offended his host. There would be more offenses to come.

Meanwhile, we have two conflicting sources on Dostoevsky's first visit to Baden-Baden and his experience at Bénazet's casino. Perhaps sensing that her companion might one day be famous, Suslova kept a diary of their travels together. Given that their relationship was more often tempestuous than tender, her account of the Baden-Baden phase of the trip is curiously upbeat. "The journey here [to Baden-Baden] with F. M. [Fedor Mikhailovich] was rather entertaining . . . he spoke in verse during the entire trip, and finally, here, where we had some trouble finding two rooms with two beds, he signed the guest register 'officer,' at which we had to laugh a lot. He plays roulette all the time and is generally very carefree." If Dostoevsky was in fact "carefree"— and that is truly hard to believe—Madame Roulette brought a quick end to his insouciance. A letter from Fedor to his brother Mikhail, our second source for the writer's first Baden-Baden experience, contains the all-too-familiar revelation: "I came to the table [at Bénazet's] and in a quarter of an hour had won six hundred francs. That fired me up. Suddenly, I began to lose. I couldn't stop, and I lost everything, down to the last kopek." Dostoevsky goes on to plead with his brother to scrape together whatever money he can find and dispatch it forthwith to Turin, Italy, where the couple planned to go next. Fedor's desperate plea to his brother constitutes a much more revealing indication of his state of mind in Baden than a whistle-in-the-dark diary entry by Suslova: "F. M. has lost some money gambling and is a bit worried about not having enough money for our journey."

Despite their impoverishment, the couple did manage to continue their journey to Italy as planned. After Suslova returned to Paris in the fall, Dostoevsky began his return trek to Russia, a trip that included a stopover in yet another grand German spa, Bad Homburg. Once again, his purpose was to gamble, and the consequence was as always: small wins followed by waves of heavy losses. We know he lost badly because he sent a letter to Suslova begging her to send money immediately. The young woman was willing to help, even though she had become almost as exasperated with her lover as he was with her. In her diary she relates that, lacking ready cash to dispatch to Dostoevsky, she contemplated pawning her watch and other valuables before securing a three-hundred-franc loan from a French friend, female this time. She sent the whole lot to Homburg, where, of course, Dostoevsky immediately pissed it away. How he paid for his trip home we do not know.

We do know that Dostoevsky was not yet done with either Suslova or gambling in German spas. The two lovers traveled together during Dostoevsky's third trip to Europe in 1865. That journey would prove even more exasperating than the one in 1863, in part because the intervening year, 1864, had been a terrible one for Dostoevsky, even by his exacting standards. His wife finally passed away, sending him into convulsions of guilt; he also lost his beloved brother Mikhail, which produced paroxysms of pain. His struggling journal *Time* went belly up, leaving him with a pile of debt. Undeterred, he launched a new journal, *Epoch*, to which he hoped Turgenev would contribute. To that end, he wrote the older writer a rather lame letter of apology for his earlier rude behavior in Baden-Baden, which he attributed to his tough luck at the gambling tables. He would be "very ashamed" of himself, he added, if he didn't have "the hope of something more intelligent in the future."

When it came to gambling in German spas, Dostoevsky's experience in 1865 showed that he had not wised up one bit. On the other hand, he genuinely *did* have hopes of doing "something more intelligent" in the immediate future. He wanted to write "a long story"—and to do so, he intended to travel abroad once again. The "long story" turned out to be *Crime and Punishment* (1866), a tale he started writing in Wiesbaden, site of plenty of past crimes and self-punishment on his own part. It may seem odd that Raskolnikov, that quintessential self-loathing St. Petersburg intellectual, first came to life in a German spa. But perhaps it's not so strange after all: given what the spas did to Dostoevsky's state of mind, they were the perfect places in which to think about murder. Moreover, clichéd as it may sound, Dostoevsky seems to have drawn creative energy and inspiration from suffering and self-loathing, and he undoubtedly knew, if only unconsciously, that he was likely to find both of these spiritual afflictions in the same place he passionately sought (financial) redemption: German spa land.

And he *did* seek redemption once again at Wiesbaden. No sooner had he hit town and checked into the Hotel Victoria than he scurried around the corner to the main casino, where he was to spend most of his time at the spa. At the risk of becoming tedious, I have to report that this third pass through Wiesbaden was same old, same old. He won a few francs on the first day and then over the next four days lost everything, including the 175 rubles he had set aside for his journey through Europe with Suslova. She in fact joined him in Wiesbaden for a couple of days, only to get so fed up with his feckless behavior that she rushed back to Paris.

Alone and without money even to pay his hotel bills, Dostoevsky unleashed a volley of anguished pleas for help to everyone he could think of, including the much-put-upon Turgenev. His appeal to the squire of Baden-Baden was a tour de force of obsequious flattery and self-abasement:

> I arrived in Wiesbaden only five days ago, and I have lost everything already, just everything, including my watch, and I even owe money to the hotel.
> I feel loathsome, and ashamed to be bothering you with my affairs. But I really have no one else right now to whom I can turn and, in the second place, you are much more intelligent than the others, and so it is morally easier for me to turn to you. Here is what I have in mind: I am asking you, as one human being to another, for 100 thalers. . . . It is quite unlikely that I can pay you back before *three weeks*; then again, it might be earlier. In any case, a month at the latest. I feel horrible inside (I thought it would be worse) and, above all, I'm ashamed to bother you, but what can you do when you are drowning?

Turgenev, ever the enabler, promptly sent fifty thalers, not the requested hundred. His loan was enough to warrant a thank-you note from Dostoevsky and a promise "to pay you back very soon." A false promise, as it turned out. Dostoevsky would stiff his benefactor, adding another bone of contention to an increasingly contentious relationship.

Meanwhile, from Wiesbaden Dostoevsky dispatched a plea for help to yet another Russian literary luminary, the great socialist thinker and critic Alexander Herzen, who was then living in exile in Geneva. But Herzen, suffering hard times himself, begged off. So there was nothing for it but to turn once again to poor Suslova, who had barely been able to finance her return to Paris and who had rushed away screaming that she wanted nothing more to do with her underperforming gambler-junkie lover.

If it had been humiliating to go begging to Turgenev, Dostoevsky's renewed appeal to Suslova must have felt like sewer crawling. "My affairs are in a lamentable state," he cried. "It is not possible to sink any further." Yet perhaps further degradation *was* possible, for he quickly added:

"Down deeper there must be another zone of misery and filth of which I have no inkling yet." If that deeper zone of misery indeed existed, Wiesbaden would be the place to find it: "I am tormented by my inactivity . . . by this waste of time, and by this *accursed Wiesbaden*, which has so sickened me that it makes me disgusted with life!" But even now he was not down so far that he couldn't crawl lower: "I have asked you to help me out if you can borrow from someone or other. I am not very optimistic, Polya, but if you can, do it for me! You must agree that it would be quite difficult to find anyone in a more troublesome and painful predicament than I am in at this moment."

Yet another abject appeal went out to an old family friend, Baron A. E. Wrangel, a sometime visitor to Wiesbaden who was then Russia's emissary to Denmark. Throwing himself on Wrangel's mercy, Dostoevsky stated bluntly that because of recent gambling losses he desperately needed a loan of one hundred thalers. "I have nothing," he lamented. "I owe money to the hotel, I have no credit, and I am in a frightful situation. It is always the same thing as before, the only difference being that it is now twice as bad." As usual, he promised to repay the loan in short order, since his literary ship was about to come in. "I count on my story [the as-yet-unnamed *Crime and Punishment*], which I am writing day and night. But instead of three folio sheets it is spreading out to six, and the work is not yet finished." (Wrangel did send the one hundred thalers, though this infusion proved to be only a down payment on the sum Dostoevsky owed his avaricious landlord, who had even cut off the supply of candles the writer depended on to work through the night—thereby, perhaps, unwittingly adding to the darkness of *Crime and Punishment*.)

Although in his various pleas for financial help Dostoevsky typically insisted that the person to whom he was writing was his last and only hope in the world, he actually found a new benefactor in—of all places— "accursed Wiesbaden." The benefactor in question was Father I. L. Yanishev, the priest in charge of Wiesbaden's Russian Orthodox Church. That the German spa town should have its own Orthodox Church and priest was a testament to the impressive size and influence of the resident Russian community, which was significantly augmented each summer by legions of Slavic visitors seeking a cure, a gambling fix, or both. The tendency of Russian spa patrons to spread their custom among all the grand German Kurorte meant that Wiesbaden was not alone in having an Orthodox Church: so, too, did Baden-Baden, Bad Homburg, and Bad Ems. (Karlsbad and Marienbad had them as well.) In each case, the job of the local priest was to do for his flock's souls what the thermal waters were supposed to do for their bodies. (Which of these ministrations was the more dubious is a question of infinite interest—but, alas, probably unanswerable in the end.)

With Dostoevsky, of course, Father Yanishev had his work cut out. The writer came to him full of stories of woe and a plaintive plea for a monetary bailout so that he could resolve his debts in Wiesbaden and return to Russia. Yanishev, who was unusually cultivated for an Orthodox priest (he had studied physics and mathematics along with theology), not only supplied Dostoevsky with an emergency loan but engaged him in learned discussions of free will and "charitable love"—themes that were to preoccupy the writer in his greatest work, *The Brothers Karamazov*. (In that work, the latitudinarian priest, Father Zosima, echoes the teachings of Father Yanishev.) Dostoevsky remained for the rest of his life in close contact with his spiritual benefactor, whom he praised as a man "of angelic purity and a *passionate* believer." It was Father Yanishev who presided at Dostoevsky's funeral in 1881. Clearly, the writer had found a lot more in Wiesbaden than his embittered letters would suggest.

It was also in Wiesbaden—and to a lesser extent in Baden-Baden and Bad Homburg—that Dostoevsky found the inspiration and material for a short piece of fiction he originally titled *Roulettenburg* but then changed to *The Gambler*. Like Turgenev's *Smoke*, *The Gambler* is not among its creator's better-known works, but it is without doubt (in Joseph Frank's words) "one of the liveliest, brightest, and most amusing of [Dostoevsky's] shorter creations." It also, again like Turgenev's little novel, opens a window on life, in this case mainly low life, in German spa land at a time when gambling was the primary attraction for many of the patrons.

This work's backstory is almost as interesting as the story itself. In the fall of 1866, Dostoevsky found himself in a new and particularly nasty bind. Pressure from his creditors had forced him to sell the rights to all his previous works plus an as-yet-unwritten book of "not less than ten printed sheets" (160 pages) to his publisher, Feodor Stellovsky, for three thousand rubles. If he failed to produce this new work by November 1, Stellovsky would have the right to reprint all Dostoevsky's past and future work with no payment to the author. (In the long, sad history of publisher-author relations, this has to be one of the sadder moments.) Dostoevsky had to grind out a new novel, or at least a novella, within one month or give up writing as gainful employment. How could he possibly accomplish this feat? What topic might lend itself to a one-month literary blitzkrieg? Gambling, which Dostoevsky had fatefully seen as a source of financial salvation, had helped get him into this mess in the first place; perhaps gambling, not *doing* it but *writing* about it, might help extricate him from the merde. For some time he had been toying with the idea of writing a story about gambling. Now, in early October 1866, with less than a month to go before Stellovsky's deadline, the writer decided to give it a try.

To make what seemed an impossible task a little less impossible, Dostoevsky decided to *dictate* this new work rather than to write down every word himself in his usual fashion. On the recommendation of the director of Russia's first shorthand school, the writer engaged the services of a twenty-year-old stenographer named Anna Grigoryevna Snitkina to capture his cascade of words in shorthand and then transcribe these hieroglyphics into legible prose. Dostoevsky and Anna worked together every day from noon to 4:30 p.m. for two weeks. At the end of this arduous process, Dostoevsky had a manuscript for Stellovsky, just in time. In Anna Grigoryevna he also had a new partner—and one who would shortly become his second wife.

Although the conditions of its gestation were hardly optimal, *The Gambler* must have been fun for Dostoevsky to write. It not only allowed him to analyze (and in a way to rationalize) his gambling addiction as an ineluctable trait in the Russian character, but also to dump a bucketful of bile on the Germans and their damned spas. It is his portrait of "Roulettenburg" that is of most interest to us here. Of course, the portrait in question is nothing like one might find in a guidebook or travelogue; there is nothing remotely objective about it. While the novella is not, strictly speaking, autobiographical, the central character and narrator, Alexei, can be said to speak for Dostoevsky in his colorful castigation of "the roulette towns on the Rhine."

The Russian newspapers may rave about the magnificence of the German spa town casinos, says Alexei, but in reality "there is no splendor whatsoever in those sordid rooms." The players and croupiers are sordid, too:

> As to the mob, their way of gambling is really quite repulsive. I wouldn't even mind saying that a lot of plain stealing goes on around the table. It is very hard on the croupiers, who sit at the end of the tables, watch the stakes, collect the money, and make the pay-offs. And they, too, are a quite unsavory lot. Mostly French.

Dostoevsky plays a lot with the stereotype of the Russians as inveterate gamblers, incapable of resisting the siren call of the round black bitch with her spinning ball. And yet, to our narrator Alexei, the Russian predilection with reckless gambling is vastly preferable to the ethos prevailing among the German burghers in their awful little spa burgs: dogged accumulation of capital by slavish work and dutiful saving. "I'd rather spend my life like a nomad under a tent than worship the German idol," proclaims Alexei. "What idol?" he is asked. And he answers:

> The German method of accumulating wealth. I haven't been here very long, but what I have already managed to observe and check is enough to outrage my Tartar nature. I assure you, I want none of their virtues! Yesterday, I went for a six- or seven-mile walk through the town and the countryside, and it all looked to me exactly like the illustrations in those little German manuals of moral principle. Every house here has its *Vater*, a frightfully virtuous and infinitely honorable man. In fact, he's so honorable that it's frightening to come too close to him. Well, I personally can't stand people who are that honorable! And each of these *Vaters* has a family, and in the evenings they all sit together and read wholesome, edifying books. And above the housetops, elms and chestnuts rustle, a stork nests on the roof, and the sun sets behind it, and everything is so supremely poetic and touching.

I repeat, the character Alexei is *not* simply a stand-in for Dostoevsky; and, to be sure, the author is having quite a lot of fun with his fictional creation's rantings. Yet, just as with his own earlier rantings in *Winter Notes*, the jaundiced take in *The Gambler* on the penny-pinching, anal-retentive Teutons and their storybook spa towns is every bit as serious as it is amusing.

Showdown in Baden-Baden

One might imagine that by writing extensively and honestly about the gambling bug, Dostoevsky would have purged that bug from his system. After all, do not the mental therapists tell us that by bringing a problem out into the open and discussing it candidly we can rid ourselves of said problem? But Dostoevsky's "issue" was rather too complicated for the pat answers of psychology. Although in *The Gambler* he does not prettify or romanticize the gambling addiction, by making it a quintessentially *Russian* trait he gives his protagonist, and ultimately himself, an all-too-convenient explanation for this self-destructive behavior: throwing fortunes down the old gambling rat hole is, alas, *just what Russians do.*

And Dostoevsky would continue to do just that for another five years following the publication of *The Gambler* in 1866. The summer of the next year, 1867, found him for a second time in Germany's premier spa town, Baden-Baden. He went there for an unusually long stay of five weeks, and this time he was in the company of his new wife, Anna, who was pregnant with their first child. The Baden-Baden sojourn proved to be exceptionally trying for poor Anna because Fedor gambled incessantly, periodically winning just enough to keep at it, day after day, night after night, until finally all was lost, including Anna's wedding ring, a brooch Fedor had given her as a wedding present, and even her shawl and spare frock. Unlike Dostoevsky's earlier consort, Suslova, Anna loved her man so deeply that she forgave him for his recklessness and stuck by him. (More than that: she reportedly rewarded him with sex and caviar every time he added a new chapter to his work in progress!) Ivan Turgenev, on the other hand, with whom Dostoevsky was to have an epic showdown near the beginning of the Baden visit, finally washed his hands of his difficult friend. Their fiery quarrel drew not merely on long-simmering personal pique but on the much larger ideological antipathies attending that ongoing uncivil war back in Russia between westernizers and Slavophiles.

Before plunging into this seminal donnybrook between these two great writers, I must, in the interest of sadomasochistic verisimilitude, spend a few moments with the newlyweds on their honeymoon from hell in Baden-Baden.

The Dostoevskys arrived in Baden-Baden on July 5. According to Anna, the weather was "horrid and gloomy," with buckets of rain. Nonetheless, Fedor went off promptly to the Conversation House, taking with him "some thalers and fifteen ducats" and promising, on his honor, "not to play." At the end of three hours, reports Anna, "Fedor came back and told me he had lost all the money he had taken with him." That first day set the pattern for the rest of their stay. Anna would dole out some of their precious savings. Fedor would promise to stop playing the moment he had lost a small, prearranged sum—and then return home hours later having lost everything he had taken with him. Sometimes, however, he did win modest amounts, but this was worse than constant losing because it encouraged him to keep playing, day after day, prolonging the agony.

Anna rarely accompanied him to the gambling rooms. She stayed "home" by herself, first in a hotel room that was far too expensive for them and then in a shabby flat over a smithy, where she had to put up with the din of constant hammering from below. On occasion, at Fedor's prodding, she went to the Reading Room in the Conversation House, but she disliked doing so because she was embarrassed to be seen wearing one of her unfashionable threadbare frocks. Soon she had only one dress to wear because, in order to feed her husband's gambling habit, she had to pawn most of her wardrobe to a German Jew who, in her view, cheated her mercilessly. During the first phase of their stay, she suffered almost every day from morning sickness. But even worse was the dreadful loneliness and nagging fear that she and Fedor would soon be left entirely destitute or that—in his anguish over losing at the tables—her husband would commit suicide, which he sometimes cruelly threatened to do. Instead of pulling the plug on his life, Fedor made Anna's life miserable with his incessant self-castigation, his passive-aggressive whining "that he was not worthy of me, he was a swine and I was an angel, and a lot of other foolish things of the same kind." Anna always reassured him of her love and, as if to prove it, parceled out a few more francs or ducats for him to lose. On those occasions when he won a little money, he would bring her flowers or fruit, and she would fall over herself in gratitude: "This thoughtfulness on Fedor's part pleased me enormously, especially as it was such a surprise.... How grateful I am to my darling, precious Fedor for his attentiveness to me!" But since Fedor's "attentiveness" more typically involved leaving her alone for hours on end while he gambled away the grocery money plus the money she'd scraped together by pawning her clothes, Anna was often on the edge of breaking down entirely. "We went to get a meal [after visiting the pawnshop] as I was terribly hungry. I had suffered beyond words, waiting for Fedor. I cried, and cursed myself, Roulette, Baden-Baden, and everything on earth."

During his previous stay in Baden-Baden, Dostoevsky, we'll recall, had called upon Turgenev to hit him up for a loan—a loan he had neglected to repay. Still unwilling (and unable) to make good on his obligation, he hoped to avoid encountering Turgenev on his second visit to the town. But not long after his arrival, he ran into Goncharov in the street and, after pressing the writer for a small loan, learned from him that Turgenev was already aware of his presence in the city. Now there was nothing to do but to call on his erstwhile benefactor lest he, Turgenev, suspect (correctly) that Dostoevsky was trying to avoid him because of the unpaid loan.

We have two sources for the epochal showdown in Baden-Baden between Dostoevsky and Turgenev: an entry in Anna's diary set down the day after the meeting and a letter from Fedor to his friend Apollon Maikov written a month later. Although the two sources concur on many points, Anna's account is considerably less harsh than Dostoevsky's own, probably because the writer spared his wife some of the more grisly details. Relating what Fedor told her of the meeting, Anna reports that Turgenev (who was still too tactful to say anything about the unpaid loan) was "embittered, even to the point of being venomous," about the hostile reception in Russia accorded his novel *Smoke*. Fedor, fully sharing that negative opinion of *Smoke*, "treated [Turgenev] none too gently," telling him archly "to procure a telescope" so that he might see more accurately what was going on in Russia. Anna reports also that "Fedor declared he found the Germans extremely stupid and very apt to be dishonest." Turgenev took grave offense at this comment, assuring Dostoevsky that he, the rude visitor, "had irreparably insulted him for he himself had now become, not a Russian anymore, but a German." Yet Anna concludes her account by insisting that "on the whole, [the two writers] parted as friends."

Dostoevsky's letter to Maikov makes clear that there was no such friendly parting and that the exchanges between the two men were even more bruising than he had led Anna to believe. Matters became truly ugly when the conversation switched from *Smoke* to the bitter westernizer-Slavophile debate. "[Turgenev] criticized Russia and the

Russians monstrously, horribly . . . [he] said we ought to crawl before the Germans, and that all attempts at Russianness and independence [were] swinishness and stupidity." Dostoevsky relates that it was at this point that he told Turgenev to get himself a telescope, since as a perpetual exile he was clueless about actual conditions prevailing in his homeland. Referring to his own brief stay in Germany, Dostoevsky complains in the letter of having to reside in a place without "Russian thoughts, Russian books, and even friendly faces." Referring to Turgenev's decision to hole up in Baden, Dostoevsky tells Maikov that he asked the older man how in heaven's name he could live abroad, for "to be without one's native land—it's suffering, honest to God!" As for those Germans Turgenev so fawningly loved, Dostoevsky insists he denounced the whole pack of them as "rogues and swindlers . . . much worse and more dishonest than ours." Turgenev might bang on about superior German civilization, but, says Dostoevsky, he told him in short order that "civilization [had] done nothing for them" whatsoever.

According to Dostoevsky's report, Turgenev then "flew into a paroxysm of rage," shrieking that Fedor had offended him *personally*. "'You should know that I have settled here permanently,' he fumed, 'that I consider myself a German, not a Russian, and I'm proud of it.'" Drawing himself up to his full five-foot-three height, Dostoevsky announced that he was sorry if he had offended his host and promptly took his leave. "I vowed never again to set foot at Turgenev's." Turgenev, for his part, hoped he had seen the last of Dostoevsky: he sent a card by his lodgings the next morning saying as much.

For once, both men were as good as their word. It was Anna, though, who had the last word. Regarding Turgenev's insistence that he felt more German than Russian, she wrote in her diary: "Of all the curious men— how could he possibly be proud of being a German instead of a Russian? No Russian writer should . . . declare himself a *German*!"

Do Svidaniya to Deutschland

Four years after this agonizing Baden-Baden visit, Dostoevsky finally kicked the gambling habit for good. This happened in Wiesbaden, where it had all started almost ten years earlier. On April 5, 1871, Dostoevsky went to the main casino in town, determined simply to have a look around. Once there, he began to "play mentally," with great success. This inspired him to play physically, and lo and behold, he won eighteen thalers. Then, as he related sadly in a letter to Anna, who awaited him in Dresden, the usual happened: "By half-past nine I had lost everything and I left the tables in a stupor." He pleaded with her for thirty thalers, promising that he would use the money only to come to her. And he added:

> Anya, I lie at your feet, I kiss them and I know you have a perfect right to despise me and to think, "he will gamble again." By what shall I swear to you that I won't, *I won't*? For I have deceived you before. But my angel, do understand: I know you would die if I were to play again. I am not absolutely mad. I know I should be lost if that were to happen. I won't gamble, I won't, I won't. I shall come back *at once*. Believe me *for the last time* and you will not regret it.

Anna proved unable to send the requested money, which may have been a good thing. Dostoevsky nonetheless found a way to get to Dresden and, more importantly, also found a way, for the first time, to hold true to his promise to his wife. Anna confirmed the blessed turnaround in her affectionate memoir/portrait of him: "I, of course, could not all at once believe in such great happiness as Fedor's indifference to roulette. . . . But this time the happiness was realized. That indeed was the last time he played roulette. . . . He returned from Wiesbaden cheerful and calm, and immediately sat down to the continuation of his novel, *The Devils*."

However firm his vow of gambling abstinence might have been, Dostoevsky, one imagines, could very easily have suffered a relapse were it not for some help from the new German kaiser, Wilhelm I. On his orders, casino gambling was banned across the entire German Reich, effective October 1872. It happens that Dostoevsky returned to German spa land four more times before his death—in 1874, 1875, 1876, and 1879. Anna could not be by his side on any of these occasions, but, perhaps more crucially, neither could Madame Roulette.

Dostoevsky confined himself on these last four spa visits to one Kurort: Bad Ems. These trips were all actually motivated by the reason he had given for his earlier excursions to Germany: bad health. As I noted earlier, Dostoevsky suffered from respiratory ailments, and in those days Bad Ems was *the* place to go for this malady. The writer had a referral to an emphysema specialist named Dr. Orth, who prescribed regular doses of the famous mineral water and also forbade his patient from writing, on grounds that the excitement this generated offset the calming effect of the healing waters. But Dostoevsky had deadlines to meet and bills to pay, and so he scribbled away in his hotel room, all the while sucking for air. That he kept coming back to Ems was a testament to his desperation and also to his conviction that the "cure" was keeping him alive. "Had I not gone to Ems this past summer, I would surely have died in the [subsequent] winter," he wrote in 1875.

That his visits to Ems were, in Dostoevsky's view, a *necessary* evil, did not make them any less evil. His letters to Anna from the spa constitute a litany of complaints about the changeable climate, high cost of living, ridiculous rules and regulations, obnoxious fellow patients, officious doctors—and, of course, those God-awful Germans all over the place. Bad Ems, he noted in his first letter, had "boomed [in the past five years] and people have started to come here from all corners of Europe." Too many damn people! The crush had resulted in a shortage of decent lodgings and consequent price gouging on the part of landlords. Dr. Orth had ordered him to drink from the *Kesselbrunnen* spring on grounds that its waters would do wonders for his lungs as well as his diarrhea, but in fact he suffered from *constipation* rather than diarrhea and now feared (correctly as it turned out) that "there may be some ill effect . . . from the Kesselbrunnen spring." The diet Orth put him on cannot have helped: "I am to eat more acid things and take vinegar with salad . . . and to eat meat with fat. I am also to drink red wine, either from France or the local wine." Problem was, the Medoc was out-of-sight expensive, while the local red "is first-rate vinegar and [still] costs 20 groschen a bottle." As for the mineral water he was required to drink: "[Its] taste is sour like salt and it smells slightly of rotten eggs." Listening to the spa band was a "bore," since the group played Lutheran hymns and other German "rubbish" like Wagner, "a most dull German dog in spite of all his fame." Nor was shopping a relief: "The shops are abominable. I wanted to buy myself a hat. I only found one wretched little shop where the goods were rather like those we can buy in our market. All the goods are exhibited with pride, the prices are exorbitant, and the shopkeepers turn up their noses at the customers."

It goes on and on like this letter after letter. Clearly, that Russian chip on the shoulder that Dostoevsky had carried on his first visit to Germany was still firmly in place. Ems cannot have been all *that* bad!

On the other hand, it is true that Ems was the last of the great German Kurorte to really take off, and when Dostoevsky went there in the 1870s, the place still had some significant altitude to gain.

During Dostoevsky's last visit to Ems, when, healing waters or no, his emphysema had gotten ever worse and he suffered terribly from a sore throat, night sweats, gout, and constipation, he took out his anger and frustration on a target that was becoming lamentably popular in late nineteenth-century Russia (and, to a lesser degree, in Germany, too): the Jews. Wealthy Jews were becoming a mainstay at all the grand Central European spas, a development that Dostoevsky, along with many others, found detestable. The fact that he personally had to reside right next door to some rich Russians Jews in the Hotel d'Alger was just too much. As he wrote Anna:

> For four days I sat and put up with their conversations behind my door (the mother and son), they talk pages on end, whole volumes of talk, on and on without the slightest pause, and, above all, they don't only shout, they *squeal* as if they were in an Israelitic consistorium, or a synagogue, and they don't pay the slightest attention to the fact that they are not the only people in the hotel.

Then there were the Jewish shopkeepers in town, who "swindled" him at every turn. As he informed Anna: "We have never had such swindling shopkeepers in Russia as there are nowadays in Germany. They are all Jews, the Jews have got hold of everything and they swindle you all the time, literally, they rob you."

"At last I am leaving Ems," Dostoevsky informed his wife in a letter dated August 27. He thought his *do svidaniya* to Germany was only temporary, that he would return to Ems the following year. But he never went back, and he was dead two years later.

Turgenev had said goodbye to Baden-Baden even earlier. Throughout the rest of the 1860s he continued to lead a comfortable life in the luxury Kurort—perhaps *too* comfortable. In 1870, at age fifty-two, he observed in a letter that a "Russian writer who has settled in Baden by that very fact condemns his writing to an early end." Turgenev had continued to write, but he came to believe (echoing Tolstoy and Dostoevsky) that his life was *so* easy and *so* divorced from the gritty realities of contemporary Russia that it could not provide the fodder for cutting-edge literature. He was thus in a restless frame of mind when outside events conspired to bring an end to his comfortable idyll in Baden-Baden. The war between France and Prussia in 1870 forced the Viardots out of their adopted home. They were French citizens, and quite suddenly, the Rhinelanders had discovered their German patriotism and turned anti-French. Although Turgenev took the German side in this conflict because he passionately hated Napoleon III, his loyalty to the Viardots was greater than his newfound identification with Germany or his love for Baden-Baden. When they left, he decided to follow them—first to London and then back to Paris.

In 1879 Turgenev returned to Russia for a time and discovered to his astonishment that the radical younger generation loved him. He gave a speech in St. Petersburg in which he naively stated that the generational rift as described in *Fathers and Children* had now been bridged. Two years later, a band of young radicals assassinated Czar Alexander II.

When Turgenev went back to Paris in 1881, he was diagnosed with cancer of the spine. He lived two years longer in great pain, nursed by his beloved Pauline (whom, in a fit of delirium, he confused with Lady Macbeth). When he died on September 3, 1883, at age sixty-four, he was rambling on in Russian, complaining about not being able to get an erection and imagining (rather like Tolstoy) that he was a holy Russian peasant. His body was shipped back to St. Petersburg and buried in the sprawling Volkovo Cemetery, whose "Writer's Walkways" section also contains the grave of Ivan Goncharov, now in a state of permanent "Oblomovism."

CHAPTER FIVE

~

Politics on the Promenade

A nineteenth-century German encyclopedia recommends that diplomats should commence their meetings only *after* having taken the water cure, as "the well-being of thousands might depend on the state of the politicians' livers." This was sound advice, and nineteenth-century European diplomats frequently took it—though one wonders whether concern for the well-being of thousands could really compete with concerns for their own livers. In any event, the men who politicked at the grand spas were certainly the very sort who had to worry about dodgy livers and other health consequences of upper-crust living. As one commentator observes, "Policy-making on the [spa] promenade reminds us of the extent to which politics was still being made by dynastic rulers and a narrow political class in the European age of high capitalism." In other words, high-level policy got made by the same clique of gout-ridden, inbred royals and aristocrats who went regularly to the spas and who went there whether or not they had a political chore to perform. But if they *did* have such a chore to do, there is no question that being able to do it in comfortable surroundings was not an added bonus: it was a *necessity*. No nineteenth-century policy maker in his right mind would have dreamed of conducting his political business in a squalid place (though, to be fair, this rule of the game applies to other eras as well, including our own).

Like having famous artists on the premises, hosting political gatherings and royal tête-à-têtes added greatly to the spas' cachet; such events also helped prop up commercial viability after casino gambling was banned across the German Reich. The spas that dominated Europe's promenade politics were mostly in Central Europe. Napoleon III might have schemed with Piedmont's Camillo Cavour at Plombières (France) in 1858 to push the Austrians out of northern Italy, but overall, as a French historian concedes, "German spas surpassed the French" when it came to diplomatic gatherings, treaty negotiations, and other high-level political machinations in the nineteenth century. The men of influence favored the Central European Kurorte not only because these places had luxurious facilities but also because their relative seclusion allowed the leaders to convene in peace, far from the madding crowds.

A Line in the Water

The long war to break the hold by Napoleonic France over much of Europe was still raging when, following a victory over French forces at Kulm in northern Bohemia on August 29–30, 1813, the three principal Allied leaders—Emperor Franz I of Austria, Czar Alexander I of Russia, and Prussian King Friedrich Wilhelm III—met at the nearby spa town of Teplitz to reaffirm their commitment to bringing down the Corsican upstart. The old Bohemian spa was not its usual graceful self as the monarchs and their staffs commenced their meetings in early September. Instead of wealthy civilian curists, the handsome town was filled with military riffraff. Some of the elegant hostelries had been converted into temporary hospitals for wounded soldiers. Early fall rains and marching troops had turned the streets into churning rivers of mud, impeding the progress of legions of camp followers, including bedraggled prostitutes competing for military custom. Everyone could have used a bath, but only those with means, officers and diplomatic gentlemen, could avail themselves of the thermal pools. Austrian minister of state Prince Clemens von Metternich, the real power behind the Austrian throne, was obliged to admit that "Toeplitz is now a sad place. Everywhere is full of wounded; in the redoute hall they have been amputating arms and legs." Ugly, too, was the state of morale among the Allied forces at this point in the long struggle. Infighting among the coalition partners and heavy battlefield losses conspired to put everyone under strain. Often the only bond uniting the Allied leaders, apart from their common hatred of Napoleon, was the French language they employed in communicating with one another.

Yet Metternich decided to be optimistic about the prospects of hardening the anti-French alliance, which was his main goal in the Teplitz discussions. "Everything is going well, beyond expectation," he wrote to his then-lover, the thrice-married seductress Princess Wilhelmina of Sagan. "Everything is beautiful, perfect, and God appears to be protecting His cause." And in fact, whether it was the Almighty's doing or not, Metternich and the three monarchs were able, after considerable wrangling, to agree to a new strategic arrangement committing the powers to continue military operations together until a peace founded on "a just balance" and common conservative principles had been achieved.

The agreements signed in Teplitz on September 9, 1813, held up, more or less, until Napoleon's final defeat at Waterloo in June 1815. They can be considered the beginning of a long series of subsequent efforts, some also hammered out at Central European spas, to repress any and all recurrences of the radical ideas embodied in the French Revolution and then perpetuated (but also greatly subverted) by Napoleon. Thus one can say that the conservative powers drew their line against revolutionary change not in the sand but in the water.

It quickly became apparent, however, that the French Revolution had unleashed forces for change that were difficult to stifle, whatever the Allies might have envisaged at Teplitz or at the much larger Congress of Vienna two years later. Not only had France's armies carried the transformative ideals of the revolution into neighboring states, but in their crusade against France, conservative rulers, especially the Germans, had been obliged to take pages from the French book, mobilizing ideas such as constitutionalism, parliamentary empowerment, and, above all, nationalism to generate popular enthusiasm for the campaign. Once Napoleon had been shipped off to exile in St. Helena in 1815, the German authorities tried to pack their dangerous ideological weapons back into the airtight trunks of ancien régime absolutism. Yet those supposedly trusty packing crates proved no more able to contain their combustible contents than the proverbial genie bottle could contain its impetuous imp.

The genie of German nationalism roamed most adventurously in the venerable German universities, whose students (and some professors), having imbibed the ideals of both Enlightenment rationalism and romantic-nationalist identity politics, were clamoring for the establishment of a new German nation based on constitutional and ethnic-communal principles. These activists had been deeply disappointed by the post-Napoleonic program of restoration, which, in the German region, had brought forth a loose association of states dubbed the German Confederation. "Where is the Germany," asked a student patriot who had fought against Napoleon, "that was worthy of our common struggle?" To promote their cause the students formed *Burschenschaften* (fraternities), the first one founded in Jena in 1815. Unlike the archconservative fraternities of imperial Germany, famous for beer swilling, saber dueling, and Jew baiting, the early Burschenschaften agitated courageously, if often confusedly, for a unified nation infused with democratic principles. Decked out in the red-black-gold colors of one of the student-volunteer units that had fought against the French, the Burschenschaften held boisterous rallies proclaiming their nonnegotiable demands.

The most famous and provocative of these rallies was the Wartburg Festival, held on October 18, 1817. This date was pregnant with meaning for the young Germans: it was the three-hundredth anniversary of Martin Luther's Ninety-Five Theses and the fourth anniversary of the bloody "Battle of the Nations" against Napoleon near Leipzig. After solemnly marching to the Wartburg Castle, where Luther had translated the Bible into German, the students built a huge bonfire upon which they cast books and pamphlets authored by "reactionary" opponents of their ideals. A book-burning party by university students might strike us as odd—and certainly it was ominous: as Heinrich Heine famously wrote in 1821, "Where they burn books they will ultimately also burn people."

The nationalistic students of the Wartburg generation did not burn people, but one of them did resort to political assassination. On March 15, 1819, a mentally unbalanced theology student from Jena named Karl Sand stabbed to death August von Kotzebue, the playwright whom we briefly encountered earlier in this journey as the author of two plays scored by Beethoven. Kotzebue had also penned several political essays deemed worthy of burning at Wartburg and, even worse, had served as an agent for the hated Russian czar. "Thank you, God, for the victory!" cried Sand as he knelt over the bloody corpse of Kotzebue and tried futilely to strike out his own life. At his trial, Sand called Kotzebue a "traitor to the [German] nation." Convicted of murder, he was promptly beheaded.

For the rattled defenders of the status quo, who saw Karl Sand's bloody deed as a sign of widespread corruption among the educated youth, simply lopping off the miscreant's head did not seem an adequate counterrevolutionary measure. Friedrich Gentz, a conservative intellectual and advisor to Prince Metternich, warned the latter, "The murder . . . is an unmistakable symptom of the *degree of virulence* which the pestilential fever of our day has reached in Germany." Fully agreeing with Gentz, Metternich leaped on the Kotzebue assassination as a justification for seeking new measures to curb the kinds of "subversive" activity and speech that threatened the existing monarchical order. Seeing the German universities and Burschenschaften as the heart of the problem, the Austrian minister called together a conference of representatives from various German states to draw up a set of emergency restrictions and regulations. The meeting was set for early August 1819. The proposed venue was Karlsbad.

Why Karlsbad? In part, Metternich chose it for the same reason that grand spas would host a whole series of major political events over the following decades. Karlsbad was supremely comfortable, possessed of excellent lodging options and fine eateries; it abounded in medicinal waters for gouty bodies; and it had tranquil parks and secluded paths perfect for that private diplomatic walk in the woods. For Metternich personally, it was a known quantity: he had cured there often before and loved the place. He prized it not only for its manifold comforts but also for the sociopolitical cosmopolitanism of its clientele and culture—internationalist values that he hoped to shore up against those fierce winds of nationalism that might, if left unchecked, blow apart polyglot structures like his cherished Habsburg Empire.

On the eve of Karlsbad Conference, Metternich met briefly with King Friedrich Wilhelm of Prussia in Teplitz, where the latter was taking his annual cure. Metternich's object was to establish with Prussia a common program for Karlsbad. This would ensure that the upcoming conference progressed as smoothly and predictably as the magnificent wall clocks the Austrian chancellor collected to symbolize his brand of statecraft. Having Prussia on board would also protect against that state's going its own way, an option Metternich always feared. As Henry Kissinger, a great admirer of Metternich, relates in *A World Restored* (1973), at Teplitz the Austrian minister acted like a "stern teacher," reminding Friedrich Wilhelm that he had always warned against the dangers of constitutionalism and radical nationalism. Having induced his royal pupil to sign on to the Convention of Teplitz, which formalized a common agenda for Karlsbad, Metternich boasted that he had strengthened "the most active element in the King's soul, a tendency toward paralysis," virtually guaranteeing that he would "hardly dare to take the boldest of all steps, that of introducing a constitution [for the German Confederation]."

The Karlsbad Conference itself opened on August 6, 1819. It stayed in session until the end of the month, even though most of the work had been completed in the first few days. The delegates stayed on after their task was effectively over because they had come to the conference also *to play*, and Karlsbad was an excellent place in which to do this. For three solid weeks the spa's thermal pools, card parlors, dancing rooms, restaurants, and up-market brothels were full of jovial ministers of state determined to let down their hair following their stressful parlays. (Goethe, by the way, arrived in Karlsbad toward the end of the conference but did not have any part in the proceedings.)

And what did the Karlsbad delegates accomplish? Compared to the draconian policies and practices of twentieth-century police states, the so-called Karlsbad Decrees seem fairly mild, but they were repressive enough by the standards of the day. Divided into three sections, the decrees embraced higher education, the press, and ideological "subversion" generally. More specifically, they required the individual states of the confederation to place agents in the universities to monitor classes, enforce discipline, and remove from office "all teachers who propagate doctrines hostile to public order or existing governmental institutions." Students expelled as "subversive" from one university were not eligible for admission to any other institution of higher learning in the confederation. Furthermore, all "secret and unauthorized societies in the universities" (Burschenschaften as well as politicized sports groups called *Turner*) were to be disbanded immediately. With respect to the press, new rules gave the Austrian-controlled Diet of the Confederation powers to suppress on its own authority any writings "inimical to the honor of the union, the safety of individual states, or the maintenance of peace and quiet in Germany." Finally, Karlsbad provided for the establishment of "an extraordinary commission of investigation" to thoroughly examine "the facts relating to the origin and manifold ramifications of the revolutionary plots and demagogical associations directed against the internal peace both of the union and the individual states."

Under the authority of the Karlsbad Decrees, police across the confederation arrested scores of students and sentenced some of them to long jail terms. A few professors were summarily fired. Of course, this was precisely what Metternich had wanted. In his view, Karlsbad was a great success and one for which he had only himself to thank. Upon the conference's conclusion he dashed off a characteristically self-infatuated letter to another of his lovers:

> Here I am, thank God, delivered of my great work. The labor passed off happily, and the child has come into the world. I have every reason to be satisfied with the result, and I ought to be, for all I wished has come to pass. Heaven will protect an enterprise so worthy of its support, for it concerns the safety of the world. What thirty years of revolution could not produce has been brought about by our three weeks' labor at Karlsbad. It is the first time that a number of measures have appeared together so anti-revolutionary, so just, and so preemptory.

Not everyone was as enthusiastic about Karlsbad as Metternich. Fired now with even greater contempt for the conservative status quo, nationalistic student groups went underground, determined to subvert the system despite constant monitoring by government spies. Liberal elements not only in Germany but elsewhere in Europe expressed outrage over Metternich's work. Britain's House of Commons formally condemned the Karlsbad Decrees, and the letters section of the *Times* bristled with hoots of derision.

None of this bothered Metternich, but it did bother some of the hospitality entrepreneurs of Karlsbad, and for good reason. Although grand Kurorte like Karlsbad were happy enough to host august political gatherings, spa functionaries generally hoped to avoid having their towns associated with any one political faction or orientation: better to remain "neutral," like any good transnational enterprise. Yet via Metternich's machinations the name Karlsbad now became virtually synonymous with invasive spying, pettifogging regulations, small-minded censorship, and governmental repression. This understandably undercut the spa's appeal to more progressive curists from the German states, France, and Britain—

and thereby the very *internationalism* that Metternich so prized. Local business figures estimated that it would take a full generation for the spa to live down the repressive, antiliberal, and anti-intellectual decrees now associated with the Kurort. Karlsbad town fathers may have welcomed Metternich to their gilded precincts, but his "line in the water" was a legacy they could well have done without.

The German Question(s)

The task for the grand spas, then, was to strut prominently upon the stage of high-level politics without being typecast in any one political role. Most of the Kurorte managed to achieve this feat up to a point, although in the end all these would-be islands of neutrality were swamped by the waves of national and imperial enmity sweeping across Europe in the late nineteenth and early twentieth centuries.

One of those tides of discord—indeed the major one to bedevil Europe in the second half of the nineteenth century—welled up from an active political fault zone known as the German Question. In its initial iteration, the German Question had to do with the German region's ongoing disunity: Could (or should) that disunity be overcome? If so, how might that be achieved, and under whose leadership? Later, once Germany had become unified under Prussian leadership, the question changed to: Can the old European balance of power hold up with this new heavyweight on the scales? And if this giant tried to throw his weight around, how might he be held in check by the other bullies on the block? We know how the various versions of the German Question would be answered over the years. What is less well known is the role played by the grand Central European spas in the formulation of those answers.

In June 1860 Baden-Baden served as the stage for a conference among the leaders of the German Confederation. If hosting delegates to the Congress of Rastatt back in 1797–1798 had launched Baden-Baden's career on the diplomatic stage, the so-called Fürsten-Kongress (Princes' Congress) of 1860 confirmed its place at the pinnacle of promenade politics. As mentioned earler, this conference provided the convenient occasion that Richard Wagner adroitly exploited to lobby for an end to his political exile from German territory. Baden-Baden itself may not have been much to Wagner's liking, but it certainly appealed to the principal player at that gathering, King-Regent Wilhelm I of Prussia.* Ever since 1849, when he had visited the spa town following the suppression of the Baden revolution of that year, Wilhelm had been a regular summer patron. He loved the place for its natural beauty; its *Ruhe und Ordnung* (quiet and orderliness); its splendid hotels; and, last but not least, its healing waters, since he, too, was afflicted with gout and respiratory problems. Another important draw for him was the town's Prussian connection, confirmed most recently by his daughter Luise's marriage to Grand Duke Friedrich I of Baden. Where better, then, to bring together the other major and minor potentates of the German Confederation in order to reassure them, rumors to the contrary, that Prussia had no desire to engineer a shotgun marriage between the German states with Prussia holding the gun?

In early June, the first distinguished invitees began to arrive. Grand Duke Friedrich and Luise coached down from Karlsruhe and lodged in the Neue Schloss. Wilhelm and his wife, Augusta, settled into the Maison Mesmer, along with a brace of Prussian generals. The kings of Bavaria, Württemberg, and Saxony took quarters in the splendid Hotel d'Angleterre. The King of Hannover and the Grand Duke of Saxony-Weimar also found opulent quarters; so, too, did the Duke of Nassau and the Duke of Saxony-Cobourg. All these worthies were just making themselves comfortable and starting to work up their talking points when an unexpected gate-crasher descended upon the town: Emperor Napoleon III of France. Modern man that he was, Napoleon arrived by train, a fast special direct from Paris. Grand Duke Friedrich greeted the emperor at the station and escorted him and his retinue of gaudily clad imperial guards to the magnificent Hotel Stefanie overlooking the River Oos.

Why had Napoleon III stuck his Gallic nose into this hitherto all-German party? Like Wilhelm I, he wanted to reassure the world—or at least the German world—that he was not a power-hungry despot with aspirations to expand his power at the expense of peaceable German princelings. The princelings had reason to worry: Just recently, after

---

*Wilhelm was a royal regent at this point because his brother, Friedrich-Wilhelm IV, had suffered a stroke in 1857 that left him mentally incapacitated (a condition some thought he had displayed well before his stroke). Wilhelm became Prussian king on his brother's death in 1861.

helping the Kingdom of Piedmont-Sardinia to expel the Austrians from Lombardy, Napoleon had rewarded himself by annexing the Italian border provinces of Nice and Savoy. (This had been part of the secret deal worked out with Cavour at Plombières.) Now rulers of the territories along Germany's Rhine frontier with France worried that their holdings might be next. More precisely, they worried that Napoleon and King Wilhelm might be inclined to strike a diabolical bargain at their expense: Wilhelm might give his blessing to French expansion into the Rhineland area in exchange for Napoleon's acceptance of Prussian domination over the rest of Germany. Napoleon had come to Baden-Baden to say, in effect, "Not to worry, princelings; I'm done expanding for the time being." As for Wilhelm, he was pleased with Napoleon's presence at the gathering because it would help him, Wilhelm, quiet his fellow Germans' fears about a possible backstairs bargain: The king and emperor would hardly be hatching any secret plots when surrounded day and night by other leaders with their ears pressed firmly to the ground and their eyes glued on the two principals' every move.

On the other hand, the sheer concentration of powerful (and semipowerful) potentates in one place led curious outsiders to wonder what might be going on inside those opulent hotel suites. This and other fancy spa conferences raised the quintessential voyeuristic question: "What if those walls could speak?" Most likely, those walls would have relayed nothing but the usual banalities, backbiting gossip, and pillow talk, but even that would be of interest to the historian looking for insights into the mind-set of the time. Too bad, perhaps, that there were no electronic bugs at the Princes' Conference in Baden-Baden as there later would be (along with regular bugs) in the once-grand hotels of Marienbad and Karlsbad during the Soviet era.

We do know what transpired in the diplomatic sessions at the Neue Schloss and Maison Mesmer. A series of carefully constructed conversations led in fairly short order to the above-mentioned diplomatic reassurances. Much of the action took place *after* the talking sessions were over, just as had been the case at Karlsbad. According to a contemporary account, "during the evenings the Conversation House shimmered wonderfully in a sea of multicolored torches like a fairy palace. Inside, ivory balls of luck rolled merrily and chips of gold danced brilliantly across the green tables." On Sunday morning, Napoleon III and his retinue walked to Mass along streets filled with gawkers; the *Stiftskirche*, for the first time in ages, was filled to capacity. During the afternoons, the diplomats took their ritual peregrinations along the Lichtentaler Allee and the Promenade in the *Kurpark*. There was plenty of time, too, for excursions to the Old Castle and other must-see destinations in the region. And of course, the spa facilities did a land-office business, what with all those gouty bodies and plenty of strong-armed young masseuses to minister to them.

In the very next month, King-Regent Wilhelm carried his message of reassurance personally to Emperor Franz Josef of Austria. The historic first meeting between these two sovereigns took place, appropriately enough, in Teplitz, a spa as dear to Austrian royals as Baden-Baden was to the Prussians. As reported in gushing tones by a Leipzig newspaper correspondent, Franz Josef himself was on hand at the Teplitz station when Wilhelm's special train steamed in at 5:30 p.m. sharp on July 25, 1860. Standing patiently on the platform, the thirty-year-old Austrian monarch cut an impressive figure with his signature muttonchop whiskers and his lithe frame decked out in the uniform of a Prussian regiment of which he was an honorary member. The emperor removed his hat when Wilhelm, after some delay, stepped down from his carriage and strode briskly up to his Austrian host. The Prussian monarch likewise was in uniform, in his case an *Austrian* one, such military cross-dressing being standard procedure among sovereigns of the day. As for the figure he cut: "His whole bearing is manly, soldierly, without being stiff; his facial features radiate rectitude and honesty." The leaders exchanged a protracted Teutonic handshake. "The two men stood silently together for a long time, clearly moved by the importance of this moment. And we saw precisely how the emperor's face changed color several times while the introductions of the respective retinues continued," rhapsodized the Leipzig reporter.

Manly greetings completed, the sovereigns climbed into a stately horse-drawn carriage and drove off through cheering crowds to the Gasthof Stadt London, where Franz Josef stood his guest to a welcoming lunch. Then it was off to the Hotel Prince de Ligne, the elegant hostelry where Wilhelm and his sizable retinue would be quartered and the sovereigns' private tête-á-tête would take place on the following day. In the meantime, a ceremonial high tea was laid on for Wilhelm at the castle of Prince Clary, a local notable who often hosted Emperor Franz Josef when he was in town. At Castle Clary a regimental band played the Prussian and Austrian anthems (the tune for the latter eventually taken over by the Germans, like so much else).

Our Leipzig reporter had little to say about the actual talks on July 26 between the two sovereigns and their top ministers, which transpired behind closed doors guarded by armed soldiers from both powers. Throughout the five-hour meeting, "a huge crowd waited almost breathlessly beneath the windows of the room where the secret discussions were taking place," confided the reporter. Apparently, though, there was not too much to be breathless about. As was his intention, Wilhelm sought to reassure Franz Josef that Prussia had no intention of supplanting Austria as the leading power in the German Confederation, much less lead a charge toward German unification. Apparently, too, the sovereigns got along well together. They had much in common: a fundamentally conservative outlook, a distrust of parliaments and constitutions, a manly addiction to hunting, and, of course, a love of grand spas. It is safe to surmise that on that July afternoon in Teplitz in 1860 these two leaders could not have imagined that, a mere six years hence, they would be at war with each other.

As it turned out, Wilhelm was lucky even to be around for that war. In the following summer this august personage, now officially King of Prussia, was the target of an assassination attempt in, of all places, Baden-Baden. On July 14, 1861, Wilhelm took his usual early morning constitutional along the Lichtentaler Allee; also as usual, he had no bodyguards. Near the Cistercian Cloister he ran into Count Flemming, Prussia's emissary to Baden, who joined the king on his walk. A few minutes later a young man overtook the two gentlemen, greeted them politely, then stood aside as they went on their way. No sooner had they done so than two shots rang out from behind. The first of the bullets whizzed over the king's head into the distance, but the second grazed his neck, opening a flesh wound. More surprised than badly injured, Wilhelm spun around clutching his neck, while his companion eyed the young man and asked, "Who fired?" "I did," replied the man calmly, before being hauled away by some irate citizens who had hurried to the scene.

After receiving first aid at a gardener's cottage near the cloister, Wilhelm was able to return to the Maison Mesmer under his own power. Later that evening he stood on the hotel's balcony as a parade of well-wishers passed below, thanking the heavens for His Majesty's salvation.

Wilhelm also saw God's will at work here, writing shortly afterward that "the protecting hand of Divine Providence had miraculously deflected" the assassin's bullet.

The would-be assassin, it turned out, was a twenty-two-year-old student of Russian-German heritage named Oskar Becker, who had come to Baden-Baden the previous day with the express intention of killing the Prussian monarch. At his trial, Becker explained that he had decided on regicide because Wilhelm, as Prussian king, was doing nothing to foster German unity. Due to a personal appeal for clemency from Wilhelm, Becker got a twenty-year prison sentence rather than a blade through his neck.

Attesting to Wilhelm's immense popularity with the Baden-Baden citizenry, the site of his brush with death became a local shrine. A stately oak tree in which the miraculously deflected bullet had lodged soon needed to be fenced off because scores of Wilhelm-worshipers were tearing off pieces of bark as sacred talismans. The cottage where Wilhelm received his first aid achieved status as a protected historical site.

All this piety might seem a bit much for a flesh wound, but the episode reflected genuine shock among the locals over what had transpired in their town. The citizens of grand Kurorte like Baden-Baden were proud that royals and other dignitaries typically walked their streets and parks without bodyguards, confident in the security of their surroundings. Actions like Oskar Becker's obviously challenged that image and might, if repeated, undermine or even eliminate the spa towns' desirability as summer haunts for national rulers and other personages of high political importance.

This terrible prospect, it turned out, failed to materialize: The spa towns did not become popular shooting galleries with strolling potentates as targets (which is not to say that there would not be plenty of shootings, stabbings, and bombings of world leaders elsewhere over the course of the next half-century). Still, even though Wilhelm was spared the fate of many of his counterparts around the world, and Baden-Baden itself escaped the taint attached to some assassination sites (think Ford's Theater and Sarajevo), the comfortable notion that this Kurort, and by extension other grand spa towns, constituted oases of security in a dangerous world, had with Becker's brazen action taken a slug rather more serious than the one that grazed King Wilhelm's neck and lodged in a Lichtentaler oak.

Baden-Baden's obvious reverence for the Prussian royal house notwithstanding, this town (and the state of Baden more generally) stood for relatively liberal politics within the German Confederation. When King Wilhelm was in residence there, he found himself subjected to national-liberal influences, not least from his son-in-law Grand Duke Friedrich, as well as the latter's foreign minister, Franz von Roggenbach. While in no way wishing to undermine the sovereignty of the individual states of the confederation, these liberals advised the king to pursue a tighter federal union with a common parliament elected by the people and a Prussian executive. Had the king followed this advice, German, European, and even world history might have taken a different course than it did. But the king was not by nature a liberal, and the option desired by his son-in-law was hardly the only one being pushed on him at that time.

Another came from Otto von Bismarck. This larger-than-life (and just plain large) figure was not yet Prussian prime minister—that would come in late 1862, when King Wilhelm called him in to resolve a stalemate between the Crown and Prussian legislature over military spending. Nonetheless, from his post at that time as Prussian ambassador to Russia, Bismarck kept a sharp eye on German Confederation politics, and from previous visits to Baden-Baden he knew quite a lot about the political landscape there. Worried about what Wilhelm might be getting up to among all those liberals in spa land, Bismarck rushed there himself in July 1861, arriving just in time to see his king almost removed from the scene by Becker's bullet. Settling into the Hotel d'Angleterre, where General Albrecht von Roon was also staying, he pulled from his briefcase a memo on the German Question he had drafted in St. Petersburg. Because Bismarck presented this memo to the king in Baden-Baden, and because it was in that spa town that Wilhelm first became fully acquainted with his soon-to-be prime minister's thoughts on the German situation, this memo is known as the Baden-Baden Memorial.

What did it say? Briefly, it recommended a highly revealing twist on that other advice being proffered to the king in Baden-Baden. Bismarck, who was first and foremost a *Prussian* patriot, argued that the German Confederation as it was then constituted did not give Prussia enough clout, especially in matters military. Moreover, the confederation was too loosely configured to satisfy a growing clamor for national unity spreading across the land. Therefore, Prussia should publicly proclaim its support for "a national assembly of the German people."

So far, this sounded very much like the advice Wilhelm was getting from the Baden liberals. But Bismarck proposed that this prospective assembly be chosen by the *state legislatures*, not by any kind of electoral franchise, even a restrictive one. By having the assembly members selected by the legislatures, Prussia could be sure of these delegates' "intelligence and conservative outlook." Because Austria would never accept such a "reform" to the confederation, Bismarck favored a "small" German federation modeled on the existing Prussian-dominated customs union (*Zollverein*), but with extended powers. The Habsburgs, effectively kicked out of the union, would no longer be able to exert their malign influence over German affairs.

Aware of King Wilhelm's fundamental conservatism, Bismarck went on in his memo to argue that this approach, while accommodating— indeed exploiting—liberal desires for German unity, would produce a solidly *conservative* federal union. Above all, within this new Germany, Prussia would actually enjoy enhanced power and influence. Prussia would also be more secure in the world than would be the case if it continued to try to stem the tide of German unity. In effect, then, Bismarck was proposing that the Prussian crown steal nationalism from the liberals and turn it into a conservative property. Soon enough, exactly this plan would be actualized, and we know the long-term result: nationalism would "belong" to the political right for many decades hence in Germany (though not only in Germany).

When Bismarck presented this memo to the king in Baden-Baden, he fully understood that whatever Wilhelm might think of it, most of the other confederation leaders, not just the Austrians, would vehemently oppose it. He may have already sensed that it was going to take more than words, more than well-argued memos, to engineer German unity under Prussian domination. But in Baden-Baden, the future "Iron Chancellor" wanted to lay the foundation for what he saw as the optimal solution to the German Question, whether that be achieved through peaceful means or (more likely) through war.

The road to German unity would indeed be paved not by "speeches and majority decisions," but by "iron and blood," as Bismarck famously put it in a condescending oration before the Prussian Landtag in 1862. Central Europe's grand spas did not get significantly caught up in the actual fighting during the subsequent wars of German unification; characteristically, however, some of the spas were very much part of the diplomatic wheeling and dealing attending these conflicts. Indeed, in two of the German-unity wars, diplomatic initiatives emanating from grand spas actually helped set the stage for the bloodletting. In other words, not only did Europe's leaders draw lines of ideological defense in the water, they also drew their swords there.

The first of the unification wars, in early 1864, pitted Prussia and Austria together against Denmark, the casus belli being who should control the duchies of Schleswig and Holstein—the Danish Crown or the German Confederation. The Danish War was a lopsided, mercifully quick conflict, one the Danes should never have allowed Bismarck to goad them into. Nor, for that matter, was it a wise decision on Emperor Franz Josef's part to join this war on the side of the Prussians, for it made Austria look like a Prussian toady and undermined its status among anti-Prussian elements in the German Confederation. (One wonders whether Franz Josef's fatal penchant for working together with his "good friend" Wilhelm was not in part a product of the convivial times the two men spent together in the baths at Teplitz, Karlsbad, and Bad Gastein.)

The German-Danish War turned out to be a great boon for Prussia, whose troops did most of the fighting on the German side. By beating up on the hapless Danes, Prussia effectively put itself forward as a champion of *German* interests, thereby winning the hearts and minds of liberal nationalists across the confederation. Even the radical left was impressed: Karl Marx argued that the German victory over the Danes amounted to a "victory of civilization over barbarism." The German-Danish War was also a great personal success for Bismarck, who had orchestrated the conflict.

Yet an even greater success for Bismarck and Prussia came *after* the war, when Austria and Prussia addressed the task of figuring out how to divide and administer the spoils of their joint victory. Bismarck knew this would be agonizingly difficult, and he relished the prospect of matching wits with his Austrian counterparts on the diplomatic chessboard. As it happened, the opening of the diplomatic match coincided with the beginning of spa season in June 1864, when Europe's leaders all abandoned their capitals for the baths. Thus there was nothing for it but to take the verbal maneuvering to the waters, not a bad thing, actually. Between June 19 and June 24, the Austrians and Prussians met for a negotiating session at Karlsbad, with Foreign Minister Count Johann Rechberg representing Austria and Bismarck moving the pieces for Prussia. Nothing much was resolved at this meeting, but Bismarck believed he was making good progress toward a checkmate. On June 27 he wrote his sister that "politically things are going so well that it makes me nervous, '*pourvu que cela dure*.'"

Bismarck achieved his checkmate a little more than a year later at another high-level meeting at yet another spa: Bad Gastein.

This alpine health resort may have been on Austrian territory, but it was familiar turf for the Prussians, too. Field Marshal Helmuth von Moltke had started taking the waters regularly there in 1859 (as he would do for the rest of his life) and recommended the place to his sovereign, King Wilhelm. The king made his first visit in 1863 and was so impressed that he, too, made Gastein one of the stops on his annual rounds of the grand spas of Central Europe. All told, he would cure there some twenty times, attributing his "sound physical constitution" to the spa's thermal springs. Quaintly, while curing at Gastein, Wilhelm tried to keep a lower profile by registering as "Graf von Zollern." Of course, nobody was fooled, especially since Wilhelm insisted on staying at the Badeschloss (Bath Palace) and typically met with other royals, including Franz Josef in 1863 and 1864. Moreover, Wilhelm did not travel light: according to a local chronicler, the king always arrived "with many baggage wagons because he even brought along the court silver from Berlin."

Sometimes the king also brought along Bismarck, which was the case in summer 1865 when Franz Josef, desperate for an acceptable end to the political squabbling between Austria and Prussia over how to manage the two duchies they had claimed from Denmark, sent his latest foreign minister, Count Gustav von Blome, to negotiate a deal. Blome thought himself quite clever, but Bismarck, more accurately, considered him an idiot with his "outmoded Byzantine-Jesuitical method of negotiating, full of tricks and dodges." During the daily negotiations at the Hotel Straubinger, Bismarck regularly outfoxed his opponent and then, in the evenings, insisted on playing cards with poor Blome so that he could terrify him with the violence of his play.

The treaty, or Gastein Convention, that emerged from this lopsided match of wits diabolically split the administration of the two duchies between Austria and Prussia: Austria would rule over Holstein and Prussia over Schleswig. The arrangement was diabolical because it would, as Bismarck well knew, be difficult to maintain and undoubtedly generate friction between the two administering powers, especially if one of those powers kept poking a stick in the eye of the other. "I never imagined I could find an Austrian who would put his name to such a document," said Bismarck later (regarding Blome and the Gastein Convention).

Bismarck could not be sure that what he had achieved at Gastein would turn out to be a springboard for a final reckoning with Austria, but knowing the Austrians, he believed that to be the case.

And he was right. In 1866 escalating disputes over the administration of Schleswig and Holstein culminated in all-out war between Prussia and Austria, the latter allied to most of the other states of the German Confederation. The details of this German civil war, fortunately neither as long nor as costly as the fratricidal bloodbath just completed over in America, need not detain us here. Suffice it to say that Prussia, exploiting superior armaments and military organization, trounced Austria and its allies after some seven weeks of hard fighting. The key battle occurred on July 3 at the Bohemian town Königgrätz. Located due east of Prague, the battlefield was a comfortable distance from Karlsbad and Marienbad, which avoided getting swept up directly in the fighting. Nonetheless, the spas did suffer a significant loss of revenue in 1866 because foreign visitors naturally wanted to avoid taking their cures anywhere near a conflict zone. A Marienbad doctor pleaded to the Austrian War Ministry to have his Kurort and all other major Austrian spas officially declared neutral and thus out of bounds for any military activity. His plea went unanswered.

The political consequence of the 1866 war, as Bismarck had hoped, was the expulsion of Austria from German affairs and the creation of a new Prussia-dominated entity, the North German Confederation. This short-lived constellation embraced all the states north of the River Main. Among the smaller entities annexed outright by Prussia were the Duchy of Homburg-Hesse and the Duchy of Nassau, which included the spa towns of Homburg, Wiesbaden, and Bad Ems.

Still, though Prussia had now greatly expanded its power, including its spa power, Bismarck's goal of a Prussia-dominated Germany was not yet completed, for the southern states, including Bavaria and Baden, remained outside the fold. Bringing them in would require yet another war, a third and final one. And as it would turn out, this crucial conflict would also originate in a grand German spa.

That spa was Bad Ems. This Kurort, which lies in a narrow valley on the River Lahn, not far from the junction of the Rhine and Mosel Rivers at Koblenz, is the smallest of the grand spa towns treated in this book. Many Germans today associate it exclusively with the "Ems Telegram" and the origins of the Franco-Prussian War. I'll turn to this story shortly, but a little introduction is in order before I give this town its heady moment on the stage of promenade politics.

Ems had been functioning as a *Bad* since the fifteenth century, but it was not really until the mid-1800s that it began gaining international notice as a worthy cure destination. The town itself grew accordingly: in 1818 it had only 912 inhabitants; by 1858 that number had climbed to 2,953. As one of the city's historians has written, a resident of Ems in 1800 would have felt as if he had landed on a different planet were he to be dropped into the town a century later: "The village and its once-remote bath complex had grown together into a modern city, with large multi-storied houses, paved streets, gas lighting, sewers, commercial enterprises and factories."

The changes culminating in this transformation began in earnest during the years immediately following the Napoleonic Wars. The newly created Duchy of Nassau, to which Bad Ems (along with Wiesbaden) now belonged, invested extensively in modern facilities, including a splendid new *Kurhaus* (cure house). A contemporary book on Germany's thermal spas praised Ems's waters as wonderfully effective against lung diseases and also useful in promoting fecundity: perfect, in other words, for a tubercular lady trying to get pregnant.

The combination of well-publicized healing waters, idyllic setting and mild climate, proximity to the Rhine, excellent rail connections starting in the late 1840s, and the usual gambling concessions brought foreign patrons to Bad Ems in ever-increasing numbers. As early as 1830, some 40 percent of the patrons were foreign, most of them from France and England.

In 1821 Grand Duke Nicholas of Russia and his Prussian wife, Charlotte, visited the spa; Nicholas I later returned once as czar, while

Charlotte came back several times after her husband's death in 1855. Predictably, the Russian royal family's imprimatur popularized the banya with that nation's aristocracy, which added Ems to the list of grand Central European spa towns they traveled among every summer. Czar Alexander II showed up there in 1876 to help consecrate a Russian Orthodox Church. While at the spa, he also issued the "Ems Decree," which banned the use of the Ukrainian language in the Russian Empire. Together with the French and English, this infusion of Russian guests ensured that by 1847 more than half of the patrons at Ems were foreign.

Also largely because of that Russian presence, the percentage of patrons of royal or upper-aristocratic lineage was very high, even by grand Kurort standards. In an irreverent 1872 essay collection on the German spas, *Satans Mausefallen* (*Satan's Mousetraps*), travel writer Hans Wachenhusen claimed that "In Bad Ems no one counts unless he wears a crown or is in the retinue of a royal." In Ems, Wachenhusen went on to say, ordinary tourists *did* show up from time to time, but there they constituted "only a few weeds among the wheat."

The influx of foreigners to Ems, blue-blooded or not, dropped off sharply in the summer of 1866, when the town was briefly occupied by Prussian troops (though no actual fighting occurred there). In 1867 the North German Confederation, with prudish Prussia at the helm, announced that no gambling casinos would be allowed to operate on its territory starting in the year 1873. (That ruling would be superseded by the Reich-wide ban on casino gambling imposed by the new imperial government in 1872.) As if trying to cram in as much play as possible before the roulette wheels stopped spinning, gamblers from all over Europe streamed into Ems in 1868 and 1869. Ironically, patronage from France reached a record high in 1869, the year before France and Prussia went to war—a war kicked off in Bad Ems.

Every good story has a backstory, and the one behind the *Emser Depesche* (Ems Telegram) is complicated even by the standards of nineteenth-century diplomacy. What follows here is a highly abridged version.

When the Spanish throne fell vacant in 1868 following a military *pronunciamiento* against Queen Isabella II (herself the beneficiary of a similar coup in 1843), the crown was offered by the Spanish Cortes to Prince Leopold of Hohenzollern-Sigmaringen, a South German Catholic branch of the Prussian ruling dynasty. The prospect of a Hohenzollern,

Catholic or not, on the throne of Spain thoroughly alarmed France. Napoleon III had been watching the rise of Prussia with considerable trepidation, and, having recently suffered several embarrassing setbacks in the arena of foreign affairs (the collapse of his Mexican Empire comes to mind), was disinclined to suffer another one in the form of a *Boche* ruler on his southern border. On cue from the imperial government, the French press howled in protest. But the howls faded when it became known that Prince Leopold, on the advice of his father Karl Anton, had rejected the Spanish offer. Karl Anton worried that allowing his son to take power in Madrid would cause outrage in France. Prussian King Wilhelm I, head of the Hohenzollern clan, agreed with this assessment and encouraged the rebuff of Madrid.

Bismarck was another story. In the aftermath of the Austro-Prussian War and the creation of the North German Confederation, he had been casting about for another "crisis" that might help him complete the unfolding of German unification. He knew that to bring all the Germans together an outside agent would be needed, a foreign foil against which every patriotic Teuton would willingly grapple. What better bogeyman than France, a country that for generations had fomented and exploited German disunity? Observing France's apoplexy over the prospect of a German on the Spanish throne, Bismarck was sorely disappointed when Karl Anton, backed by Wilhelm, seemingly dashed this prospect for good.

Yet it soon turned out that the so-called Hohenzollern candidature was *not* dead. The Spanish junta behind the original offer to Leopold, not wanting to take no for an answer, approached Karl Anton again in March 1870. Young Leopold himself was dazzled by the prospect of being a Hohenzollern equivalent to the worldly Habsburgs, perhaps even a new Charles V. Bismarck, for his part, immediately wrote a memo to King Wilhelm arguing that Leopold's ascension to the throne of Spain would be a great boon for all of Europe. The king, however, remained skeptical: What did the Hohenzollerns want with some broken-down Catholic country that was subject to the whims of excitable Latin juntas? Prodded by Wilhelm, Karl Anton once again sent regrets on behalf of Leopold to Madrid.

Bismarck was so angry over the king's behavior that he considered resigning—something he actually threatened quite often. Instead of tendering his resignation, however, he resorted to another gambit that he deployed even more frequently: he lied. In May 1870 he told Karl Anton that he had finally persuaded King Wilhelm that acceptance of Madrid's offer was the right way to go after all. Shortly thereafter, Prince Leopold sent a formal letter of acceptance to Spain, which was made public on July 2, 1870. At this point, Bismarck hustled off to his country estate at Varzin in remote Pomerania, hoping that in his absence the brazen fiction he had dropped on his sovereign's doorstep would turn into fact.

Even if that did not happen, Bismarck knew as he left Berlin that he had gotten the pot gloriously boiling. Indeed, the day after Leopold's acceptance of the Spanish crown was made public, French foreign minister Duke Antoine de Gramont (himself a caricature of Latin excitability) told the Chamber of Deputies that a Hohenzollern on the throne in Madrid represented a threat to France and *absolutely could not be tolerated*. He hinted at war.

Bismarck now had his envisaged "crisis." The final act of our drama played out not in Berlin or Paris but in little Bad Ems, for July after all was the height of the summer spa season, and the players had all headed off to the baths. Wilhelm, as was his wont, had repaired to Ems for the second phase of his annual cure program, settling into a suite in the Kurhaus. Bismarck was prepared to go to Ems if need be, but for the time being he thought it best to stay out of his sovereign's immediate reach at Varzin, where he had a small spa of his own. (Count Alfred von Waldersee, chief of the Prussian general staff, complained in his diary that Bismarck was off "taking the waters" in Varzin instead of tending shop in Berlin as war with France loomed on the horizon.) France's ambassador to Prussia, Count Vincent Benedetti, had gone off to take the waters at Wildbad (a small spa in Baden) but shifted to Ems when he received orders from Gramont to go there immediately and pressure Wilhelm to beat a retreat on the Hohenzollern candidature. (Leopold himself, by the way, was off on an air- and water-cure vacation in the Austrian Alps.)

Benedetti arrived in Ems on July 9. He had a hard time finding accommodations because everything was booked up. Finally a French family moved out of the Hotel Ville de Bruxelle to make room for the ambassador. When he met with Wilhelm at the Kurhaus on the following day, Benedetti did not know that the king had just dashed off a letter to Karl Anton, urging him to persuade his son to withdraw his name for the Madrid job. Karl Anton acted at once, and on July 12 it was publicly announced that Leopold had done as his father wished: he was not going to Spain after all. At the same time, Wilhelm sent a telegram to Bismarck at Varzin instructing him to come to his sovereign's side at Ems.

Bismarck had in the meantime returned to Berlin, and it took a while for news of Wilhelm's actions at Ems to catch up with him. Of course he was furious—once again he thought of resigning. It was just *so hard* to work with a king who worried about other sovereigns' feelings and failed to see the big picture. Instead of going to Ems as ordered, he stayed in Berlin and stewed.

What Bismarck did not know as he fumed helplessly in Berlin was that the French were already deciding on actions that would save the day for him and ultimately deliver the military confrontation he thought he needed to bring the Germans together. Not content with Prussia's having backed down in the Spanish throne crisis, Gramont, and behind him Napoleon III, now pursued a splashier diplomatic victory for France in the form of a public promise from Wilhelm *never again* to revive the Hohenzollern candidature.

Benedetti was given the unhappy task of presenting this demand to Wilhelm at Ems. Unlike Gramont, the ambassador was smart enough to be uncomfortable with this assignment, but he nonetheless manfully saw it through. On the morning of July 13, he confronted Wilhelm on his walk along the Promenade next to the River Lahn. Despite his brush with death in Baden-Baden, the king walked without bodyguards. Dressed in his usual spa getup of civilian suit and top hat, Wilhelm carried a cane in one hand and a drinking glass in the other, for like any good curist he was making the rounds of the town's thermal fountains. Contrary to some popular accounts, the king was not shocked by Benedetti's approach, which was polite enough. But as the ambassador relayed Gramont's demands, Wilhelm became increasingly agitated. Such impertinence, and on the Promenade, no less! Politely but firmly, Wilhelm told Benedetti that he could not accommodate the demands from Paris. And when Benedetti asked whether he could see the king later that day to discuss this matter further, Wilhelm said *nein*—or rather *non*, since they were conversing in French. (Today, there is a marker at the very spot where Wilhelm and Benedetti had their fateful encounter, but in my various visits to Ems I have never seen any riverside strollers pausing to take in the spot's sobering historic weight.)

Had Wilhelm's rejection of the French demands been left as it was delivered that morning at Bad Ems, Paris would certainly have been irritated, but Napoleon probably would have found ways to live with the rebuff. After all, the Hohenzollern candidature had been scotched, and the chances of its revival were unlikely in the extreme. Yet the matter did not end as Wilhelm and Benedetti had left it on the Promenade at Ems.

Fatefully, King Wilhelm sent Bismarck a telegram outlining what he had told Benedetti and through him the French government. He requested that Bismarck comment on his actions at Ems, asking him also whether "the new [French] demand and my refusal should not be communicated to our embassies abroad and to the press." Bismarck instantly realized that the French, via Wilhelm, had given him the means with which to shift the simmering stew of Franco-Prussian relations from a low-burning flame to a white-hot one. Rather than simply comment on Wilhelm's telegram, he "edited" it in such a way as to make the king's actions appear much more offensive than they actually had been. He put particular emphasis on Wilhelm's rejection of a further meeting with Benedetti, making this sound as if the king wanted nothing more to do with the French, period. In Bismarck's nimble phrasing, it was as if the king of Prussia had told the emperor of France to put his demands where the sun doesn't shine and then to bugger off. Of course, this poisonous missive, instantly known as the Ems Telegram, was indeed made public to the entire world.

France's ensuing declaration of war against Prussia produced precisely the kind of conflict Bismarck wanted, one that soon drew in the other German states. Out of this fraternal Teutonic neck-ringing of the Gallic rooster emerged a new German Reich, forged, just as Bismarck had predicted, by iron and blood, the latter predominantly French.

But what of the little spa town where the final fuse had been lit? In the short run, the German-French war was bad for business. For a time, the English and even the Russians stayed away—not to mention the French. But Europe's wealthy foreign curists, again with the exception of the French, soon started coming back to Bad Ems, and by the late 1870s, even with casino gambling no longer available, the spa was setting new records for patronage.

It has to be said, though, that the *majority* of the new guests were German, primarily Prussian. The Prussian (and now also imperial German) capital of Berlin became the leading supplier of curists to Ems after 1871.

For many imperial subjects hailing from Prussia, curing at historic Bad Ems became almost an act of patriotic devotion, akin to visiting one of the Franco-Prussian War memorials that were sprouting up all over the new nation. At Ems one could literally bathe in German glory.

Leading the Prussian pack was Wilhelm himself, now emperor of Germany. With the exception of 1878, when he was badly injured by a would-be assassin's shotgun blast in Berlin, Wilhelm cured every summer at Ems until 1887, the year before his death. Indeed, Ems came to rival Gastein as his favorite spa. Although Wilhelm liked to think of himself as a modest-living fellow, he always traveled to Ems by special train, and his arrivals there invariably occasioned much fuss among the townfolk and other curists. Count Harry Kessler, later to figure prominently in Weimar German culture, witnessed as a precocious child the kaiser's arrival at Ems while visiting with his family in 1880. "The whole of Ems is in mirth today for the Emperor is coming," he wrote in his diary on June 19. "We place ourselves behind the school children who have lined up all down the way the emperor must pass. As the festive hour approaches the crowd gets greater. Soon a shriek as if everybody was at least being murdered reaches our ears but it presently appears to be the emperor's train that has arrived. Now the emperor's carriage comes and a hail of bouquets comes down upon it."

As for Wilhelm's daily routine at Bad Ems, Prince Bernard von Bülow, a future German chancellor, claimed that this "could not have been simpler." In reality, it could have. True, Wilhelm worked alone every morning on a terrace of the Kurhaus, *even opening and sealing his own envelopes.* As always when on vacation, he dressed in civilian clothes and continued to take his daily constitutionals on the Promenade, where (per Bülow) "he greeted acquaintances cheerfully, sometimes with a little joke, [behaving] absolutely naturally without any stiffness or pose." But as was the case with his other spa sojourns, Wilhelm resided in only the finest accommodations and dined off the court silver he had brought along from Berlin. His "simplicity" was a little like Queen Marie Antoinette's playing milkmaid at the Palace of Versailles. Yet there *was* rather less pomp in the kaiser's routine at Ems compared with his life in Berlin, and that relative ease of living was certainly one of the Kurort's chief attractions for the aging king/emperor, as it was indeed for many other high-level spa patrons.

Among the many supreme sovereigns who flocked to Ems in the 1870s was Czar Alexander II, who (as mentioned earlier) visited in 1873 to consecrate the local Orthodox Church; he then returned every summer for the next three years. Alexander's curing at Ems was a way of solidifying his relationship with the new German kaiser, an important ingredient in the alliance arrangements between Germany and Russia inaugurated by Bismarck in the 1870s. It is to this complicated alliance system—and the role played in it by Central Europe's grand spas—that I must now turn.

Five Balls over the Waters: Bismarck's Alliance System

"Summers brought no break from work, because monarchs went to the grand spas to take the waters and make treaties," writes historian Jonathan Steinberg in his masterful biography of Bismarck. The new German Reich was barely eight months old when, in summer 1871, Kaiser Wilhelm I repaired as usual to Bad Gastein for (part of) his annual cure program. Aware that the kaiser intended to meet Emperor Franz Josef in Bad Gastein, Bismarck hurried to the Alps to be with his monarch. He wanted to ensure that any discussions between the sovereigns helped to repair the severely damaged relations between the two Central European empires, for he now saw Austria-Hungary as the first link in a new conservative alliance system dedicated to preserving the status-quo. Bismarck well knew that France, having lost Alsace-Lorraine to Germany in 1871, hoped to overturn that status-quo as soon as possible and therefore needed to be isolated. Russia, too, was a potential problem, for the existing power relationship in the Balkans was not at all to its liking: Russia hoped to become the major player there in place of the fading Ottomans and instead of the equally ambitious Austrians. Ultimately, thought Bismarck, Russia would need to be kept in check, ideally through an alliance, but the first order of business was mending fences with Austria.

And where better to do that than in Gastein, a place where both emperors had conferred together before? On the eve of the sovereigns' tête-à-tête at Gastein's venerable Hotel Straubinger on August 24, Bismarck piously instructed German missions abroad to announce that this meeting between the monarchs would show the world that "the disturbance in friendly relations, to which both lands, in contrast to the feelings of the two rulers, had been pushed by their historic developments, must now be seen as a completed and finished episode." "Pushed by historic developments" may perhaps have been a slightly euphemistic phrase for a bloody civil war engineered by Bismarck, but never mind, the two sovereigns did indeed rekindle their "good feelings" for each other at Gastein, thereby helping forge the first link in Bismarck's conservative diplomatic chain.

The addition of Russia to that chain in October 1873, yielding the so-called Three Emperors League, occurred in Berlin rather than at a spa, but Franz Josef had prepped for the Berlin summit through informal chats with Czar Alexander II and Emperor Wilhelm I at his summer villa in Bad Ischl. There, in addition to thermal bathing and strategizing, he and his guests hunted wild game and undertook carriage drives in the hills.

Bismarck would spend the years after German unification frantically trying to prop up his conservative alliance system. Despite all his machinations, his intricate diplomatic arrangement ultimately foundered on the intractable rivalry between Russia and Austria-Hungary in the Balkans. Deep-seated German contempt for "barbaric" Russia also played a role here.

The chancellor's stressful foreign-policy juggling act inevitably took a terrible toll on his health, which was also undermined by his penchant for eating, drinking, and smoking on a scale considered heroic even by the generous standards of the day. According to one of his top aides, Christoph von Tiedemann, a typical lunch for trencherman Bismarck consisted of "roast beef or beef steak with potatoes, cold roast venison, fieldfare, fried pudding, etc." Dinner was "six heavy courses plus dessert." To wash all this down, Bismarck drank copious glasses of wine with every meal, including breakfast. In the afternoons he added beer and champagne (generally two bottles of the latter), then more beer along with brandy after dinner. Revealingly, the chancellor's bedchamber had to be equipped with *two* enormous chamber pots to accommodate his mighty output. As he ate and drank, so did he smoke: an unbroken chain of big black cigars from morning to night. Eventually, not content with the effects of one Havana stogie at a time, he devised a special multipronged cigar holder that allowed him to consume three big Cubans at once. He bragged that when he fired up this formidable machine at the dinner table he would be so "fogged in" by smoke that no one could see him, much less plague him with stupid chatter.

Although Bismarck was quite proud of his prodigious appetites, his doctors, understandably, became alarmed. They did not fail to make a connection between their patient's lifestyle habits and his chronic insomnia, piles, stomach pains, heartburn, gout, and nervous irritability. His escalating irascibility was especially worrying. Frequently he would fly into wild rages, hurling abuse, and sometimes heavy objects, at anyone unfortunate enough to be in range. When his physicians appealed to him to cut back on both work and consumption, he upbraided them as "dolts" who "made elephants out of gnats." (Apropos elephants, Bismarck, at six feet, four inches in height, topped out on the scales at 280 pounds in his mid-sixties.)

Notwithstanding his contempt for physicians, Bismarck did accept one piece of their advice: Starting in the early 1870s he regularly visited spas to decompress, shed a pound or two, and take in the salubrious waters. His favorite Kurort was Bad Kissingen, a resort in the Franconian region of Bavaria. There he stayed in a private apartment and walked to the Kurhaus each morning along a route heavily guarded by local police (in 1874 he was slightly wounded by a would-be assassin as he left his Kissingen quarters). Bismarck avoided encountering other curists and ogling vacationers by bathing in private and returning to his apartment in a closed carriage supplied by Bavaria's King Ludwig II. In the end, Bismarck was convinced that this Kissingen regimen was doing him a world of good, whatever his "dolt" doctors might say. "I owe my health to a loving God and the healing waters of Bad Kissingen," he liked to claim.

At Kissingen, Bismarck did try to cut down on work, instructing Christoph von Tiedemann not to send him any "business" when he was curing. Upon leaving for the spa in June 1876, he told his young aide that he hoped "to bring back a skin color as fresh as your own."

But Bismarck could not entirely avoid "business," even in Kissingen. In July 1877 he took time away from his cure routine to compose an outline of his foreign policy called the Kissingen Diktat (Kissingen Decree). Here he admitted to suffering from what the French newspapers called his "*cauchemar des coalitions*" (nightmare of coalitions)—the nightmare of being surrounded by hostile powers. More specifically, he worried that Austria might slip its German moorings and tie up with Russia or France, or perhaps France would combine with Russia. He concluded his decree by stating that his ideal diplomatic scenario involved "an overall political situation in which all the Powers except France need us and are held apart from coalitions against us by their friendly relations with each other."

By virtue of his stays at Kissingen, Bismarck may indeed have felt healthier, but his mental state, haunted by those nightmare coalitions, did not improve very much. In late summer 1877, he was no sooner back in Berlin following his Kissingen cure than his doctors ordered him to take an extended medical leave at Bad Gastein. Although he tried to evade this enforced vacation by claiming that the trip would prove too hard on his old dog Sultan (an indispensible companion trained to bite on command, as none other than Richard Wagner once discovered), Bismarck ended up actually enjoying his time in the mountains. According to Tiedemann, who joined him and his family at Gastein in late summer 1877, Bismarck fell into a pleasant routine involving daily thermal baths, frequent carriage rides with his family, dinners with friends, and healthful walks around town. On one of these walks Bismarck pointed out to Tiedemann various points of interest, including the *very bench* on which King Wilhelm had sat when he, Bismarck, briefed him on the Gastein Convention. Surrounded by beautiful alpine scenery, breathing crisp mountain air, and wrapped in the bosom of family, Bismarck apparently cast off some of his usual irascibility. Here, at the grand Austrian spa, he showed that he could be, in Tiedemann's words, "a most charming" fellow, a regular mensch. For Tiedemann himself, just being with Bismarck and his family in such a special place had "all the effects of a good water-cure."

As Bismarck had indicated in his Kissingen Decree, his hope was to ensure Germany's security through alliances with other conservative powers, meanwhile keeping potential enemies, above all France, isolated. By the late 1870s, his original constellation of Germany, Austria-Hungary, and Russia was already stumbling due to new upheavals in the Balkans that further weakened the Ottomans and thus intensified the race between Russia and Austria to fill the power vacuum in the region. Bismarck saw that he had to make a choice between Austria-Hungary and Russia as his primary partner.

The choice proved not all that difficult, since both domestic and strategic factors argued for Austria: Most Germans favored ties to their kindred eastern neighbor over Slavic Russia, and Bismarck himself believed that the two Central European powers together constituted an impregnable bastion. As he remarked in 1879, "If Germany and Austria were united, they would be, together, a match for any enemy, France or Russia."

Out of this calculation came a new (or, more precisely, reinforced) link in Bismarck's diplomatic chain, the Dual Alliance between Germany and Austria-Hungary, forged in late 1879. As was only fitting, this deal was negotiated and sealed at Bad Gastein, a place Bismarck now knew intimately. So did Austria-Hungary's chief representative at the talks, Count Julius Andrassy; he had often cured at the resort. The alliance that these two veteran curists worked out between repeated trips to the baths amounted essentially to a defensive pact. Both powers were committed to helping each other in the event of a foreign attack (which the Austrians interpreted to mean a *Russian* attack). Once again, a defensive line had been drawn in the water, this one strategic.

Roughly a year before Bismarck had tightened Germany's ties to Austria-Hungary at Gastein, he had started negotiations that would culminate in 1882 with another strategic arrangement: the Triple Alliance among Germany, Austria-Hungary, and Italy. This compact, designed mainly to secure Austria-Hungary's southern flank and prevent Italy from cozying up to France or Britain, was signed in Berlin. The preliminary negotiations, however, began in the summer of 1878 in—where else?—Bad Gastein.

To the pairing of Bismarck and Andrassy a third player was added in the person of Francesco Crispi, Italy's foreign minister. Crispi was a newcomer both to Bismarck's ongoing diplomatic chess tournament and to that tourney's premier alpine arena. The Italian never became a Gastein regular, but he enjoyed his time in the Alps with Bismarck, who, as usual, showed off all the local attractions as if they belonged to the German Reich (which indeed they would between the years 1938 and 1945). By adding Italy to his diplomatic chain, Bismarck seemed to have strengthened it, but in reality Italy was a very weak link and an unreliable one at that. When push came to shove in World War I, Italy adroitly cut its ties to the Central Powers in favor of a new fighting alliance with those Powers' Western foes. After all, Britain and France promised Rome what Berlin and Vienna could not or would not: Habsburg South Tyrol. Francesco Crispi, it seems, was not the only Italian who developed a taste for Austrian alpine scenery.

There were other parts of Bismarck's alliance system that had no connections to grand spas and therefore need not be elaborated upon here. But before leaving this topic I might note that Bismarck's intricate diplomatic arrangement was fully in shambles by the time he was forced from power by Kaiser Wilhelm II in 1890. His successor, Count Leo von Caprivi, admitted that, unlike Bismarck, he "could not [juggle] five glass balls in the air at one time": two balls was his limit.

Vicky, Willy, Nicky, Bertie, and Franz Josef

If Bad Gastein had been a prominent venue in the making of Central European diplomacy during the years following German unification, another grand spa, Bad Homburg, stepped into the political limelight from the time of Kaiser Wilhelm I's death in March 1888 to the First World War. In 1866, King Wilhelm I had established Homburg as the Hohenzollern family's principal summer residence; forty-six years later, in 1912, his grandson, Kaiser Wilhelm II, got the town officially designated as a "Bad." Yet another Hohenzollern emperor, Friedrich III, who ruled very briefly in 1888, also prized Homburg, where, like his father and son, he summered virtually every year of his adult life. During his brief rule, an elegant avenue abutting the Kurpark was designated "Kaiser-Friedrich-Promenade," the name it still holds today.

Formally known as Bad Homburg vor der Höhe, this handsome Kurort sits at the foot of the Taunus Hills just north of Frankfurt, to which it was connected by a railway line, the Homburger Bahn, in 1860. Homburg's thermal waters, like those of its peers, had been in use since Roman times, though they were relatively late to attract more than local attention. Much of the credit for this goes to a local physician named Edward Christian Trapp, who "rediscovered" the Elisabethbrunnen (Elisabeth Fountain), the spa's principal spring, in 1834. This and another nearby spring achieved greater renown when Germany's most famous chemist, Justus Liebig, gave them a scientific thumbs-up shortly thereafter. Homburg's Quellen owed their first significant development to Princess Elizabeth, daughter of King George III of England, who married a Landgrave of Homburg-Hessen and devoted her dowry to sprucing up the springs.

But even with its fine thermal waters Homburg would not have moved quickly into the first rank of Central European Kurorte without an equally fine casino, which, like the one in Baden-Baden, was the product of French inspiration. In 1840 two gambling entrepreneurs, François and Louis Blanc, showed up in Homburg and signed a mutually satisfactory contract with the Landgrave of Homburg-Hessen. Out of this deal the Blanc brothers obtained the right to build a casino and keep half the proceeds for themselves; the other half would go to the Landgrave. But the Blancs did more than just establish a casino; they financed an elegant Kurhaus to which, like their entrepreneurial counterparts at other grand spas, they invited Europe's best artists. Among them was the singer Adelina Patti, who, fortunately for François Blanc, gambled away the entire five-thousand-gulden fee he had paid her for a single night's performance. Of more lasting importance was the endowment of what became the most expansive and beautiful of all the Central European Kurparks. To lay out the park's extensive gardens, lawns, brooks, and artificial ponds, François Blanc (Louis died in 1850; François himself later moved to Monte Carlo and established the fabled casino there) brought in Prussia's premier landscape artist, Peter Joseph Lenné. In subsequent decades Lenné's magnificent improvement on nature—something "God might have done, if He'd had any money," local wags crowed—became even more magnificent with the addition of ornate drinking fountains and, in 1890, the palatial Kaiser-Wilhelms-Bad, hailed by *The World* newspaper as "the most modern, luxurious, and comfortable" thermal bath complex in Europe.

Homburg's Kurpark ministered to the soul as well as the body. On one corner rose an onion-domed Russian Orthodox Church, its cornerstone laid in 1896 by Russia's new ruler, Czar Nicholas II. The church testified to the extent to which Homburg, like Ems, Wiesbaden, and Baden-Baden, had become a prized pit stop for the Russian nobility in the second half of the nineteenth century. (Also like those other spa churches, Homburg's Orthodox Chapel would be closed down during World War I, things Russian having fallen out of favor.) A rather different, and even more exotic, spiritual edifice graced another corner of the park: a crimson and gold, winged-roof Siamese temple, shipped in pieces to Homburg by King Chulalongkorn (known at home as the "Royal Buddha") as a thank-you gift for the king's successful cure visit in 1907. Alas, Chulalongkorn died in 1910—his cure wasn't *that* successful—and because it took almost seven years to reassemble and erect the elaborate temple, its benefactor could not be present for the dedication ceremony, at least in his most recent incarnation.

In truth, Bad Homburg had never been overrun by Buddhist Thais, but it certainly *was* heavily patronized by sport-worshiping Englishmen, who left their own mark on the Kurpark in the form of Continental Europe's first tennis courts and golf links. The latter facility was too small to be more than a glorified putting green, but it offered a little light exercise for out-of-shape curists and an attractive space for afternoon conversations (not to mention refreshing après-golf drinks in the adjoining clubhouse). As for the Homburg tennis courts, they became the site of a major annual tournament in August, a high point in the international tennis calendar. Like the Russians, the English would soon lose favor in Homburg, but *their* temples never fell completely out of use, war and changing politics notwithstanding.

Apropos politics, it was the Hohenzollern presence at the spa that made Homburg an important arena in that domain during the last decades before World War I. Before becoming emperor on March 9, 1888, Crown Prince Friedrich spent summers at the spa in the company of his father and mother. After marrying Princess Victoria ("Vicky"), the eldest daughter of Britain's Queen Victoria, in 1856, Friedrich brought his young wife regularly to Homburg. Like him, Vicky prized the town for its natural beauty and salubrious climate. A love for Homburg was hardly their only mutual affinity: both were liberals. This was not terribly strange for Vicky, whose father, Prince Albert, had a strong liberal streak, but for Friedrich it was a genuine departure from tradition, and one that caused a deep rift within both the Hohenzollern family and the Prussian political establishment. Conservatives like Bismarck and Count Waldersee despised Friedrich and fretted over what would happen to Germany once the throne passed to him and his English-born wife.

As fate would have it, Bismarck and his ilk need not have worried too much about Friedrich's occupancy of the throne, for he was so sick with throat cancer when he took power that he could accomplish very little. Moreover, he was able to do that very little for a mere ninety-nine days; he died at age fifty-six on June 15, 1888.

Obviously, no spa could have cured Friedrich III's cancer, but this did not stop him from trying to arrest the disease through a month-long water cure at Bad Ems in April 1887. Friedrich's spa treatment for this severe malady was not as ridiculous as it might strike us today. Conventional cancer treatments in those days were not much, if any, better than medicinal hot waters, and they were a lot more painful. Nor was it even easy to diagnose cancer. In Friedrich's case, the ominous growth on one of his vocal cords was not definitively diagnosed as cancerous for several months. His German doctors suspected that cancer might be present, but Professor Rudolf Virchow's famous pathology laboratory at the Charité Hospital in Berlin, to which tissue samples from the growth were sent, initially found no signs of the dread disease.

Meanwhile, in addition to relatively benign spa treatments, Friedrich underwent fruitless efforts to remove the growth by knife and even a burning-hot wire—all with only doses of cocaine as an anesthetic. In desperation, Vicky called in a famous specialist from London's Harley Street, Morell Mackenzie, much to the dismay of Friedrich's German physicians. Mackenzie believed that Friedrich's growth was benign and continued to insist that this was the case even as the tumor grew apace and impeded Friedrich's breathing, speech, and eating. When Mackenzie finally realized that his patient had cancer, it was too late to operate (perhaps a blessing, given that additional surgery would have been very painful and probably ineffective).

After Emperor Friedrich III's death, former empress Victoria ended up staying on in Homburg or its immediate vicinity for the rest of her life. First from the Royal Castle in town and then from her villa Friedrichshof in nearby Kronberg, she bombarded Queen Victoria with letters sharply critical of Germany's new sovereign, her own son Wilhelm—Kaiser Wilhelm II, a.k.a. "Willy." Vicky developed an extremely difficult relationship with her eldest son once it became clear that young Willy, despite her best efforts to turn him into an English-style liberal, was becoming, in her words, "hopelessly Prussian"—conservative and militaristic to the core. For this bad turn she blamed evil influences back in Berlin (above all, Bismarck) and the garrison town of Potsdam, where Willy learned to play soldier and adore military uniforms. Seeing her son in one of those uniforms on his tenth birthday appalled her: "Poor Willy in his uniform looks like some unfortunate little monkey dressed up standing on top of an organ," she wrote her mother. By the time Emperor Friedrich was sick with cancer Vicky's distrust of Willy was so great that when he advised surgery for his dying father, she interpreted this as a ploy to bump him off immediately so that he, Willy, could more quickly grab the reins of power.

Now, it *is* certainly true that Willy was exceedingly anxious to take power and not at all hesitant to show it. It is also true that he had little respect for his father and even less for his mother, who, he claimed, had "besmirched" Germany and "brought [it] to the brink of ruin." It is *not* true, however, that Wilhelm II was a typical reactionary Prussian; rather, he was a new-school imperialist who instead of perpetuating the Bismarckian status quo wished to turn Germany into a "world power"—one that could rival his mother's native land. (Wilhelm's ambitious foreign policy, which he expected to control himself, was a bone of contention with Bismarck and one of the reasons he sacked the Iron Chancellor in 1890.)

Wilhelm's famously volatile personality and equally famous imperial quest may well be traced, at least in part, to a physical deformity he carried from birth. Willy was a breach baby, and nineteenth-century medicine was not much better at handling complicated births than it was at treating difficult diseases like cancer. Willy's case had the added complication of being royal: court protocol forbade obstetricians from looking directly at the center of their operations; they had to work by feel under a heavy flannel nightgown. As it happens, the obstetrician doing the feeling here, per Vicky's express instructions, was Sir James Clark, personal physician to the queen of England. Struggling to extract Willy, a difficult fellow even then, from his confinement, Sir James pulled too forcefully on the forceps. Willy came out with a badly damaged left arm, which remained for the most part useless ever after. Later, Kaiser Wilhelm would declare to all who would listen: "One English doctor killed my father and another one crippled my arm. And for that we have my mother to thank, who would never consult a German doctor." Perhaps it is not overdoing the pop psychology to suggest that Willy spent the rest of his life trying to compensate for—and to get even for—what had happened to him at birth.

On the other hand, Willy's animosity toward his mother did not spill over to Bad Homburg, her ongoing residence and veritable nest of perfidious Albion. Despite a love for travel—he was dubbed the "Traveling Kaiser" or "Wandering Willy"—Wilhelm II continued to summer regularly in Homburg as well as at other German grand spas. As a testament to his affection for Homburg, he commissioned in 1901 a huge Lutheran church, the Erlöserkirche, built partly in the Byzantine style he had come to admire during a visit to Constantinople.

Wilhelm's schedule in Homburg was almost as frenetic as in Berlin. If he was not commanding a parade of zeppelins launched from the spa he was overseeing a motorcar race or laying the cornerstone for a nearby replica Roman fort called the Saalburg. Fancying himself a latter-day Lenné, he loved to walk briskly through the Kurpark, snapping his fingers as he passed by trees he wanted cut down in favor of different varieties. He attended many golf and tennis matches, although he desisted from playing either game on account of his withered arm. At Homburg he socialized with visiting plutocrats from Germany and abroad: Krupps and Opels, Harrimans and Goulds. He even hobnobbed with wealthy Jews, something he was hesitant to do back in Berlin. Among his Jewish associates in Homburg were members of the Frankfurt-based Rothschild banking dynasty, who had (and still have) an enormous estate near the spa.

But most of all, Kaiser Wilhelm hosted fellow sovereigns and other high-ranking political figures while he was resident in Homburg, thus making the Kurort a kind of second court for the Wilhelmian Empire. Among the sovereigns he greeted there was Czar Nicholas II, his cousin by marriage. After laying the cornerstone for the local Orthodox church in 1893, Nicholas, along with his new German-born wife, Alexandra, returned to the spa in 1896 to preside over the church's official consecration. On both these occasions Wilhelm II took time from his busy schedule to entertain his cousin.

Unlike Bismarck, however, Kaiser Wilhelm II was not a believer in the importance of maintaining Germany's Russian alliance, and he therefore let lapse the so-called Reinsurance Treaty that Bismarck had engineered with Russia in 1888. Yet Wilhelm *did* want to stay on friendly terms with "Cousin Nicky," believing that good relations at the top would be enough to prevent the two nations from ever coming to blows. His personal opinion of Nicky as a man, though, was no higher than his estimate of the Russians as a people. He routinely referred to his cousin as a "ninny" and a "whimperer," a uxorious weakling who let his wife wear the pants and was fit only "to live in a country house and raise turnips." Thus, while Willy dutifully entertained Nicky when the latter showed up at Homburg, he did not invite him to come for long visits, much less put him up in the Royal Castle.

The foreign sovereign who came most frequently to Homburg was Albert Edward ("Bertie"), Prince of Wales from 1841 until the death of his mother in January 1901, and King Edward VII from then until his own death in 1910. Bertie's reason for coming to Homburg was not to see "Willy," his nephew, but to visit his sister Vicky—and to enjoy himself in ways he could not do at home.

Bertie, as it happens, fully shared Vicky's less-than-positive take on her son. Like her, he came to fear that this impetuous young man might actually be mentally unbalanced. (Bertie, by the way, did not have much respect for Nicky either; he described his Russian relative as "weak as water.") Bertie was deeply put off by Willy's insensitive treatment of his dying father, and when the young fellow became kaiser and started banging on about how Germany would challenge Britain for world leadership, especially on the high seas, Bertie was positively contemptuous.

On the other hand, once he, too, became a sovereign, Edward saw it as his duty to promote harmonious relations between Britain and the other European powers, including bellicose Germany. King Edward did not enjoy the same policy-making powers as Wilhelm or Nicholas, but like them he believed that foreign affairs were best regulated from the top, among "royal colleagues" who could rise above the rancor of petty, popularity-obsessed politicians. Wilhelm, while agreeing with his uncle on the proper role of sovereigns in foreign affairs, deeply resented Bertie's tendency, as he saw it, to treat him like a naughty little boy and, in general, to assume a God-given superiority of Britain over upstart Germany.

Not surprisingly, then, the various meetings between the two men, whether in Homburg or elsewhere, were cordial enough on the surface but at bottom infused with deep mutual distrust. As one British Foreign Office official reported of a meeting between Edward and Wilhelm in Wilhelmshöhe in 1907: "Although the king was outwardly on the best of terms with the German emperor . . . I could not help noticing that there was no real intimacy between them." This was an understatement.

Fortunately for Edward, and perhaps for Wilhelm, too, the Englishman had more on his plate (literally and figuratively) than faux-cordial get-togethers with his nephew. When Bertie as crown prince visited Homburg and other grand German spas such as Baden-Baden, he lived large, like his size. (He lived well back home in London, too, but there he had his censorious mother looking over his shoulder; on the Continent, he felt he could throw most restraints to the wind.) His appetite for food, drink, and cigars was as prodigious as Bismarck's—not for nothing was he nicknamed "tum-tum." His dinners normally consisted of twelve courses, starting with gut busters like whole piglets stuffed with truffles and fois gras and then tapering off to "light" items such as roast beef and Yorkshire pudding. Like the Iron Chancellor, Bertie sometimes used tobacco as a weapon, in his case to irritate his parents; his idea of rationing his tobacco intake was to limit himself to one cigar and two cigarettes before breakfast. When his London club, White's, refused to allow smoking in its morning room, Bertie bolted and formed Marlborough Club, where smoking was encouraged *everywhere*.

Meanwhile, his only form of exercise, apart from a little golf and lawn tennis, was vigorous sex, not necessarily, or even usually, with his wife Alexandra. From early on he dallied with a host of mistresses, among them Lady Susan Vane, whom he impregnated, and an Italian lady named Giulia Barveci, a grand horizontal who proudly described herself as "the greatest whore in the world." Speaking of whores, Bertie was a regular patron at Le Chabanais, a luxury bordello in Paris where he had a room all to himself furnished to accommodate his special needs. The furnishings included a large copper bathtub that Bertie filled with champagne to bathe in with prostitutes. But the pièce de résistance was the prince's fabled *fauteuil d'amour*, a made-to-order love seat in rococo style featuring reinforced legs and two handles protruding from the top for extra purchase. In this formidable contraption, Bertie could be serviced by two ladies at once; they performed their duties on top, lest they be crushed to death.

Bertie's appetite for gambling was, fortunately, rather less prodigious than his lust for food and sex, but even his casual gambling forays at Baden-Baden and Homburg were problematical because casino gaming was illegal in England and his indulging in it reinforced a growing image of him back home as a wastrel. A London newspaper reporting on his gambling junkets at Homburg waxed indignant over the prince's frittering away national treasure that had been wrung from the sweat and toil of British working men and women.

But whatever the toll his Continent-centered indulgences took on his domestic reputation, Bertie clearly was a man who *needed*—and loved—spas. His love affair with Central European water-cure resorts continued to blossom during his long tenure as crown prince. "Wales," as the Prince was (aptly) called in Europe, took his bloated body from one spa to another every summer, womanizing, gluttonizing, and gaming as he went.

At Homburg, though, he sometimes tried seriously to cure—and to lose weight. He had his own massage room at the Kurhaus. It is said that he once lost forty pounds in two weeks, only to gain it all back when he went home. In truth, he could have gained the weight back even while curing, for his regular regimen at Homburg invariably included grand dinners, parties, and picnics—*lots* of picnics.

He also found time to shop. Famously, on one of his shopping expeditions in Homburg he spied a fedora that struck his fancy at a local haberdashery; he ordered some minor changes to the design and popularized the headgear as the "Homburg." This was just one of his sartorial innovations. He made it fashionable for men to crease their trousers at the side rather than in the front. Due to his wide girth, a physical feature quite common among gentlemen of his day, he popularized the custom of leaving open the lower button on his suit and sport coats.

Edward loved Homburg and the other German Kurorte he patronized, but starting soon after his assumption of the throne in 1901 he shifted his spa custom to sites in Bohemia: Karlsbad and (above all) Marienbad. One of the reasons Edward settled on Marienbad involved his health, or, more precisely, his alarming obesity. Marienbad, whose waters were quite gaseous, was said to be the best spa in Europe for weight reduction. As one curist noted in 1890, "Many of the patients at Marienbad pass their days in serious fashion. They live to grow thin. If they arrive resembling Falstaff, many hope to depart resembling Cassius in appearance." The weight-reduction record at Marienbad was proudly established by an Egyptian, El Gamel Bey, who lost fifty-three kilograms during his cure.

Edward did not outdo Gamel Bay and certainly would never end up looking like Cassius, and in any event the *main* reason for his shift from German to Austrian spas was political. To put it bluntly, Edward became profoundly exasperated with the Germany of Kaiser Wilhelm II. His own exasperation with Germany tied in with a growing antagonism toward the Kaiser and his Reich on the part of Britain's political class and general public. (British foreign secretary Sir Edward Grey said prophetically of Wilhelm II that he was "like a battleship with steam up and screws going, but with no rudder, and he will run into something some day and cause a catastrophe.") Bitter controversy over the kaiser's decision to build a blue-water navy that might in time challenge Britain's maritime supremacy lay at the heart of this Anglo-German antagonism, but both sides soon found many additional reasons to distrust each other.

King Edward had no qualms about shifting his spa patronage from one German-speaking Central Power to another because, like many Englishmen of his day, he made a clear distinction between Germany and Austria. (France's fiery Germanophobe politician Georges Clemenceau made the same distinction: he would happily cure in Austrian Bohemia but *never* in Germany.) Desiring to exploit this emerging bias, some Bohemian Kurorte, including Marienbad, now placed advertisements in French and British newspapers touting not only their miraculous waters but also their "inestimable advantage of not being in Germany." Marienbad, where Edward ended up spending seven summers, turned out to be a perfect fit for the king because there he could not only *play* to his heart's content but also do a little "work" in the form of conferring with Kaiser Franz Josef, whom he came to admire. In this cosmopolitan atmosphere he could readily keep his finger on the pulse of European politics. Perhaps from his comfortable Bohemian base, Edward might even help shape world affairs by coaxing Austria-Hungary to mediate between Britain and Germany. That, at least, was the king's hope.

We can follow Edward on his sojourns at his favorite spa through a contemporary chronicle entitled *King Edward at Marienbad,* penned by one Sigmund Münz, a Vienna-based newspaper reporter who traveled with the king in Austria. With respect to Edward's daily routine in Marienbad, Münz felt bound to tell his readers that the Briton, his worrisome rotundity notwithstanding, did not seriously diet—"he had no desire to pose as a penitent"—nor did he stint on his wardrobe. He brought along dozens of elaborate outfits, and "his taste in the cut and colour schemes of his clothes was impeccable." Marienbad's waters, as they had done for the aged Goethe, seemed able "to renew [Edward's] perennial youth"—that is, his youthful libido. His retinue at the spa always included "a number of ladies, some of whom could boast that they had once basked in the sunshine of Royal favor in the past, while others could still claim that prerogative in the present."

On the political side, King Edward's meetings with Franz Josef provided singular relief after his unhappy jousts with capricious Wilhelm II. "King Edward could not complain that on any day of his many visits he had been embarrassed by any Imperial caprice or manifestation of Hapsburg megalomania." Perhaps the soothing thermal waters did their part here: "Never, as long as King Edward was drinking the healing waters of the *Kreuzbrunnen* and taking the baths, was he guilty of the slightest lapse in the respect due to the venerable Emperor, whose friendship for England had endured for sixty years." While at the spa Edward always took care to toast Franz Josef's birthday (August 18), putting on his Austro-Hungarian Hussar uniform and hosting a lavish dinner at the Hotel Weimar, where he kept a suite of rooms. (This hotel is now defunct, but one can see a replica of Edward's Weimar suite in the town museum next door. Unfortunately, the fabled fauteuil d'amour is not there; it's in private hands somewhere in Paris, and apparently still in use.)

For the historic Marienbad meeting between the two sovereigns in 1904, the little spa pulled out all the stops.* "At night the picturesque town was brilliantly illuminated, the main street displaying a huge arch of incandescent lamps spelling out the names of the Emperor and King," reported Münz. When Franz Josef held court in the Kursaal, all Marienbad turned out to greet him: "first the nobility, then the Roman Catholic clergy, the Army, the municipal and provincial authorities, the heads of the Protestant clergy, and the leading Jews."

Münz's mention here of "the leading Jews" merits further comment. Unlike many Victorian gentlemen, Bertie was not a knee-jerk anti-Semite; early on he had included wealthy Jews like the Rothschilds in his inner circle and valued their advice on financial matters. In Bohemia, he shared with Franz Josef a reputation of being "well disposed" toward Jews. His engagement on behalf of Russian Jews suffering under government-condoned oppression earned him great respect among Jewish refugees in Austrian Bohemia. Münz could write with justification: "It was obvious that not only the distinguished, but also the humbler Russian Jews in

---

*The town is still striving to capitalize on this historic meeting. In May 2014, civic leaders unveiled a life-sized bronze sculpture of the two potentates standing together in a central square.

the Bohemian spas were full of admiration for King Edward, for they expressed it by contributing generously to his philanthropic schemes."

What Münz failed to mention in his laudatory reportage on the philo-Semitic king's Marienbad meeting with Franz Josef, no doubt because he did not know about it, was that a typhus case had surfaced in Edward's hotel just four weeks before his arrival. A local spa doctor, Enoch Heinrich Kisch, conveniently determined that this case had been imported from elsewhere and therefore need not be made public. Why "ruin the Kurort's reputation" on the eve of its big moment in the spotlight? Kisch reasoned.

Festive as this royal encounter between the two potentates may have been, one might well ask whether it, or a similar meeting between the two sovereigns at Bad Ischl in 1908, did very much to further Edward's hopes of getting Franz Josef to mediate with Wilhelm II or, more boldly, to split Austria away from Germany? The answer must be a resounding "no." To the extent that Edward may have actually influenced high-level policy, he managed this not vis-à-vis Austria but with France, his first foreign love. Edward's state visit to Paris in 1903, called by one commentator "the most important royal visit in modern history," smoothed the way for the Entente Cordiale between the two imperial rivals. On the other hand, when it came to constructing a friendship with Austria-Hungary strong enough to prevent it from making serious mischief alongside its German ally, neither the friendly ministrations of King Edward nor the soothing waters of Marienbad or Bad Ischl proved much use.

King Edward, it must be said, was less interested in peace per se than in helping put together an alliance system directed against Germany. By contrast, another frequent Marienbad curist, Austrian pacifist Berta von Suttner, whose visits sometimes overlapped with Edward's, used her spa stays to push for a comprehensive military stand-down among the Great Powers. In a speech at the Marienbad Kursaal in 1905 she passionately advocated the substitution of law for armed force in international relations, something that had already been attained, she noted, in the domestic affairs "of every civilized state." The civilized Kursaal crowd clapped politely but hardly seemed galvanized by her wise words: People "found peace propaganda boring," averred Herr Münz, a member of the audience.

Many people also found Emperor Franz Josef boring. Novelist Robert Musil quipped that the Austrian monarch was like one of those stars that had already died by the time their light reached earth. He was certainly less lively and charismatic than King Edward VII, his bon vivant friend. Franz Josef worked as hard as Edward played. Whereas the Englishman had a small army of mistresses, the dour Austrian monarch had but one: Katharina Schratt, a well-known actress. Although Franz Josef had a gentle side, he could be famously strict, especially with his family. He was also given to melancholy, and God knows he had much to be melancholic about: his brother Maximilian was executed by rebels in Mexico; one of his daughters died in infancy; his only son, Crown Prince Rudolf, committed suicide along with his young lover at Mayerling; his wife Elisabeth was stabbed to death by an Italian anarchist in Geneva; and his nephew, Crown Prince Franz Ferdinand, was assassinated by a Bosnian nationalist in Sarajevo, an event that linked Habsburg family tragedy to world tragedy.

Franz Josef coped with the manifold stresses and sadness in his life by retreating every summer to beautiful Bad Ischl. It was in Ischl in 1853 that the twenty-three-year-old kaiser met his wife-to-be, Elisabeth ("Sisi"), a fifteen-year-old Bavarian princess who had journeyed to the spa along with her mother and older sister, Helene. Mama Ludovika was promoting Helene as a bride for Franz Josef, but the young emperor had eyes only for Sisi, who even then was quite an eyeful. Tall and slim with long brown hair, she projected an aura of quiet simplicity that seemed fully at one with the rustic beauty and freshness of Ischl. Soon after that first encounter, Sisi and Franz Josef became formally engaged, also at Ischl. Upon their marriage a year later, Franz Josef's mother gave the young couple the perfect wedding gift: a Biedermeier-style villa in Ischl, surrounded by a spacious park. For the rest of their lives, both Franz Josef and Sisi would treasure this place as their bolt-hole of first resort.

While Sisi spent her long summers at Ischl reading novels, writing poetry, and maniacally exercising in order to maintain her famous "wasp waist" (she even installed a gym next to her bedroom), Franz Josef used the villa mainly as a base from which to hunt wild game. He is said to have killed 50,556 game animals over the course of his sixty-six summers in Ischl. With the exception of Sisi's private quarters, the walls at the villa were (and are still—the place is now a museum) completely covered with glassy-eyed animal heads and rustic antler displays.

Franz Josef's favorite room in the villa was his comfortable study, suitably equipped with a large desk, leather wing chairs, a giant globe, and a capacious humidor along with a state-of-the-art electric cigar lighter. (He allowed himself such gadgets only in Ischl; his Hofburg study back in Vienna was strictly candlelit.) Atop a shelf near his desk stood another modern marvel, an electric fan made by Siemens. This was a gift from Katharina Schratt, whom Franz Josef had set up in Ischl with a small villa of her own. (Schratt, by the way, was tolerated by Elisabeth because the empress had lovers of her own—many of them. Moreover, after her fourth pregnancy, she withdrew from sexual relations with her husband to the relief of both.)

For Kaiser Franz Josef, summers at Ischl were not principally about policy making—he did that back in Vienna. The emperor did, however, enjoy hosting fellow monarchs like King Edward at the villa, along with a plethora of visiting dignitaries from all over the world. Among these was former American president Ulysses S. Grant, whom Franz Josef received at Ischl in 1878. During their chat in Franz Josef's study, Grant, waving one of his host's Havanas, declared out of the blue that he was sick of military parades, indeed sick of all things military, above all war. Franz Josef, though no militarist himself, was so astonished that a great general could utter such heresies that he could only laugh. It was a revealing laugh—and given what was soon to come, a laugh that makes one want to cry.

CHAPTER SIX

Modernization and Its Discontents

The three or four decades before World War I—those heady years when the fin de siècle segued into the Belle Époque—stand as the true salad days for Central Europe's grand spa towns. True, the crowds munching on their fancy Kurort salads no longer consisted so heavily—and reassuringly—of gouty aristocratic *Stammkunden* (regulars), the archetypal spa clientele of old. Yet patronage was increasing steadily across the board, a welcome development due largely to an influx of new bourgeois visitors, a good many of whom were Jewish and/or American. The visitor count went up despite the ban on casino gambling imposed by the imperial government in newly unified Germany. For the German spas, the shocking casino closure proved not to be the death blow that many feared. Whether or not they had to compensate for the loss of casino gaming—not an issue at the Habsburg spas because they generally lacked large casinos in the first place—the Central European Kurorte made themselves more attractive by adding splendid new bathing and hospitality facilities. The spas also worked to strengthen the "scientific" component of their therapeutic offerings in order to compete effectively with conventional hospitals and clinics profiting from major new breakthroughs in medical science and health-care delivery.

Yet the materially changing environment at the spas—their physical modernization, therapeutic "medicalization," and broadened clientele base—brought deep unease to those patrons who cherished the more traditional, tranquil, and homogeneous atmosphere at the old Kurorte. Looking back after World War I on the unsettling changes that had transformed his beloved Wiesbaden in this period, the travel writer Alfons Paquet wrote: "The Wilhelmian era emptied over the city a cornucopia of brilliance, riches, and prosperity, but also a rush toward unlimitedness, a wholesale succumbing to get-rich fever. . . . A dazzling influx of international visitors was paraded daily before the eyes of old and young alike." Other commentators complained of "Überfremdung" (excess of foreign influence), a widening gap between rich and poor, and a rift between those who profited from the modernized cure enterprises and those who emphatically did not. Not surprisingly, this undercurrent of malcontented commentary did not go unnoticed by newcomers to the spas—especially by those latest Kurort patrons, the Jews and Americans, on whose heads much of the odium was unloaded. Some of these visitors proved quite capable of adding dissonant notes of their own to the ambient hum of discontent accompanying the modernization of the grand Central European spa towns.

Innovations

Among the most important innovations at the major German and Austrian Kurorte in the decades before the war was the addition of so-called *Badepaläste* (bath palaces) to the water-cure infrastructure. And *palatial* these structures certainly were! Just as in the age of imperial Rome, in late nineteenth-century Central Europe enormous state-financed bathing establishments followed each other in rapid succession, each more opulent than the last. The trend started in Baden-Baden with the opening in 1877 of the spectacular Friedrichsbad, named after Grand Duke Friedrich of Baden. Eight years in the making, this huge (62.5 by 50 meters) sandstone temple to the senses directly emulated in its interior spaces the great Baths of Caracalla and Diocletian, while its exterior façade evoked the Italian High Renaissance, making it a true gallimaufry of historicist eclecticism. The Friedrichsbad was an instant hit. Attracting some sixty thousand visitors a year, it soon outgrew its capacity and had to be expanded. The State Bathing Authority also felt obliged to commission two more bath palaces in quick order: the Landesbad in 1888 and the magisterial Augustabad in 1890. And as if these improvements were not enough, the authority added a state-of-the-art *Inhalorium* for patients with severe respiratory diseases. Commissioned in 1897, this facility completed an astounding makeover of Baden-Baden's publicly financed water-cure industry.

Competition for custom being fierce among the grand Central European spas, Baden-Baden was hardly alone in throwing up new, and ever more luxurious, bath palaces. Bad Homburg got into the game with the above-mentioned Kaiser-Wilhelms-Bad, completed in 1890 after three years' construction. Although named after Kaiser Wilhelm I, whose statue stands out front, the facility's Italian Renaissance exterior and vaguely Orientalist interior replete with Moorish mosaics seemed more suited to the garish taste of Wilhelm II. That emperor indeed loved the place so much that he demanded an entire section all to himself. Bertie, the Prince of Wales, bathed there, too, though presumably not in the company of Willy.

Given the era in which Homburg's Kaiser-Wilhelms-Bad went up—a period not exactly known for its financial probity—it's not surprising that charges of corruption attended the building's gestation. When an entire wing collapsed during construction, some local worthies, including the haberdasher who manufactured the Homburg hat, accused the chief architect, Louis Jacobi, of using inferior materials in order to pad his own pockets. Indignant, Jacobi sued the haberdasher for libel. Fortunately, peace among the litigants was restored by the time the building was completed in 1890, and the legions of curists who subsequently flocked there to bathe were presumably undisturbed by any hint of foulness in the firmaments.

Wiesbaden, Homburg's larger neighbor to the southwest, was not about to be outdone in the bath palace department by any of its German rivals. In Wiesbaden's case, the need for a more "representative" bathing establishment was especially acute because the existing cluster of Quellen around the Kranzplatz, including the beloved Kochbrunnen, were relatively dowdy. That situation changed with a vengeance in the new century with the erection in 1910–1913 of the magnificent Kaiser-Friedrichs-Bad, the last grand *Badepalast* to go up in Germany before World War I. Coming late in the game as it did, this structure could incorporate the most recent developments in spa technology, along with the dernier cri in interior design: Art Nouveau, or what the Germans call Jugendstil. (Fortunately, when the complex was renovated in 1999, the original interior appointments were saved.)

Impressive as these new bath palaces were, they were outdone both in sheer size and technological gadgetry by a plethora of new super-luxury hotels. In America and Europe, the last decades of the nineteenth century signaled the dawn of a golden age of grand hotels that stretched into the 1930s. Gilded Age America produced monuments to excess like New York City's Waldorf Astoria and Plaza; Chicago's Palmer House; and San Francisco's Palace (perhaps the most opulent of all). In Europe, Berlin had its Kaiserhof, Esplanade, and Adlon; Paris its Crillon, Plaza Athenée, and Georges V; London its Claridge's and Connaught; Vienna its Imperial, Bristol, and Sacher; and Lausanne its wonderful Beau Rivage Palace. Yet nowhere in the world was the phenomenon of the grand hotel more at home, thicker on the ground, than in the great Central European spa towns.

Wiesbaden, as the largest of the *Kaiserreich* Kurorte, with some eighty thousand guests in the 1883 season and ninety thousand ten years later, offered the most impressive array of luxury hotels in German spa land. Karlsbad and later Bad Gastein enjoyed this distinction among the Habsburg Empire Kurorte. Unfortunately, we can stop in at only a couple of these magnificent hostelries—and even then, we can merely cast a quick look around rather than settle in for a multiweek stay as a dedicated curist of old would have done.

Undoubtedly the crown jewel in Wiesbaden's luxury hotel collection was the Nassauer Hof (it still is). Requiring an entire decade (1897–1907) to fully complete, this splendid pile, located directly across the Wilhelmstrasse from the Kurhaus, had over three hundred rooms, all equipped with private baths. The hotel also boasted easily accessible elevators; airy social spaces and restaurants; a marble-clad ballroom; the "Orangerie" for daily concerts and five o'clock teas; an adjoining garage for automobiles; and a concert/travel ticket office.

But most impressively, the Nassauer Hof had its own subterranean thermal spring, which provided hot, medicinal water both for the private baths and two expansive in-house spas. In these spa zones a curist had a choice of Moorish baths, electric-light baths, blue-light treatments, alternating current baths, steam baths, cold-water baths, suction and hot-air treatments, and vibration and pneumatic massage. Those in need of industrial-strength enemas had access to a contraption looking similar to an electric chair, bolted to the floor, which could pump a dozen liters of water through the colon in under two minutes. There was also a health club/gymnasium complex where, "under strict medical supervision," a guest could undergo "electro-shock therapy." (In 1903, when the facility was still under construction, Kaiser Wilhelm II and Czar Nicholas II had a brief tête-a-tête at the Nassauer Hof. Neither potentate seems to have availed himself of the electroshock treatment, forgoing thereby a possible life—and history—changing experience.)

Early on, in the Nassauer Hof's mirror-clad main dining room, most guests ate table d'hôte—that is, at assigned places around large tables with other hotel guests, as on an ocean liner. This arrangement could be enjoyable or trying, depending on the company. Invariably, the meal times amounted to exacting sizing-up exercises, with diners pressing each other over family backgrounds, employment, cultural preferences, and other crucial information. Like the seating arrangements, menus for the multicourse meals came down from on high, in this case from the head chef, who was absolute master of his universe. Until the post–World War II era, when Kurort hotel chefs finally began to realize that an endless parade of heavy dishes may not have been the best thing for ailing, overweight guests and accordingly phased out the table d'hôte, curists who ate regularly at the Nassauer Hof and other grand spa hotels probably lopped years off their lives. On the other hand, these guests may not have been aware that they were shortening life spans they had come to the spas to prolong; and in any event, it's entirely possible that their many hours of trencherman bliss were worth those few lost years.

Habsburg Austria's best answer to hospitality meccas like Germany's Nassauer Hof was the Grand Hotel d'Europe in Bad Gastein. Opened two years after the Nassauer Hof, this ten-story pomposity stood (and still stands, though no longer as a hotel) on a rocky site overlooking the deep gorge that runs through Gastein. Construction at this spectacular location was not easy nor very safe: clearing space for the foundations required extensive dynamite blasting, shocks from which blew out the windows of neighboring hotels, much discomforting the guests. When it opened on May 29, 1909, the Grand Hotel d'Europe justifiably touted itself as the most modern hostelry in Austria-Hungary (and could with equal justice have expanded this claim to include the entire world). Every one of its 148 rooms had a private bath with hot and cold running water, electric lighting, and a telephone—this last feature a true sensation.

The public men's room off the lobby featured urinals with little mirrors strategically placed on the bottom, allowing especially stout gentlemen to admire their equipment—not to mention avoid peeing on their shoes. The building also had central steam heating and electric-powered elevators. This being a cure hotel, there were fourteen in-house thermal bath cabins whose waters were piped in from Gastein's famous high-radon-content thermal springs.

Fittingly, the Grand Hotel d'Europe's first officially registered guest was a retired k. und k. Field Marshal, Seine Exzellenz Herr Emanuel Edder von Rehberger. This august personage was followed by legions more of his ilk—so many that the hotel's *Herrensalon* came to resemble an outpost of the imperial court in Vienna. Quickly enough, though, the hotel became "internationalized" with an influx of blue bloods from all over Europe.

Yet it was not just the usual clapped-out Euro–blue bloods who turned up at this fabulous hostelry. The hotel's cutting-edge modernity made it especially attractive to industrial and banking magnates from America. Railroader E. H. Harriman, a sometime curist at Homburg, switched to Gastein in 1909 in a desperate last-ditch effort to fend off metastatic cancer. For a five-week cure visit to Gastein that summer, Harriman booked twenty-two rooms in the Grand Hotel d'Europe for himself, his wife, and a large retinue of servants, aides, and pets. (The cure clearly did not have much effect on Harriman's cancer: he died on September 9, 1909.) Intriguingly, the guest list two years later included Dr. Heinrich Ernst Göring, an upstanding German diplomat. Dr. Göring's more famous son Hermann never managed to stay in the Grand Hotel d'Europe, but his hated rival Joseph Goebbels certainly did, along with many other top Nazis at a time when Gastein's waters ran among the "brownest" of all the Kurorte in the expanded German Reich (more on this later).

While grand hotels added immensely to the prestige and appeal of all the major Central European Kurorte, they alone could not have kept the visiting curists happily entertained, especially when a growing proportion of those visitors could not afford them in the first place, and even those who could naturally wanted additional diversions outside their gilded quarters.

Going to watch "the sport of kings"—horse racing—provided one such escape. Baden-Baden happened to have a thoroughbred racetrack at nearby Iffezheim, founded by Édouard Bénazet in 1858. Expansions and refinements over the years made Iffezheim one of the Continent's finest facilities for this sport. Structural improvements to the complex as well as prize purses were financed largely from gambling proceeds at Bénazet's money-spinning Conversation House. When the casino closed in 1872, it seemed for a moment that Iffezheim might have to close down, too, but a group of wealthy horse-loving aristocrats prevented that from happening by placing the track under the aegis of their newly founded International Club, which sponsored the races from then on. (Apart from the passion of its sponsors, what kept Iffezheim viable was the fact that racetrack betting, as opposed to casino gambling, was not prohibited by the Reich government.) As in Baden-Baden, visitors to Wiesbaden had easy access to a good thoroughbred track at Erbenheim, some six kilometers away. Here, too, wealthy patrons stepped in to keep the facility afloat after the local casino closed.

Horse racing, of course, had been around since antiquity, but motor-car racing, and motoring in general, represented a hugely exciting new divertissement for spa guests at the turn of the century. A pioneering figure here was the American expatriate writer Edith Wharton, who undertook thrilling "motor-flights" around France in a luxurious Panhard-Levassor in 1905–1907. Due to occasional bouts of ill health, Wharton sometimes chose spas like Aix-les-Bains as pit stops during her tours. Yet it was in the spas of Central Europe, not France, where motoring became truly fashionable. Baden-Baden, not surprisingly, was on the inside track here, sponsoring a "test run" for automobiles from Mannheim to the spa town starting in the early 1890s. (Ever after, Baden-Baden has had a love affair with autos, or at least with extremely valuable antique ones, hosting popular "old timers' reunions" every summer. At these occasions today, there's always a toss-up between the cars and the car admirers as to antiquity of vintage.)

By the turn of the century, some of the wealthiest cure guests were motoring down to the spas in their own luxury Maybachs, Bugattis, Daimlers, Hispano-Suizas, and Panhards. Once having driven *to* the spas, these motoring enthusiasts naturally wanted to drive around *in* them, and here the darker side of the motoring craze immediately became manifest. Some drivers resembled Mr. Toad in *The Wind in the Willows*: they were every bit as incompetent as passionate. Even the competent drivers disturbed the peace with their extraordinarily noisy and smelly progress through town and the tendency to raise dust storms wherever they went. Steering mechanisms being what they were on these early autos, even practiced drivers often ran into or over other cars, cows, horses, trees, and fences—along with pedestrians and their little toy dogs. A collision between an automobile and a horse at Marienbad's Kreuzbrunnen in 1908 resulted, in addition to one dead horse, a one-year prohibition on auto traffic around the Kreuzbrunnen. Given what was soon to transpire along the once-peaceable lanes of Marienbad and other spa towns, one can only regret the brevity of that early auto-traffic suspension.

Soon the machine-generated noise around spa land occurred not just on the ground but also up in the air. Not long after Kaiser Wilhelm II sponsored a zeppelin parade over Bad Homburg, Baden-Baden established a zeppelin port down the road at Oos. (Tellingly, one of that spa's early promotional posters shows a big, fat zeppelin floating placidly over the town.) Zeppelins had very noisy engines and were susceptible to crashes because of their extreme vulnerability to the elements. No question about it, these were fascinating machines, a wonder to fly in and to behold from the ground, but you never knew when they might come crashing down—and, as one authority on zeppelins has noted, for "sheer terror," nothing could beat the crash of a zeppelin.

By the early twentieth century, the skies over Central Europe, especially Germany, were dotted here and there with fixed-wing aircraft as well as blimps and dirigibles. As historian Peter Fritzsche tells us in *A Nation of Fliers*, early twentieth-century Germany embarked on a perilous romance with aviation. Primitive airstrips sprouted up all over the place, and adventuresome young men (and a few young women) took to the skies in brittle wood and canvas contraptions. The inevitable crashes these pioneers experienced were perhaps not as spectacular as airship dives, but there were a lot more of them given the craze for birdlike flight in the Belle Époque. Because the zeppelin port near Baden-Baden also had facilities for fixed-wing aircraft, that Kurort witnessed its full share of crashes, one of them just missing the Friedrichsbad. As with other facets of the man-machine romance in this relatively innocent era, the one with aircraft would lose some of its luster during World

War I as civilians got their first taste of aerial bombardment. However, one imagines that for some of the elderly, less-than-forward-looking spa visitors, a diminution of enthusiasm for these modern machines might have begun rather earlier.

The most popular diversions at the Central European spas were firmly rooted to the ground and as old fashioned as they were up to date: exercise and sport. Walking had long been part of the cure regimen at Baden-Baden; indeed, spa doctors there had pioneered serious walking as a healthful, stress-reducing activity. But in the late nineteenth century, *all* the grand spas got caught up in, and helped to further, an exercise and sport craze that went well beyond mere walking (or, for that matter, horseback riding). Across Europe and North America people threw off their sedentary ways and began, with varying degrees of enthusiasm, to hike long distances, climb mountains, swim in seas and lakes, ride bicycles, do gymnastics, and play golf, tennis, soccer, and other competitive sports.

Soccer was by nature communal, but in fact, the whole exercise craze was highly organized, with hiking clubs, mountaineering clubs, shooting clubs, archery clubs, gymnastic clubs, swimming clubs, and bicycle clubs sprouting up all over the place. For sports fanatics with the desire and ability to transcend duffer status, there was a plethora of new high-level competitions, most notably the modern Olympic Games, inaugurated in 1896, and the Tour de France (whose early riders set the tone for later competitors by using performance-enhancing drugs like strychnine; some competitors also dropped tire-bursting tacks as they rode, a tactic that fortunately passed out of fashion).

It is not surprising that the Central European spas should have been in the thick of all this activity. As always, they attracted the healthy as well as the hoping-to-be-healthy, and many of these folks were also reasonably wealthy and highly mobile: the jet-setters of their era. Come the sad day when curists could no longer play roulette, why not play at something else?

Bad Homburg, as I mentioned earlier, boasted Continental Europe's first tennis courts and golf links. (These Homburg tennis courts, which charged a small usage fee, racked up so much money for the newly instituted Cure Administration that the first *Kurdirektor*, an amiable chap named Alexander Schultz-Leitershofen, could for years skim money off the top for himself. Eventually he got caught and would have gone to jail had not fellow Freemasons in the tennis club intervened with the authorities on his behalf.) Baden-Baden also experimented briefly with a golf facility in the Lichtentaler Allee, but this tree-lined area proved too constricted for a decent game, and strolling curists made a fuss over being beaned by low-flying balls. Eventually the course had to be moved out of town, where an expanded version of it can be found today.

Also on the outskirts of Baden-Baden was a new health institute, the Naturheilanstalt Lichtental, where "patients" played sports in the nude or near-nude. Playing games naked was nothing new—the ancient Olympians had done that—but what the ancients lacked and the Naturheilanstalt Lichtental proudly possessed was an elaborate "scientific" theory extolling the health benefits of full-body exposure to fresh air and sunlight.

Meanwhile, Baden-Baden's archrival, Wiesbaden, was populous enough to offer *all* the popular new sports in fancy facilities. In addition to lawn-tennis courts and an eighteen-hole golf course, Wiesbaden had rifle and pistol shooting ranges, an archery range, a fencing facility, two splendid swimming clubs on the banks of the Rhine, a hot-air balloon launching site, and one of Germany's first football clubs, *Weißes Rössl*, founded in 1889.

As for the Bohemian spas, their lack of a need to fill a gap created by a sudden loss of casino gambling did not prevent them from plunging pell-mell into the new sporting craze. Marienbad, for example, boasted Austria-Hungary's first tennis court, established in 1883 in the gardens of the misnamed Hotel Casino (there was never a real casino there) by the hotel owner's son. This innovation took some doing. All the equipment had to be ordered from England, and the first shipment of racquets eventually made its way through Austrian customs only because puzzled officials at the *Zollamt* decided that the strange-looking paddles must be some kind of musical instrument. Once in place, the new court was a huge success, bringing in six hundred gulden in its first year of operation, one thousand in its next. Marienbad's Hotel Casino accordingly became the venue for Austria's first tennis tournament, presided over by—whom else?—Bertie, the Prince of Wales.

Sport-loving Marienbad curists did not have to restrict themselves to tennis: by the beginning of the century, the town had its own velodrome, shooting range, trotting-horse course, riding stables, outdoor swimming pool, multipurpose stadium, and a large gymnasium operated by the German Gymnastics Association. It also had a magnificent new golf course, inaugurated by the unavoidable Bertie. (These days, a five-kilometer wooded trail leading from the town center to the golf links bears the name "King Edward Path," but it is hard to imagine Bertie himself having walked the entire distance.)

Not every spa patron wanted to pound a tennis ball, ride a bike, walk a golf course, sweat up a storm in a gym, or even shoot a target pistol. Thus, the long-established high-cultural divertissements continued to have a firm place at the grand spas; indeed, the performing arts achieved even greater importance at the major Kurorte once gambling was no longer an option.

One can see this especially in Wiesbaden, where at the urging of Kaiser Wilhelm II, a frequent cure-guest there, a splendid new Royal Court Theater opened its doors in 1894. Located on the Warmer Damm opposite the Kurhaus, the theater had 1,300 seats and a special *Kaiserloge* for His Imperial Majesty. Wilhelm II used the loge some one hundred times during his thirty-year reign—a source of much pride to the kaiser's local following but a curse for those who would have preferred a more adventurous repertoire. Because the kaiser despised everything modern in the arts, drama included, the new court theater offered up nothing but the most conventional fare. Heinrich Ibsen once cured at Wiesbaden, but none of his works made it into the court theater's repertoire on Willy's censorious watch.

Wilhelm's writ did not extend to Marienbad, which in Central Europe pioneered that most modern of art forms: cinema. In Austria, as in Germany, "moving pictures" moved in more ways than one: presenters transported their wares, along with the bulky equipment necessary to show them, from town to town, rather like a traveling circus. Starting in 1906, an entrepreneur named Georg Eckert operated a fourteen-wagon cinema-circus in Bohemia that included all the major spas on its itinerary. In 1910, tired of pulling his train from stop to stop, Eckert set up a permanent "Kino" in Marienbad, where he had found his most enthusiastic audiences. His initial 250-seat facility was such a success that he built a much bigger one in 1914. (Despite the ensuing wars, sociopolitical chaos, and constantly changing cinema technology, Eckert's Kino soldiered on through the years, albeit under varying managements and with repeated renovations. Now called the Slavia, it still stands on its original location just off the Hlavní třída, Marienbad's main avenue.)

Not every turn-of-the-century grand spa had a permanent cinema, but all of them had luxury shopping—more of it in these salad days than ever before. The fin de siècle/Belle Époque was the signature era not only of grand hotels but of grand department stores, or *Warenhäuser* as the Germans called them. It was thoroughly fitting that the inauguration of the department store coincided with the revival of the Olympic Games, since many of the customers who descended into these gilded commercial arenas seemed to regard shopping as an Olympic sport, aggressively elbowing each other aside in scrums around the cosmetics counter.

Baden-Baden had boasted a luxury shopping scene in its early days as a destination spa; that commercial culture continued to develop apace as the town grew, but store owners could not compete with gambling as a source of tax revenue for the state and municipality. As a consequence, there was little pressure to modernize the local emporia, and some of them became downright dowdy over time. This was especially true of a collection of wooden stalls arrayed directly in front of the Conversation House; initially meant to be provisional, they remained in place year after year, selling everything from comestibles to clothing. As soon as Baden-Baden's casino closed, however, orders came down from the new municipal Cure Administration to replace the sheds with permanent structures housing fine shops capable of pulling in the kind of money formerly dropped at the roulette tables.

Yet it was not Baden-Baden but Wiesbaden that brought shopping to its apogee as an art form (and athletic event) in the decades before World War I. By the 1880s, Wiesbaden promoters were proudly making the claim that London and Paris had nothing on their town when it came to high-end shopping: Whether the purchases involved jewelry, watches, artwork, clothing, cosmetics, or cigars, Wiesbaden provided only the very best. For a time, most of this high-end shopping still could be found in small specialty shops, but in the first decade of the new century Wiesbaden added two spectacular department stores, both located in the Old Town, to its commercial infrastructure.

Significantly, one of these new emporia was Jewish owned, as were many of the *Warenhäuser* going up in the larger cities across Central

Europe. As it happened, Seligmann Blumenthal, the complex's owner, had launched his commercial career in Wiesbaden with a small notions shop some twenty-five years earlier, but his deep roots in the town did not prevent him from being attacked as a rapacious interloper bent on pushing smaller "German" shops out of business. An editorial in the local newspaper sought to assuage the populist anger by arguing that new *Warenhäuser* like Blumenthal's were "legitimate projects of modern urban commerce," which would no more supplant small and medium-sized businesses than "the locomotive and automobile had eliminated [horse-drawn] carriages and push-carts." In fact, these latter relics of an earlier age *were* being phased out, just as some of Wiesbaden's smaller shops were being squeezed out by the *Warenhäuser*—the "big box stores" of their day. Like so many innovations in this tumultuous time, the modernization of shopping generated its fair share of discontent.

Medicalization: "It's Not Just about the Waters Anymore!"

To the grand Central European spas caught up in the promises and perils of modernization, far-reaching changes in medical science and health care during the waning nineteenth century seemed to level a major blow, if not a coup de grâce, to their age-old mission as primary ports of call for the sick and injured. After all, in the realm of healing, spas had profited for centuries from a lack of appealing or useful alternatives. But what if conventional medicine could actually *cure*? What if city hospitals and clinics, instead of being "anterooms to the graveyard," became way stations to wellness and longevity? In the longer run, ongoing breakthroughs in biological and medical science would indeed pull the rug out from under the spas' long-proclaimed status as cure-all centers for serious disease. Yet in the half-century before World War I, the grand spas' apogee, new challenges on the conventional medical front actually *helped* the Kurorte to thrive because they spurred a renewed and enhanced focus on healing, an effort that claimed to make the spas every bit as "scientific" and up to date as any health institution in the world.

In 1882 Professor Robert Koch of the University of Berlin discovered the tubercle bacillus, thereby paving the way, finally, for truly effective treatment of tuberculosis (and, in the process, ultimately undercutting the popularity of Kurort inhaloriums and high-elevation air-cure sanatoria like Davos, the model for the sanatorium in Thomas Mann's *Magic Mountain*). Koch also isolated the waterborne bacillus responsible for cholera, a disease that had periodically wreaked havoc in the Kurorte. Spa doctors who rejected Koch's discovery of a waterborne killer-germ hoped vainly for reinforcement from Koch's bitter rival, Bavaria's Max Pettenkoffer, who rashly sought to discredit Koch's theory by ingesting a sample of cholera-infected water from the Berlin professor's lab; Pettenkoffer caught the bug and almost died. Over in France, Louis Pasteur was making his own contributions to the germ theory of disease through his pioneering work in bacteriology. Over time, preventative measures such as pasteurization and vaccination would turn out to be the best new medicine against old medicine—that is, against late-in-the-day surgical procedures for infectious diseases.

If surgical intervention *did* prove necessary to deal with diseases or injuries, better to have it done under optimally hygienic conditions, something that had never been the case until another great medical pioneer, England's Joseph Lister, applied Pasteur's ideas to his own field of surgery by insisting on a sterile operating environment. Lister admonished surgeons not only to *wash their hands* (a radical concept) but also to sterilize instruments and wounds with carbolic acid.

Like Koch's germ theory of disease, Lister's promotion of antisepsis encountered early resistance among his peers, especially in America. A tragic victim of this medical obscurantism was President James Garfield, who in 1881 succumbed not to the bullets fired into his chest by a deranged assassin but to a raging infection unleashed throughout his body by dirty-fingered doctors who had pooh-poohed the novel notions of Joseph Lister. By the turn of the century, however, most hospitals in the industrialized world were adopting Lister's methods, thereby turning these hitherto foul-smelling and disease-spreading institutions into (generally) safer places for medical treatment.

Another huge change came in the realm of pain management. The nineteenth century, especially its second half, brought a series of breakthroughs in mankind's age-old battle against pain, including the often overpowering pain attending medical operations. (Apropos operation-induced pain, one need only recall the mastectomy undergone by English novelist Frances Burney in 1811 with only wine as an anesthetic. Of this harrowing experience the poor woman wrote: "When the dreadful steel was plunged into the breast—cutting through veins, arteries, flesh, nerves—I needed no injunctions not to restrain my cries. I began a scream that lasted unintermittingly during the whole time of the incision—and I almost marvel that it rings not in my ears still!—so excruciating was the agony.") The premier painkiller of the later nineteenth century, opium, called "God's own medicine" by the great Sir William Osler because of its miracle-working natural properties, underwent various chemical refinements leading from morphium to heroin, which was initially thought to be nonaddictive and therefore widely prescribed. Another new "miracle" drug was cocaine, which young physicians like Sigmund Freud hailed as perfectly safe and beneficial in every way. Freud was so crazy about cocaine that he prescribed it liberally for pain and anxiety and even used it extensively himself as a confidence builder (not least for sex with his fiancée), exclaiming after his first dose, "There is nothing at all one need bother about!" Freud's view on this matter changed as first his patients and then he himself fell into severe addiction. Yet the obvious darker side to these new drugs should not obscure the fact that they constituted an important part of the larger revolution in medical science that was transforming the ways people looked at health care and their treatment options at times of illness or injury.

In Europe, especially Central Europe, the physicians and surgeons working at the major urban medical centers in the era of Koch, Pasteur, Lister, and Freud had undergone years of university study, practical training, and common licensing procedures. This in itself was something of a revolution. Taking Germany as an example, until the 1870s there had been no commonly accepted curriculum for medical education across the region. Among the German states there were widely differing classes of medical practitioners, the major distinction being between Ärzte (physicians) and Wundärzte (surgeons). In most German hospitals the medical personnel consisted primarily of the Wundärzte, who had little or no academic training. The social esteem of medical practitioners was accordingly quite low—certainly a far cry from the exalted status doctors would later come to enjoy.

The German physicians' transformation from glorified barbers to dignified men of science came about rapidly in the last decades of the nineteenth century, as the doctors underwent a self-generated process of professionalization. In 1873 German doctors established their own professional association, the Deutscher Ärztevereinsverband (German Medical Association—GMA), which pulled together a number of previously existing state and regional organizations. The GMA immediately set about creating uniform standards for physician training and licensing across the Reich. Borrowing from its American counterpart, the American Medical Association, the GMA drafted a code of medical ethics and behavioral norms designed less to protect the public than to promote a clear distinction between their own university-trained members and assorted paramedical practitioners like village herbalists, midwives, and chiropractors. Tellingly, the GMA's code included a rejection of advertising along with free or reduced-price treatments, the prescription of patent medicines, and (above all) any public criticism of other doctors' performances. The GMA also promised to discredit and eventually root out tenacious residues of what it derisively called *Kurpfuscherei* (quackery).

Did this campaign against quackery mean to include practitioners at the grand spas? Some spa doctors certainly thought so and were thrown on the defensive. But how, more precisely, did the major Kurorte and their medical staffs respond to the manifold challenges to their enterprise inherent in the dramatically altered conventional medical landscape?

Well, in the first instance, they sought to fight fire with fire. As the nineteenth century drew to a close, the larger Central European Kurorte increasingly opened their doors to private clinics providing cutting-edge conventional medical treatments and procedures. A pioneer in this domain was, once again, Baden-Baden, which sanctioned in 1892 the establishment of the Frey/Gilbert Klinik. Among this institution's specialties was radiology, that new medical science deploying the discovery of electromagnetic radiation (X-rays) by Germany's Wilhelm Röntgen. (The Frey/Gilbert Klinik, by the way, lives on today in Baden-Baden as the Dr. Franz Dengler Klinik für Innere Medizin und Orthopädie, a fabulously upscale enterprise offering both hydropathic treatments and the latest wrinkles in orthopedics, sports medicine, and internal medicine.) Another addition to Baden-Baden's health-care landscape was the privately owned Sanatorium Höhenblick, which specialized in rheumatism (it, too, continues to function, albeit now as a branch of Baden-Württemberg's State Institute for Respiratory Diseases). Needless to say, Baden-Baden's welcome mat for private clinics was quickly put out just as avidly by other major Kurorte across Germany and the Habsburg Empire.

Along with private clinics, municipal hospitals became an integral part of the medical infrastructure at the grand spas. Tellingly, though, like the municipal cemeteries, these forbidding institutions tended to be located well outside the core thermal-spring "cure districts" so as not to distract or discomfort ordinary spa guests.

Much as traditional cure-guests might have wished to avoid the local Krankenhäuser, not to mention the cemeteries, having full-service hospitals relatively close to hand made good sense because spa doctors were often the first to diagnose serious illnesses calling for hospitalization. Once so diagnosed, patients who had come to the Kurort for a hydropathic pick-me-up could simply be shifted from one part of town to another.

Increasingly, the doctors on call at the better spas in Central Europe were no slouches when it came to diagnosing all manner of diseases because they had been trained in the same newly rigorous fashion as their peers at university hospitals and major urban clinics. Both in Germany and the Habsburg Empire, laws introduced in the 1870s required all spas to operate under the control of university-trained physicians and according to "scientific" principles. Many of the younger spa physicians, in fact, divided their time between seasonal employment at the Kurorte and junior faculty positions at university hospitals in Vienna, Prague, or Berlin. Far from seeing their summer jobs as a larkish break from their "real" work, these ambitious young practitioners brought to the spas (in the words of one authority) "new therapies and applications from the big city, which often had nothing to do with the local mineral springs," thereby turning the spas "into large-scale laboratories for medical fashions of the day while introducing diverse innovations." The Kurorte were perfect for this lab function because unlike normal urban or even small-town spaces, they offered relatively closed environments where patients' diets and habits could be regularly monitored (if not always successfully controlled) by the spa physicians.

Not all the "scientific" spa doctors were young eager beavers working their way up the greasy pole of academic medicine. Josef Seegan, an early specialist in modern balneology and the author of an influential textbook titled *Handbuch der allgemeinen und speziellen Heilquellenlehre*, taught a regular course on hydrotherapy at the University of Vienna every winter semester for thirty years between 1854 and 1884. For much of that same period Seegan spent his summers in Karlsbad, where he maintained a busy medical practice situated off the Alte Wiese near the center of town. Along with hydrotherapy, Seegan was an acknowledged expert on metabolic diseases such as diabetes, which he insisted was treatable with Karlsbad waters whose exact chemical composition he had subjected to rigorous analysis. These waters' chief component, *Glaubersalz*, had in his view a significant and controllable influence on human metabolism. (Seegan also maintained that diabetes was a particularly *Jewish* disease, a contention that I'll take up later in my discussion of Jews at the Central European spas.)

Scientific modernization at the grand Kurorte was not confined to the primary thermal-spring facilities and/or associated hospitality and entertainment industries. While much of the new bath architecture was unabashedly historicist, spa towns avidly embraced the latest developments in urban design and hygiene, from municipal electric lighting and sewage systems through water purification facilities and the monitoring of foodstuffs for infectious diseases. The spa towns were also full of new gadgets for keeping track of things—itself a fin de siècle fetish (and one still very much with us today, of course). Writing of Marienbad—though this observation applies to other Kurorte as well—historian Mirjam Zadoff points to a plethora of innovations, including "Meteorological Pillars; hydrometers; informational booths relating the mineral contents of the local springs; scales for checking weight [especially important in kilo-conscious Marienbad]; countless clocks to facilitate timely movement from one medical treatment to another; and, last but not least, English-style water closets, urinals and toilets." (More recent German toilets would come equipped with little shelves, allowing one to inspect and measure production before flushing.)

All these modern innovations notwithstanding, the grand Kurorte did not escape disparaging put-downs from academic physicians and commentators who debunked these places as holdovers from a prescientific age—their "cures" a function of "superstition and wishful thinking." Such rude dismissals, threatening as they were to the very essence of the spas' medicalization project, thrust many a Kurort doctor into an openly combative posture. The spa physicians' feisty counteroffensive offers a revealing window into the Kurort practitioners' self-image at a crucial juncture in their institutions' historical development.

The Viennese physician Wilhelm Winternitz, often called (not least by himself) the father of scientific hydrotherapy, admitted that when he broke into this field in the early 1860s it was "frowned upon by orthodox medicine as unworthy." But Winternitz insisted that he and other like-minded practitioners had greatly refined their discipline over the years. Now, they were able to measurably demonstrate the precise effect of various medicinal waters on "the heart, blood vessels, and the circulation of blood through the skin, nervous system and lungs." Claiming that with cold-water treatments he could alter tension levels within the arteries and thereby affect blood circulation, Winternitz developed an array of "cooling apparatuses" such as "cool caps, heart hoses, rectum and vaginal coolers," along with the formidable "Psychrophor"—a "water-cooled catheter that helped tone the urinary tract." In addition to working at spas, Winternitz founded his own Wasserheilinstitut in the Vienna Woods in 1865 and in 1862 set up a hydrotherapy station in the newly opened Allgemeine Wiener Polyklinik.

Like Winternitz, Dr. Heinrich Will, a physician practicing in Bad Homburg in the 1880s and 1890s, admitted that there were all sorts of "scientific controversies" surrounding the medical effectiveness of mineral-water Quellen. He noted sadly that some contemporary critics were debunking the waters' health-giving properties as "improvable"—just "a raft of fantasies that [belonged] in the dustbins of superstition."

Such criticisms, attested Dr. Will, had increased notably in recent years (he was writing in 1880): "No era has done more than the present one, armed as it is with the latest scientific insights from physics and chemistry, to slice a merciless scalpel through many a pretty prejudice." But the very discoveries of modern science, Will went on to insist, had now supplied "a natural physical underpinning for various water-healing effects that previously had been attributed to the mystery of God." At the same time, Will cautioned that "we medical rationalists must not make the all-too-common error of pushing rationalism so far that it stops being rational" and "abandons age-old observations and experiences simply because at this moment in time their inner-workings remain hidden to us and unsusceptible to strict rationalistic interpretation." But above all, counseled Will, spa doctors must make absolutely clear to their patients that their water-cures were *not* some wonderful Lourdes-like divine gift requiring no effort on their part to carry out their doctors' orders and injunctions.

While Dr. Will conceded that some of the thermal waters' secrets might still remain hidden to science, a more typical posture among spa doctors was to proclaim that the waters' efficacy had been as thoroughly dissected and substantiated by chemical research as any other therapeutic resource. A Karlsbad "consulting physician" named J. Kraus published an exhaustive analysis of the local waters in 1880 that detailed the specific effects of particular aquatic components on various human organs and physical functions. With respect to "movements" in the gastrointestinal tract, for example, Kraus confidently postulated that within a short period after ingestion, the waters of Karlsbad "induce one or several fluid motions, which in common with the flatus, have a strong smell of sulphuretted hydrogen [presumably a good thing]. These excretions, especially at the beginning of the cure, are of a dark brown, sometimes green color, which is caused by the increased secretion of thick bile."

Several Kurort doctors advanced the argument that the fast-paced modern age, rife as it was with tension, anxiety, and stress, made protracted spa visits more necessary than ever—and more imperative for a broader class of curists. Writing in 1909, a Bad Nauheim doctor named Friedrich Hirsch could observe: "Whereas in earlier days the bathing-trip was a prerogative of the 'upper ten thousand' . . . today it is almost commonplace [for members of the professional classes] to devote several weeks each year to rehabilitation. Increased productivity demands in the workplace, testing the very limits of creative capacity and the nervous system, make a period of rest and recovery more mandatory than ever."

Not surprisingly, growing numbers of spa doctors made the psychological diseases of the modern era their specialty. In Germany, Wiesbaden emerged as crack-up central: *the* place to go for crises of the nerves and other emotional afflictions collectively called (in the parlance of the day) "neurasthenia." As one British visitor stated flatly in 1901: "Wiesbaden means relief to the victim of nerves." For Kurorte like Wiesbaden, a major advantage of nervous diseases was not only that they were ever more frequent but also that they were hard to discount or dispute on observable physical grounds (much like one of today's versions of neurasthenia:

chronic fatigue syndrome). Our British visitor to Wiesbaden noted wryly: "An attack of nerves is no improbable affliction even for the most robust-looking of individuals, and if you solemnly declare that you have it, not all the doctors in the world can prove the contrary. 'So Wiesbaden would be just the thing for me, Herr Doktor, nicht wahr?'" Another Englishman, this one making the rounds of the Bohemian spas in 1890, noted that at Karlsbad, Marienbad, and Franzensbad the doctors required their high-strung, hyperbusy patients to occupy their fevered minds with nothing but purposefully active care regimens. They must "refrain from every form of mental worry and from all thoughts of business"—a program of distraction-deprivation similar to the strict ban on smart phones and iPads at some wellness centers today.

And indeed it *was* probably the case that fin de siècle spa visits for the "neurasthenic" could be as trying as they were, say, for sufferers from gout. At least this is the impression one gets from a witty satire on this subject written by the French travel writer and novelist Octave Mirbeau in 1901. Entitled *Les Vingt et un Jours d'un neurasthénique*, this autobiographical novel chronicles the tribulations of a big-city intellectual at an unnamed spa in the Alps. Anticipating Woody Allen ("I'm at two with nature"), Georges Vasseur, the protagonist, whines on at great length about the *horrors of the outdoors*—all those towering mountains, murky lakes, and endless trees! Vasseur's fellow curists come from all over the world yet manage to be universally provincial, ugly, and fat. "Amidst all these ugly visages and sagging bellies, I hardly ever experienced the surprise of seeing a pretty face or thin frame!" cries Vasseur. (Much the same complaint can be made about some of the spas today.)

Yet Mirbeau was clearly an outlier when it came to his distaste for turn-of-the-century spas, alpine or otherwise. People, including big-city dwellers, not only flocked to the Kurorte in record numbers but also seem to have taken seriously the strict rules and regulations set down by the local doctors. Because these rules allowed only the most modest partaking in after-hours diversion, the medicalized spas were considerably more subdued and quiet during the evenings than had hitherto been the case. Curists still went to the opera and theater, but these institutions now shut their doors sharply at 9:00 p.m., allowing guests to be safely tucked into their beds shortly thereafter. In a novel set partly in Karlsbad, *Their Silver Wedding Journey* (1899), the American writer William Dean Howells makes nighttime at this "supreme type of a German health resort" sound like something only a librarian could love: "By nine o'clock everything is hushed; not a wheel is heard at that dead hour; the few feet shuffling stealthily through the *Alte Wiese* whisper a caution of silence to those issuing with a less guarded tread from the opera; the little bowers that overhang the stream are as dark and mute as the restaurants across the way which serve meals in them by day; the whole place is as forsaken as other cities at midnight."

Midnight at 9:00 p.m. might not seem like a recipe for success, but apparently it was. All the major Central European Kurorte not only expanded their patient bases but also substantially augmented their in-house staffs in this era. Spa doctors, beleaguered though some of them might have felt, were much in demand. Wiesbaden, that mecca for mental cases, boasted more doctors per capita than any other city in Germany; it also attracted so many retirees, many of them faithful spa-goers, that it became known as "Pensionopolis" (a distinction, by the way, that it shared with Baden-Baden). Without doubt, the spas' timely medicalization was an integral part of this success story. With this and other innovations, the grand old Central European spas revealed a capacity to adapt to new circumstances without completely turning themselves inside out. In the end, the captains of spa land seem successfully to have internalized a famous piece of wisdom expressed in Giuseppe di Lampedusa's great nineteenth-century novel, *Il Gattopardo* (*The Leopard*): "*Se vogliamo che tutto rimanga come é, bisogna che tutto cambi*" (If we want things to stay as they are, things will have to change).

A Jewish Space

A notable feature of the grand Central European spas in the late nineteenth and early twentieth centuries was a greatly expanded Jewish presence. A much higher percentage of the spas' clientele now hailed from the Jewish plutocracy and upper-middle classes; their medical staffs became heavily Jewish; their religious and hospitality infrastructures boasted (or were blighted by, depending on one's point of view) synagogues, kosher restaurants, and "Jewish" hotels and cafés; and their repertory of target diseases included complaints thought to be preponderantly Jewish, such as diabetes and neurasthenia.

The campaign to "medicalize" the grand spas was to a considerable degree a Jewish project, as was indeed that broader modernization of conventional medicine of which the innovations at the spas constituted an important part (both Seegan and Winternitz were Jewish). According to one medical historian, some 75 percent of the physicians who pursued new directions in internal medicine at the University of Vienna in the late nineteenth century were Jewish, and those from that group who chose to work summers at the Bohemian Kurorte were *all* Jewish.

Jewish physicians were almost as thick on the ground in the medical schools and Kurorte of the German Kaiserreich. At the turn of the century, some 50 percent of Jewish students studying in the Reich universities were pursuing medical degrees; many of these students focused on newer specialties like internal medicine, gynecology, psychiatry, and cosmetic surgery—fields in which the professorates were also heavily Jewish.

Echoing this development, the medical staffs at spas like Baden-Baden and Wiesbaden resembled outposts of the Neurology Department of Berlin University. By 1909, over 6 percent of the doctors in Baden-Baden were Jewish, compared to only 1.4 percent of the town's overall population. The reason for this situation is easily explained: facing entrenched opposition to their advancement in older, more established fields of study and in more traditional venues of employment, Jews sought opportunity on the new frontiers. Among those new frontiers, the recently medicalized grand spas of Central Europe were perhaps the most attractive of all.

Attractive, but not without challenges and frustrations—as a lengthy memoir by one of those fin de siècle Jewish spa doctors makes abundantly clear. Enoch Heinrich Kisch, the Marienbad physician who uncovered, and then promptly covered up, the typhus case in King Edward VII's hotel in 1904, was, along with Seegan and Winternitz, a pioneer of balneology who fought assiduously to get his field recognized as a bona fide scientific enterprise. But it was not easy. Kisch toiled *for thirty-seven years* as an untenured assistant professor (*Privatdozent*) at the University of Prague before finally, as a gray-haired senior citizen, getting promoted to associate professor (he never did make Ordinarius, or full professor). With respect to his career as a *Badearzt* in Marienbad, Kisch tells us that it was only after decades of hard work that he attained "professional and scientific respect." Initially he encountered resentment as an interloper, and his early successes as a researcher and clinician provoked no little envy among his older colleagues. What seems to have irritated the older gentlemen was the fact that Kisch and other highly trained newcomers were aggressively establishing new and demanding parameters for the profession of Badeartz. As a result of their influence, Kisch noted proudly, by the late nineteenth century a "conscientious" spa doctor had to stand "at the very peak of his science, and be familiar with all the latest accomplishments, research and viewpoints." Additionally, he had to have assiduously studied chemistry, physics, and geology and be a master of many foreign languages. Moreover, dealing as he did with often querulous patients who typically arrived with diagnoses from their family doctors and high expectations of immediate cures, the spa physician had to be particularly "sensitive" and "psychologically adroit" (in other words, had to possess what we would call today a winning bedside manner).

Was anti-Semitism among non-Jewish colleagues and the Gentile world in general another of those "challenges" faced by modernizing spa physicians like Enoch Kisch? Our memoirist, deeply assimilated and diplomatically cautious, said nothing directly about this issue, but a vague mention of "painful events and unhappy conditions" attending his professional career might well point in that direction.

After all, anti-Semitism *was* a reality of life for spa doctors across the Central European landscape—despite, and indeed in part because of—their higher numbers and significant accomplishments. Like their fellow medical specialists in major urban centers, Jewish spa physicians drew fire from various conservative circles for plunging medical care into the fragmented and highly compartmentalized confusion of modern life and for exploiting their fancy new expertise to make pots of money—offenses supposedly totally foreign to "German" (i.e., Gentile) doctors. "The German physician," proclaimed one right-wing newspaper, "is completely immune both to exaggerated specialization and to prevailing trends toward self-enrichment." Another anti-Semitic periodical, *Frei-Deutschland*, accused Jewish spa doctors of subjecting unsuspecting Gentile patients to their latest "scientific" experiments, including hypnosis and autosuggestion. Yet another knock against the Jewish spa doctors brought their patients into the smear: these overspecialized, hyperintellectual physicians were said to attract and to feed off anxiety-ridden, insomniac, big-city bookworms—in short, those "neurasthenic" whiners who were alleged to be "predominantly Jewish."

The oft-voiced canard that Jews were by nature prone to nervous diseases and other mental disorders undoubtedly overshot the mark (which is not to deny that Jews themselves often parroted this stereotype or that there were good reasons for Jews to be nervous). On the other hand, the equally ubiquitous complaint that the grand Central European spas were being "overrun" by Jews was true enough in the sense that from the 1870s on, Jewish patrons *did* constitute a significantly higher percentage of the clientele at the major Kurorte—especially but by no means exclusively those Kurorte relatively close to great Mitteleuropa metropolises with burgeoning Jewish populations like Berlin, Vienna, Budapest, Prague, and Warsaw. Although not based on any congenital disposition, this influx undoubtedly derived in part from Jews' concentration in large urban areas and their overrepresentation in modern occupational pursuits associated with high stress. As one contemporary Jewish commentator put the matter: "It must not be forgotten that Jews are often salespeople or academics and that they wear out their nervous systems in stressful jobs. Added to that is the fact that Jews are preeminently urbanites. For these reasons they frequent the spas more than others."

Among the major Central European Kurorte, Austria's Baden-bei-Wien became a kind of poster child for the so-called Jewified water-cure resort. Not only did this bucolic little town just south of Vienna become a favored summer haven for Viennese Jews, in the period between 1870 and 1938 it housed the third-largest Jewish *Gemeinde* (municipal community) in all of Austria.

Extremely wealthy Vienna-based Jewish families like the Ephrussis, Wittgensteins, Gallias, and Jellineks were frequent visitors to Baden-bei-Wien. The businessman Moriz Gallia, who maintained an enormous Renaissance-style palazzo in Vienna's Wohllebengasse, liked Baden so much that he built an imposing villa there in 1890. (This was the first purchase Moriz made upon acquiring great wealth as director of the Austrian Gas Glowing Light Company.) Gallia's neoclassical villa, with an external staircase flanked by two stone lions, was said to reflect "an appetite for conventional trappings of wealth and power" typical of the Central European Jewish plutocracy.

Emil Jellinek was another Viennese tycoon who spent a good part of his time in a Baden villa. Scion of Adolf Jellinek, the chief rabbi of Vienna, Emil Jellinek amassed a large fortune in insurance, stock trading, and the new automobile industry, this last enterprise bringing him a seat on the board of directors of the Daimler-Maybach Automobile Corporation. While working as a salesman and race-car driver for Daimler-Maybach on the French Riviera, Emil Jellinek promised the company a substantial order of cars if Daimler would design a sporty new auto line named after his ten-year-old daughter, Mercedes. Jellinek stipulated that the new auto had to be the most advanced thing on wheels. "I don't want a car for today, or tomorrow, it will have to be the car for the day after tomorrow," he exclaimed. Daimler's new thirty-five horsepower "Mercedes," introduced in 1901, proved to be just that.

But naming a new car after Mercedes was not the only way Jellinek reportedly sought to immortalize his daughter. As one of the sponsors of a decorative fountain called the Undinebrunnen in Baden-bei-Wien's Kurpark, Jellinek apparently asked the sculptor, Joseph Kassin, to model the face of the fountain's principal figure, the beautiful water nymph Undine, after Mercedes. According to the Undine myth, the nymph longs for a human soul, which she can acquire only through the faithful love of a mortal man. Alas, no sooner does she find a knightly human lover than her beau turns untrue, damning Undine to her soulless water world. Presumably Emil Jellinek did not have such a sad fate in mind for Mercedes, but he may have unwittingly cursed her: she went on to have two disastrous marriages, was forced to beg for food on the streets of Vienna at the end of World War I, abandoned her husband and children in the 1920s, and died of bone cancer, impoverished, at age thirty-nine. As far as we know, she never drove a Mercedes.

Baden-bei-Wien's Jewish clientele at the turn of the century did not consist exclusively, or even primarily, of palazzo-owning plutocrats like the Gallias and Jellineks. Profiting from a generalized rise in economic well-being among Central Europe's professional and commercial middle classes, prosperous bourgeois Jews from cities like Vienna made spa going an integral part of their annual routines. Such spa patrons belonged to the "ten or twenty thousand" Viennese Jewish families living "quiet and comfortable lives," as novelist Stefan Zweig writes in his endearing memoir, *The World of Yesterday*. For many of these folks, Baden-bei-Wien was *the* destination summer resort, their very own stomping ground.

"Destination" is used here in an almost literal sense, for bucolic Baden was the end of the line for a new interurban tram service, the Badener-Bahn, which carried many a Viennese curist from the Ringstrasse to the spa. Once there, middle-class Jewish visitors did not generally rub shoulders with the superrich Gallias or Jellineks, who, of course, sheltered in private villas. The bourgeois guests carved out their own spaces, patronizing a new crop of mostly Jewish cafés, food shops, restaurants, Gasthäuser, and hotels (the leading example of the latter being the Hotel Schey, which maintained an acceptably kosher kitchen). Observant Jews came together in a new synagogue (founded in 1873) in the Grabengasse, while more assimilated Jews went for Sabbath strolls and tended to avoid the kosher venues. Baden-bei-Wien, in other words, cannot be said to have been much of a "melting pot" or social leveler among Jewish patrons of varying income levels or degrees of faith—and even less a commingling arena for Jews and Gentiles. There was not yet much overt anti-Semitism at Baden in this era—that would have been frowned upon by the town fathers—but there was not much mixing among Jews and Gentiles either.

The same was true of the grand Bohemian Kurorte, Karlsbad and Marienbad, which, like Baden-bei-Wien, saw a dramatic growth in Jewish patronage in the late nineteenth century. Although Vienna was a feeder city for these spas, too, the majority of their Semitic clientele hailed from heavily Jewish neighborhoods in Prague, Budapest, and Warsaw—or even points farther east. Their variegated experiences in fin de siècle Bohemian spa land are imaginatively reconstructed in *Marienbad* (1982), a witty novel published originally in Yiddish by the Polish-Russian master Sholom Aleichem. This deliciously satiric novel consists of some three dozen letters, love notes, and telegrams recounting the intricate interplay between urban life and Kurort existence among nouveau-riche Jewish businessmen and their grasping, social-climbing wives. In one of the letters, a moderately wealthy Jewish businessman named Kurlander complains to a friend that his wife, Beltzi, has got it into her head that she *must* go immediately to Marienbad. "Why so suddenly to Marienbad? . . . She says she's not well and must go [to the spa]. . . . But confidentially, I'll tell you *I* understand what's behind Marienbad. If [the very rich] Madam Tchopnik goes to Marienbad, why shouldn't Madame Kurlander also go to Marienbad?" Another correspondent comments on the superiority of Marienbad over Karlsbad as a marriage market for "our kind of people." "Although I personally have never been to Marienbad, according to respected opinion Marienbad is a place for pleasure and luxurious living. Those who go there are the kind of people who do not feel in exactly perfect health or, quite the opposite, those who are in too good health and whose main purpose is nothing more than to trim off a few pounds like our friend Chaim Soroker, a person of sizable proportions, or the kind of people who find their satisfactions in simply looking on as others enjoy worldly pleasures. Accordingly, it is far easier to find a decent match there than in the other place."

As Mirjam Zadoff argues in her study of Jewish identity in the Bohemian spas, Jewish experiences in those places mirrored the manifold diversity of Jewish life outside the Kurorte. In fact, just as the hothouse atmosphere in nineteenth-century German spas tended to aggravate ideological rifts among Russian curists, prolonged stays at Karlsbad and Marienbad magnified differences among the Jews flocking to Bohemia. Pressed together in constricted spaces, Jews from differing socioeconomic backgrounds and ideological camps—people who back home could and did largely ignore one another—now could not avoid one another's company. Against this backdrop, various coteries closed ranks and showed their colors more aggressively: Zionists became more Zionist, socialists more socialist, observant Jews more observant, wealthier Jews more conspicuously wealthy. (The same tendency, by the way, would soon manifest itself among Jewish communities and other refugee groups thrown together in exile.)

In the major Bohemian spas at the turn of the century, the primary distinction among Jewish patrons was the huge gap between highly assimilated Jews from Western and Central Europe and so-called *Ostjuden* (Eastern Jews), hailing from Poland, Galicia, and Russia. The cultural divide between these two broad groupings was notable enough in metropolises like Berlin, Munich, and Vienna, but at Karlsbad and Marienbad it could take on, in Zadoff's words, "a grotesque dimension." Among the assimilated Western Jews, close proximity with long-bearded, caftan-wearing, and Yiddish-speaking Ostjuden triggered "a mixture of strangeness, confusion, and fascination." What generated confusion was not so much the shtetl garb—Western Jews had seen that often enough in the ghettos of Mitteleuropa—but the fact that these Eastern Jews were clearly *rich*, or at least rich enough to spend time at a costly spa.

Yet another disorienting factor had to do with context: it was quite odd to see caftan-clad Ostjuden disporting themselves against a backdrop of alpine grandeur, as opposed to their usual urban haunts. As one Jewish Marienbad patron from Munich put the matter: "In Marienbad . . . the rich Polish and Galician Jews exhibited a material opulence that was completely new to us. . . . For me their whole appearance and in part also their animated gesticulations simply seemed comical, especially when one encountered a procession of such long coats in the middle of the forest or on the promenade." Sigmund Münz, the Viennese reporter who followed Edward VII around Marienbad, was likewise struck by the sheer incongruity of Ostjuden at a grand spa: "Groups of Galician or Polish Russian Jews, among them many men with wasted, drawn faces, long beards, and side-curls, stood about [the fountains] in long *kaftans*, as if they had met for morning prayer. Their faces bore an expression of melancholy. They might have been standing beside the Wailing Wall of Solomon's Temple at Jerusalem, or by the waters of Babylon."

Meanwhile, some of the Gentile curists and commentators observing the influx of Jews into Central European spas were struck not so much by any social or cultural distinctions among these visitors but by the very existence of the influx, which they castigated as a *"Verjudung"* (Jewification) of semisacred territory. In 1900 the prominent Austrian Christian Social legislator and priest, Joseph Schleicher, lamented: "You can't spit without hitting a Jew. All the summer resorts, baths, and water-cure locales—everyplace is overrun by Jews." This sense of being under alien siege applied primarily to the established constituencies at smaller and less costly spas that were now being frequented in some cases by a poorer class of Jews, some of them Ostjuden who had found sanctuary in Central Europe courtesy of well endowed German-Jewish welfare organizations. Yet at the turn of the century, even venerable Bad Ems, known since the Franco-Prussian War for its heavily Prussian and strongly nationalist clientele, suddenly found its precincts "defiled" by Eastern Jews of the poorer sort (their visits presumably paid for by their wealthy sponsors). In 1904 that Kurort's Bath Commissioner complained in his annual report about "the socially unacceptable" appearance of raggedy Ostjuden at his establishment. He vilified these people as "a plague" and "bunch of scum" and urged that henceforth they be turned away.

An urge to bar the door to Jews—not just to poorer Ostjuden, but to *all* Jews—was starting to take hold among the smaller spas of Central Europe in the first decade or so before World War I. In 1903, the Berlin-based Verein zur Abwehr des Antisemitismus (Association for the Prevention of Anti-Semitism) could register with alarm that at the dawn of the new century Germany alone harbored some sixty Kurorte which had officially declared themselves off-limits to Jews—or "*judenrein*" (Jew-free) in the poisonous parlance of the day. Observed the Verein: "Whereas [Gentile] citizens planning a cure visit need consider only questions such as location and cost, Jewish citizens have to make sure that their haven of choice has not suddenly declared itself '*judenrein*.'" This ugly trend started, said the Verein, with the North Sea island spa of Borkum and then quickly expanded as aggressive anti-Semites promised local cure directors greater patronage if they would guarantee their premises to be free of Jews. Such promises of commercial gain typically turned out to be illusory, but once having gone down the *judenrein* garden path, it was hard to turn back. So far, conceded the Verein, only a small sampling of Germany's smaller, less prestigious Kurorte had taken this route, but if the anti-Semitic plague continued to advance, *all* the less costly spas would soon be affected, leaving only the large luxury resorts open to Jews. Of course, this would deprive less wealthy Jews of the all-important cure experience. This development was all the more lamentable, concluded the Verein, because if there was "any place in the world where political, social and religious distinctions should be put aside, it is the baths."

A decade later the situation seemed to have only gotten worse, at least in the view of the Verein zur Abwehr des Antisemitismus. Anti-Semites were now celebrating "orgies" of Jew hatred at the spas they controlled, contended the association. And by further reducing the number of spas where Jews could go, they were inadvertently creating a few spas which were essentially *all* Jewish—the very apotheosis of the "Jewified spa." Most of the grand luxury spas were still holding out as cosmopolitan refuges, but they also were under pressure from the racists, and one had to wonder, agonized the Verein, "when they too might fall prey to the increasing barbarism."

Taking the Waters with Marx/Twain

Conservative malcontents and racist ideologues were not the only observers of Central Europe's spa scene to find reasons for discontent as the grand Kurorte reached the apogee of their influence and popularity in the years between 1870 and 1914. Along with the legions of ordinary bourgeois and aristocratic spa patrons, many of that era's preeminent intellectual movers and shakers made pilgrimages to the Kurorte in hopes of finding a cure for what ailed them. Instead, to varying degrees, they often found reasons to be irritated or even distressed by their experiences at the spas.

In the summer of 1880, Friedrich Nietzsche spent a very unhappy two months in Marienbad. He was hoping, after a long stay in Venice, to find relief from his chronic migraines in the shady, higher altitudes of Bohemia. But as he wrote his mother soon after his arrival at the spa: "I had a very bad journey, looking for woods and mountains: *everything* was disappointing, or rather it was impossible for my eyes. . . . I shall not be able to bear it here for more than four weeks." In fact he stayed for an additional four weeks in Marienbad because he was simply too ill to get back on the road. In a despairing letter to a friend back in Venice (Peter Gast), he wailed that the journey had damaged his health, the local mountains seemed "pointless and nonsensical," and the thermal waters were aggravating his headaches. "Think carefully before leaving Venice. The people are so ugly here, and a steak costs 80 kreuzer. It is like being in an evil world." Nor was Nietzsche pleased to discover, as he informed his mother, that three-quarters of the Marienbad guests were Jewish. When some Polish tourists mistook him for a fellow Pole he was outraged, declaring himself to be Swiss. Finally, it hardly helped that he was frequently dreaming about Wagner, with whom he'd recently had a bitter falling out. As he wrote Gast: "How often I dream about [Wagner], and always in the spirit of our former intimacy. . . . All that is now over, and what use is it to know that in many respects he was in the wrong?" Nietzsche was aware that another of his cultural idols, Goethe, had loved Marienbad, but even the hovering ghost of the great poet did not prove inspirational. Upon leaving Marienbad, Nietzsche grumbled: "Certainly no one in this place has done as much thinking as Goethe did, and even he seems not to have let anything truly profound go through his head while he was here—same also for me."

Like Nietzsche, Sigmund Freud was put off by the high cost of *his* favorite spa, Bad Gastein—an expenditure he tried to justify by citing his pressing need for summer recuperation in the mountains following the nasty Viennese winters. (Freud would continue summering in Gastein despite the high prices.) On one occasion (in 1913), Freud varied his routine by going to Marienbad, but his brief stay there was a disaster. Not only did he find no cure for the gastrointestinal problems he had picked up on a recent visit to the United States, but the cold, wet weather pitched him into near terminal melancholia.

Freud's fellow Viennese, the writer (and sometime physician) Arthur Schnitzler, savored his occasional stays in Bad Ischl, where, like Gustav Mahler, he rode his bicycle all over the place—and also enjoyed invigorating trysts in the woods with lady riders. Yet Schnitzler was profoundly irritated by the local cycling club's racist credo that only those of "pure German blood" could manage to ride bikes. He also grew to detest the "vacuous health-babble" of his "lame-brained" fellow curists (a curse that is still very much evident in today's major spas). As for Karlsbad, Schnitzler found that grand spa overly pretentious; he preferred homey Marienbad, where the guests "were not so proud to be there as in Karlsbad."

Theodor Herzl, yet another Viennese Jew—and the founder of modern Zionism—had perhaps the most disagreeable spa experience of all. Long suffering from heart trouble, Herzl went to Franzensbad in May 1904 in the hope that a good long rest, completely free of stressful political work, would put him to rights. Because he arrived at the spa before the season properly got under way, he did indeed find plenty of quiet, and at first the total lack of action seemed restorative—"I suck on boredom like someone else on pleasure"—he graphically wrote. But soon the boredom became, well, boring, and he plunged back into his work with a vengeance, doctor's orders be damned. His heart be damned, too, for Herzl's health actually *worsened* at the spa, prompting him to break off his cure after only two and a half weeks instead of the prescribed six. Not long after his return to Vienna, he fell ill with pneumonia and died. Franzensbad may not have killed Herzl, but it cannot have done him much good.

Let me conclude this little parade of malcontents with Stefan Zweig, who as a child summered regularly with his family at Marienbad. Stefan's father, a wealthy textile merchant based in Vienna, went to Marienbad primarily to humor his wife, Ida, a sufferer of many maladies, real and imagined. While the elder Zweigs seem to have enjoyed their annual cures at the spa, which involved lengthy stays at the luxury Hotel Gütt, young Stefan was less enthusiastic because he was unable to join his parents at meals (the hotel dining room, like the main thermal baths, was off-limits to children). Stefan's less-than-happy memories of his childhood summers in Marienbad provided the fodder for his best known novella, *Brennendes Geheimnis* (*The Burning Secret*), in which a young lad on vacation at an unnamed spa discovers that a gentleman who had befriended him did so only to gain access to his beautiful mother, whom the faux friend seduces. That searing experience, though hardly putting Zweig off spas—he eventually became a regular at Baden-bei-Wien, Bad Ischl, and Bad Gastein—may have been a source for his apparent inability to enjoy a "normal" sex life as an adult. Although his stories deal frankly with sexual matters, he was deeply inhibited in his physical contact with women. His friend, playwright Carl Zuckmayer, recalled: "[Zweig] loved women, adored women, loved to talk about women, but 'in the flesh' . . . he tended to avoid them." In his later visits to grand spas, Zweig seems to have avoided women altogether, perhaps because he identified these places with archetypal sexual betrayal.

The Kurort complaints of our intellectual heavyweights from Nietzsche through Zweig are instructive, but a lack of extensive firsthand documentation of their visits makes them less useful to the chronicler of spa life than the experiences of two other big-name contemporary curists, Karl Marx and Samuel Clemens (a.k.a. Mark Twain). Following Marx/Twain on their peregrinations into Central European spa land is as good a way as any (and a lot more fun than most) to assess the "cure" experience for hyperobservant health pilgrims at this crowning moment in Kurort history.

Karl Marx made three successive trips to Karlsbad in the years 1874, 1875, and 1876; in 1877 he switched his cure custom to the small Rhineland spa of Bad Neuenahr. A grand spa like Karlsbad may be considered a rather unlikely destination for one of Europe's most famous enemies of the ruling classes. And indeed, for most of his adult life Marx had vowed to steer clear of such places, which he dismissed as degenerate playgrounds of the haute-bourgeoisie and aristocracy: opiates of the upper classes. As late as 1869 he rejected a suggestion that he repair to Karlsbad for his health: that spa, he huffed, was "boring and expensive" (a judgment based on no actual experience at that point).

Yet for all his fulminations against conspicuous consumption, and despite a life that nobly sacrificed material success on the altar of low-paying literary toil ("If only my Karl had *made* some capital instead of writing a book about it!" his mother once lamented), Marx harbored a secret love of luxury, especially luxury hotels (completely forgivable, in my view). Unlike some of today's middle-class and upper-middle-class Marxists who suck down to the working classes, trying to be "one with the people," Marx had as little to do with working-class people as possible, preferring the company of fellow bourgeois intellectuals. He especially enjoyed the company of his wealthy friend and benefactor, Friedrich Engels, courtesy of whose largesse he was able on occasion to indulge his taste for high living (it was "Fred" Engels who financed his trips to Karlsbad).

Marx had yet another character trait that made his excursions to Karlsbad less incongruous than they might appear at first glance: lifelong hypochondria, along with a corollary conviction that his ailments demanded only the very best medical treatment available. Moreover, practicing as he did a daily grind full of hard work and bad habits, it was not long before Marx suffered from some very real health problems to go along with his fanciful ones. By the early 1870s he had acquired the obligatory gout and bad liver, to which he added spells of dizziness, frequent headaches, insomnia, and painful carbuncles on his butt.

Nevertheless, Marx required one more factor in his life situation to warrant a major departure from routine like a trip to Karlsbad: a very sick daughter. In 1874, Karl's beloved nineteen-year-old daughter Eleanor ("Tussy"), long vulnerable to bouts of ill health, was refusing to eat and spitting up blood. For some time Karl's own doctor had been urging him to take an extended cure visit to Karlsbad, and now Tussy, too, seemed desperately in need of healing waters. There was nothing to be done but to head for the hills of Bohemia.

Marx and his daughter traveled by train from London to Karlsbad in summer 1874. By this stage in his tumultuous life, Marx was well established as a radical journalist and political activist; he had experienced numerous run-ins with the law over the years, resulting in forced exile to France, Belgium, and, most recently, London; he was certainly quite well known to police authorities all over Europe. In fact, while traveling to Karlsbad he complained to his wife, Jenny, that his name had "figured again JUST NOW in trials [of radicals] in Petersburg and Vienna" and that some "ridiculous RIOTS in Italy [had been] connected not only with the International . . . but directly with me."

This explains one of the more curious—and amusing—aspects of Marx's visit to the Bohemian spa: his decision to check into his hotel, the Kurhaus Germania, as "Charles Marx, Squire of London, and daughter." Registering this way meant spending more than necessary for his quarters, since "gentlemen" invariably paid a premium, yet Marx was prepared to go that extra mile to keep the police off his back. Nonetheless, if "Squire Charles" thought he was fooling anybody with this ridiculous *nom de voyage*, he was sorely mistaken.

The local police were onto Marx from the beginning and anxious to find some reason to send him packing back to London. But Marx was careful not to give them any cause. Whether out of fear of being rousted by the authorities or, more likely, genuine hope that his and Tussy's health problems might be alleviated by a completely focused cure regimen, devoid of political distractions, he and Eleanor (who shared his radical views) did nothing but concentrate on their cure. Karl wrote Engels at the start of their stay: "Dear Fred, . . . We are both living in strict accordance with the rules. We go to our respective springs at 6 every morning, where I have to drink seven glasses. Between each two glasses there has to be a break of 15 minutes during which one marches up and down. After the last glass, an hour's walk, and finally coffee. Another cold glass in the evening before bed." For Marx, Karlsbad was about carbuncles, not class war.

Intriguingly, one of Marx's fellow lodgers at the Germania was Ivan Turgenev. The two famous figures must have known of each other's presence there, but neither man mentions the other in his correspondence. (Marx may have wanted to avoid Turgenev because the Russian writer was close to the anarchist Michael Bakunin, whom he despised.) Yet Marx was no wallflower at Karlsbad. He and his daughter socialized regularly with other curists from the educated classes—mainly a bevy of German and Polish professors. He wrote Engels that "half the local medical faculty" had gathered around him and his daughter—"all very acceptable people for my present purpose when I have to think little and laugh often." Marx even made a new friend in the person of a Polish aristocrat named Count Plater.

As part of his "gentleman" guise, Squire Charles had taken care to dress so well that another guest, when asked to identify which figure was a count, Marx or Plater, guessed the former. Observing this blossoming friendship between Marx and Plater, a local journalist wrote fancifully that the "Chief of the [Socialist] International" was consorting with the "chief of the nihilists" (poor Plater!). By contrast, the resident police official charged with monitoring Marx's activities at Karlsbad felt obliged to report, no doubt with some disappointment, that his quarry was behaving as a model curist and engaging in no political activity whatsoever.

Marx's conscientiousness as a patient seems to have paid off. He firmly believed that his Karlsbad cure had done him a world of good. He reported to Engels that he had lost some weight and could feel an improvement in his liver. "I believe that I have finally achieved my purpose in Karlsbad, at least for a year."

That was the wonderful thing about spas: If the cure didn't work, you'd have to come back and try again; if it *did* work, you'd want to come back to keep the improvements going for another year. Marx's second and third cure visits to Karlsbad hewed to the pattern he set during his first stay, though in 1875 he went to the spa alone, without Tussy in tow.

What impressions and perceptions, collectively, did Marx take away from his three extended stays at this grand Bohemian spa? Interestingly enough, Marx's experience in Karlsbad brought out a dimension in his character and thinking that has generally been overlooked or downplayed in the reams of commentary written about him: a concern for the effects of industrialization on the natural environment, especially forests and rivers. Marx was at heart something of a naturalist; as a boy he had enjoyed walking in the hills overlooking the Mosel River near his birthplace in Trier, and as an exile in London he sought refuge from smoky Soho in the leafy expanses of Hampstead Heath. Acutely interested in all aspects of modern life, he was undoubtedly familiar with the early stirrings of the "conservation" movement in the United States and Europe—with John Muir's epic trek through the Sierra Nevada in the late 1860s, the creation of Yellowstone National Park in 1872, and the foundation of a flurry of *Naturschütz* (nature preservation) groups in Germany and Austria in the early 1870s. During his first stay in Karlsbad he rhapsodized to Engels about the "very beautiful surroundings here" and his wonderful walks over the wooded granite mountains. Yet he could not help adding that there "are no birds here," surmising that they were repelled by the sulfurous vapors of the thermal springs.

After his third visit to the region, Marx had become painfully aware that the environmental problems around Karlsbad went far beyond stinky springs and a lack of bird life. What he had once called "the pestilential breath of civilization" in Britain now seemed to be encroaching on relatively rural Bohemia. He took worried note of extensive logging and mining operations in the nearby Erzgebirge, which were deforesting the hills surrounding the spa and polluting the local rivers. As he wrote Engels in 1876: "The Tepl [River] looks as though it's almost completely drained. Deforestation has reduced it to a sorry state; at times of heavy rain (as in 1872) it floods everything, in hot years it disappears altogether." Although the air in Karlsbad was far better than in London (hardly a high standard), occasional smoke from coal-burning stoves and mining operations turned the atmosphere a "brownish-yellow color." When a lack of funds in 1877 forced Marx to transfer his now-annual spa pilgrimage from Karlsbad to Bad Neuenahr, he took consolation that "the air [in the Rhineland spa] is always admirable." (Had Marx miraculously fetched up in Western Bohemia a century later, when it belonged to the Soviet Empire's paradise of workers and farmers, he would have discovered that the disturbing environmental developments of his own day had mushroomed into full-scale ecological dystopia.)

During his stays in Karlsbad, Marx naturally kept a critical eye on the region's sociopolitical scene as well as on environmental matters. He could not have precisely timed the political destruction of the Habsburg Empire forty years hence, but he was quite prophetic about its ultimate fate. Having experienced at close hand the incompetence and corruption of *k. und k.* officialdom in Karlsbad, he wrote Engels: "The more one sees of Austrian conditions, the more one is convinced that this state is nearing its end."

Mark Twain may seem at first glance to have little in common with Karl Marx—the American writer was certainly no communist and had little patience with grand socioeconomic theorizing—yet Twain was in his own way as much a rebel as Marx. Over the course of his long career, he carried out a one-man rebellion against linguistic convention and the long-established imperative that American artists piously genuflect before the altar of European Culture. He was, in the words of one of his biographers, a pioneering "American Vandal" who swaggered about the European continent full of aggressive confidence, more than happy to give a good licking to any local fop "who dared assert a higher claim on history." In *Innocents Abroad*, his often farcical account of a journey he took to Europe and the Holy Land in 1867 with a group of American religious pilgrims, Twain became more contemptuous of things European the deeper he traveled into the Continent. What struck him in Paris was the squalor of the Faubourg St. Antoine, full of dirty children, "greasy, slovenly women," "filthy dens" selling third-hand clothing, and "little crooked streets [where] they will murder a man for seven dollars and dump his body in the Seine." (On a return trip to France ten years later, Twain was even more disgusted with the place, summing up his view of that nation's men-folk in one memorable line: "A Frenchman's home is where another man's wife is.") In *Innocents* he tells us that Italy's tobacco was unsmokeable; its towns crawled with fat priests who "looked like consummate famine breeders"; the baths in Milan had no soap; Italian women grew not just mustaches but *full beards*; Lake Como's waters were "dull compared with the wonderful transparence of Lake Tahoe"; and the Italian countryside, even more priest-ridden than the towns, constituted "the heart and home of priestcraft—of a happy, cheerful, contented ignorance, superstition, degradation, poverty, indolence, and everlasting uninspiring worthlessness." (Twain's take on the Middle East was even more disparaging: "Christ been once, will never come again.")

On the other hand, Twain's initial impression of Germany, which he saw for the first time during the same late-1870s European trip that occasioned his jaundiced quip about French males, was surprisingly positive (or perhaps not so surprising: Many Americans are impressed with Germany after having just visited France). "What a paradise this land is!" he rhapsodized in a letter to his friend William Dean Howells, remarking on the locals' "prosperity, contentment, clean clothes and good faces." He even liked Berlin, calling it "a German Chicago," which for him was a compliment. Yet this admiration for things German did not survive more extensive acquaintance with that country. It was not long before Twain was grousing about the omnipresent cuckoo clocks ("the most hateful things in the world"); the "eternal hotel fashion of noisy pets"; the yodeling ("Drat this stupid yodeling!"); the loudly clanging church bells ("I wish that church would burn down!"); Wagnerian opera ("*Lohengrin* gave me a headache"); and, above all, the "awful German language," rife with words so long they had a "perspective"—looking at them from front to end was like looking down "the receding lines of a railway track." (Twain was absolutely right: from its starting point one can barely see the end of *Donaudampfschiffahrtsgesellschaftskapitänsmützenabzeichen*, "Danube Steam Navigation Company Captain's Cap-badge," the German language's longest word.)

It was a visit to Baden-Baden that most decidedly put Twain off Germany. The writer had not gone to Germany to take the waters in Baden but to hunker down in some out-of-the-way place and do some serious writing. "I want to find a German village where nobody knows my name or speaks any English & shut myself up in a closet 2 miles from the hotel & work every day without interruption. . . ." he wrote his mother. But shortly after arriving in Germany his wife, Livy, who was traveling with him, became ill and wished for a cure-stay in famous Baden-Baden. To indulge her, but also because he himself had a touch of rheumatism in his joints, Twain decided to take the waters with her. In the end, the writer resolved not to tarry at the spa; he moved on after a little more than a week, leaving Livy behind to continue her cure on her own. Nonetheless, his encounter with Baden-Baden was lengthy enough for him to make some firm judgments. These he wrote down on the spot and then refined for later publication in another of his travel books, *A Tramp Abroad* (1879).

The section on Baden-Baden in *A Tramp* is one long catalogue of complaints—some of them, perhaps, inserted for humorous effect, but most of them undoubtedly heartfelt. The town was charming and pretty enough, he conceded, but the curists there were a very dull lot, walking up and down the Promenade, trying hard not to look bored yet failing in this. "It [the Promenade walk] seems like a rather aimless and stupid exercise." Of course, many of these people *did* have a "real purpose" for being there, he admitted: They were "racked with rheumatism" and were in Baden "to stew it out in the hot baths." Some of the curists also drank the hot medicinal waters with a pinch of imported Karlsbad salt—"a dose not to be forgotten right away." Twain was disquieted not only by the thermal waters' sulfurous taste but also by the slatternly fountain maid who served him his drink. She took forever to draw his water and then refused to give him a clear answer—an *American* answer—when he asked the price. "*Nach Belieben*" (what you wish), she said repeatedly, counting on his ignorance and liberality to pay too much. Eventually, sorely exasperated, Twain gave her a silver twenty-five-cent piece instead of the going price of a penny or tupence, adding sarcastically, "If it isn't enough, will you stoop sufficiently from your dignity to say so?" But instead of shriveling in shame, the woman ostentatiously *bit* his coin to check its genuineness and then waddled languidly back to her post. "She was the victor to the last, you see."

The fountain maid's manner and tactics were typical of Baden-Baden vendors in general, Twain discovered. "The shop keeper there swindles you if he can, and insults you whether he succeeds in swindling you or not." Same for the keepers of the baths. The "frowsy woman" selling tickets at the august Friedrichsbad not only "insulted [Twain] twice every day," but also "with rigid fidelity to her great trust," cheated him regularly. "Baden-Baden's splendid gamblers are gone, only her microscopic knaves remain," he concluded. On the other hand, Twain claimed that the baths themselves had helped clear away his rheumatism. "I fully believe I left my rheumatism in Baden-Baden. . . . I would have preferred to leave something that was catching, but it was not in my power." Yet it *was* in his power to get his revenge on the town with a devastating bit of advice for fellow American travelers to Europe: "See Naples and then die—but endeavor to die *before* you see Baden-Baden!"

Twain was indulging in poetic license when he claimed to have left his rheumatism in Baden-Baden; it turned out that he had no more left his affliction in the town than lost his heart to the place. Worse yet, over the next ten years, owing to relentless hard work and all the usual vices, he wore down his constitution to the point that a truly serious cure seemed in order. Livy, having ministered doggedly to her husband's every need, was worn out, too, and was suffering from severe heart strain. In 1890 her doctor suggested that both she and her husband would profit from a lengthy cure-stay at a European thermal-spring spa.

Of course, if thermal waters were all they needed, Twain and his wife could simply have moseyed up the road to Saratoga Springs, Gilded Age America's best answer to the grand spas of Europe. However, as a health destination, Europe had more appeal to the couple than any local spa for a reason that Americans these days might find astounding: it was significantly *cheaper* than the United States! This consideration was crucial to Twain because he had recently lost much of his fortune on ill-advised investments, including a publishing house that put out, apart from Grant's best-selling memoirs, mostly money-losing tomes; an unworkable typesetting machine; and a "miracle" health food called Plasmon that brought health only to the wallet of its maker. (As much as he discredited miracles from the heavens, Twain was a sucker for "miracle" products offered up by earthly hucksters.) Thus, for the sake of their physical and financial health, Mark and Livy decided there was nothing for it but to "*absquatulate*" (his wonderful word) to Europe for a good long spell.

Close to the beginning of a European stay that would end up lasting a full *nine years*, Twain and his wife stopped for five weeks at Aix-les-Bains for a thorough workup. The thoroughness of the treatments notwithstanding, Aix's waters could not heal Livy's heart condition, nor could they do much for Twain's rheumatic right arm, which unhappily was also his writing arm. Yet at least the stay at Aix provided fodder for a humorous put-down of French spas entitled "Aix—the Paradise of the Rheumatics."

From Aix it was on to a pilgrimage site of a different sort, Germany's Bayreuth, mecca for Wagner fans the world over. Bayreuth was Livy's choice—and as if to punish her Wagner-hating husband for pulling her out of Aix, she dragged him to *nineteen* performances of the master's work. This (for Twain) butt- and brain-numbing experience was grist for another piece of satirical invective: "At the Shrine of St. Wagner's."

Because Livy remained ill, and because Twain felt he deserved a relieving bit of quiet time after the Wagner ordeal, they moved directly from Bayreuth to Marienbad. Like his previous stops, Twain's visit to Marienbad yielded a humorous sketch, "Marienbad—A Health Factory." The humor here, however, proved somewhat gentle compared with most of his missives from Europe, especially those from Germany. No question about it, like so many Yankees (and British), the American Vandal preferred Austria to Germany.

The short jaunt from Bavarian Bayreuth to Bohemian Marienbad meant moving from one world to another, claimed Twain, "from the very old to the spick and span new; from an architecture totally without shapeliness or ornament to an architecture attractively equipped with both; from universal dismalness as to color to universal brightness and beauty as to tint; from a town which seems made up of prisons to a town which is made up of gracious and graceful mansions proper to the light of heart and crimeless." That these comparisons were gratuitous and heavy-handed only underscores Twain's disappointment with Deutschland (excepting Berlin, which he continued to admire). Other distinctions between Bavaria and Bohemia, rather more significant and less the product of jaundice, quickly caught Twain's eye: in Bohemia, military uniforms were "rare" (so rare that "we might have been in a republic"), and there were more Polish Hassidic Jews. About the latter Twain was quite approving, although his impression that such approval was widely shared in the region was undoubtedly too generous, at least with respect to the native ethnic Germans and Czechs: "Almost the only striking figure is the Polish Jew. He is very frequent. He is tall and of grave countenance and wears a coat that reaches to his ankle bones, and he has a little wee curl or two in front of each ear. He has a prosperous look, and seems to be as much respected as anybody."

In his sketch of Marienbad, Twain claims that he did not go to the famed spa to take the waters but merely to look around—implying that this pit stop was also primarily for Livy. However, very much like Hans Castorp in Thomas Mann's *Magic Mountain*, no sooner had the visitor arrived at the spa than old hands around the place began throwing out "hints" that he might be a bit gouty and liverish, "and pretty soon I was a good deal concerned about myself."

Thus—again like Hans Castorp on the Magic Mountain—Twain subjected himself dutifully to the daily routine of the gout-ridden curist at Marienbad: making the rounds of the fountains with a drinking glass hanging at his belt; slugging down the "dreadful water with the rest"; "tramping about the hills for an hour or so"; eating "only the food [he] didn't want"; and drinking at night "one glass of any kind of liquor [he had] a prejudice against." This routine was repeated day after day without moderation. "I don't see any advantage in this over having the gout," he ruefully concluded.

It is hard to believe that in reality Twain was anywhere near as dutiful a curist as he claimed to be in his essay (mostly for comic effect). More likely he was one of those "independent" and less-than-serious patients of whom spa doctors incessantly complained. Yet even supposing that he was not the model patient he said he was, he clearly went through enough of the numbing ritual to thoroughly dislike it—and indeed to deeply resent it. His ringing indictment of the hypercontrolling ideology behind the spa protocol comes across as quite heartfelt—and, I might add, quintessentially American:

> They make you drop everything that gives an interest to life. Their idea is to reverse your whole system of existence and make a regenerating revolution. . . . They spare nothing, they spare nobody. . . . They say they can cure any ailment, and they do seem to do it; but why should a patient come all the way here? Why shouldn't he do these things at home and save the money? No disease would stay with a person who treated it like that.

Twain claims in "Marienbad" that he personally emerged from his treatment at the spa in better shape, sort of. "I am said to be all right now, and free from disease, but this does not surprise me. What I have been through in the two weeks would free a person of pretty much everything in him that wasn't nailed down there. . . . And if I don't say but that I feel well enough, I feel better than I would if I was dead, I reckon."

The sad fact is that the Marienbad "cure" had no significant effect on Twain's health, which continued to deteriorate. But it does seem to have put him off this particular Bohemian "health factory." Although he occasionally visited other spas during the almost twenty years remaining of his life, he never returned to Marienbad.

I would be remiss in leaving Twain to his fate and eventual return to America without contrasting his impression of a widespread "respect" for Polish Hassidic Jews in Marienbad with his observation on the status of *all* Jews in Vienna some years later. Revealingly enough, when the writer visited Vienna in 1898, he came under sharp attack from the local right-wing press, which assumed that anyone with a first name like "Samuel" must be a Jew. He got his revenge with a humorous but biting account of his visit to the Austrian Parliament, which at the time was debating a Socialist initiative to allow the use of Czech as one of the officially sanctioned languages of the Austro-Hungarian bureaucracy (only German and Hungarian were then permitted). But all the participants in this linguistic debate understood that the real matter at issue here was tolerance for ethnic minorities in the empire, including that most beleaguered of minorities, the Jews. Accordingly, German nationalists attacked the proposed language reform in a hail of anti-Semitic slurs. Fistfights broke out inside the parliament building and then spread to the streets outside, engulfing the elegant Ringstrasse in bloody rioting. In his punchy piece about the parliamentary dustup, Twain noted that the debaters were all "earnest and sincere men"—and that most of them "hated the Jews." Regarding the street fighting, he observed a little later in a letter that "in some cases the Germans [were] the rioters, in others the Czechs—and in all cases the Jew had to roast, no matter which side he was on."

Clearly, while the grand spas of Germany and Austria might still be *relatively* tolerant and tranquil at this juncture, the great cities of Central Europe were not. Although Mark Twain could not have known it, what he was witnessing in Vienna in 1898 was a small-scale rehearsal for the horrific violence and mass killing that would engulf the bloody century about to begin.

CHAPTER SEVEN

Trouble in Paradise

Spa-Town Life from World War I to the Triumph of Hitler

The trouble with apogees is that it's all downhill from there, though not necessarily a straight drop. Having reached their peak of influence and appeal in the half-century before World War I, Central Europe's grand spas went into sharp decline—a decline from which they would never entirely recover. The downturn was by no means uniform or universal: there would be plenty of signs of vitality, especially in the cultural realm, and at times economically. (This was true not only of the Central European spas. Belgium's Spa enjoyed a brief resurgence in 1932 when it hosted the International Pageant of Pulchritude, popularly known as the Miss Universe Contest.) Moreover, the major spa towns remained "slices of paradise" (in the words of one curist) for many residents and visitors alike. Yet there was definitely trouble in paradise throughout the period between World War I and the beginning of the Third Reich. Growing economic malaise, insularity, xenophobia, and racism foreshadowed even greater problems to come under the Nazis.

The Grand Spas at War

Grand spas provided stages both for the beginning and for the end of World War I: Bad Ischl owned this dubious distinction for the launching of hostilities in the Balkans, while Baden-bei-Wien and Belgium's Spa shared it for the Great War's end. This rather prominent role in one of the most terrible human tragedies of modern times was not the fault of the spas. As always, the spa towns were just pleasant nests in which to do occasional bad business—rather like Somerset Maugham's Monaco: "a sunny place for shady people." Had world leaders taken seriously the bath towns' ethos of internationalism and peaceful coexistence—of putting profits before national and ethnic rivalries—the war might never have come about at all.

On the morning of June 28, 1914, Austrian Crown Prince Franz Ferdinand should by all rights have been off hunting either at his own shooting lodge, Schloss Blühnbach near Salzburg, or at the Kaiser Villa in Bad Ischl, where, like his uncle Franz Josef, he loved to decimate the local game population.* Instead, he was sitting in the back seat of an open-top Graef and Stift coupé as the big car, part of a six-automobile motorcade, rolled majestically down the Appel Quay in Sarajevo. Next to him in the car sat his pregnant wife, Sophie, a Czech-born lady whose relatively low dynastic status had mandated that her marriage to Franz Ferdinand be morganatic.

The crown prince had been dispatched to the Bosnian capital by his uncle to preside over military maneuvers designed to show the neighboring Serbs, who considered Bosnia part of *their* patrimony, that Vienna remained firmly in charge of a region it had annexed some six years earlier. The date chosen for the archduke's parade through Sarajevo constituted an additional poke in Serbian eyes: June 28, 1914, was the 525th anniversary of the Field of Blackbirds Battle in Kosovo, where the Ottoman Turks had crushed the Serbs and put an end to their own Balkan empire. In Serbian eyes, the blackbirds were still cawing for redemption from this humiliation.

Six operatives affiliated with the Black Hand, a secretive, hypernationalist hit squad run from Belgrade, stationed themselves along the Appel Quay, Sarajevo's main avenue, waiting for Franz Ferdinand to roll by. Each terrorist carried a small bomb to throw at the archduke, as well as poison to swallow in case of failure. Four of the terrorists might

---

*Franz Ferdinand was every bit as avid a hunter as his uncle. He is said to have killed a total of 274, 889 wild animals during his life, taking some of the larger creatures on his world travels. His greatest sorrow, apart from getting bagged himself, was to have missed downing a grizzly bear during a trip to the American West in 1882. Moreover, the cowboys made fun of him.

just as well have swallowed their poison in advance: paralyzed with fear or indecision, they didn't even throw their bombs.

The only conspirator who actually launched his grenade managed to miss the archduke's car and hit another auto, wounding two soldiers riding in it. In shame, this fellow duly swallowed his poison and jumped off a bridge, but the poison was not strong enough to kill him, and his envisioned death leap landed him in a pile of cushioning mud. The lone remaining would-be assassin, a young man named Gavrilo Princip, left his post on the Appel Quay, despairing of his chances for a glorious date with destiny. Rather than giving up entirely on the assassination plan, however, Princip took up a new post on Franz Josef Street, part of the route the archduke was scheduled to take on his departure from the city.

Franz Ferdinand might well have escaped his own disastrous date with destiny that day had not Austrian bungling surpassed even that of the Black Hand terrorists. After visiting City Hall as scripted, the crown prince decided to pay a hospital call on the soldiers injured in the attack; this plan involved a return route directly down the Appel Quay, skipping Franz Josef Street. Franz Ferdinand's driver, however, was not apprised of the change of plan, so he turned onto Franz Josef Street, per his original instructions. Upon being informed of his error he stopped the car, which, lacking a reverse gear, had to be pushed back to the Quay. Princip, armed with a revolver, happened to be standing a few meters from where the car stopped. All he had to do was walk a few paces, draw his gun, and fire point blank at the imperial sitting ducks. Sophie bled to death fairly quickly, while Franz Ferdinand, shot through the neck, succumbed en route to the hospital. His last words were, "Sopherl, Sopherl, don't die! Stay alive for the children!"

Had Franz Ferdinand himself stayed alive that day, it's possible that the roughly 8.5 million men who died in World War I might have lived on as well. As for Princip, he tried to shoot himself, but a crowd surging in around him knocked away his pistol; he swallowed some cyanide but threw it up before it could take effect. He was imprisoned in the Austrian military fortress at Theresienstadt, later to be converted by the Nazis into a "model" concentration camp decorated to look like a spa. Princip died there of tuberculosis in 1918.

Habsburg action now shifted to Bad Ischl, where Emperor Franz Josef was firmly ensconced in his villa, settling down for the summer spa season. The emperor received the news of his nephew's assassination with something less than tearful anguish. After a few moments of deep thought, he said: "Dreadful! The Almighty does not allow Himself to be challenged! A higher power has restored an order of things that I was unable to uphold." In Franz Josef's view, God clearly disapproved of Franz Ferdinand's marriage to a woman of less-than-satisfactory pedigree. No doubt the Deity, like his self-proclaimed chief emissary in Central Europe, also frowned on the archduke's oft-stated aspiration, upon assuming power, to give the Slavs greater powers within the Dual Monarchy. (Viewed from the hindsight of one hundred years, this sensible political program looms as one of the twentieth century's most tragic missed opportunities, for it might, just might, have helped keep the Habsburg Empire from stumbling into war.) Alas, Franz Ferdinand's assassination only hastened that stumble because in Franz Josef's eyes, this brazen transgression against Habsburg authority had to be punished. Indeed, the emperor and his advisers understood that the Black Hand's deed offered Austria a welcome opportunity to strike decisively against Belgrade, long a major thorn in Habsburg flanks.

For the next three weeks Bad Ischl buzzed with activity as imperial officials descended on the little spa town to plot Vienna's retribution against Belgrade. In the end it was decided that an ultimatum should be sent to the Serbs—and a very harsh and humiliating ultimatum at that. Rather than handing their adversaries a Mafioso-style "offer they couldn't refuse," the Austrians would hand them an offer they couldn't accept. Among other nonnegotiable demands, the ultimatum required Belgrade to allow Vienna to participate in the investigation of Franz Ferdinand's murder, a clear assault on Serbian sovereignty. Belgrade's expected rejection would justify an Austrian declaration of war.

The bustle of activity at the Bad Ischl Kaiservilla in the wake of Franz Ferdinand's assassination did not significantly affect day-to-day life at the spa itself—the season went on as usual, though some guests went out of their way to cheer Habsburg officials as they came and went. Similarly, in Baden-bei-Wien, news of the Sarajevo killings caused momentary excitement but no great consternation, much less prophecies of doom. Stefan Zweig happened to be sitting in Baden's Kurpark reading a book about Tolstoy and Dostoevsky when a message about the murders went up on the bandstand:

My mind was instinctively distracted from my reading when the music abruptly stopped. . . . A change also seemed to come over the crowd promenading among the trees like a single pale entity flowing along. It too stopped walking up and down. Something must have happened. . . . I stood up and saw the musicians leaving the bandstand. . . . Coming closer, I saw that excited groups of people were crowding around a communiqué that had just been pinned up on the bandstand. . . . More and more people came up, thronging around this notice. The unexpected news passed from mouth to mouth. But to be honest, there was no special shock or dismay to be seen on the faces of the crowd, for the heir to the throne had not by any means been popular. . . . Two hours later there was no real sign of grief to be seen. People were talking and laughing, later that evening musicians performed in the cafés again.

Similar scenes unfolded in other Austrian spas and indeed across the whole Habsburg Empire. When some foreign papers expressed concern that the Sarajevo tragedy might bring destabilizing sanctions against Serbia, Vienna's *Neue Freie Presse* reassuringly commented: "The political consequences of this are being greatly exaggerated."

In reality, behind the scenes at Bad Ischl and Vienna, Franz Ferdinand's not-entirely-unwelcome demise was taking on ominous significance. The incident also preoccupied Kaiser Wilhelm II's government in Berlin since Emperor Franz Josef and his military commander-in-chief, Franz Conrad von Hötzendorf, wanted to make sure of German backing before going ahead with any action against Serbia that might bring war. After all, Belgrade had the support of France and (above all) Russia; Vienna needed Germany to put pressure on St. Petersburg to stay out of the conflict and/or to come to Austria's aid should Russia jump into the fray. Austrian foreign minister Count Leopold von Berchtold accordingly sent a letter to his counterpart in Germany asking for support in "neutralizing" Serbia as "a power factor." Without delay, Wilhelm let his friend and frequent cure partner Franz Josef know that if push came to shove, Berlin had the Austrians' back.

This fateful reassurance from Germany has gone down in history as the "blank check," but in actuality it was considerably more than that: it was a kind of marching order from Berlin to take swift action against the Serbs. A cable to Vienna from Austria's embassy in Berlin read: "[His Majesty] quite understands that . . . if we really recognize the necessity of military measures against Serbia, he would deplore our not taking advantage of the present moment, which is so favorable to us."

Spa guests at Ischl and other ordinary citizens of Central Europe might be forgiven for acting as if nothing very momentous was transpiring in the days following Franz Ferdinand's assassination; after all, many top Austrian and German officials were also behaving in *their* normal fashion—that is, going off on vacation or taking the cure at their favorite spas. While Emperor Franz Josef resolutely stayed put in Bad Ischl, his chief of staff Conrad repaired to an air-cure spa high in the Dolomites. Kaiser Wilhelm set forth on a planned sea cruise off Norway; German foreign minister Gottlieb von Jagow embarked on a honeymoon jaunt to Lake Lucerne; Reich war minister Erich von Falkenhayn went off for two weeks to the North Sea island of Juist; and German army chief of staff Helmuth von Moltke insisted on taking the waters at Karlsbad, which he always did this time of year. (Moltke, a nephew of the great Franco-Prussian War general of the same name, was of a surprisingly frail constitution, both physically and mentally.) As it happened, Moltke began his Karlsbad cure on the very day that Franz Ferdinand met his untimely end. Roman Emperor Nero is said (apocryphally) to have "fiddled while Rome burned"; of Moltke it can reliably be said that he bathed while the fuse of war was being lit.

The fuse turned out to be fairly short. On July 21, in Bad Ischl, Franz Josef approved the text of Austria's ultimatum to Serbia; on the following day, Berlin (in the person of von Jagow) did the same; and one day later, at 6:00 p.m. sharp, Vienna gave Belgrade forty-eight hours to accept Austria's terms or face the consequences. Military attack was not explicitly set forth as one of those consequences, but this was understood by all. Tellingly, when Russian foreign minister Sergei Sazonov saw the contents of the ultimatum, he cried, "This means war!" Kaiser Wilhelm's commentary was equally revealing: "Bravo. . . . Now [it is imperative] to stomp down hard on the feet of the rabble."

From what we know now, it seems probable that Belgrade would actually have accepted the Austrian ultimatum in its entirety, despite its severity, had not the Russians stiffened Serbian backs at the last moment by promising support in case of war with Austria-Hungary. Armed with this crucial assurance (and contrary to the widely held view that Belgrade's eventual response came within a hair of capitulation), Serbia answered Austria's ultimatum with a brilliantly composed amalgam of equivocations, obfuscations, denials, and half-acquiesces that boiled down to a demand that Vienna *prove* its allegation of Serbian complicity in the Black Hand attack. When Serbia's foreign minister delivered this document to Austria's man in Belgrade, Baron Wladimir Giesl von Gieslingen, it took the Austrian only a moment to see that the reply would not be acceptable to his superiors. Realizing that war between Serbia and Austria-Hungary was imminent, Giesl promptly left Belgrade, his bags having already been packed.

Although war still could have been avoided if Belgrade elected to back down, there was little chance of that, and Austria was not about to give Serbia much time for reconsideration. On the morning of July 28, exactly one month after Franz Ferdinand's assassination, Emperor Franz Josef signed Austria's declaration of war against Serbia.

The location for this fateful action was Franz Josef's manly study in the Kaiservilla at Bad Ischl. The Kaiser signed the order with an ostrich-feather quill—a typical anachronism for him but an ironic one, too, given that the war he was signing into being would deploy the very latest in killing technology. Franz Josef scratched his name to the war order while seated at his big desk beneath a pure white bust of his dead wife, Sisi. In addition to the war declaration, Franz Josef signed an "Appeal to My Peoples" calling for the entire polylinguistic, multiethnic, and mutlifaith Habsburg Empire to come together as one in this hour of trial.

Austria's bumbling incompetence in the war to come manifested itself even before the first shots were fired. Because Vienna had melodramatically closed its embassy in Belgrade after Franz Ferdinand's assassination, Foreign Minister Berchtold lacked an emissary in town to hand-deliver Franz Josef's declaration of war (by custom, such documents were to be presented with a certain style). Germany refused to relay the message because it was pretending not to know Vienna's intentions. Finally, Berchtold was reduced to sending the war declaration via telegram, a recourse so low-rent and ridiculous that Serbian prime minister Nikola Pašić thought it was a joke. Alas, it was not, but Jaroslav Hašek, author of the satirical war novel *The Good Soldier Svejk*, might well have written the script for the opening act of this piece of tragicomedy. "A monarchy as idiotic as this ought not to exist at all," says trooper Svejk of the aged empire he pretends to fight for.

Less than laughable wartime realities were also foreshadowed by the scene in Bad Ischl in the immediate wake of Austria's declaration of war. Notices went up around town announcing imminent restrictions on train travel for civilians and the curtailment of nonofficial telephone conversations between Ischl and Vienna. Although most of the townspeople, like folks elsewhere around the empire, openly welcomed the news of war against Serbia, many foreign spa guests rushed to the railway station to book their departures while they still could. Over the next two days the few trains still offering civilian accommodation were crammed with curists abandoning the baths. The local cure director could only hope that the Austrian generals were right when they promised a quick and victorious end to the conflict.

The conflict failed not only to end quickly but also to stay local, as the Austrian leaders had hoped it would. The Austro-Serbian dustup segued into a wider war as the cluster of so-called entangling alliances among the Great Powers kicked in. It must be said, though, that these entanglements could easily have been undone—Italy was to throw off its treaty obligation to Germany and Austria-Hungary in 1915 without a qualm—and a wider war was no more necessary or inevitable than was the smaller Balkan scrap. Indeed, during the week between Austria's attack on Serbia and opening day of the long shooting season to come, many a martial hothead—even Kaiser Wilhelm—experienced bouts of cold feet. But unfortunately, in violation of Clausewitz's wise dictum that war is too important to be left to generals, civilian leaders across Europe allowed their top military men, who worried primarily about invasion timetables and the imperatives of a quick strike, to call the shots. What these civilian leaders arguably *should have done* is retreat to some grand spa—say, Bad Gastein or Baden-Baden—where between relaxing massage treatments and soothing hot baths they could have worked out their disagreements in a civilized fashion. Here we have yet another intriguing "what if?" moment in the annals of our spa-centered history of the modern world.

As an all-encompassing industrial conflict, World War I was fought on the home fronts as much as on the battlefields. The Central Powers, short on important natural resources and therefore highly dependent on imports, were not in a strong position to weather a long conflict fought in several theaters. As their troops marched off to battle in early August, few of the leaders expected a long slog. Kaiser Wilhelm famously told his boys that they would be home "before the leaves [had] fallen from the trees." Central Europe's grand Kurorte constituted a small but intriguing slice of this crucial home front scene, and following their fate through the protracted wartime carnage is one way of tracking the process through which the center fell out of the Central Powers between 1914 and 1918.

Just as residents of Bad Ischl (and, for that matter, other k. und k. Kurorte) welcomed Austria-Hungary's initial salvo against Serbia in late July 1914, the German spas celebrated lustily when their nation plunged into a wider war against France, Russia, and Britain. Between August 1 and August 4, with church bells ringing incessantly in the background, the Kurorchester in Baden-Baden played the national hymn over and over again at the demand of patriotic zealots. Young women rushed to the railway station at Oos to press hot drinks and flowers into the hands of newly enlisted soldiers passing through town in the first troop trains. Similarly, in Bad Homburg the Kurorchester, along with the volunteer firefighters' band, played stirring marches like *Preussens Gloria*, *Torgauer*, and *Fridericus Rex*. "With song and sound, Homburg's finest marched off to war in a delirium of joy," recalled a local memoirist.

At Bad Homburg and other German spa towns, the sudden exodus of so many young men, festive as it might have been, brought a problem for the cure industry in the form of labor shortages. Bath attendants, hospital orderlies, and even spa doctors were rushing off to the front. These labor shortages might have been even more problematic had they not coincided with similar shortages of guests. In the case of Bad Homburg, curists from enemy nations left voluntarily; in Bad Ems, the British, French, and Russian citizens were summarily expelled.

Interestingly enough, in Baden-Baden some cure guests from the Entente countries thought they could tarry a bit before abandoning their precious baths. They soon found themselves interned in the Kurort along with enemy nationals rounded up in other parts of Baden. A town famous for its cosmopolitanism seemed to have become a hotbed of xenophobia overnight. This nativist turn also manifested itself in a series of hasty name changes: hotels, restaurants, shops, and public buildings previously bearing French or English designations now bedecked themselves in proper German nomenclature—Conversation House, for example, became Kurhaus. Yet another sign of the times was the sudden cancellation of musical and theatrical events with an internationalist or foreign taint.

Iffezheim's annual thoroughbred "Race Week," a major international draw every August, was called off for 1914: after all, a different kind of race, the German rush across Belgium, was already in full swing.

"You may not be interested in war," Trotsky is supposed to have said, "but war is interested in you." He was right. The 1914–1918 war was so "interested" in able-bodied young men that it wanted their company—on the plate—for breakfast, lunch, and dinner. There are 525,600 minutes in a year. In World War I, almost five (on average) soldiers died in every one of those minutes over the course of the four-year conflict. Germany alone suffered eight hundred thousand casualties in the first six months of fighting. Germany's grand spas were accustomed to frequent death, but not on this scale, and not involving their own young men. The first Bad Emser to die in the war fell on August 20 in Belgium; by the end of the conflict, he had been followed to the grave by another 184 local lads. Baden-Baden, about three times the size of Ems, lost a total of 510 men at the front; the first Baden-Badener to die (on August 9, 1914) was named Max Krieg, appropriately enough.

The war consumed raw materials and money as greedily as young male meat. It was not long before the voracious war machine, combined with the constrictive effects of a tight Allied naval blockade, brought serious shortages of everything from bullion to beer (this last deficiency a special indignity for the Bavarians). The grand German Kurorte suffered from the shortages along with other towns and cities, though arguably they felt the pinch even more acutely because they had grown accustomed to a greater array of imports for their pampered foreign guests. During the war it was not just English jams, Russian caviar, and French wines that were hard to find. Already by mid-1915 supplies of coal and basic food staples were running dangerously low, necessitating strict governmental rationing. In Baden-Baden, during the fall of 1916, adult citizens were restricted to a weekly quota of 1,400 grams of cereal grains, 125 grams of dried fruits, and 200 grams of sugar (all this about one-third of what people would have normally consumed). Entire school classes were sent out into the Black Forest to harvest berries and mushrooms. Baden-Baden's soccer pitches were converted to vegetable gardens.

With supplies of money running short, too, and the German government unwilling for morale reasons to impose income taxes to keep up with the costs, Berlin resorted to war bonds drives to pay for the conflict.

Another money-raising stratagem involved erecting a huge wooden statue of Field Marshal Paul von Hindenburg near the Reichstag; patriots could pound a nail into the statue's flanks for one mark. Individual cities often had their own versions of this tactic. Baden-Baden chose for its fund-raiser a model of Baden's state animal, the griffin, a creature about as authentic as some of the town's cures. Propped up at the entrance to the city's commercial district, the Baden-Baden griffin brought in twenty-four thousand marks over the course of the war.

Not all citizens of Germany's spa towns suffered equally in the conflict, any more than did the citizenry elsewhere. The rich were naturally in a better position to pay the larcenous prices charged by black marketeers and opportunistic farmers. Guests at the better hotels had access to larders kept reasonably well stocked by enterprising quartermasters.

An especially egregious example of wartime high living in the spas involved Kaiser Wilhelm II. He suffered no privations at all when he was in residence at Bad Homburg. The emperor was there quite often because from March 1917 until early 1918 this royal spa town became his personal headquarters. Every morning while the Kaiser was in residence at Homburg, a local baker brought fresh rolls to the Stadtschloss kitchen. Loads of high-quality anthracite coal for the castle ovens also arrived regularly, although the shipments typically came in after nightfall so as not to arouse envy among heat-deprived ordinary citizens. But this obfuscation did not work. "People began to doubt," wrote one local critic, "if members of the imperial family were even aware of how much the general populace, including the Homburgers, were suffering under the difficult wartime conditions." Nor were ordinary Homburgers much amused when they recognized their local *Schlosspark* as the backdrop for a Berlin magazine cover photo showing "the Kaiser in the Field." Observing that the Kaiser's conspicuous consumption was generating "considerable antipathy" among ordinary townsfolk, one of the emperor's aides, Admiral Georg von Müller, suggested delicately that His Majesty might want to display some strategic Spartanism in his daily habits. According to von Müller, Wilhelm got the message: he "showed understanding" for local sensibilities by heroically limiting himself to *one pat of butter on each slice of toast*. On the other hand, there were no notable cutbacks on "Austria Day," April 3, 1917, when Wilhelm invited the new Austrian Kaiser, Karl, along with Field Marshal

Hindenburg, General Erich Ludendorff, and Chancellor Theobald von Bethmann-Hollweg to Homburg for some fruitless strategizing. About a year later, Wilhelm and his family abandoned Homburg—for good as it turned out. The Kaiser shifted his headquarters to Spa in Belgium. One can safely presume that ordinary Homburgers were happy to see His Royal Backside disappear down the road.

Long before the Kaiser decamped from Homburg, the beds left empty by cure-guests departing from various clinics, sanatoriums, and hotels across Central European spa land had been filled by a different kind of clientele: wounded soldiers undergoing medical treatment as well as military families enjoying subsidized spa vacations. Baden-Baden began receiving soldiers wounded in the fighting in Belgium as early as August 22, 1914. These men were put up in the Landesbad, which had been hastily converted to a military hospital. Although Baden-Baden was never officially declared a *Lazarettstadt* (military hospital city) during the war, virtually all its sanatoriums and clinics served the army in various capacities from 1915 on. Bad Ems, which was taken over by the Prussian War Ministry as a hospital station, went into full military mode, with nightly blackouts and special guard units posted at all bridges and railway crossings. Bad Homburg also took in wounded soldiers, although by dint of a triage system the men sent to this spa tended to be less severely injured. "Reserve Lazaretts" for soldiers with light wounds were established at Homburg's Sanatorium Dr. Baumstark and in several area hotels. A special foundation funded by a local hotel owner enabled noncommissioned officers and enlisted men, along with their families, to spend one-week vacations at the Hotel Augusta. Many of the Augusta vacationers were of working-class background, and their subsidized stays in Homburg amounted to first encounters with a grand spa. Although these wartime flings were brief and frugal by Homburg standards, they pointed toward a rather different future for this and the other opulent old Kurorte of Central Europe.

This is not to say that there were not aspects of the German spa scene that remained familiar to curists and vacationers who resolved to keep visiting their favorite Kurorte, war or no war. Felix Gilbert, a native of Baden-Baden who had moved to Berlin as a child (and later became a distinguished historian in the United States), went with his mother for short vacations in Baden-Baden every spring for the first three years of the war. He recalls in an evocative memoir that many other upper-middle-class Berlin families did the same. True, Gilbert and his mother could not help noticing that some of the great hotels had closed while others had been converted into hospitals. They also saw fewer strollers on the Lichtentaler Allee and, more ominously, heard gunfire in the distance and occasionally spied French airplanes overhead. "But," Gilbert concludes, "for many [visitors], vacations in Baden-Baden were not very different from what they had been in peacetime."

Wiesbaden's war experience was slightly different from that of Baden-Baden and other smaller German Kurorte because its cure industry was embedded in an unusually large urban landscape. Also, in 1914 this spa had an exceptionally high percentage of foreign patronage. Although Wiesbaden embraced Berlin's official line that the war was a necessary defense against Russian aggression, city spokesmen were careful to insist that their town bore no hostility towards foreigners—even French, British, and Russian foreigners. As one newspaper commented: "The residents of this city understand full well that not all English and French citizens agree with the aggressive policies of their governments. [Furthermore], they know the Russian people well enough to realize that the best of that nation is absolutely not in agreement with its Czarist dictatorship; surely hundreds of thousands of citizens of the giant Russian imperium hold in their hearts the hope that Russia does not emerge victoriously from a war imposed on Europe by a lunatic despotism."

Unlike its counterparts in the German spa world, Wiesbaden did not expel or intern all enemy-nation curists as soon as hostilities began. The Kurort harbored hundreds of stranded French, British, and Russian guests in fine hotels. Moreover, although the outbreak of hostilities certainly curtailed foreign visits—travel difficulties alone made that inevitable—some visitors from neutral nations continued to make their way to the spa. Not surprisingly, local hotel owners and bath entrepreneurs hoped to keep the foreign faucets open as long as possible (after all, hosting foreign visitors paid a great deal better than putting up wounded soldiers or penny-pinching military families). But taking care of stranded enemy nationals, not to mention attracting new guests, was getting harder and harder as Wiesbaden started experiencing the same food and coal shortages affecting the rest of the country. To cater to their large contingent of foreigners, local cure-industry leaders petitioned the Prussian government to loosen food rationing restrictions and to allow extra shipments of provisions.

Normally, Wiesbaden's municipal authorities supported whatever the cure industry wanted, but the seemingly endless war was imposing enormous stress and suffering on a large working-class population in no mood to see rich foreigners accorded special privileges. In April 1917, hoping to calm populist anger, the police chief banned newspaper advertisements for oysters, caviar, and other delicacies. Shortly thereafter, the mayor wrote a letter to the Prussian government calling attention to the special needs of the cure industry, upon which hundreds of jobs depended, and also to the desperate plight of the city's poor, most of whom had no connections to the spa world and whose animus against the cure entrepreneurs and their patrons was threatening to tear the city apart. Convinced that the situation was worsening by the day, the mayor proposed that the Prussian government *either* provide extra rations for Wiesbaden's cure community *or* suspend access to the city for all foreign nationals excepting business travelers. Undoubtedly aware that the first option was out, Wiesbaden's mayor was in effect turning against the local cure industry, an extraordinary thing to do.

Berlin had more pressing problems on its plate than the tribulations of the Wiesbaden mayor and his warring constituencies—though these miseries mirrored a broader climate of discontent spreading across the entire country. The Hessian State Archives contain no evidence of any response from Berlin to the mayor's proposal, and in any event, Wiesbaden soon had other problems on its plate as well. In the last two months of the war it fell under bombardment by French aircraft, the only major German Kurort to suffer this indignity.

The Austro-Hungarian grand spas were rather less affected by World War I (at least in its early stages) than were the major Kurorte of western Germany. The fighting was far away—no sounds of gunfire or enemy aircraft overhead—and citizens of Prague and Vienna continued to take their accustomed summer cures at Gastein and Ischl, Karlsbad, and Marienbad.

When Franz Kafka, then a hardworking insurance man based in Prague, needed a vacation and possible cure for his persistent headaches and weak lungs (he would be diagnosed with tuberculosis in 1917), he sought out Marienbad. Having been there on business trips before the war, he succumbed once again to the little town's seductive charms. And apropos seduction, he also saw Marienbad as a perfect place to revive his on-again, off-again love affair with Felice Bauer, a young Jewish woman he had met in 1913 through his friend Max Brod. Shortly after meeting Felice, he wrote her that he "wouldn't mind staying alone [in Marienbad] for several months to take stock of my position," but by 1916 he wanted to share this charming place with his fiancé. He selected Marienbad over Karlsbad as a love nest because, as he wrote Felice in May of that year, "Karlsbad is rather pleasant, but Marienbad is unbelievably beautiful." "A long time ago," he further confided, referring to Marienbad's fame as a fat farm, "I ought to have followed my instinct which tells me that the fattest are the wisest [Kafka himself, a devotee of the hundred-chews-a-minute doctrine of health food guru Horace B. Fletcher, was rail thin]. After all, one can diet anywhere, no need to pay homage to mineral springs, but only here can one wander about in woods such as these."

Alas, when Franz and Felice finally managed to rendezvous in Marienbad for ten days in July 1916, the beautiful setting could not fully compensate for the challenges of prolonged proximity. Unused to being together for more than a day or two at a time, the couple quarreled incessantly, and when they tried to escape their claustrophobic quarters in the Hotel Schloss Balmoral with walks in the woods, it rained heavily. Franz sought solace in the Bible, but that didn't help either. A frustrated entry in his diary for July 5 reads: "The hardships of living together. Forced upon us by strangeness, pity, lust, cowardice, vanity, and only deep down, perhaps, a thin little stream worthy of the name of love, impossible to seek out, flashing once in a moment." Nor did Marienbad cure his headaches, much less his lung disease: "I am miserable," he confessed in his diary on July 4, "I have two little boards screwed against my temples."

The fact that Kafka was Jewish allows me to segue to the question of what World War I meant to the situation for Jews in Central Europe, and more specifically for Jewish curists in Central Europe's grand spas. In general, Jewish citizens of Germany and Austria-Hungary were just as quick to embrace the war as were their Gentile countrymen—indeed even more so, because they saw participation in the conflict as an opportunity to demonstrate their patriotism, their belongingness. The Centralverein deutscher Staatsbürger jüdischen Glaubens (CV) called on German Jews to dedicate themselves to the Fatherland "*über das Maß der Pflicht hinaus* [beyond the usual measure of duty]." Baden-Baden's chapter of the Israelitische Frauenverein (Jewish Women's Association) urged its members to do whatever they could, such as volunteering as nurses, to support the nation in its hour of peril. Over in Austria, Sigmund Freud experienced at the war's outbreak an unexpected spasm of patriotism: "Perhaps for the first time in thirty years," he wrote his brother Abraham, "I feel myself an Austrian, and would like just once more to give this rather unpromising empire a chance." Freud was gratified to encounter similar sentiments among fellow Austrian Jews at Karlsbad, where he was curing at the start of the war. Poignantly, the July/August 1914 newsletter of the Austro-Israelite Union proclaimed: "In this hour of danger we [Jews] consider ourselves to be fully entitled citizens of the state. . . . We want to thank the Kaiser with the blood of our children and with our possessions for making us free; we want to prove to the state that we are its true citizens, as good as anyone. . . . After this war, there cannot be any more anti-Semitism. We will claim full equality."

A more illusion-filled prophecy is hard to imagine. The long war *intensified* anti-Semitic agitation rather than moderating it, much less wiping it out. The fact that German and Austrian Jews, just as their lobby groups commanded, did their full part for the war effort, including dying in high numbers at the front, did not spare them from being castigated as shirkers and profiteers. For Germany, the inglorious acme of wartime anti-Semitism came in summer 1916 with a so-called *Judenzählung* (Jew census), organized by the Prussian War Ministry. This project was supposed to document Jewish underrepresentation at the front. When the census takers discovered that the opposite was true, they suppressed the results.

The German-Jewish press reported, sadly, no lessening of anti-Semitic policies and practices. The CV had to continue putting out its "Warning List" of racist spas throughout the war. None of the previously blacklisted anti-Semitic resorts had cut back on racist hostility; on the contrary, these places joined lustily in the widespread defamation of Jews as draft dodgers and war profiteers. Although the luxury Kurorte continued to steer clear of open and aggressive anti-Jewish hate mongering during the war, that prolonged crisis, in the view of the CV, delivered no grounds for hope that even this relative toleration might survive the bloodletting.

The grand Habsburg Empire spas also remained relatively free of the aggressive anti-Semitism infecting large cities like Vienna and Budapest, whose streets were flooded with Galician Jewish refugees expelled by the Russian army. When the war broke out, Jewish banker Viktor Ephrussi sent his wife and children to Bad Ischl for safety. Wartime Bad Gastein harbored a few Bavarian Jews who had gone there to escape growing anti-Semitic hostility at home. But one had to wonder whether Austria would retain *any* safe havens for Jews if the Habsburg Empire, which historically had tried to protect its various minorities, did not survive the fighting.

As the war dragged on, the survival of the empire indeed seemed increasingly doubtful. Put bluntly, the nearly 750-year-old Habsburg monarchy was falling apart like a cheap suit. Many of those who believed in the imperial enterprise had died in the first years of the war. Starting in 1916, the Habsburg realm was crippled by strikes, mutinies, and separatist agitation among the subject nationalities. Kaiser Karl, who succeeded Franz Josef in November 1916, was no match for this situation, which called for extreme competence rather than the bumbling banality that characterized this figure. Among the empire's many last straws was its humiliating loss to the Italians at the Battle of Vittorio Veneto in late October 1918.

Fortunately for my purposes in this book (if not necessarily for the Austrian war effort), the Austro-Hungarian imperial command moved to one of the Habsburg grand spas, Baden-bei-Wien, in the last phase of the conflict. Like so many of its counterparts, this spa had become a Lazarettstadt early on, caring for some fifteen thousand wounded and sick soldiers. Soon after becoming emperor, Karl established his personal headquarters in the "Kaiserhaus" on the Marktplatz, while the military high command took over a parish school. Kaiser Karl, decked out smashingly in a German general's uniform, hosted Kaiser Wilhelm, costumed in Austrian military finery, at the Baden Rathaus in early 1918. There were the predictable exchanges of mutual resolution and respect, but the Austrians soon began plotting an early exit from the war. As for Baden-bei-Wien, it had suffered serious wheat and coal shortages in 1917 and early 1918, but the presence of the kaiser and imperial high command improved matters significantly on the food front: after all, these worthies needed to keep up their strength for the surrender to come.

While Baden-bei-Wien was seeing off the Habsburgs, Belgium's Spa provided the luxury trapdoor through which Hohenzollern control over Germany dropped from sight in November 1918. In March of that year, Kaiser Wilhelm shifted his personal headquarters from Bad Homburg to Spa, where the German Supreme Command (OHL) was already bunkered down. Having gotten there first, the OHL claimed the best quarters, the Hôtel Britannique, one of the finest hostelries in Europe (comfort trumped negative nomenclature). Comforts aside, the Belgian spa town offered little in the way of enjoyment to the German military commanders. General Ludendorff's last-ditch summer offensive had failed, and the Allies, with crucial assistance from thousands of recently arrived American Doughboys, had staged powerful counteroffensives in August and September. Interestingly enough, Ludendorff blamed the failure of his last offensive in part on another new arrival, the "Spanish" influenza epidemic, which indeed was adding significantly to the misery of life for everyone on the western front. (Some Americans, meanwhile, were claiming that the *Germans* had started the epidemic and brought the disease to the United States by submarine!)

By autumn 1918, Ludendorff was cracking up. At Spa he got treatment for severe depression from local therapists as well as from Dr. Albert Hochheimer, the OHL's chief physician. Hochheimer ordered regular thermal bathing, long walks, and plenty of rest. Although Ludendorff's condition continued to worsen, he remained astute enough to convince Kaiser Wilhelm to institute political reforms at home, changes which significantly strengthened the power of the Reichstag. Ludendorff pushed this course of action so that it would be *civilian* parliamentarians rather than military bosses who would have to sign the armistice which the general knew was coming. Thus it was in the historic cure-town of Spa that the seeds were sown for the postwar *Dolchstosslegende* (stab-in-the-back legend)—that fateful fable which blamed Germany's humiliating defeat in World War I on civilian "traitors" at home rather than on the actual military culprits.

Spa was no happier a place for Kaiser Wilhelm, who, in addition to catching a light dose of the Spanish bug himself, had to face the sad fact that his hope for a long imperial "day in the sun" for Germany was coming to an end in the rainy gloom of Belgium. Worse, fed-up citizens back home in Germany and President Wilson in Washington were making it clear that neither Wilhelm nor any of his Hohenzollern heirs could expect to maintain power in the Reich. Fearing that if he returned to Berlin he might end up hanging from a lamppost, Wilhelm said goodbye to Spa and fled over the Dutch border into exile on November 10, one day after Socialist leader Philipp Scheidemann proclaimed a new German republic from a balcony of the Reichstag.

German Spa Towns and the Weimar Republic

The revolution that broke out in the closing days of World War I and swept away Germany's "Second Empire" made its presence felt in the country's grand spas, though not as bloodily as in larger cities like Berlin, Hamburg, and Munich. Just as in those big cities, however, a Workers' and Soldiers' Council controlled Bad Ems for a few weeks right after the war. In a speech he delivered before this militant body at the Ems Kursaal on December 1, 1918, Mayor Eugen Schubert opportunistically aligned his administration with the revolution but also appealed, in best Kurort fashion, for political calm and social stability. Wiesbaden, too, fell briefly under the power of a revolutionary Council. In Baden-Baden, local radicals, of which there were only a few, played a less active role, power being exercised primarily by the established *Stadtrat* (municipal council). With lingering historical memory of previous revolutionary convulsions, Baden-Baden's citizenry hastened to establish a "*Selbstschutz*" (self-defense) unit, whose main purpose was to ward off any communist uprisings of the sort occurring in Berlin, Munich, and parts of central Germany.

It would be the sad lot of Baden-Baden to fall under harsh French military occupation following World War II; in the aftermath of World War I, however, it was the citizens of Bad Ems and Wiesbaden who suffered that fate. These towns belonged to the large region in western Germany occupied by France—the left bank of the Rhine as well as right-Rhine bridgeheads around Mainz, Koblenz, and Cologne—as a guarantee for reparations payments and a buffer against possible Boche aggression. In the case of Bad Ems, the French must have seen their occupation as gratifying payback for a certain telegram dispatched from that spa town in 1870. Paris rubbed salt in German wounds by deploying black and Arab colonial troops among its occupiers. German residents, fearing for their "racial purity," decried this tactic as the "*schwarze*

Schmach am Rhein" (black shame on the Rhine). In Bad Ems, where the occupation lasted ten years, some four thousand troops commandeered schools, hospitals, large hotels, and many private villas as lodging for their troops. The new inhabitants did not treat their quarters kindly; soon many a villa began to look more like a beat-up barracks or student rental than a once-grand private residence.

For the Bad Ems cure industry, the loss of crucial hotel space, not to mention the presence of marauding soldiers, was devastating. Bath visits dropped to almost nothing. The same was true for Wiesbaden, which the French occupied until 1925 before handing over this duty to the British. As in Ems, the four- to five-thousand-strong French occupation force in Wiesbaden commandeered all the better hotels, along with numerous hospitals, schools, and private residences—some eight hundred of the latter. To ensure that their forces got enough food and coal, French authorities in Wiesbaden sharply curtailed coal deliveries to the resident population and imposed a food-rationing system that made wartime allocations seem generous. They also restricted travel in and out of the area for natives and forbade any transfer of capital. Finally, just to remind the locals who was boss, France's occupation authority required all citizens of Wiesbaden and Ems to salute French officers whenever and wherever they encountered them. Occasionally French vacationers came to town to revel in this spectacle and to take advantage of the enormous buying power of their own currency (a rare occurrence, not to be missed), but otherwise, there were precious few civilian visitors to the famous Wiesbaden baths.

The violence of wartime battlefronts found a new outlet in peacetime Germany in the form of political assassinations and putsches from both left and right. Although all of the putsches failed, they, along with a rash of murderous attacks by right-wing hit squads on figures connected with the hated new "Weimar" Republic, dangerously destabilized that entity in its fragile early years of existence.

The grand German Kurorte were not directly caught up in this mayhem, but it is worth noting that one of the more notorious postwar political assassinations took place in Bad Griesbach, a small Black Forest spa town not far from Baden-Baden. On August 26, 1921, Matthias Erzberger, one of the signers of the 1918 armistice, was gunned down by two nationalist fanatics as he was taking his morning constitutional. The killers found sanctuary in Munich, which after the crushing of a short-lived "Soviet Republic" in spring 1919 became the favored stomping ground for right-wing enemies of the republic, including Adolf Hitler. Serial political murder rarely being a draw for tourism, health related or otherwise, these attacks did their part to wreak havoc on the German cure industry's bottom line.

Apropos economics, the putsches and assassinations also helped to undermine a national currency already seriously weakened by reckless wartime borrowing. In the period between late 1918 and late 1923, Germany experienced a total meltdown of its once-formidable mark, a hyperinflation on a scale never before seen in the modern world (and, thankfully, not seen again since, though some nations are working on it). No need here to retell tales of million-mark beers and prostitutes who spurned wads of high-denomination bills in favor of a cigarette. Of course, like all the other horrors of the early Weimar years, the catastrophic inflation added to the woes of the spas. Lacking a viable currency with which to do business, the Kurorte, like many other German towns, began printing promissory notes of their own called *Notgeld*. This emergency money, usable only locally, was backed by whatever assets the towns controlled. For example, Baden-Baden deployed its great thermal baths as chief collateral to produce Notgeld worth 1,465 billion Reichsmarks as of October, 1923. The town used this water-backed currency to pay municipal employees and to subsidize social services for the thousands of ethnic Germans expelled from Alsace following France's reannexation of that territory in 1919. In Bad Ems and Wiesbaden there were forms of Notgeld printed by French-sponsored separatist movements whose goal was an "independent Rhineland" tightly shackled to France. The existence of this competing currency further weakened the mark. On November 20, 1923, citizens of Bad Ems had to pay 1.5 million Reichsmarks for a pound of ghastly margarine and 3 million for a small bushel of potatoes. Paris did not mind the mark meltdown because German reparations had to be paid in gold and material goods. French tourists did not mind the currency crash either, for it meant supercheap sprees in Germany, including German spa land. Yet relatively few French tourists or curists were inclined to slum in Germany while nationalist zealots were spewing anti-French slogans—an outcry that became even louder in early 1923, when French troops occupied the Ruhr Valley, Germany's industrial heartland, in retaliation for German defaults on reparation payments.

Meanwhile, German citizens were in no position to make up for the shortfall in foreign visitors to the spas. As early as January 1919, before the mark had entered its true death spiral, a British reporter passing through Wiesbaden noted that prices for staples were already stretching the budgets of anyone obliged to pay in marks. A pound of butter, he noted, cost a whopping thirty marks—though in actuality the price didn't mean much because butter could only be procured through barter for an equally precious commodity, such as tobacco. In any event, would-be German curists were hardly likely to spend money on a thermal bath when they could barely afford butter.

Germany's catastrophic era of hyperinflation came to a welcome end in late 1923 with the introduction of a new currency, the Rentenmark, backed by mortgaged governmental land and industrial assets—and, more importantly, by the willingness of a shell-shocked populace to trust it. Because political violence around the country had begun to wane while the old currency was still sprouting zeros, however, there was a brief period when foreign tourists could take advantage of Germany's surreal economic predicament without too much danger of getting beaten up or shot. The British trickled back—although almost exclusively *bourgeois* British, the landed gentry being too busy at home trying to save their country estates from crippling death duties, soaring maintenance costs, and other modern-day horrors. Even French tourists ventured over to the Rhineland Kurorte, though, as with the Brits, these visitors were a far cry from the free-spending aristos of old, and most of them stayed only a few days. Nonetheless, this modest infusion of foreign patronage meant that the grand spas began to recover economically somewhat sooner than the rest of the country.

Once the new currency managed to gain traction and recoup some of its prewar strength, British and French spa visitors, although now thicker on the ground, took a backseat to Americans at the grand German Kurorte. By 1926, more than half the guests staying in Baden-Baden at the luxurious Brenner's Park Hotel were American. Some of those Brenner's Americans had even brought their own cars from home—this being a time when rich Americans still drove American cars and liked to show them off.

The Yank spa visitors were part of a much larger invasion. From late 1922 through 1929, Americans descended on Europe, including Germany, "by the crazy boatloads," to use F. Scott Fitzgerald's happy phrase. This American preeminence in European tourism, including health tourism, is hardly surprising. After all, in those days the dollar was king. Both Britain and France were deeply in hock to the United States. Newly sovietized Russia was hemorrhaging refugees, some of whom were wealthy enough to scoop up Kurort villas from their impoverished German owners, but Russia was no longer a dependable source of health pilgrims. In the end, it is perhaps only fitting that the grand German Kurorte, supreme microcosms of the nation that they were, should have been pulled back into relative prosperity by the same folks whose banks were helping to salvage the German economy as a whole through desperately needed loans. Of course, such economic dependence had its downside: What if Mr. Moneybags went belly up himself?

At the German spas in the middle years of the Golden Twenties there was little inclination to dwell too much on the possibility of future calamity: there were plenty of challenges in the present, including that of retaining cultural vitality at a time when all the artistic action seemed to be shifting to Berlin. With the capital sucking up talent from all corners of the country (including dumbed-down, right-wing Munich), there was a real possibility that the great water cure resorts would end up as nothing *but* water—and *back*water to boot.

This did not happen—at least not quite—because opportunistic cure directors and hospitality entrepreneurs refused to let it happen. Exhilarating Weimar culture, it turned out, manifested itself not only in the famously louche capital but also in the grand spa towns. In 1919, a year of tumult, the Kurhaustheater in Baden-Baden mounted major productions of Wagner's *Tristan und Isolde* and *Der fliegende Holländer* along with Engelbert Humperdinck's *Hänsel und Gretel*. In subsequent years, the Mannheim Nationaltheater opera company made stops in Baden-Baden, as did the Berliner Staatsoper under Bruno Walter and New York's Metropolitan Opera under Erich Kleiber. Italy's Pietro Mascagni came to town with his *Cavalleria Rusticana* in 1925. And, most important, Baden-Baden became a vibrant outpost of the Weimar avant-garde when, every summer between 1926 and 1929, the German Chamber Music Festival, directed by Paul Hindemith, made that spa town its home.

In 1927 the Chamber Music Festival premiered, along with innovative works such as Darius Milhaud's *Rape of Europa* and Hindemith's own

Hin und Zurück, the very first collaboration between those two Weimar icons, Berthold Brecht and Kurt Weill. The piece in question was the *Songspiel Mahagonny*, later known as *Das Kleine Mahagonny* to distinguish it from the duo's longer opera, *Aufstieg und Fall der Stadt Mahagonny*. It is hard to imagine bad-boy Brecht, who smoked stinky stogies and wore a tattered leather jacket in a grasping attempt to come across as a working-class bloke, showing up at all in sedate Baden-Baden, much less performing there; and indeed his and Weill's work seemed an odd fit for the town. Basically, the piece was a collection of raucous songs about life in "Mahagonny," an imaginary Wild West fool's paradise (*Blazing Saddles* meets Jack London's Klondike) where gold-rush suckers spend their days and nights fighting, whoring, gambling, and glugging gallons of whiskey. On the other hand, given the work's "American" setting, and given 1920s Baden-Baden's dependence on Yankee gold, perhaps the town was a fitting venue after all.

In any event, Baden-Baden's authorities were undeniably suspicious of Brecht, and they became truly alarmed when they heard that he intended to have his two female leads, one of them Weill's wife, Lotte Lenya, appear naked on the stage. They quickly vetoed this idea. Yet even without nudism, *Mahagonny* ended up shocking many of the spectators. To their astonishment, the stage consisted of a boxing ring into which various tough guys named Jim, Jake, Bill, and Joe climbed to belt out their numbers, and to belt each other. Behind the ring was an expressionist screen depicting scenes of violence and greed. Following the tough guys came equally tough gals seeking "the way to the next whiskey bar" in their signature *Alabama Song* (a way later trod by Jim Morrison and the Doors). Even before Lotte Lenya, singing "in a hoarse voice with lascivious inflections," finished her solo, people in the audience were on their feet, some cheering, some booing and whistling. Fisticuffs broke out, life imitating art. The singers retaliated by shaking their fists and blowing on pennywhistles they pulled from their pockets. Even Brecht climbed into the ring and whistled away. Baden-Baden hadn't seen anything like this since Lola Montez lifted her dress and mooned the Conversation House back in 1845.

The twenties in Wiesbaden, occupied by the French and then the British, did not generate anything in the cultural realm quite as exciting as *Mahagonny*, but the town did boast a lively avant-garde visual arts scene around the Russian-born painter Alexej von Jawlensky. After having worked in Munich with the famed Blaue Reiter school of painters at the turn of the century, Jawlensky was expelled from Germany as an enemy alien in 1914, only to wash up in Wiesbaden in 1921.

Wiesbaden made sense for Jawlensky because after World War I, that spa town became a major haven for Russians fleeing the Bolshevik Revolution and civil war. Jawlensky was also enticed by the town's thermal waters, for he was already suffering from the arthritis that would soon cripple him so badly that he could barely hold a paintbrush. Yet, like the Weimar Republic itself, Jawlensky enjoyed a few productive years in the mid-twenties when he produced some of his best work—primarily his "Constructivist Heads" series—and even formed a coterie of fellow abstract artists called the Blaue Vier, in homage to the Blaue Reiter. The Blaue Vier managed to transplant to Wiesbaden something of prewar Munich's progressive spirit at a time when that spirit had been almost wholly extinguished in Munich itself.

Despite his increasing enfeeblement, or perhaps because of it, Jawlensky stayed on in Wiesbaden even after the Nazis came to power and included some of his works in their infamous Exhibition of Degenerate Art in 1937. Impoverished and under constant threat of persecution, Jawlensky died in his adopted home in March 1941, just three months before the Wehrmacht attacked his native land.

As always, a lively arts scene helped draw patrons to the grand Kurorte, but in the 1920s the spas needed to transcend their old business model—basically one of offering culturally enhanced cure vacations—if they wanted to remain commercially viable. One promising angle involved the growing "convention market." Some of the spa towns began to put themselves forward as ideal venues for various international congresses. Leading the pack in this domain was Bad Homburg, which today touts itself as "Germany's Convention Capital." In the 1920s Bad Homburg could not yet claim that distinction—many more professional associations gathered in Berlin—but the town managed to attract one or two major meetings each summer from 1924 through the early thirties. In 1925, for example, the International Psychoanalytic Association came to town. By all accounts, the psychiatrists took their annual congresses seriously but also found time to kick back and amuse themselves. Sigmund Freud was very sorry to have to miss the Homburg Congress on account of his jaw cancer, for which he wore a painful and unsightly prosthesis. He sent his daughter Anna in his stead.

Although congress hosting constituted an important new addition to the major spa towns' commercial draw, *curing* (or the promise thereof) remained their core business—this despite ongoing gains by conventional medicine that increasingly made trips to one's local hospital, clinic, or GP a more useful option. The sad reality, though, was that in the twenties many diseases or injuries that later on could easily be treated with drugs remained killers or cripplers. This was true even in America, where conventional medicine had achieved its greatest advances. Tennis great Bill Tilden almost died from a small infection on his middle finger in 1924; President Calvin Coolidge's son *did* die from a similar infection two years later.

When the Swiss-based German writer Hermann Hesse came down with a painful case of sciatica in 1924, he sought relief not at his local clinic but at Switzerland's most famous spa, Baden. As he relates in a delightful memoir about his stay at the spa, he was hardly the only sciatica sufferer there:

> I saw getting off the same train three or four colleagues, sciatics, clearly indicated as such by the nervous tightening of their buttocks, the insecure step and rather helpless and tearful expressions which accompanied their cautious movements. . . . There and then I had discovered, in the very first minutes, one of the great secrets and spells of all spas and I savored my discovery with true delight: companionship in suffering, *'socios habere malorum.*

In his memoir about his Baden stay, Hesse had nothing to say about political and social tensions there—this was Switzerland, after all—and it was not long before profound ennui set in. Had the writer gone to *Germany* for his treatment, he might have been less bored. In particular, the anti-Semitism that had fouled some of Germany's thermal baths in the Wilhelmian era, especially during the war years, continued to escalate in the 1920s. As before, German Jews planning a spa visit could consult the CV for information on anti-Semitism at specific resorts. But by the late twenties, the list of no-go resorts and hotels had grown so long that the agency began identifying which places were *willing* to take "Semites" rather than which were not. Not surprisingly, one of the areas in Germany with the fewest number of Jew-friendly spas was Bavaria, birthplace of the Nazi Party.

During the years when the CV was still identifying anti-Semitic spas, the resorts that ended up on the agency's no-go list did not seem to mind forgoing potentially lucrative Jewish business. On the contrary, one small spa town, Masserberg in the Thuringian Forest, complained when it was *left off* the CV's warn list for 1926: "With deep resentment we have seen that in your blacklist number 19 of May 7 our resort was not mentioned. [In fact], our spa is also one of those places that prefer to see Jews' behinds rather than their fronts. Also, our climate is not suited for tribes that come from southern areas." Like Bavaria, the North German region of East Prussia and some of the East Frisian vacation islands in the North Sea became well known for their anti-Semitic atmosphere—one imagines the hotels and restaurants there bearing little swastikas rather than stars in a Nazi version of the *Michelin Guide*. Rejecting a friend's invitation to cure on the East Frisian island of Langeoog, Stefan Zweig fulminated:

> I can't bear to be anywhere near these Pan-German louts! . . . These people are the scum of the earth! . . . So L[angeoog] is not on. I'm not going to excuse myself and be "tolerated," especially when I'm paying good money. I'd rather go to a spa with 700,000 Galician Jews! I can do without that—I'd rather go to Marienbad or Italy, if I can't find the right thing here. If I'm breathing the same air as them, they're stinking out the whole of nature for me—I feel for this lot what I normally don't allow myself to feel—utter hatred.

Even at spas where cure directors and hotel owners were anxious to attract Jewish custom, it sometimes proved difficult to prevent anti-Semitic staff members or local racists from fouling the atmosphere. Jewish hotel guests might find swastikas printed on their napkins; strolling around town, Jewish tourists might see "No Entry for Jews!" signs posted at bath entrances, Nazi flags in shop windows, and anti-Semitic graffiti carved into park benches.

Increasingly, it was not only the smaller Kurorte that were infected with race hatred. Wiesbaden, much to the frustration of the local cure administration and major hotel owners, was becoming "Nazified" in the late 1920s. Hitler himself delivered a speech in the town in January

1929, attracting a sizable crowd. For five days prior to his visit, shop windows in town overflowed with Nazi posters. Shocked, the CV instructed its members to warn Wiesbaden officials that they risked a Jewish boycott of their city in light of the brown flood. But all the civic authorities could do, or would do, was impose a ban on public marches and demonstrations by uniformed Nazis. And soon they would not be willing or able to do even that.

Weimar Germany's mid-1920s economic recovery turned out to be as brief as it was spotty—many middle-class families had lost everything in the earlier currency collapse and never recovered. The implosion of the American economy following the Crash of 1929 brought new devastation to Germany; bankruptcies proliferated, unemployment skyrocketed, soup kitchens and squatter camps sprang up across the country. German spa land did not escape this tide; indeed, the grand spa towns' dependence on domestic stability and American patronage put them on the frontlines of the ensuing economic chaos.

As it happened, a group of international bankers was meeting in Baden-Baden's Hotel Stephanie at the very moment when the walls of Wall Street came crashing down. The bankers were working on modifications to Germany's reparations obligations—a task that a few weeks later would in retrospect look about as useful as the proverbial deck-chair rearrangement on the sinking *Titanic*. Those bankers had barely abandoned their suites at the Stephanie when a wing of the hotel had to be closed for want of guests. Worse, in 1930 the entire Europäischer Hof, Baden-Baden's largest hotel, went on the auction block due to insolvency. It was purchased for peanuts by a Munich developer named Albert Steigenberger, who made it the first link in a long chain of luxury hotels. In that same year, Baden-Baden registered the highest per capita indebtedness of any municipality in Germany—perhaps the only distinction about which local boosters did not brag.

Anyway, all the other German Kurorte had similar claims to misery. Take Bad Ems, for example. The thermal baths there might just as well have dried up because their customer base of well-heeled curists certainly had. Another source of livelihood for the town, a nearby lead and silver mine, closed down in 1931, throwing 180 workers on the dole. By the winter of 1932–1933, more than one-quarter of Ems's inhabitants lived on welfare.

For Weimar Germany, the political consequences of the economic depression were immediate and catastrophic. A populace thrown into material uncertainty so soon after the previous malaise provided easy pickings for radicals offering simple explanations—and simple remedies—for the crisis. At the cost of the political center, Communists on the far left and Nazis on the far right surged in popularity. It was the latter who ultimately proved most adept at aggravating and exploiting the socioeconomic meltdown. During the era of relative calm in the mid-1920s, the Nazis had posed no major threat on the national level and even less of one in the major Kurorte, where their xenophobic pitch was rightly understood to be bad for business. But between 1930 and 1933, even spa land betrayed a weakness for extremism, particularly, but by no means exclusively, of the rightist variety. In Baden-Baden a panicky electorate awarded the Nazis 20.5 percent of the total vote in the Reichstag elections of September 1930; in the national elections of July 1932, that figure shot up to 30 percent, almost as much as the long-dominant Catholic Center Party. As for Bad Ems, in the Reichstag elections of 1928, the last pre-Crash tally, the KPD and NSDAP had together gained less than 5 percent of the total vote; but in July 1932 these parties gleaned over 50 percent, with the Nazis outpolling the Communists by some 5 percent.

The ensuing total collapse of Weimar democracy was not inevitable, but it would have taken a very firm hand on the tiller to keep this vessel off the rocks. Tragically, the one political helmsman who possessed this kind of skill, Foreign Minister (and former chancellor) Gustav Stresemann, died in October 1929, just as the ship of state started to go down. Stresemann's untimely death—he was only fifty-one—was caused by high blood pressure, the sort of affliction easily treatable with drugs today. But not then. During August 1929, Stresemann had spent two weeks in Baden-Baden taking the waters and undergoing various other spa treatments for his illness. Baden-Baden failed him and in failing him can be said (perhaps a bit melodramatically) to have failed Germany.

Two years after Stresemann's death, Weimar democracy experienced an intimation of its own mortality at the spa town of Bad Harzburg. This small Kurort in Lower Saxony had in the 1920s already become infamous for its anti-Jewish racism. There was hardly a bench in town without a swastika or anti-Semitic slogan engraved on it; the municipal swimming pool was likewise littered with slurs against Jews. It was in this (for antidemocratic racists) welcoming spa that a coalition of prominent nationalists calling themselves the Harzburg Front met on October 11, 1931, to denounce the current conservative government of Chancellor Heinrich Brüning (which itself was no paragon of democracy). In the eyes of this hastily formed front, which included such notables as publishing magnate Alfred Hugenberg, banker Hjalmar Schacht, and Nazi leader Adolf Hitler, the Brüning government was far too accommodationist toward the Allied Powers and not nearly tough enough toward Germany's resurgent left. The Harzburg coalition was anything but a solid alliance—Hitler and Hugenberg despised each other—but the much publicized meeting in October 1931 foreshadowed a fateful cooperation among antidemocratic forces in placing Hitler in power some fifteen months later. Once the Führer was at the helm, Bad Harzburg city fathers placed a plaque at the site of the 1931 meeting, duly marking their town's "historic" role in the death of Weimar and birth of the Third Reich.

Rump Austria

If, in the eyes of many observers, Germany's Weimar Republic appeared doomed at birth to live but a brief and unhappy life, Austria's "First Republic" seemed even less likely to survive. The new, post-treaty republic retained only 23 percent of the territory and 26 percent of the population of the Cisleithanian (Austrian) half of the defunct Dual Monarchy; some 3 million of the country's populace lived in Vienna. In other words, rump Austria was a "dwarf state" with a "water-head" capital—badly disabled, one might say, rather in the fashion of that inbred Habsburg dynasty which had ruled the place for so long but was now gone for good. Like Germany, republican Austria was crippled with huge debt, an increasingly useless currency, and high unemployment. Also like Germany, but actually a lot more so, the new nation suffered from a legitimacy crisis at home: A significant portion of its citizens believed either that the state could not survive or did not deserve to. Given the opportunity, a majority of Austrians would have opted to join Germany, but the Allies forbade that opportunity in the postwar treaty system. The citizens of Austria's westernmost province, Vorarlberg, actually tried to join *Switzerland*, but the Swiss wouldn't have them. Republican Austria managed, again like

Germany, to achieve a partial economic recovery in the mid-1920s, but even in these (brief) better times, a goodly portion of citizens wished they could be citizens of somewhere else.

Given the state of things in the Republic of Austria, one might assume that the condition of the country's great spa towns would have been equally precarious, especially since the clientele that these places had largely depended on—the titled aristocracy, European plutocracy, and upper bourgeoisie—had been hit hard by the war and postwar inflation, while the spa-loving Habsburg civil service bureaucracy had vanished entirely. And suffer the spas certainly did—in the beginning. There was even widespread fear that these luxury enclaves might collapse and fall into ruin, much like the great Roman baths after the imperial decline. Nonetheless, in fairly short order, more rapidly than the nation as a whole, republican Austria's major spa towns not only recovered but went on to prosper—a development that engendered considerable jealousy and ill-will among less favored sectors around the country. More than ever, major Austrian cure complexes like Baden-bei-Wien, Bad Ischl, and Bad Gastein seemed to be places apart, islands or oases of relative stability and privilege. Yet appearances could be deceptive, and in the end, Austria's fabled spa towns had more in common with their less grand surroundings than the spa denizens who valued that apartness might have desired.

Baden-bei-Wien's close proximity to Vienna accentuated the sociopolitical differences between Kurort and capital. Whereas Vienna in the twenties gained the sobriquet "Das Rote Wien" (Red Vienna) by dint of its huge and assertive working-class population and Socialist city government, Baden opted from the outset for the conservative Christian Social Party, which had the backing of both the Catholic and Jewish establishments. To revive the town's fortunes amid high inflation and a serious fall-off in patronage from the East, local entrepreneurs opened a plethora of dance halls and nightclubs. Hitherto stuffy hotels and coffeehouses brought in jazz bands and cabaret acts to woo younger audiences. The center of this new hip scene in Baden was Rudolf Sternberg's Schlosshotel Bellevue, which opened its doors on June 29, 1920, with a charity jazz concert. The bathing society "Badenia" launched a new amusement park replete with canoe rentals, open-air cinema, merry-go-round, and hippodrome. Keeping up with the times, in the mid-1920s this fun park added a minicar race track, roller coaster, and Punch and Judy show. Baden now had its own version of Vienna's famed Prater Park; characteristically, the Baden version was *klein aber fein*—"small but refined" (if ever an amusement park can be considered as such).

Casino gambling remained illegal in Austria through the twenties, just as it had been in the old empire, but local authorities in Baden-bei-Wien, mindful of the need to spur international tourism, turned a blind eye to the many small gambling operations that sprouted up in hotels, nightclubs, and private villas. After the ban on casino gambling was lifted in 1930, following Austria's plunge into economic depression, Baden-bei-Wien (in 1934) opened the republic's largest casino. The new facility effectively tapped into a spirit of devil-may-care adventurism that was a by-product of the Crash of 1929. Hedonism replaced health as Baden's principal draw.

Yet even before this happened, during the period when Baden-bei-Wien was clawing its way back to relative prosperity, the town had its full share of have-nots—enough of them, indeed, that in 1923 the local police chief warned dog owners to keep a close eye on their pets lest hungry citizens dognap them for food. In November 1920, employees of the town *Sparkasse* (savings bank) went on strike; shockingly for sedate Baden, some angry citizens took advantage of the strike to blow up the town gate and loot local stores. Two years later, municipal service employees walked off the job, leaving uncollected garbage all over the streets. In an ominous political sign of the times, on October 10, 1920, local Nazis took over the Kurhaus for a rally. They invited one "Adolf Hitler from Munich" to be their keynote speaker. Herr Hitler, however, had to beg off due to inflammation of his vocal chords. The future Führer's presence, though, might not have been of much use to Baden's Brownshirts because even in the chaotic inflation years, they languished far behind the Christian Socials and Socialists in popularity. On the other hand, relative weakness did not prevent Baden's Nazis from acting as if they owned the place: In 1924 they loudly demanded that all Jewish cure guests leave town immediately and that resident Jews decamp to Palestine.

In early 1924, Austria finally brought an end to the ruinous inflation with the introduction of a new currency, the *Schilling*. In Baden-bei-Wien the currency stabilization proved particularly stimulative. A host of new public buildings and monuments went up in the mid-twenties, recasting the built environment in the manner and scope it retains to this day. Among the more notable innovations was a sprawling new cure facility, the Strandbad. Drawing on the high-volume Marienquelle, this (still extant) institution pulled in hundreds of bathers daily. Two additional bathing complexes, the Johannesbad and Ferdinandsbad, along with a municipal art museum, came on line at the same time. Finally, a splendid new Kurpark was laid out in 1927, replete with a domed Beethoven Temple and smaller Mozart Temple to remind guests of Baden's illustrious musical heritage.

Yet even amid such promising developments there remained signs of future trouble, signs of Baden's proximity to restive Vienna. In 1926 and 1927, Vienna-area Nazis poured into Baden's normally placid precincts to fight street battles against members of the Republikanischer Schutzbund, the Socialists' party army. In 1928, local Nazis set off a stink bomb in the new Beethovenkino to protest the screening of a pacifist film, *Zwei Welten*. Later that year a coalition of *völkisch* groups staged a rally in front of the Kurhaus. Their purpose was to proclaim their bitter hostility toward the internationalism and social inclusiveness favored by the local cure industry.

On October 17, 1929, just before the Wall Street Crash, Badeners and their guests were treated to the inspiring sight of the *Graf Zeppelin*, Germany's magnificent new dirigible, floating majestically overhead. Looking like a huge silver cigar, the machine cruised in circles for about an hour before vanishing over the horizon. In the year of the zeppelin overflight, Baden-bei-Wien attracted more than fifteen thousand foreign cure-guests, a record. Like the big blimp, those visiting hoards would soon vanish.

Even more than Baden-bei-Wien, Bad Ischl, Kaiser Franz Josef's summer residence, had been closely bound up with the old Austrian imperial establishment and all it stood for. In a polemical memoir, *Verlorenes Paradies* (Lost Paradise—1924), Vienna *Neue Freie Presse* journalist Emil Löbl saw Bad Ischl as *the* "symbol of old-Austria with its incomparable charm and jittery weakness, its very formal culture and aggravating sloppiness, its sharp wit and humdrum routine, its wonderful affirmation of life and mawkish cult of death." Some of this old atmosphere lived on tenaciously in Ischl after the Habsburg collapse, but in the "Golden

Twenties" the handsome Alpine spa town became more closely identified with the country's "new rich," especially its new *Jewish* rich, and for a high-living, free-spending foreign clientele. Bad Ischl became *the* place to go for Austrians who had found ways to thrive amid the turmoil of the postwar era—and also for foreigners who could selectively dip into that turmoil to savor the best that battered little Austria had to offer. In stark contrast to most of its neighbors, Bad Ischl boomed in the twenties: twenty-two thousand guests came in 1922 and twenty-six thousand in 1928, a record for the spa.

Ischl's salubrious waters remained a chief attraction, but so did its culture, especially its musical culture. Having become a major outpost of Vienna's frothy operetta scene at the turn of the century, Ischl actually supplanted the capital as "operetta central" in the twenties and thirties. The main reason for this achievement, if achievement it was, involved the residency of operetta king Franz Lehár, who now spent most of his time in the spa town and oversaw the performance of his own and other composers' works at the local theater. Lehár wrote all of his last twelve operettas in his stately new villa on the River Traun (now a museum and a must-see attraction for Lehár *Liebhaber* the world over).

As the composer told a journalist in 1939, he could do technical work in Vienna, but for inspiration he needed Ischl: "I have written thirty stage works so far, yet I must confess I always have the best ideas in Ischl. This must be due to the air there."

But the hills above Ischl were filled with more than the sound of operetta music. Postwar Alpine Austria was a hotbed of anti-Semitic sentiment and ethnic German nationalism. Many of the smaller spas around the province of Salzburg, in which Ischl lay, banned Jews entirely. Jews throughout the province were forbidden to wear traditional mountain garb such as *Lederhosen*, bone-button Loden coats, and feathered Alpine hats. As for Ischl itself, the fact that many of those "new rich" visitors who flocked there in the twenties were Jewish made it a special target for racist abuse. Among regional anti-Semites the town became known as Bad Ischeles ("eles" being a typical Yiddish usage). In 1920 the Upper Austrian Teachers' Association decried Jewish guests at Bad Ischl as "black-marketers and plunderers of the people." Even the above-cited Emil Löbl, a relatively sophisticated Viennese, plunged into his poison pot of racist slurs and nativist bilge when he described the "new" Ischl as a hive of "big earners with Nigger lips and Cyclops hands, easy women pulled toward money like iron filings to a magnet, fabulous automobiles [owned by] horse traders, and colorful creeps from currency-strong foreign lands taunting us with their wealth." Not surprisingly, the blow delivered by the Crash of 1929 brought an escalation of anti-Jewish rhetoric in Ischl. The Nazi movement there gained enough new adherents to start putting out its own party organ, the *Ischler Beobachter*, in 1930. This paper promptly called for a ban on Jewish visitors to the spa.

Like Bad Ischl, although even more so, Bad Gastein continued in the post–World War I era to trade effectively in its health-giving thermal waters, its self-proclaimed status as *"die Quelle ewiger Jugend"*—a fountain of eternal youth. The local waters' high radon-gas content had long been a particular claim to fame, but new research commissioned by the city's cure industry in the 1920s touted that gas's capacity to repair damaged tissues and organs, clear clogged arteries, restore movement in arthritic joints, and, most miraculously, arrest the spread of cancer. Conventional cancer treatment being what it was in that era—essentially just painful surgery—cancer patients continued to flock to Gastein to bathe in the radon-laced waters and to sit four hours in special "radon compartments" filled with the gas.

Among those desperate curists was Sigmund Freud, a longtime Gastein enthusiast. He remained a loyal patron in the twenties and early thirties. For him, the beautiful mountain resort south of Salzburg continued to be a necessary haven from the noxious scene in Vienna—now more noxious than ever due to incessant noisy quarreling between the Reds and the Blacks, the Socialists and Christian Socials. He looked forward to the "delicious quiet" of his annual summertime stays in Gastein, days "free and fair," enlivened by "the glorious air, the water, the Dutch cigars, and the good food, all resembling an idyll as closely as one can get in this Central European hell."

But those Dutch cigars presented a problem, and Freud knew it. Even in his day, it was understood that smoking could cause cancer, and when Freud detected a lesion on his palette he was alarmed—alarmed, however, not so much for what this lesion might mean for his health as for his future as a six-cigar-a-day smoker. He was desperately afraid that if he informed his personal physician of his lesion, the doctor would forbid him his stogies. He kept his affliction secret for a long time, and when he finally sought treatment for his festering lesion he opted for a cosmetic scrape-over rather than the serious intervention he really needed. Moreover, Freud did not stop smoking, about which he had a useful theory. In his view, this habit, like just about every other male addiction, was a "substitute for masturbation." Having (presumably) given up the latter, or at least cut back on it, he saw no reason to ditch the former. In any event, regular sittings in the Gastein radon box would, he hoped, soon set him to rights. (Eventually, Freud did give up his beloved cigars, but not before it was far too late.)

During his cure visits to Gastein, Freud never stayed in the superexpensive Grand Hotel de l'Europe, but this luxurious hostelry did not want for glittering names during the Golden Twenties, which were especially golden for its resourceful owner, Viktor Sedlacek. King Ferdinand I of Bulgaria (traveling incognito as "Count Murany") lodged there three times between 1924 and 1926. Apart from lolling in the baths, Ferdinand's passion while in Gastein was to drive his big Bentley into the hills at night and, from the comfort of his car seat, plug away at deer transfixed by his headlights. When the municipality banned auto traffic after 8:00 p.m., Ferdinand indignantly refused to continue patronizing a town that "treated [him] in such a thankless manner."

No matter, there were many more travel-heavy types where he came from—or, more precisely, from India, then a major supplier of some the world's richest curists. From the fabled subcontinent came three megaspenders in the 1920s: the Maharaja of Baroda; Prince Amarjit Singh of Kapurthala; and (most impressive) Maharaja Khengarji III of Kutch, a personal friend of Queen Victoria during the last years of her reign. All these potentates landed in Sedlacek's hotel with entourages that took up much of the building, stretching housekeeping and kitchen staffs to their limits.

On the heels of these pro-British Indian princes came a subcontinent guest of similar eminence but far different political persuasion: Subhas Chandra Bose, champion of Indian independence. Hailing from a wealthy family himself, Bose lived only a little less grandly than the princes he despised.

Finally, as colorful and demanding as these Indian curists was King Faisal I of Iraq, who stayed for several weeks in the summer of 1930 to cure his gout (and, according to whispered rumor, to treat a nasty case of syphilis he had picked up who knew where).

One cannot really picture Ferdinand, Faisal, or the Indian Maharajas skiing down a snow-covered slope, but starting in the 1920s this rigorous winter sport was on offer at Gastein and other major Alpine Kurorte for those who wanted it. Bad Gastein, along with St. Moritz in Switzerland and Chamonix in France, pioneered the rapid spread of this craze across the Alpine region. Along with St. Moritz, Gastein had the signal advantage of providing visiting skiers (the majority of whom in those early days were British) with both snow *and* thermal water: hence the epic delight of being able to soak in a hot mineral bath after a long, cold day on the slopes. Gastein also boasted one of the world's first ski schools—staffed by English-speaking teachers. Nearby Bad Hofgastein harbored Austria's biggest ski jump, a marvel rendered instantly famous on January 5, 1922, when, for the first time in history, a man jumped over forty meters and lived to tell the tale. The town's evolution as a destination ski resort was much enhanced by the construction of a new auto road into the area that was passable in winter as well as in summer. In the summer, Gastein also pulled in "spillover" custom from the popular Salzburg Music Festival—some visitors, like Mark Twain, perhaps desiring a cure after their opera.

Foreign visitors to Gastein, winter or summer, most likely paid little attention to the area's political atmosphere, though this spa town was by no means immune to the tensions gripping the Austrian First Republic in the early twenties and then again after the Crash of 1929. In 1921, Tyrol and Salzburg provinces (Gastein and Ischl both belonged to Salzburg) voted over 90 percent in favor of joining Germany. In part this was a protest against "Red Vienna." Whatever the motives behind the vote, its rejection by the Allies further fanned Alpine Austrian hostility toward the Western victors, including those lofty British crowding the ski slopes. Anger over the treaty system combined with an affinity for some of the ideals propagated by Adolf Hitler, himself of course an Austrian, fueled the establishment of Nazi grouplets throughout the region in the 1920s.

Yet it must be said that all through this decade, despite persistent pro-Anschluss sentiment, Austrian Nazis had virtually no influence on the political shape of the new nation. The Austrian Socialist Party naturally had no use for the Brownshirts, and the conservative Christian Social Party, which dominated national politics after 1922, saw Nazi radicalism as a danger to economic recovery and the Catholic Church. As for Gastein itself, during the twenties its tiny Nazi chapter gained no more traction than did the far Left. The town's most influential businessman, hotelier Viktor Sedlacek, stepped forth as a Republican loyalist despite lingering affinity for the old monarchy. He documented his political stance in July 1927 by giving free lodging at his grand hotel to ten Viennese policemen injured in antigovernmental rioting in the capital. By dying in December 1937, Sedlacek avoided by a few months having to witness his country's annexation by Hitler, a man he despised.

In the end, rump Austria's First Republic was as much dependent on sustained economic recovery as was Germany's Weimar equivalent. Actually, Austria was especially vulnerable because its economy depended on loans not just from America but also from France. In 1931, to punish Austria for discussing a possible customs union with Germany, France pulled its huge deposits from Austria's largest bank, the Credit Anstalt, causing that bank to fail. With credit suddenly unavailable, companies across the land shut down; breadlines and soup kitchens proliferated.

There were no soup kitchens in Bad Gastein, but in the years between 1930 and 1938 there were plenty of vacant hotel rooms, near-empty restaurants, and batherless baths. One finds clear evidence of sudden hard times in the proceeds at Sedlacek's Grand Hotel de l'Europe: gross income in 1930 was 1,235,330 schillings; by 1932 it was already down to 711,535. Yet things were soon to get even worse—worse not just for Sedlacek's hotel but for the rest of Gastein and indeed for the entire Austrian cure/tourism industry.

As they did in Germany, Austria's Nazis profited immediately from widening economic misery. In the parliamentary elections of 1930, Austrian Nazis won 110,000 votes—not bad for a party that two years earlier had counted only 4, 800 members nationally. Regional elections in April 1932 in Vienna, Lower Austria, Salzburg, Styria, and Carinthia brought the Nazis even more impressive gains, with legions of younger, first-time voters opting for the Austrian branch of Hitler's party. When, some seven months later, native son Hitler took power in Germany, Austria's Nazis believed that their hour had come: They demanded that their government step aside and let Hitler take control, the postwar treaty system be damned.

As it happened, Hitler himself was not yet prepared to heed this call, but he was not averse to pumping up pro-Anschluss sentiment and doing what he could to further destabilize the Austrian Republic. In May 1933 he sent a fellow Nazi, Minister of Justice Hans Frank, to Austria on a propaganda visit. Vienna responded by expelling Frank. The Austrian government also banned the wearing of "political" uniforms (i.e., Nazi uniforms) in all vacation areas. The stage was now set for a half-decade of Austro-German rancor that is of interest for many reasons—not least for what it did to the Austrian tourist industry and to grand spa towns like Bad Gastein.

Determined to teach Vienna a lesson for its ouster of Frank, on June 1, 1933, Hitler's government imposed a thousand-mark tax on any German citizen traveling to Austria for vacation or cure. This *"Tausend-Mark-Sperre"* virtually ended German holiday and cure visits to the Austrian Alps, a favored destination. Given that Austria at this point drew more cure and holiday visitors from Germany than any other foreign land, Hitler's tactic was a harsh blow indeed—and one also quite illustrative of the rancor this man harbored for his native land.

Bad Gastein, for all its internationalism—all its popularity among Indian Maharajas, British skiers, and American health pilgrims—suffered from the German drought along with the rest of the Austrian tourism industry. On the day after Berlin imposed its punitive tourism tax, representatives of the Austrian Hotel Association met in Bad Gastein to discuss what they feared would be "an economic catastrophe of unprecedented proportions." Their fears turned out to be fully justified. Even the Grand Hotel de l'Europe was by no means immune. As of June 17, 1933, Sedlacek was complaining to the municipal government that, as a result of the German tax, he had only forty guests in his hotel as opposed to 109 at the same time the previous year. He had been forced to cancel the hotel's nightly dance entertainments because there was not a dancing pair in sight; nor had anyone shown up for the traditional five o'clock teas. In the following summer, the Nazi newspaper *Alpenwacht* could report with considerable Schadenfreude: "There are in all Bad Gastein [this season] only 200 guests rather than the usual 6,000. In the town's flagship hotel, the Grand Hotel de l'Europe, there are some 95 employees waiting on a single guest—the King of Belgium—along with two additional paying guests and a couple house detectives registered as guests. In other local hotels we see a similar full complement of personnel but only a handful of patrons. Custom is way down across the board."

Slouching toward Berlin: Karlsbad and Marienbad in the Twenties and Thirties

For all its liabilities in the postwar period, the Austrian First Republic had the putative advantage of relative ethnic, linguistic, and cultural homogeneity. The same cannot be said for the new state of Czechoslovakia. Like Yugoslavia, with which it would share a long-term fate of coming apart at the seams, the Czechoslovakian Republic was an artificial creation of the Western Allies, cobbled together out of disparate ethnic, religious, and linguistic groups that had no profound tradition of mutual love. Czechoslovakia's founding fathers tried to overcome this deficiency by proclaiming their new republic in front of the Liberty Bell in Philadelphia, as if that locale's supposed spirit of "democratic brotherliness" would rub off. Unfortunately, Philly's *actual* spirit of class and ethnic acrimony seems to have taken hold in this Central European cooking pot: Not a whole lot of brotherly love bubbled up over the years between Czechs, Slovaks, Germans, Poles, Ruthenes, Hungarians, and Jews.

Ethnic Germans who held sway in the country's westernmost Sudeten region, home to old Bohemia's principal spa towns, were anything but pleased to be part of the new Czech nation. Referencing Woodrow Wilson's "Fourteen Points," which included the right of "self-determination among nations," German speakers in the Sudetenland tried to negotiate a union with their Austrian brothers. Foiled in this endeavor by the Allies and believing themselves "racially" and culturally superior to the Slavs who dominated the new central government in Prague, Sudeten Germans chafed under Prague's efforts to impose control. The heavily German grand spa towns of Karlsbad and Marienbad, much as they liked to think of themselves as worldly enclaves devoid of petty ethnic rivalries, became thoroughly caught up in these antagonisms. The grand spas also came to embrace, albeit with a certain ambivalence, the anti-Semitic prejudices that typically accompanied heightened ethnic consciousness in Central Europe.

The rift between Prague and the Sudeten spas manifested itself early on in a conflict over nomenclature. Czechoslovakia's central government insisted that Karlsbad and Marienbad now go by their official Czech names, Karlovy Vary and Mariánské Lázně. Determined to retain as much of their old *k. und k.* cachet as possible, German-speaking town leaders protested vehemently. In the end, they dealt with the name problem by ignoring it, doggedly continuing to use the old designations in their dealings with the outside world. (And, one must admit, they had a certain point: *Last Year in Mariánské Lázně* simply doesn't resonate.)

Whatever they called themselves, the Sudeten-German spa towns suffered economically in the postwar period more intensely and more lastingly than their peers elsewhere in Central Europe. This is not surprising. The Bohemian Kurorte had been highly dependent on the upper and upper-middle classes of the Austrian and Russian empires for their custom—golden geese now dead and gone. Bourgeois Germans, destitute themselves, were no longer regularly popping over to Bohemia for health tune-ups, much less month-long cures. Nor were the British and the French showing up in useful numbers despite the fact that the luxury Orient Express train now made stops in Karlsbad during the summer spa season. In 1913 Karlsbad had registered around sixty-five thousand cure-guests and Marienbad some forty-five thousand; during the twenties and thirties, Karlsbad averaged around forty thousand visitors and Marienbad about thirty-five thousand a year.

Disturbing as these numbers were, though, the Sudeten grand spas were at least still kicking, still open for business. The Arabs are known to have saved important parts of the Greco-Roman patrimony from extinction in the Middle Ages; it was the *Jews*, of all people, who served this function for the grand Bohemian spas in the challenging years after World War I. Jews had been prominent for some time in Karlsbad and Marienbad, both as patrons and as residents. But in the twenties and thirties they became *absolutely crucial* for the spas' survival. German and Eastern European Jews faithfully took the Sudeten waters when other groups did not. (These "other groups," by the way, included Americans—vital for the sustenance of German and Austrian Kurorte in this era but largely absent from the Czech scene, as indeed they are today.) In the end, then, grand spas like Karlsbad and Marienbad were never more "Jewish" than in the twenty-year period between 1918 and 1938.

Ironically, the Sudeten-region spas, even lofty Karlsbad and Marienbad, became more openly anti-Semitic at the very moment they became more dependent on Jewish patronage. How did local anti-Semites negotiate the tricky waters between the Scylla of their prejudice and the Charybdis of economic necessity? In general, they hid their anti-Jewish hatreds under welcoming smiles during the summer spa season only to vent them with added gusto, often against resident Jews, during the off-season. Frustration over their need to display even short-term, strategic tolerance may have been one of the factors in the rise of openly anti-Semitic political groups like the German-National Party, the German National Socialist Workers' Party (Sudeten Nazis), and Konrad Henlein's Sudeten German Home Front (renamed the Sudeten German Party in 1935), which enjoyed significant electoral success both in Karlsbad and Marienbad in the twenties and thirties.

This conjunction between the spa towns' dependence on Jewish business and their underlying distaste for the hand that fed them constituted a dilemma also for Jewish organizations like Germany's Centralverein deutscher Staatsbürger jüdischen Glaubens, which continued to monitor anti-Semitism in Bohemian holiday resorts and Kurorte and to instruct Jews on which places to avoid. If the CV were to highlight anti-Semitic sentiment in the Sudeten spas, it risked disrupting the flow of crucial Jewish custom to these locales—a development that would undoubtedly make life much harder for resident Jews, some of whom were themselves owners of hospitality businesses. After much internal agonizing, the CV opted not to include Karlsbad and Marienbad on its no-go list.

These spas' ability to retain their "Jew-friendly" reputation despite growing undercurrents of anti-Semitism explains in part why the executive committee of the World Zionist Organization decided in 1921 to make Karlsbad the site of its epochal Twelfth Congress, the first one after World War I and the 1917 Balfour Declaration promising British support for a "national home for the Jewish people" in Palestine. There were other reasons for this decision as well. First, Zionist pioneer Theodor Herzl had himself cured in the town, making it politically kosher for his followers to gather there (much like that other "Zionist" patriarch, Brigham Young, had made Salt Lake City acceptable for his compatriots). Moreover, the new Czech government actively supported Zionism. Then there was the lure of Karlsbad itself—one of the world's grandest spas, a place famous for luxury, yet now amazingly cheap due to a weak national currency and low demand. Lodging in Karlsbad was not only inexpensive but also abundant: more than thirty thousand hotel rooms and virtually all of them readily available for the two-week, off-peak period in early September when the congress was to assemble. To sweeten the pot, the municipality offered discounts on public transport and relief from the "cure tax" imposed on visitors. Finally, Karlsbad's fabled waters came into play as a good reason to gather there: Did not Jews have their share of bodily aches and pains? Did they not need soothing soaks? As the congress was about to meet, one attendee proposed a less literal and more floridly grandiose connection between this highly important Jewish gathering and Karlsbad's function as a much-celebrated healer of human affliction: "Carlsbad is now on the cusp between two seasons: the time of those who came to heal their body has come to an end, and they are slowly leaving town. And the people of the Congress, who are coming here to heal the soul of the nation, are filling up the hotels and private rooms."

The Zionists, 540 of them from forty-two nations, met in Karlsbad from September 1 to September 15. As conventioneers are wont to do, they divided their time between business and pleasure. On the business end, in addition to contending with numerous internal squabbles, they addressed the knotty problem that their prospective "national home" in Palestine was already occupied, and occupied by people less than enthusiastic about sharing their space with hordes of newcomers. Although the congress predictably condemned recent violence by Palestinian Arabs against Jewish settlers, Zionist leader Chaim Weizmann also emphasized the imperative of "peaceful cooperation between the Jews and the Arabs for the well-being and blessing of the land and its entire population." A resolution was duly passed declaring "harmony and mutual respect between Arabs and Jews" as a goal of the new state.

As it happened, the Zionist conferees and the non-Jewish residents of Karlsbad coexisted rather more peacefully than Jews and Arabs in Palestine, though admittedly the bar here was not very high. When not attending business sessions in the Grand Hotel Schützenhaus (the former home of a *k. und k.* shooting club), the conventioneers threw themselves into the pleasure side of their visit: they took in a special Jewish art exhibit organized for their benefit; they walked in the woods, bathed in the thermal waters, gulped the salty *Sprudel*, and sat around in kosher cafés eating *Kuchen* and solving the problems of the world. If they encountered anti-Semitic bath attendants or waiters, the latter seem to have minded their manners, bit their tongues, and flashed fake smiles. In fact, the Zionists liked Karlsbad so much that they returned there for their Thirteenth Congress in 1923, despite an unsettling rumor (hotly and truthfully denied by local authorities) that the town had added a swastika to its municipal coat of arms.

Yet, putative swastikas aside, not all Zionists viewed Karlsbad as an appropriate gathering place for their movement. After all, grand European spas like Karlsbad symbolized the past—and a decadent, anxiety-ridden past to boot. One of the congress attendees, German journalist Arthur Holitscher, argued that it was "scarcely tolerable" that Zionists, strong-willed Jews with their eyes firmly fixed on the future, should convene in a place where gouty geezers gathered to hand-wring about their health and wax nostalgic about the past.

The Zionists did not return to Karlsbad, but through the rest of the twenties and much of the thirties, Jews continued to pour into that spa town, along with its smaller sister spa Marienbad and a few other choice Sudeten resorts. This influx became even greater after Hitler's seizure of power in neighboring Germany led to the outright banning of Jews from one Reich Kurort after another. Now, so many German Jews were hopping over the Czech border for cures that Marienbad enjoyed a brief boost to its economy after three years of terrible drought engendered by the Crash of 1929. (Marienbad in 1929 welcomed 41,226 cure-guests; by 1933, that figure had dropped by about half, to 21,503. In 1936, though, the spa hosted the International Psychoanalytic Society, which was heavily Jewish, for its annual congress.)

Yet, if the flow of German marks was certainly welcome in the Sudeten spas, the German Jews spending that money were generating even greater antipathy among pro-Nazi Sudetendeutsche, who bristled at the notion that their region was being used as a sanctuary by people the Mother Reich wanted no part of. Why couldn't *they* treat the Jews the way Hitler did? Well, it turns out they *could*—even if their first effort along these lines was limited to a single prominent victim.

The victim in question was Theodor Lessing, a Berlin-born polymath (philosopher, poet, physician, and psychologist) who had fled to Czechoslovakia in March 1933 shortly after Hitler's assumption of power. He stayed briefly in Prague before moving on to Marienbad, about which he had heard wonderful things. Pleased to have landed in what he called "one of the most beautiful and healthy places in Europe," a paradise combining the "advantages of a world-class spa with those of country living," Lessing was shocked to read in a local newspaper one day in June 1933 that the German government had put a bounty of eighty thousand marks on his head. This article, the same paper admitted a couple days later, had been a "joke," but Lessing was less than amused (and, in fact, the German government *did* want him dead, for he was continuing to write anti-Nazi polemics from his Bohemian sanctuary). Although understandably worried that some local Nazi knuckle dragger might see the newspaper article as an invitation to do Germany's bidding, Lessing rejected all suggestions that he seek refuge elsewhere. He even refused to relocate to securer quarters than his rooms in the Villa Edelweiß, which lay on the outskirts of Marienbad near a remote spring called the Waldquelle. "If a fanatic tries to kill me, I only pray that it may be quick," he said.

Lessing did not even get that humble wish. On the night of August 30, 1933, two thugs from the region shot him in the head through an upstairs window—they had purloined a ladder—as he sat writing in his comfortable study; he died an agonizing three-and-one-half hours later in the hospital. The killers fled to Bavaria, where they were celebrated as heroes and given a small financial reward by Joseph Goebbels for their services to the Reich. Marienbad Nazis were also very pleased with the murder, greeting it as a justified response to "goings-on among the emigrants."

Lessing's murder shocked Czechoslovakia, which, unlike Germany, was not used to political assassinations. The Czech government banned the *Marienbader Zeitung* for six months for printing the "joke" article on Lessing. On September 3, the poet/philosopher was buried under strong police guard in the local Jewish cemetery. (His grave can still be visited today, though doing so requires a long hike through the woods to the outlying burial ground.) The killing also had a huge impact on the town of Marienbad, which had always regarded itself as a safe haven for all, including Jews. Hundreds of horrified cure-guests, not just Jews, immediately fled the city, and many preregistered guests canceled their reservations.

For Marienbaders worried about their town's economic plight, Lessing's murder was hardly the only source of concern. German *Jews* might be throwing marks around Marienbad, but few *other* Germans were coming to the Czech spas due to the "anti-German" policies of the government in Prague. In response to Berlin-backed separatist agitation among members of Henlein's Sudeten German Home Front, Prague banned the Reich flag and Nazi Party publications from Czechoslovak soil. Prague also banned the Czech chapter of the Nazi movement. These steps in turn produced a boycott of Czechoslovakia by Hitler-loyal Germans. The mayor of Karlsbad protested that his town had lost five thousand German cure-guests in 1934 alone, a devastating blow to the local economy. Spa-town appeals to Prague to lighten up on the Hitlerites went unanswered—another sign of the government's "unconcern for the plight of the Sudeten cure industry," as local advocates put it.

Yet another sign of this neglect, according to Sudeten cure-industry representatives, was the government's refusal to allow casino gambling at the spas, and this at a time when both Germany and Austria were relaxing their restrictions on this highly profitable enterprise. No wonder the Sudeten spas were hurting!

By the mid-1930s, Prague and Berlin had mended fences somewhat, and the Sudeten spas were hoping fervently for some spillover from the 1936 Berlin Olympics (as were, for that matter, major spas in Germany and Austria). Maybe even the rich Americans would find their way back to the lovely Sudeten spas! Alas, although the Olympic Torch Relay passed through Teplitz (where local Nazis greeted it with "Heil Hitler" salutes), not many tourists included the Sudeten spas in their Olympics itineraries. In July–August 1936, Karlsbad actually reported a *drop* in visitors compared with the same period the previous year. As for Marienbad, it had to make do with a pre-Olympics swim meet between the Czechoslovak and Yugoslav Olympic teams. To land this mighty prize, Marienbad had to put up a seven-thousand-crown guarantee and house the competitors gratis with local families.

In light of the ongoing hard times, both Marienbad and Karlsbad competed vigorously for convention and congress business. In September 1934 Marienbad was pleased to host the Second Internationale Kongress für Förderung medizinischer Synthese und ärztlicher Weltanschauung— a program combining holistic medicine and eugenics. For the assembled medical practitioners, the take-home message from this meeting was expressed by a professor from Königsberg who urged his peers to do their part to address a fatal demographic imbalance in growth rates between the dim-witted and the bright—the latter breeding far too little, the former far too much. "No nation with a sound racial consciousness can accept the relentless proliferation of the untalented," he warned. The eugenics doctors found Marienbad so much to their liking that they decided to reconvene there in 1936.

Yet neither Marienbad's attractiveness to racists—or, for that matter, memories of the Lessing murder—could entirely undercut the spa's ongoing appeal to Jews. Word was out among Central European *Judentum* that Jewish entrepreneurs in Marienbad desperately needed patrons. In August 1936 the Executive Council of the World Association of Orthodox Jews met in Marienbad's National Hotel to discuss the dire situation for Jews in Germany and to plan for their upcoming 1937 World Congress, which they decided to hold in the beleaguered spa town. Before dispersing, the Orthodox leaders proclaimed their determination to resist Nazi efforts to "douse the flame of the Jewish people." That flame would continue to burn not just in Germany, they promised, but also in Palestine. "Palestine is Jewish, not Arab, and the Jewish people will live on there forever," said a spokesman.

The Jewish flame indeed burned brightly that next summer in Marienbad, when the Third World Congress of Orthodox Jewry gathered at the spa as planned. For a couple of weeks the little town was so filled with men in long cloaks and black felt hats that it might have passed for a shtetl in Poland. Yet this Lvov-like look did not go down at all well with a good portion of the local population. A representative of Henlein's party denounced the vice mayor, who was Jewish, for bringing down this black-clad scourge upon the Sudeten people. He urged that nothing like it ever be allowed to blight the town again.

And in fact there were no more Jewish congresses in Marienbad or Karlsbad in subsequent years—or decades for that matter. The next major meeting to transpire in a grand Sudeten spa was of a far different nature indeed: a gathering of Henlein's Sudetendeutsche Partei at Karlsbad on April 23-24, 1938. On April 24, Henlein issued his "Karlsbad Program," which called for complete autonomy for the Sudeten region—a steppingstone to secession from Czechoslovakia and coupling with Germany. The manifesto also demanded "full freedom [for Sudeten Germans] to demonstrate their German racial identity and affinity for German [i.e., Nazi] ideology." Henlein was obviously inspired by Germany's recent annexation of Austria; if Austria could "go home to the Reich," why not the Sudetenland? Indeed, Hitler had personally told Henlein as much in a meeting on March 28 in Berlin, where he instructed the Sudeten leader to stir up trouble back home so as to justify German military intervention. At about the same time, Hitler mooted with his generals an invasion of Czechoslovakia codenamed "Plan Green."

With Hitler's blessing, Henlein's forces embarked on an insurrectionary campaign designed to provoke a full-blown crisis in the Sudetenland. Much of this campaign focused on the grand spa towns, with their significant Jewish populations and assets. Nazi thugs ran through the streets of Karlsbad and Marienbad, breaking shop windows and beating up Jews. Marienbad Nazis imprisoned over a dozen Jewish citizens in the basement of the Café Egerland (now Hotel Monty). Not surprisingly, Jews began fleeing the two towns in droves, most of them heading for Prague. As the violence expanded to include Czech targets and even anti-Nazi ethnic Germans, Prague declared martial law in the region and, in late September, ordered a general military mobilization. Because the Western Powers had earlier committed to protect Czechoslovak sovereignty, the whole world braced for war.

War was averted at the last minute by the infamous Munich Agreement, through which Britain and France bought peace by ceding the Sudetenland to Germany (a gift that was not theirs to give). In justifying this pact, Britain's Neville Chamberlain famously said that the West could not be expected to go to war "because of a quarrel in a far-away country between people of whom we know nothing." Chamberlain's much celebrated "peace for our time" ended up lasting eleven months. In the interval between the Munich Agreement and Germany's invasion of Poland on September 1, 1939, Hitler gobbled up the rest of Czechoslovakia.

The Czechs, who had not been party to Munich, were naturally livid over the loss of the Sudetenland, though some found a silver lining in the fact that what remained of Czechoslovakia would be free of German influence. "We have only one consolation," averred a Prague patriot. "We won't need to maintain a German university in Prague and a technical college in Brno [anymore]. We'll purge our Czech air of every bit of the German virus."

Meanwhile, most of the ethnic Germans in the Sudetenland were overjoyed by Munich. The *Marienbader Zeitung* editorialized on September 30: "The injustice of Versailles has been set aside and Adolf Hitler has given his people a unified state such as the French and British people have enjoyed for centuries and the Italian people for decades."

Yet be careful what you cheer for—especially if you are a resident of a Sudetenland spa town. Even before German troops marched into the area to claim Hitler's new booty, Karlsbad and Marienbad were showing signs of acute distress. With virtually all the foreign guests having abandoned the baths, the towns' economies were in worse shape than ever. City streets and squares had completely lost their famous cosmopolitan flair. Even the fabled Grand Hotel Pupp, Karlsbad's most luxurious hostelry, looked neglected and forlorn.

For a good eyewitness glimpse of Karlsbad at this nadir in its long history, I'll leave you with a few lines from Maurice Hindus, a now-forgotten American journalist who visited that spa town on September 16 while covering the Czech crisis for various American newspapers:

> We reached Carlsbad. From the window of the train the station looked empty and gloomy. Only two porters came to meet the passengers, so most of us carried our own baggage. . . . None [of the hotel porters] could remember when the hotel lobby, even toward the end of the tourist season, looked so empty and so desolate. . . . It was past midnight when I turned out the light in my room. Sleep failed to come. I looked out the window. Carlsbad! I remembered that Czar Alexander III had visited it, and Turgenev. Kings and writers, artists, bankers, princes and charlatans had gone there, sometimes for their health, sometimes to start or to consummate national and international conspiracies. A city of doom or promise; which was it to be now? The streets were silent and gloomy; the stars that glittered through the haze with niggardly brightness held in them more darkness than light, more threat than promise.

CHAPTER EIGHT

Brown Waters

Grand Spas under the Third Reich

Hitler's promised "Thousand-Year Reich" lasted a mere twelve years (admittedly, twelve years too many), but for Central Europe's grand spas, that twelve-year stretch was the most momentous and destructive period in their entire history. True, the Kurorte had been battered about by the Great War and the Great Depression. But the Third Reich brought a wrenching degradation, a perversion of principles, in which the spas themselves were highly complicit. By the time the Nazi-instigated Second World War brought home to the Reich the same kinds of misery that Hitler's Germany was inflicting on its European neighbors, the grand spas were essentially a branch of the German war machine, their waters figuratively stained brown by Nazi ideology and blood-red by the patronage of wounded Wehrmacht soldiers, their primary clientele.

Nazis and Spas

National Socialism's perspective on Germany's spas was not without ambiguity, rather like the Hitler government's attitude toward other venerable institutions such as the army, churches, and universities. Certainly the grand Kurorte, at least at their epitome, were not compatible with Nazism's populist, racist, xenophobic ideology. Early on, Nazi ideologues had criticized luxury water-cure resorts as elitist, degenerate, and un-German—privileged precincts for wealthy snobs, many of them foreign and/or Jewish, who frittered away their time playing silly games, betting on horses, and engaging in illicit sex. (The fact that women had a prominent place in grand spa life was not lost on the misogynistic Nazis: shortly before Hitler took power a pack of Brownshirt thugs harassed society ladies for smoking in public in Baden-Baden.) Committed as they were, at least in principle, to breaking down class differences, expelling the Jews, eliminating "excessive foreign influences," and purging German culture and society of "unwholesome" practices, the Nazis, one imagines, would have gone after the Kurorte at the earliest opportunity. Yet their dealings with German spa land showed inconsistency because the leadership lacked uniform views on and experiences with spa life; moreover, the grand Kurorte themselves, or at least Baden-Baden, exploited an internal rift between ideology and pragmatism that ran through the entire history of the Third Reich.

Unlike Bismarck and the three "Second Reich" kaisers, Hitler was no spa aficionado, though God knows he could have used a good cure, replete with every kind of therapy, physical and psychological, in the grand Kurorte armory. By the time he took power, at age forty-four, he was already suffering from severe stomach cramps and attacks of nervous anxiety. The cramps convinced him (alas, incorrectly) that he had cancer and would soon die—hence his great hurry to put into practice the plans he had spelled out in *Mein Kampf*. But instead of sensibly dealing with his pains and anxieties with stress-reducing water cures—and perhaps a bit of brain-numbing electroshock therapy—he tried to stay healthy by taking lots of drugs and becoming a vegetarian and near-teetotaler, troubling signs in themselves. True, he sipped a beer now and then in order to appear folksy, but his liquid refreshment of choice was that old spa specialty, gaseous mineral water—in particular Fachinger Sprudel, crates of which he carried with him wherever he went. So partial was Hitler to Fachinger that when his long-time valet, Wilhelm Krause, served him an alternative brand during the Poland campaign, Hitler sacked him on the spot. The Führer was also a personal hygiene fanatic: he bathed every day, sometimes more than once. Fearing exposure to germs, he shied away as much as possible from shaking hands, much less hugging or cheek kissing in the Italian/Slavic style. He also harbored a phobia about being seen undressed; thus he refused to disrobe fully for medical exams (and perhaps also for sex, though we don't know that for a fact).

Given these phobias, one can hardly imagine Hitler sitting naked or near-naked in a thermal pool with dozens of other folks, "Aryan" or not. Nor might he even have enjoyed lolling alone in a spa bath, since said bath would not have been free of "pollutants" from previous bathers. In the end, when it came to unwinding, Hitler preferred his "Berghof" mountain retreat on the Obersalzberg near Berchtesgaden—though his Berghof stays cannot have been all that relaxing due to his habit of making key policy decisions there and haranguing houseguests for hours on end. (Hitler's presence at Berchtesgaden helped to make a nearby spa, Bad Reichenhall, very popular with top Nazis and various supplicants trying to curry favor with the Führer. The Jewish society columnist Bella Fromm, who cured regularly at Reichenhall, complained in her diary that Hitler's proximity "poisoned the mountain air" and attracted bothersome panjandrums like Alfred Krupp, who splashed about in the waters while awaiting an audience on the mountain.)

Not surprisingly, we have no record of Hitler's visiting spas for his health. Once he became Reich chancellor, he occasionally showed up at Kurorte, including grand ones, but solely for political reasons. For example, on June 30, 1934—the "Night of the Long Knives"—he, along with Goebbels, hastened down to Bad Wiessee, a small spa on the Tegernsee south of Munich, to put an end to what to what he claimed (falsely) was an incipient putsch against him by his old friend, SA commander Ernst Röhm. Hitler personally stormed into Röhm's room in the Pension Hanslbauer and placed him under arrest. The Führer later indignantly claimed that he had found Röhm in bed with a naked boy, but this was untrue, and in any event Hitler had known of his friend's homosexuality for years. Röhm, his "cure" abruptly over, found himself packed off to prison in Munich, where, refusing to shoot himself, he was shot dead by his SS guards. (A warning: Night of the Long Knives buffs traveling to Bad Wiessee in hopes of, say, booking Röhm's room at the Pension Hanslbauer can forget that dream: the pension in question no longer exists, though one can find "historic postcards" of it on eBay.) Following Germany's annexation of Sudetenland in October 1938, Hitler paid visits to Franzensbad and Karlsbad. In the former spa he and Heinrich Himmler drank glasses of mineral water drawn direct from the Franzen Quelle (a deviation from Fachinger necessary to please the locals). In Karlsbad, Hitler led an honor guard down the main street and addressed cheering crowds from a balcony of the opera house. Roughly one year later, in 1939, the Führer showed up in Bad Ems to celebrate Christmas with the SS *Leibstandarte Adolf Hitler*, which was based at the spa during Germany's preparations for its invasion of the Low Countries and France (about which more below). Given Bad Ems's historic association with humiliating France, virtually all the top Nazis visited that grand spa at one time or another, either to take the waters or simply to bask in the perceived glorious aura of the place.

Heinrich Himmler was sometimes at Hitler's side during the latter's spa appearances, but the SS leader also visited Kurorte on his own both for political purposes and to cure. Every bit as hypochondriac as Hitler, Himmler as a youth had spent many a summer at a spa on Bavaria's Staffelsee, where he dutifully bathed in hopes of improving his uncertain health and strengthening his puny body. Later in life he enthusiastically embraced hydropathy, along with other forms of Naturheilkunde, as the most ideologically acceptable "medical" recourse for race-conscious Germans. He was not alone. "Natural healing" was more popular during the Third Reich than at any other moment in German history, with the possible exception of our own credulous times. Although not quite as alcohol adverse as Hitler, Himmler aped his master in making a big thing of preferring mineral water over beer—some Bavarian *he* was! As head of the SS, Himmler saw to it that this enterprising and omnipresent state-within-the-state gained control over 75 percent of Germany's mineral water production.

Hermann Göring, by contrast, was emphatically *not* a water-over-beer man, and among the top Nazis he had the greatest affinity for high life at the luxury spas. There was no grand Kurort in Central Europe that he did not visit at one time or another. Among his favorites were Baden-Baden, in whose Augustabad he liked to loll with a cigar in one hand, a glass of champagne in the other, and Bad Gastein, which he patronized at least three times. When it came to spa connoisseurship, as well as sybaritic rotundity, Göring might be seen as Nazism's best answer to King Edward VII, though to see him as such would be to set aside an opportunistic inhumanity and brutality on his part that contrasted sharply with Edward's fundamental decency.

Göring's rival, Joseph Goebbels, not only hated the fat field marshal but also despised his lollygagging about in luxury spas. During the war year 1943 Goebbels grumbled in his diary that Göring seemed to do nothing with his time but take vacations and hang around in grand water resorts. In the wake of Germany's disastrous defeat at Stalingrad in February 1943, Goebbels even demanded that the luxury Kurorte be shut down. On the other hand, the dwarfish, womanizing propaganda minister did not exactly eschew luxury spas himself. Like Göring, he was partial to Baden-Baden and Bad Gastein, where he liked to frolic with his starlet mistresses. (Goebbels is said to have had no sexual intercourse whatsoever before age thirty-three and then to have made up for his late entry by exploiting his position as chief of Nazi German film production to bed no fewer than thirty-six actresses.) Perhaps because of his clubfoot and dwarfish stature, Goebbels steered well clear of the spas' thermal pools and public baths. Moreover, as a loyal Rhinelander, he was partial to Riesling rather than mineral water.

Although Central Europe's luxury spas could be (and were) attacked by some Nazis as "un-German" due to their moneyed cosmopolitan clientele, Germany's vast array of smaller and less pricey Kurorte found a favored place in the Third Reich's social and cultural infrastructure. In principle, the Nazi regime committed itself to replacing a hierarchical society based on heritage and income with a classless *Volksgemeinschaft*.

To that end, among other initiatives, Nazi Germany established Kraft durch Freude (KdF, Strength through Joy), a Reich-wide tourism and leisure-time agency whose stated goal was to end regional, religious, and class conflict. Run by Labor Service boss Robert Ley, an old Hitler crony who devoted much of his own leisure time to hitting the bottle and then to detoxing in luxury spas, the KdF made available to the working and lower-middle classes all sorts of activities previously open only to the better-off: horseback riding, sailing, skiing, seaside vacations, even ocean cruises.

Another KdF project was the "People's Car," a.k.a. Volkswagen. Inspired by Henry Ford's mass-produced Model T and designed by Ferdinand Porsche, the VW enjoyed Hitler's personal backing. In fall 1938, the KdF sent three prototype VW Beetles on a promotional tour through Germany. The cavalcade made a brief stop in Bad Ems, enticing many a local to put down a hefty deposit on one of these fabulous new buggies, deliverable in 1941. All told, some 340,000 Germans paid 275 million marks in prepayments on VW Bugs. In the end, only 640 of the KdF cars were ever produced, most of them going to party bosses. In

1940 the production line was shifted to military vehicles, and the Nazi government kept all the deposits as "contributions" to the war effort.

Spa visits also figured prominently among KdF offerings. Between 1933 and 1939, some 67 percent of all KdF holiday trips led to Kurorte or to similar recreation/beauty spots. As one might imagine, the majority of the spas in the KdF inventory were of the less distinguished variety—and, of course, "Jew-free." Borkum in northern Germany was a favored KdF seaside spa, while Eppstein in the Taunus Hills was a prized *Luftkur* destination, drawing three hundred Strength through Joy vacationers every weekend during the summer months. Eventually, even haughty Baden-Baden deigned to take in a few KdF tours, though these folks were relegated to the down-market eastern end of town.

For wealthy Nazis, the foreign Kurort of choice was Switzerland's Davos—erstwhile inspiration for Thomas Mann's *Magic Mountain* but known widely during the Third Reich as "Das Hitlerbad" (even though Hitler himself was not a regular there). Where today Bill Clinton, Bill Gates, Tony Blair, and the peripatetic Bono solve the world's problems at the annual Global Economic Forum, during the 1930s the most prominent visitors were upper-crust Germans with impeccable Nazi credentials. The nearby tuberculosis sanatorium Deutsches Haus catered exclusively to racially approved Reich-German patients. Between 1932 and 1937, some 189 Davos residents joined their local branch of the NSDAP. It was here that Wilhelm Gustloff, chief of the NSDAP Foreign Association in Switzerland, met his end on February 4, 1936, at the hands of a young Croatian Jew named David Frankfurter. (Enraged by Hitler Germany's attacks on the Jewish people, Frankfurter went to Gustloff's home and shot the Nazi leader five times in the head, neck, and chest; he then called the local police to confess his deed.) Hitler personally ordered a state funeral for Gustloff in his home town, which helped to put this handsome Alpine village on the map of Nazi martyrology.

But back to the KdF plebeians. During the Second World War, once the Germans had conquered Russia's Crimean Peninsula, Robert Ley put forth a plan to turn the entire area into "one big Kurort" for the German masses. Hitler concurred in the plan. "Crimea," the Führer announced, had to be "cleared of all foreigners" and made available exclusively for German settlement and recreation needs. For the duration of the war, however, total ethnic cleansing had to be put on hold.

Himmler, who took over the resettlement operation, ordered that the Crimean Tartars, many of whom had already been expelled by Stalin, be spared further deportation because they had collaborated with the Wehrmacht in vanquishing the Red Army. Thankfully, due to the war's outcome, Ley, Hitler, and Himmler never realized their dream of converting Crimea into a giant German Kurort. And if these days Vladimir Putin has plans to turn the territory into one big banya for Russian vacationers—at times he has indicated as much—he's got his work cut out: the peninsula's infrastructure is in terrible shape, its baths broken down, its hotels severely substandard.

"Germany's Visiting Card"

When it came to actually setting down some sort of national policy on spas, especially luxury ones, Hitler's government had to contend not only with differing perspectives among top leaders but also with the fact that basic bread-and-butter needs did not necessarily harmonize well with hallowed ideological precepts. A conflict between pragmatism and ideology bearing implications for the spas had shown up early on when the Reich had to decide whether or not to host the 1936 Olympic Games. In the 1920s, Nazi ideologues, including Hitler himself, had attacked the Olympic movement for its internationalist, peace-loving ethos and its inclusion of "inferior races" like blacks and Jews. The International Olympic Committee (IOC) had awarded the 1936 Summer Olympics to Berlin in 1931, but when Hitler came to power in 1933, many observers assumed he would disavow the games, forcing the IOC to move the festival elsewhere. Yet figures close to Hitler, above all Goebbels, convinced him that hosting the Games (including the Winter Olympics in Garmisch-Partenkirchen) would bring in large amounts of desperately needed foreign currency—and also allow the Nazis to show the world a friendly, cosmopolitan, and sophisticated Third Reich. Pragmatism trumped ideology, and the German Olympic Games went on as planned. This same line of pragmatic thinking applied, at least for a time, to Germany's premier Kurort, Baden-Baden.

Noble spa town that it was, Baden-Baden waited two days before staging a "spontaneous" torchlight parade to celebrate Hitler's accession to power. The town waited two full months before hoisting the swastika flag above city hall. Such tardiness was not a function of serious opposition to Hitler; rather, Baden-Baden simply wished to display a decorous reserve in its embrace of the new order—after all, one could not know whether it would even last.

Crucially for Baden-Baden in the early days of the Third Reich, the man who assumed control over the area, *Kreisleiter* Kurt Bürkle, was an "old fighter" (pre-1923 member of the NSDAP) with close ties to Hitler's inner circle. Bürkle might have used that clout to impose a hard-line Nazi agenda on the city but instead took the position that the best way for Baden-Baden to achieve an economic turnaround was to revive its standing as a first-rank international cure destination. More specifically, Bürkle, backed by the city council, proposed to have the town center officially designated a *Bannmeile* (neutral zone), free of political demonstrations, intimidation of foreigners, and even anti-Semitic repression. At a rally on April 7, 1933, Bürkle proclaimed: "The new administration of Baden-Baden will take pains to ensure that within the Kurort Bannmeile a complete civil truce prevails. . . . [The regional government] will always operate on the premise that Baden-Baden is a cure center and residential enclave where hospitality toward *all* visitors—especially *foreign* visitors, independent of religion or race—will be observed." In coming to Baden-Baden, Bürkle promised, foreigners would encounter a Germany that was friendly, tolerant, safe, and prosperous. In short, the outside world would be able to look upon Baden-Baden as "[Nazi] Germany's Visiting Card."

Central to Bürkle and company's vision for their special turf was a return of casino gambling to the spa town. Baden-Baden had never reconciled itself to the loss of what had once been one of its largest sources of revenue. Throughout the 1920s city boosters, along with their cohorts in other grand German spas, had campaigned hard to bring back the money-spinning wheels of yore. Despite being more liberal than the Kaiserreich in virtually every domain, Weimar Germany had retained the defunct empire's ban on casinos. Would the Nazis retain it as well? From the standpoint of ideology, it certainly appeared that they would. After all, casino gaming had an elitist image—it seemed about as compatible with beer-belly Brownshirt taste as, say, champagne. On the other hand, Hermann Göring was known to *love* champagne: perhaps he—or, more to the point, Hitler—could be induced to stomach a little roulette.

In May 1933, a Baden-Baden delegation led by Kurt Bürkle met personally with Hitler in Berlin and pled their case for a resumption of casino gambling. Painting a bleak picture of their town's current economic condition, they argued that starting the roulette balls rolling again at the spa was key to the region's recovery in general. At the conclusion of the meeting, Hitler promised to consider the matter.

The Führer didn't ponder the question very long. In July 1933 the Reich Interior Ministry announced that casino gaming would be permissible in Germany but *only* in cities that, in the period between 1924 and 1930, had registered at least seventy thousand visitors a year, of whom no less than 15 percent had to be foreign. Additionally, said cities had to be situated close to the border of a foreign nation that offered gambling. In so framing its casino conditions, Berlin clearly had Baden-Baden in mind, for the old Black Forest spa was quite demonstrably the *only* Kurort in Germany that could meet them.

Baden-Baden received notification of its special status on August 18, 1933, when the Reich Interior Ministry officially granted the town permission to open a casino. Grateful city officials promptly made Adolf Hitler an honorary citizen of the town. They also renamed the main square after the Führer and planted a "Hitler Oak" in the Lichtentaler Allee.

Town leaders planned to open Baden's new casino as early as October 1933, but to do so they needed to locate someone who could actually *run* such a facility—no easy task in a country that hadn't had any casinos for over sixty years. Unable to find any qualified German operators, Baden-Baden had to turn to *France* for its casino talent. The town had done this before, back in the 1830s, but since then a lot of very dirty water had passed under the Franco-German Bridge. To make matters even more ticklish, the French concessionaire that won the Baden contract was "racially tainted." The group's technical director, Georges Wormser, and his chief assistant, Carol Nachmann, were Jewish, as were the primary financial backers; only the firm's front man, an industrialist named Paul Salles, was a Gentile. On being apprised of this situation, the Reich Interior Ministry developed serious second thoughts regarding its licensing of a casino to Baden-Baden. The ministry could be persuaded to accept Baden's choice of a gambling concessionaire only on the condition that all the Jews involved stayed in the deep background. Furthermore, to avoid any direct dealings with the "tainted" concessionaire, the ministry would maintain contact with Baden's new gaming operation via a "study group" set up by the municipality. And finally, the Kurort's new casino venture was put on a one-year probation: it must prove its worth in that time or relinquish the spinning balls to another contender (Wiesbaden was first on the list).

As it happened, Baden-Baden had no difficulty surviving its probation year. Profits at the tables exceeded expectations by a good margin, and in 1934 the town's casino license was extended for ten years. However, when the Salles group's own contract expired at the end of 1935, it was *not* renewed; news of the firm's Jewish connections had gotten out through a French newspaper article embarrassingly titled "Les associes juifs d'Hitler." Not surprisingly, this revelation yielded unwelcome criticism from Nazi zealots. Baden-Baden's Cure Administration now took over all casino operations on its own, having in the meantime been able to train some homegrown talent.

Not just Baden-Baden's new casino was on a roll. In the brief period between late 1933 and the end of 1936, visitor numbers at the spa town shot up, reaching 125,000 in 1936. A substantial percentage of the new patronage was foreign—a very welcome development given that Hitler's coming to power had sparked an international movement to boycott all things German, including German spas (and the 1936 Berlin Olympics). Baden hotel owners and restaurateurs, happy to be flush again, echoed municipal politicians in profusely thanking their honorary *Bürger*, Adolf Hitler, for granting them their life-saving casino.

While the advantage of having Nazi Germany's sole casino certainly contributed to Baden-Baden's remarkable rejuvenation, gaming was not the only reason for the turnaround. More broadly, what stood behind the old Kurort's commercial comeback in the early years of the Third Reich was its status as a "neutral zone" in politics and culture—a unique privilege that allowed the city both to welcome a diverse foreign crowd and, as a necessary corollary, largely to eschew racist discrimination on the municipal level.

Baden-Baden, I hasten to emphasize, was not without its own Nazi activists, and shortly after Hitler came to power local Brownshirts harassed a Jewish department-store owner named Ludwig Lipsky, forcing him temporarily to close down. Moreover, under a Reich-wide measure carrying the Orwellian title "Law for the Restoration of the Professional

Civil Service," imposed on April 7, 1933, two Jewish members of the town council were summarily dismissed. During the nationwide boycott of Jewish businesses and services on April 1, 1933, SA thugs (now dressed in fancy Brownshirt ensembles designed by future German couture king Hugo Boss, who also supplied the swankier SS outfits) stood outside Jewish-owned stores warning customers to stay away. The April boycott, however, proved an even greater failure in Baden-Baden than elsewhere across the Reich. More importantly, Baden-Baden witnessed no physical attacks on Jews in the early Nazi years and no efforts to ban them from municipal services, including cure and bathing facilities. This was unusual, even for Germany's major Kurorte. Bavaria's Bad Kissingen had imposed its own ban on Jews in July 1934; Bad Ems did so in December of that year; and Bad Homburg followed suit in June 1935.

This relatively "moderate" treatment of Baden-Baden Jewry during the opening years of the Third Reich had significant consequences not only for the town's economy but also for its social makeup. Between 1933 and 1937, German Jews sought out Baden-Baden as a refuge from the active persecution they were experiencing in other parts of the Reich. Some 320 German-Jewish citizens resettled in the spa town during this period. Interestingly enough, 40 percent of these newcomers were over fifty years of age: no doubt they regarded a move to Baden-Baden as less stressful and risky than migration to a foreign land (we must remember that most foreign countries were either closing their doors to Jews entirely or making settlement on their soil extremely difficult). Also interesting is that 5 percent of the Jewish migrants to Baden-Baden bought property there—a testament to their confidence in the town as a long-term sanctuary.

This influx of German Jewish residents (along with, by the way, significant numbers of foreign Jewish cure visitors) did not go unnoticed by Nazi zealots across Germany. In 1936 a Nazi hate sheet called *Der Führer* complained that Baden-Baden's "Jew-friendly" policies threatened to turn that spa town into "an outpost of Palestine." On the other hand, the Olympic Games were coming to Germany in 1936, and the Hitler government was determined to show the world a kinder and gentler Third Reich—"Nazism lite," one might say. Put in yet another way, what the Nazi leadership wanted to achieve during the "Olympic year" was to present the entire nation as one big Baden-Baden, a picture postcard of German amiability.

Baden-Baden itself certainly got the message. Indeed, the city, highly conscious of its allure to foreigners, hoped that many of the *Ausländer* heading to Garmisch and Berlin for the games would make a detour to the Black Forest in order to get a physical tune-up and/or to take in some of the special cultural and sporting attractions the spa town was laying on for that year. The most notable of these special events was an international golf tournament that would transpire on the town's lush links immediately after the Berlin Olympics had concluded. Baden's proposed golf tourney gained Hitler's personal blessing inasmuch as there was to be no golf competition at the Berlin Olympics and the Führer was anxious to show off Germany as a first-rank golfing power (never mind that only a handful of Germans had ever broken eighty in a traditional eighteen-hole competition). Hitler was so confident in Germany's victory that he endowed a brass salver engraved with the words "*Golfpreis der Nationen, Gegeben vom Führer und Reichskanzler Adolf Hitler*." His idea was to motor down to Baden-Baden in order to present personally this cherishable keepsake to the happy winners.

Amazingly, among the seven nations competing on Baden-Baden's par-sixty-eight course over two thirty-six-hole days, the two German contestants actually took a five-stroke lead at the end of the first day of competition. Diplomat Joachim von Ribbentrop, who was watching the action, gleefully wired Hitler that Deutschland could expect a glorious victory. Hitler accordingly summoned his Mercedes for the drive down to Baden-Baden, which heretofore he had scarcely visited. Alas, on the tourney's final day the British contenders seemed to remember that *their* part of the world, not Germany, had invented golf (the powerful Yanks hadn't invented golf either, but they weren't playing) and took a lead not just over the Germans but also over a surprisingly competent French duo. The British completed the tournament with a five-stroke victory over France and a twelve-stroke advantage over the third-place Germans, who had completely choked in the final going. Knowing that the Führer would *not* be pleased, Ribbentrop raced off by car to interrupt him before he could reach Baden-Baden. Hitler promptly turned around and headed back to Berlin. Ribbentrop, not Hitler, presented the British players with perhaps the least known (and least prized) international golf trophy ever, the "Hitler Cup."

For the duration of the Berlin Olympics, Hitler's government famously put a damper on public displays of anti-Semitism—not just in

Berlin and Garmisch but across the Reich. After all, some of those Olympics tourists could be expected to travel elsewhere in Germany. Once the games were over, however, anti-Jewish actions and policies resumed with a vengeance—and in this second, more intense phase of persecution, Baden-Baden became fully caught up in the horror. That elegant spa town's days as a haven of relative tolerance, as "Germany's Visiting Card," were definitely over.

For Baden-Baden's Jews, the new harsh times were preceded by changes in local and district political leadership: Kurt Bürkle stepped aside as Kreisleiter for a Nazi zealot named Wilhelm Altenstein, while another hard-liner, Hans Schwedhelm, took over as *Oberbürgermeister*. Both these men were completely on board with Berlin's stepped-up efforts to drive German Jews into emigration by making life for them increasingly miserable at home. On January 20, 1937, the *Reichsstatthalter* for Baden, Robert Wagner, announced new anti-Jewish measures for that state. He seemed to have Baden-Baden specifically in mind, for the regulations included a prohibition on Jewish real-property purchasing; the exclusion of German Jewish citizens from all thermal pools and cure facilities; and the placement of signs saying *"Juden unerwünscht"* (Jews Unwanted) at the ticket windows of bathing complexes (this to deter foreign Jews).

Not surprisingly, Baden-Baden's *Kur* operators, luxury shop owners, restaurateurs, and hoteliers were appalled over these harshly discriminatory policies—so appalled, in fact, that they took the unusual step of leveling sharp protests in Wagner's direction. In a letter dated February 9, 1937, a group of Baden-Baden businessmen fumed: "Our entire city and its citizens are in great distress over the measures related to the Jews, which are intended to ban [these people] from our healing facilities. . . . All the advantages achieved by [reopening] the Spielbank Baden-Baden will be eliminated by these restrictions. . . . Those affected [by the decree] and their friends will now shift their patronage to baths in Switzerland and France, and Baden-Baden will be the big loser." A little later, Baden-Baden's hoteliers weighed in with a protest of their own: "The regulations affecting Jews also affect our hotels and will mean the *ruin of our beautiful bath-city!!!* News of the [imposed measures] hit our town like a bolt of lightning!"

Reichsstatthalter Wagner and Baden-Baden's Nazi leadership remained unmoved by these cries of alarm. In fact, Oberbürgermeister

Schwedhelm expressed relief that the city would no longer have to live with the reputation of being "an oasis for Jews in Germany." Moreover, he and his colleagues were convinced that excluding Jews from Germany's premier spa town would not harm its economy one bit. Non-Jewish foreigners would continue to patronize the spa, they believed, and the town would see a greater influx of "good Germans" now that Jews were no longer "polluting" the waters.

This confidence proved misplaced, to put it mildly. Over the short period between early 1937 and early 1940, guest visits, both by foreigners and overall, dropped steadily. Foreign patronage, having reached a high of about 35,000 in mid-1936, fell to 20,000 at the end of 1937 and to 10,000 in 1939. The overall decline was equally relentless, from a high of 125,000 in 1936 to about 45,000 in 1940.

With foreign visitors making themselves increasingly scarce in Baden-Baden, one might imagine that German Jewish residents would also have gotten themselves out of there as quickly as possible. Perhaps because they had enjoyed relative security early on, however, Baden-Baden's Jews proved less willing to emigrate than their cohorts elsewhere in the Reich. The vast majority sat tight as they were stripped of their citizenship per the infamous 1935 Nuremberg Laws and then forced to "sell" businesses and other assets through the Nazis' "Aryanization" program, which amounted to state-sanctioned theft. Ludwig Lipsky, the aforementioned owner of Baden-Baden's largest department store, reluctantly handed over his business to Aryan ownership in August 1938. Starting in that same summer, all German Jews, Badeners included, were made to add "Sara" or "Israel" to their names and to carry identity cards marked with the letter J. Also in 1938, Baden-Baden's Jews were banned from walking in the Kurpark. The Holländische Hof, one of the larger hotels in town, put up a sign on its restaurant door saying "No Entry for Jews or Dogs." SA thugs now patrolled the few remaining Jewish-owned shops, taking the names of all who dared to patronize them.

Yet worse, much worse, was to come. On November 9–10, 1938, Hitler's government orchestrated the Reich-wide pogrom known to history as *Reichskristallnacht* (Night of the Broken Glass). If any Baden-Baden Jews still harbored the illusion that their town was somehow "above" the worst Nazi excesses, this day and night of horror shattered that belief. In the early morning hours of November 10, Baden-Baden police officers and SS men rounded up all Jewish men over eighteen years of age and frog-marched them to police headquarters in Sophienstrasse. According to one of the victims, a high school teacher named Arthur Flehinger, the majority of Baden-Baden's Gentiles chose to stay indoors during the roundup, ashamed perhaps to look their Jewish neighbors in the eyes. Once assembled at the police H.Q., the Jews set off under guard for the local synagogue, where a gauntlet of young thugs "escorted" them up the steps and into the building. An SS man forced Flehinger to sing the *Horst Wessel Lied*, the Nazi anthem. When Flehinger did not sing loudly enough, he was made to repeat the ordeal. After that he was ordered to read aloud passages from *Mein Kampf*, and when once again his performance was thought muted, he was encouraged to speak up by blows across his neck. The Jews were held captive in their temple for several hours. Those who needed to relieve themselves were made to do so on the floor, right where they stood. Finally, the guards cleared the building, but not before stealing precious religious artifacts and then setting the entire structure ablaze. As elsewhere in Germany, Baden's Jews later received a bill for the damages and cleanup costs associated with Reichskristallnacht.

While their temple was still burning, Baden-Baden Jews under the age of sixty underwent yet another forced march to the railroad station at Oos, where they were packed into trains destined for Dachau, the Reich's pilot concentration camp just north of Munich. Most spent about a month at the camp before being allowed to return home—a "home" they now knew was no longer theirs, and one they had best flee immediately lest they be deprived of the opportunity to leave at all.

Between January 1, 1937, and the end of 1939, some 218 Baden-Baden Jews (from a total population in 1937 of 385) fled Nazi Germany to foreign lands. Those who stayed in town were primarily older people, for whom the rigors of emigration were simply too much. On the morning of October 20, 1940, most of these holdouts, 120 of them, were deported to Gurs, a grim internment camp in the French Pyrenees. Two years later, the inmates who had survived the horrors of Gurs were packed into boxcars and sent to extermination camps in the East. A similar fate befell the handful of Jews still hanging on in the spa town. They thought they were sacrosanct because they were married to "Aryans," but their immunity proved brief. As of summer 1942, Baden-Baden, that erstwhile haven for Jews, was "judenrein."

Meanwhile, during the last two years of peace, Baden-Baden, its Jewish population decimated and its foreign patronage sharply in decline, exchanged its vaunted cosmopolitan flair for a thoroughly German atmosphere—or, more precisely, a *Nazi* German atmosphere. Swastika flags bedecked all public buildings and most hotels. The vast majority of the guests at those hotels were Germans or citizens of the Reich's "Axis" allies.

No hotel in Baden-Baden registered the political vicissitudes of this era more clearly than the above-mentioned Brenner's Park, a local landmark that had emerged as the town's preeminent hostelry starting in the early twentieth century. Operated in the 1920s and 1930s by two grandsons of the original owner, Alfred Brenner, who had acquired the fabled Hotel Stephanie in 1872 and added to it a pair of equally magnificent wings, this enormous pile of stone overlooking the River Oos became in the twenties *the* place to bunk for globe-trotting plutocrats. Brenner's was particularly attractive to nouveau riche tourists from America, who could deposit their fancy autos in the building's underground garage, the first of its kind in Europe. (Those autos were treated by Brenner's garage attendants to the same Teutonic loving care that their owners received upstairs.) Because the hotel depended so heavily on American custom, however, Brenner's occupancy rate plunged like the New York Stock Exchange after the Crash of 1929. Serious thought was given to closing down. Yet due to the ongoing loyalty of Germany's own plutocracy and fashionable entertainment community, the hotel managed to hang on. In summer 1930 its guest list included Franz Lehár, Jewish torch-singer Richard Tauber, and Berlin Philharmonic conductor Wilhelm Furtwängler. The reopening of Baden-Baden's casino three years later sparked a new boom at Brenner's, which became the favored lodging for high-rolling *Spieler*. During the early years of the Third Reich, wealthy foreigners once again constituted a mainstay for the business. *Ausländer* comprised 63 percent of Brenner's clientele in 1936, the high-water mark for foreign patronage. Among the foreign notables was Walt Disney, who stayed at the hotel during a European tour in summer 1935. Although not a Nazi sympathizer (as is sometimes alleged), Disney admired some of the things Hitler was doing, such as putting down the Communists. In turn, Hitler had a weakness for Walt, screening his Mickey Mouse cartoons ad nauseam at the Berghof.

Naturally, the subsequent post-1937 drop-off in foreign visits to Baden-Baden also hurt Brenner's bottom line. However, at least until the war, the hotel compensated for a scarcity of outsiders with an influx of insiders: Brenner's became a favored stomping ground for Nazi *Bonzen* (big wigs) like Göring, Goebbels, and Himmler. The SS leader showed up often, as his omnivorous organization maintained close ties to the Bielefeld-based family firm that owned considerable stock in the Brenner's Park Corporation—and would assume controlling interest in 1938. The firm in question, Oetker and Sons, started out as a pudding manufacturer and went on to produce all kinds of edibles. During World War II the company became a major supplier to the Wehrmacht, providing the troops with such delicacies as synthetic sausage made from recycled garbage. Company patriarch Rudolf Oetker boasted of his membership in a business lobby called "Der Freundeskreis Reichsführer SS," (Friends of the SS Leader), which between 1935 and 1944 donated about one million marks a year directly to its SS "friend." (The Oetker firm still owns Brenner's, and while spending a few days and mountains of Euros at this Schwarzwald Xanadu to conduct research for this book—anything for science—I discovered that the staff is *not* inclined to discuss their institution's role in the Third Reich, if indeed they are curious about it at all.)

Baden-Baden, it turns out, was not only Nazi Germany's lone casino town at this point (the Greater German Reich would later include Baden-bei-Wien's Spielbank), but also its sole "visiting card." As if feeling guilty for allowing a degree of tolerance, even temporary, in that famous Kurort, Nazi authorities showed no similar restraint in their dealings with other grand spa towns. Nor, apart from Baden-Baden, did representatives of the Kurorte themselves make much effort to keep Nazi ideology at bay.

Let's look briefly at Bad Ems as a case in point. The NSDAP was quite strong in this spa town even before Hitler came to power, winning 35 percent of the votes in the Reichstag elections of November 1932, the highest of any party in the city. Town leaders threw a big party for Hitler soon after his accession to power and named him an Honorary Citizen on March 31, 1933—a distinction the city did not repeal until *1989!* Even Bad Ems's Cure Administration was quick to jump on the Nazi bandwagon. After leading the torchlight parade celebrating Hitler's assumption of the Reich chancellorship, local spa administrators erected a man-sized swastika atop the dome of the Kursaal, the iconic center of the Cure Quarter. Nearby, in front of the huge statue of Kaiser Wilhelm I, Bad Ems organized one of the largest book burnings in the Nazi Reich. On May 10, 1933, schoolkids tossed thousands of books and pamphlets purged from public and private collections on an enormous bonfire. Fueling the blaze were works of Marx, Heine, Kafka, Tucholsky, Helen Keller, and Thomas Mann, among others. (Mann himself, having recently fled Germany to escape possible arrest for making anti-Nazi speeches, was denounced at the book burning as an "enemy of Germany"—although early on in his exile he had muted his criticism of Hitler's regime in a deluded hope that his books might remain available there and his property unmolested.)

With "un-German" writings safely up in flames, Bad Ems's bosses turned their attention to unacceptable people. The Ems police rounded up forty members of various organizations considered hostile to the new order and paraded them through town en route to prison (and later deportation to camps). Bearing a large sign saying *"Wir sind die Lumpen von Bad Ems!"* (We are the dregs of Bad Ems), the men endured volleys of curses, spit, and even blows from fellow townsfolk lining the street.

Ems's Jewish population also suffered persecution as soon as the Nazis took power; for them there was no temporary reprieve, as happened in Baden-Baden. A prominent early target of Nazi harassment was one Emil Königsberger, a wealthy merchant and the sole Jewish member on the city council. Despite his archconservative German Nationalist political credentials, Königsberger came under such harsh public abuse from local Nazis that he suffered a fatal heart attack in March 1933. Poignantly, he fell dead among his supposed friends at his *Stammtisch* (regular table) at the Goldenes Fass tavern. Königsberger's council seat immediately passed to a member of the Nazi Party. A week after Königsberger's death, his fellow Ems citizens joined heartily in the April 1 Reich-wide boycott of Jewish shops. Here, at least, local Nazis could crow with some legitimacy that the boycott was a success.

Significantly, the boycott action extended to the hospitality businesses within Ems's historic cure quarter. A special decree issued on that malignant April Fools' Day by Ems's new Nazi mayor, Hermann Messerschmidt, and promptly endorsed by local hoteliers and restaurateurs, stated that Jews "must not be served at any facilities operating in the cure quarter." In spring 1933 Jewish spa doctors also came under fire. The Prussian Interior Ministry, now under the leadership of Hermann Göring, dispatched a hack bath physician named Wolfgang Klaue to Bad Ems with orders to purge the Kurort of Jewish practitioners. Klaue took to his task with such zeal that the town's spa operations were judenrein within a few months. (Göring, I should add, had his eye on Ems not so much because of its vaunted thermal waters but because valuable lead mines nestled cheek to jowl with the Quellen, which they were polluting. Instead of protecting the waters, as most Emsers naturally wanted, Göring, already thinking of arms-production needs, ordered an expansion of the mining operations. "I am not interested in asthmatics," he huffed, "I only care about the ore. We've got plenty of water in Germany, we don't have enough lead.")

One of the sadder aspects of Ems's anti-Jewish campaign was the alacrity with which many ordinary townspeople took it up. Hardly a week went by without some vigilant citizen denouncing a neighbor to authorities for infractions like tipping one's hat to a Jew, consorting with Jews, or patronizing Jewish services. For example, some zealot informed Julius Streicher's anti-Semitic rag *Der Stürmer* that Bad Ems's Hotel Römerbad was secretly taking meat deliveries from a local butcher named Salomon. Another citizen denounced the reputable Ems-based spa physician Dr. Siegfried Cohn as a *Schieber* (racketeer).

Inevitably, Cohn was one of the prime targets of Ems's version of Reichskristallnacht. Groups of SA thugs broke into his house on the night of November 10, 1938, threw furniture out the windows, and drove the Cohn family into their backyard garden, where they huddled fearfully in a toolshed for hours. Although Dr. Cohn could not have known it, regional Nazi bosses had decided to hit his town especially hard because Ems housed the largest Jewish Gemeinde in the Lower Lahn River area. It was time, the Nazis said, to make this "historic" German Kurort "judenrein." Accordingly, they trashed virtually every remaining Jewish business in town and wrecked dozens of private homes along with Cohn's. Local thugs even pillaged an upscale hotel whose Gentile owner was regarded as Jew-friendly. Although the orders for this pogrom had come down from Berlin, the actors in the Ems violence were predominantly local and included craftspeople, schoolteachers, and town notables—a very "democratic" affair. As SA pillagers stormed through the streets, some bystanders cheered them on or even joined in. Although most ordinary folk did not take part in the pillaging and looting, apparently not a single Emser raised an objection to what was going on.

"Ein Volk, Ein Reich, Ein Führer"

When it comes to ideological rigidity, an empire's borderlands are often more zealous than the heartland, more Catholic than the pope. So it was with the Third Reich—and with the Third Reich's late-acquired and briefly held grand spa towns in Austria and the Sudetenland. Places that had once celebrated their separateness from surrounding small-mindedness now became citadels of conformity in the Greater German Reich.

After Hitler came to power in Berlin it took him a mere five years to bring his native nation *"heim ins Reich"* (home to the Reich). But this half-decade seemed an eternity to his fanatical followers in Austria. In July 1934 they mounted a coup in Vienna designed to force an immediate *Anschluss* with Germany but succeeded only in murdering the Catholic conservative chancellor, Engelbert Dollfuss (a man so large in self-esteem and so small in stature that he was known as "Mini-Metternich"). Dollfuss's successor, Kurt von Schuschnigg, sought to perpetuate Mini-Metternich's policy of Austrian independence; he re-outlawed the Nazi Party and saw to the trial and execution of Dollfuss's assassins. His own party, the Fatherland Front, imposed authoritarian rule over the land. But Schuschnigg, a dry, uninspiring, and weak-willed figure, was ultimately no match for Hitler, who in February 1938 bullied him into lifting the anti-Nazi measures and naming a prominent Austrian Nazi, Arthur Seyss-Inquart, to his cabinet. Then, as if ashamed of his capitulation, Schuschnigg tried to save the day by announcing a referendum on Austrian independence. Enraged, Hitler demanded that Schuschnigg call off the vote. Even though the Austrian leader hastily complied and stepped down, on March 12, 1938, German troops poured over the border under the pretext of "restoring order." Although technically an invasion, the German takeover of Austria was more akin to strolling through an open door.

On March 11, 1938, Seyss-Inquart's hometown of Baden-bei-Wien was bedecked with the red-white-red banners of the Fatherland Front in preparation for Schuschnigg's referendum. The chancellor's resignation speech that same evening brought an immediate change in political coloration: out came the black-red-white colors of Nazi Germany, along with cries of "*Ein Reich, Ein Volk, Ein Führer.*" To the cheers of crowds below, a man on the roof of the Rathaus pulled down the Austrian flag and hoisted the swastika banner. A Nazi zealot named Franz Schmid, who would become Baden's new mayor the following day, climbed atop the Ferdinand Fountain in the Kurpark and announced that his town's glorious return to the Reich meant an end to twenty years of weakness and humiliation imposed by the Western powers.

No sooner had Baden-bei-Wien changed its political spots than it went from being the favored Kurort of Austrian Jewry to a model spa town of the new order, much prized by top Austrian Nazis. (The fact that the town had a casino was definitely *not* a detraction here.) Seyss-Inquart, now Reichsstatthalter for the Ostmark (Austria's designation in Greater Germany) had much to do with this transformation. He honored his hometown with a personal visit on March 20, 1938, thereby helping to make the spa fashionable for other leading Nazis. Hermann Göring came down on April 9 to inspect a new barracks complex being built for Wehrmacht Flak Regiment Number 25, whose presence signaled Baden's emergence as a Nazi *Garnisonstadt* (garrison city). Naturally, the sybaritic field marshal took this opportunity to try the local waters, which he found much to his liking (though he would not return to the spa until the war years). By the time Göring graced the town, Baden-bei-Wien had already engineered some requisite place-name alterations: Hauptplatz became Adolf-Hitler-Platz; the old Pfarrgasse, having been rechristened Dollfussgasse in 1935, now bore the name of one of the chancellor's executed assassins, Otto-Planetta-Strasse. The day after Göring's visit, April 10, 1938, Baden residents cast their votes in a plebiscite to validate Austria's annexation by Germany. Baden-bei-Wien's tally of 15,877 "ja" votes versus 35 "nein" pretty much matched the nationwide result of 99.75 percent in favor of the Anschluss.

During its brief moment in the brown sun, Baden-bei-Wien traded vigorously on its ties to Beethoven, whom the Nazis adopted as one of their own, as they had Richard Wagner. In the Third Reich the only politically correct way to see Beethoven was (in the words of one Nazi pundit) "as a representative of his Volk; as the highest embodiment of his race." Mirroring Bayreuth's Nazified Wagner Festival, in 1938 and 1939 Baden-bei-Wien mounted much-heralded Beethovenfestspiele that placed both the great composer and his erstwhile summer refuge firmly in the National Socialist cultural orbit. As in Bayreuth, the musical quality of the festival performances was quite high (Hitler himself demanded the deployment of the best players and conductors), but only a true believer could have enjoyed the ancillary exhibitions and symposia designed to reveal Beethoven as a thoroughly *völkisch* artist—a Nazi waiting to happen. The town whose police had once arrested Germany's greatest composer as a "lump" smothered itself during the festivals in a sea of Beethoven imagery and swastika flags. Along with the inevitable Beethoven beer steins, souvenir shops offered special "Festspiel" tea-towels bearing the likenesses of Beethoven and Hitler side by side—two "Great Germans" on one rag.

When Beethoven was alive and composing in Baden-bei-Wien, he had found considerable support and admiration among the town's substantial Jewish population. That community was already disintegrating under intense governmental persecution by the time Hitler and Beethoven showed up on the souvenir tea towels. On July 2, 1938, the Nazified *Kreisleitung* forbade Austrian Jews from settling in Baden and ordered recently arrived Jews to leave the town immediately. Jews with deep roots in the area, of whom there were many, also faced harsh measures designed to force them out. In the fall of 1938, local schools banished Jewish students to separate classrooms; in 1939, Jewish kids were banned from public education altogether. As in Germany, Jewish business owners were forced to offload their properties for pennies on the mark (that currency having replaced the schilling in April 1938). Jewish-owned villas—erstwhile summer havens for families like the Galas, Jellineks, and Ephrussi—became vacation retreats for Nazi bosses or local headquarters for Nazi institutions. Meanwhile, on the water-cure front, Mayor Schmid's administration set aside one isolated thermal bathing facility for Jews in April 1938, only to take even that away a year later, when it barred Jews from all bath and cure facilities in the town.

The majority of Baden-bei-Wien's Jews got the Nazis' message clearly enough and took flight from the town (and Ostmark) in whatever way they could. By 1940, after just two years of Nazi control, the spa town's once vibrant Jewish Gemeinde had essentially disappeared.

The few Jews who could not or would not leave soon disappeared as well—or rather, *were* disappeared.

Hitler's Austrian followers had attempted to force an Anschluss on Bad Ischl and the Salzkammergut some four years before the Führer brought his former homeland "heim ins Reich." On July 25, 1934, just as Vienna-area Nazis were storming the chancellor's office in the Ballhausplatz and gunning down "Mini-Metternich," a band of alpine Brownshirts tried to take over Ischl only to be turned back by local police and elements of the army. Two of the putschists, Franz Saureis and Franz Unterberger, happened to hail from Bad Ischl itself. Like their counterparts in Vienna, the two Franzes paid for their impatience by going before a military firing squad. In March 1938, with Austria safely home in the Reich, Bad Ischl honored its Nazi "martyrs" by renaming a major street Saureis-Unterbergerstrasse. The most important name change, however, was reserved for the true hero of the hour: "Adolf-Hitler-Platz" replaced "Kreuzplatz" on signs for the town's central square.

The name alterations portended more significant changes on the social-political front in the alpine Kurort. A *Kurdirektion* that heretofore had welcomed Jews, or at least rich ones, now fell over itself to display its newly brown credentials. In time for the 1938 summer cure season it decreed that Jewish visitors must be quartered separately in the least desirable hotels and pensions. Jewish guests would not be allowed to enter the central cure area during concerts by the Kurorchester. A year later Ischl banned Jewish cure-guests entirely—a largely symbolic move, since Jews were no longer coming to this deeply inhospitable Kurort anyway.

As for resident Jews, they, along with their counterparts all across Austria, faced increasing pressure to vacate their homeland. The Jewish owner of the Hotel Franz Karl, one of the grand hostelries of the k. und k. era, folded his tent and fled the country. Jewish artists such as Oscar Straus and Emmerich Kálmán, preeminent operetta composers who had helped put Ischl on Austria's musical map, emigrated as well (Straus to a successful career on Broadway). Even Franz Lehár, Central Europe's beloved operetta king, came under scrutiny by the Gestapo because he had a Jewish wife. Yet in the end Lehár was allowed to stay around: after all, one could hardly expel the composer of *Die lustige Witwe*, Hitler's all-time favorite operetta.

The great Franz Lehár's presence notwithstanding, Bad Ischl became something of a backwater during the Nazi era because it failed to catch on with the Ostmark's new elite. This was definitely not the case with nearby Bad Gastein. Once the Reich had absorbed Austria, Reichsdeutsche streamed back to their favorite alpine Kurort in numbers large enough to compensate for the missing foreign visitors. Popular in particular with Nazi Bonzen, German plutocrats, and stars of the state-controlled cultural industry, Gastein became (in the words of one commentator) "the premier *Heilbad* for Aryan Teutons."

Bad Gastein's permanent residents, or most of them anyway, greeted the Anschluss with wild enthusiasm. A ten-year-old witness to the raucous celebration on the night of March 12, 1938, recalled being awakened by a loud noise. He ran to his window to see a long torchlight parade snaking through town, the demonstrators crying (what else?): "*Ein Volk, Ein Reich, Ein Führer! Sieg Heil, Sieg Heil!*" at the top of their lungs. The next day, recalled the youngster, many Gasteiners were too hoarse to speak.

The townsfolk had another opportunity to cheer the new order on April 5, 1938, when Hitler himself made an appearance in town. Actually, his appearance lasted only a few seconds, amounting merely to a wave from the window of his special train as it sped through town. (Hitler was on a swing through Austria to drum up enthusiasm for the April 10 Anschluss plebiscite.) The brevity of Hitler's "visit" did not prevent hundreds of Gasteiners from crowding the train station to "Sieg Heil" as their Führer whizzed by.

In preparation for the upcoming plebiscite, Gastein's newly Nazified municipal leadership ordered all householders to bedeck their residences with swastika flags. The larger the house, the bigger and more numerous the banners had to be. As expected, Gasteiners voted overwhelmingly in favor of the Anschluss—2385 "ja" votes to just one "nein." That one negative ballot might have been an embarrassment, since fully *fifty* Gemeinde in Salzburg Province registered no dissenters at all. Yet, rather than simply discarding its lone nein, as one might have expected, Gastein's bosses decided to exploit it for some good Nazi fun. They rustled up a donkey from a local farm, attached a sign to the animal saying "I voted no," and paraded the beast through town to the accompaniment of a brass band. Gasteiners found this spectacle hugely entertaining—and perhaps instructive as well.

Not long after the dissenting donkey show a very different creature—a true Nazi "*hohes Tier*" (big shot)—made a stopover in Gastein.

None other than Propaganda Minister Joseph Goebbels rolled into town for a brief stay at the Grand Hotel de l'Europe—and a brief tryst with his latest mistress, Czech-born actress Lída Baarová. (Hitler later made Goebbels give up Baarová "for the good of the Reich" after the randy minister's wife, Magda, complained to the Führer that "the Slav slut" was ruining her model German marriage—a marriage that dutifully produced six blond children, every one of whom Magda would murder with cyanide-laced bedtime treats as Russian soldiers closed in on their refuge in Hitler's bunker.) As they did during their donkey spectacle, Gasteiners lined the streets and cheered for Goebbels. On hand for the German's historic visit was Edmund Glaise-Horstenau, an Austrian army general and assistant to Seyss-Inquart. Glaise thought (wrongly) that by embracing Nazism, a conservative Catholic nationalist like himself could preserve a measure of autonomy and influence for Austria within Greater Germany. But the Third Reich had no use for Ostmark "particularism," preferring instead the hyper-Nazi zeal displayed by most Austrians. In short order, Glaise and his ilk were "pushed into the background," as he bitterly complained. Unsurprisingly, though, the prickly Austrian kept his discontent to himself during Goebbels's Gastein visit, readily joining the minister in his triumphal drive through town. Only in his postwar memoirs did Glaise reveal his "true" feeling about having to interrupt his annual Gastein cure to honor the oily German shrimp:* "Goebbels was once in Gastein and I was forced to join his triumphal motorcade down the Hauptstrasse. The [townspeople's] enthusiasm for the guy was revolting."

Gasteiners indulged in yet another burst of Nazi enthusiasm a few weeks later in connection with one of those ceremonial name changes then transpiring across Austria. A prominent street that in July 1934 had been altered from "Reichstrasse" to "Dr. Dollfussstrasse" was rechristened again, on April 21, 1938, to "Strasse der SA." This was a magnificent moment for the local storm troopers, prompting an hour-long parade. (Once the Nazis were gone from the scene, "Strasse der SA" unsurprisingly struck local leaders as "*unzeitgemäss*"—inappropriate to the new age. Today the street bears the designation "Kaiser-Franz-Josef-Strasse"—part of a strategic *k. und k.* nostalgia makeover that afflicts the entire region.)

---

*Even at the time, some critics of Goebbels thought the little propagandist personified Thomas Hobbes's definition of life: "nasty, brutish, and short."

If, as I've said, Gastein in the Third Reich became a Heilbad for top Teutons, just who, apart from Goebbels, were those illustrious visitors? The list of major Nazi patrons included Goebbels's hated rival, Hermann Göring, who first stayed at the spa in September 1940 with his daughter Edda and wife Emmy, a former actress. Frau Emmy, it seems, suffered from various afflictions, including chronic sinus infections, which she hoped to remedy at Gastein. The Göring ménage rented an entire seventeen-room floor in the elegant Kaiserhof Hotel for their three-week visit. Not content with the hotel's accoutrements, Emmy had her big brass bed and favorite carpets shipped to Gastein from Berlin. Göring returned to Gastein three more times in 1941 to stay with his ailing wife and daughter. Again, they resided either at the Kaiserhof or the Hotel Regina—definitely *not* the Grand Hotel de l'Europe, which was rendered off-limits for them by the lingering taint of Goebbels.

In August 1940, just before Göring's first visit, Alfred Rosenberg, a self-infatuated ideologue who headed the Foreign Department of the Nazi Party, settled into the Kaiserhof for a three-week cure. A more regular visitor was *Reichsleiter* Walter Buch (the Nazi Party's top judge), who cured there with his wife on three occasions between 1938 and 1942. Yet another Nazi-era heavyweight was Franz Ritter von Epp, who was Hitler's Reichsstatthalter for Bavaria. Epp loved Gastein because it reminded him of Bavaria without being *in* Bavaria, where he had to deal daily with low-rent Hitler hangers-on whom he loathed. As if the golden-brown luster cast by Goebbels/Göring, Rosenberg, and Epp were not enough, Gastein could also boast a host of only slightly less distinguished luminaries of Hitler's government in the years between 1938 and 1943: Education Minister Bernard Rust, Agriculture Minister Walter Darré, Labor Minister Franz Seldte, Transportation Minister Julius Dorpmüller, and Post Minister Wilhelm Ohnesorge. Along with these figures came a gaggle of *Gauleiters*, an orgy of *Obergruppenführer* SS, and such leading lights of the Wehrmacht as U-boat Admiral Karl Dönitz, Army General Alfred Jodl, Field Marshal Paul von Kleist, Rear Admiral Hans Bütow, and many, many more.

Gastein had long been a favored water-resort for globe-trotting financiers and industrialists; during its Nazi years the spa continued to attract this breed, albeit now an exclusively German variant thereof. As if to make up for the smaller feeder-pool, virtually all the big-name German industrialists with profitable ties to the Hitler regime showed up at the

Alpine spa. Between 1938 and 1940 the town's Kurliste included, inter alia, Fritz Thyssen, Carl Bosch, Ferdinand Porsche, Peter Klückner (a mining and metals magnate), Gustav Krupp von Bohlen, Wilhelm von Opel, Willy Messerschmitt, and Ernst Heinkel. (Examining Gastein's Kurliste, one can speculate that if the British had just dropped a few timely bombs on this one little spa, they might have wiped out a good part of the German military-industrial machine.)

For Gastein locals—and even, no doubt, for some of the visiting generals and industrialists—appearances at the spa by entertainment-industry celebrities of the Third Reich provided the highest pitch of excitement. Admittedly, Nazi Germany's performance culture lacked the verve and sophistication of Weimar days, but it was still something to spot actresses Lil Dagover and Olga Tschechova frolicking in the baths. Leading men showed up as well: Willi Bürgel, Hans Thimig, and Wolf Albach-Retty, to name just three long-forgotten Nazi-era matinée idols. At Gastein these film stars could mix not only with Reich-government cabinet ministers (a perhaps less-than-thrilling option) but also with genuine brownish blue bloods like Prince Joachim Albrecht von Preussen, Prince Philipp von Hessen, and Countess zu Eulenberg. It was all so very, very chic—or at least what passed for chic in Hitler's Reich before it all went up in flames.

It would be unfair to Nazi-era Gastein to give the impression that it *entirely* lacked illustrious foreign clientele. The problem, though, was that such foreign patronage had to be limited pretty much to Berlin's principal allies, Italy and Japan. In the end, the former nation proved to be about as useful to Gastein as a supplier of paying curists as it did to Nazi Germany as a military ally. Virtually no Italians of distinction came north to cure because even the wealthy and influential among them felt looked down upon in Nazi Austria, and Rome lived in constant fear that Hitler might any day bring the Italian Alto Adige (South Tyrol) *"heim ins Reich"* alongside its former Austrian owners. Moreover, despite Mussolini's opportunistic alliance with Hitler, the Italians had many old bones to pick with the Austrians and Germans; most Italians wanted as little to do with the arrogant Tedeschi as possible. (Even Mussolini combined his admiration for the Germans' military power with contempt for their culture, observing early on that their ancestors were still "baying at the moon" while Rome was civilizing the Mediterranean world.)

That left Japan, a nation with its own magnificent water-cure culture and no record of affection for the distant and (in Japanese eyes) probably unhygienic thermal waters of Central Europe. Nonetheless, perhaps out of a sense of duty, a few Japanese diplomats paid visits to Gastein in the early 1940s. First to arrive, as if to test the waters, was Le Je Wen, an ethnic Chinese emissary to Berlin from Japan's puppet-state of Manchukuo. He was followed by the Japanese ambassador to Italy and then, the crowning glory, Tokyo's ambassador to Berlin, Hiroshi Oshima, with wife in tow. Under Oshima's aegis, a mixed-gender Japanese tour group also showed up at the spa, all elegantly dressed in the latest European fashions. The Japanese diplomats stayed at the Grand Hotel de l'Europe, now run by Viktor Sedlacek's son Alfred, who, "purely for business reasons," joined the Nazi Party in May 1938. (One imagines the recently deceased Viktor Sedlacek, a Nazi foe, turning over in his grave.)

Along with the Japanese, a sprinkling of other foreign diplomats turned up in Gastein—this paucity of foreign patronage itself being a telling sign of Greater Germany's isolation and diminished status in the larger scheme of things. Ankara's ambassador to Berlin cured in Gastein in 1942, staying at the Grand Hotel de l'Europe. (During World War II, Turkey remained neutral until near the end of the conflict, when it joined the Allies. Before that, however, it maintained close ties with Germany, which it supplied with vital raw materials like chromite.) On the heels of the Turk came Vojtech Tuka, minister-president of Slovakia, a clerical-fascist client state of Nazi Germany, carved (like Sudetenland) out of the corpse of republican Czechoslovakia. Tuka visited Gastein twice, in 1943 and 1944, and he, too, stayed at the Grand Hotel de l'Europe, obviously *the* place to lodge for visiting emissaries. But Tuka's stay was a last hurrah for Alfred Sedlacek's posh hostelry; soon it would become a hospital for wounded and dying soldiers.

Well before World War II visited devastation on Gastein and other Central European spa towns, the Nazi takeover in Austria spelled escalating torment for Gastein-area Jews, just as it did for Ostmark Jews in general. In Gastein's case, the attack on resident Jews was preceded by the newly Nazified municipality's decision, right after the Anschluss, to close city doors to any and all foreign Jewish visitors. The reason given for this foreign Jewish ban was that the Kurort "regrettably lacked" sufficient facilities to provide "separate bathing arrangements" for Jews and Gentiles as required by the laws of Greater Germany. Shortly after this pronouncement, city leaders announced that, per a Reich Interior Ministry decree of July 27, 1938, Gastein was obliged to get rid of all "Jewish" place names. Lacking any significant offenders in this domain, the spa town contented itself with changing the name of a woodsy footpath from "Meyerbeer-Weg" to "Holzweber-Weg" (Franz Holzweber being another of the Dollfuss assassins whose execution by Schuschnigg's regime instantly brought them martyr status among area Nazis).

Having dutifully exorcized the ghost of a long-dead Jewish musician (and frequent Gastein curist) from their woods, town fathers turned to the more serious task of ridding their community of its extant Jewish residents by making their lives unlivable. At first they compelled Jewish business owners to place large signs on their premises saying "*jüdisches Geschäft.*" Next, in June 1938, a local law forbade Jews from renting or purchasing property, commercial or residential. A Jewish jeweler from Salzburg who for years had rented a small space in the city center during the summer spa season was informed by letter that "Jews are not wanted in Gastein at any time or in any capacity." Accordingly, Nazi mayor Josef Würther's administration now turned its attention to long-established Jewish property owners, pressing them to sell up immediately and leave town for good. As of late October 1938, if Jews refused to liquidate their holdings, their property could be *zwangversteigert*—that is, auctioned off by governmental fiat. Würther also enlisted local bankers—ever-trusty allies in Nazi skullduggery—to do his dirty work. For example, when the Polish-Jewish owners of the Hotel Bristol refused to give up their business, Würther induced a bank to foreclose on the property. The next day Gestapo agents showed up at the Bristol and ordered the Jews to leave town within three hours or face incarceration. After brief internments in Salzburg and Vienna, the Bristol Jews eventually managed to immigrate to Chile. In their absence, the Hotel Bristol was auctioned off to the Gestapo, which turned the building into its local headquarters. A similar fate befell the property of a much-loved spa doctor, Anton Wassing, who, his many years of devoted service to the community notwithstanding, was forced to "sell" his spacious Kurhaus to an "Aryan" buyer for a small fraction of its market value. Wassing and his wife fled to Vienna, where he died of heart disease before he could be shipped east; his wife died in Theresienstadt in 1943.

By the time the infamous Night of the Broken Glass descended on Austrian Jewry, the anti-Semitic persecution campaign in Gastein had proved so effective that there were no more Jews left in town to beat up or kill—surely a disappointment to local Nazi brutes. The thugs therefore had to content themselves with trashing Jewish properties recently abandoned by their owners. Not realizing that Dr. Wassing's Kurhaus had already passed into new Aryan ownership, Kristallnacht vandals included that elegant property in their orgy of plunder. Even Mayor Würther had to admit that the lads might have gotten a bit too enthusiastic.

What happened in Bad Gastein during Reichskristallnacht was rather tame compared to the riotous pogrom that convulsed Karlsbad, which, like Marienbad and other predominantly ethnic-German communities in the Sudetenland, saw this occasion as an opportunity to celebrate their region's recent annexation by Hitler's Germany. While local police looked passively on, SS and SA men went from house to house rounding up any Jews they could find. The Nazis herded their quarry down the main street to a small hotel, where trucks stood waiting to transport them to the central police station. From the station they were dispersed to several regional prisons, there to undergo several days of physical and mental torture designed to teach them that there was no place for them in the "new" Karlsbad. Actually, they must have already gotten this message during their humiliating parade through town. As one participant in that sad march recalled: "We trudged through our beautiful and beloved hometown, cursed and abused by crowds of onlookers. What a transformation for Karlsbad—a Kurort to which people from all over the world had once come for healing! Goethe was often here, Beethoven too, and many others. Now an inhuman delirium rules the streets."

The same could be said of Marienbad. As in Karlsbad, Nazis there targeted Jewish property as well as people. Marienbad's majestic synagogue, the largest in the Sudetenland, went up in flames at the same time as Karlsbad's and some thirty other Jewish temples across the region. (Today there's a gaping void where the synagogue once stood and a small monument across the street attesting to the temple's fate and the broader destruction of Marienbad Jewry.)

As the events of November 9–10, 1938, made abundantly clear, Sudetenland's grand spas slipped seamlessly into their new role as showplaces of Nazi ideology and practice. As early as November 16, 1938, just six weeks after the German annexation, the *Marienbader Zeitung* could proudly proclaim the spa town "judenfrei." The paper went on to promise that "everything which today is still reminiscent of Jewish influence will soon be cleared away."

To actualize the "promise" of a Jewish-influence-free Marienbad, a host of Nazi agencies set up shop in town. Local Brownshirts took over the Hotel Casino, while units of the SS and Gestapo moved into the Rathaus. So many Marienbader joined the NSDAP that the party divided itself into two chapters, one for the western side of town, another for the east. Between these two Nazi turfs ran Marienbad's Hauptstrasse—now rechristened (but of course!): *Adolf-Hitler-Strasse*.

With the conclusion of that Nazi *annus mirabilis* 1938, ethnic-German citizens of Karlsbad and Marienbad looked forward to a bright future under national socialism. The *Marienbader Zeitung* published a New Year's greeting to Sudetenland's leader in Berlin: "Unser Führer! The Kurort of Marienbad commemorates at the end of the historic year 1938 your act of liberation and pledges to you anew our vow of unconditional loyalty and best wishes for your prosperity in the year 1939!" Marienbad's "liberated" Kurdirektion hastened to integrate the town's thermal-spring operations into the new order. Ever since their initial commercial exploitation in the early nineteenth century, Marienbad's principal Quellen had been owned by the Tepl Monastery. In January 1939 Marienbad's National Socialist mayor, supported by the *Kreisleitung*, "requested" of the Tepl abbot that he cede control of the springs to the regional government, headquartered in Eger. Not surprisingly, the abbot rejected this demand—and, equally predictably, the Nazi government confiscated the Quellen "in the public interest." Meanwhile, in the Hotel Weimar, the new director removed a picture of Franz Josef from Edward VII's former suite and replaced it with a portrait of Sudeten-Nazi boss Konrad Henlein.

At a meeting of Sudeten cure-industry functionaries in Marienbad in January 1939, the region's new rulers outlined their vision for water-cure operations under national socialism. Here one sees the influence of Heinrich Himmler, that passionate devotee of Naturheilkunde, who had visited Marienbad earlier that month to discuss spa doctrine, commune with his inner Visigoth, and deliver a public lecture entitled "The Police: Your Friend, Your Helper." Under the rubric "The Role and Tasks of Healing Baths," a visiting spa doctor from northern Germany called for a greater emphasis on the "natural" healing properties of thermal waters as opposed to a recent "obsession with science." In any assessment of hydropathic efficacy, said this expert, "*Naturgegebenheit* and *Naturgebundenheit* [fundamental, built-in *naturalness*] must always remain paramount. . . . *Bäderheilkunde* [healing therapy by thermal baths] is the purest and best form of Naturheilkunde," he concluded, in that it produces "a renewal of the life-force that never fails to surprise."

Alas, just as in Germany and Austria, in Sudetenland opportunities for achieving life-force renewal via Bäderheilkunde at the spas were about to become scarce, at least for civilians.

A Coda: Badenheim 1939

The Central European spa scene on the eve of World War II is the subject of Israeli novelist Aaron Appelfeld's best-known work, *Badenheim 1939*. As a child growing up in the Bukovina (northeastern Romania), Appelfeld had gone with his parents to various Central European Kurorte, which he remembered without fondness, although the spas must have been pure heaven compared to the labor camp to which he was sent as a teenager by the Nazis, as well as to the bleak forest in which he hid out for three years before being rescued by the Red Army. Some fifty years later, in a conversation about his recently published novel with the American writer Philip Roth, Appelfeld justified what Roth called *Badenheim 1939*'s "ahistorical" quality by noting that the work derived from a "child's vision preserved within me." And "ahistorical" the novel technically is, for it depicts a Marienbad-like spa town filled with Jewish curists in the summer of 1939—a time when the Central European spa scene was largely devoid of Jews. Yet if we push the chronology back just a year or so, *Badenheim 1939* does offer an accurate portrait of Jewish life in the major Kurorte at the very moment that scene was about to vanish forever.

In the novel, middle-class Jews from across Mitteleuropa pour into Badenheim, settle into their lodgings, tuck into their pink ice creams and heavy pastries, anticipate impending entertainments ("The Festival Program is full of surprises this year!"), and plunge into little love affairs and infatuations, all the while oblivious to the operations of the "Spa Sanitation Department," which is quietly sorting out the Jews from Gentiles and erecting barriers at the city gates. Soon the Jews are placed under quarantine, sedated with drugs, and subjected to daily inspections. Word filters down that free transit to Poland is in the offing. "There's nothing to be afraid of," assures physician/impresario Dr. Pappenheim. "There are many Jews in Poland. In the last analysis, a man has to return to his origins." Yes indeed—dust to dust, ashes to ashes. Clearly, or in fact not quite so clearly to many of the inmates, the "spa" is becoming a kind of concentration camp, something on the order of Theresienstadt: bucolic gateway to points east.

With its murky atmosphere of impending doom lurking behind blinkered frivolity and willful self-deception, *Badenheim 1939* is manifestly an allegory on the condition of Central European Jewry on the cusp of its annihilation. In a broader sense, though, it also amounts to a dissection of European society about to plunge yet again into an orgy of self-destruction—an echo of Thomas Mann's portrait in *The Magic Mountain* of a fevered, sickness-suffused social order on the eve of World War I. Yet for the spa historian, *Badenheim 1939* is yet one thing more: although its author may not have intended it as such, the novel can be read as a kind of antivaledictory for the fabled Central European spas themselves. Like the Jews to whom these places had once catered, the grand Kurorte, full of illusory hopes and empty promises, were sliding irrevocably into catastrophe.

Wartime

With respect to Western Europe, the first phase of World War II is known as the "phony war" (*drôle de guerre*; *Sitzkrieg*), because, in contrast to World War I, Germany focused its predations on the east, leaving all quiet on the western front. But for the grand spa towns of Central Europe, especially those clustered near the French border, the opening months of hostilities were more upsetting than droll. Even before the German attack on Poland, Wehrmacht troops moved into a new bunker complex near Baden-Baden designed to serve as headquarters for military operations in the west. Unlike in August 1914, the outbreak of fighting on September 1, 1939, brought no public celebration in Baden-Baden—and in truth there was nothing much to celebrate. Wehrmacht troops now occupied the town proper, commandeering hotels, pensions, and private villas. This time around no foreign guests had to be booted out to make way for the military: British and French curists had long since vanished; and even citizens from friendly or neutral nations, sensing war in the air, had stopped coming to the spa. The Spielbank, its recent opening hailed as a gift from the Führer, shuttered its doors, another gift from the Führer. The palatial Augustabad also closed, as did the municipal theater. Even more unsettling were the preparations for potential air attacks: citizens were commanded to darken their houses at night and to prepare cellar rooms as bomb shelters. The Sanatorium Dr. Dengler was designated a public shelter. Flak batteries took up position in the hills around town.

Bad Ems, with its strategic location near Das Deutsche Eck ("German Corner") at Koblenz, became overnight a Lazarettstadt—a function that all the major Kurorte would assume over the course of the war. From the air, Ems took on the look of one big hospital complex, with large red crosses painted on the roofs of prominent buildings. Here, too, Wehrmacht troops swarmed in, some in transit to Hitler's "Westwall," some to take up quarters in commandeered public buildings and hotels. Hastily imposed blackout regulations in Ems included the tiny *Grablampen* (grave lamps) in local cemeteries—lest these little lights for the dead provide a beacon for enemy bombers and add to the number of graves. Scarily enough, on the night of September 11, air-raid sirens jolted Bad Emsers out of their beds, though the planes overhead turned out to be friendly (which, however, did not necessarily mean there was no danger: the first bombs to fall on Freiburg in the war came from a Luftwaffe crew who thought they were hitting Colmar in France). Not only the Bad Ems dead suffered under these blackout regulations: dogs could no longer enjoy their nightly walks because passersby might trip over their leashes or, worse, slip in piles of unseen doggy business on the sidewalks. Drowning one's fears and sorrows in drink suddenly became more expensive because, as of September 4, a pfennig surcharge was tacked onto every liter of alcohol purchased in bars or stores. The first Emser to beat this tax by dying in combat was not some lowly private, as one might have expected, but a general named Roettig, ex-chief of the Ems Police Academy.

While Bad Emsers could not fail to notice these intrusive wartime regulations, they remained largely unaware that, as autumn 1939 gave way to winter 1940, preparations for a massive attack on the Low Countries and France were secretly taking shape in cordoned-off woods and valleys nearby. On the other hand, it became clear in late December that something big was up because word filtered down that the Führer himself intended to pay a Christmas visit to his "own" unit of SS men, the SS-Leibstandarte Adolf Hitler (LAH), stationed in Bad Ems. Word also had it that Hitler would bring along SS leader Heinrich Himmler, SS security chief Reinhard Heydrich, NSDAP-Reichsleiter Martin Bormann, and Luftwaffe field marshal Erhard Milch.

Hitler had celebrated Christmas with the LAH before, but this year was special because, unbeknownst to Bad Emsers, he wanted to give the troops his personal blessing before their participation in Germany's western offensive (scheduled for January 1940 but ultimately postponed until spring). Aware only that the Führer was paying their town a signal honor, townsfolk stood in the cold for hours on December 23 awaiting the arrival of their master's Mercedes G4 limousine. One wit shouted, "*Lieber Führer komm doch bald, unsere Füsse werden kalt*" (Dear Führer, come soon please, our poor feet are about to freeze). Finally, a big black Mercedes whizzed down the Lahnstrasse and screeched to a stop at the Kurhaus, site of the LAH party. No one got out, though: the car was a decoy, part of the tight security Hitler now deployed following a failed attempt on his life at a Munich beer hall in November 1939. A second limousine turned out to contain Heinrich Himmler, another disappointment. Hitler himself, political rock star that he was, waited yet another hour before showing up and then made his entrance through a back door.

The SS men assembled inside the Kurhaus had it better than the crowd outside: no cold feet. No warm bellies either, though, because the troopers were not allowed to eat or drink until Hitler arrived. In a short speech, Hitler told the LAH that they stood on the Westwall, poised to win Germany the *Lebensraum* (living room) it had been denied by England. "You, the soldiers of my Honor Guard, are the chosen few of destiny, the guarantors of Germany's victory!"

While they awaited their moment of destiny on the other side of the Westwall, the LAH settled down to a generally amicable relationship with the Bad Ems population. Civilians and soldiers staged joint cultural evenings and sporting events, including an SS versus townie boxing match. Despite a strict sexual conduct code prevailing in the SS—unmarried men were meant to remain chaste apart from state-sanctioned coupling with approved brood mares—the lads enjoyed many a "cure bath" with local girls, who cheekily began referring to the Führer's finest as the "*Unterleibstandarte*" (Lower Body Service). Yet not all was harmonious between town and brown (or black): in time-honored fashion, the soldiers trashed their hotel and villa lodgings, even tossing antique furniture into fireplaces for extra heat. Property owners complained of punched-in walls, torn curtains, soiled carpets, and pilfered accoutrements. The director of the *Stadtbad* wondered whether his property would ever be usable again, what with the depredations caused by all those coed frolics in the tub.

And then, one fine May morning, the LAH suddenly vanished, plunging over the Westwall along with the other military units that had been gathering nearby for months. Hitler's belated *Drang nach Westen* (western campaign) was finally on.

In stark contrast to Germany's push west a quarter-century earlier, this one did *not* stall out. After storming through Luxemburg, Holland, and Belgium in a matter of days, the Germans descended on their principal target, France. The French were expected to be a tougher adversary but famously proved a relative pushover, Paris falling on June 14 and the entire "Grande Nation" on June 22. The Germans went through France "like shit through a goose," complained the British, before themselves vacating the Continent through the orifice of Dunkirk.

The Wehrmacht's astonishing victory over France generated jubilation across Greater Germany, including Greater German spa land. "Hitler's war" suddenly seemed not such a bad idea after all, and the Führer himself looked like a military genius. (He would have appeared even more a genius if, as many Germans hoped, Britain would now come to its senses and accept "honorable" peace terms with Germany, ceding her control of the Continent.) As we know, Prime Minister Winston Churchill refused to see the light of Anglo-German amity and vowed to fight on. Yet as Germany girded its loins for a final showdown with Britain, many Reich citizens, including Baden-Badeners, expressed optimism regarding the eventual outcome. "Our victorious army will shortly be lords of London," predicted a local paper. The town's Kurdirektor assured his staff that the Reich's coming victory over England would mean "new glory in Greater Germany" for Baden-Baden.

In the meantime, residents of Germany's premier spa town paused to enjoy fully the fruits of victory in the west. For Baden-Baden in particular, the year or so following the fall of France, rather than the first months of hostilities, constituted the real "phony" war, the true Sitzkrieg. The town's Wehrmacht lodgers having moved on, luxury hotels could reconvert to civilian accommodation. The Spielbank reopened, as did the opera, theater, and great bath palaces. Civilian guests streamed back into town, determined to "cure" while they still could. True, the patrons were almost all from Greater Germany, but this was a sizable feeder zone, and in 1942 Baden-Baden actually welcomed more registered cure-guests (27,849 in July alone) than ever before in its history. Locals could almost get the impression that no war was going on at all.

Yet even during this brief period of *gute Zahlen* (nice numbers) and frantic frivolity, there were plenty of signs that not all was well. Even in luxury hotels like Brenner's, civilian curists had to share space with badly wounded soldiers, which must have been somewhat off-putting for the paying guests. (Injured and dying men would soon take over *all* the space at Brenner's, as they would at eleven other local hostelries.) Fuel and some foodstuffs were already being rationed in 1942, with the restrictions becoming tighter by the month—a development Hitler had hoped to avoid lest it undermine morale, as it had in World War I. As of late 1941, another unsettling sign of the times was the sudden appearance in town of lice-ridden, typhus-infected Russian prisoners of war. Housed in a primitive camp on the southeastern edge of the city, the prisoners often marched through town on their way to various work details. Some 235 of these wretches died in captivity over the course of the war. No "cure" for them in Baden-Baden.

Roughly two hundred kilometers north of Baden-Baden, at the Hessian spa town of Bad Nauheim, embassy officials of the United States, Moscow's new ally against Nazi Germany, were experiencing an internment of their own, albeit nowhere near as harsh as that suffered by the Russian POWs.

Upon declaring war on the United States following Axis-partner Japan's attack on Pearl Harbor, Hitler ordered the internment of Washington's Berlin embassy staff within Germany instead of allowing their repatriation back home as they had expected. German officials chose Bad Nauheim for the confinement largely because the spa town possessed a lodging facility, Jeschke's Grand Hotel, large enough to accommodate the 115 internees (Foreign Service officers, military attachés, spies, journalists, several wives, a few children, five dogs, a cat, and three canaries). Opened in 1912, the four-hundred-room Grand Hotel in its heyday had hosted the likes of Charles Schwab and William Randolph Hearst. But it had fallen on hard times in the 1930s and had closed in 1939 with the onset of war. As for Bad Nauheim, it, too, had seen better days. The spa had gained international fame in the early twentieth century for its distinctive salt springs that were used to treat heart and nervous diseases. James Roosevelt had visited Bad Nauheim repeatedly in the early 1900s in a fruitless effort to cure his ailing heart; it was there that his young son Franklin learned to speak German—and learned to hate Germans.

Conditions for the American internees in wartime Bad Nauheim were admittedly not what a peacetime curist would have experienced. There were no thermal baths or soothing massages. The rooms at the hastily reopened Grand Hotel were freezing cold in winter, since fuel was severely rationed. Food was rationed, too. The regular fare consisted of a mostly vegetarian stew that had been cooked to a pulp in order, complained the Americans, to remove all taste. But unbeknownst to the whining Yanks, their food ration was actually 150 percent (later 200 percent) of the ration allowed German civilians. Moreover, the Americans could obtain wine and spirits from their hotel's well-stocked cellar. Although the internees were largely confined to the hotel and its grounds, they were given considerable latitude by their German minders to amuse themselves as they saw fit. (Aware that their own diplomats were undergoing similar confinement at a water-cure resort in West Virginia, White Sulphur Springs, German officials hoped to avoid a mutually injurious spa spat with the Americans.) Under the direction of their resident chief, the brilliant diplomat and Russia expert George Kennan, American internees set up an informal institution of higher learning they called "Badheim University" with the motto: "Education for the Ignorant by the Ignorant." In fact, Kennan himself, anything but ignorant, taught a months-long course on Russian history, wherein he argued that contemporary Soviet leaders harbored the same "Oriental" despotic instincts, the same distrust of the outside world, as the czars of old. In his view, this raised the question of "whether Russia [was] to be the confusion or the salvation of the Western European continent" once it came time to make peace with Germany. On the lighter side, to amuse themselves, the internees played indoor football games in which they substituted ceramic spittoons for pigskins, and staged outdoor baseball games using socks rolled around champagne corks in place of balls.

Undoubtedly these diversions would not have kept the restless Americans amused for very long—but fortunately for them, unlike the Russians POWs, they were confined at their German spa for only five months before a reciprocal agreement between Washington and Berlin allowed them to return home. (For Americans, Bad Nauheim would later assume renewed interest as the headquarters in 1945 for General George Patton and, in 1959, as the US Army home of Elvis Presley, who used the town's Burgpforte on the cover of his hit record "A Big Hunk o' Love.")

While the American internees could return to a land of bounty, Germany slid ever deeper into destitution and disarray. As the conflict dragged on and Germany's opponents reversed initial setbacks in the field and began pummeling Reich cities with bombs, the privations of the Sitzkrieg era appeared in retrospect almost like privileges. Baden-Baden, it is true, avoided serious damage from bombing until December 1944, when an American raid destroyed two hundred houses and killed thirty-six civilians, but starting in 1943 the town had to accommodate hundreds of refugees from Karlsruhe and the Ruhr district who had been bombed out of their houses by the British. Another spa town casualty was Wiesbaden, which lost some 1,700 of its citizens and one-quarter of its buildings to British and American bombs. (For the British, bombing German civilian targets, including spa towns, was perceived as legitimate payback for the Luftwaffe's Blitz on London and the notorious "Baedeker raids" on English beauty spots like Exeter, Canterbury, York—and Bath.) Increasingly, Badeners also had to cope with losses of their own on various fields of battle, as Germany's ill-fated campaign to conquer Soviet Russia proved far more costly than its campaign in the west. By war's end, some one thousand Baden-Baden men had been killed or severely wounded, most of them on the eastern front.

In the wake of Germany's horrific defeat at Stalingrad in early 1943, Goebbels demanded a cessation of "frivolities" like thermal bathing, cabarets, and gambling. As it happened, the Baden-Baden baths never closed down entirely—wounded soldiers could use them, not to mention stressed-out Nazi functionaries—but the prospects looked grim for the town's beloved casino. The director of the Spielbank wrote a beseeching letter to Berlin listing the reasons why, Goebbels notwithstanding, roulette wheels should continue to spin at the spa. Baden and Germany desperately needed the revenues from gaming, he pointed out, and no personnel essential to the war effort were employed in this enterprise (the croupiers were all Italians, hardly useful on the front). Showing once again a triumph of pragmatism over ideology, Berlin extended the Spielbank's license for a year, during which time a surreal atmosphere prevailed in the gilded halls. Recalled one Spieler: "I can still see the well-dressed ladies, the very distinguished company sitting around the tables. . . . [Actors] Lil Dagover and Karl-Ludwig Diehl and other film greats, officers in mufti, the director of Daimler-Benz with his thin, striking mistress, puffing elegantly on a cigarette encased in a silver holder."

Lacking a casino, Bad Ems did not display scenes quite as surreal as that of Baden-Baden's Spielbank, but this town likewise experienced a wartime roller-coaster ride from hubristic pomp through muddling along to full-blown disaster. Predictably, France's capitulation brought crowds of townsfolk to the "Ems Telegram" memorial on the River Lahn, a perfect place to celebrate yet another Teutonic triumph over the Gallic "archenemy." Homeowners covered their residences in swastika banners and church bells rang out for seven days straight. Yet as early as May 1942 those same church bells disappeared from their belfries to be melted down into munitions. The little iron fences surrounding grave sites met this same fate. As an official Lazarettstadt from early on, Bad Ems took in so many casualties (over thirteen thousand) that every one of its thirteen hospital stations was filled to capacity by late 1942.

Yet it was not only wounded soldiers who were "cared" for in Ems's commandeered hotels and sanatoria. Per orders from Berlin, local citizens with significant mental disorders underwent forced sterilization to prevent them from adding to the Reich's *"lebensunwertes Leben"* (life unworthy of living). For some severely handicapped citizens, the "treatment" went beyond sterilization. An undetermined number of Ems residents were put to death or subjected to medical experimentation at the "cure center" of Hadamar.

While wartime Bad Ems was certainly a site of horror for many, it also, at least for a brief period, remained a place of relaxation and blissful curing for a privileged few. Like Baden-Baden, Bad Ems attracted its full share of *Goldfasane* (golden pheasants, i.e., high Nazi officials wearing uniforms covered in honorary bling). Bad Ems's Hotel Löwen, owned by the local SA chief, catered to the likes of Victor Lutze, successor to Ernst Röhm as national storm trooper chief. Lutze strolled daily on the Promenade, bombarded with sycophantic "Sieg Heils" and autograph requests from lesser Brownshirts. A yet more prominent visitor was Prince August Wilhelm of Prussia, a genuine blue-blood Nazi who was keeping up the Hohenzollern tradition of curing at Ems. In terms of star power, however, neither golden pheasants nor Nazi blue bloods could hold a candle to Olga Tschechova, Hitler-Germany's best-known actress (star of such hits as *Die Drei von der Tankstelle* and *Menschen im Sturm*). In November 1940 Olga came to Ems because, as she admitted, she desperately needed a place where she could find "true quiet after all my stressful work."

Ems's era of relative quiet, of hosting golden pheasants and brownish film stars, came to an end with the onset of extensive Allied bombing across the Reich. Like Baden-Baden, Ems itself suffered only minor damage until December 1944, but, again like its larger peer, the town had to take in hundreds of refugees from more severely bombed regions nearby. Unlike Baden-Baden, Bad Ems, starting in 1943, also sheltered crucial industrial and military research operations transplanted thither from the devastated Ruhr region. Preeminent among these was the Dortmund-based Kaiser Wilhelm Institute for Labor Physiology, whose main research division moved to a former sanatorium known as Das Haus der Türme. The researchers' primary task was to investigate the human capacity for sustained labor under adverse conditions, such as minimal nourishment. The Reich needed to know just how much, or rather *how little*, it could feed its millions of slave laborers without their dying off like flies. Also of interest was which nationalities could work the longest and hardest with the least nourishment. To answer these questions, institute scientists, led by a Nazi Party member named Dr. Heinrich Kraut (!), experimented on thousands of Polish slave laborers and Russian POWs, putting them through backbreaking days of lead-mine work while essentially starving them with per-diem diets ranging from 1,000 to 1,500 calories. Dr. Kraut's assistants regularly recorded the workers' weight, musculature, health, and bodily excretions. A high rate of expiration among the workers was no cause of concern to Kraut because discovering the absolute limit of human endurance was the whole point of his study—and anyway, there was no shortage of "*Versuchstiere*" (research animals).*

The major Austrian grand spas, integral additions to Gross Deutschland that they were, shared just as fully as their German sisters in the Reich's wartime triumphs and miseries. For a considerable time, Baden-bei-Wien basked mainly in the celebratory side of things. After all, it had the only casino in the Austrian part of the expanded Reich, so it was a magnet for the Ostmark's political leaders and moneyed classes. Figures for overnight stays remained quite high for 1939 and 1940: 378,935 and 394,832, respectively.

Yet a great many "visitors" to the town were in no position to gamble or otherwise enjoy their stay. Baden-bei-Wien started taking in wounded soldiers in 1940 and became an official Lazarettstadt following Germany's invasion of the Soviet Union in June 1941. By 1944 so many wounded soldiers were flooding in from the meat-grinder eastern front that, along with all the major hotels, every school, gymnasium, and public building of any size was conscripted for hospital use. As of late 1944, local high school kids had no need for classroom space anyway because they were being called up for duty in the so-called *Volksturm*, Nazism's last-ditch home guard composed of the very young and the very old. Baden-bei-Wien's Volksturm "volunteers" took their oath to defend the Reich to the death in front of the Trinkhalle, which instead of serving Sprudel to curists now dispensed drugs to wounded soldiers.

When it became clear that, mighty Volksturm or no, Baden-bei-Wien was soon going to fall to the approaching Russians, local Nazi chiefs made plans to escape westward, leaving the town to fend for itself. (This kind of cowardice was by no means unusual: Nazi leaders all across the eastern part of Hitler's collapsing empire were doing the same thing.) To cover this opportunistic retreat, Baden's Nazi Bürgermeister announced the evacuation of the main city hospital; he and his ilk then

---

*Dr. Kraut learned that the Russians were able to do the most work under the worst conditions; the average "eastern worker" required 100 fewer calories per day than a typical German; and *no one* could work effectively on fewer than 1,100 calories per diem. The importance of Kraut's work impressed not only his Nazi bosses but also the conquering Americans, who after the war kept his Bad Ems operation afloat with new research opportunities. Kraut himself became a member of the Allied Commission on Rationing and Food Supply.

joined the exodus of doctors and patients heading west. Lucky them. Not long thereafter, Baden-bei-Wien was hit by its first major air attacks of the war. Two raids in early April 1945 killed seventy-two civilians and wounded thirty-one. With 184 buildings destroyed, including all but one of its bath complexes, and no electrical power or running water, Baden-bei-Wien no longer looked much like a resort, even a *last resort*.

In Bad Gastein the transition from gloating over early victories to griping over wartime sacrifices came very quickly. Bath-facility operators saw their civilian patrons disappear as early as August 1939, when the Reichsbahn (National Railway) announced that train service for civilians would soon be discontinued. On September 3, two days after the onset of hostilities, the municipality informed cure-guests that they had forty-eight hours to leave Gastein for their homes, wherever they might be. At the same time, all area hotels and guest-houses were ordered to make themselves ready to receive refugees.

Following Germany's victories in Poland and Western Europe, Gastein's cure and hospitality industry got the green light to resume business—though not quite business as usual: hotels had to save space for wounded soldiers because this spa town, too, was now an official Lazarettstadt. Among the commandeered facilities was the venerable Hotel Straubinger, where Bismarck had once played his diplomatic chess games against the overmatched Austrians. In winter 1942–1943 some 735 of the town's inventory of 2,030 guest beds—about 35 percent—were in military use. By late 1944, that figure would reach almost 100 percent, with every large hotel serving Wehrmacht "guests." By that time, city streets also crawled, sometimes literally, with wounded soldiers. Shortly before war's end, the wife of Kurdirektor Zimburg described the scene to her since-conscripted husband: "You wouldn't recognize Gastein as it is now. One sees in the streets practically only wounded men . . . some missing both legs."

The requirement to house wounded soldiers was not the only wartime burden experienced by Gastein hoteliers: they, along with local restaurateurs, faced significant labor shortages as the war dragged on. The Reich sought to remedy this problem by shipping in POWs and slave laborers. Gastein restaurateurs fought over a small cache of French POWs to serve as cooks and waiters; for scullery and other menial tasks, they exploited a ready supply of Poles and Ukrainians. According to

Kurdirektor Zimburg, Gastein could not have remained "open for business" during the war without this imported slave labor.

Meanwhile, heavy work on the city's roads, bridges, and sewer system was entrusted to some thirty Russian POWs, whose tightly guarded quarters on the edge of town resembled a concentration camp. Another group of forty Russians toiled in nearby gold mines. These men lived (and died) on a starvation diet of the kind prescribed by Dr. Kraut at Bad Ems. To combat typhus, the prisoners took one bath a week—always at an isolated facility where there was absolutely no chance they would come in contact with Germans or other "Nordics."

As the war progressed, or regressed, Gastein's native population also experienced cuts in calorie intake, albeit nothing like those imposed on the Slavic *Untermenschen*. In April 1942 the weekly per capita meat ration was reduced by fifty grams, the bread ration by 250 grams. Now Gasteiners subsisted on 2,000 grams of bread, 206 grams of fat, and 300 grams of meat per week. Kurdirektor Zimburg noted that on this diet the average Gasteiner was losing between *ten and twenty kilos* (the same transformation for which legions of overweight peacetime spa patrons had once paid hefty sums). As of late 1940, Gasteiners were also doing a lot more walking than driving because, due to fuel shortages, only the Bürgermeister, chief doctor, and building inspector were permitted to use private cars. For a good many Gasteiner, the most painful privation of all began in winter 1941: *no more skiing* in the nearby mountains!

There was no more skiing at Bad Ischl, either. Yet the wartime privations of the Ischl natives paled in comparison to the sufferings experienced by residents of the Ebensee concentration camp just down the road. A subcamp of the Mauthausen network, Ebensee housed Jews and slave laborers who worked on a huge underground tunnel system meant to shelter arms and munitions factories, including the Peenemünde V-2 rocket facility (it stayed north, however). Due to its incredibly harsh living and working conditions, Ebensee became known as one of the "worst" camps in a system where the bar for bad was stratospherically high. Roughly twenty thousand inmates died at this hellhole during its two-year existence between 1943 and 1945.

Unlike the Austrian and old-Reich Kurorte, the Sudeten grand spas did not enjoy even a temporary boomlet during the war, which for them remained unphony from start to finish. No sooner had the war started than Karlsbad's Nazi overlords dismantled the town's art-nouveau iron and glass pavilions, which joined Marienbad's bronze Goethe statue as matériel for munitions. Neither Karlsbad nor Marienbad had much in the way of civilian clientele between 1940 and 1945. Virtually all the "guests" were military, most of them soldiers wounded in fighting on the eastern front. In 1940 Reich authorities registered both spa towns with the International Red Cross as hospital cities, duly plastering public buildings with the requisite insignia visible from the air. Not every building so designated actually housed wounded men, but *all* the major hotels certainly did, including the ones where Marx and Edward VII had stayed. In Karlsbad even the central railway station became a Lazarett.

Interestingly enough, one of the injured German soldiers who received treatment in Marienbad was a young Waffen-SS trooper named Günther Grass. (The future Nobel Prize laureate in literature kept his SS service secret until the publication of his memoir, *Beim Häuten der Zwiebel—Peeling the Onion—*in 2006, when he revealed that he had been conscripted into a Waffen-SS tank division as a teenager. Since the writer later became known for his left-wing views, German conservatives made much of this belated admission, insisting it undercut his "smug" moral authority.)

As Grass tells the story of his injury and treatment in *Zwiebel*, on April 20, 1944, Hitler's birthday, he was standing in line for chow, hoping for some chocolate or brandy to mark the occasion. Instead he got a nasty gift from an attacking Russian tank unit in the form of shell-shrapnel in his right leg and left shoulder. Packed into a cattle-car train with other wounded soldiers, Grass lay on piss-covered straw for an overnight trip from hell to Meissen, where he was off-loaded and handed orders to get himself, however he could, to the hospital station at Marienbad, many miles away over the Erzgebirge (Ore Mountains).

Grass dutifully set off for the fabled Bohemian Kurort, which, literate German he was, he knew to be "a spa for the rich and famous, much celebrated in literature," the place where "old Goethe had fallen in love with a young thing, been given the brush-off, and sublimated his grief in a 'Marienbad Elegy.'" Grass somehow managed to get himself over the mountains, traveling sometimes by train but mostly by horse-cart, never deviating from his marching orders. His trek was briefly interrupted in that other famous Bohemian spa, Karlsbad, where he fell to his knees in the street, shaking with fever. A military policeman picked him up and, seeing his orders, slung the unconscious trooper over the backseat of his motorcycle and drove him on to Marienbad. For Grass, Marienbad meant salvation, a truly genuine cure. He spent the last days of the war recovering from his wounds "in a freshly made bed." It was in his wonderful spa sack that he learned "the Führer was no more," and that he was about to fall into the hands of the Americans rather than the Russians, another cause for celebration.

Needless to say, many of the thousands of wounded soldiers who ended up in Marienbad or Karlsbad during the war did not fare so well as Günther Grass, and even the civilian populations of these towns suffered considerably. Food rationing, first imposed in 1940, became ever more restrictive as the conflict wore on, the draconian cuts eventually yielding widespread malnutrition. Despite an absence of able-bodied men, the spa towns had more mouths to feed than ever due to an influx of refugees escaping the advancing Red Army. On the other hand, even the refugees had it better than the legions of French, Dutch, Polish, Ukrainian, and Russian slave laborers, housed in primitive camps outside the towns. In late 1943, Marienbad also became the temporary home of Berlin's enormous Robert Koch Hospital, whose entire staff and patient population moved to this supposedly bomb-free sanctuary.

For most of the war, both Marienbad and Karlsbad did manage to avoid the horrors of aerial bombardment. But in spring 1945 the American air force began hitting the Sudetenland hard in order to speed the advance of General George Patton's Third Army, which aimed at conquering the whole Bavarian/Bohemian mountainous region before it could be turned into an "Alpine fortress" for bitter-end Nazi fighters. (This "Alpine redoubt" idea remained largely a Nazi fantasy and Allied nightmare, but given what the Allies were learning about Hitler's minions, any horror scenario seemed plausible.) In the case of Marienbad, the bombers focused on transportation hubs like the train station and nearby airfield, leaving most of the town unmolested. Karlsbad, on the other hand, got hit hard by the USAF on September 12, 1944, and again on April 17 and 19, 1945. The attacks did severe damage to the northern part of the city and, tragically, destroyed the train station-cum-hospital, killing over one hundred patients. (Had Günther Grass stayed on in Karlsbad rather than following his marching orders to Marienbad, the postwar German literary scene might have been a lot less lively—no Oscar the dwarf beating his *Tin Drum*.) Luckily for future curists, Karlsbad's gracious cure quarter survived the war more or less intact.

Although both Karlsbad and Marienbad housed their full share of Nazi fanatics, who exploited the heightened wartime "racial consciousness" to persecute and eventually drive the remaining Slavic populations from the region, the towns made no heroic last-ditch stands against advancing enemy forces. Marienbad capitulated peacefully on May 6 to one of General Patton's divisions. Karlsbad, which lay a little closer to the onrushing Soviets, was in a hurry to make a deal with the Yanks before the dreaded "Ivans" arrived. Accordingly, a representative of the Kreisleitung drove out to the American headquarters at Eger, pleading for the Americans to get a move on and to spare Karlsbad any further bombardment. After all, the town was a hospital station and an architectural gem to boot! The American officer in command was happy enough to oblige; it turned out that he had vacationed in Karlsbad himself and did not want to see "the beautiful old spa" destroyed. Accordingly, the Americans rolled into town unopposed on May 8. Like the Marienbaders, the Karlsbaders now fervently hoped that they would be subjected to a bubble-gum, Hershey bar, and Camel cigarette occupation by the Americans. But it was not to be. Per agreement already made between Washington and Moscow, Karlsbad was scheduled for Soviet occupation. On May 11, 1945, the Red Army replaced the Americans as lords of the manor.

It turned out that the Russians would not stay long in Karlsbad, nor would the Americans tarry in Marienbad. As the victors pulled out of Sudetenland in 1945, the inhabitants of these grand Bohemian spa towns, proud bastions of ethnic-German domination, could hardly have known that they were in for a whole new spate of changes, as (literally) unsettling as any that had gone before.

CHAPTER NINE

A New Beginning

Think of the ninety-year stretch between 1900 and 1990 as a kind of world-political soccer match, albeit a lot less tedious than the athletic variety and with some actual points scored, including many own goals. One would think that the first half of this brutal contest might have provided more than enough drama for one game, what with two world wars and the destruction of four major empires, but the second half proved almost as gripping. For example, contemporaries witnessed the emergence of a protracted Cold War that at various moments threatened to turn hot; the spectacular resurgence of World War II's principal losers, Germany and Japan; the appearance of two new global superpowers, the United States and the USSR, with the latter embarrassing the former by launching the first artificial satellite, dog, and cosmonaut into space—and the United States retaliating with its even more spectacular moon landings; the equally astonishing collapse in the late 1980s of the Soviet Union's Eastern European satellite system and the demise in 1990 of the USSR itself; a corollary spread of liberal-capitalist values around much of the world—and a simultaneous critique of those values in some of the very places they achieved their greatest triumphs.

Against the backdrop of these epochal developments, the goings-on at Central Europe's major spas between 1945 and 1990 might seem rather less weighty—and let's face it, they *were* less weighty. Yet the show put on by our grand water-cure resorts over the course of this forty-five-year period is quite intriguing and certainly highly *revealing* as a small-arena version of the larger drama transpiring simultaneously on the world stage.

Postwar

At the end of World War II one had to wonder whether Central Europe's grand old spas would survive at all as cure destinations, much less recover any of their former glamour and prosperity. A return to "normalcy," whatever that might mean, seemed out of the question. What historian Ian Buruma writes of Europe as a whole in *Year Zero—A History of 1945* applies in spades to the spa towns: "The world could not possibly be the same. Too much had happened, too much had changed, too many people, even entire societies, had been uprooted."

In 1945, as Central Europe swarmed with liberated Jews, displaced persons, and demobilized soldiers, the region's major spa towns all fell under occupation by Allied forces, some for only short durations, others for longer stretches. Regardless of duration, conditions were harsh.

As they had after World War I, the French took over in Baden-Baden. This time, however, they made that largely intact Black Forest jewel the capital of their military occupation zone in Germany. (Say what you want about the French: they have good taste and know how to take care of themselves.) In Baden-Baden, the French took care of themselves by commandeering every desirable property in sight while ensuring that most of the available food, especially the better items, went into their bellies rather than into those of the vanquished Boche. As late as 1947–1948, German residents of Baden-Baden received 200 grams of meat per month; the French got 225 grams *per day*. Fans of thermal waters themselves, the French were determined to "make a little Vichy" out of Baden-Baden, replete with imported French food and prostitutes. (Some of the French administrators, it turned out, had actually served in the collaborationist Vichy regime during the war; they were hastily removed when this was revealed in the Communist press.) Regardless of their previous experience, the French occupiers took full advantage of Baden's amenities. "Eight hundred colonels," announced a contemporary report, "are enjoying casino living in Baden in 1945."

France also assumed control in Bad Ems following a brief occupation there by the American army, which overran the city. Given Ems's role in Franco-German relations, seizing overlordship in that town must have been especially gratifying for the French, who in addition to commandeering all the major hotels expelled more than two thousand natives and German refugees from the area. Germans remaining in the city were forbidden, on pain of expulsion, from speaking their own language in the streets.

Bad Homburg and Wiesbaden, as part of America's much larger occupation zone, fell under US Army administration. The Americans were more lenient toward the natives than the French—though, at least early on, not significantly so. According to US occupation policy, Germany was to be treated as a "defeated" nation rather than as a "liberated" one. There was to be no "fraternization" with the natives, including the females. (Resourceful GIs, however, managed to get around this restriction, arguing that "copulation without conversation" did not amount to fraternization.) In Bad Homburg, which the Germans surrendered without a fight, the US Army established its headquarters in the Stadtschloss, erstwhile summer palace of the Hohenzollerns. Higher-ranking officers settled into the Hotel Ritter (now the Steigenberger), which during the war had been a rest-and-recreation facility for the Wehrmacht.

Like the French, the Americans did not mind rubbing the natives' noses in their misery. In the graceful Kurpark, where they established their mess tents, the GIs ate heartily and tossed copious leftovers into a fire pit, all before the tearful eyes of starving Homburgers. Similar scenes unfolded in Wiesbaden, where the American general in charge imposed a strict civilian curfew excepting only the hours from seven to nine in the morning and three to six in the afternoon. The Americans took over most of the housing in the central city, including the Nassauer Hof and the newer Hotel Rose, cordoning off the entire area with barbed wire. In September 1945 the US Air Force moved into Wiesbaden, which became its European headquarters for the next three decades.

Luckily for the Wiesbadeners, Homburgers, and all the other inhabitants of America's military zone, Washington's tough, no-nonsense approach to military occupation did not last long. It soon dawned on US policy makers that holding down the Germans without letting them do anything on their own was going to be *very* expensive, rather like running a huge prison. Moreover, as relations between the United States and its wartime Soviet ally deteriorated, ushering in the Cold War,

Americans realized that they might need "their" Germans in a potential conflict with the USSR and *its* Germans. Hence Washington curbed its zeal for de-Nazification, promoted the establishment of German-administered political institutions, assisted in economic rejuvenation (culminating in the Marshall Plan, the largest foreign aid package in history), and even pushed the West Germans to rearm. (To their dismay, US officers soon discovered that most Germans had no desire whatsoever to rearm, having had enough of things military; and when the West Germans finally *did* start planning a new army they insisted it must be thoroughly *democratic*! The "quality of the soldiers in the new German army might not be as high as those of the Third Reich," worried General Alfred Gruenther, one of the American officers on the scene. Where were those Nazis when one needed them?)

Grand Kurorte in the US zone benefited significantly from America's occupation policy turnaround and material largesse. As early as 1946, money was made available for the restoration of bathing and other cure facilities in Bad Homburg and Wiesbaden. As the European headquarters for the American Air Force, Wiesbaden became a major launching pad for the famed *Luftbrücke*—the military airlift of food and supplies to West Berlin when that entity was blockaded by the Soviets in 1948–1949.

With all those US airmen in the neighborhood, flush with dollars and needing places to part with them, the long-shuttered Wiesbaden Spielbank beckoned enticingly. The US authorities gave a green light to casino gambling in April 1946, though the roulette balls could not start rolling again until November 1948 due to "moral reservations" about gaming in Hesse's state government. Wiesbaden's gaming license extended to Homburg, which opened a smaller casino under the aegis of Wiesbaden's Spielbank. Thus, courtesy of the Americans, an old Kurort tradition suspended by the prudish Prussians and only minimally revived by the Nazis once again became a vital and lucrative dimension of grand spa life in (Western) Germany.

Like Germany, Austria came under Four-Power Allied occupation after the war—with the United States taking control of the Salzkammergut and its major grand spas, Bad Gastein and Bad Ischl. Right from the beginning, American occupation officers tended to treat the Austrians more indulgently than they did the Germans, having made an agreement with their Allied partners in 1943 to consider Austria "Hitler's first victim." Albeit dubious in terms of Austria's actual role in the Third Reich, this arrangement seemed prudent given that nation's strategic location in Central Europe and the Allies' desire to separate the country from Germany. Of course, this victim label immensely pleased the Austrians, who made it an integral part of their postwar image—one that presented the Alpine nation to the world as an extended von Trapp family full of doughty anti-Nazis. (When I lived in Vienna in 1964–1965, *The Sound of Music* played in my neighborhood cinema *the entire time*. The locals could not get enough of it.)

Bad Gastein welcomed the American army as fervently as it had recently welcomed the Wehrmacht, treating the Allies as "liberators from Prussian oppression." The GIs, for their part, were pleased to find themselves in such a posh place after the rigors of their trek across Germany. This was especially true of the lucky soldiers who scored quarters in the commandeered Grand Hotel de l'Europe. A member of the 101st Airborne Division wrote that the hotel "seemed like a paradise. It was great to sleep in a bed again . . . and to eat prepared meals served in a dining room." Another soldier rhapsodized about "the hot baths and lovely city atmosphere."

The splendors of the Grand Hotel were not the only surprise in store for the Americans in Bad Gastein. Upon their arrival, they learned that the entire staff of the Japanese embassy was in residence, having been relocated to the Alpine spa in the last weeks of the war. Even more astonishing was the news that a train filled with gold and valuables looted from Hungarian Jews was parked in the nearby Tauern Tunnel. The train had traveled from Budapest to Gastein along with Nazi officers fleeing the Red Army. The Americans quickly seized the booty-filled boxcars and shifted them to Salzburg for safekeeping. Many US officers opportunistically "requisitioned" valuables from the "gold train" as it stood in the Salzburg depot.

Over the next few years the region around Gastein and Ischl became a happy hunting ground for treasure seekers on the lookout for Nazi loot supposedly hidden at the bottom of mine shafts and dark mountain lakes. The search for treasure seems to have preoccupied the American occupiers at least as much as de-Nazifying the natives, a program the Yanks never pushed very hard anyway (thereby helping to foster postwar Austria's emergence as a haven for fugitive Nazis). The American authorities did, however, manage to punish the Gastein spa doctor who had treated Emmy Göring for her maladies during the war: for that reason they took away his license to practice medicine. The physician in question had never been a member of the Nazi Party and was much loved in the community for his technical expertise and caring ways. Deprived of the right to pursue his livelihood, the man committed suicide.

Like the Americans, the Russians had agreed in 1943 to treat the Austrians as "victims" of Nazism, but in the end the Soviet occupiers did not administer their part of Austria much differently than they did their zone in Eastern Germany. They saw the land and its people as war booty, to be exploited to the fullest. They dismantled entire factories and shipped them east, along with Austrian POWs destined for slave labor in the USSR.

On the other hand, when it came to the one major Austrian Kurort in their district, Baden-bei-Wien, the Soviets behaved a bit more circumspectly than elsewhere. They had decided before the war's end that this once-idyllic spa town close to Vienna would be their zonal headquarters, so they strove to make the place as livable as possible. This took some doing due to the town's pitiable condition in the spring of 1945. Like their Western wartime partners, the Soviets immediately commandeered the best of what was still intact by way of housing and put up a wooden fence around their compound. In fairly short order, Russian officers imported their wives, mistresses, and families, so that by 1946 there were almost as many Russians living in the town as Austrians. The Soviet compound boasted Russian schools, stores, and cinemas. The occupiers erected imposing monuments to Stalin and Lenin in the Kurpark and changed "for all time" the name "Kaiser-Franz-Ring" to "Stalin-Ring."

There was not much to russify when it came to cure facilities because only one bath complex had survived the war intact. Baden-bei-Wien would not see any non-Soviet curists until 1948, when the partly restored Strandbad and Johannesbad reopened for business. A year later, Baden's Pfarrkirche (parish church) installed a new set of bells to replace the ones the Nazis had melted down for munitions. By this time, the natives were finding a modus vivendi with their occupiers, which did not stop them from dreaming of the day when "Ivan" would pack up and go home.

For the major Bohemian Kurorte, Karlsbad and Marienbad, military occupation by the Soviets and Americans, respectively, proved too short to have much of an impact. What *did* convulse these spa towns, however, was the postwar expulsion of the ethnic German population from the Sudetenland.

Edvard Beneš, a veteran political leader (and former champion of multiethnicity) who headed the Czechoslovak Republic's wartime exile government in London, stated ominously in 1945 before returning to Prague: "Woe, woe, thrice woe to the Germans, we will liquidate you." Beneš did not quite fulfill this promise, but he did his best. With Stalin's blessing, the non-Communist but Soviet-friendly Czechoslovak leader presided over an orgy of German purging that stretched from Prague through the Sudetenland. In Prague itself, Czech ethnic cleansers packed more than ten thousand German speakers into the Strahov soccer stadium and machine-gunned many of them for sport. In an echo of September 1938, but with different perpetrators and victims, young Czech zealots ran through the streets of Karlovy Vary and Mariánské Lázně (now the spas' definitive names) beating up Germans and smashing their shops. Imitating Nazi treatment of the Jews, Czechs barred Germans from public places, including the baths; they made Germans wear armbands with the letter N (for *německé*); they forbade them from buying fresh fruits and vegetables and meat; they threw them into camps where they were routinely tortured and made to sing and dance for the amusement of their guards. Unblushingly, Beneš called these actions "the final solution of the German question" (or *"konečné řešení německé otázky"* in Czech).

Ethnic Germans who survived the initial persecution and bloodletting became victims of a brutal expulsion from their homes orchestrated by the Czech government. Slightly over two million Sudeten Germans, carrying nothing but a few portable possessions, were forced across the German border, some on foot, some in cattle cars, joining millions of fellow expellees from Poland and other parts of Eastern Europe. Arguably, these Germans were, as one British correspondent wrote, "reaping from the seeds they had sown," but their plight was nonetheless pitiable, especially since most of the refugees found themselves in new "homes" in destitute Germany that were hardly more welcoming than the ones they had been forced out of in Bohemia. Lucky were the few hundred expellees from Marienbad who ended up in relatively wealthy Bad Homburg, which went on to adopt Mariánské Lázně as a "partner city" in 1953. But there had been absolutely no sense of German-Czech partnership in the czechified grand spas during the immediate postwar period.

Given enough time, the Czech spas might have been able to crawl out of their parochial hole—Czechoslovakia, after all, was one of the few Eastern European nations not occupied by the Red Army or locked directly in the icy embrace of Comrade Stalin. But Karlovy Vary and Mariánské Lázně were not allowed time to throw off their insularity because, in February 1948, Stalin sanctioned a coup by restless Czech Communists, who quickly moved this land firmly into the Soviet orbit.

A month after the coup, Foreign Minister Jan Masarýk, a lone holdout from Beneš's pre-Communist regime, died from a fall out his office window. The Czech authorities claimed he had "jumped to his death." This athletic feat (Masarýk somehow managed to close his office window during his "jump") is best understood as the "Third Defenestration of Prague"—a third historic case of tossing hated or inconvenient political figures out of high windows, albeit not invariably to their death.*

The Czech spas' hopes for rapid rejuvenation and expanded patronage crashed to earth in 1948 along with Masarýk's body. Shortly after the defenestration, Klemens Gottwald's Communist regime nationalized all the baths and major hotels in Karlovy Vary and Mariánské Lázně.

Recovery

Like battered Europe itself, the grand spas of Mitteleuropa "came back," after a fashion, starting in the 1950s and 1960s. Yet there was a huge difference in the degree of recovery between the Kurorte on the western side of the Iron Curtain and those in the east. There had always been variations in style and feel between, say, Baden-Baden and Marienbad. But from the early 1950s to the end of the 1980s these places were worlds apart.

In West Germany the grand spas' rejuvenation went hand in hand with that nation's economic recovery—its fabled *Wirtschaftswunder*.

---

*The First Defenestration of Prague took place in 1419 and involved the killing of seven Catholic city council members by followers of the radical religious reformer Jan Hus. The Second Defenestration amounted to some more Catholic tossing, this time in 1618, when disgruntled Czech Protestants pitched two Habsburg imperial governors and their scribe out the sixteen-meter-high window of the Bohemian Chancellery. All three survived their fall because they landed in a cushioning pile of horse manure. Although spared by the "holy shit," the men's fate is said to have helped kick off the Thirty Years' War.

This astonishing revival derived from a number of factors—political stability, surprisingly intelligent governmental policies, currency reform, Marshall Plan aid, an abundant supply of trained labor, the Korean War boom—but the key to it all was the German people's sheer determination to dig out from the ruins and rebuild their lives on a new footing. Everyone in bombed-out Wiesbaden was "incredibly hardworking," noted the American fighter pilot (and future novelist) James Salter on a short visit to that spa town in 1950. Indeed they were.

A prime symbol of this recovery was the Volkswagen Beetle, which now really *did* become a "people's car" (albeit early on primarily a white-collar people's car as opposed to a blue-collar bug). Another sign of better times was a landscape of bustling spas, a terrain which itself was crawling with shiny new Käfer (Beetles).

This fundamentally new turn in the history of German spas came courtesy of a national health insurance program that had its origins in Bismarck's pioneering social security system but was vastly more generous and inclusive. A national system of *Krankenkassen*—semiautonomous insurance agencies funded by the state and mandatory contributions from employees and employers—allowed West German citizens to spend subsidized three-to-four-week stays at an accredited spa simply on the say-so of a friendly family GP. There was also a subsidized week-long *Nach-Kur*, or follow-up cure, so that curists would not have to plunge abruptly and rudely back to work without a period of adjustment and quiet reflection at home. Rare was the physician who refused to write a prescription for a spa stay to "cure," say, a spot of rheumatism, poor circulation, migraines, lower back pain, or whatever else the patient complained of. Not every sufferer ended up in an upscale spa like Bad Homburg or Baden-Baden because the *Krankenkassen*, not the patient, usually selected the Kurort. However, if a medical specialist insisted that only Baden-Baden would "work" for a particular ailment, then Baden-Baden it would be.

Naturally, the West German spa industry was *very* happy with this arrangement, and so, too, were the West Germans. As we know, the Germans had always been enthusiastic spa lovers, but in the past only the better-off among them could patronize these places, or at least the luxury ones. Now a pipe fitter, backed by the right physician, might find himself sharing a thermal pool in Bad Homburg with a corporate lawyer.

Across the West German spa landscape, visitor numbers increased at a steady pace from the mid-1950s to the early 1980s, reaching over six million in 1981. Starting in the mid-1960s, patronage by foreigners also rebounded, for by then the major spas had refurbished their facilities and were able to cash in on a growing health and fitness craze throughout the Western industrialized world. Many of those foreign visitors came (once again) from the United States, a nation whose own spa scene, rather like its passenger railway system, suffered grievously from a lack of German-style public spiritedness on the part of its policy makers.

Alas, the West German system of spa subsidization was too good to last. Small-minded bean counters from Bonn blanched at the high cost. And it *was* expensive, contributing in no small way to the large deficits which most of the Krankenkassen were running up by the late 1970s. Under pressure from the insurance agencies and Finance Ministry bureaucrats, the government of Chancellor Helmut Schmidt, a Social Democrat no less, took the scalpel in 1982 to health-care benefits, including the spa subsidies. Cruelly, new regulations limited subsidized cure visits to one every three years (except for the truly sick) and required patients to contribute ten marks a day out of their own pockets toward their medical costs. Physicians were instructed to prescribe fewer spa visits or lose their Krankenkassen privileges.

The consequence of these measures was a sharp slump in trade, especially for the lower-cost spas that depended entirely on subsidized visits. Overall, there was a 25 percent plunge in West German spending on spa treatment between 1980 and 1983, according to a spokesman for the German Spa Association in Bonn. Some of the newer and lesser-known spas went under. On the other hand, the grand old luxury Kurorte, with their casinos, social cachet, and world-famous waters, managed to weather this crisis and soldier on.

Take Bad Homburg, for example. In 1984, two years into the new era, ten thousand curists took the waters (compared to an annual average of twenty thousand in the late nineteenth century and about fifteen thousand in 1980, Homburg's best year in the post–World War II recovery era). Despite the cuts on spa spending by the government, some 95 percent of Homburg's guests in 1984 were on doctor-prescribed treatments. Not all were wealthy. "Now we get everybody from business executives to restaurant waiters taking the cure," said Homburg's spa director, Erich

Gunkel. The German patrons at Homburg and other major Kurorte were willing to pay more for their spa visits in large part because they increasingly believed the waters were useful not only as healing agents but as a *prophylactic* measure against serious disease. They firmly subscribed, it seemed, to the old (but often neglected) adage, "Prevention is better than healing." In 1985, Homburg's spa director was confident that a growing commitment to preventative health-care regimens would keep the better German Kurorte in business. "Today, we cannot call it a renaissance, and the red ink continues," director Gunkel averred, "but we find an improvement owing to a greater proportion of people going to the spas just to stay healthy."

For the smaller and somewhat less prestigious Bad Ems, which by the 1970s was doing well enough to expand its cure facilities, survival after the government cuts was a close-run thing and derived less from the local waters, whether prophylactic or healing, than from ancillary entertainments. "Ems stands before bankruptcy," cried the *Lahnzeitung* in 1983. Fortunately for Ems, its Spielbank finally reopened in 1987, and this brought in a new wave of tourists who sometimes took the waters while losing their shirts at the tables. The town's historic cure complex, while hardly the bustling scene of old, did not go under after all.

Along the road to recovery, the grand West German spas managed to resume some of their salad-day functions as promenades for high-level diplomacy and political decision making—and also as watering holes for global potentates and plutocrats. Wiesbaden, for example, became an important player in postwar West German politics via its role as capital of the newly created federal state of Hesse. The city also became the home of two new federal agencies: the Federal Criminal Office and the Federal Office for Statistics. With the establishment in 1957 of the Rhein-Main-Hallen, Wiesbaden joined Frankfurt as one of the FRG's premier trade-fair cities.

Baden-Baden, largely because of close ties to West German chancellor Konrad Adenauer, an "honorary citizen" of the town, won the right to host the fledgling federal republic's coming-out party on the postwar diplomatic stage. In August 1953, the foreign ministers of the European Coal and Steel Community, a precursor to the Common Market and European Union, met at the Black Forest resort to discuss common economic and political strategies.

In 1955 Baden-Baden was graced—or blighted, if you will—by a visit from the dictatorial ruler of Iran, Shah Mohammad Reza Pahlavi, a true connoisseur of the high life. The Shah was the first reigning monarch to cure at the spa in sixty years, and both he and his hosts reveled in the experience. (Some twelve years later, in June 1967, the Shah's visit to West Berlin provoked a violent demonstration that tragically yielded the death of one of the student protestors, Benno Ohnesorg.)

In 1962 Konrad Adenauer, together with his French counterpart Charles de Gaulle, met at Baden's Brenner Park Hotel to lay the groundwork for the Franco-German Friendship Treaty—a surprisingly successful fence-mending operation that anchored the crucial postwar Franco-German rapprochement more generally. Eighteen years later, Brenner's reprised this historic tête-à-tête by hosting a meeting between French president Valery Giscard d'Estaing and German chancellor Helmut Schmidt. Unfortunately, neither man took the waters, as their nineteenth-century predecessors surely would have done. (Schmidt, a chain smoker, was apparently not a devotee of preventative medicine.)

Finally, in 1981, Baden-Baden sealed its status as a premier gathering place for the world's movers and shakers by providing the stage for the Eleventh Congress of the International Olympic Committee (IOC). The delegates met in the Kurhaus, not far from a bust of the modern Olympics founder, Baron Pierre de Coubertin. The bust of Coubertin had been put up by the Nazis in 1938 to commemorate the first German-hosted Olympic Games in 1936. In 1981 the IOC, led by Spain's Juan Antonio Samaranch, a former Francoist, was still a classic old-boys' club made up of wealthy businessmen and lower-level aristocrats. The delegates spent two weeks in September choosing venues for the 1988 Winter and Summer Games (Calgary and Seoul, respectively), and discussing ways to "market" the Olympics more effectively. Outside the Kurhaus stood a small group of anti-Olympic protesters from Nagoya, Japan, which was competing with Calgary for the 1988 Winter Games. "No Olympics for Nagoya," read signs carried by the protestors. So busy were the IOC Congress attendees dodging protesters and coming up with new commercial strategies for the games that they reportedly had "little time to loll around in the [Baden] baths."

By the 1970s the major West German spa towns fully embodied the larger material success of the federal republic: they exuded prosperity and confidence. While older West German citizens, spa-town dwellers or not, were on the whole proud of their nation's economic success, a younger generation coming of age in the 1960s—or some of them, anyway—emphatically did *not* share this enthusiasm.

Even stately Baden-Baden nurtured a few radical "68'ers" in its midst. In January of 1968, that year of youth revolt across the West, two Baden-Baden-bred university students invited "Red" Rudi Dutschke, a leader of West Germany's leftist student movement, to deliver one of his inflammatory speeches in Baden's august Kurhaus, the very belly of the capitalist beast. Baden-Baden's mayor, a member of the conservative Christian Democratic Union Party, denied use of the Kurhaus for the event, obliging the students to hold their rally outside in the cold. Not surprisingly, the rally turned violent, demonstrators pelting the police and the Kurhaus with ice. Among the few Baden-Baden elders who came out to support the protesters was famed conductor Pierre Boulez, a part-time resident of the spa town.

In the 1980s Bad Homburg, which had become the FRG's wealthiest town per capita due to the plethora of Frankfurt-based bankers residing there, witnessed firsthand the degeneration of West Germany's idealistic sixties protest movement into bloody terror. At the very end of this terror-ridden epoch, in November 1989, Red Army Faction (RAF) terrorists descended on Homburg to murder Alfred Herrhausen, chief of the Deutsche Bank, with a remote-controlled car bomb.

The RAF was also responsible for attacks against American targets in the Wiesbaden area. On August 31, 1981, activists burned seven cars at a US military housing complex in the spa town. Four years later, RAF militants detonated a car bomb at the Rhein-Main Airbase near Wiesbaden, killing two American servicemen. While it cannot be said that German spa land in this era was unusually dangerous for Americans or anyone else, the grand spas hardly escaped the antimaterialist crusading and intergenerational antagonism that constituted the flip side of West German prosperity.

The Second Republic of Austria also managed an impressive postwar revival, though the rebound took a little longer to gain traction than in West Germany. Of enormous help to Austria's recovery was a remarkable *Staatsvertrag* (state treaty) in May 1955 that brought an end to

Four-Power Allied occupation—most crucially an end to the crippling presence of the Russians. Austria had been compelled to pay a large part of the occupation costs incurred by the Soviets, who had also confiscated much of the nation's industrial and food production—some 63 percent of the latter between 1947 and 1955. According to a tenacious legend, Austrian treaty negotiator Leopold Figl induced Soviet foreign minister Viacheslav Molotov to forgo any mention of Austria's Nazi past in the preamble to the state treaty by getting him drunk on some deceptively potent Heurigen wine he'd brought with him to Moscow. In reality, Molotov didn't give a damn about Austria's brown past and hoped that the neutrality that came along with Austrian independence would allow a continued Russian influence in the area while preventing any political or military alliances between Austria and the West.

No Austrians were happier to see the Soviet occupiers go than the native residents of Baden-bei-Wien, whose cure and hospitality industry could not even begin to revive while, as Viennese visitors complained, one "couldn't walk the streets without tripping over a Russian." On the very day of the Soviet pullout, September 19, 1955, Badeners gleefully tore down the high wooden fence encircling the Russian compound and began repairing damages to stately old buildings caused by the war and occupation. In many cases, the devastation was severe, the departing Russians having stripped the structures of everything of value, including copper wiring, light fixtures, and toilets (though, according to a local canard, the Russians had made scant use of the latter, preferring the floors). No question about it: reestablishing Baden-bei-Wien as a major cure destination with up-to-date facilities was going to be a herculean task, one requiring massive investment from the newly independent federal government in Vienna.

Anxious to attract visitors—especially wealthy West Germans—to its noble Kurorte, Vienna did invest some serious money in Baden's restoration effort, but the real hero of that spa town's comeback was one Viktor Wallner, Bürgermeister from 1965 to 1988. Bürgermeister Wallner pursued the restoration of Baden's extensive cure infrastructure with tireless zeal, overseeing a complete overhaul of the Marienquelle and the Josefsbadquelle. Yet Wallner understood, better than most, that handsome thermal baths would not by themselves guarantee commercial viability in the new era since fewer people were indulging in the extended water-cure rituals of old. (Austria, moreover, did not institute a government-funded spa subsidy program as generous as West Germany's—the country was too poor—although some private health plans included Kurort visits.)

On Wallner's watch, Baden-bei-Wien successfully reinvented itself as a "convention destination" with the conversion of its old Kurhaus into a "Kongresshaus" (convention center). Conventioneers and other overnight visitors had an array of upscale hotels to choose from, among them former public buildings recently sold off to private entrepreneurs. To accentuate Baden's bucolic ambiance, the town core became a pedestrian-only zone, its cobbled lanes lined with boutiques and wine shops specializing in the local product. A magnificently renovated Stadttheater (municipal theater) showcased Austrian playwrights along with the music of Beethoven, whom Baden-bei-Wien continued to tout as one of its own despite the rather less-than-cordial treatment it had accorded the composer during the time he lived there. In 1980 the old spa town proudly celebrated the five hundredth anniversary of its municipal incorporation. The city was "back," crowed local boosters.

That most fabled Austrian Kurort, Bad Gastein, experienced a similar comeback, although the secret of this achievement resided not so much in its healing waters—hyped as those certainly were. Much more than in the post–World War I era, Gastein's post–World War II recovery derived from its Alpine terrain—those towering mountains in which folks could hike in the summer and ski in the winter.

Above all, it was the latter activity, Alpine skiing, which fueled and shaped modern Gastein's reincarnation. (An American parallel is Aspen, Colorado, a former mining town that had gone into a sharp decline until a timely exploitation of powdery "white gold" in the hills brought new recreational riches—and eventually a deluge of movie stars bearing their own white powder.) Just as in Aspen, in the Gastein area downhill skiing was still a pastime for the hardy few in the immediate post–World War II era—many enthusiasts, some missing a leg from the war, actually *walking* up the ski runs rather than taking the rudimentary lifts—but starting in the mid-1950s, skiing became a true *Volkssport* (mass sport), attracting ever greater hordes to the slopes. Gastein and nearby Bad Hofgastein met the increased demand with a growing array of sophisticated chairlifts and gondolas. While legions of duffers gracelessly executed their *Sitzmarks* and face-plants, "ski cannons" shot down the more demanding runs in one World Cup race after another. (In 1958, Gastein hosted the World Alpine Ski Championships.) Between its winter and summer visitors, the Gasteinertal (Gastein Valley) tourist industry boomed as never before: 97,598 visitors showed up in 1955–1956; by 1994 that number had climbed to 305,000.

Of course, not everyone who came to Gastein wanted to hike or ski. Some visitors, especially elderly ones, simply wished to treat their aches and pains in the thermal waters, as curists had done for centuries. Among these senior-citizen health pilgrims was Thomas Mann, who in August 1951, at age seventy-six, stopped in Gastein for two weeks during the fourth of his five postwar trips to Europe. (Mann had become an American citizen during his prolonged exile in the United States, but his adopted nation's sharp turn to the right in the early Cold War era—the shameful posturing of Senator Joseph McCarthy, the witch hunts launched by the House Un-American Activities Committee, and *Life* magazine's denunciation of the writer as a "Communist Dupe"—caused Mann to rethink his allegiances and to consider spending his last years back in Europe. Ultimately he decided to move to Switzerland, settling near Zurich in 1952 and dying there three years later.)

In that European summer of 1951, Mann hoped that Gastein's "Fountain of Youth" waters might alleviate his painful arthritis, but they ended up doing more than that. Although the bath ritual was demanding for him, the writer felt rejuvenated enough to plunge fully back into *Die Bekentnisse des Hochstaplers Felix Krull* (*The Confessions of Felix Krull, Confidence Man*), a youthful work he had begun way back in 1911 and then put aside, only to return to, albeit fitfully, in 1950 after reading Gore Vidal's homosexual novel *The City and the Pillar*. Gastein proved a perfect setting in which to make good progress on the novel. More still, the stimulation from the thermal bathing—along, perhaps, with the pleasure of swimming in his own entrancing prose—produced miraculous morning erections. He even managed to masturbate again, an achievement he found "ridiculously satisfying." Whatever the source of Mann's erotic/creative rejuvenation, the novel that emerged from it proved to be a true comic masterpiece—and one, I should add, that is rife with spa themes such as the pursuit of luxury and fashion, sexual adventurism, physical vanity, sloth, roguery, and a world of alluring promises underpinned by artifice, beauty, and eternally returning hope.

Mann's visit to Gastein turned out to be a harbinger of things to come. Notables of all sorts once again found their way to the glittering Alpine Kurort, although cultural luminaries now took a backseat to global potentates and politicos atop the Kurliste scrupulously maintained by Cure Director Heinrich Zimburg.

In summer 1962 no less a figure than King Ibn Saud of Saudi Arabia descended on Gastein with a retinue of sixty-four lackeys. He and his entourage stayed in the opulently refurbished Parkhotel Bellevue, which now rivaled the Grand Hotel de l'Europe as Gastein's premier address. Unfortunately, Saud and his troop limited their stay at the spa to one week, a disappointment to local businesspeople. In 1966 Soviet president Nikolai Podgorny and Austrian chancellor Josef Klaus interrupted their bilateral talks in Vienna with a refreshing break at Bad Gastein, although apparently neither leader took the waters. By contrast, Iran's peripatetic Shah Pahlavi, an avid skier as well as spa connoisseur, spent *his* two weeks at Gastein in February 1965 both soaking and skiing. The shah chose to stay at the Grand Hotel de l'Europe rather than the Bellevue because the Grand was the only place in town large enough for his eighty-person-strong entourage, bristling with Savak secret police.

The shah's stay was a welcome shot in the arm for hotelier Alfred Sedlacek, whose high-maintenance institution was finding it hard to compete with newer, more efficient establishments. In 1967 Sedlacek hosted Sheik Ali Bin Abdullah Al-Thani of Qatar for a one-week stay, which proved the hotelier's last hurrah. Running a deficit of 175,809 schillings in 1967–1968, Sedlacek closed down his fabled hotel at the end of 1968.

Yet this was not quite the end for Gastein's most famous hostelry. In 1982 Reinhardt Stefan Tomek, a self-described resuscitator of moribund businesses, reopened the hotel after sinking 150 million schillings into its renovation. Infatuated with publicity, Tomek orchestrated a series of live Austrian/German television broadcasts of New Year's celebrations from his hotel. The first New Year's bash in 1983 featured American singer Liza Minnelli, to whom Tomek paid 5.4 million schillings, a typical extravagance. (Later Grand Hotel New Year's stars included Shirley Bassey and Charles Aznavour.) Tomek's hotel also hosted the Miss Europe contest in 1984 and, as a display of urbanity, awarded actor Peter Ustinov a $10,000 "Epicure of the Year" prize. Determined to make Bad Gastein the

"Monte Carlo of the Alps," Tomek in 1985 moved the town's casino to gaudy new quarters on the first floor of his hotel.

From the outset, Tomek's expenditures far exceeded his profits, and when Austrian tourism took a nosedive in the mid-1980s as a combined result of a weak dollar, the Chernobyl disaster, and the Waldheim affair,* Tomek was forced to declare bankruptcy. The Grand Hotel de l'Europe closed its doors for good in 1988—a terrible setback for a new generation of historic hotel buffs like me who were tragically denied the opportunity to stay there.

Gastein never quite managed to become the "Monte Carlo of the Alps," but it weathered the crisis of the mid-eighties sufficiently to hold its own as Austria's premier Alpine Kurort. Among the foreign eminences who stayed there every summer for long stretches in the late 1980s and 1990s was German chancellor Helmut Kohl, a figure of Bismarckian dimensions (both physically and historically) who required regular cures every bit as much as the Iron Chancellor. Yet since annual weeks-long cure stays of the sort undertaken by Kohl were hardly standard practice anymore, Gastein, like other grand Kurorte, had had to rework what it meant to be a spa.

If the West German and Austrian Kurorte were proud showcases of their nations' postwar socioeconomic systems, so, too, were the major *lázně* (baths) of Communist-ruled Czechoslovakia, Karlovy Vary and Mariánské Lázně. Czechoslovakia's new rulers could have shut down these "culturally decadent" remnants of the old order, as they did most of the ornate coffee palaces and up-market bordellos in Prague, yet instead they decided to retain them and use them for their own purposes.†

That a new ideology—and new imperial "protector"—now dominated the scene became clearly evident in structural nomenclature and

---

*During his campaign for the Austrian presidency in 1986, Kurt Waldheim, a former secretary general of the United Nations, was accused of having committed crimes against Jews and others while serving as a Wehrmacht officer in the Balkans during World War II. Waldheim denied the charges and went on to win the presidency, in part by exploiting a domestic backlash against his accusers. However, the revelations about Waldheim's past and the resurfacing of anti-Semitism during his electoral campaign prompted boycotts of Austria by some foreign tourists, especially Americans.

†Among the bordello-purge victims was the chandeliered suite of rooms in Prague's elegant Hotel Paris. Dubbed "The Department of Internal Medicine" by the women who worked there, this fabled cathouse catered mainly to fruit and vegetable brokers from the neighborhood. The scene is lovingly re-created in Bohumil Hrabal's historical novel, *I Served the King of England* (1971).

usage at both spa towns. Karlovy Vary's Greek-revival Kurhaus turned into the "Colonnade of Czechoslovak-Soviet Friendship" and served mainly as a site for political meetings and party rallies. Later on, in 1975, Karlovy Vary's rebuilt Thermal Colonnade was rechristened "Yuri Gagarin's Hot Spring Colonnade" to honor the pioneering Soviet cosmonaut who died testing a MiG-15 in 1968. (A large bronze statue of Gagarin, erected in front of the Colonnade in 1975, was shifted to the airport in 1992. It is still there.) The former Hotel Pacific, a faded Belle-Époque beauty, bore as of 1950 the inspirational moniker Úspěšný Února ("Successful February") in homage to the February 1948 Communist coup in Prague. The building in which Karl Marx dutifully met with his spa physician during his stays at Karlovy Vary became "The Karl Marx Museum." Here one could see the *very glass* from which the great revolutionary had sipped his daily dosage of healing waters. (Alas, this experience is no longer available: the Marx Museum vanished in 1994.)

For its part, Mariánské Lázně now boasted a Maxim-Gorky Colonnade (the Russian writer had cured there in the early 1920s) and a Gottwald Square, named after the Stalinist president of Czechoslovakia from February 1948 to 1953.

More important than these alterations in nomenclature was a fundamental change in clientele at the Czech spas. Karlovy Vary and Mariánské Lázně became state-subsidized rest and recreation centers for industrial laborers and toilers on the country's newly collectivized factories and farms. Party leaders and bosses of state-run unions also cured at the spas, where the finest hotels (such as Karlovy Vary's Grand Hotel Pupp and Mariánské Lázně's Esplanade) maintained suites reserved for the political elites' exclusive use.

Such party privileges notwithstanding, Communist-era Karlovy Vary and Mariánské Lázně were strongly egalitarian in their social makeup, a completely new development for them. The social leveling at these fabled resorts went further than in their postwar West German counterparts because state subsidies at the Czech spas covered virtually everything, from transportation to meals, and embraced family dependents as well.

There was certainly something to be said for this new order of things. For the first time, a class of people who had been present at the spas only as hired help now appeared as guests, taking the waters and getting their massages just like their "social betters" of old. By all accounts, they made good use of this new opportunity, claiming their places with their fellow workers every season on the dates and in the spaces assigned them by a centralized spa bureaucracy. And God knows they had as much need for this experience as any rich curist of old, what with their cigarette-smoke-damaged lungs, cerotic livers, and assorted afflictions related to highly fatty, starch-laden diets.

Commendable as it undoubtedly was, maintaining the grand old Czech spas as fully subsidized R and R depots for deserving workers was a serious financial challenge for a nation that (unlike West Germany) was anything but wealthy. Thus it was not long before the Czech authorities concluded, rather like the Nazis with Baden-Baden, that in Karlovy Vary and Mariánské Lázně they had a valuable resource which, handled properly, might generate revenue via foreign tourism. And the foreign tourists they had in mind were rich Westerners—definitely *not* the shallow-pocketed visitors from other East-bloc states who were already arriving in droves.

Along with sporadic investments in infrastructure refurbishment, the government in Prague sought to make the nation's once-glamorous water-cure resorts more attractive to the outside world by expanding a modest summer film festival inaugurated by Czech filmmakers in 1946 into a splashy international extravaganza on the model of Cannes and Venice. Staged initially both in Mariánské Lázně and Karlovy Vary, the Czech film festival moved exclusively to the latter spa town in 1950. The event *did* pull in some foreign patrons, but not nearly as many as the organizers had hoped because the ruling Communist Party could not resist imposing ideological controls on both the selection of films and the list of invitees. Nor was the physical setting a truly convincing answer to Cannes or Venice. After attending the Karlovy Vary festival in 1953, American newspaper columnist Art Buchwald reported, to the chagrin of his hosts, that most of the grand buildings were "shabby" and "sadly deteriorated."

Among the least "shabby" structures in Karlovy Vary was the Grand Hotel Pupp, which had been occupied (and duly trashed) by the Red Army after the war but then extensively renovated in 1948–1949. In 1948 the hotel was able to welcome its first distinguished foreign guest in many years—the Maharaja of Dharampur, no less. As the principal site for Karlovy Vary's annual cinematic exhibition from 1950 to the mid-1970s, the

Hotel Pupp sponsored the crowning of a "Miss Film Festival Beauty Queen" every July—a major event in the national cultural calendar.

As with the film festival more generally, however, the demands of ideological conformity limited the Pupp's appeal among non-Communist visitors. Saddled as of 1951 with a new name, Grandhotel Moskva-Pupp, the hostelry became a kind of private clubhouse for top political and union functionaries, a gilded setting for dreary party meetings and socialist convocations. A Karlovy Vary "cultural" newspaper, *Lázněský časopis*, could toot proudly in 1950: "Today's guests at the Hotel Pupp no longer wear monocles or Belgian spats, but they carry in their heads the latest decrees of the Ninth Congress of the Communist Party of Czechoslovakia!" An official guidebook to Karlovy Vary published in the following year derided at length the pre-Communist-era Pupp as an embodiment of everything sinful and degraded in capitalist/imperialist society, while celebrating the "Pupp of today" for its hosting of Young Pioneer meetings, regional (party) conferences, and May Day festivities. "While taking its place in the service of the toiling masses, the Hotel Pupp has not lost its [earlier] reputation as one of the best and most comfortable hotels in Czechoslovakia. On the contrary, it has discovered in this new service to the nation its true role and mission," boasted the guidebook.

For all its exemplary political correctness, the new Pupp looked much like the old Pupp and could not, it was felt, fully "represent" the achievements of Czechoslovakian Communism. As a physical icon of the forward-looking new order, and as a more up-to-date stetting for the International Film Festival, Karlovy Vary's Communist bosses ordered the construction of a mammoth new bath/hotel/entertainment complex on the edge of the historic cure district. Begun in 1967 and completed nine years later, the Cure Hotel Thermal was a fifteen-story modernist tower block soaring high over the town. It would be hard to imagine a structure more out of harmony with its surroundings. Yet for that very reason the Thermal symbolized, certainly more boldly than the renovated Pupp, the reality that Karlovy Vary stood firmly under new management. (The Cure Hotel Thermal still stands today as a massive eyesore, a hideous blight on the landscape; inferior materials and shoddy workmanship resulted in periodic renovations rather than the demolition that should have been its fate.)

Lacking a major annual event on the order of Karlovy Vary's International Film Festival, Mariánské Lázně struggled more grievously than its larger peer under regime-imposed parochialism. Discriminating foreign guests had little reason to visit the place. To put it bluntly, wealthy Westerners (above all, wealthy West Germans, the primary foreign target audience for the spa) would travel to the ends of the earth before splashing about with Czech and Polish bricklayers in a dilapidated Communist-controlled East European health resort. Even fastidious Czechs could find the Warsaw Pact atmosphere prevailing in Mariánské Lázně (and for that matter, Karlovy Vary) hard to take. Returning in the 1950s to a grand spa (clearly Mariánské Lázně) where she had worked long ago, the Czech heroine (Tereza) in Milan Kundera's novel *The Unbearable Lightness of Being* is appalled by the changes: "The streets and buildings could no longer return to their original names. As a result, a Czech spa had suddenly metamorphosed into a miniature imaginary Russia, and the past that Tereza had gone there to find turned out to be confiscated."

One development in the early 1960s that helped revive foreign interest in Mariánské Lázně had nothing to do with the official efforts to attract Westerners. This was the production in 1961 of the most famous spa film ever made, Alain Resnais's *L'Année Dernière à Marienbad* (*Last Year in Marienbad*). This paean to melancholy and loss was (largely) a succès d'estime in the United States and Western Europe, winning a Golden Lion in Venice in the year of its appearance. Soon the film became something of an object of worship among cineastes. Enthusiasts went to see it several times, convinced that only repeated viewings could bring out its complicated and deep meaning (just as grand spas required repeated visits to fully work their magic). And sure enough, the movie drew significant numbers of fans to Mariánské Lázně—folks determined to walk the very baroque halls and manicured paths down which a mysterious tuxedoed man stalks a beautiful woman with whom he thinks he had an affair at the spa in the year past.

In actuality, due to opposition from the Communist authorities, this piece of nostalgic Western "decadence" could not be filmed in Mariánské Lázně at all, but instead had to be shot in Munich's Schloss Nymphenburg, birthplace of "Mad" King Ludwig II (which might partly explain the film's slightly deranged murkiness). Had they been thinking more creatively, the Czech authorities would have designated one of Mariánské Lázně's baroque bath palaces as the "true" film location and populated it with gowned and tuxedoed actors standing motionless, lost in profound silence, eyes fixed on an unfathomable past. But of course, they did not do this—and far from allowing the film a profitable run in its nationalized cinemas, the Czech government banned it from screens across the nation. Czech audiences did not get a chance to see *Last Year* until the 1968 "Prague Spring"—and then only briefly before the Curtain came down again and stayed down until 1989.

Although *Last Year in Marienbad* was denounced by a few Western critics (most notably Pauline Kael) as pretentious nonsense, a central notion conveyed by the film—namely, that this particular place, this hauntingly elegant *Marienbad*, has a strong capacity to evoke nostalgia—cannot be easily dismissed. Milan Kundera's Tereza found only a tainted, "confiscated" past in Communist-era Mariánské Lázně, but then she had lived there in a different era. For visitors to the town in the 1960s and 1970s who "knew" its older incarnation only through literature or film—visitors like me—this place, for all its obvious deterioration, still had the capacity to take one back in time to a more refined and decorous age. I can certainly muse along with another literary character, "Marie" in W. G. Sebald's evocative novel *Austerlitz* (2001), who during a brief stop at the spa in 1972 imagines what it must have been like in the fin de siècle:

> I can just see in my mind's eye, said Marie, a set of very corpulent men disregarding their doctor's advice and giving themselves up to the pleasures of the table, which even at a spa were lavish at that time, in order to suppress, by dint of their increasing girth, the anxiety for the security of their social position constantly stirring within them, and I see other patients, most of them ladies and rather pale and sallow already, deep in their own thoughts as they walk along the winding paths from one of the little temples which house fountains to the next, or else in elegiac mood, watching the play of clouds moving over the narrow valley from the viewing points of the Amalienhöhe or Schloss Miramont.

EPILOGUE

The Grand Spas Today

"They step out of the shadows into the light: the Kurorte of Germany. Having struggled [to stay afloat] after the national health care reforms, they have now fully taken advantage of the booming market in personal well-being and fitness. . . . An aging population is becoming ever more conscious of health issues and is prepared to invest out-of-pocket in wellness and preventative care."

So stated a German spa-industry press release in 2008—and, oddly for a publication of this sort, it contained a large measure of truth. As I pointed out earlier, the grand West German Kurorte had managed to weather the steep cuts in government spa subsidies in the early 1980s. In fact, in the early years of the new twenty-first century, the German spa industry could have legitimately made even bolder and broader claims regarding its status than the one cited above. Most of the major German Kurorte had done quite a bit more than merely exploit the health and fitness fetishism of aging baby boomers, though God knows they had done that. Acutely aware for some time that they had to be about more than just "healing waters" to survive, the spas these days have successfully revitalized a somewhat dormant ancillary strength: high culture. Also, more than ever, they push an attraction that helped save them in the 1950s and 1960s—casino gambling—opening it up to a truly global audience of the sort one finds in Las Vegas and Monte Carlo. Within the confines of their revitalized *Badekultur*, the contemporary German spas are vigorously capitalizing on a unique (though hardly new) social feature: naked coed bathing. And finally, on the ever-crucial patronage front, the collapse of the Soviet Empire has allowed the German spas to draw again on a once-valued clientele: Eastern European, especially Russian, cure-guests. Moreover, China's booming economy and "opening" to the West (at least for its elites) has provided a whole new stream of free-spending visitors, especially to the casinos.

Yet it must be emphasized that not all today's grand German Kurorte have profited equally in the new era, any more than they did in earlier spates of rejuvenation. (I should mention, by the way, that no spa town situated in the former East German territory absorbed into the West in the 1990 national reunification stands on the list of major German Kurorte today.) As has always been the case with Germany's luxury spa world, it is not only the spas' thermal waters that betray varying properties but their social and cultural scenes as well.

"The real secret to today's Baden-Baden lies in the friendly people, young and old," boasted a Baden booster in 2006. "We laugh a lot and enjoy life here more than in any other place in Germany." The cheerfulness bar may not be terribly high in hard-working, anxiety-prone contemporary Germany, but Baden-Badeners *do* have good reason to feel pleased with their lot. Their town has amply confirmed its status not only as the leading Kurort in Germany but as the premier spa in Europe and probably the entire world.

One reason for this supremacy is very old, dating back to the Roman Empire: Baden-Baden is far and away the best place on the planet to get naked in public without being arrested or packing sand in one's crevices. More specifically, you need only drop in at Baden-Baden's palatial Friedrichsbad on the days of the week (Sunday, Tuesday, Wednesday, and Friday) when naked mixed bathing is not only available but *required*. Being German, the Friedrichsbad has lots of rules for bathers. You probably won't be lashed if you deviate from these regulations, but you'll certainly warrant a disapproving look almost as severe as if you had shown up wearing a swimsuit. There are *seventeen* stages to go through—various pools, showers, sweat chambers, steam chambers, "deep" massages, and skin scrapings—each with a precise time limit. Should you wish to try the medicinal waters at one of the fountains situated throughout the complex, you'll be firmly warned to confine your intake to 175 milliliters. Even on days when men and women bathe separately in the thermal pools, they come together, like it or not, in the central whirlpool.

If my experiences with mixed naked bathing at the Friedrichsbad are a reliable indicator, most of the patrons are quite satisfied with this system. The whole process is supposed to be about *health*, not sex, but that didn't stop a few of the younger couples in my purview from playing their naughty little games—or prevent loners like myself from discreetly ogling the action. It continues to be claimed, as it was in ancient Rome, that naked bathing is a great "leveler." This may be true in terms of social class, but it is patently false when it comes to pulchritude. And if one finds oneself excluded from the more frolicsome side of the naked bathing experience, one can, as I did, mentally gauge the physical attributes of one's tubmates.

Getting naked—and healthy—in the Friedrichsbad is not cheap. In 2012, a minimal three-hour stay, sans any specialized personal attentions, cost about sixty dollars, while the "luxury package," replete with fruit salad, ran closer to one hundred dollars. Interestingly enough, if you want to bathe in Baden-Baden without dropping your drawers, you typically pay *less*, though not a lot less. For example, in the sparkling new Caracalla Spa, a two-hour visit (again at 2012 prices) cost thirty dollars. Here the patron has a choice of five different saunas, including an "aroma sauna" (not advisable) and a "meditation sauna" (even less advisable). Caracalla's pièce de résistance is a domed sixty-person sauna called the "Spectaculum"—though its towels-over-privates policy renders it rather less spectacular, albeit perhaps also less alarming, than the "textile-free" precincts of the Friedrichsbad.

One of the more notable changes in Baden-Baden's contemporary cure culture involves a sharp decline in *drinking* the medicinal waters as opposed to bathing in them. Modern tastes being what they are, few spa visitors these days will tolerate heavy doses of the mineral-laden, urine-warm waters bubbling up from the Quellen. Baden-Baden's majestic, multicolumned nineteenth-century Trinkhalle, one of the town's most impressive edifices, now receives relatively few visitors, and some of these (like myself) simply cruise the place, while watching others dip their three-euro souvenir glasses into the fountains. On one occasion I observed an elderly Chinese gentleman attempting the *Trinkkur*. Asians are said to be able to ingest just about anything, but this fellow no sooner took a bit of water into his mouth than he disgustedly spat it out.

As is well known, most Chinese have no similar aversion to gambling. To accommodate them, and more generally to expand its clientele beyond the lounge-lizard, Eurotrash crowd that came to play in the 1950s and 1960s, Baden-Baden's gilded, Louis XIV-style casino has updated its policies. Men no longer have to wear a jacket and tie on the playing floor; women don't have to wear frocks. Ordinary townsfolk and tour guides are no longer excluded, as they once were. In addition to roulette and blackjack, the gaming palette now includes poker tournaments featuring No-Limit Texas Hold 'em. For the ladies there are fashion shows and "glamour parties." The casino's restaurant offers three-course "culinary festival" dinners every evening.

Intriguingly, to assuage some ongoing hand-wringing regarding gambling's darker side, self-aware "problem gamblers" or people who fear they might be can impose on themselves specific betting and time-of-play limits, which they register in advance with the casino. Should a registered *Spielsperre* (play-locked) patron attempt to transcend these limits, house authorities will immediately intervene, and no amount of Dostoevsky-like tantrums will gain a reprieve.

Fully aware of my own cluelessness around games of chance, I lamely confined myself to a guided tour of Baden-Baden's magnificent casino. There I learned, to my enduring disbelief, that fully 97 *percent* of the gambling intake goes back to the players, leaving a mere 3 percent for the house. Less incredible (I could see this for myself) was the claim that Baden-Baden's casino is thriving today, with 1,500 patrons on a typical summer weekend.

Another fact I picked up on my casino tour: Only 1.7 percent of the regular gamblers at Baden-Baden's casino are Russian! This surprised me not only because of the well-known proclivity for gaming among these folk but because these days Baden-Baden is positively crawling with Russians. As in the past, wealthy Russians come in droves to take the waters and sport about in what has always been their favorite European *banya*. What is notable now is the existence of a very substantial permanent population of Russians—so many that the spa town has been recently labeled, as it was in the mid-nineteenth century, "the only Russian city outside Russia." (Nowadays the designation is even more apt.)

Notable also is the social composition of the Russian contingent: it is largely middle- and upper-middle-class. Why are these bourgeois Russians residing in Baden-Baden and not, say, Berlin? The ones I talked to in the streets all said they didn't want big-city excitement, they wanted security and calm, and Baden-Baden offered these assets aplenty. "We feel completely comfortable here," is the way one paterfamilias put the matter.

By and large, the "Russians" in question are not citizens of the Russian Federation living as expatriates in Germany. Rather, they are former citizens of the Soviet Union or post-Communist Russia whose ancestors had settled in the Volga region under Catherine the Great in the eighteenth century. With the relaxation of travel/emigration restrictions beginning under Mikhail Gorbachev, and the subsequent disarray surrounding Soviet Communism's collapse and Russia's rocky transition to free-market capitalism, thousands of ethnic-German Russians decamped to Germany, where they could gain automatic citizenship by virtue of their "German blood." A somewhat smaller faction of Baden-Baden's new Russian community consists of Jews who had immigrated to Germany either from Russia proper or one of the former Soviet republics. As Jews, they also get preferential treatment in today's Germany.

The influx of Russians, whatever their ethnicity or religion, has hardly gone unnoticed by the natives. The fact that some of the wealthier Slavic newcomers have been buying up villas and haunting the casino has generated some grumbling about a "takeover" by "vulgar Mafiosi." In 2001, when the "Russian wave" was picking up steam, Germany's tabloid press spilled a lot of ink over an alleged "Mafia convention" at Schloss Bühlerhöhe, a luxurious hilltop hotel outside Baden-Baden.

Yet with time the town seems to have come to terms with its Russian-born residents and visitors, who, after all, dutifully pay their taxes and/or park plenty of euros with local businesses. Some Baden-Baden hoteliers even find it "touching" that the more cultivated Russian visitors—tourists carrying copies of Turgenev's *Smoke* or Dostoevsky's *The Gambler*—are treading in the footsteps of their illustrious literary forebears.

Apropos culture, splendid artistic amenities of the sort that once attracted Turgenev and his set are again part of Baden-Baden's appeal. In addition to its older Staatliche Kunsthalle (the municipal art museum that incorporated Louis Viardot's personal collection), Baden-Baden boasts the new Richard Meir–designed Museum Frieder Burda, founded in 2004 by the eponymous publishing magnate to house his enormous trove of German expressionists and American abstract expressionists and to provide space for traveling exhibitions. (When I visited in summer 2013, the Burda featured a magnificent show of Emil Nolde's color work.)

Today's Baden-Baden is also very ambitious on the classical music front, an old strong point for the spa. Since 1998 this smallish city of roughly 55,000 inhabitants offers discriminating opera fans cutting-edge productions in its magisterial Festspielhaus, one of Europe's largest opera houses. In 2004 and 2006 the spa town, having 140 years earlier unsuccessfully wooed Richard Wagner with the offer of a personal theater, sponsored glittering productions of his *Ring* cycle produced by St. Petersburg's Kirov Company. When it comes to Wagner, contemporary Baden-Baden is rivaling Bayreuth and Munich, and it offers restorative après-opera massages to boot! (Tellingly, Baden-Baden took the lead in a collective campaign launched by the major Continental European spa towns in 2012 to gain recognition for their historic contribution to global culture as UNESCO World Heritage Sites.)

As part of an ongoing effort to move seamlessly from the hallowed nineteenth century directly into the twenty-first—largely forgetting the dark interval between—modern Baden-Baden has worked hard to create a lively social scene, complete with globe-trotting celebrities and a jumping nightlife.

The city has made some notable achievements on this front. During the 2006 German-hosted football World Cup, the English team made Baden-Baden its base, and not because of the soothing waters or romantic vistas. Unsurprisingly, the English footballers trashed their digs at Schloss Bühlerhöhe, but the hotel needed renovating anyway. David Beckham and company could, and did, also kick up their heels in new nightspots like Max's Dance Club and the Bombay Rooms, both located on swinging Kaiserallee.

That quintessential baby boomer, Bill Clinton, visited Baden-Baden both before and after his presidency. In 1991 he went there to attend the annual Bilderberg Conference, a gathering of political, financial, media, and academic luminaries designed to "foster dialogue between North America and Europe." Clinton returned to Baden-Baden a couple of times after leaving office, finding the place, as he said, "so nice you have to name it twice" (an old joke). On both occasions, Mr. Clinton reportedly spent plenty of time at the Brenner's Hotel bar—though not nearly as many hours as President Boris Yeltsin of Russia apparently logged there during visits in the 1990s.

Frank Sinatra, whom Marlene Dietrich called "the Mercedes among men," also graced Brenner's in the early 1990s, pronouncing Baden-Baden his favorite European watering hole. The elderly singer's accolade was double-edged, though: although it has had some success catching on with the young, Baden-Baden would remain, at bottom, a refuge for men and women of a certain age.

This is even truer of the other grand Kurorte in today's Germany. Apart from their ongoing corporate convention and congress-hosting business, which often pulls in younger crowds, the primary grand spa clientele these days tends to be elderly, even ancient (a cohort mercilessly mocked by younger Germans as *"Grufties"*—folks with one foot in the *Gruft*, or "grave"). Like Baden-Baden but not quite with the same level of success, Bad Homburg, Wiesbaden, and Bad Ems try to keep one foot on terra firma by organizing endless rounds of special attractions, especially during the peak summer cure season.

For example, Bad Homburg sponsors an annual *Luftschiffparade* (dirigible overflight) at the site of the original *Reichsluftschiffparade* of 1910. There are frequent vintage auto rallies and car shows. In 2009 I witnessed a splendid Porsche exhibition—"Vom Volkswagen zum Traumwagen"— at Homburg's Central Garage. And speaking of garages, Homburg puts on an annual Girls' Day at local auto repair shops, where "girls of all ages" learn to handle a screwdriver, clean carburetors, and change motor oil— then repair to the thermal baths for tune-ups of their own.

In its relentless campaign to remain a lively tourist and curist destination, Bad Homburg (and the same can be said for Wiesbaden) has the advantage of close proximity to Frankfurt and its huge airport, the largest in Germany. Long-distance air travelers are known (and I am one of them) to make a beeline for the Homburg baths immediately upon extracting their sore butts from airplane seats in Frankfurt.

Bad Ems, somewhat out of the way and more rural in character, has had a harder time maintaining its status as a top Kurort. Additional cuts in governmental health-care subsidization in 1996 hit Ems especially hard, causing a plunge in cure visits from ten thousand annually in the early nineties to fewer than six thousand at the end of the decade. In

1997, a major private clinic, Dryander-Klinik, had to close shop, and in 1999 the venerable Kurhaus ceased operations and sold off its physical plant to a private hotelier. A *Gesundheitszentrum* (health center) at the principal thermal spring, having been expanded in the sixties, had to be drastically downsized in the nineties to remain solvent. Most of Ems's medical business these days takes place not in the historic cure district but in modern clinics located on a hill behind the town.

Bad Ems boosters justifiably tout their city's historic baths and Belle Époque architecture as worthy of a visit. They speak of "tradition newly interpreted" against a backdrop of ravishing natural beauty. Ems hosts summer music festivals, art exhibitions, and boating excursions on the River Lahn.

Yet, if I may extrapolate from my own experiences there, visitors to Ems these days should be prepared for a somewhat less-than-riveting experience, something on the order of a field trip to an old folks' home.

Like most German thermal bath hotels, Bad Ems's graceful Häckers Kurhotel, where I stayed, offers nude coed sauna baths. I dutifully performed this ritual during my visit, but since I was the *only one* in the room I could be neither excited nor repelled. It was a bit odd, too, to find myself virtually the only guest in the hotel (admittedly, this was the off-season) and also one of the few strollers in the streets who got around without the aid of a cane or walker. Running in the morning was out: I would have felt too guilty. Repairing to the municipal historical museum, I watched a vintage film clip showing bustling street scenes from 1914; a greater contrast to today would be hard to imagine. Mark Twain said of Baden-Baden that one should die *before* going there. Of Bad Ems I would say, more charitably, that while one may not want to put this spot atop one's "bucket list," it might be a very pleasant place in which to kick the proverbial pail.

"*Senectus ipsa morbus*" ("Aging is itself a disease") wrote the Roman playwright Terence (d. 159 BCE). No grand spa has taken this aphorism closer to heart than Austria's Bad Gastein, with its claim to be the "source of eternal youth." Gastein continues to be heavily patronized by people hoping to stay forever young by sitting hour after hour in radon-laced thermal baths or steam chambers. Alas, many if not most of these seekers have little or no youth left to retain, and going to Gastein to rekindle a vanished *Jugend* is akin to visiting the Virgin Islands to recover sexual innocence. The well-established connection between radon gas and lung cancer has had surprisingly little effect on patronage, nor has it prevented Gastein from actually touting a level of radioactivity in its air "significantly higher than the European average." Lest visitors get the idea, however, that simply sniffing the local *Luft* is sufficient to turn back the clock, a recent guidebook on the *Gasteiner Kur* advises that radon levels in the air are too low to be "therapeutically useful"—and that even loitering on the famed Waterfall Bridge amid its invigorating mists is "no replacement for a full-on *Radonkur*."

Unfortunately for a spa trying to celebrate eternal youth, Gastein these days is looking a bit long in the tooth itself. Of course, most grand spas *choose* to cultivate a retro look—vintage "k. und k." in the case of the contemporary Austrian and Czech spas—but crucial parts of Gastein's historic core are blighted by ghostly dereliction as opposed to scrupulously maintained historicism. Three formerly majestic structures in the center of town—the famed Hotel Straubinger, Hotel Austria, and the Badeschloss—stand vacant behind chainlink fences, their façades crumbling and their windows broken or boarded up. On a tour of the city in 2013, I learned from my indignant guide that a pair of "Viennese real estate speculators" had purchased the properties with a promise to renovate and reopen them. Apparently lacking the funds to do so and unwilling to offload them to better-fixed purchasers (various offers had been deemed too low), the Viennese investors simply sat on their assets, letting them fall ever further into decay.

These crumbling old edifices are not the only eyesore in today's Gastein, however. Nearby squats another abandoned structure of much more recent vintage: a concrete and glass convention center designed by the modernist architect Gerhard Garstenauer and completed (to some accolades and many groans) in 1974. While certainly fulfilling Garstenauer's professed aspiration to "create a contrast" to Gastein's prevailing nineteenth-century aesthetic, this brutalist monstrosity also broke new ground in shoddy workmanship, starting to fall apart almost as soon as it came together. Once it became unusable, it, too, fell into the hands of the Viennese speculators, who promptly enhanced their acquisition's charm by fencing it off. Along with its ghostly neighbors, the broken-down Kongresszentrum represents a particular insult to Gastein's elderly cure guests, who would prefer that their surroundings not look like they feel.

Fortunately, such lamentable blight of its historic core, albeit a huge problem for the city, is not the whole story when it comes to the architectural landscape of contemporary Gastein. The town boasts a bevy of new boutique hotels, most notably the Hotel Miramonte, a remarkable reincarnation of a 1960s-era hostelry that had gone to seed along with the hipsters who once frequented it. Prized for its spectacular views over the Gastein Valley (every room has a balcony), the Miramonte also features an in-house spa, sauna, and "Yoga-Raum."

The Miramonte was built on the premise that Gastein could attract actual young people in addition to the oldsters hoping to recapture their youth. If one can trust various 1980s newspaper stories touting Gastein as an Alpine getaway for big-city twenty- and thirty-somethings, then the Miramonte premise has certainly paid off.

Yet more recent reports, confirmed by my own experiences in today's Gastein Valley, would suggest that much of the "action" has moved from Gastein proper to nearby Bad Hofgastein. This is where the region's most luxurious hotel, the Grand Park, is situated, along with the best restaurants, cafés, and sports outfitters.

Bad Hofgastein is also, I might add, where the majority of the area's Russian tourists can now be found (should one have any desire to find them). When I stayed at the Grand Park during a recent off-season visit to the area, almost all the other guests at the hotel were Russian—and, by the look of them, the very sort of Russians that many Germans complain about these days. Here they finally were, packed around the hotel bar: big shaven-headed bruisers dressed in designer track suits with lots of bling. Their female partners were likewise right out of central casting: tall, blond, big-breasted women wearing spiked heels that could kill. (When the Russians left the bar, I asked the bartender about them. He said he personally didn't like them very much and preferred refined American guests like myself.)

Russians apparently also flock to the Gastein Valley in the winter to ski—or at least to après-ski. Downhill skiing, which was so instrumental to Bad Gastein's (and also to Bad Ischl's) recovery in the fifties and sixties, still pulls in affluent crowds. Every winter, the grand Alpine spa towns are jammed with people combining the delights of soaking and schussing. Yet there is a danger on the horizon for relatively low-lying mountain resorts like Bad Gastein (altitude 1,002 meters), Bad Ischl, and also famed Kitzbühl in the Tyrol: global warming. Rising temperatures have not yet knocked out an entire ski season, but climate change is often forcing later opening dates on the slopes and extensive use of snow-making equipment. "Christmas on the Roof of the World"—the kind of snow-filled Alpine skiing experience that Ernest Hemingway wrote about back in the day—may soon be a thing of the past at Bad Gastein.

Baden-bei-Wien does not have to worry about snow—or, rather, the lack of it. Although primarily a summer resort, its proximity to booming Vienna brings in visitors all year around. Baden's patronage, though, is heavily Austrian, and many of the visitors are day-trippers who come down from Vienna on the Badener-Bahn. When I made this delightful little excursion in 2011, I seemed to be the only nonnative aboard.

Missing from the Baden-bei-Wien of today is not only the bustling contingent of foreigners who once crowded the streets but, sadly, its once-large permanent population of Jews. The Nazis strove to make this spa town judenrein in the 1930s, and while there are no Nazis in (plain) sight today, there are also very few Jews.

American and Western European visitors to the Czech grand spas during the first days of their pupa-like reemergence from their Communist-era cocoons often expressed mild disappointment: try as they might to portray themselves as vital reincarnations of their nineteenth-century selves, the spas seemed to be having trouble throwing off postwar shabbiness and insularity. A West German visitor to Mariánské Lázně and Karlovy Vary in 1989 acknowledged a pleasing contrast between these towns' lingering Habsburg-era "glow" and surrounding Soviet-style "gloom" but noted, too, that the old façades were crumbling away and the social atmosphere reeked of melancholy. Just after the Berlin Wall came down, provoking wild celebrations across Germany, an American visitor found Mariánské Lázně suffused with "a feeling of quiet solemnity," the streets filled with old folks sipping mechanically from their mineral-water cups, and the once-grand casino, "portrayed in advertisements as a Czech Monte Carlo," almost empty most of the time, "with only a few West German and Arab visitors playing at the three blackjack and roulette tables on a Friday night." A *New York Times* reporter visiting Mariánské Lázně in November 1991 found that town a sad testimony to a "half-century of neglect" and a barrage of Communist social engineering that had turned "sumptuous dining rooms into canteens" and partitioned "spacious living quarters for the few into compartments to accommodate many." The reporter cited local complaints regarding the low-budget German tourists and day-trippers who now constituted the town's primary foreign patronage: "They come because one mark buys them three beers here and not even one at home. The ones from old East Germany, who are not so rich and very economical-minded, come here to buy their food, because it's cheaper." The *Times* man could not help wondering how this once-glamorous spa town, and its older sister resort, Karlovy Vary, would further evolve once privatization came into effect in 1992 and the "market economy" became fully established.

Now we have a pretty good answer. Over the twenty-five-year period since the collapse of Communism in Eastern Europe, the great Czech spas have managed a thorough physical rejuvenation, one characterized not so much by the construction of gleaming new cure facilities (as was often the case in Germany and Austria), but by the loving restoration of old institutions. All the grand Central European spas afford visitors a certain sense of time warp, but none more so than today's Karlovy Vary and Mariánské Lázně.

Living in the past, though, has its price. The Czech spas have had a hard time attracting a young and hip clientele—harder even than their Austrian and German rivals. With the exception of Karlovy Vary's two-week-long International Film Festival each summer, which brings in the likes of Scarlett Johansson and Antonio Banderas, affluent young Americans and Western Europeans seem not to include Czech spa land in their frenetic travels. The majority of visitors these days consists of middle- or even lower-middle-class vacationers from Eastern Europe (along with the unavoidable busloads of low-budget tourists from Germany).

The only visitors among this group with serious money to spend are the Russians. Once again, Russians are streaming back to Karlovy Vary and Mariánské Lázně, as they are to Baden-Baden. But unlike the Baden "Russians," many of the Russians who descend on the Czech spas these days are not ethnic Germans or Jewish émigrés but wealthy oligarchs (reportedly a few gangsters among them) in search of a second home, a Western bolthole should conditions turn against them at home. By all accounts, these folks are not particularly cherished by the locals, despite (and in part because of) their big-spending ways. Mindful of the Russians' track record in Czechoslovakia during the Soviet era, a Karlovy Vary art gallery owner named Marcela Balounova complained to a *New York Times* reporter in 2010: "The Russians invaded us before and they are invading us again," referring to the Soviets' suppression of the "Prague Spring" in 1968. "I still remember crying when the Russians came here. And here we are more than forty years later and this place has become a little Moscow."

"Little Moscow" may be an exaggeration, but Karlovy Vary natives grouse that real estate investments by wealthy Russians have pushed up local property values by 40 percent and that borscht is supplanting *knedliky* (Czech dumplings) on restaurant menus around town.

One reason for the Czech spas' failure to draw wealthy Westerners may be that, for all their dedication to restoration, they have not managed to restore that special sense of exclusivity and privilege that they exuded in their heyday. Even less have they re-created their salad-days status as vital centers of action, whether that action be diplomatic, social, or cultural. A British journalist, J. M. Ledgard, summed up the scene in Mariánské Lázně as follows: "The post-Communist period has been depressing. Most of the tea rooms catered for the budget-conscious German pensioner. The apple strudel was dry, tea came on a string. The council flats in the rich villas were broken down and stood out like black teeth among the restored buildings. 'This is a place for people that are tired of life,' a tourist guide told me. 'There are no young people here. Nothing happens.'"

Or, as another British visitor, publisher/historian Simon Winder, put it about Mariánské Lázně in his 2013 history of the Habsburg monarchy, *Danubia*:

> [The Communist-era people's spa] has been set aside now in favour of trying to recreate the pre-1914 Europe's playground atmosphere. Once more people parade up and down the old Kaiserstrasse as they admire the hotels, buy jewels and amber and stop for a cake and ice-cream. Once again, genuinely dying people and mere malingerers hiss at each other across dining rooms, fortunes are lost at roulette and nannies and mistresses clutter the parks. . . . Of course, it is profoundly boring here. You can only sip nasty water, munch chocolate cake or buy amber bracelets for a certain percentage of the day. Rubbing out a key underworld rival with a silenced machine-pistol in a mud bath—with bullets

making different sounds as they clack into the tiling or plonk into the mud—does not take much *time*.

My own experiences in Karlovy Vary and Mariánské Lázně left me with a somewhat less jaundiced view. During my stays in the latter spa I saw no Russian mobsters dodging bullets in the mud baths. In fact, I saw surprisingly few other bathers at all during my visits to the famed *Kreuzquelle* pool. Between soaks I got a massage from a youngish Russian woman who said she had narrowly escaped the clutches of the human traffickers who had arranged her migration to Czechoslovakia from a small town in Siberia. She was happy to be massaging rather than hooking.

I can confirm the presence (both in Mariánské Lázně and Karlovy Vary) of one upscale jewelry store after another and also the monotony this repetition evokes. I wondered who would want to browse through these same-looking shops, let alone buy anything. Apparently the answer is no one, or at best a precious few. During repeated visits I never saw more than a handful of shoppers in the fancy boutiques, and in fact, most of the people strolling up and down the main commercial avenue did not look to be the sort of people who would, or could, buy amber bracelets or Patek Philippe watches.

Judging from the strollers' clothing styles and snippets of conversation I overheard, the majority of visitors were Eastern European, predominantly Czech, with a sprinkling of Poles and Russians. Many were seriously overweight, looking like models for Fernando Botero paintings. This was especially true of the guests in Mariánské Lázně. Old Marienbad, of course, had been famous as a fat farm, but from the way folks at the restored spa were tucking into their dumplings at sidewalk restaurants, I guessed that they had not come to town to lose weight. "I beat anorexia," proclaimed a T-shirt worn by a stout lady diner.

In his novel *The Farewell Party* (1976), set in a Marienbad-like spa during the 1970s, Milan Kundera writes of a childless woman coming to the spa "in the hope of gaining fertility," as so many women had done in the nineteenth century. I saw several young ladies who might have fallen into this category, and I imagined them to be eyeing me as a potential solution to their problem—the grandiosity of the architecture will do that to a fellow.

In Mariánské Lázně I stayed at the château-like Esplanade overlooking the town, and in Karlovy Vary I lodged in the even more prestigious Grand Hotel Pupp—again, anything for science. While both these places proved quite comfortable and cosseting, they did not come up to the standards set by five-star luxury establishments like Baden-Baden's Brenner's Park Hotel and Spa or Wiesbaden's Nassauer Hof (any more than Mariánské Lázně's little neighborhood ski hill represents much of a threat to Bad Gastein).

This latter point is an observation, not a complaint. One should not, in my view, go to today's Mariánské Lázně or Karlovy Vary in search of the most refined luxury, as many curists in the fin de siècle and Belle Époque most certainly would have done. Nor should one look for the latest developments in popular culture; they just aren't there. Moreover, the grand Czech spas these days are definitely *not* in the political thick of things, as they once were.

Yet for the historian this very lack of centrality is of considerable interest and importance. It is an integral part of the spa towns' larger story of engagement with and adjustment to the outside world—a story of rising and falling "relevance." Like their gilded sisters in Germany and Austria, the Bohemian/Czech water-cure resorts never were and are not today "timeless." As I have stated often enough during this long journey, the grand spas are watery mirrors reflecting ever-changing faces—smile lines, dimples, wrinkles, warts, wounds, and all.

Acknowledgments

Often more of a talker than a doer, I talked for many years about writing a book on the grand spa towns of Central Europe before actually settling down to do it. Thus my first words of thanks must go to all those friends and colleagues who for years on end lived under the threat of a "Large-on-Spas" book without complaint, or at least without complaint to my face. Decades ago one of my Smith College colleagues, Howard Nenner, presented me with a book titled *The Spas of Bulgaria*—either to get me going or to shut me up. In Montana my good friends Adrienne Mayor, Josh Ober, Michelle Maskiell, and Billy Smith listened to endless spa-project plans, sometimes asking plaintively, "Why don't you just do it?!"

Now that I *have* finally done it, I owe thanks to the many people and institutions who helped bring this enterprise to fruition.

My editor at Rowman & Littlefield, Susan McEachern, took the project on, no doubt wondering what in God's name she was doing with a book about baths. She provided much-needed encouragement and editorial advice as I stumbled from spa to spa. (Like many of my enablers and abettors in this operation, Susan generously offered to be my research assistant in the field, not realizing how harrowing and self-sacrificial spa sleuthing can be.)

Many thanks as well to colleagues and friends who took the trouble to read draft chapters and to make suggestions for improvement. They include Archie Alexander, Peter Bloom, Klaus Böll, Howard De Nike,

Jürgen Förster, Peter Hayes, Guenter Lewy, Dale Martin, Peter Range, Jonathan Schneer, Billy Smith, Hans Vaget, and Tom Wessel. Special thanks to Adrienne Mayor, a superb scholar and literary stylist, who subjected several chapters to a stern editorial vetting. Jürgen Förster, an old friend and former colleague at the Militärgeschichtliches Forschungsamt (then in Freiburg), spotted some embarrassing factual errors and sent me useful literature on military aspects of the spa story. My friend Klaus Böll supplied me with needed materials from Germany when I could not get there myself and provided hospitality and guidance during my research visits to spas in the Frankfurt area. Yet another very good friend, Howard De Nike, a lawyer, anthropologist, and Jesuit-trained grammarian, applied his singular set of skills to the entire manuscript, as indeed he did with my previous project on the 1972 Olympic Games. In both cases Howard's assistance proved invaluable.

Along with friends and colleagues, I ruthlessly pressed various members of my family into service on the spa front. As I always do, I made my son Josh, himself a professional historian, read and comment on parts of the manuscript. He did not allow filial loyalty to compromise his critical acumen. My sisters-in-law, Kristen and Kate Wheeler, read draft chapters and offered encouragement. Kate, a fine novelist and teacher of writing, tried her level best to improve the opening section of this book, though I proved a somewhat recalcitrant student. My physician wife, Margaret, who is not only a gifted healer but an expert on the history of healing, gave me advice on the medical side of the spas saga—advice I sometimes actually took. An author in her own right, Margaret also worked hard to elevate the tone of my presentation (alas, a thankless task). Finally, I need to thank my twelve-year-old daughter Alma for showing (mostly) patience and good humor in the face of my frequent foul moods and shameful lack of attention to her own needs during the writing of this book.

Courtesy of Billy Smith and Michelle Maskiell, I was allowed to present some of my early findings to fellow Montana State University scholars at one of their fabled "salons" in Bozeman, Montana.

Thanks are due as well to the staffs of the archives, libraries, and museums in which, when not actually "taking the waters" myself in the cause of science, I spent many a fruitful hour. These institutions include the Baden-Baden Stadtbibliothek; Baden-bei-Wien Stadtbibliothek;

Bad Gastein Stadtmuseum; British Library, London; Bundesarchiv, Berlin; Gemeindearchiv, Bad Ischl; Doe Library, University of California, Berkeley; Gemeindearchiv der Gemeinde Bad Gastein; Greene Library, Stanford University; Hessisches Staatsarchiv, Wiesbaden; Museum im Gottischen Haus, Bad Homburg; Městské Museum Mariánské Lázně; Öffentliche Bibliothek der Pfarre, Bad Ischl; Österreichische Staatsbibliothek, Vienna; Renne Library, Montana State University; Stadtarchiv, Wiesbaden; Stadtarchiv, Bad Ems; Stadtarchiv im Historischen Museum, Baden-Baden; Státni Okresni Archiv Karlovy Vary; Stadtbibliothek, Wiesbaden; Sterling Library, Yale University; and Widener Library, Harvard University. Thanks also to the proprietor of the Ischler Bücherladen Antiquariat in Bad Ischl, who supplied me both with hard-to-get books and firsthand information about the region. He was just one of the many local figures—spa functionaries, masseurs and masseuses, tour guides, hoteliers, and bartenders—who filled my head with lore on their locales.

For help in putting together the spa map for this book, I am grateful to Michele Angel. Thanks once again to Michelle Maskiell, this time for assistance with assembling the book's cover art.

Finally, a hearty *Dankeschön* many times over to my old friend and Smith College colleague, Hans Vaget, a world authority on Goethe, Wagner, and Thomas Mann—and indeed on all things German. Hans painstakingly vetted the entire manuscript, catching me in numerous errors and imbecilities and proposing additions and refinements that greatly improved the final product. A native of Marienbad, Hans also shared with me insights gleaned from his own family's expulsion from the Sudetenland following World War II. It is to Hans Rudolf Vaget that this book is admiringly dedicated.

Principal Sources and Suggestions for Further Reading

The information contained in this book is derived from a variety of sources: personal experiences at the relevant spa towns; interviews; unpublished archival materials; newspapers; and printed imaginative literature, correspondence collections, memoirs, and secondary studies.

I made use of the following archives and museums: Hessisches Staatsarchiv, Wiesbaden; Stadtarchiv Wiesbaden; Stadtarchiv Baden-Baden; Stadtmuseum Baden-Baden; Stadtarchiv Bad Ems; Museum im Gottischen Haus, Bad Homburg; Gemeindearchiv der Gemeinde Bad Gastein; Stadtmuseum Bad Gastein; Stadtmuseum Bad Ischl; Městské Museum Mariánske Lázně (Municpal Museum Marienbad); Státní Okresni Archiv Karlovy Vary (Archive of the Karlsbad Region).

Principal Newspapers: *Badener Zeitung, Badeblatt* (Baden-Baden), *Frankfurter Rundschau, International Herald Tribune, Karlsbader Kurliste, Karlsbader Tageblatt, Karlsbader Zeitung, Lahnzeitung* (Bad Ems), *Manchester Guardian, Mitteilungen aus dem Verein zur Abwehr des Antisemitismus* (Berlin), *Neue Freie Presse* (Vienna), *New York Times, Niederösterreichische Nachrichten, Selbstwehr, Völkische Beobachter, Die Welt, Wiener Zeitung, Wiesbadener Kurier, Wiesbadener Tageblatt.*

The following list of references, organized by chapter, is restricted primarily to easily accessible printed sources.

Chapter 1

Useful works on medicinal waters and the global spa phenomenon include: Sylveyn Hähner-Rombach, ed., *'Ohne Wasser kein Heil': Medizinische und kulturelle Aspekte der Nutzung von Wasser* (Stuttgart, 2005); Garnot von Hahn and Hans-Kaspar von Schönfels, *Wunderbares Wasser: Von der heilsamen Kraft der Brunnen und Bäder* (Stuttgart, 1986); Roy Porter, ed., *The Medical History of Waters and Spas* (London, 1990); William A. R. Thomson, *Spas That Heal* (London, 1978); George Ryley Scott, *The Story of Baths and Bathing* (London, 1939); Joseph Wechsberg, *The Lost World of the Great Spas* (New York, 1979); Alev Lytle Croutier, *Taking the Waters: Spirit, Art, Sensuality* (New York, 1992); Vladimir Křižek, *Kulturgeschichte des Heilbades* (Stuttgart, 1990); Burkhard Fuhs, *Mondäne Orte einer vornehmen Gesellschaft: Kultur und Geschichte der Kurstädte 1700–1900* (Hildesheim, 1992); David Blackbourn, "Taking the Waters: Meeting Places of the Fashionable World," in Martin Geyer and Johannes Paulmann, eds., *The Mechanics of Internationalism* (Oxford, 2001); and Susan C. Anderson and Bruce H. Tabb, eds., *Water, Leisure, and Culture: European Historical Perspectives* (Oxford, 2002).

The cult of "healing waters" in the preclassical ancient world is deftly treated in Hahn and Schönfels, *Wunderbares Wasser*; and in the opening chapter of Křižek's *Kulturgeschichte des Heilbades*. These two volumes are also useful for classical Greece and Rome. Lore on the hygiene habits of the Scythians comes from Adrienne Mayor, "Beauty Secrets of the Ancient Amazons," www.wondersandmarvels.com/2012/09. Public bathing in Egypt is touched upon in Stacy Schiff, *Cleopatra* (New York, 2010). For my treatment of bathing in the ancient West, I've relied above all on Katherine Ashenburg, *The Dirt on Clean* (New York, 2007), along with Robert Hughes, *Rome* (New York, 2011); R. J. B. Bosworth, *Whispering City: Rome and Its Histories* (New Haven, 2011); Julian Marcuse, *Bäder und Badewesen in Vergangenheit und Gegenwart* (Stuttgart, 1903); Michael Matheus, ed., *Badeorte und Bäderreisen in Antike, Mittelalter und Neuzeit* (Stuttgart, 2001); Ralph Jackson, "Waters and Spas in the Classical World," in Roy Porter, ed., *The Medical History of Waters and Spas*; Jerome Carcopino, *Daily Life in Ancient Rome* (New Haven, 1940); J. P. V. D. Balsdon, *Life and Leisure in Ancient Rome* (New York, 1969); Garrett G. Fagan, *Bathing in Public in the Roman World* (Ann Arbor, 1999); Fikret

Yegül, *Bathing in the Roman World* (Cambridge, 2010); and Roy Bowen Ward, "Women in Roman Baths," *Harvard Theological Review* 85, no. 2 (1992). The bathing culture in ancient Pompeii is taken up in Mary Beard, *The Fires of Vesuvius: Pompeii Lost and Found* (Cambridge, MA, 2008). My account of Baiae comes largely from Tony Perrottet, *Pagan Holiday* (New York, 2003). For views on and the consumption of opiates and alcohol by the ancients, see Martin Booth, *Opium: A History* (New York, 1996); and Iain Gately, *Drink: A Cultural History of Alcohol* (New York, 2008). Two guidebooks to the ruins of ancient Bath proved useful: *Hot Bath* (Bath, 2003); and *The Essential Roman Baths* (Bath, 2006). Ancient Aquae is explored at the beginning of Dagmar Kircherer's useful short history of Baden-Baden, *Kleine Geschichte der Stadt Baden-Baden* (Braunschweig, 2008); and in the first volume of Rolf Gustav Haebler's exhaustive *Geschichte der Stadt und des Kurortes Baden-Baden*, 2 vols. (Baden-Baden, 1969).

For information on medieval and Renaissance hydropathy and public bathing, I turned to the aforementioned volumes by Ashenburg, Porter, and Matheus, as well as Marie Guérin-Beauvois and Jean-Marie Martin, *Bains Curatifs et Bains Hygiéniques en Italie de L'Antiquité au Moyen Age* (Rome, 2007); Jeffrey L. Singman, *Daily Life in Medieval Europe* (Westport, CT, 1999); Thomas Smethurst, *Hydropathia, or The Water Cure* (London, 1843). On Cardinal Bibbiena's pornographic bedroom, see Tony Perrottet, "The Secret City," www.slate.com/vatican-inside-the-secret-city, 2011. Most of my commentary on Poggio di Bracciolini comes from Stephen Greenblatt's *The Swerve: How the World Became Modern* (New York, 2011). For Montaigne, I relied on the author's *Travel Journal* in *The Complete Works*, translated and edited by Donald Frame (London, 2005); and the excellent biography of Montaigne by Sarah Bakewell, *How to Live, or A Life of Montaigne* (New York, 2010). The complaint about Bath by Samuel Pepys comes from *The Diary of Samuel Pepys—Complete Edition* (London, 2011); Smollett's commentary on Bath is in his autobiographical novel *Humphrey Clinker*, first published in 1771. Bergeron's views on Spa are in Russell T. Barnhart, *Gamblers of Yesteryear* (Las Vegas, 1983). Thomas Coryat's jaundiced views of Baden come from Michael Strachan, *The Life and Adventures of Thomas Coryat* (London, 1962). For more on Coryat and his travels, see Tim Moore, *The Grand Tour* (New York, 2001). The quotation on Karlsbad from Simon Winder comes from Winder's *Danubia: A Personal History of Habsburg Europe* (New York, 2013). On early Karlsbad, see Wechsberg, *Lost World*; Alfred Niel, *Die großen k.u.k. Kurbäder und Gesundbrunnen* (Graz, 1984); and Petr David and Vladimir Soukup, *Wonders of Czech Spas* (Prague, 2006). For the Karlsbad *Trinkkur* and the commentary of Dr. Tilling, see W. Fraser Rae, "Life at the Bohemian Baths," *Blackwood's Edinburgh Magazine* (October 1890).

For the Grand Tour, I relied on Christopher Hibbert, *The Grand Tour* (New York, 1969); Winfried Löschburg, *A History of Travel* (Leipzig, 1979); Chloe Chard, *Pleasure and Guilt on the Grand Tour* (Manchester, U.K., 1999); Brian Dolan, *Ladies of the Grand Tour* (New York, 2001); and the Grand Tour entry in Anthony Grafton, et al., eds., *The Classical Tradition* (Cambridge, MA, 2012). On Aix-les-Bains and French spas, useful are Wechsberg, *Lost World*; Douglas Peter Mackaman, *Leisure Settings: Bourgeois Culture, Medicine, and the Spa in Modern France* (Chicago, 1998); and Eric T. Jennings, *Curing the Colonizers: Hydrotherapy, Climatology, and French Colonial Spas* (Durham, NC, 2006). For Georgian Bath and the Pump Room, I used Thomas Hinde, *Tales from the Pump Room: Nine Hundred Years of Bath: The Place, Its People and Its Gossip* (London, 1988); J. A. Patmore, "The Spas of Britain," in R. P. Beckinsale and J. M. Houston, *Urbanization and Its Problems* (New York, 1968); Kenneth Young, *Music's Great Days in the Spas and Watering Places* (London, 1968); and Ian Bradley, *Water Music: Music Making in the Spas of Europe and North America* (Oxford, 2012). Benjamin Silliman is quoted in Roy and Lesley Adkins, *Jane Austen's England* (New York, 2013), which is also an excellent source for Austen in Bath, as is Claire Tomalin, *Jane Austen: A Life* (New York, 1997); and Katherine Reeve, *Jane Austen in Bath* (New York, 2006). A useful correspondence collection is R. W. Chapman, ed., *Jane Austen's Letters to Her Sister Cassandra and Others*, 2 vols. (London, 1932). The relevant Austen novels, *Northanger Abbey* and *Persuasion*, are both available in the Wordsworth Classics series. For the rush to the English seaside, I recommend J. A. R. Pimlott, *The Englishman's Holiday: A Social History* (London, 1976); and J. Walton, *The English Seaside Resort: A Social History, 1750–1914* (Leicester, 1983).

Principal Sources and Suggestions for Further Reading ~ 415

Chapter 2

For general studies on nineteenth-century Baden-Baden, I relied upon the above-cited Kircherer and Haebler volumes, as well as Peter Martin, *Salon Europas: Baden-Baden im 19. Jahrhundert* (Konstanz, 1983); and Eugène Guinot's classic *L'Été a Bade* (Paris, 1868). The quotation about mediocre meals comes from Klaus Fischer, *Faites votre Jeu: History of the Casino Baden-Baden* (Baden-Baden, 1975). An excellent study of Pyrmont in the eighteenth century is Reinhold Kuhnert, *Urbanität auf dem Lande: Badereisen nach Pyrmont im 18. Jahrhundert* (Göttingen, 1984). An insightful comparison of rising German and declining English spas can be found in William Bacon, "The Rise of the German and the Demise of the English Spa Industry: A Critical Analysis of Business Success and Failure," *Leisure Studies* 16 (1977). For a specific comparison of Baden-Baden and Bath, I suggest Rolf Derrenbach, *Frühe Hauptstädte der Geselligkeit: Aufschwung und Glanz der Städte Bath und Baden-Baden* (Bonn, 2006). On the spread of the French Revolution to German territory, I relied largely on T. C. W. Blanning, *The French Revolution in Germany* (Oxford, 1983), from which the French lieutenant's comment comes. The quotation from Aloys Schreiber is in Kircherer, *Kleine Geschichte*. Baden's international dynastic connections can be followed in Haebler, *Geschichte*. For Baden-Baden's infrastructural and cultural improvements and its emergence as a center of nineteenth-century romanticism, see Heinrich Berl, *Baden-Baden im Zeitalter der Romantik* (Baden-Baden, 1981). Johann Cotta's Badischer Hof is profiled in Bernhard Fischer, *Der Badische Hof, 1807–1830* (Marbach, 1997); Cotta's career as an entrepreneur and impresario is examined in Bernhard Fischer, *Johann Friedrich Cotta: Verleger—Entrepreneur—Politiker* (Göttingen, 2014). The *Morning Paper* quotation is in Fischer, *Faites votre Jeu*.

Gaming in Baden-Baden in the age of Bénezet is treated extensively in Fischer, *Faites votre Jeu*, and in Barnhart, *Gamblers of Yesteryear*. An excellent essay focusing on art and culture in Baden-Baden is Monika Steinhauser, "Das europäische Modebad des 19. Jahrhunderts: Baden-Baden—Eine Residenz des Glücks," in Ludwig Grote, ed., *Die deutsche Stadt im 19. Jahrhundert* (Munich, 1973). The chapter on Baden-Baden and other spas in David G. Schwartz, *Roll the Bones: The History of Gambling* (New York, 2007) is also highly useful. The Hebel quotation comes from Fischer, *Faites*. On Lola Montez, see David Clay Large, "Life, Liberty and the Happiness of Pursuit: Lola Montez in Bavaria," in John Merriman, ed., *For Want of a Horse: Choice and Chance in History* (Lexington, MA, 1985). Gladstone's travails in Baden-Baden can be followed in Bernhart, *Gamblers of Yesteryear*, and Bradley, *Water Music*.

The information and quotations for the section on August Granville's Baden-Baden come from Granville's *The Spas of Germany*, vol. 1 (London, 1837). On Boerhaave, Tissot, and Priessnitz, see Smethurst, *Hydrotherapia*; on spa walking, Gudrun M. König, *Eine Kulturgeschichte des Spaziergangs: Spuren einer bürgerlichen Praktik 1780–1850* (Vienna, 1996). For Jews in Baden-Baden, I relied primary on Angelika Schindler, *Der verbrannte Traum: Jüdische Bürger und Gäste in Baden-Baden* (Bühl-Moos, 1992). For David Marx, see Kircherer, *Kleine Geschichte*.

Granville's *Spas of Germany* has much to tell us about travel to Baden-Baden in the 1820s and 1830s. For the railroad story, see above all Wolfgang Schivelbusch, *Geschichte der Eisenbahnreise: Zur Industrialisierung von Raum und Zeit im 19. Jahrhundert* (Munich, 1977). On "railway spine," see Tom Zoellner, *Trains* (New York, 2014).

The Revolution of 1848 in Baden-Baden is deftly handled in Kircherer and Haeble. Useful for the revolution across Germany are James J. Sheehan, *German History 1770–1866* (Oxford, 1989); and Thomas Nipperdey, *Deutsche Geschichte, 1800–1866* (Munich, 1983). For anti-Semitism in the Baden revolution, see Manfred Gailus, "Anti-Jewish Emotion and Violence in the 1848 Crisis of German Society," in Christard Hoffmann, Werner Bergmann, and Helmut Walser Smith, eds., *Exclusionary Violence: Antisemitic Riots in Modern German History* (Ann Arbor, 2001). Crown Prince Wilhelm's comment about returning to Baden as a friend comes from Reinhard Schneider, *Der Balkon: Aufzeichnungen eines Müßiggängers in Baden-Baden* (Wiesbaden, 1957). The long Rumbold quotation is from Horace Rumbold, *Recollections of a Diplomatist* (London, 1903).

Chapter 3

The quotation on the Viennese coffee houses comes from Charlotte Ashby, Tag Gronberg, and Simon Shaw-Miller, *The Viennese Café and Fin-de-siècle Culture* (New York, 2013). Goethe's inquiry about Wiesbaden is in Detlev Schaller and Hans Dieter Schreeb, *Kaiserzeit—Wiesbaden und seine Hotels in der Belle Epoque* (Wiesbaden, 2011). Goethe's aborted trip to Baden-Baden is discussed in Berl, *Baden-Baden im Zeitalter der Romantik*. For Goethe's many excursions to Karlsbad, I relied on *Conversations of Goethe with Johann Peter Eckermann* (London, 1998); Johannes Urzidil, *Goethe in Böhmen* (Zurich, 1965); Nicholas Boyle, *Goethe: The Poet and the Age*, vol. 2 (Oxford, 2000); Richard Friedenthal, *Goethe: His Life and Times* (New Brunswick, 2010); Hans Rudolf Vaget, *Goethe: Der Mann von 60 Jahren* (Königstein, 1982); Hermann Bausinger et al., *Reisekultur: Von der Pilgerfahrt zum modernen Tourismus* (Munich, 1991); and John Armstrong, *Life, Love, Goethe* (New York, 2006). Goethe's comments about his first visit to Karlsbad come from Urzidil. His description of his cure routine is in Bausinger, *Reisekultur*.

For the Goethe-Beethoven connection, see, in addition to Urzidil and Friedenthal, Edmund Morris, *Beethoven: The Universal Composer* (New York, 2005); and John Suchet, *Beethoven: The Man Revealed* (New York, 2012). For Beethoven's ailments and spa visits, I also consulted Barry Cooper, *Beethoven* (Oxford, 2000); and Martin Cooper, *Beethoven: The Last Decade, 1817–1827* (Oxford, 1970).

A good history of Baden-bei-Wien is Raimund Wieser, *Baden: Ein kleines Wien* (Baden, 1990). On Beethoven in Baden, see Stadtgemeinde Baden, ed., *Beethovens Wohnstätten in Baden* (Baden, 1947); and Alfred Willander, *Beethoven und Baden* (Baden, 1989). For Beethoven's arrest in Baden, I consulted "Beethoven als 'Lump' von der Polizei verhaftet," *Wiener Zeitung*, Dec. 8, 2010.

On early Marienbad, I used David and Soukup's *Wonders of Czech Spas*; and Vladimir Křižek and Richard Svandrik, *Marienbad* (Prague, n.d.). For Goethe in Marienbad, see Urzidil. A good account of Goethe's last love is Hellmut Wilke, *Das Mädchen und der Dichter* (Frankfurt, 2013).

The best source for Baden-Baden's cultural life in the romantic era is Berl, *Baden-Baden im Zeitalter der Romantik*. On Musset and Sand, I also relied on George Sand, *Lettres d'un Voyageur* (London, 1987). For Victor Hugo, I consulted André Maurois, *Victor Hugo and His World* (London, 1986).

For music and musicians in the spas, see Berl, *Baden-Baden*; Bradley, *Water Music*; Heinz Biehn and Johanna Baronin Herzogenberg, *Grosse Welt reist ins Bad* (Munich, 1960); Friedrich Baser, *Grosse Musiker in Baden-*

Baden (Tutzing, 1973); *Johannes Brahms in den Bädern Baden-Baden—Wiesbaden—Bad Ischl—Karlsbad* (Exhibition Catalog, Baden-Baden, 1997); Malcolm MacDonald, *Brahms* (New York, 1990); *Clara Schumann—Johannes Brahms Briefe aus den Jahren 1853–1896*, 2 vols. (Leipzig, 1927); *Clara und Robert Schumann in Baden-Baden und Carlsruhe*, Exhibition Catalog (Baden-Baden, 1994); Derek Watson, *Liszt* (New York, 1989); Erich Kloss, ed., *Briefwechsel zwischen Wagner und Liszt*, 2 vols. (Leipzig, 1910); Richard Wagner, *Mein Leben* (New York, 1983); *Selected Letters of Richard Wagner*, translated and edited by Stewart Spencer and Barry Millington (New York, 1988); Martin Gregor-Dellin, *Richard Wagner, Sein Leben, sein Werk, sein Jahrhundert* (Mainz, 1995); Robert W. Gutman, *Richard Wagner* (Harmondsworth, 1968); Barry Millington, *Wagner* (London, 1984); Hector Berlioz, *The Memoirs of Hector Berlioz* (New York, 2002); Hector Berlioz, *Mémoires comprenant ses voyages en Italie, en Allemagne, en Russie et en Angleterre, 1803–1865* (Paris, 1870); Peter Bloom, *The Life of Berlioz* (Cambridge, 1998); Jacques Barzun, *Berlioz and His Century* (Chicago, 1956); Gustav Mahler, *Briefe* (Vienna, 1982); Derek Cooke, *Gustav Mahler* (New York, 1980); Helmut Brenner and Reinhold Kubik, *Mahlers Welt: Die Orte seines Lebens* (Salzburg, 2011); Alma Mahler-Werfel, *Mein Leben* (Frankfurt, 1963). Liszt's sometime paramour Marie Duplessis is the subject of an insightful biography by Julie Kavanagh, *The Girl Who Loved Camellias: The Life and Legend of Marie Duplessis* (New York, 2013). On musicians gambling in the spas, see Barnhart, *Gamblers of Yesteryear*.

Chapter 4

Russian patronage and gambling at the great Central European spas is treated in Barnhart, *Gamblers*; Schwarz, *Role the Bones*; Schaller and Schreeb, *Kaiserzeit*; Kircherer, *Kurze Geschichte*; Berl, *Baden-Baden*; Klaus Fischer, *Russen in Baden-Baden* (Baden-Baden, 1981); and Diethard Schlegel, *Russische Vergangenheit und Gegenwart in der Stadt Baden-Baden* (Baden-Baden, 2012). For Gogol, I consulted Vladimir Nabokov, *Nikolai Gogol* (New York, 1971); Isaiah Berlin, *Russian Thinkers* (New York, 1978); D. S. Mirsky, *A History of Russian Literature* (Evanston, 1999); Edyta M. Bojanowska, *Nikolai Gogol: Between Ukrainian and Russian*

Nationalism (Cambridge, MA, 2007); Nikolai Gogol, *Works* (New York, 1995); and Nikolai Gogol, *Dead Souls* (New York, 1971).

For Turgenev's background, I drew on Mirksy, *A History*; Berlin, *Russian Thinkers*; V. S. Pritchett, *The Gentle Barbarian: The Life and Work of Turgenev* (New York, 1977); Leonard Schapiro, *Turgenev: His Life and Times* (New York, 1978); Harold Bloom, ed., *Ivan Turgenev* (New York, 2003).

On Turgenev and Tolstoy, I used Fischer, *Russen*; Pritchett, *Gentle Barbarian*; A. N. Wilson, *Tolstoy* (New York, 1988); Rosamund Bartlett, *Tolstoy: A Russian Life* (Boston, 2011); and Tolstoy's novel *Anna Karenina*. For the writer's ménage à trois in Baden-Baden, I consulted, in addition to Berl, Pritchett, and Fischer, Ute Lange-Brachmann and Joachim Draheim, eds., *Pauline Viardot in Baden-Baden und Karlsruhe* (Baden-Baden, 1999). Turgenev's relationship with Flaubert is best followed in their letters, collected in Barbara Beaumont, ed., *Flaubert and Turgenev: A Friendship in Letters; The Complete Correspondence* (New York, 1985). I also drew heavily on the author's Baden-Baden novel, *Smoke* (1867), and on his 1862 masterpiece, *Fathers and Children*.

For Dostoevsky's psychic/physical odyssey, I relied above all on Joseph Frank's magnificent five-volume biography, *Dostoevsky* (Princeton, 1976–2002). Also useful was Michael Minihan, *Dostoevsky, His Life and Work* (Princeton, 1967); and Rachel Polonsky, *Molotov's Magic Lantern: Travels in Russian History* (New York, 2010). The writer's experiences in Germany can be followed in Fischer, *Russen in Baden-Baden*; Berl, *Baden-Baden*; Karla Hielscher, *Dostoevsky in Deutschland* (Frankfurt, 1999); and Leonid Tsypkin, *Summer in Baden-Baden: From the Life of Dostoevsky* (New York, 1989). I made extensive use of Dostoevsky's own novels and correspondence, especially: *Winter Notes on Summer Impressions* (New York, 1995); *The Gambler* (New York, 1981); *The Brothers Karamazov* (New York, 2011); *Selected Letters of Fyodor Dostoevsky* (New Brunswick, 1987); *Letters of Dostoevsky to His Family and Friends* (London, 1961); *The Letters of Dostoevsky to His Wife* (New York, 1930); and *Dostoevsky Portrayed by His Wife: The Diary and Reminiscences of Mme. Dostoevsky* (London, 1926). Freud's "Dostoevsky and Parricide" is an introductory article to a scholarly collection on Dostoevsky's *The Brothers Karamazov* that was published in 1926. For Dostoevsky's fraught relationship with

Turgenev, I used Frank, *Dostoevsky, The Stir of Liberation, 1860–1865*; and Pritchett, *The Gentle Barbarian*, as well as Dostoevsky's letters and the memoir of his wife, Anna. The information about Anna Dostoevsky's reward of sex and caviar to her husband comes from James and Kay Salter, *Life Is Meals: A Food Lover's Book of Days* (New York, 2010).

Dostoevsky's last visit to Wiesbaden is chronicled in his letters to his wife and her memoir. For Turgenev's goodbye to Baden-Baden, see Pritchett, *Barbarian*.

Chapter 5

High-level politicking at the grand spas is touched on in Winfried Löschburg, *A History of Travel*, from which the German encyclopedia advice comes, and in David Blackbourn, "Taking the Waters," which is the source for the comment on the persistence of dynastic rulers in the European age of high capitalism. Armand Wallon, *La Vie Quotidienne dans les Villes d'Eaux 1850–1914* (Paris, 1981), treats diplomacy in both the French and German spas. I also consulted Otfrid Pustejovsky, "Politik und Badewesen," in the Exhibition Catalog, *Grosse Welt reist ins Bad, 1800–1914, Ausstellung des Adelbert Stifter Vereins* (Munich, 1980). For Metternich in Teplitz, I drew on Adam Zamoyski, *Rites of Peace: The Fall of Napoleon and the Congress of Vienna* (New York, 2007). On rising German nationalism and the Burschenschaften, I used James Sheehan, *German History*; and the first volume of Paul Wentzcke et al., eds., *Darstellungen und Quellen zur Geschichte der deutschen Einheitsbewegung im neunzehnten und zwanzigsten Jahrhundert*, 10 vols. (Heidelberg, 1957–1978). On Karl Sand, see Sheehan, *German History*, and Robert Wesselhöft, ed., *Carl Ludwig Sand, Dargestellt durch seine Tagebücher und Briefe von einigen seiner Freunde* (Altenburg, 1821). Metternich's response to the Kotzebue murder and the lead-up to the Karlsbad Conference are treated in Donald Emerson, *Metternich and the Political Police* (The Hague, 1968); and Henry Kissinger, *A World Restored* (New York, 1973). For the Karlsbad Conference and Karlsbad Decrees, see Sheehan; Emerson; and especially Prince Richard von Metternich, ed., *Memoirs of Metternich, 1815–1829* (New York, 1970).

The so-called Prince's Conference of 1860 is treated in Kircherer, *Kleine Geschichte*; Otto Pflanze, *Bismarck and the Development of Germany*, vol. 1: *The Period of Unification 1815–1871* (Princeton, 1963); and Jonathan Steinberg, *Bismarck, A Life* (New York, 2011). Firsthand descriptions of Baden-Baden during the meeting can be found in Schneider, *Der Balkon*; and the memoirs of Duke Ernst II of Sachsen-Coburg-Gotha excerpted in Biehn and Herzogenberg, eds., *Grosse Welt reist ins Bad* (Munich, 1960). The Leipzig newspaper account of Wilhelm I's meeting with Emperor Franz Josef in Teplitz is reprinted in the Exhibition Catalog, *Grosse Welt reist ins Bad, 1800–1914*. Schneider's *Der Balkon* contains an account of the assassination attempt on Wilhelm I and is the source for Wilhelm's thanking Divine Providence for his salvation. For Bismarck's Baden-Baden "Memorial," I relied largely on Otto von Bismarck, *Gedanken und Erinnerungen* (Munich, 1932); and Pflanze. My account of Bismarck's negotiations with Austria's Count Johann Rechberg in Karlsbad is derived from Steinberg. Wilhelm I's curing at Gastein is covered in Sabastian Hinterseer, *Gastein und seine Geschichte* (Bad Hofgastein, 2012), and Alfred Niel, *Die grossen k. und k. Kurbäder und Gesundbrunnen* (Graz, 1984). Steinberg, along with Otto Friedrich, *Blood and Iron* (New York, 1995), are my principal sources for Bismarck's negotiations with Gustav von Blome and the Gastein Convention.

Useful for the history of Bad Ems are Hans-Jürgen Sarholz, *Geschichte der Stadt Bad Ems* (Bad Ems, 1994); Sarholz, *Bad Ems: Steifzug durch die Geschichte* (Bad Ems, 2004); Ludwig Spengler, *Der Kurgast in Ems* (Bad Ems, 1859); and Hermann Sommer, "Stationen eines Kurbads im 19. Jahrhundert—Bad Ems," in Matheus, ed., *Badeorte*. Hans Wachenhusen's *Satans Mausefallen* (Berlin, 1872) offers a witty contemporary take on Ems, Wiesbaden, and Bad Homburg.

My account of the "Ems Telegram" derives from Steinberg, *Bismarck*; Planze, *Bismarck and the Development of Germany*, vol 1; David Wetzel, *A Duel of Giants: Bismarck, Napoleon II and the Origins of the Franco-Prussian War* (Madison, 2001); Roger Price, *The Second Empire: An Anatomy of Political Power* (New York, 2001); and the dated but still useful Hermann Oncken, *Napoleon III and the Rhine: The Origins of the War of 1870–1871* (New York, 1928). Harry Kessler's account of Wilhelm's visit to Ems comes from *Journey to the Abyss: The Diaries of Count Harry Kessler 1880–1914* (New York, 2011). Bülow is quoted in Schönfels, *Wunderbares Wasser*.

For the spas' role in Bismarck's alliance system, I relied heavily on the memoirs of the chancellor's aide, Christoph von Tiedemann, *Sechs*

Jahre Chef der Reichskanzlei (Leipzig, 1910), along with Steinberg and Otto Pflanze, *Bismarck and the Development of Germany*, Volume II: *The Period of Consolidation, 1871–1880* (Princeton, 1990). Bismarck's comment regarding the impregnability of an Austro-German combination and Caprivi's complaint about juggling glass balls come from Brendan Simms, *Europe: The Struggle for Supremacy from 1453 to the Present* (New York, 2013).

Bad Homburg's rise to prominence in the era of Wilhelm II can be followed in Wechsberg, *Lost World*; Harald Fechtner, *Das alte Bad Homburg 1870–1920* (Villingen, 1963); Barbara Dölemeyer, "100 Jahre Bad Homburg von der Höhe—Wie erreichte die Stadt ihre Namensänderung?" *Mitteilungen des Vereins für Geschichte Bad Homburg von der Höhe* 61 (2012); and especially the memoir by Leila von Meister, *Gathered Yesterdays* (London, 1963).

Empress Frederick ("Vicky") and Homburg are discussed in Hannah Pakula, *An Uncommon Woman* (New York, 1995). For Vicky's troubled relationship with her son, I relied on her extensive correspondence, especially with her mother: Frederick Ponsonby, ed., *The Letters of Empress Frederick* (London, 1928). For Kaiser Friedrich III's untimely death, I consulted Wilhelm Treue, ed., *Drei deutsche Kaiser, Wilhelm I—Friedrich III—Wilhelm II: Ihr Leben und ihre Zeit 1858–1918* (Würzburg, 1987). A good short biography of Kaiser Wilhelm II is John C. G. Röhl, *Kaiser Wilhelm II* (Cambridge, 2014); I also consulted Wilhelm's own *The Kaiser's Memoirs* (New York, 1922); and Lamar Cecil, *Wilhelm II*, 2 vols. (Chapel Hill, 1989–1996). For the relationship between Wilhelm, Czar Nicholas II, and the Prince of Wales, later Edward VII, see Catherine Clay, *King, Kaiser, Tsar: Three Royal Cousins Who Led the World to War* (New York, 2006). An excellent new biography of "Bertie" is Jane Ridley, *The Heir Apparent: A Life of Edward VII, the Playboy Prince* (New York, 2013). On Edward, I also consulted David Fromkin, *The King and the Cowboy: Theodore Roosevelt and Edward the Seventh, Secret Partners* (New York, 2008); and Roy Hattersley, *The Edwardians* (London, 2006). My central source for Edward in Marienbad is the firsthand report compiled by the Viennese journalist Sigmund Münz, *King Edward VII at Marienbad* (London, 1934). Also useful is Niel, *Die grossen k. und k. Kurbäder*. For Emperor Franz Josef and his bride, "Sisi," I drew on Steven Beller, *Francis Joseph* (Harlow, 1996); Brigitte Hamann, *Elisabeth: Kaiserin wider Willen* (Munich, 1998);

and Martina Winkelhofer, *The Everyday Life of the Emperor: Francis Joseph and His Imperial Court* (Innsbruck, 2012).

Chapter 6

The Paquet quotation comes from Schaller and Schreeb, *Kaiserzeit*, which is a good source for the modernization of Wiesbaden in general. Indispensible for changes across the spa landscape in the late nineteenth century are Kircherer, *Kleine Geschichte*; Klaus Fischer, *Baden-Baden: Personen—Orte—Begebenheiten* (Baden-Baden, 2010); Sarholz, *Bad Ems*; Hinterseer, *Gastein und seine Geschichte*; Křižek, *Marienbad*; Kostanze Crüwell, *Von Fürsten, Quellen und Roulette: Kleine Promenade durch die Bad Homburger Geschichte* (Frankfurt, 1996); and a contemporary account, William Harbutt Dawson's *German Life in Town and Country* (New York, 1901). The Hessian State Archive has extensive files on urbanization issues in Ems, Wiesbaden, and Homburg. The scandal surrounding the construction of Homburg's Kaiser-Wilhelms-Bad is treated in Gerta Walsh, *Tatort Bad Homburg: Von grossen und kleinen Sündern aus vier Jahrzehnten* (Frankfurt, 2001). For the rise of grand hotels at the spas, I consulted Schaller and Schreeb, *Kaiserzeit*; Laurenz Krisch, *Die Geschichte des Grand Hotel de l'Europe in Bad Gastein* (Bad Gastein, 2009); Habbo Knoch, "Das Grandhotel" in Alexa Geisthövel and Habbo Knoch, eds., *Orte der Moderne: Erfahrungswelten des 19. und 20. Jahrhunderts* (Frankfurt, 2005); and Elaine Denby, *Grand Hotel: Reality and Illusion* (New York, 1998). E. H. Harriman's experience in Gastein is treated in the biography of his son, Averell, by Rudy Abramson, *Spanning the Century: The Life of W. Averell Harriman, 1891–1986* (New York, 1992). On Edith Wharton's "motor-flights," see Wharton's own *A Motor-Flight through France* (New York, 1908); and Hermione Lee, *Edith Wharton* (New York, 2007). Aviation is covered in Guillaume de Syon, *Zeppelin! Germany and the Airship, 1900–1939* (Baltimore, 2002); and Peter Fritzsche, *A Nation of Fliers: German Aviation and the Popular Imagination* (Cambridge, MA, 1992). Sport at the spas is treated in Kircherer, *Kleine Geschichte*; Schaller and Schreeb, *Kaiserzeit*; and Křižek, *Marienbad*. On the Homburg tennis court scam, see Walsh, *Tatort*. For Marienbad's pioneering tennis court and cinema, see Křižek, *Marienbad*. I relied largely on Schaller and Schreeb, *Kaiserzeit*, for Wiesbaden's shopping scene and the battle over Blumenthal's department store.

Robert Koch's discovery of the cholera bacillus and Max Pettenkofer's abortive effort to discredit the discovery are treated in David Clay Large, *Where Ghosts Walked: Munich's Road to the Third Reich* (New York, 1997). On antisepsis and the death of Garfield, see Candice Millard, *Destiny of the Republic: A Tale of Madness, Medicine and the Murder of a President* (New York, 2011). Fanny Burney's painful mastectomy is described in Frances Burney, *Journal and Letters* (London, 2001). For innovations in pain management, cocaine, and Freud, I consulted Booth, *Opium*; Harvey Cushing, *The Life of William Osler*, 2 vols. (Oxford, 1925); and especially Howard Markel, *An Anatomy of Addiction: Sigmund Freud, William Halsted, and the Miracle Drug Cocaine* (New York, 2011). My chief source for the professionalization of German medicine is Charles McClelland, *The German Experience of Professionalization* (New York, 1991). For "medicalization" at the spas, especially those of Bohemia, I relied on Mirjam Zadoff, *Next Year in Marienbad: The Lost Worlds of Jewish Spa Culture* (Philadelphia, 2012), which is the source for the comments on new measuring gadgets and the spas as medical laboratories.

Wilhelm Winternitz is quoted in Wolfgang Krauss, "Die Hydrotherapie: Über das Wasser in der Medizin," in Herbert Lachmayer, Sylvia Mattl-Wurm, and Christian Gargerle, eds., *Das Bad: Eine Geschichte der Badekultur im 19. und 20. Jahrhundert* (Vienna, 1991). The quotations from Heinrich Will come from Dr. Heinrich Will, *Der Kurort Homburg vor der Höhe: Seine Mineralquellen und klimatischen Heilmittel* (Homburg, 1880). J. Kraus's comments on "fluid motions" appear in his study *Carlsbad and Its Natural Healing Agents* (London, 1880). Dr. Hirsch is quoted in Schaller and Schreeb, *Kaiserzeit*. The British doctor's comments on Wiesbaden as a cure center for nervous disorders is in Dawson, *German Life in Town and Country*. W. Fraser Rae, "Life at the Bohemian Baths," is the source for the advice on refraining from business activity at the spas. I used a German translation of Mirbeau's novel *Die Badereise eines Neurasthenikers* (Budapest, 1902).

For scholarly studies of the great spas as a "Jewish space," I relied above all on Zadoff, *Next Year*; Krauss, "Die Hydrotherapie;" Schindler, *Der verbrannte Traum*; John M. Efron, *Medicine and the German Jews: A*

History (New Haven, 2001); Frank Bajohr, *"Unser Hotel ist judenfrei": Bäder-Antisemitismus im 19. und 20. Jahrhundert* (Frankfurt, 2003); and Lothar Bembenek, *Das Leben der jüdischen Minderheit in Wiesbaden-Bieberich bis zum Ersten Weltkrieg* (Wiesbaden, 2010). My most useful primary source is the memoir by Enoch Heinrich Kisch, *Erlebtes und Erstrebtes: Erinnerungen von Dr. E. H. Kisch* (Stuttgart, 1914). I also used the *Mitteilungen aus dem Verein zur Abwehr des Antisemitismus*, a journal which chronicles German Jewry's battle against anti-Semitism in the spas and elsewhere. See especially "Jüdische Ärzte," *Mittelungen*, no. 4, Oct. 27, 1894; "Der Beruf des Ärztes," *Mitteilungen*, no. 43, Oct. 24, 1896; and "Die Juden in den Bädern," *Mitteilungen*, no. 13, Aug. 4, 1903.

For Baden-bei-Wien's Jewish community, I consulted Wieser, *Baden: Ein kleines Wien*. An excellent portrait of the Ephrussi family is Edmund de Waal, *The Hare with Amber Eyes: A Hidden Inheritance* (New York, 2011). The Gallia family is portrayed in Tim Bonyhady, *Good Living Street: Portrait of a Patron Family, Vienna 1900* (New York, 2011). For the Wittgensteins, see Alexander Waugh, *The House of Wittgenstein: A Family at War* (New York, 2008). On Emil Jellinek, I recommend the memoir by Guy Jellinek-Mercedes, *My Father Mr. Mercedes* (London, 1966); and on Emil's daughter Mercedes Jellinek, see "Her Name Still Rings a Bell," *New York Times*, Oct. 19, 2001. Stefan Zweig's memoir, *The World of Yesterday* (Lincoln, 1942), is a nostalgic but penetrating picture of Central European Jewry from the late nineteenth century to World War II. Sholom Aleichem's satiric novel *Marienbad* (New York, 1982) opens a window on Jewish life at the great Bohemian spas, as does the above-cited study by Zadoff. Joseph Schleicher is quoted in Robert Kriechbaumer, ed., *Der Geschmach der Vergänglichkeit: Jüdische Sommerfrische in Salzburg* (Vienna, 2002). For anti-Semitism at Bad Ems, see Bajohr, *"Unser Hotel ist judenfrei."* The lament about the growth of "judenrein" spas in Germany appears in "Die Juden in den Bädern," *Mitteilungen*, no. 13, Aug. 5, 1903; the complaint about "orgies" of anti-Semitism ten years later comes from "Bäderantisemitismus," *Mitteilungen*, no. 14, July 3, 1912.

For Nietzsche in Marienbad, I consulted Friedrich Nietzsche, *Chronik im Bildern und Texten* (Stiftung Weimarer Klassik, Munich, 2000); Ronald Hayman, *Nietzsche: A Critical Life* (New York, 1980); Peter Bergmann, *Nietzsche: The 'Last Antipolitical German'* (Bloomington, 1987); and David Farrell Krell and Donald L. Bates, *The Good European: Nietzsche's Work*

Sites in Word and Image (Chicago, 1997). On Freud in Gastein and Marienbad, see Křižek, *Marienbad*; and Peter Gay, *Freud: A Life for Our Time* (New York, 1988). Schnitzler's biking experiences in Bad Ischl are discussed in Johannes Sachslehner, *Bad Ischl: K. u. k. Sehnsuchtsort im Salzkammergut* (Vienna, 2012); see also Arthur Schnitzler, *Tagebuch 1893–1902* (Vienna, 1989). For Schnitzler's impressions of Karlsbad and Marienbad, see Arthur Schnitzler, *Briefe 1875–1912* (Frankfurt, 1981). Herzl's brief sojourn at Franzensbad is treated in Zadoff, *Next Year*. For Stefan Zweig, I relied on his short novel *Burning Secret* (London, 2008); Oliver Matuschek, *Three Lives. A Biography of Stefan Zweig* (London, 2011); and Gert Kerschbaumer, *Stefan Zweig. Der Fliegende Salzburger* (Salzburg, 2003).

I consulted the English-language edition of Marx and Engel's *Collected Works*, 50 vols. (New York, 1975–2004) for Marx's correspondence from Karlsbad. His and his daughter's visits to Karlsbad are examined in Egon Erwin Kisch, *Karl Marx in Karlsbad* (Berlin, 1968); and Walt Contreras Sheasby, "Marx at Karlsbad," *Capitalism, Nature, Socialism* 12, no. 3, September 2001. For more general background studies on Marx, his health, and his habits, I relied on Jonathan Sperber, *Karl Marx: A Nineteenth Century Life* (New York, 2013); Mary Gabriel, *Love and Capital: Karl and Jenny Marx and the Birth of a Revolution* (New York, 2011); David McLellan, *Karl Marx: His Life and Thought* (New York, 1973); and Jerrold Siegel, *Marx's Fate: The Shape of a Life* (Princeton, 1978).

My discussion of Mark Twain in the Central European spas is based largely on Twain's travel books *The Innocents Abroad* (New York, 1996) and *A Tramp Abroad* (New York, 1996), as well as his essays collected in *The Complete Essays of Mark Twain* (New York, 1991), and *The Complete Humorous Sketches and Tales of Mark Twain* (New York, 1961). For background on Twain I relied on the excellent Twain biography by Ron Powers, *Mark Twain: A Life* (New York, 2005); Justin Kaplan, *Mr. Clemens and Mark Twain* (New York, 1966); Ben Tarnoff, *The Bohemians: Mark Twain and the San Francisco Writers Who Reinvented American Literature* (New York, 2014); and K. Patrick Ober, *Mark Twain and Medicine* (Columbia, MO, 2003).

Chapter 7

Among the many treatments of the assassination of Archduke Franz Ferdinand and the outbreak of World War I, most useful and up-to-date are Christopher Clark, *The Sleepwalkers: How Europe Went to War in 1914* (New York, 2012); and Margaret MacMillan, *War That Ended Peace: The Road to 1914* (New York, 2013). Amusing and insightful is Ivo Banac, "Sarajevo 1914: Wrong Turn at the Appelquai," in John Merriman, ed., *For Want of a Horse*. For Bad Ischl at this crucial moment, see Sachslehner, *Bad Ischl*. Zweig's observation comes from his memoir, *The World of Yesterday*. Stig Föster, "Russische Pferde: Die deutsche Armeeführung und die Julikrise 1914," in Holger Afferblack, ed., *Kaiser Wilhelm II als Oberster Kriegsherr im Ersten Weltkrieg* (Munich, 2005) is my chief source for the actions of Germany's leaders in July 1914. Jaroslav Hašek's novel *The Good Soldier Svejk* (New York, 1974) is a wonderful send-up of Austrian bumbling in the war. On Baden-Baden at the war's ouset, see Kircherer, *Kleine Gesichichte*; for Bad Homburg, I used Crüwell, *Von Fürsten*; and Yitzhak Sophoni Herz, *Meine Erinnerungen an Bad Homburg und seine 600-Jahre jüdische Gemeinde* (Homburg, 1981). A very thorough study of modern Bad Ems is Wilfried Dieterichs, *Die Stadt: Herrenjahre in der Provinz; Bad Ems 1914–1964* (Weilburg, 2013). Felix Gilbert's memoir *A European Past: Memoirs 1905–1945* (New York, 1988) is good on wartime Baden-Baden. Wiesbaden's unique war experience is chronicled in Antina Manig and Hartmann Wunderer, eds., *Wiesbaden im Ersten Weltkrieg* (Wiesbaden, 2013). I also made extensive use of the police and mayoral files in the Hessian State Archive.

For Franz Kafka's wartime spa experience, I used his *Letters to Felice*, edited by Erich Heller and Jürgen Born (New York, 1973); Beate Borowka-Clausberg, *Damals in Marienbad* (Berlin, 2009); and a novel by Jacqueline Raoul-Duval, *Kafka in Love* (New York, 2011). The German-Jewish wartime experience is treated in Schindler, *Der verbrannte Traum*; Bajohr, *Unser Hotel ist judenfrei*; Zadoff, *Next Year*; and De Waal, *The Hare*. The Freud quotation comes from Gay, *Freud*; the Austro-Israelite proclamation is from De Waal, *The Hare*. On Ludendorff at Spa, I consulted Robert B. Asprey, *The German High Command at War* (New York, 1991); and Nick Lloyd, *Hundred Days: The Campaign That Ended World War I* (New York, 2014).

The revolution of 1918–1919 and early postwar period in German spa land are covered in Dieterichs, *Die Stadt*; Sarholz, *Bad Ems*; Kircherer, *Kleine Gesichichte*; Manig and Wunderer, *Wiesbaden*. The best study of the hyperinflation is Gerald D. Feldman, *The Great Disorder: Politics, Economics, and Society in the German Inflation 1914–1924* (New

York, 1993). The newspaper report on inflation in Wiesbaden is "Wiesbaden Still a Luxury Town," *Manchester Guardian*, June 28, 1919. On Brenner's Park Hotel in the 1920s, see Fischer, *Baden-Baden*. For Brecht and Weill in Baden-Baden, I used John Fuegi, *Brecht & Co: Sex, Politics, and the Making of Modern Drama* (New York, 1994); and Ronald Sanders, *The Days Grow Short: The Life and Music of Kurt Weill* (Hollywood, CA, 1991). For Jawlensky in Wiesbaden, I consulted Schaller and Schreeb, *Kaiserzeit*; Clemens Weiler, *Alexej von Jawlensky: der Maler und Mensch* (Wiesbaden, 1955); and "Alexei Jawlensky and His Son, Andreas," *New York Times*, May 1, 1987. Bill Bryson, *One Summer: America, 1927* (New York, 2013) is the source for Bill Tilden's infection. The Hesse quotation is in Hermann Hesse, "A Guest at the Spa," *Autobiographical Writings* (New York, 1972). For anti-Semitism at the German spas, I consulted Bajor, *Unser Hotel*; and Jacob Borut, "Antisemitism in Tourist Facilities in Weimar Germany," *Yad Vashem Studies* 28 (2000). The Zweig complaint is in Matuschek, *Three Lives*. On Stresemann and the Harzburg Front, see Henry A. Turner, *Stresemann and the Politics of the Weimar Republic* (Princeton, 1963).

Austria's First Republic is treated in Barbara Jelavich, *Modern Austria: Empire and Republic 1815–1986* (Cambridge, 1987); Bruce Pauley, *Hitler and the Forgotten Nazis* (Chapel Hill, 1981); and Evan Bukey, *Hitler's Austria* (Chapel Hill, 2000). Baden-bei-Wien in the 1920s is recalled in a memoir by Victor Wallner, *Badener Betrachtungen* (Baden, 1987); and in Wieser, *Baden: Ein kleines Wien*. The *Badener Zeitung* is also invaluable. For Bad Ischl, I consulted the memoir by Emil Löbl, *Verlorenes Paradies* (Vienna, 1924); Sachslehner, *Bad Ischl*; Bradley, *Water Music*; Dieter Neumann and Rudolf Lehr, *Menschen, Mythen, Monarchen in Bad Ischl* (Bad Ischl, 2008); and Margit Bachler-Rix, *Die klingende Stadt: Rund um die Ischler Operette* (Bad Ischl, 1977). For Bad Gastein, see Hinterseer and Krisch, *Gastein und seine Geschichte*; Hermann Greinwald, *Die Gasteiner Kur* (Bad Gastein, 2011). Howard Markel, *An Anatomy of Addiction*, is my source for Freud's smoking and health. Patronage at Gastein's Grand Hotel is chronicled in Krisch, *Die Geschichte des Grand Hotel de l'Europe*. On skiing in the Gastein Valley, see Sebastian Hinterseer, *Bad Hofgastein und die Geschichte Gasteins* (Salzburg, 1977); and Jim Ring, *How the English Made the Alps* (London, 2000). The rise of the Nazis in Austria and Hitler's "Tausend-

Mark-Sperre" are ably treated in Pauley, *Hitler and the Forgotten Nazis*. Sedlacek's lament is in Krisch, *Grand Hotel*.

The travails of Karlsbad and Marienbad in the 1920s and 1930s are examined in Zadoff, *Next Year*; Bajohr, *Unser Hotel*; Jörg Osterloh, *Nationalsozialistische Judenverfolgung im Reichsgau Sudetenland 1938–1945* (Munich, 2006); and Heinz Schubert, *Karlsbad: Ein Weltbad im Spiegel der Zeit* (Munich, 1980). The World Zionist Organization meeting in Karlsbad is discussed in Zadoff, *Next Year*. On the Lessing murder, see Zadoff; Theodor Lessing, "Mein Kopf," in Lessing, *Bildung ist Schönheit: Autobiographische Zeugnisse und Schriften zur Bildungsreform; Ausgewählte Schriften*, vol. 1 (Bremen, 1995); and Richard Švandrilik, *Juden in Marienbad* (Marienbad, n.d.). The pre-Olympics swim competition and holistic medical conference are reported on in the *Marienbader Zeitung*. On Henlein's "Karlsbad Program," see Osterloh, *Nationalsozialistische Judenverfolgung*. The "German virus" comment is quoted in Osterloh. The Hindus quotation comes from Maurice Hindus, *We Shall Live Again* (New York, 1939).

Chapter 8

For examples of Nazi hostility to "elitist" resorts and other upper-crust institutions, see Hans Brandenburg, "Nationalsozialismus und Bürgertum," *Blut und Boden*, no. 3, 1933; Andreas Pfenning, "Das Eliten-Problem in seiner Bedeutung für den Kulturbereich der Wirtschaft," *Zeitschrift für die gesamte Staatswissenschaft*, July 1936; and Walther Darré, *Blut und Boden: ein Grundgedanke des Nationalsozialismus* (Berlin, 1935). For Hitler's health and hygiene habits, a good recent source is Volker Ullrich, *Adolf Hitler: Die Jahre des Aufstiegs* (Frankfurt, 2013). On Bella Fromm and Bad Reichenhall, see her *Blood and Banquets: A Social Diary* (London, 1942). Hitler's assault on Bad Wiessee is chronicled in David Clay Large, *Between Two Fires: Europe's Path in the 1930s* (New York, 1990); Hitler's Christmas visit to Bad Ems is treated in Dieterichs, *Die Stadt*; for his trips to Karlsbad, see Geoff Walden, "Third Reich in Ruins," www.thirdreichruins.com/czech.htm. Himmler's heath and bathing habits are examined in Bradley F. Smith, *Heinrich Himmler: A Nazi in the Making, 1900–1926* (Stanford, 1971). On Nazism and homeopathy, I consulted Detlef Bothe, "Die Homöopathie im Dritten Reich," in Sigrid Heinze, ed., *Homöopathie 1796–1996: Eine Heilkunde und ihre Geschichte* (Berlin,

1996). For Göring, I relied largely on Richard Overy, *Goering: The 'Iron Man'* (London, 1984); and Werner Maser, *Hermann Göring: Hitlers janusköpfiger Paladin; die politische Biographie* (Berlin, 2000). The best biography of Goebbels is Ralf Georg Reuth, *Goebbels* (New York, 1993). An excellent short study of the KdF is Shelley Baranowski, "Strength through Joy," in Shelley Baranowski and Ellen Furlough, eds., *Being Elsewhere: Tourism, Consumer Culture, and Identity in Modern Europe and North America* (Ann Arbor, 2001). On the Volkswagen, see Bernhard Rieger, *The People's Car: A Global History of the Volkswagen Beetle* (Cambridge, MA, 2013). Davos under Nazism is profiled in "Das Hitlerbad," www.zeit.de/2007/04/A-Davos. On the idea of making Crimea Nazi Germany's "Riviera," see Shelley Baranowski, *Strength through Joy: Consumerism and Mass Tourism in the Third Reich* (New York, 2007).

Baden-Baden's special status in the early years of the Third Reich is treated in Kircherer, *Kleine Geschichte*; Achim Reimer, *Stadt zwischen Demokratien: Baden-Baden von 1930 bis 1955* (Munich, 2005); and Rolf Rößler, *Baden-Baden unter dem Hakenkreuz* (self-published manuscript, n.d.). Specifically for the Jewish situation, see Schindler, *Verbrannte Traum*. Details on the "Hitler Cup" can be found in George Peper, "Cup of History," www.linksmagazine.com/best_of_golf/cup-of-history-olympics-golf. Arthur Flehinger's ordeal is discussed in Schindler, *Verbrannte Traum*. For Brenners Park Hotel under Nazism, I used Fischer, *Baden-Baden: Personen-Orte-Begebenheiten*; and "Brenners Park-Hotel and Spa," de.wikipedia.org/wiki/Brenners_Park-Hotel_%26_Spa.

The best source for Bad Ems in the Third Reich is Dieterichs, *Die Stadt*. Also useful is Sarholz, *Streifzug*. For Bad Homburg, see especially Arbeitsgemeinschaft der Jungsozialisten in der SPD, ed., *Das Hakenkreuz über Bad Homburg: Eindrücke und Erlebnisse Bad Homburger Sozialdemokraten* (Bad Homburg, 1982). A useful source for Wiesbaden is Lothar Bembenek and Axel Ulrich, *Widerstand und Verfolgung in Wiesbaden 1933–1945* (Giessen, 1990).

The rise of Nazism in Austria is thoroughly discussed in Pauley, *Hitler and the Forgotten Nazis*. For the Nazification of Baden-bei-Wien, see Wieser, *Baden: Ein kleines Wien*. Beethoven's exploitation by the Nazis is treated in David B. Dennis, *Beethoven in German Politics, 1870–1989* (New Haven, 1996). For Bad Ischl in this period, I relied primarily on Sachslehner, *Bad Ischl*. An excellent study on Bad Gastein under

Nazism is Laurenz Krisch, "Bad Gastein während der NS-Herrschaft," *Mitteilungen der Gesellschaft für Salzburger Landeskunde* 147 (2007). See also Gert Kerschbaumer, *Faszination Drittes Reich: Kunst und Alltag der Kulturmetropole Salzburg* (Salzburg, 1988). The commentary on Goebbels and Baarova comes from Mariusz Szczygiel, *Gottland* (Brooklyn, 2014). Glaise-Horstenau's account of Goebbels's visit to Gastein can be found in his memoir, *Ein General im Zwielicht: die Erinnerungen Edmund Glaises von Horstenau* (Vienna, 1980).

For Nazified Karlsbad, see Osterloh, *Nationalsozialistische Judenverfolgung*; Karl Josef Hahn, "Kristallnacht in Karlsbad," in Harald Salfellner, *LeseReise Karlsbad* (Tesin, 2005); and Stanislav Burachovič, *Die Geschichte vom Grand Hotel Pupp* (Karlsbad, 2010). For Marienbad's embrace of Nazism, I relied chiefly on the *Marienbader Zeitung*; Svandrlik, *Juden in Marienbad*; J. May, *Marienbad: Der Weltkurort mit den Gemeinden des Landkreises* (Geisenfeld, 1977); and *Marienbad: Der Führer durch die Stadt und ihre Umgebung* (Cheb, 2009).

Aharon Appelfeld's novel *Badenheim 1939* (Boston, 1980) is an evocative meditation on Jewish self-deception as the Holocaust descends. Appelfeld's interview with Philip Roth is contained in the latter's *Shop Talk: A Writer and His Colleagues and Their Work* (Boston, 2001).

The German spas during World War II are treated in Kircherer, *Kleine Geschichte*; Reimer, *Stadt zwischen Demokratien*; Rößler, *Baden-Baden*; Dieterichs, *Die Stadt*; and Bembenek and Ullrich, *Widerstand und Verfolgung*. Goebbels's denunciation of the grand spas can be found in Elke Fröhlich, ed., *Die Tagebücher von Joseph Goebbels: Sämtliche Fragmente*, 4 vols. (Munich, 1987). On the American internment in Bad Nauheim, see Charles B. Burdick, *An American Island in Hitler's Reich: The Bad Nauheim Internment* (Menlo Park, CA, 1987); and John Lewis Gaddis, *George F. Kennan: An American Life* (New York, 2011). For the Austrian Kurorte at war, I relied on Wieser, *Baden*; Krisch, "Bad Gastein"; and, for Bad Ischl and Ebensee, Edeltraud Kendler, *Nie Wieder! Das Konzentrationslager Ebensee* (Bad Ischl, n.d.). The Allied bombing and invasion of the Salzkammergut is discussed in Katharina Hammer, *Glanz im Dunkel: Die Bergung von Kunstschätzen im Salzkammergut am Ende des 2. Weltkrieges* (Altaussee, 1996).

Günther Grass's Marienbad experience is recorded in his memoir, *Beim Häuten der Zwiebel* (Göttingen, 2006). On the capitulation of

Karlsbad and Marienbad, see Karl L. Lippert, "Erlebnisbericht 1945," in Salfellner, ed., *LeseReise Karlsbad*.

Chapter 9

Europe in 1945 is brilliantly analyzed in Ian Buruma, *Year Zero: A History of 1945* (New York, 2013). Also excellent is Gregor Dallas, *1945: The War That Never Ended* (New Haven, 2005). For Baden-Baden under French occupation, I relied on Kircherer, *Kleine Geschichte*; Reimer, *Stadt zwischen Demokratien*; and F. Roy Willis, *France, Germany and the New Europe 1945–1967* (London, 1968). The French occupation of Bad Ems is amply covered in Dieterichs, *Die Stadt*. On the American occupation and American-zone spas, I consulted Anni Baker, *Wiesbaden and the Americans 1945–2003* (Wiesbaden, 2004); Esther Knorr-Anders, *Wiesbaden für alte und neue Freunde* (Bamberg, 2011); Erhard Niedenthal, *Das Spiel in Wiesbaden* (Wiesbaden, 1997); Petra Goedde, *GIs and Germans* (New Haven, 2003); Detlef Junker, ed., *GIs in Germany: The Social, Economic, Cultural, and Political History of the American Military Presence* (Cambridge, 2013); and David Clay Large, *Germans to the Front: West German Rearmament in the Adenauer Era* (Chapel Hill, 1997). For Austria and the Austrian spas under American and Russian occupation I used Jelavich, *Modern Austria*; Krisch, "Bad Gastein"; Krisch, *Grand Hotel*; Hammer, *Glanz im Dunkel*; Wieser, *Baden*; Nina Stadelmann, *Baden in Zwei Tagen* (Baden, 2010); and Tony Judt, *Postwar: A History of Europe since 1945* (New York, 2005). The Czech scene and the Sudeten German expulsion are discussed in Buruma, *Year Zero*; Judt, *Postwar*; Burachovič, *Grandhotel Pupp*; Ben Shephard, *The Long Road Home* (New York, 2011); Giles MacDonogh, *After the Reich: The Brutal History of the Allied Occupation* (New York, 2007); and "Expulsion of Germans from Czechoslovakia," http://en.wikipedia.org/wiki/Expulsion_of_Germans_from_Czechoslovakia. Insightful also is Szczygiel, *Gottland*; and the novel by Bohumil Hrabal, *I Served the King of England* (London, 2009).

Useful for the West German economic miracle and German spa recovery are Kircherer, *Kleine Geschichte*; Fischer, *Baden-Baden: Personen*; Rieger, *People's Car*; John Ardagh, *Germany and the Germans* (London, 1987); and Werner Abelshauser, *Deutsche Wirtschaftsgeschichte seit 1945* (Munich, 2004). On the Baden-Baden IOC meeting, see Herb Weinberg,

"The Olympic Selection Process: Baden-Baden 1981," *Journal of Olympic History*, Winter 2001. For the Wiesbaden bombings, see Baker, *Wiesbaden*. A good history of the Austrian Staatsvertrag is Rolf Steininger, *Der Staatsvertrag. Österreich im Schatten von Deutscher Frage und Kaltem Krieg 1939–1955* (Vienna, 2005). On Baden-bei-Wien's recovery, I consulted Wieser, *Baden: Ein kleines Wien*; and Stadelmann, *Baden*. Gastein's modern cure scene is discussed in Heinrich Thaler, *Gasteiner Kurbüchlein* (Bad Gastein, 1968). Post–World War II Austrian alpine skiing is treated in Hinterseer, *Bad Hofgastein*; and Friedrich Fetz, *Franz Hopplicher: Sein Leben und Wirking für den alpinen Skilauf* (Innsbruck, 2006). For Thomas Mann's postwar odyssey, I relied on Hans Rudolf Vaget, *Thomas Mann, der Amerikaner* (Frankfurt, 2011); and Ronald Hayman, *Thomas Mann: A Biography* (New York, 1995). The final years of Gastein's Grand Hotel de l'Europe are chronicled in Krisch, *Grand Hotel*. Communist-controlled Karlovy Vary is recalled in Wechsberg, *Lost World*; and Art Buchwald, *I'll Always Have Paris* (New York, 1996). The Hotel Pupp's role in this period is handled in Burachovič, *Geschichte vom Grand Hotel Pupp*. The Czech fate of the film *Last Year in Marienbad* is treated in Křežek and Svandrlik, *Marienbad*.

Epilogue

Material in the epilogue was derived largely from interviews with spa workers, officials, and patrons; city tours and personal cure experiences; contemporary newspaper and magazine stories; and official publications of spa town press departments, tourist offices, bath facilities, and casinos. For the report bolstering the grand spas' UNESCO "World Heritage Site" application, see Katharina Herrmann, Tamara Klemm, and Markus Mayer, eds., *Internationalität in ausgewählten Kunststädter des 19. Jahrhunderts* (Baden-Baden, 2012). Also useful are city guidebooks with strong historical components. I recommend, inter alia, *Karlsbad: Reiseführer durch das Zentrum*; *Marienbad: Der Führer durch die Stadt und Ihre Umgebung*; *Baden [Baden-bei-Wien] in Zwei Tagen*; *Kurpark Bad Homburg v. d. Höhe: Ein Spaziergang durch Geschichte und Gartenkunst*; *Wiesbaden für alte und neue Freunde*; *Bad Ems: Streifzug durch die Geschichte*; and *Baden-Baden zum Kennenlernen: Eine Reise- und Stadtführer*. A handy guide to German Kurorte in general is Gerhart Eckert, *Heilbäder und Kurorte: 270 Ziele für Kur und Erholung* (Düsseldorf, 1988).

Index

Aachen, Germany, 26, 34
Adenauer, Konrad, 377–78
The Adventures of Chichikov (Gogol). See *Dead Souls*
De aere, aquis et locis/On Air, Water and Local Conditions (Hippocrates), 14
Agrippa, Marcus, 18
Aida (Verdi), 19
AIDS, 33n
On Air, Water and Local Conditions (Hippocrates), 14
air cure, 2, 238, 274
Aix-la-Chapelle/Aachen, Germany, 26, 34
Aix-les-Bains, France, 4, 44, 231, 265, 414
Alabama Song, 292
Albach-Retty, Wolf, 345
Albert, Prince (husband of Queen Victoria), 213
Albert Edward, Prince of Wales. See Edward VII, King of England

alcohol consumption, 4n, 44, 413. See also wine
Aleichem, Sholom, 251–52, 425
Alexander I, Czar of Russia, 57–58, 182
Alexander II, Czar of Russia, 145, 155, 158, 179, 200, 206–7
Alexander III, Czar of Russia, 317
Alexander the Great, 16
Alexandra, Queen Consort to Edward VII, 216, 218
Allgemeine Wiener Polyklinik, 243
Allies/Allied forces: World War I, 278, 286, 298, 305, 308; World War II, 346, 359–60, 364, 378–71, 379–80, 431
"Alpine redoubt" idea, 364
Alps, Austrian, 132, 202, 206, 210, 245, 301–2, 305, 307, 400–401. See also Gastein; Ischl
Altenstein, Wilhelm, 331
Amarjit Singh of Kapurthala, Prince, 304

Amélie (loved by Berlioz), 128
American occupation and American-zone spas. See under United States
Anchmolus, 17
the ancient West, 12–29
Andrassy, Count Julius, 210
Anna Karenina (Tolstoy), 150, 156, 419
L'Année Dernière à Marienbad. See *Last Year in Marienbad*
anti-Semitism, 8, 86, 134n, 248–49, 254, 284–85, 294, 425; the Berlin Olympics and, 330–31. See also Centralverein deutscher Staatsbürger jüdischen Glaubens (CV); "judenrein" spa towns; racism; *specific countries, regions, and cities*, e.g., Austria; German Kurorte; *specific spa towns*
apodyteria, 19
Appelfeld, Aaron, 350–51, 431
April 1 Reich-wide boycott of Jewish shops, 336
aquae, 18
Aquae Albulae, 24, 35
Aquae Cutilae, 24
Aquae (settlement east of the Rhine), 28, 49
Aquae Sulis, 27, 33
Arabs, 32–33, 81, 287, 309, 311, 315, 383, 401
archeology, 19, 26
Archimedes, 13
Armenbad (bath for the poor), 80
Arnim, Bettina von, 98–99, 100
art/artists, 91–135, 235, 292–293, 395–96. See also *individual artists*; *specific genres*, e.g., musicians; writers
Asclepius, 15

Asia, 5, 69, 393
Aspen, Colorado, 381
Auden, W. H., vi
Aufstieg und Fall der Stadt Mahagonny (Brecht and Weill), 292
Augustabad, 226, 322, 352
Augusta of Saxe-Weimar, Empress of Germany/Augusta of Prussia, Princess-Regent, 88, 118, 121–22, 189
Augustus, Emperor, 18, 24
August Wilhelm of Prussia, Prince, 359
Austen, Jane, 47–48
Austerlitz (Sebald), 389
Austria, 108, 371; anti-Semitism/rise of Nazis in, 135, 265, 267–68, 284–85, 301–7, 346–48, 384n, 428–30; First Republic of, 298, 305–6, 308, 428; as "Hitler's first victim," 370–71; Jews, Austrian, 284, 339–40, 348; occupation forces in, 101, 370–72, 379–80; Ostmark (Austria's designation in Greater Germany), 339–40, 342–43, 360; postwar revival, 379–80; rump Austria, 298–308; Second Republic of, 379–80; *Staatsvertrag* (state treaty), 379–80, 433; under the Third Reich, 338–41, 346–48, 371, 430; tourism in, 300, 306–7, 384; Twain and, 265, 267–68. See also Austria-Hungary; Austrian Kurorte; Habsburg Empire; *specific cities and other locations*, e.g., Alps; *specific time periods*; *specific topics and events*, e.g., Gastein Convention
Austria-Hungary, 206–7, 209–10, 220, 222, 229, 234, 274–77,

Index ~ 437

282–85; Baden bei Wien, imperial command in, 285. *See also* Habsburg Empire
Austrian Hotel Association, 307
Austrian Kurorte/spa towns, 198, 219, 226, 273, 299, 384, 431, 432; American and Soviet occupation of, 101, 371–72; anti-Semitism in, 135, 302–3, 346–48; clientele of, 309. *See also* Baden-bei-Wien; Gastein; Ischl
Austrian Socialist Party, 305–6
Austrian War Ministry, 198
Austro-Prussian War, 201
automobiles/driving craze, 231–32, 237. *See also specific automobiles*, e.g., Volkswagen
"Axis" allies, 334, 355
Aznavour, Charles, 383

Baarová, Lída, 343
Bacon, William, 415
Bad Ems, Germany, 4, 67, 131, 137, 139, 169, 198–206, 214, 277–78, 280, 377, 423; anti-Jewish campaign in, 337, 425; and casino gambling, 64, 200, 358, 377; clientele of, 124–25, 200, 204–6, 212, 253, 359; Dostoevsky in, 175–78; the Ems Telegram, 199–204, 358; history of, 178, 199; Hitler's Christmas visit to, 322, 353, 429; occupation forces in, 287–88, 368–69; under the Third Reich, 322–23, 329, 335–37, 352–53, 358–60, 362, 429–30; today, 397–98; Wagner in, 124–25; Weimar Republic and, 287–89, 296–97. *See also* German Kurorte/spa towns

Baden, Switzerland, 11, 26, 33–34, 39–40, 51–52, 293–94
Baden-Baden, Germany, 49, 51–89 and *passim*; and anti-Semitism, 86, 326, 416; Brenner's Park Hotel in, 290–91, 334–35, 355, 378, 396–98, 405, 428, 430; clientele of, 54, 57–58, 60, 81, 89, 91, 108–15, 132, 212, 246, 277; and the Crash of 1929, 296; as "Europe's Summer Capital," 6, 51–89; Friedrichsbad in, 9, 13, 74, 226–27, 232, 264, 392–93; German Confederation leaders in, 188–91; as "Germany's Visiting Card," 326–31; getting to, 81–84; Granville's, 69–79; horse-racing in, 230–31; IOC meeting in, 378, 432; the "Jewish Question," 79–81; music and musicians in, 122–32, 291–92, 396; occupation forces in, 287, 368; private clinics in, 240–41; Revolutions of 1848–1849 in, 84–89, 416; Romantic-Era writers in, 108–15, 417; Russian community in, 57, 394–95; Russian writers/clientele in, 137–79 *passim*, 212; shopping scene in, 236; sports in, 234; theater in, 79, 127, 131, 291–92, 352, 355; under the Third Reich, 320, 322–36, 351, 354–55, 357–59; today, 393–97; Turgenev in, 7, 122, 129, 141, 143, 145, 149–58, 178, 395; Twain in, 263–64; Wilhelm I, and assassination attempt, 88, 192–93; World War I and, 278; xenophobia in, 277–78. *See also* German Kurorte/spa towns; *specific topics, events, and time periods*

Baden-Baden, casino gambling in, 6, 61–69, 80–81, 87–88, 108–10, 125–27, 132, 164–65, 218, 368; the Third Reich and, 326–28, 331, 334–35, 352, 355, 357–58; today, 394. *See also* casino gambling
Baden-Baden, Conversation House in, 59, 78, 81, 112–13, 131–32, 148–49, 156, 173, 190, 292; the Bénazets and, 61–68, 87–88, 110, 113, 115–17, 125–29, 132, 231; changed to Kurhaus, 277; closing of, 231, 236
Baden-Baden Memorial, 194–95
Baden-bei-Wien, Austria, 4, 101, 269, 272, 299–301, 417, 433; Austro-Hungarian imperial command in, 285; Beethoven and, 101–3, 381; and casino gambling, 300, 335, 339, 360; clientele and residents of, 101, 249–51, 257, 340, 401; as convention destination, 381; Jewish community/clientele in, 101, 249–51, 340, 401, 425; as Lazarettstadt, 285, 360; Soviet occupation of, 372; Stadttheater (municipal theater) in, 381; under the Third Reich/during World War II, 338–39, 360–61, 430; today, 401
Badenheim 1939 (Appelfeld), 350–51, 431
Baden-Württemberg's State Institute for Respiratory Diseases, 240
Badepaläste. *See* bath palaces
Badeschloss, 197, 399
Bad Gastein, Austria, 4, 35, 108, 132, 196–98, 205–7, 209–11, 228–30, 381–84; and anti-Semitism, 346–48; Bismarck's negotiations in, 197–98, 421; and casino gambling, 383–84; clientele of, 285, 303–5, 307, 342–45, 381–84; Freud in, 256–57, 303–4; Grand Hotel d'Europe in, 229–30, 304, 306–7, 343–44, 346, 356, 371, 383–84, 423, 428–29, 432–33; Jewish patronage of, 285; occupation forces in, 370–72; post-World War I era, 276, 282, 285, 299, 303–7; and radon gas, 230, 303, 398–99; skiing in, 305, 381–82; under the Third Reich, 322–23, 342–48, 361–62; today, 398–401, 405; Wilhelm I and, 205. *See also* Alps
Bad Griesbach, Germany, 288
Bad Harzburg, Germany, 297–98, 428
"Badheim University," 356
Bad Hofgastein, 305, 381, 400
Bad Homburg, Germany, 4, 169, 230, 232, 293, 329, 369, 373, 375–77, 421–23, 427, 430; casino gambling in, 87, 131, 137, 139, 165–66, 169, 211–12, 218, 370; clientele of, 137, 211–19; as "Germany's Convention Capital," 293; Hohenzollern family in, 211, 213–17, 369; Kaiser-Wilhelms-Bad in, 10, 212, 227, 423; King Edward VII in, 217–19; occupation forces in, 369–70; RAF attack in, 379; tennis and golf in, 213, 233–34, 423–24; thermal waters of, vi, 211, 243; today, 397; World War I and, 277, 279–80, 286
Badischer Hof, 60, 75, 92, 109, 415
Bad Ischl, Austria, 4, 108, 256–57, 299, 301–3, 305, 426–28, 430–31; anti-Semitism in, 135, 302–3;

clientele of, 132–35, 285, 301–2;
Franz Josef I and, 132, 135, 223–
24, 271–75, 301; Jewish patronage
of, 135, 285, 302–3; music and
theater (and musicians) in,
132–35, 302; occupation forces in,
370–71; politics and, 207, 222–24;
under the Third Reich, 341, 362;
today, 400–401; World War I and,
269–77, 282, 285
Bad Kissingen, Germany, 150, 329
Bad Nauheim, Germany, 244, 355–
57, 431
Bad Neuenahr, Germany, 257, 261
Bad Pyrmont, Germany, 49, 52, 64,
415
Bad Reichenhall, Germany, 321, 429
Bad Wiessee, Germany, 321, 429
"Baedeker raids," 357
Baiae resort, Italy, 25
Balfour Declaration (1917), 310
Balkans, 206–7, 209, 269–70, 276,
384n
balneology, 2
Balounova, Marcela, 403
Balzac, Honoré de, 65
Bären Hotel, 115
Baroda, Maharaja of, 304
Barveci, Giulia, 218
Bassey, Shirley, 383
Bath, England, 4, 26–27, 32, 40, 52,
54, 59, 70, 357, 413–15; gambling
in, 46, 61; good and bad years
of, 48–49; hygienic situation in,
37–38; Pump Room of, 46–49
bath palaces, 5, 197, 226–28, 355, 389
Bathsheba, 12
Battle Creek, Michigan, 4, 74
"Battle of the Nations," 184
Baudelaire, Charles, 163

Bauer, Felice, 282–83
Bauer-Lechner, Natalie, 133
Bavaria, Germany, 57, 66, 121–24,
150, 189, 199, 208, 223, 238, 265–
66, 278; anti-Semitism in, 285,
295; Gastein and, 285, 344; as Nazi
Party birthplace, 295, 313; Patton's
Third Army and, 364; Staffelsee
in, 322; under the Third Reich,
329, 344, 364. *See also specific cities/
locations*, e.g., Munich
Bayreuth, Germany, 124, 265, 396;
Wagner's theater in, 122–25, 265,
340, 396
Beard, Mary, 18, 21, 413
Béatrice et Bénédict (Berlioz), 128
Beauharnais, Stéphanie de, 56–57
Beau Rivage Palace, 228
Becher, Dr. David, 94
Becker, Oskar, 193–94
Beckford, William, 45
Beethoven, Ludwig van, 6, 66, 116,
123, 129, 184, 348, 381; arrest of,
102–3, 417; in Baden-bei-Wien,
101–3, 340, 381; Goethe and, 98–
101; Nazi exploitation of, 339–40,
430
Beethovenfestspiele, 340
Beethovenkino, 301
"Beethoven's disease," 99
Beethoven Temple, 301
*Beim Häuten der Zwiebel—Peeling the
Onion* (Grass), 363–64
Belgiojoso, Cristina, 117
Belgium, 83, 258, 278, 280, 307, 354.
See also Spa, Belgium
Belgrade, Serbia, 270, 272–75
Belle Époque, 225, 232, 236, 385,
398, 405
Bellow, Saul, 160

Bénazet, Édouard, 68, 87–88, 115, 125–29, 132, 231
Bénazet, Jacques, 61–68, 108, 110, 113, 115–17, 132, 148–49
Bénazet's Conversation House. *See* Baden-Baden, Conversation House in
Benedetti, Vincent, Count, 202–4
Beneš, Edvard, 373–74
Berchtold, Count Leopold von, 273, 275
Bergeron, Pierre, 38–39
Berlin, Germany, 67, 80, 89, 123, 142–43, 160, 197, 202–10 *passim*, 214, 216, 228, 273–74, 278–82; and Henlein's Sudeten German Home Front, 314, 316; Jewish population of, 249, 252–54; professional associations gathered in, 293; under the Third Reich, 327, 337–38, 344–46, 349, 355–58, 364; Twain and, 262, 266; Washington's Berlin embassy staff, 355–57; Weimar Republic and, 287, 291
Berlin, University of, 237–38, 241, 247
Berlin, West, 370, 378
Berlin Olympics (1936). *See* Olympic Games (1936)
Berlin Philharmonic, 334
Berlin Wall, 401
Berlioz, Hector, 6, 65, 68, 118, 123, 125–30
Berlusconi, Silvio, 25
"Bertie." *See* Edward VII, King of England/Albert Edward, Prince of Wales
Bethmann-Hollweg, Theobald von, 280

Bibbiena, Cardinal, 31
Biedermeier style, 101–2
Bilderberg Conference, 396
Bismarck, Otto von, 122–24, 194–98, 201–18 *passim*, 320, 361, 375, 384, 421; alliance system, spas' role in, 206–11; the Ems telegram, 200–204; Rechberg, negotiations with, 197, 421
Black Forest, Germany, 29, 69, 76, 114, 130, 278, 288. *See also* Baden-Baden
Black Hand terrorists, 270–72, 275
Bladud, 26–27
Blanc, François and Louis, 212
Blaue Reiter school of painters, 293
Blaue Vier (abstract artists), 293
Blome, Count Gustav von, 197–98
Bloom, Peter, 128
Blumenthal, Seligmann, 237, 424
Boerhaave, Herman, 73
Bohemia, 33, 40–41, 73, 119, 133–34, 219–22, 234–35, 255, 258–61, 265–67, 308–10, 313, 405; Battle of Königgrätz, 198
Bohemian Kurorte/spa towns, 220, 245, 365; and anti-Semitism, 308–10; and casino gambling, 234; clientele of, 251–52, 309, 425; Goethe in, 92–108; Jewish patronage of, 251–53, 309, 425; "medicalization" at the spas, 247, 424; postwar expulsion of ethnic German population from, 372–74; under the Third Reich, 363–65. *See also* Czech spa towns; Franzensbad; Karlsbad; Marienbad; Teplitz
Boieldieu, François-Adrien, 119
Bolshevik Revolution, 293

bombardment, aerial, 233, 282, 352
Bonaparte, Napoleon/Napoleonic Wars, 56–58, 60, 63, 69, 80, 98, 101, 182–84; post-Napoleonic period, 82, 137, 143, 184
Bonaparte, Napoleon III. *See* Napoleon III
Bonn, Germany, 66–67, 116, 376
Borkum spa, 254
Bosch, Carl, 345
Bose, Subhas Chandra, 304
Bosnia, 223, 270, 272–73
Boss, Hugo, 329
Botero, Fernando, 404
Boyle, T. Coraghessan, 4n
Bracciolini, Poggio, 34, 40
Brahms, Johannes, 6, 129–34
Brecht, Berthold, 292
Brennendes Geheimnis/The Burning Secret (Zweig), 257
Brenner, Alfred, 334–35
Brenner's Park Hotel, 290–91, 334–35, 355, 378, 396–97, 405, 428, 430
Brentano, Antonie, 99
Brighton, England, 48
Bristol Hotel, 228, 347
Britain, 26, 39, 45, 57, 144, 187, 210, 261, 291; and the "Hitler Cup," 330; the Munich Agreement, 316–17; occupation by, 288, 292; physicians, British, 69–70; spa clientele, British, 67, 79, 244–45, 277, 281, 290, 305, 307, 309; spas in, 9, 15n, 48, 54; travelers, British, 42–49, 82. *See also* England; *individual sovereigns*, e.g., Edward VII; *specific events*, e.g., World Wars I and II
Britannique, Hôtel, 286

Brod, Max, 283
brothels. *See* prostitution
Browning, Edgar Alfred, 107
Brownshirts, 300, 306, 328, 341, 349, 359
Brühl, Moritz, 95
Brühl, Tina, 95
Brun, Friederike, 97
Brüning government, 298
Budapest, Hungary, 9, 249, 251, 285, 371
Bukovina, Romania, 350
Bülow, Cosima von, 117, 123
Bülow, Hans von, 117
Bülow, Prince Bernard von, 205
Burda, Frieder/Museum Frieder Burda, 395–96
Bürgel, Willi, 345
Bürkle, Kurt, 326–27, 331
Burney, Frances, 239–40, 424
The Burning Secret (Zweig), 257
Burschenschaften (fraternities), 184
Buruma, Ian, 368
business activity, refraining from, 245, 424
Bütow, Hans, 344
Byron, Lord, 45, 78

Caer Baden, 26–27
Caesars, 18, 24, 26
caldarium, 19
cancer, 3, 133, 179, 213–15, 230, 238–39, 294, 303, 320, 399
capitalism, 181, 367, 379, 387, 395, 420
Caprivi, Count Leo von, 211
Caracalla, Baths of, 18–19, 226
Caracalla, Emperor, 18, 29, 68
Caracalla Spa (today), 393
Carinthia, Austria, 135, 306

Carl August, Duke of Saxe-Weimar, 92, 94, 96, 106, 108
Carlisle, Earl of, 44
Carlsbad, Czechoslovakia. *See* Karlsbad
Casablanca, vi
casino gambling, 6, 61–68, 87–88, 110, 163, 376, 391–92; bans on, 64, 87–88, 132, 176, 182, 200, 204, 218, 225, 234, 300, 314, 326–27; Hitler and, 327–28; Russians and, 137–79 *passim*, 394–95. *See also* Baden-Baden, casino gambling in; *other spa towns, regions, and countries*, e.g., France
Castorp, Hans, 2, 266
Catherine Braganza, 38
Cato, 23
Cavour, Camillo, 182, 190
Celsus, 24–25
Celts, 26–27
Central Europe, 3–11
Central Powers, 210, 276–77
Centralverein deutscher Staatsbürger jüdischen Glaubens (CV), 283–84, 294–96, 310
Chabert, Antoine, 62–65, 77–78
Chamberlain, Neville, 316
Chamber of Deputies, 64, 202
Chamonix, France, 305
Charlemagne, Emperor, 34
Charles II, 38
Charles (or Karl) IV, 41
Charles VI, Holy Roman emperor, 93–94
Chateaubriand, François-René de, 128
Cheltenham, England, 4, 48
Cheville, L., 62
Chico Hot Springs, Montana, 4

China, 5, 392–93
Chinati Hot Springs, Marfa, Texas, 2
Chopin, Frédéric, 6, 110, 112, 122
Christianity, 30–31, 32, 147
Christian Social Party, 253, 299–300, 304, 306
Christmas, 43, 401; Hitler's visit to Bad Em, 322, 353, 429
Chulalongkorn, King, 212
Churchill, Winston, 354
Ciceri, Pierre-Luc-Charles, 65
cinema, 235–36, 299, 371–72, 386, 389, 423
civil war, German, 198, 207
Clark, Sir James, 215
Clary, Prince, 191–92
Clemenceau, Georges, 220
Clemens, Olivia "Livy," 263–66
Clemens, Samuel. *See* Twain, Mark
Clement of Alexandria, 23–24
climate change, 401
clinics, private, 240–41, 398
Clinton, Bill, 324, 396
cocaine, 214, 239, 424
Cohn, Dr. Siegfried, 337
Cold War, 367, 369–70, 382
Cologne, Germany, 160–61, 287
Colorado (Aspen), 381
La Comédie Humaine (Balzac), 65
Communism, 287, 297, 334, 368, 382; Czech spas and, 373–74, 384–89, 401–4, 433. *See also* Soviet Union
concentration camps, 271, 333, 336, 347, 351, 362
Conrad, Joseph, 69
Constantine, Emperor, 30
Conversation House, Baden-Baden. *See* Baden-Baden, Conversation House in
Coolidge, Calvin, 294

Coryat, Thomas, 39–40, 51, 413
Cotta, Joachim, 92
Cotta, Johann Friedrich, 59–61, 75, 108–9, 415
Coubertin, Pierre de, 378
Counter-Reformation, 31
Crash of 1929, 296, 300, 303, 305, 312, 334
Crime and Punishment (Dostoevsky), 166, 168
Crimean War, 145–47
Crimea/Russia's Crimean Peninsula, 324–25
Crispi, Francesco, 210
Croatia, 324
Crusades, 33
cure centers. *See Kursaal*
Cure Hotel Thermal, 387
CV (Centralverein deutscher Staatsbürger jüdischen Glaubens), 283–84, 294–96, 310
Czechoslovakia, 2, 105, 266–68, 270, 308–17, 432–33; Communist-era, 373–74, 384–89. *See also* Bohemia; Prague; Sudetenland
Czech spa towns, 308–10, 314, 343, 346, 374, 414, 417; clientele in, 385, 402–3; Communist-era, 373–74, 384–89, 433; today, 399, 401–5. *See also* Karlsbad (Karlovy Vary); Marienbad (Mariánské Láznì)

Dachau, 333
d'Agoult, Marie, 117
Dagover, Lil, 345, 358
Daimler-Maybach Automobile Corporation/Daimler-Benz, 231, 250, 258
La dame aux camélias (Dumas), 117n

Danish War, 196
Danubia (Winder), 403–4
Darwin, Annie, 15n, 74
Darwin, Charles, 15n
Daumier, Honoré, 110
David, King, 12
Davos, Switzerland, 324
Dead Souls (Gogol), 139–41
Death in Venice (Mann), 107
Defenestrations of Prague, 374 and 374n
Defoe, Daniel, 46
de Gaulle, Charles, 378
Degenerate Art, Exhibition of (1937), 292
Dengler, Dr. Franz, 240, 252
Denmark, 168, 196–97
depression, economic, 297, 300; the Great Depression, 319. *See also* Crash of 1929
depression (melancholy), 42, 130, 146, 286
Das Deutsche Eck, 352
Deutsches Haus tuberculosis sanatorium, 324
Dharampur, Maharaja of, 386
Dietrich, Marlene, 397
Diocletian, Baths of, 226
Diocletian, Emperor, 19, 31–32
dirigibles, 232, 301, 397
Disney, Walt, 334
Disraeli, Benjamin, 68
doctors, spa, 69–70, 240–42, 246–49
Dolan, Brian, 45
Dolchstosslegende (stab-in-the-back legend), 286
Dollfuss, Engelbert, 338–39, 343, 347
Domitian, Emperor, 19
Donaudampfschiffahrtsgesellschaftskapitänsmützenabzeichen, 263

the Doors, 292
Dostoevsky, Fedor, 6–8, 138, 141, 158–78, 272, 394–95, 419–20; psychic/physical odyssey of, 158–78; wife Anna, 170, 172–78, 420
Dostoevsky, Marya Dimitrievna, 163
Dostoevsky, Mikhail, 161–63, 165–66
Drang nach Westen (Hitler's western campaign), 354
Dresden, Germany, 160, 176
Dryander-Klinik, 398
Dual Alliance between Germany and Austria-Hungary, 210
Dual Monarchy, 272, 298
Dumas, Alexandre, fils, 117n
Duplessis, Marie, 117, 418
Duval, Jeanne, 163

Eastern Europe, 367, 373–74, 392, 402–4; Jews, Eastern European, 309
Eastern Jews (*Ostjuden*), 252–54
East Germany, 392, 402
Ebensee concentration camp, 362, 431
Eckert, Georg, 235–36
Edward VII, King of England/Albert Edward, Prince of Wales, 217–24, 234–35, 247, 253, 322, 349, 363, 422; at Marienbad, 219–22
Egerland, Café, 316
Egmont (Beethoven), 99
Egypt, 12–13, 219, 412
electromagnetic radiation (X-rays), 240
"electro-shock therapy," 229
Elisabethbrunnen, Bad Homburg/ Princess Elisabeth, vi, 211
Elisabeth ("Sisi"), Empress of Austria, 223–24

Elizabeth Christine, Holy Roman Empress, 93
Elizabeth I, Queen, 37
Ems. *See* Bad Ems, Germany
Engels, Friedrich, 258
England, 4, 357. *See also* Britain; specific spa towns/locations, e.g., Bath
the Enlightenment, 45, 183–84
Entente Cordiale, 222
Entente countries, 277
Ephrussi, Viktor/Ephrussi family, 249, 285, 340, 425
Epicurean values, 35
Epidaurus, 15
Epp, Franz Ritter von, 344
Eppstein in the Taunus Hills, 324
Erlöserkirche, 216
Erzberger, Matthias, 288–89
Eschenbach, Wolfram, 120
Esplanade Hotel, 228, 385, 405
Essenes, 12
ethnic cleansing, 324, 373
eugenics, 314–15
Eulenberg, Countess zu, 345
Europa (journal), 140
Europäischer Hof, 118, 296
Europe, continental, 36–37, 39, 42–43, 45, 51, 77, 82, 213, 218, 231, 233, 262, 354, 396
exercise, 74, 233–34. *See also* sports

Fabricus, 23
Faisal I, King, of Iraq, 304–5
The Farewell Party (Kundera), 404
"fat farm," Marienbad's fame as, 283, 404
Fathers and Children (Turgenev), 155–57, 179, 419
Faust (Goethe), 113

Ferdinand Fountain, 339
Ferdinand I, Emperor, 93n
Ferdinand I, King, of Bulgaria, 304–5
Ferdinandsbad bathing complex, 301
Festspielhaus, 124, 396
Field of Blackbirds Battle in Kosovo, 270
Figl, Leopold, 380
First World War. *See* World War I
Flaubert, Gustav, 6, 153–55, 419
Flehinger, Arthur, 333, 430
Flemming, Count, 192
Fletcher, Horace B., 283
Der fliegende Holländer (Wagner), 291
Florence, Italy, 33–34, 127
"fluid motions," 244
food rationing, 278, 281, 288, 360n, 362, 364
Ford, Henry, 323
Forty-Eighters, 86n, 121
France, 4, 57, 82, 190, 203–4, 258, 289, 291; and casino gambling, 63–66, 212, 327–28; the Ems telegram, 200–204; First Empire, 65; "July Revolution" in, 64; the Munich Agreement, 316–17; occupation by, 287–88, 292, 368–69; spa clientele, French, 44–45, 54, 60, 110, 204, 277, 281, 309; tourism in, 44; Vichy regime, collaborationist, 368; World War II and, 322, 354, 358. *See also individual sovereigns; specific cities, spa towns, and other locations,* e.g., Aix-les-Bains; Evian; Vichy; *specific events and time periods,* e.g., French Revolution; World Wars I and II
Franco-Prussian War, 154, 179, 205, 253–54

Frank, Hans, Nazi Minister of Justice, 307
Frank, Joseph, 159, 169, 419
Frankfurt, Germany, 10, 85–87, 89, 92, 161, 211, 216, 377, 379, 397, 408
Frankfurter, David, 324
Franzensbad, Czechoslovakia, 98, 104, 245, 256, 321, 426
Franz Ferdinand, Crown Prince and Archduke of Austria, 270–75, 426; assassination of, with wife Sophie, 223, 270–72, 275
Franz Josef I, Emperor/Kaiser, 101, 211, 219–20, 223–24, 285, 421–22; at Ischl, 132, 135, 223–24, 271–75, 301; "Kaiser-Franz-Josef-Strasse," 343; King Edward and, 220–24, 349; Wilhelm I and, 191–92, 196–97, 206–7
Fraser, George MacDonald, 66
Freiburg, Germany, 86, 352, 408
French Revolution, 43, 45, 53, 77, 80, 183, 415
French revolutions of 1789–1799 and 1830, 84
Freud, Abraham, 284
Freud, Anna, 294
Freud, Sigmund, 135, 159, 163, 239, 284, 293, 419, 424, 426–28; at Gastein, 256–57, 303–4
"Der Freundeskreis Reichsführer SS," 335
Frey/Gilbert Klinik, 240
Friedrich, Grand Duke Karl, 51–59, 62
Friedrich I, Grand Duke of Baden, 189, 194, 226
Friedrich III (kaiser of Germany), 211, 213–14, 422

Friedrichsbad, in Baden-Baden, 9, 13, 74, 226, 227, 232, 264, 392–93
Friedrich Wilhelm III of Prussia, 182, 185–86
Friedrich Wilhelm IV of Prussia, 57, 86, 189n
frigidarium, 19, 31
Fritzsche, Peter, 232–33
Fromm, Bella, 321
Fürsten-Kongress (Princes' Congress), 188–89, 420
Fürth, Germany, 83
Furtwängler, Wilhelm, 334

Galen, 14
Galicia, 252–53, 285, 295
Gallia, Moriz/Gallia family, 249–51, 425
The Gambler (Dostoevsky), 169–70, 395
gambling. *See* casino gambling
El Gamel Bey, 219
Garcia, Pauline Viardot-. *See* Viardot-Garcia, Pauline
Garfield, President James, 238, 424
Garmisch-Partenkirchen, Germany, 325
Garstenauer, Gerhard, 399
Gast, Peter, 255
Gastein Convention, 197–98
Gasteiner Symphonie in C major (Schubert), 132
Gastein. *See* Bad Gastein, Austria
Gasthaus Hirsch, 80
Gasthof Stadt London, 191
Il Gattopardo/The Leopard (Lampedusa), 246
Gentz, Friedrich, 185
German civil war, 198, 207

German Confederation, 184, 186, 188–92, 194, 196, 198, 200–201
German-Danish War, 196
Germania, Kurhaus, 259
German Kurorte/spa towns, 7, 49, 52–53, 55, 70, 125, 182, 219, 226, 288, 420, 427–28, 431–33; and anti-Semitism, 86, 254, 294–98, 337, 425, 438; and casino gambling, 64, 138, 171, 225, 391–92; clientele of, 290–91, 309; luxury hotels in, 228; national health insurance program and, 375; Russian writers in, 7, 137–79; under the Third Reich, 320, 325–26, 328, 354, 357; today, 391–92; Weimar Republic and, 287–98; West German spa industry, 375–79; World War I and, 277–82. *See also* Baden-Baden; Ems; Homburg; Wiesbaden; *specific topics*, e.g., mud baths
German nationalism. *See* nationalism, German
German Question(s), 188–206, 373
German Spa Association, 376
German Supreme Command (OHL), 286
Germany: and anti-Semitism, 284; and the Crash of 1929, 296; Dual Alliance with Austria-Hungary, 210; German people as hardworking, 375; Germans as spa patrons, 204–5; Greater, 339, 343, 346–47, 354–55; Hohenzollern control over, 286; imperial, 184; Jews, German, 80, 173, 253, 283–84, 294, 309, 312–13, 329, 331–32, 424–25, 427; the Munich Agreement, 316–17; the

New German School, 130; the revolution of 1918–1919, 286–89, 427; "Second Empire" of, 287; the Third Reich, 319–65; the Triple Alliance, 210, 276; unification of, 86–87, 124, 184, 188, 192, 195–96, 201, 207, 211, 225, 317, 392; the Versailles Treaty, 317; Weimar Republic, 287–98. *See also* German Kurorte; West Germany; *specific cities and other locations; specific events,* e.g., Berlin Olympics; *specific topics,* e.g., medicine; rail travel

Gibbon, Edward, 44
Giesl von Gieslingen, Wladimir, 275
Gilbert, Eliza. *See* Montez, Lola
Gilbert, Felix, 280–81
Giscard d'Estaing, Valery, 378
Gladstone, Helen, 67–68
Gladstone, William, 67–68
Glaise-Horstenau, Edmund, 343
Global Economic Forum, 324
global warming, 401
Goebbels, Joseph, 230, 313, 321–23, 325, 335, 357–58, 430–31; as denouncing the grand spas, 322–23; Gastein, visit to, 343–44; wife Magda and children of, 343
Goethe, Johann Wolfgang von, 5–6, 113, 117n, 127–28, 131, 161, 416–17; Beethoven and, 6, 98–101, 417; in Bohemia, 6, 92–108, 111, 186, 220, 255, 348, 363, 417
Gogol, Nikolai, 138–41, 145–46, 161
Golden Balls boardinghouse, 104
golf, 1–2, 5, 213, 216, 218, 233–35, 330, 430
Goncharov, I. A., 154

gonorrhea, 29, 147
The Good Soldier Svejk (Hašek), 427
Gorbachev, Mikhail, 395
Gorchakov, Prince, 118
Göring, Edda, 344
Göring, Emmy, 344, 372
Göring, Heinrich Ernst, 230
Göring, Hermann, 322–23, 326, 335, 337, 339, 344
Gottwald, Klemens, 374
Graf Zeppelin, 301
Gramont, Duke Antoine de, 202–3
Grand Budapest Hotel (Anderson), 9
Grand Hotel d'Europe. *See under* Gastein: Grand Hotel d'Europe in
Grand Hotel Pupp, 317, 385–87, 405, 433
Grand Park Hotel, 400
Grand Tour, 42–49
Grant, Ulysses S., 224, 265
Granville, Augustus Bozzi, 69–79, 82, 161, 416
Grass, Günther, 363–65
Great Britain. *See* Britain
Great Depression, 319
Great Powers, 222, 276
Great War. *See* World War I
Greece/Greeks, 11, 13–18, 20–22, 69, 385
Grey, Sir Edward, 220
Griesbach. *See* Bad Griesbach, Germany
Grillparzer, Franz, 108
Gruenther, Alfred, 370
Gully, Dr. James, 15n, 74
Gunkel, Erich, 376–77
Gurs internment camp, 333
Gustloff, Wilhelm, 324
gymnasia, 16–17, 20

Habsburg Empire, 41–42, 185, 195, 201, 210, 241, 271–73, 275, 298–99, 401, 403–4; the Defenestrations of Prague, 374 and 374n; the Habsburg family, 93n, 298; *k. und k.*, 230, 261, 277, 309, 311, 341, 343, 399; leading spas of Habsburg Austria, 101, 132, 225, 229, 285. *See also* Austria-Hungary; *individual sovereigns*
Häckers Kurhotel, 398
Hadrian, Emperor, 21–22, 27
Hamburg, Germany, 287
Hamilton, William Alexander Anthony Archibald Douglas (Eleventh Duke of Hamilton), 57
Handbuch der allgemeinen und speziellen Heilquellenlehre (Seegan), 241
Hänsel und Gretel (Humperdinck), 291
Hanslbauer, Pension, 321
Harriman, E. H., 230
Harzburg. *See* Bad Harzburg, Germany
Harzreise (Goethe), 131
Hašek, Jaroslav, 275, 427
Das Haus der Türme, 359
health insurance program, German, 375
Hearst, William Randolph, 356
Hebel, Johann Peter, 63, 80, 109
Hecker, Friedrich, 85–86
Hegel, Georg Wilhelm Friedrich, 143
Hegelians, Left, 143
Heine, Heinrich, 68, 83, 113, 144, 184, 336
Heinkel, Ernst, 345
Henlein, Konrad, 310, 314–16, 349
Henri IV, King, 44
Herodotus, 412
heroin, 239, 388

Herrhausen, Alfred, 379
Herzen, Alexander, 167
Herzl, Theodor, 256, 310, 426
Hesse, Germany, 85, 113, 370; federal state of, 377
Hesse, Hermann, 294
Hessen, Prince Philipp von, 345
Hibbert, Christopher, 43–44, 414
High Renaissance, Italian, 226
Himmler, Heinrich, 321–22, 325, 349, 353, 429
Hindemith, Paul, 291–92
Hindenburg, Paul von, 279–80
Hindus, Maurice, 317
Hippocrates, 14
Hirsch, Friedrich, 244
Hirsch hotel, 80
Hitler, Adolf, 86, 300, 305–7, 312–64 *passim*, 370, 429–31; Christmas visit to Bad Ems, 322, 353; health and hygiene habits of, 320–22; at Kurorte, 321–22; the Third Reich, 319–65; as Wagner fan, 125, 340; Weimar Republic and, 289, 295, 298
the "Hitler Cup," 330, 430
Hochheimer, Albert, 286
Hofgastein. *See* Bad Hofgastein
Höhenblick, Sanatorium, 240
Hohenlohe-Ingelfingen, Prince Kraft von, 88
Hohenzollern, House of, 88, 211, 213, 286–87, 359, 369; the Ems telegram, 200–204. *See also individual sovereigns*
Hohenzollern-Sigmaringen, Prince Karl Anton of, 57, 201–2
Hohenzollern-Sigmaringen, Prince Leopold of, 200–203
Holitscher, Arthur, 312

Holland, 149, 322, 354
Holländische Hof, 85, 149, 332
Holstein, Germany, 196, 198
Homburg. *See* Bad Homburg, Germany
Homburg-Hesse, Duchy of, 198, 211–12
Homer, 13
horse racing, 230–31
horses, 4, 13, 19, 44, 60–61, 64, 83, 111, 115, 191, 230–33, 235, 237, 323, 363; horse racing, 230–31, 320
hospitals, 3, 225, 237–39, 241, 288. *See also* Lazarettstadt
Hotel Augusta, 280
Hotel Austria, 399
Hotel Casino, 234, 349
Hotel d'Alger, 178
Hotel d'Angleterre, 189, 194
Hotel Franz Karl, 341
Hotel Gellért, 9
Hotel Gütt, 256
Hotel Löwen, 359
Hotel Miramonte, 400
Hotel Monty, 316
Hotel Pacific, 385
Hotel Paris, 384n
Hotel Prince de Ligne, 191
Hotel Regina, 344
Hotel Ritter, 369
Hotel Römerbad, 337
Hotel Rose, 369
hotels, luxury, in spa towns, 228–30. *See also specific hotels*
Hotel Schey, 251
Hotel Schloss Balmoral, 283
Hotel Steigenberger, 369
Hotel Stephanie, 189, 296, 334
Hotel Straubinger, 197, 206, 361, 399

Hotel Victoria, 166
Hotel Ville de Bruxelle, 202
Hotel Weimar, 221, 345, 349
Hötzendorf, Franz Conrad von, 273–74
Howells, William Dean, 245–46, 262
Hugenberg, Alfred, 298
Hugo, Victor, 114–15
Humperdinck, Engelbert, 291
The Hunchback of Notre-Dame (Hugo), 114
Hungary, 308, 371. *See also* Austria-Hungary; Budapest
A Hunter's Notes (Turgenev), 145
Hus, Jan, 347n
Hutton, Mr., 70
hydropathy, 2
hydrotherapy, scientific, 243
hyperinflation, 289–91, 427–28

Ibsen, Heinrich, 235
Iffezheim, Germany, 231, 278
Iliad (Homer), 13
Imperial Hotel, 228
India, 1, 304
Indonesia, 5
inflation, 289–91, 427–28
Inhalorium for patients with severe respiratory diseases, 227
Innocents Abroad (Twain), 262
innovations, 226–37
"The Inspector General" (Gogol), 140
International Olympic Committee (IOC), 325, 378
International Spa Association, 1
IOC. *See* International Olympic Committee
Iran, Shah of, 378, 383
Iraq (Faisal I, King of), 304–5

Iron Chancellor. *See* Bismarck, Otto von
Isabella II, Queen, 200
Isabella Lubomirska, Princess, 95
Isayeva (Dostoevsky), Marya Dimitrievna, 163, 166
Ischl. *See* Bad Ischl, Austria
Italy, 33–34, 36–37, 44, 47, 56, 58, 96, 131, 182, 259, 262, 285, 291, 295; Baiae resort in, 25; and the Third Reich, 345–46; the Triple Alliance, 210, 276. *See also* Renaissance, Italian; *specific cities/ locations*

Jacobi, Louis, 227
Jagow, Gottlieb von, 274
Japan, 345–46, 355, 367, 371, 378
Jawlensky, Alexej von, 293, 428
Jellinek, Emil, 250, 425
Jellinek, Mercedes, 250
Jerome, St., 30
Jeschke's Grand Hotel, 355–56
Jews/Jews of Central Europe, 246–54, 368, 371; Balfour Declaration (1917), 310; Hassidic, 266–67; Jewish presence, expanding, 246–54; the "Jewish Question," 79–81; "judenrein" spa towns, 8, 254, 333, 337, 401, 425; *Judenzählung* (Jew census), 284; Orthodox, 315; *Ostjuden*, 252–54; as spa clientele, 225, 246–54, 283, 295, 309–10, 312; World War I and, 283–84. *See also* anti-Semitism; *under* Baden-Baden and other spa towns; Third Reich; *specific countries and regions; specific events*
Jodl, Alfred, 344

Johannesbad bathing complex, 301, 372
Josephine Friederike Luise, Princess, 57
the "July Revolution" (France), 64

k. und k. *See under* Habsburg Empire
Kael, Pauline, 389
Kafka, Franz, 108, 282–83
Kaiserhof Hotel, 344
Kalergis-Moukhanoff, Marie von, 122
Kálmán, Emmerich, 341
Kapurthala, Amarjit Singh, Prince of, 304
Kapuzinerkloster, 60
Karl Anton of Hohenzollern-Sigmaringen, Prince, 57, 201–2
Karl I, Kaiser, 285
Karl Louis. *See* Louis, Karl
Karl (or Charles) IV, 41
Karlovy Vary. *See* Karlsbad
Karlsbad Conference, 185–86, 420
Karlsbad Decrees, 186–87
Karlsbad (Karlovy Vary), 4–6, 33, 92–104, 106, 133, 274, 282–84, 372–74, 424, 429, 433; and anti-Semitism, 308–12, 316; clientele of, 93–94, 108, 119, 251–53, 284, 309–12, 314; Communist-controlled, 190, 384–88, 433; Goethe in, 92–98, 103–4, 186, 417; Grand Hotel Pupp in, 317, 385–87, 405, 433; history and legend of, 40–42, 93–94; Jewish patronage of, 251–53, 284, 309–12; luxury, fame for, 310–11, 317; Marx in, 258–59; modernization and, 228, 242, 244–45, 256–61, 263, 426; occupation forces in,

365, 372; Peter the Great in, 42, 93, 137; politics and, 169, 185–88, 190, 196–98, 197, 219, 421; salt content of waters, 94; theater in, 93, 96; and the Third Reich, 316–17, 321, 348–49, 363–65; today, 401–5; in the twenties and thirties, 308–17; World Zionist Organization meeting in, 310, 429. *See also* Bohemian Kurorte; Czech spa towns

"Karlsbad Program," 315–16

"Karlsbad water," 59

Karlsruhe, Germany, 59, 68, 81–82, 85, 126–27, 189, 357

Kassin, Joseph, 250

KdF. *See* Kraft durch Freude (KdF, Strength through Joy)

Kellogg, John Harvey, 4, 74

Kennan, George, 356

Kent, William, 44

Kessler, Harry, 205

Khengarji III of Kutch, Maharaja, 304

The Kickleburys on the Rhine (Thackeray), 82

King Stephen (Kotzebue), 99

Kisch, Enoch Heinrich, 222, 247–48, 425

Kissileff, Sophie, 137–38

Kissingen Diktat (Kissingen Decree), 208–9

Kissingen. *See* Bad Kissingen, Germany

Kissinger, Henry, 185–86

Kitzbühl, Austria, 401

Klaus, Josef, Austrian chancellor, 383

Das Kleine Mahagonny (Brecht and Weill), 292

Klüber, Johann Ludwig, 59–60

Klückner, Peter, 345

Koblenz, Germany, 9, 199, 287, 352

Koch, Robert, 237–39, 364, 424

Kochbrunnen hot spring, Wiesbaden, 227

Kohl, Helmut, 384

Kölreuter, W. W., 59

Königgrätz, Battle of, 198

Königsberger, Emil, 336

Korean War, 375

Kosovo, 270

Kotzebue, August von, 99, 184–85, 420

Kraft durch Freude (KdF, Strength through Joy), 323

Kramer, Dr., 70, 73–76

Krankenkassen system, 375

Kraus, J., 244, 424

Krause, Wilhelm, 320

Kreisleitung, 340, 349, 365

Krieg, Max, 278

Kristallnacht, 348

Krupp, Alfred, 321

Krupp von Bohlen, Gustav, 345

Kundera, Milan, 404

Kunst, Wilhelm, 79

Kurliste, signing of, 94

Kurorte ("cure-towns"), 41, 225. *See also specific time periods; specific towns and general regions* (e.g., Austrian Kurorte; Bohemian Kurorte; German Kurorte)

Kursaal (cure center), 161, 221–22, 287, 335

Kutch, Khengarji III, Maharaja of, 304

The Lady of the Camellias (Dumas), 117n

LAH (SS-Leibstandarte Adolf
    Hitler), 353–54
Lampedusa, Giuseppe di, 246
Langeoog island, 295
Last Year in Marienbad (Resnais),
    388–89, 433
laudanum abuse, 67–68
Lausanne, Switzerland, 228
Lazarettstadt (military hospital cities),
    280–81, 285, 352, 358, 360–61
Ledgard, J. M., 403
Left Hegelians, 143
Legouvé, Ernest, 128
Lehár, Franz, 132, 302, 334, 341
Lehrer, Tom, 144n
Leipzig, Germany, 184, 191–92, 421
Lelia (Sand), 111
Lenné, Peter Joseph, 212, 216
Lenya, Lotte, 292
Leopold, Grand Duke, of Baden,
    64–65, 85–86
Leopold, Prince, of Hohenzollern-
    Sigmaringen, 200–203
Les Misérables (Hugo), 115
Lessing, Theodor, 312–13, 315, 429
Levetzow, Amalie von, 98, 106
Levetzow, Ulrike, 98, 105–8
Ley, Robert, 323–24
Liberty Bell in Philadelphia,
    Pennsylvania, 308
Lichtental (Baden-Baden), 115,
    129–30
Lichtentaler Allee, 53, 115, 132,
    191–92, 234, 281, 327
Liebig, Justus, 211
Lipsky, Ludwig, 328, 332
Lister, Joseph, 238–39
Liszt, Franz, 6, 66–67, 116–18, 122–
    23, 130
Löbl, Emil, 301–3

London, England, 2, 46, 68–69,
    179, 214, 218, 228, 258–61, 292,
    354; Czechoslovak Republic's
    wartime exile government in, 373;
    Luftwaffe's Blitz on, 357
Louis, Karl, 56–58
Louis Philippe, King, 64, 84, 110
Low Countries, 322, 352
Lubomirska, Princess Isabella, 95
Lucca baths in Italy, 36
Lucretius, 34
Ludendorff, General Erich, 280, 286,
    427
Ludwig I of Bavaria, 66
Ludwig II of Bavaria, 121–23, 125,
    208, 388
Die lustige Witwe (Lehár), 132, 341
Luther, Martin, 184
Lutze, Victor, 359
Luxemburg, 354
Lyme Regis, England, 48

MacDonald, Malcolm, 129–30
Mackenzie, Morell, 214
The Magic Mountain (Mann), 2, 238,
    266, 324, 351
Mahagonny (Weill), 292
Mahler, Alma (Schindler), 134–35
Mahler, Gustav, 6, 133–35, 256
Maikov, Apollon, 174–75
Mainz, Germany, 287
Malvern, England, 4, 15n, 74
Mann, Thomas, 2, 106, 238, 266,
    324, 336, 351, 382, 409
Mannheim, 231, 291
Marcellinus, 21
Marfa, Texas, 2
Mariánské Lázně. *See* Marienbad
Maria Theresa, Holy Roman Empress,
    93–94

Marie Amelie Elisabeth Karoline, Princess, 57
Marienbad (Mariánské Láznì), 4, 33, 120, 169, 198, 232, 242, 245, 247, 372–74, 417, 423–26, 429; and anti-Semitism/racism, 308–10, 312–16; beauty and charm of, 105, 256, 282–83; clientele of, 108, 251–57, 282–83, 295, 309–15; Communist-controlled, 190, 384–86, 388–89; as "fat farm," 283, 404; Goethe and, 6, 92, 98, 104–8, 111, 255, 363; history of, 104–5; Jewish community/clientele of, 221–22, 251–53, 255, 283, 295, 309–13, 315; King Edward in, 219–22, 422; *Last Year in Marienbad*, 388–89, 433; occupation forces in, 365, 372; sports in, 234–35, 423–24; and the Third Reich, 316–17, 348–50, 363–65; today, 401–5; Twain in, 265–67; in the twenties and thirties, 308–17. *See also* Bohemian Kurorte; Czech spa towns
Marienbad (Aleichem), 251–52, 425
"The Marienbad Elegy" (Goethe), 107
Marshall Plan, 375
Martial, 22
Marx, David Raphael, 81
Marx, Eleanor ("Tussy"), 258–59
Marx, Karl, 81, 255–68, 336, 363, 385
Mary, the Virgin, 104–5
Masarýk, Jan, 374
Mascagni, Pietro, 291
Masserberg, Germany, 295
Maugham, Somerset, 270
Mauthausen concentration camp network, 362
Maximilian I of Mexico, 223
Maximilian Joseph I, King, 57
McCarthy, Joseph, Senator, 382
Medici, Catherine de, 162
medicine/"medicalization," 8, 225, 237–47, 424. *See also* doctors; hospitals; pain management
medieval period, 3, 31–34, 41, 413
Meir, Richard, 395
Meissen, Germany, 363
Mendelssohn, Felix, 161
Menshikov, Prince, 148
Mercedes, 250, 330, 353, 397
The Merry Widow (Lehár), 132, 341
Mesmer, Maison, 189–90, 192
Messerschmidt, Hermann, 336
Messerschmitt, Willy, 345
Metternich, Prince Clemens von, 182–83, 185–88, 338, 341, 420
Mexico, 223
Michelangelo, 31
Michelet, Jules, 32
Michigan, Battle Creek. *See* Battle Creek, Michigan
Middle East, 262
MiG-15, 185
Milhaud, Darius, 192
mineral water, 11, 14, 24, 27, 36–37, 41–42, 70, 73, 94, 119–20, 155, 177, 243; Hitler's preference for, 320–22; Royal Mineral Water Hospital for Rheumatic Diseases, 47
Minerva (Sulis Minerva), 27–28
Minnelli, Liza, 383
Mirbeau, Octave, 245, 424
Miss Universe Contest, 269
mixed-gender bathing, 20, 23–24, 33–34, 40, 392–93, 398
modernization, 225–68
Molotov, Viacheslav, 380

454 · Index

Moltke, Helmuth von (Franco-Prussian War general), 124, 197, 274
Moltke, Helmuth von (German army chief of staff), 274
monasteries, 31, 104, 349
Montaigne, Michel de, 36–37, 96, 413
Montana (Chico Hot Springs), 4
Monte Carlo, 61, 212, 384, 391, 401
Montez, Lola, 66–68, 116–17, 123, 292, 416
morphium. *See* opiates
Morrison, Jim, 292
Moschus, 17
Moscow, Russia, 57, 80, 138n, 141–42, 145, 380
Mosel, River, 199, 260
Mozart Temple, 301
mud baths, 75
Müller, Georg von, 279
Munich, Germany, 67, 122–23, 252–53, 287, 289, 291, 293, 296, 300, 388; under the Third Reich, 321, 333, 353; today, 396
Munich Agreement, 316
Münz, Sigmund, 220–22, 253, 422
music and musicians, 91, 115–35. *See also individual names; specific spa towns, e.g., Baden-Baden*
Musil, Robert, 222
Musset, Alfred de, 6, 110–13, 417
Mussolini, Benito, 19, 345

Nabokov, Vladimir, 139, 418
Nachmann, Carol, 327
Naples, Italy, 25, 35, 43, 264
Napoleon. *See* Bonaparte, Napoleon
Napoleonic Wars, 60, 63, 199
Napoleon III, 83, 126, 151, 179, 182, 189–91, 201, 203–4

Nash, Richard "Beau," 46
Nassau, Duchy of, 189, 198–99
Nassauer Hof Hotel, Wiesbaden, 228–29, 369, 405
National Hotel (Marienbad), 315
nationalism, German, 86, 183, 195, 302, 420
National Socialist German Workers Party (NSDAP), 297, 324, 326, 335, 349, 353. *See also* Nazi Party
A Nation of Fliers (Fritzsche), 232–33
"natural cure," 73–74
Natural History (Pliny the Elder), 18
On the Nature of Things (Lucretius), 34
Naturheilanstalt Lichtental, 234
Naturheilkunde, 74, 322, 349–50
naturopathy. *See* Naturheilkunde
Nauheim. *See* Bad Nauheim, Germany
Nazi Party, 295, 303, 313–14; and spas, 319–29. *See also* National Socialist German Workers Party (NSDAP); Third Reich; *specific topics and events, e.g., Olympics*
Nero, 19, 25, 274
Nerval, Gérard de, 6, 112–14
nervous disorders, 244–46, 424
Nestroy, Johann Nepomuk, 108
Neuenahr. *See* Bad Neuenahr, Germany
Neue Schloss (New Palace), Baden-Baden, 55, 189–90
"neurasthenia," 244–45
New German School, 130
New York City, 1, 18
New York State (Saratoga Springs Resort), 4
Nicholas I, czar of Russia, and wife Charlotte, 143–44, 199–200

Nicholas II, czar of Russia, 212, 216, 229, 422
Nietzsche, Friedrich, 108, 255, 425–26
Night of the Broken Glass. *See* Reichskristallnacht
"Night of the Long Knives," 321
Nolde, Emil, 396
North Sea, 254, 274, 295
Notgeld currency, 289
NSDAP. *See* National Socialist German Workers Party; Nazi Party
nudity, public, 20, 33–34, 234, 392. *See also* mixed-gender bathing
Nuremberg Laws (1935), 332
Nymphenburg Palace (Schloss Nymphenburg), 388

Oblomov (Goncharov)/"Oblomovism," 154
Octavian (Caesar Augustus), 18
Odyssey (Homer)/Odysseus, 13
Oetker, Rudolf/Oetker and Sons, 335
Offenbach, Jacques, 68, 131
Ogier, Mr. (banker), 147–49
OHL (German Supreme Command), 286
Ohnesorg, Benno, 378
Olympic Games (1936), 16–17, 19, 29–30, 233, 236, 314, 325, 328–31, 330–31, 378, 408
Oos River/Valley, 28, 49, 53, 68, 83, 112–14, 123, 148, 151–53, 189, 232, 277, 333–34
Opel, Wilhelm von, 345
operettas, 131, 302, 341
opiates, 14–15, 20, 67–68, 128, 239, 413
Oppenheimer, Spielbank, 80
Orel province (Central Russia), 141

Orth, Dr., 176–77, 177
Orthodox Church, Russian. *See* Russian Orthodox Church
Orthodox Jews, 315
Oshima, Hiroshi, 346
Osler, Sir William, 239
Ostjuden (Eastern Jews), 252–54
Ostmark (Austria's designation in Greater Germany), 339–40, 342–43, 360
Otto-Planetta-Strasse, 339
"The Overcoat" (Gogol), 140

Paganini, Nicolo, 6, 63
Pagello, Pietro, 111
Pahlavi, Shah Mohammad Reza, 378, 383
pain management, 214, 238–39, 424
Palestine, 300, 310–11, 315, 329
Palladio, Andrea, 47
Pan, 31
Paquet, Alfons, 226, 423
Paracelsus, 35
Paris, France, 3, 43, 45, 58, 60, 63–68, 83–84, 88, 110, 112–14, 119, 122, 125–26, 140, 144, 146–47, 153, 160–67 *passim*, 179, 189, 218, 221–22, 228, 262, 354
Parkhotel Bellevue, 383
Pasteur, Louis, 238–39
Patti, Adelina, 212
Patton, George, 357, 364
Payer, Monsieur, 62
Pearl Harbor, 355
Pepys, Samuel, 37, 413
Peter the Great, 42, 73, 93, 137, 142
Pettenkofer, Max, 238, 424
"Phantoms" (Turgenev), 164
Philadelphia, Pennsylvania, 308
physicians, spa. *See* doctors

Pius IX, Pope, 31
Planetta, Otto, 339
Plasmon, 265
Plater, Count, 259–60
Pliny the Elder, 18, 23–25
Plombières-les-Bains, France, 36, 182, 190
Podgorny, Nikolai, Soviet president, 383
Pohl, Richard, 123
Poland, 252, 253, 266–67, 315–16, 322, 351, 361, 373. *See also* Warsaw
politics, 181–224, 420–23
Pompeii, 21
Porsche, Ferdinand, 323, 345
Prague, Czechoslovakia, 41, 198, 241, 247, 282, 308, 312, 384–86, 389; and anti-German policies, 314–16, 373; Defenestrations of, 374 and 374n; Jewish population of, 249, 251; "Prague Spring," 389, 403
Presley, Elvis, 357
Preussen, Prince Joachim Albrecht von, 345
Priessnitz, Vincent, 73–75, 416
Prince's Conference of 1860, 188–89, 420
Princip, Gavrilo, 271
Prisoners of War (POWs), 361–62; Austrian, 372; Russian, 355, 357, 359, 362
propaganda, 70, 222, 307, 323, 343
prostitution, 19–20, 33, 43, 56, 65, 67, 110, 130, 153, 182, 186, 218, 268, 288, 384n
Prussia, 57, 86–89, 98, 118, 121, 280–84, 295, 337, 359, 370–71; Austro-Prussian War, 201; Franco-Prussian War, 154, 179, 205, 253–54; politics, the spas and, 123–24, 185, 188–205, 212–15; spa clientele from, 204–5, 253. *See also individual sovereigns*, e.g., Friedrich Wilhelm III of Prussia
Prussian War Ministry, 280, 284
"Psychrophor" catheter, 243
Purna Kumbh Mela festival, 12
Putin, Vladimir, 139n, 325
Pyrenees, France, 64, 333
Pyrmont. *See* Bad Pyrmont, Germany

Qatar, 383
Quellen, 71, 101, 161, 211, 227, 243, 337, 349, 393
Quelle zum Greifvogel, 80

racism/race hatred, 8, 254–56, 269, 284, 295–98, 302, 314–15, 319, 328. *See also* anti-Semitism
radon gas, 230, 303, 398–99
RAF (Red Army Faction), 379
rail travel, 48, 65, 115, 122, 160, 189, 191, 199, 205, 211, 235, 237, 242, 258, 276–77, 294, 309, 317, 376; to Baden-Baden, 83–84; "railway spine," 84, 416; the Third Reich and, 333, 342, 361, 363–64
Rape of Europa (Milhaud), 192
Raphael, 31
Rastaat, Germany, 55–56, 58, 78, 88
Rastaater Congressblat (Schreiber), 56
Rastatt, Congress of, 188
Red Army, 325, 350, 364–65, 371, 374, 386
Red Army Faction (RAF), 379
Rehberger, Emanuel Edler von, 230
Reichenhall. *See* Bad Reichenhall, Germany
Reichskristallnacht, 332–33, 337, 348

Reinsurance Treaty, 216
Renaissance, Italian/Renaissance era, 31–32, 34–35, 127, 226–27, 249, 413
Rentenmark, 291
Resnais, Alain, 105, 388
respiratory ailments, 2–3, 155, 176, 189, 227, 240.
  See also tuberculosis
Revolutions of 1848–1849, 84–89, 121–22
Rhine, River, 28–29, 56, 66, 82–83, 119, 148, 160, 170, 190, 287; proximity of Ems and Wiesbaden to, 199, 234, 288
Rhineland region, 114, 179, 190, 257, 261, 290, 323; "independent Rhineland" goal, 289
Ribbentrop, Joachim von, 330
Richards, Keith, 117
Ring des Nibelungen (Wagner), 124
The Road to Wellville (Boyle), 4n
Röhm, Ernst, 321, 359
Rolling Stones, 117
Roman Empire, 20, 30, 44, 392
Romania, 350
romanticism/Romantic Era, 108–15
Rome, city of, 141, 412; ancient, 15–35, 226, 393; Rome Olympics (cancelled), 19
Roon, Albrecht von, 124, 194
Roosevelt, Franklin, 356
Roosevelt, James, 356
Rosenberg, Alfred, 344
Roth, Philip, 350, 431
Rothschild banking dynasty, 216, 221
roulette. See casino gambling
Royal Mineral Water Hospital for Rheumatic Diseases, 47
Rudolf, Crown Prince of Austria, 223

The Ruins of Athens (Kotzebue), 99
Rumbold, Sir Horace, 88–89
Russian Orthodox Church, 168–69, 200, 206, 212, 216
Russia/Russians: and Austrian POWs, 372; at Baden-Baden, 57, 394–95; the Bolshevik Revolution, 293; and casino gambling, 137–79 *passim*, 394; civil war in, 293; in Czech spa towns today, 402–3; German attitude toward, 207; Jews, Russian, 221, 253; Napoleon's invasion of, 57, 101; POWs, Russian, 355, 357, 359, 362; Russian writers at the grand German spas, 7, 137–79; as spa clientele, 57, 212, 277, 281, 394–95; Wiesbaden as haven for, 293. See also Soviet Union; *individual names*, e.g., Turgenev; *specific cities and other locations; specific events and time periods*, e.g., Crimean War; World Wars I and II
Rust, Bernard, 34

Saalburg fort, 216
Sacher Hotel, 228
Salles, Paul, 327
Salmen inn, 55
Salter, James, 375
Salzburg, Austria, 270, 302–3, 305–6, 342, 347, 371
Salzburg Music Festival, 305
Salzkammergut, Austria, 134, 341, 370, 431
Samaranch, Juan Antonio, 378
Sanatorium Höhenblick, 240
Sand, George, 6, 110–12, 117, 417
Sand, Karl, 184, 420
San Francisco, California, 33n, 228

Sarajevo, 193, 223, 270, 272–73
Saratoga Springs Resort (New York State), 4
Satans Mausefallen/Satan's Mousetraps (Wachenhusen), 200
Saud, King Ibn, 383
saunas, 33, 74, 393, 398, 400
Savonarola, 33
Saxe-Weimar, Duke Carl August of. *See* Carl August, Duke of Saxe-Weimar
Saxony, Germany, 49, 52, 121, 189, 297
Sazonov, Sergei, 274
Schacht, Hjalmar, 298
Schiller, Friedrich, 97
Schindler, Alma, 134–35
Schivelbusch, Wolfgang, 83
Schleicher, Joseph, 353
Schleswig, Germany, 196, 198
Schloss Bühlerhöhe, 395
Schmid, Franz, 339–40
Schmidt, Helmut, 376, 378
Schnitzler, Arthur, 256, 426
Schratt, Katharina, 101, 219–20, 223–24
Schreiber, Aloys, 56, 415
Schubert, Franz, 117, 132
Schubert, Mayor Eugen, 287
Schultz-Leitershofen, Alexander, 233
Schumann, Clara, 129–31
Schumann, Julie, 130–31
Schumann, Robert, 129–30
Schuschnigg, Kurt von, 338–39, 347
Schwab, Charles, 356
Schwedhelm, Hans, 331–32
scientific hydrotherapy, 243
Scipio Africanus, 23
Scythia, 13, 412
Sebald, W. G., 389

Second World War. *See* World War II
Sedlacek, Alfred, 346, 383
Sedlacek, Viktor, 304, 306–7, 346
Seegan, Josef, 241–42, 247
Seneca, 22–23
Serbia, 270, 272–77
sexual license, atmosphere of, 20, 24–25, 34, 40, 91, 393
sexually transmitted diseases, 29, 33, 39, 147, 153, 305
Seyss-Inquart, Arthur, 338–39, 343
Sheridan, Richard, 46
shopping, luxury, 236–37, 424
Siberia, 158–59, 404
Silliman, Benjamin, 46–47
Sinatra, Frank, 397
Sixtus V, Pope, 31
Skalnik, Vaclao, 105
skiing, 305, 323, 362, 381–83, 400–401, 405
Slavia, 236
Slavophiles, 7, 143, 150, 158, 172, 174–75
Slovakia, 346
Smoke (Turgenev), 156–58, 169, 174, 395, 419
Smollett, Tobias, 38, 413
Snitkina, Anna Grigoryevna (wife of Dostoevsky), 170, 172–78, 420
soccer, 233, 273, 278
Songspiel Mahagonny (Brecht and Weill), 292
The Sorrows of Young Werther (Goethe), 94
The Sound of Music, 371
Soviet Union, 101, 190, 261, 289, 291, 367, 369–70, 372–74, 383, 385, 392, 401, 403; Communism's collapse in, 395; occupation by, 101, 365–66, 372, 380; World War

II and, 356–57, 360, 365. See also Russia
Spa, Belgium, 1n, 4, 26, 33, 40, 45, 52, 59, 269; gambling in, 61; Kaiser Wilhelm in, 286–87
Spain, 69, 200–203
Spartans, 17
The Spas of Germany (Granville), 69
spa towns. See Kurorte ("cure-towns"); *specific towns*
"Spectaculum" sauna, 393
Spielbänke (casinos). See casino gambling; *specific casinos and locations*
sports, 233–34. See also Olympics; *specific sports*
SS-Leibstandarte Adolf Hitler (LAH), 353–54
St. Moritz, Switzerland, 305
St. Petersburg, Russia, 89, 140, 142–47, 152, 161–63, 166, 179, 194, 259, 273, 396
Stadtschloss at Homburg, 279, 369
Staffelsee (Bavaria), Germany, 322
Stalin, Joseph, 138, 325, 372–74
Stalingrad, Battle of, 323, 357
Steigenberger, Albert, 296
Stein, Charlotte von, 95
Stellovsky, Feodor, 170
Stephenson, George, 84
Sternberg, Rudolf, 299
Stoicism, 23
Storm, Theodor, 154
Strabo, 25
Strandbad cure facility, 301, 372
Strasbourg, France, 51, 63, 82–83, 127
Straus, Oscar, 341
Strauss, Johann II, 129, 131–32
Streicher, Julius, 337

Strength through Joy. See Kraft durch Freude (KdF, Strength through Joy)
Stresemann, Gustav, 297
strigils, 17, 22
Struve, Gustav von, 85–86
Stufetta del Bibbiena, 31
Styria, Austria, 306
subsidization, West German system of, 376, 397
Sudeten-German spa towns, 309
Sudetenland, Czechoslovakia, 308–17, 338, 346, 348–50, 362, 364–65; ethnic German expulsion from, 373, 409, 432; Germany's annexation of, 321
Sulis, 26–27
Sulis Minerva, 27–28
"Sumbul" (Asiatic remedy), 69
Suslova, Apollinaria, 162–68, 172
Suttner, Berta von, 222
Swinburne, Henry, 45
Switzerland, 2, 36, 85, 114, 121, 147, 298, 305, 324, 331, 382. See also Baden, Switzerland
syphilis, 33, 305

"Das Tagebuch" (Goethe), 104
Tannhäuser (Wagner), 119
Taras Bulba (Gogol), 138n, 140
Tauber, Richard, 334
Taunus Hills, 211, 324
Telemachus, 13
tennis, 5, 213, 216, 218, 233–34, 234, 294, 423
tepidarium, 19
Teplitz, Convention of, 186
Teplitz, Czechoslovakia, 92, 108, 119–20, 191, 314; Allied leaders meeting in, 182–83; Beethoven's

meeting with Goethe in, 98–101; Metternich's meeting with Friedrich Wilhelm of Prussia in, 185–87, 420; Wilhelm I's meeting with Franz Josef in, 191–92, 196, 421

Tepl Monastery, 104, 349
Tepl [River], 261
Terence, 398
Texas, 2, 394
Thackeray, William, 82
Thailand, 2, 5
Thani, Ali Bin Abdullah, Sheik Al-, 383
theater, 16, 59, 152, 245, 291–92; Wagner's personal, 119, 121–25, 265, 296, 396. See also cinema; operettas; *specific spa towns/ locations*, e.g., Baden-Baden
Their Silver Wedding Journey (Howells), 245–46
Theodosius, Emperor, 30
Theresienstadt, 271, 347, 351
thermae, 18–20, 22–25, 29
Theroux, Paul, 9
Thimig, Hans, 345
Third Reich, 298, 319–65, 425. See also *individual names; specific topics, events, and locations*
Thirty Years War, 104, 374n
Three Emperors League, 207
Thyssen, Fritz, 345
Tieck, Ludwig, 109
Tiedemann, Christoph von, 207–9
Tilden, Bill, 294, 428
Tilling, Dr., 41, 414
Tissot, Samuel-Auguste, 73, 416
Titus, Emperor, 19
Tivoli, Italy, 24, 35

Tolstoy, Countess Alexandra, 148
Tolstoy, Leo, 6–8, 138, 146–51, 156, 158, 161, 164, 178–79, 272, 419
Tomek, Reinhardt Stefan, 383–84
Tour de France, 233
tourism tax, 307
trains. See rail travel
Trajan, Emperor, 19, 29
A Tramp Abroad (Twain), 263
transportation, 4, 115, 237; to Baden-Baden, 81–84. See also rail travel
Trapp, Edward Christian, 211
La Traviata (Verdi), 117n
Tristan und Isolde (Wagner), 119, 291
Trollope, Anthony, 82
Trotsky, Leon, 278
Tschechova, Olga, 345, 359
tuberculosis, 2, 15n, 117n, 150, 163, 199, 271, 282, 324; discovery of tubercle bacillus, 237
Tuka, Vojtech, 346
Tunbridge Wells, Britain, 70
Turgenev, Ivan, 6–7, 129, 138, 141–58, 161–62, 169, 178–79, 419–20; background of, 141–46; in Baden-Baden, 7, 122, 129, 141, 143, 145, 149–58, 178, 395; Dostoevsky and, 158, 164, 166–67, 172, 174–75; Flaubert and, 153, 419; Gogol and, 141, 145; in Karlsbad, 259, 317; Tolstoy and, 146–51, 156, 158, 164, 178–79, 419; Westernization of, 142–43. See also *Fathers and Children; Smoke*
Turgenev, Varvara Petrovna (Lutovinova), 142
Turin, Italy, 165
Turkey, 32, 69, 270, 346
Turkish baths, 20

Twain, Mark, 6, 114, 255–68, 305, 398
Tyrol, Austria, 305, 401

Ukraine, 138–40, 200, 361, 364
Undinebrunnen fountain, 250
UNESCO World Heritage Sites, 396
United States, 86n, 121, 296, 382; American internees in wartime Bad Nauheim, 355–57; American occupation and American-zone spas, 365, 368–72, 432; Americans as tourists/spa clientele, 225, 290–91, 307, 309; Gilded Age in, 228; Washington's Berlin embassy staff, internment of, 355–57. *See also* Allied forces; World Wars I and II; *specific events*, e.g., Crash of 1929; *specific locations in the U.S.*
Ustinov, Peter, 383
Utz, Jean-François, 66

Vane, Lady Susan, 218
Varro, 25
Varzin, Poland, 202–3
venereal disease, 33, 39, 147, 153, 305
Venice, Italy, 110–11, 255
Verdi, Giuseppe, 19, 117n
Verein zur Abwehr des Antisemitismus (Association for the Prevention of Anti-Semitism), 254
Verlorenes Paradies (Löbl), 301
Versailles, France, 78, 205
Versailles Treaty, 317
Viardot, Louis, 144, 151–52, 154n, 395
Viardot-Garcia, Pauline, 122, 126–27, 129, 144, 146, 151–52, 154, 179

Vichy, France, 4, 26, 44, 152–53, 368
Vichy regime, France, 368
Victoria, Princess ("Vicky")/Empress, 213–17, 422
Victoria, Queen, 213, 304
Victor of Ravenna, Bishop, 31
Vienna, Austria, 2, 43, 58, 86n, 99, 101–2, 122–23, 134, 224, 228, 241, 243, 259, 371; anti-Semitism in, 135, 265, 267–68, 285, 301, 303, 341; Baden-bei-Wien, proximity to, 299, 301, 372, 380, 401; called "Das Rote Wien" (Red Vienna), 299, 305; Jewish population of, 249–52, 256–57; operetta scene in, 302; population of, 249–52, 256–57, 298–99; spa clientele from, 89, 249–52, 251, 256–57, 282, 401
Vienna, Congress of, 58, 183
Vienna, University of, 241, 247
Les Vingt et un Jours d'un neurasthénique (Mirbeau), 245
Virchow, Rudolf, 214
Virgin Islands, 398
the Virgin (Mary), 104–5
Vittorio Veneto, Battle of, 285
völkisch movement, 301, 340
Volksturm, 360
Volkswagen/VW Beetle, 323, 375
Vulpius, Christiane, 96–97

Wachenhusen, Hans, 200
Wagner, Minna, 119–20, 122
Wagner, Richard, 6, 65, 117, 130, 133, 177, 209, 255, 263, 291; Hitler as fan/Nazi exploitation of, 125, 339–40; Kurort, trips to, 119–25, 161, 188; personal theater of, 119, 121–25, 265, 296, 396

Wagner, Robert (*Reichsstatthalter* for Baden), 331
Die Wahlverwandtschaften (Goethe), 104
Waldersee, Count Alfred von, 202, 213
Waldheim, Kurt, 384
walking, 74, 416
Wallner, Viktor, 380–81
Wall Street, 296, 301. *See also* Crash of 1929
Warsaw, Poland, 67, 249, 251
Warsaw Pact, 388
Wartburg Festival, 184
Wassing, Anton, 347
water drinkers, 17
Wehrmacht, 293, 319, 325, 339, 344, 351–52, 354–55, 361, 369, 371, 384n
Der Weiβe Hasen Hotel, 94
Weill, Kurt, 292
Weimar, Duchy of, 92, 94–95, 98–99, 107, 123, 125, 127, 130, 221
Weimar Republic, German, 205, 287–98, 326, 345, 428
Weinbrenner, Friedrich, 58–60, 62
Weizmann, Chaim, 311
West, the ancient, 12–29
Western Empire, 17, 27
West Germany/West German spa industry, 375–79, 397
West Virginia, 356
Weymouth, England, 48
Wharton, Edith, 231
Wiesbaden, Germany, 4, 6, 117, 125, 137, 139, 198–99, 377, 423, 428, 430; as becoming "Nazified," 295–96; casino gambling in, 64, 92, 166–67, 175, 231, 370; clientele of, 212, 246; as cure center for nervous disorders, 244–46, 424; Dostoevsky in, 161–63, 166–69, 175–76; Goethe and, 92, 161, 416; Hitler in, 295–96; Jawlensky in, 293, 428; as largest *Kaiserreich* Kurorte, 228; luxury hotels in, 228; modernization and, 226–28, 234–37, 244–47, 397, 423; Nassauer Hof Hotel in, 228–29, 369, 405; occupation forces in, 287–88, 292, 369–70; RAF attacks in, 379; Russians, as haven for, 293; shopping scene in, 236–37, 424; sports in, 234; theater in, 119, 235; under the Third Reich, 328, 357; today, 397; the twenties in, 292–93; Wagner and, 119; Weimar Republic and, 287–90; World War I and, 281–82; World War II and, 357, 375, 427. *See also* German Kurorte/spa towns
Wiesbadener Brunnen, 161
Wiessee. *See* Bad Wiessee, Germany
Wilhelm I of Prussia/Emperor [kaiser] of Germany, 88, 118, 189–97, 201–7, 209, 211, 227, 336; assassination attempt on, 192–93, 421; as banning casino gambling, 132, 176; the Ems telegram, 200–204
Wilhelm II, Emperor/Kaiser, 211, 214–22 *passim*, 227, 229, 232, 235, 273–80 *passim*, 285–87, 422
Wilhelmina of Sagan, Princess, 183
Will, Heinrich, 243
William Alexander Anthony Archibald Douglas-Hamilton, Eleventh Duke of Hamilton., 57
Wilson, Woodrow, 286–87
Winder, Simon, 41, 403–4, 414
Window to the West, 142

wine: as anesthetic, 239–40; drinking, 17, 21, 23
Winternitz, Wilhelm, 243, 247, 424
Winter Notes on Summer Impressions (Dostoevsky), 159–61, 171, 419
Wohllebengasse, Vienna, 249
women: in ancient Rome, 20–21, 27; and the Grand Tour, 45; and Nazi misogyny, 320. *See also individual names; specific topics*, e.g., mixed-gender bathing
Wood, John, and John, Jr., 47
The World of Yesterday (Zweig), 250–51
A World Restored (Kissinger), 185–86
World War I, 2, 8, 84, 116, 137, 210–13, 232–33, 319, 351, 355; assassination of Franz Ferdinand, 223, 270–72, 275; the decades before, 225, 227, 236–37, 254, 269, 351; the Grand Spas during, 269–87; Jews in Central Europe, meaning for, 283–84; revolution in closing days of, 287; spa-town life from World War I to triumph of Hitler, 226, 269–317, 381
World War II, 86, 107, 319, 324, 335, 346, 351–65, 384n; post-World War II, 4, 229, 287, 368–74, 381, 409; spa scene on the eve of, 350–51

World Zionist Organization (Twelfth Congress), 310, 429
Wormser, Georges, 327
Wrangel, Baron A. E., 168
wrestling, 16, 19
writers, 91; Romantic-Era writers in Baden-Baden, 108–15; Russian writers at the grand German spas, 137–79. *See also individual names*
Würther, Josef, 347
Württemberg, Germany, 189, 240

XpresSpas, 1
X-rays, 240

Yanishev, Father I. L., 168
Yasnaya Polanya, Russia, 147, 151
Year Zero—A History of 1945 (Buruma), 368
Yeltsin, Boris, 397
Yugoslavia, 308
Yushchenko, Viktor, 139n

Zadoff, Mirjam, 252, 424
Zermatt, Switzerland, 2
Zimburg, Heinrich, 361–62, 383
Zionism, 252, 256, 310–12, 429
Zöhringer, Coeur de, 72
Zuckmayer, Carl, 257
Zweig, Ida, 256–57
Zweig, Stefan, 256–57
Zwei Welten (pacifist film), 301

About the Author

David Clay Large is currently senior fellow, Institute of European Studies, University of California, Berkeley, and professor of history, Fromm Institute, University of San Francisco. Previously he taught at Smith College, Yale University, and Montana State University, Bozeman. Large's many acclaimed publications include *Where Ghosts Walked: Munich's Road to the Third Reich*; *Berlin*; *Nazi Games: The Olympics of 1936*; and *Munich 1972: Tragedy, Terror, and Triumph at the Olympic Games*. When not taking the waters in Europe, Large divides his time between San Francisco and Bozeman, Montana.